European Yearbook of Inter
Economic Law

EYIEL Monographs -
and International Eco

Volume 19

EYIEL Monographs is a subseries of the European Yearbook of International Economic Law (EYIEL). It contains scholarly works in the fields of European and international economic law, in particular WTO law, international investment law, international monetary law, law of regional economic integration, external trade law of the EU and EU internal market law. The series does not include edited volumes. EYIEL Monographs are peer-reviewed by the series editors and external reviewers.

More information about this subseries at http://www.springer.com/series/15744

Cornelia Furculiță

The WTO and the New Generation EU FTA Dispute Settlement Mechanisms

Interacting in a Fragmented and Changing
International Trade Law Regime

 Springer

Cornelia Furculiță
Chair of Public Law, European Law
and Public International Law
German University of Administrative
Sciences Speyer
Speyer, Germany

ISSN 2364-8392   ISSN 2364-8406   (electronic)
European Yearbook of International Economic Law
ISSN 2524-6658   ISSN 2524-6666   (electronic)
EYIEL Monographs - Studies in European and International Economic Law
ISBN 978-3-030-83120-2   ISBN 978-3-030-83118-9   (eBook)
https://doi.org/10.1007/978-3-030-83118-9

This Springer imprint is published by the registered company Springer Nature Switzerland AG.
The registered company address is: Gewerbestrasse 11, 6330 Cham, Switzerland

Contents

1   **Introduction**   1
     1.1   Interactions Between the New Generation EU FTA
           and the WTO DSMs in a Fragmented International Trade
           Regime   1
     1.2   Objective   2
     1.3   Overview   4
     1.4   The Research Approach   6
     References   8

Part I   Context and Concepts

2   **Setting the Context**   13
     2.1   Proliferation of RTA DSMs   13
           2.1.1   Proliferation of RTAs and Especially FTAs   13
           2.1.2   Proliferation of DSMs Contained in RTAs   15
           2.1.3   The Importance of RTA DSMs Regardless
                 of Their Risks   17
           2.1.4   Perceived Risks of Fragmentation of the
                 International Trade Law Regime   18
     2.2   The New Generation EU FTA DSMs: In Focus   20
           2.2.1   EU FTAs and Their DSMs   20
           2.2.2   The EU Commitment to the Multilateral Trading
                 Regime   22
           2.2.3   The Choice in Favor of EUKFTA, CETA,
                 EUJEPA, EUSFTA, and EUVFTA   24
     2.3   General Description of the WTO and the New Generation
           EU FTA DSMs   26
           2.3.1   Dispute Settlement Under the WTO DSU   26
           2.3.2   The Multi-Party Interim Appeal Arbitration
                 Arrangement Pursuant to Article 25 of the DSU   28

　　　　2.3.3　Dispute Settlement Under the New Generation EU
　　　　　　　FTAs   31
　　References   32

3　Conceptual Framework   35
　3.1　Fragmentation and Other Concepts   35
　　　　3.1.1　'Fragmentation' and Its Causes   35
　　　　3.1.2　The Debate on Fragmentation   37
　　　　3.1.3　The Meaning of the Term 'Fragmentation'   39
　　　　3.1.4　Assumptions Underlying 'Fragmentation'   41
　　　　3.1.5　Forum Shopping   42
　　　　3.1.6　Limited Coherence in a Fragmented International
　　　　　　　Legal System   44
　3.2　Fragmentation of the International Trade Law Regime   46
　　　　3.2.1　Types of Fragmentation   46
　　　　3.2.2　Judicial Interactions: The Original Contribution   48
　　　　3.2.3　The Critique of the Judicial Interactions
　　　　　　　Perspective   50
　　　　3.2.4　Types of Judicial Interactions Between the DSMs
　　　　　　　of the FTAs and the WTO   51
　　　　3.2.5　The Issue of the 'Same Dispute'   54
　　References   55

**Part II　Competing Interactions Between the WTO and the New
　　　　　Generation EU FTA DSMs**

4　The Changing Context   61
　4.1　The Rare Use of RTA DSMs Until Recently   61
　4.2　The Unprecedented Crisis of the WTO DSM   64
　　References   69

5　Substantive Coverage and Considerations   71
　5.1　Areas Covered by the New Generation EU FTAs   71
　5.2　Substantive Coverage of the New Generation EU
　　　　FTA DSMs   74
　5.3　Substantive Aspects Affecting the Competition Between
　　　　the New Generation EU FTA and the WTO DSMs   77
　5.4　Conclusions: Wider Consequences Resulting from the
　　　　Substantive Coverage Considerations   80
　　References   81

6　Competing Procedural Considerations   83
　6.1　Preliminary Remarks   83
　6.2　Types of Complaints   84
　6.3　Time Frames   87
　　　　6.3.1　Time Frames in the WTO DSM   87
　　　　6.3.2　Time Frames in New Generation EU FTA DSMs   91

6.3.3   Implications of the Time Frames for the Competition
Between the New Generation EU FTA and the WTO
DSMs   92
6.4   The Panel Composition Process   95
6.4.1   The Composition of WTO Panels and the AB   95
6.4.2   The Precedent Set by NAFTA   97
6.4.3   Panel Composition Under the New Generation
EU FTA DSMs   99
6.4.4   Implications of the Panel Composition Process
for the Competition Between the New Generation
EU FTA and the WTO DSMs   105
6.5   Qualifications and Obligations of Panelists, Arbitrators
and AB Members   107
6.5.1   Qualifications and Obligations of Panelists
and AB Members   107
6.5.2   Qualifications and Obligations of Arbitrators
Under the New Generation EU FTAs   109
6.5.3   Implications of Qualifications and Obligations
of Arbitrators, Panelists and AB Members on the
Preference for a DSM   110
6.6   Rules of Procedure   111
6.6.1   WTO Rules of Procedure   112
6.6.2   Rules of Procedure Under the New Generation EU
FTAs   115
6.6.3   Implications of the Rules of Procedure for the
Competition Between the WTO and the New
Generation EU FTA DSMs   118
6.7   Decisions and Reports   118
6.7.1   WTO Panel and AB Reports and MPIA Arbitral
Awards   119
6.7.2   Decisions and Panel Reports in the New Generation
EU FTAs   122
6.7.3   Implications of the Rules on Decisions and Reports
for the Competition Between the WTO and the New
Generation EU FTA DSMs   123
6.8   Appellate Stage   124
6.9   Administrative and Legal Support   130
6.9.1   Support Provided by the WTO and AB Secretariats . . .   130
6.9.2   Administrative and Legal Support to Panels Under
the New Generation EU FTAs   133
6.9.3   Implications for the Competition Between the
DSMs of the WTO and the New Generation
EU FTAs   134
6.10   Transparency   135
6.10.1   Transparency of the WTO Proceedings   136

        6.10.2 Levels of Transparency in the New Generation
                EU FTAs 138
        6.10.3 The Influence of Transparency on Choosing a DSM . . . 140
  6.11 *Amicus Curiae* Briefs 141
        6.11.1 *Amicus Curiae* Briefs in WTO Proceedings 142
        6.11.2 *Amicus Curiae* Briefs Under the New Generation
                EU FTA DSMs 143
        6.11.3 Implications of the Rules on *Amicus Curiae* Briefs
                for the Competition Between the WTO and the
                New Generation EU FTA DSMs 145
  6.12 Implementation 146
        6.12.1 Implementation of Panel and AB Recommendations
                and Rulings Under the DSU 146
        6.12.2 Implementation of Panel Reports and Rulings
                Under the New Generation EU FTAs 151
        6.12.3 The Implications for the Competition Between
                the WTO and the New Generation EU FTA DSMs . . . 156
  6.13 Conclusions: Learning Lessons 157
  References 159

7 **Competing Political Considerations** 163
  7.1   The Value of Jurisprudence 163
  7.2   Pressure to Induce Compliance 166
  7.3   Reputation 170
        7.3.1   Reputational Costs and the Risk of Immediate
                Retaliation 170
        7.3.2   Limited Role of Reputation: Other Important
                Factors for Compliance 173
  7.4   Public Opinion 176
  7.5   Likelihood of Reaching Mutually Agreed Solutions 177
  7.6   Legitimacy 180
  7.7   Previous Experience and Financial Costs 185
  7.8   Conclusions on Political Aspects 187
  References 188

8 **Conclusions on the Competing Interactions Between the
   WTO and the New Generation EU FTA DSMs** 193

Part III **Conflicts of Jurisdiction Between the WTO and the New
          Generation EU FTA DSMs**

9 **Conflicts of Jurisdiction Between the DSMs of the WTO
   and FTAs in General** 199
  9.1   Introduction 199
  9.2   Tools Available to Deal with Conflicting Jurisdictions 200
        9.2.1   Public and Private International Law Tools 201

   9.2.2 Jurisdictional Clauses 206
  9.3 Using Tools on Conflicting Jurisdictions Within the WTO 215
   9.3.1 Jurisdiction of the WTO Panels 216
   9.3.2 The Exception Under Article XXIV of GATT 218
   9.3.3 Applicable Law Within the WTO DSM 222
   9.3.4 WTO Panels Declining or Not Exercising
        Jurisdiction 227
  9.4 WTO Members' Rights to WTO Proceedings Limited by the
      Breach of DSU Good Faith Obligations 234
   9.4.1 *Argentina – Poultry* 235
   9.4.2 *EC – Bananas III (Article 21.5 – Ecuador II /*
        Article 21.5 – US) 236
   9.4.3 *Peru – Agricultural Products*: Clarity or More
        Confusion? 238
  9.5 Evaluation 243
  References 245

10 Assessment of the Jurisdictional Clauses in the New
  Generation EU FTAs 251
  10.1 Areas Presenting the Risk of Conflicting Jurisdictions Between
      the WTO and the New Generation EU FTA DSMs 251
  10.2 Introduction to Jurisdictional Clauses in the New
      Generation EU FTAs 253
   10.2.1 Types of Jurisdictional Clauses in the New
        Generation EU FTAs 253
   10.2.2 The Relevance of Choice 255
   10.2.3 The Moment of Selection 257
   10.2.4 Additional Jurisdictional Clauses on
        Countermeasures 258
   10.2.5 Preliminary Remarks 258
  10.3 Conditions for Jurisdictional Clauses 259
  10.4 The Clarity and Unambiguity of the Jurisdictional
      Clauses in the New Generation EU FTAs 260
   10.4.1 The Clarity and Unambiguity of the Relinquishment
        of the Right to Initiate WTO Proceedings 260
   10.4.2 The Clarity and Unambiguity of the Category of
        Disputes 263
  10.5 Relating to DSU Rules and Procedures 266
  10.6 'Consistent with the Covered Agreements' 267
  10.7 Not Going 'Beyond the Settlement of Specific Disputes' 269
  10.8 Jurisdictional Clauses in the Context of the AB Crisis 269
  10.9 Conclusion 272
  References 274

**Part IV   Cooperative Interactions Between the WTO and the New
           Generation EU FTA DSMs**

11   Judicial Communication 279
      11.1   The Concept and Pre-conditions of Judicial Communication . . . 279
      11.2   Functions of Judicial Communication 281
      11.3   Factors Encouraging Judicial Communication 283
      11.4   Types of Judicial Communication 287
      11.5   Increased Importance of and the Limits to Coherence in Case
             of the Communication Between the DSMs of the WTO
             and the New Generation EU FTAs 289
      11.6   Judicial Communication Within the WTO DSM 292
             11.6.1   General Attitude of the WTO DSM Towards RTAs . . . 292
             11.6.2   RTA Rulings in WTO Jurisprudence 294
             11.6.3   Reference to Other International Tribunals'
                      Jurisprudence Within WTO Proceedings 298
      11.7   Judicial Communication Within RTA Proceedings 300
      11.8   Legal Avenues for Judicial Communication Between
             the New Generation EU FTA and the WTO DSMs 303
             11.8.1   Inherent Powers as Avenues for Judicial
                      Communication 304
             11.8.2   Facts and Evidence 305
             11.8.3   Judicial Decisions Determining Customary Rules
                      and Principles of Interpretation 309
             11.8.4   FTA Judicial Decisions Under Article XXIV
                      of GATT 311
             11.8.5   Judicial Decisions in the Process of Interpretation . . . 314
      11.9   Conclusion 332
      References 336

12   Prospective Developments for Contemplation 341
      12.1   Using the WTO Secretariat for Supporting WTO Panels 341
             12.1.1   Introducing the WTO Secretariat 341
             12.1.2   Advantages and Drawbacks of the Potential Use
                      of the WTO Secretariat During FTA Proceedings 344
             12.1.3   The Relevant New Generation EU FTA and
                      WTO Legal Frameworks 350
             12.1.4   Preliminary Conclusions 354
      12.2   Using the WTO DSM to Solve FTA Disputes 355
             12.2.1   Assessing the Existing WTO Rules 355
             12.2.2   Assessing the Likelihood of FTA Disputes Being
                      Resolved Under WTO Rules 358
      12.3   Conclusion 361
      References 362

13   Conclusion 365

Chapter 1
Introduction

1.1 Interactions Between the New Generation EU FTA and the WTO DSMs in a Fragmented International Trade Regime

The international trade law regime has been characterised in the last decades by the proliferation of Free Trade Agreements (FTAs). These agreements do not only provide substantive norms, but the majority also contain dispute settlement mechanisms (DSMs) that can be used for the enforcement of FTA obligations. The trend of the proliferation of FTAs and their DSMs has not dwindled. Instead, it continues to advance and gain even more importance with FTAs currently being the main vehicle for the new rules developed within the international trade law regime.[1] More and more major trading partners that are not necessarily from the same region sign FTAs to facilitate trade between them. The European Union (EU) has the most ambitious trade agenda in the world, having concluded many such agreements and is still negotiating and set up to sign multiple new generation EU FTAs—all containing dispute settlement chapters and reflecting the EU's most recent approach to these agreements.[2] While FTAs seem to flourish, the multilateral trade regime governed by the World Trade Organization (WTO) has been struggling to update its rule book since the Doha Round of negotiations. Furthermore, with the Appellate Body (AB) being dysfunctional, the WTO is currently undergoing an unprecedented crisis, with some Members striving to establish an arbitration alternative to the appellate stage within the WTO.[3] Therefore, the international trading regime is in the process of changing.

---

[1] For more on the proliferation of RTA and their DSMs *see infra* Sect. 2.1.

[2] On the EU's ambitious trade agenda *see* Sect. 2.2.

[3] In this respect *see infra* Chap. 4.

The increasing number of FTAs and especially of their DSMs has raised fears of fragmentation leading to greater incoherence, instability, and unpredictability of the international trade regime. Furthermore, concerns that the WTO's authority is undermined and threatened are also growing. While the increasing number of FTA DSMs may pose certain risks, such as the likelihood of jurisdictional conflicts and incoherent interpretations of similar WTO and FTA norms, they could be addressed or reduced. Thus, there may be legal tools, either inspired from private or public international law or the treaties establishing the DSMs, themselves, could contain jurisdictional clauses addressing the issue of conflicting jurisdictions.[4] Moreover, the risks stemming from a fragmented international trade regime could also be alleviated by cooperation between the WTO and FTA DSMs in the form of judicial communication or other more ambitious and structural forms.[5] In the context of the AB crisis, FTA DSMs may even emerge as potential alternatives to the multilateral mechanism to solve certain categories of trade disputes.[6] Lastly, the FTA DSMs may not undermine, but rather rely on a functional WTO mechanism. Therefore, the interactions between the WTO and FTA DSMs are complex and associating them only with negative consequences is misleading.

While advancing its ambitious trade agenda, the EU has consistently expressed its support for the multilateral trading regime.[7] Therefore, the EU has to balance the multilateral and bilateral directions of its trade policy, and take care to act according to WTO rules, including Article XXIV of the General Agreement on Tariffs and Trade (GATT) regulating FTAs.[8] It needs to minimise the negative consequences and enhance the potential synergies of the interactions between its new generation EU FTA and the WTO DSMs in a fragmented and changing international trade regime, in order to uphold its credibility as a multilateralist. For this reason, the analysis of the interactions between the new generation EU FTA and the WTO DSMs is of specific interest.

1.2   Objective

In the context of the changing international trading regime, continuing proliferation of FTAs and their DSMs, the expected rise in the use of FTA DSMs, and the current crisis at the multilateral level, the interactions between the FTA and the WTO DSMs should be given renewed attention and gain increased importance. Although judicial

---

[4]On the tools dealing with conflicting jurisdictions and their likelihood of successfully addressing this issue *see* Chap. 9.

[5]This form of interactions is addressed in Chap. 11.

[6]This question is considered in detail in Part II.

[7]On the EU's support for multilateralism *see infra* Sect. 2.2.2.

[8]General Agreement on Tariffs and Trade 1994 (GATT), 15 April 1994, Marrakesh Agreement Establishing the World Trade Organization, Annex 1A, 1867 U.N.T.S 187 (1994).

interactions may not be the most common form of regime interactions, they deserve special consideration due to their increased importance in the debate on fragmentation and the difficult questions that they raise.

Since fragmentation and forum shopping are regarded as concepts free of negative connotations for the purpose of the present book,[9] the interactions that can take place between the WTO and FTA DSMs are not scrutinised merely from a negative angle. This study aims to consider not only the conflicting interactions between the DSMs analysed, but also other types of interactions that could have a potential for creating synergies. Therefore, it aims to comprehensively investigate how the new generation EU FTA and the WTO DSMs do and could interact in a fragmented and changing international trade law regime.

As the existing legal literature is mostly focused on the conflicting interactions between DSMs within the international trade law regime, other types of interactions have received less attention.[10] This work aspires to conduct a broader research and contribute to legal scholarship by investigating different ways in which DSMs do and could interact. The new generation EU FTA DSMs, which are at the centre of the present book, and their interactions with the WTO DSM have not been analysed to date in such detail. Furthermore, this study provides new and up-to-date perspectives, as it considers the interactions between the mechanisms analysed in light of the most recent changes in the international trade law regime, including the WTO dispute settlement crisis.

Three types of interactions will be analysed: **competing**, **conflicting**, and **cooperative**.[11] Competing interactions reflect the situations in which a state has a choice of forum to which a dispute can be brought, a conflicting interaction takes place when two DSMs are triggered in parallel or subsequence for the same dispute, and cooperative interactions occur when DSMs capture the synergies between them by mutually assisting each other or a DSM unilaterally engages in cooperation with another DSM. While these types of interactions reflect the approach taken that fragmentation and forum shopping are not necessarily negative phenomena, I also argue that coherence should be sought. Nevertheless, coherence should not be an absolute goal to the detriment of correctness. Limited coherence should be pursued, respecting the existing legal framework—the manifestation of the states' will.[12] Hence, the book has the objective of providing a comprehensive analysis of how the WTO and the new generation EU FTA DSMs do and could interact so that when the legal framework allows, the negative consequences are addressed and the synergies are enhanced. It intends to assess whether the new generation EU FTA DSMs could become viable alternatives to the WTO DSM, especially in the context of the WTO dispute settlement crisis and how that would affect the authority of the WTO mechanism. Thus, in certain cases, FTA DSMs could become a 'solution'

---

[9] *See infra* Sect. 3.1.

[10] *See infra* Sect. 3.2.2.

[11] For more on this classification *see* Sect. 3.2.4.

[12] On the concept of limited coherence *see* Sect. 3.1.6.

during this crisis and be used by state parties to enforce their rights.[13] Furthermore, this study will focus on how conflicts of jurisdiction could be addressed and whether the new generation EU FTAs are designed well to tackle this issue. Finally, it will analyse the avenues for communication between the new generation EU FTAs and the WTO adjudicators to bring greater coherence to the international trade regime, as well as, against the background of the AB crisis, other more ambitious and structural forms of judicial cooperation between these mechanisms and their likelihood of materialising in the future.

1.3   Overview

The book is divided into four major parts. Part I (Chaps. 2 and 3) will introduce the relevant context and concepts. Chapter 2, setting the relevant context, will describe the proliferation of Regional Trade Agreements (RTAs) and the DSMs contained therein. It will also explain the risks associated with this phenomenon and the importance of RTA DSMs. The chapter will also justify the preference for the new generation EU FTA DSMs, specifically those contained in the EU–South Korea Free Trade Agreement (EUKFTA),[14] EU–Canada Comprehensive Economic and Trade Agreement (CETA),[15] EU–Japan Economic Partnership Agreement (EUJPEPA),[16] EU–Singapore Free Trade Agreement (EUSFTA),[17] and EU–Vietnam Free Trade Agreement (EUVFTA),[18] to analyse the interactions with the WTO DSM and will present in brief the interacting mechanisms. Chapter 3 provides the conceptual framework, and will introduce the causes of and the debate on fragmentation, the concepts of fragmentation, limited coherence, and forum shopping as adopted in the present book, and the assumptions made. It will then present the types of fragmentation dealt with, and will argue in favour of the adopted judicial perspective and discuss the originality of the contribution made by this work. Finally, it will explain the types of interactions between the new generation EU FTA and the WTO DSMs studied in the following parts and will introduce the concept of 'same dispute'.

Part II (Chaps. 4–8) will deal with the first type of judicial interactions—competing interactions. Genuine competition between DSMs takes place when states

---

[13] *See infra* Chap. 8.

[14] Free Trade Agreement between the European Union and its Member States, of the One Part, and the Republic of Korea, of the Other Part [2011] OJ L 127.

[15] Comprehensive Economic and Trade Agreement between Canada, of the One Part, and the European Union and its Member States, of the Other Part [2017] OJ L 11.

[16] Agreement between Japan and the European Union for an Economic Partnership [2018] OJ L 330.

[17] Free Trade Agreement Between the European Union and the Republic of Singapore [2019] OJ L 294.

[18] Free Trade Agreement Between the European Union and the Socialist Republic of Viet Nam [2020] OJ L 186.

perceive them as being viable alternatives to each other. Part II will be dedicated to analysing how the new generation EU FTA and WTO DSMs compete, especially whether the new generation EU FTA DSMs could become viable alternatives to the WTO DSM in the current changing international trade law regime. In spite of the success that the WTO DSM has had so far and the rare use of FTA DSMs, this situation could soon change. Accordingly, Part II will analyse the competing interactions between the WTO mechanism and the new generation EU FTA DSMs, taking into consideration different aspects—substantive, procedural, and political— that may be the determinants for a party choosing in which forum a dispute is to be adjudicated. It will also consider how these factors could shape the choice in favour of a DSM and whether EU FTA DSMs could be used more often and become viable alternatives for solving trade disputes between FTA parties, especially in the context of the AB crisis and the risk of panel reports being appealed into the void. Moreover, it will also consider how competition could take place in the case of FTAs concluded between parties that have signed the Multi-party Interim Appeal Arbitration Arrangement Pursuant to Article 25 of the DSU (MPIA).[19] Based on the analysis of different considerations, this part will be indicative of the broader implications of competition between DSMs, such as whether the FTA DSMs undermine the WTO mechanism and whether positive consequences, for example learning lessons from each other, could result from competition.

Part III (Chaps. 9 and 10) will deal with the type of judicial interactions between FTA and the WTO DSMs—conflicts of jurisdictions—which are the most analysed by international trade law academics. Therefore, this part will investigate how the jurisdictions of the new generation EU FTA DSMs and the WTO mechanism could come into conflict in a fragmented and changing international trade law regime. Chapter 9 will analyse the likelihood of different private and public international legal tools, as well as jurisdictional treaty clauses, to solve these conflicts. By considering the relevant legal framework and case law, it will identify the tool that is most likely to succeed in solving the potential conflicting jurisdictions between the WTO and the new generation EU FTA DSMs and the conditions for a successful invocation. Based on the conclusions reached in Chap. 9, Chap. 10 will investigate whether the new generation EU FTAs and their jurisdictional clauses, as legal tools, comply with the conditions identified and could solve the potential conflicts of jurisdictions when invoked within WTO proceedings commenced in parallel or subsequent to FTA proceedings. It will also discuss proposals that could increase the likelihood of jurisdictional clauses contained in the new generation EU FTAs being considered within WTO proceedings to tackle the issue of conflicting jurisdictions. Furthermore, it will examine how these jurisdictional clauses would operate in the context of the changes taking place within the international trade regime, particularly the AB crisis.

Part IV (Chaps. 11 and 12) will deal with cooperative judicial interactions. Cooperative interactions could capture the positive outcomes of fragmentation and

---

[19] WTO, Multi-Party Interim Appeal Arbitration Arrangement, JOB/DSB/1/Add.12, 30 April 2020.

alleviate the potentially negative consequences. They may foster coherence in the international trade law regime and international public law. As established in the conceptual framework, coherence entails many advantages, yet it is not the ultimate goal and should be sought only within the limits established by the intentions of the parties reflected in the public international law rules agreed by them. Chapter 11 will deal with cooperative interactions in the form of judicial communication between adjudicators of the new generation EU FTAs and the WTO. It will present the preconditions, concepts, types, factors, and functions of judicial communication. It will then analyse the legal avenues for communication that the WTO and the new generation EU FTAs adjudicators could exploit, including the specific new generation EU FTA provisions on the interpretative role of WTO jurisprudence. While the WTO DSM is going through an unprecedented crisis with a paralysed AB, judicial communication could still take place at the panel level or in the context of appeal arbitration under Article 25 of the Dispute Settlement Understanding (DSU),[20] if the disputing parties are participants. In addition, Chap. 6 will examine how judicial communication could help reduce the negative consequences of a changing fragmented international trade regime even without a functioning AB. Chapter 12 will reflect on the potential for more ambitious forms of future institutional cooperation: the use of the WTO Secretariat's assistance during FTA dispute settlement and the extension of WTO jurisdiction over appeals of the new generation EU FTA reports. This chapter will contemplate future developments and discuss the opportunity to materializes them. The book will conclude with a summary of the main results of the study.

1.4 The Research Approach

In an effort to provide a comprehensive study covering different types of interactions between the new generation EU FTA DSMs and the WTO DSM, which does not only cover the conflicting ones, the book builds on a conceptual framework designed with an interdisciplinary approach to the issue of fragmentation. The conceptual framework was created based on international law, as well as international relations scholarship on fragmentation and regime interactions. Therefore, the interdisciplinary approach allowed the design of a complex and multifaceted conceptual framework on which the central parts of the book hinge. An interdisciplinary approach was preferred over a mere legal one, in order to obtain new ideas and visions inspired by international relations doctrine.

Part II on competitive interactions between the new generation EU FTA DSMs and the WTO mechanism also adopts an interdisciplinary approach. Thus, in order to

---

[20] Dispute Settlement Rules: Understanding on Rules and Procedures Governing the Settlement of Disputes, Marrakesh Agreement Establishing the World Trade Organization, Annex 2, 1869 U.N.T.S. 401, 33 I.L.M. 1226 (1994).

research how these mechanisms do and could compete, this author will conduct a legal assessment of multiple aspects that could influence states to favour one mechanism over another from the specific perspective of the states involved. Part II compares various FTA and WTO norms on dispute settlement to establish the implications and consequences for the interactions analysed. At the same time, as Part II evaluates how different political considerations may affect the choice of a state in favour of a specific forum, it makes extensive use of political science and international relations scholarship. The use of research findings from other disciplines allows a more comprehensive analysis of different considerations shaping competition between the WTO and the new generation EU FTA DSMs. A legal analysis on its own would offer an incomplete picture of what affects the preferences of states for a particular forum and in which way.

For a more robust study, the conclusions based on the use of legal analysis and political science and international relations scholarship are complemented and verified by the results acquired through elite interviews. In addition to other methods, Part II also applies a qualitative empirical method.[21] Triangulation, the technique of applying multiple methods and corroborating data obtained from different sources, helps to assess the author's presuppositions, enhances research outcomes and increases their credibility.[22] Elite interviews are to be considered those conducted with individuals with high levels of expertise and knowledge of their subject matter.[23] Therefore, the interviewees were selected so that they have the knowledge and expertise in dispute settlement under the WTO and FTA rules, especially the new generation EU FTA rules. The interviewees were a trade policymaker familiar with WTO proceedings and negotiations for the new generation EU FTA DSMs; a WTO litigator and international trade scholar who has written about FTA dispute settlement; an international trade law scholar with extensive experience in WTO litigation who has been nominated as an arbitrator by the EU for the new generation EU FTAs lists of arbitrators; an international trade law scholar with extensive experience as a WTO litigator who has acted as the chair of several WTO panels and was nominated for the chairperson's sub-lists under several new generation EU FTAs'; and a senior advisor working for an organisation representing business who is knowledgeable about the WTO and the new generation EU FTAs dispute settlement proceedings. Thus, the interviewees' knowledge of the DSMs studied made them suitable candidates to be inquired about competition between these mechanisms. Furthermore, they offer different perspectives on the subject matter due to their distinct backgrounds and insights.

The five elite interviews were conducted between July 2019 and May 2020, and each lasted about 30 min. Two of the interviews were conducted with the help of online tools and the rest took place face-to-face. Prior to the interview, the participants were given an information sheet describing the research and their rights,

---

[21] Interviews are considered qualitative empirical work (Shaffer and Ginsburg 2012, p. 4).

[22] Tansey (2007), p. 766; Shaffer and Ginsburg (2012), p. 4; Langbroek et al. (2017), p. 7.

[23] Burnham et al. (2008), p. 231.

according to the requirements of the EU General Data Protection Regulation,[24] together with a consent form. The interviews were audio-recorded only with the interviewees' agreement, otherwise the interviews were transcribed after they were conducted. All the data collected were anonymised and stored confidentially. The interviews had an in-depth semi-structured design, the conversations evolving naturally from a set of broader open questions to more specific ones depending on the context.[25] The advantage of open questions is that they allow the interviewee to engage in wide-ranging discussions and say what they think is relevant and important, rather than being constrained by the researcher's viewpoint, which increases the validity of the response.[26] Since states do not expressly declare why they choose one forum over another when they have such a choice, the data collected through elite interviews allowed me to gain insights and knowledge otherwise unavailable. Furthermore, the application of different research methods, including interviews, allowed me to corroborate the information and cross-check it, thereby increasing the reliability of the research outcomes.

Parts III and IV adopt a normative doctrinal legal approach. Thus, they analyse the law using critical reasoning, and embrace an internal approach by taking the perspective of the insiders of the system, such as adjudicators.[27] To construct the arguments, they mostly refer to primary legal sources, such as treaties, customary law, general principles of international law, as well as to existing relevant jurisprudence and doctrinal writings.[28] As the doctrinal legal approach adopted in these chapters takes an internal, normative and, sometimes, prescriptive perspective by opining on how the law should be applied or what should be the best course of action in different cases, these judgments are to be perceived through the lens of the conceptual framework.

References

Aberbach JD, Rockman BA (2002) Conducting and coding elite interviews. Polit Sci Polit 35 (4):673–676
Beamer G (2002) Elite interviews and state politics research. State Polit Policy Q 2(1):86–96
Berry JM (2002) Validity and reliability issues in elite interviewing. Polit Sci Polit 35(4):679–682
Burnham P, Gilland Lutz K et al (2008) Research methods in politics, 2nd edn. Red Globe Press, London

---

[24] Regulation (EU) 2016/679 of the European Parliament and of the Council of 27 April 2016 on the Protection of Natural Persons with Regard to the Processing of Personal Data and on the Free Movement of such Data, and Repealing Directive 95/46/EC (General Data Protection Regulation), OJ L119, 04.05.2016, Corrigendum OJ L127, 23.5.2018.

[25] This is the most common strategy according to Beamer (2002), p. 92.

[26] Aberbach and Rockman (2002), p. 674; Berry (2002), p. 681.

[27] McCrudden (2006), p. 633.

[28] These are the sources mostly used by the legal method, according to Koskenniemi (2007), para 7.

Koskenniemi M (2007) Methodology of international law. In: Max Planck Encyclopedia of Public International Law. Oxford, London

Langbroek P, van den Bos K et al (2017) Methodology of legal research: challenges and opportunities. Utrecht Law Rev 13(3):1–8

McCrudden C (2006) Legal research and the social sciences. Law Q Rev 1222:632–650

Shaffer G, Ginsburg T (2012) The empirical turn in international legal scholarship. Am J Int Law 106(1):1–46

Tansey O (2007) Process tracing and elite interviewing: a case for non-probability sampling. Polit Sci Polit 40(4):765–772

Part I
Context and Concepts

Chapter 2
Setting the Context

2.1 Proliferation of RTA DSMs

This section introduces the phenomenon of proliferation of RTAs, especially FTAs, and their DSMs. It then briefly describes the risks associated with this phenomenon and why, nevertheless, the presence of DSM chapters in RTAs is important.

2.1.1 *Proliferation of RTAs and Especially FTAs*

The proliferation of RTAs has been called the defining trade policy development of the last decades.[1] The term RTA refers to any reciprocal preferential trade agreement concluded between two or more parties from the same region or from different regions.[2] While RTAs vary in their geographical scope, the number of parties and the issues covered, the features common to all of them should be the reduction of trade barriers between state parties and seeking closer economic integration that is beyond that offered by the multilateral trading system.[3] The term RTA is to be understood, according to the WTO usage, as encompassing FTAs and Customs Unions (CUs) covering trade in goods notified under Article XXIV of GATT, Economic Integration Agreements covering services under Article V of the General Agreement on Trade in Services (GATS),[4] and regional or global arrangements for trade in goods

---

[1] Choi (2010), p. 111.

[2] WTO, Regional Trade Agreements: An Introduction <www.wto.org/english/tratop_e/region_e/scope_rta_e.htm>.

[3] Shlomo Agon (2019), p. 267.

[4] General Agreement on Trade in Services, 15 April 1994, Marrakesh Agreement Establishing the World Trade Organization, Annex 1B, 1869 U.N.T.S. 183, 33 I.L.M. 1167 (1994).

© The Author(s), under exclusive license to Springer Nature Switzerland AG 2021
C. Furculiță, *The WTO and the New Generation EU FTA Dispute Settlement Mechanisms*, EYIEL Monographs - Studies in European and International Economic Law 19, https://doi.org/10.1007/978-3-030-83118-9_2

between developing country Members under the Enabling Clause.[5] According to Article XXIV of GATT, an FTA, as a type of RTA, is 'a group of two or more customs territories in which the duties and other restrictive regulations of commerce (except, where necessary, those permitted under Articles XI, XII, XIII, XIV, XV and XX) are eliminated on substantially all the trade between the constituent territories in products originating in such territories'.[6]

Oxford Dictionaries define the term 'proliferation' as the rapid increase in the number or amount of something.[7] The rapid increase in the number of RTAs can be easily detected by comparing the number of RTAs notified during the GATT era to those notified after the creation of the WTO. During the existence of GATT, from 1948 to 1994, the organisation was notified of RTAs 124 times, while from the creation of the WTO in 1995 to 2020, the organisation has been notified of over 490 agreements.[8] In the last decades, there have been almost four times as many notifications than in the previous 46 years. While in the GATT era there were two or three notifications on average annually, the WTO receives an average of 18 notifications per year. This increase in notifications clearly shows an intensification of Members' activity with respect to conclusion of RTAs.

The number of notifications is not, however, equal to the number of RTAs, since an agreement that covers the trade in both goods and services is notified twice.[9] Thus, the total number of notifications corresponds to 302 RTAs in force.[10] About 80% of the RTAs in force are FTAs;[11] thus, the evident proliferation is mostly in FTAs. It is also important to acknowledge that the actual number of RTAs is even higher than the number notified to the WTO. A study based on searches of websites of state institutions identified 733 signed agreements between 1945 and 2009, out of which only 356 agreements have been included in the WTO list.[12] The number of identified RTAs, which is more than twice that of notified RTAs, clearly indicates that the trend of proliferation may be even more intense than identified based on

---

[5]Free Trade Agreement, as defined in para 8(b) of Art XXIV of GATT; Customs Union, as defined in para 8(a) of Art XXIV of GATT; Economic Integration Agreement, as defined in Art V of GATS; and regional or global arrangements for trade in goods between developing country members under Art 2 of the Decision on Differential and More Favourable Treatment, Reciprocity, and Fuller Participation of Developing Countries (Enabling Clause), GATT Document L/4903, 28 November 1979, BISD 26S/203 (WTO, Regional Trade Agreements Information System: User Guide <https://rtais.wto.org/UserGuide/User%20Guide_Eng.pdf>).

[6]GATT, Art XXIV:8(b).

[7]Oxford Dictionaries <https://en.oxforddictionaries.com/definition/proliferation>.

[8]WTO, Regional Trade Agreements: Facts and Figures. July-December 2019 <www.wto.org/english/tratop_e/region_e/region_e.htm#facts>.

[9]An RTA that covers both trade in goods and services is notified according to the requirements of both Art XXIV 7(a) of GATT and Art V 7(a) of GATS.

[10]WTO, Regional Trade Agreements: Facts and Figures. July–December 2019 <www.wto.org/english/tratop_e/region_e/rtajul_dec19_e.pdf>.

[11]In this respect *see* WTO, Regional Trade Agreements Database <http://rtais.wto.org/UI/publicsummarytable.aspx>.

[12]Dür et al. (2014), p. 357.

WTO data and should not be ignored. According to the 2011 WTO Trade Report based on data gathered until 2010, each WTO Member was a party to 13 RTAs on average.[13] Moreover, since June 2016, every WTO Member has at least one RTA in force.[14]

These data only confirm that the number of RTAs, especially FTAs, has grown at a very rapid pace in the last decades. Hence, the extensive theoretical literature on FTAs, as well as the continuing interest in the subject, is understandable. The present book contributes to this pool of literature with its focus on the proliferation of FTAs, with its own niche whose boundaries will be defined later.

2.1.2 Proliferation of DSMs Contained in RTAs

The proliferation of RTAs is an immense area of research with no single study being able to encompass all its aspects. Therefore, this book focuses specifically on the state-to-state DSMs contained in FTAs. DSMs are considered the set of rules designed to regulate the peaceful resolution of potential conflicts arising in relation to the interpretation of the treaty and the state parties' compliance with it.

Several studies mention that almost all RTAs contain some form of DSM.[15] According to data provided by the WTO, about 85% of the RTAs in force contain DSM clauses.[16] This percentage itself confirms that most RTAs have DSMs incorporated into their texts. However, to establish that DSMs in RTAs have proliferated, it is necessary to look at how they have evolved over time and their recent tendencies. In their analysis of 589 signed RTAs in the period 1947–2009, Todd Allee and Manfred Elsig concluded that 97% of the RTAs signed in the 2000s indicate in one way or another how disputes should be solved.[17] In conclusion, almost all RTAs concluded more recently address the issue of settling disputes. Therefore, the growth is not only in RTAs but also in the DSMs included in these agreements: both RTAs and their DSMs have proliferated.

There are different types of DSMs, and the preference for one type or another for inclusion in trade agreements has evolved over time. Thus, the question is which type has been proliferating together with RTAs. From the 1960s to 1995, most of the RTAs provided political models of DSMs that consisted solely of settling disputes through negotiations and consultations between RTA parties.[18] On the other hand, during the same period, the European model with a standing tribunal appeared, displayed by the European Court of Justice (ECJ), established in 1952 as the Court of

---

[13] WTO (2011), p. 47.

[14] WTO, Regional Trade Agreements <www.wto.org/english/tratop_e/region_e/region_e.htm>.

[15] Chase et al. (2016), p. 609; de Mestral (2013), p. 779.

[16] WTO, RTA Database: Search by Criteria <www.youtube.com/watch?v=aMTyM-p4Tp8>.

[17] Allee and Elsig (2015), p. 324.

[18] Porges (2011), p. 470; Chase et al. (2016), p. 623; McDougall (2018), p. 2.

Justice of the European Coal and Steal Community.[19] This model was followed by several other RTAs, such as the European Free Trade Area (EFTA), the Andean Community, the Economic Community of West African States (ECOWAS), the East African Community (EAC), and the Common Market for Eastern and Southern Africa (COMESA). A pattern is evident in the use of standing tribunals in all these cases—they were included in regional economic integration agreements.[20] Therefore, inclusion of standing tribunals in this type of agreement was a trend, not a general preference.

From 1995, along with the growth in the number of concluded RTAs, the incorporation of RTA DSMs providing *ad hoc* arbitration increased at the same pace.[21] Thus, the dominant model of the DSM adopted in the last two decades provides *ad hoc* third-party arbitration, with panels convened every time a dispute occurs. In this model, the arbitral awards are usually final and binding on the parties, and the majority of agreements provide mechanisms for implementation of these awards.[22] Almost all RTAs still encourage consultations as the first stage of dispute settlement similar to the models used in pre-WTO RTAs.[23] However, in the event an agreement is not reached, parties can request the establishment of an arbitration panel to decide the case. This model gained popularity after it was included in the North American Free Trade Agreement (NAFTA)[24] in 1994 and was provided in WTO's DSU which entered into force in 1995, indicating the increased confidence of countries in these models and their acceptance.[25] Familiarity with the DSU means that states understand how these proceedings work and know what to expect from them.[26] The increase in RTA DSMs providing *ad hoc* arbitration might have also been a consequence of the change in the dynamics of RTAs. They became more diverse, as more WTO Members began trading on the preferential bases offered by RTAs not only with their regional partners, but also across regions.[27] Accordingly, more complex mechanisms were needed to ensure the resolution of disputes in the event of parties being unable to reach an agreement. In addition, RTAs became more sophisticated by regulating different areas beyond borders, measures that also needed more developed approaches to dispute settlement to ensure that the benefits provided by these norms could be realised.[28] While standing tribunals can also be viewed as mechanisms to ensure effective enforcement, *ad hoc* procedures are more

---

[19] Porges (2011), p. 471.

[20] Allee and Elsig (2015), p. 328.

[21] Chase et al. (2016), pp. 623–624.

[22] Allee and Elsig (2015), pp. 336, 337.

[23] Allee and Elsig (2015), p. 324.

[24] North American Free Trade Agreement Implementation Act Public Law No. 103-182, 107 Stat. 2057 (1993).

[25] Chase et al. (2016), p. 624.

[26] Porges (2011), p. 467.

[27] Chase et al. (2016), p. 624.

[28] Porges (2011), p. 475; McDougall (2018), p. 3.

cost-effective, especially considering that the number of RTA disputes under specific agreements may be limited due to the small number of participants in these agreements.[29]

The increased number of DSMs in RTAs has raised concerns about the fragmentation of the international trade law regime. The following section will describe the risks to the international trade law regime associated with the proliferation of RTAs and their DSMs.

2.1.3 The Importance of RTA DSMs Regardless of Their Risks

Despite the potential negative consequences of multiple RTA DSMs, this section will argue that they are still indispensable for the smooth functioning of RTAs and for ensuring that there is progress in the international trade law regime.

DSMs in RTAs, as well as in other international treaties, aim to ensure that substantive obligations are complied with by the parties. Having a mechanism to enforce the obligations in RTAs is especially important in the case of RTA norms that go beyond those of the WTO. RTA norms that incorporate or replicate WTO standards can be enforced under both RTAs and the WTO dispute settlement rules, whereas for the norms providing benefits available only at the RTA level, there is no venue of enforcement other than the RTA DSM. With no DSMs, these standards risk remaining only on paper, without the parties being able to reap the benefits from them. A dispute concerning claims on norms contained only in RTAs may, however, simultaneously concern norms replicating or incorporating WTO provisions. Therefore, to be able to solve the dispute in such cases, it may be necessary for RTA DSMs to also cover claims on WTO-equal provisions. The lack of an organised way of solving disputes between parties could seriously affect their relationship. Without a peaceful means of solving a conflict, it may escalate and even result in the termination of the agreement.[30] Moreover, by including strong DSMs in their RTAs, states reaffirm their commitment to respect the agreement and their promise becomes more credible for each other, as parties to the agreement and for their own stakeholders.[31] In the context of the stalled negotiations of the Doha Round (started in 2001), RTAs became the vehicle for further developments in international trade law that could be multilateralised within the WTO in the future. Leaving these developments without any mechanism of enforcement may nullify their effect.

The WTO DSM has often been referred to as the 'crown jewel of the WTO System' because of its frequent use by the Member States and its productive

---

[29] Chase et al. (2016), p. 613.

[30] Porges (2011), p. 467; Porges (2018), p. 1.

[31] Porges (2011), p. 467; Porges (2018), p. 1.

activity.[32] It has been one of the most active international dispute settlement mechanisms in the world, with almost 600 disputes brought to the WTO and over 350 rulings issued since 1995.[33] However, the WTO DSM's success story has seen a change. It has been challenged by the increased number of disputes putting a strain on the mechanism, and it is currently undergoing an unprecedented crisis because of the AB being dysfunctional since December 2019. The crisis will be described in detail in the next part.[34] Considering the current changing situation, although RTA DSMs have litigated very few inter-state disputes until now,[35] they may come forward as potential alternative venues for trade disputes in case the WTO DSM does not function, or at least for taking a part of the burden from the WTO to unload the overwhelmed system.

In light of the necessity to enforce the more advanced RTA rules and because of the challenges the WTO DSM faces, a rise in the use of RTA DSMs in the near future is anticipated. Therefore, given the potential rise in the use of RTA DSMs and the concerns arising from it, the subject of possible interactions between RTA DSMs and the WTO DSM gains renewed attention.

2.1.4 Perceived Risks of Fragmentation of the International Trade Law Regime

The rapid increase in the number of RTAs and DSMs to enforce RTA norms has led to the crystallisation of fears of fragmentation of the international trade law regime. This section will describe the concerns associated with the proliferation of RTAs and their DSMs.

The preamble to the Marrakesh Agreement establishing the WTO provides that its aim is to promote the reduction of tariffs, on a reciprocal and mutually advantageous basis, to eliminate discriminatory treatment and create 'an integrated, more viable and durable multilateral trading system'.[36] Thus, non-discrimination and multilateralism are the key concepts that define the regime of international trade law established by the WTO. The RTAs, on the contrary, are trade agreements that facilitate trade between a small number of parties only;[37] they, therefore, also cover trade issues, but in a bilateral way, discriminating against non-FTA parties. The rationale for the existence of RTAs is to regulate trade relationships between their parties in a different, more preferential way than the non-discriminatory and

---

[32] Payosova et al. (2018), p. 1.

[33] WTO, 'Dispute Settlement' <www.wto.org/english/tratop_e/dispu_e/dispu_e.htm>.

[34] *See infra* Sect. 4.2.

[35] *See infra* Sect. 4.1.

[36] Marrakesh Agreement Establishing the World Trade Organization (Marrakesh Agreement), 15 April 1994, 1867 U.N.T.S. 154, 33 I.L.M. 1144 (1994), Preamble.

[37] GATT, Art XXIV:4.

multilateral way in which the WTO does. Therefore, overlapping with the multilateral trade regime is inherent in the nature of RTAs.

A WTO Member applies different trade rules to different states, depending on whether or not an RTA is concluded between them.[38] Thus, in an RTA relationship between trading partners, the same or similar disputes could be regulated by both regional and multilateral rules. This could create regulatory confusion because the question would arise which norm should be applicable to a particular case. Moreover, as already mentioned, most RTAs have also their own DSMs with their own scope. This means that trade-related disputes between RTA parties, if regulated by both RTAs and WTO law and covered by both DSMs, could be considered under either one of these mechanisms or both. If both DSMs rule on the same case, there is a risk of conflicting results. In addition to the same disputes being solved differently, similar disputes and issues could be dealt with differently at the RTA and WTO level, or even different RTAs could decide on similar matters distinctly. Thus, the proliferation of RTA DSMs is associated with the risk of incoherence within the international trade law regime. Incoherent rulings and interpretations are also against the principle of predictability,[39] which is enshrined in Article 3(2) of the DSU. Security and predictability in the interpretation of norms ensure that states, as signatories to the agreements, as well as economic operators, as their final beneficiaries, can rely on them. Moreover, the lack of predictability in how international trade rules are interpreted could also involve significant financial and time costs during dispute settlement,[40] if the same dispute has to be relitigated or for legal counsel that attempts to bring all possible arguments to support the case. Moreover, it may also entail significant transaction costs for economic operators that would have to navigate the complex network of international trade norms interpreted differently.[41] Hence, both states and economic operators may be confused and their expectations could be neglected. Likewise, the proliferation of RTA DSMs may be perceived as undermining the authority and centrality of the WTO DSM.[42]

These perceived risks posed by the overlap between RTA DSMs and the WTO DSM are all aspects of so-called fragmentation, a concept that will be addressed in detail in the conceptual framework.[43]

---

[38] Lee (2011), p. 633.

[39] Forere (2015), pp. 5, 41.

[40] Lee (2011), p. 635.

[41] Johnston and Trebilcock (2013), p. 627.

[42] Shlomo Agon (2019), p. 269.

[43] *See infra* Sect. 3.1.

2.2   The New Generation EU FTA DSMs: In Focus

This section will introduce the EU FTAs, their DSMs, and the EU's commitment to multilateralism. It will argue why the choice was made in favour of the new generation EU FTA DSMs, particularly those embedded in the EUKFTA, CETA, EUJPEPA, EUSFTA, and EUVFTA, to investigate the interactions with the WTO DSM.

2.2.1   EU FTAs and Their DSMs

Analysing the interactions between all FTA DSMs and the WTO DSM would result in a highly abstract study that would require neglecting the differences of each situation. Therefore, this study will limit its focus to the interactions between DSMs provided in the new generation EU FTAs, specifically the EUKFTA, CETA, EUJPEPA, EUSFTA, and EUVFTA, and the WTO DSM. This section will describe the evolution of EU Trade Policy in order to show the EU's undertaking to conclude a vast number of comprehensive FTAs, all containing DSMs.

The EU is 'the world's largest exporter and importer of goods and services taken together', and has the most ambitious trade agenda in the world.[44] The EU traditionally concluded FTAs mainly with neighbouring and developing countries until 2006, when an important shift in the EU trade agenda occurred with the communication by the European Commission of its strategy called 'Global Europe'.[45] This change was generated by the stalled negotiations within the WTO, when the EU, as well as other states, started looking for other means through which they could advance their more progressive trade agendas. The strategy marked the intention to start negotiations with new FTA parties based on their market potential, level of protection against EU export interests, and the potential partners' negotiations with EU competitors.[46] Moreover, not only did the EU Commission extend its bilateral trade agenda in 2006 to other parties than neighbouring ones, it also established that the future FTAs would be more comprehensive and ambitious.[47] Since then, the EU has repeatedly reaffirmed its intention to conclude more bilateral trade agreements.

In 2010, the European Commission published a new Communication—'Trade, Growth and World Affairs'. It confirmed that it would continue implementing the

---

[44]EU Commission, Trade for All: Towards a More Responsible Trade and Investment Policy, COM (2015) 497 final.

[45]Siles-Brügge (2013), p. 598.

[46]European Commission, Global Europe: Competing in the World. A Contribution to the EU's Growth and Jobs Strategy, COM(2006) 567 final 1, 9.

[47]Ibid. For a detailed description of the evolution of the EU trade agenda, *see* Melo Araujo (2016), pp. 13–49.

agenda set by the 'Global Europe' strategy from 2006.[48] If all the negotiations on the 2010 agenda had been concluded, EU FTAs would have covered about half of the EU's external trade.[49] The European Commission's strategy of 2015—'Trade for All', advanced a new bilateral agenda, the most ambitious in the world, referring to such FTAs as CETA, Transatlantic Trade and Investment Partnership (TTIP), EUJEPA, and the EU–MERCOSUR trade agreement.[50] According to this strategy, EU FTAs in force in 2015 covered more than a third of EU trade, and if all ongoing negotiations at that time had been successfully concluded they would have covered an impressive two-thirds of the trade.[51] Although TTIP negotiations ended without conclusion in 2016,[52] other main goals of the European Commission's agenda were accomplished and can be regarded as achievements. As of May 2021, CETA has already entered into force provisionally, the EUJEPA, EUSFTA, and EUVFTA are fully in force, and a political agreement was reached on an ambitious, balanced and comprehensive trade agreement between the EU and Mercosur states, while the negotiations on the EU–Australia and EU–New Zeeland FTAs continue.[53] All these FTAs go well beyond traditional tariff liberalisation. They are 'new generation EU FTAs', as their approach is comprehensive and they include commitments on liberalisation of trade in goods, services and investment, public procurement, subsidies, regulatory issues, competition, and sustainable development, and in the most recent agreements, such as the EUJEPA, commitments also on small- and medium-sized enterprises, information and telecommunication services, and e-commerce.[54]

Until 2000, with the exception of trade agreements relating to the European Economic Area (EEA), all other EU FTAs had only diplomatic DSMs that were based on consultations and negotiations.[55] Since 2000, the EU has included DSMs based on *ad hoc* arbitration, inspired by the WTO model, in *all* of its FTAs. The EU Commission has emphasised the importance of implementation and enforcement of norms, in order to fully benefit from the concluded FTAs.[56] Effective implementation of the EU's trade policy was the second of four specific strategic objectives of

---

[48] EU Commission, Trade, Growth and World Affairs: Trade Policy as a Core Component of The EU's 2020 Strategy, COM(2010) 612 final, 9.

[49] Ibid 10.

[50] EU Commission, Trade for All (2015), pp. 30–34.

[51] Ibid 9.

[52] EU Commission, Negotiations and Agreements <https://ec.europa.eu/trade/policy/in-focus/ttip/>.

[53] European Commission, Negotiations and Agreements <https://ec.europa.eu/trade/policy/countries-and-regions/negotiations-and-agreements/>.

[54] European Commission, Report from the Commission to the European Parliament, the Council, the European Economic and Social Committee and the Committee of the Regions on Implementation of Free Trade Agreements, Brussels, COM(2019) 455 final, 4.

[55] Bercero (2006), p. 389.

[56] Trade for All (2015), p. 15, para 2.2.1.

the European Commission for 2016–2020.[57] Implementation by way of enforcement of EU FTAs is carried out through DSMs contained therein. In the most recent trade policy review of 2021—'An Open, Sustainable, and Assertive Trade Policy',[58] responding to the developments and changes in international trading regime, the Commission establishes that 'increasing the EU's capacity to pursue its interests and enforce its rights, including autonomously where needed' is one of the three core objectives of the trade policy for the medium term.[59] Thus, after negotiating multiple deep trade agreements, the Commission stresses the importance of implementing and enforcing them in order for the EU to be able to reap the benefits stemming from them. Accordingly, enforcement through FTA DSMs is expected to be used more often by the EU as a trade policy tool.

This section showed how the EU pursues the most ambitious bilateral trade agenda in the world and how it currently focuses on implementation and enforcement of its rights under international trade agreements.

2.2.2   The EU Commitment to the Multilateral Trading Regime

The previous section described the ambitious trade agenda of the EU and EU's strive for ensuring better implementation and enforcement of its bilateral trade rights. Nevertheless, the EU is still committed to the multilateral trading regime created by the WTO. This section will argue that the EU's consistent confirmation of the support for the multilateral trading regime created by the WTO makes research on the interactions between the EU FTA DSMs and the WTO mechanism particularly interesting.

The commitment to multilateralism and observance of international law is, first of all, enshrined in the EU Treaties. According to Article 21(2)(h) of the Treaty on European Union (TEU),[60] the EU should 'promote an international system based on stronger multilateral cooperation and good global governance', while Article 3 (5) provides that the Union shall contribute 'to the strict observance and the development of international law'. Moreover, Article 216(2) of the Treaty on the Functioning of the European Union (TFEU)[61] provides that '[a]greements

---

[57] European Commission, DG Trade, Strategic Plan 2016-2020, p. 12 <https://ec.europa.eu/info/sites/info/files/trade_sp_2016_2020_revised_en.pdf>.

[58] Communication from the Commission, Trade Policy Review—An Open, Sustainable and Assertive Trade Policy, COM(2021) 66 final, 1.

[59] Ibid 10.

[60] European Union, Consolidated version of the Treaty on European Union, 13 December 2007, 2008/C 115/01.

[61] European Union, Consolidated version of the Treaty on the Functioning of the European Union, 13 December 2007, 2008/C 115/01.

concluded by the Union are binding upon the institutions of the Union and on its Member States'. Therefore, these provisions cover the WTO, as a multilateral organisation, and the international agreements that it encompasses.[62] Article II:2 of the Marrakesh Agreement establishing the WTO provides that Multilateral Trade Agreements are 'binding on all Members', and Article XVI:4 that '[e]ach Member shall ensure the conformity of its laws, regulations and administrative procedures with its obligations as provided in the annexed Agreements'. Thus, given that the EU is a Member of the WTO, according to the TEU and TFEU, it is committed to the WTO agreements that are multilateral.

The commitment to the multilateral trading regime enshrined in the EU constitutional treaties is also reflected in the EU trade strategies mentioned above.[63] Every time the European Commission has announced an ambitious trade agenda for the conclusion of an FTA, it has made sure to reaffirm its commitment to the WTO obligations.[64] In the context of the restrictive trade measures imposed by the US and the threat posed by them to the multilateral trading regime, Trade Commissioner Cecilia Malmström stated in her May 2018 speech that 'we still believe that the WTO is the fairest and best system for trade' and that 'we need to stand up for it'.[65] In her Political Guidelines for the European Commission 2019–2024, Ursula von der Leyen also stated that '[w]e will always look for multilateral solutions and I intend to lead the efforts on updating and reforming the World Trade Organization'.[66] Furthermore, even the most recent trade review based on an 'open strategic autonomy', emphasising the EU's ability to make its own choices and shape the world through its leadership, stresses that multilateralism is critical for the EU's interests and make the reform of the WTO a top priority.[67]

---

[62] 'The World Trade Organization (WTO) is a single institutional framework encompassing the GATT and all the agreements and legal instruments negotiated in the Uruguay Round: the General Agreement on Tariffs and Trade or GATT 1994 and other agreements covering trade in goods; the General Agreement on Trade in Services or GATS; the Agreement on Trade-Related Aspects of Intellectual Property Protection or TRIPs; the DSU; and the Trade Policy Review Mechanism (TPRM)' (WTO, 'Legal texts: Uruguay Round Final Act' <www.wto.org/english/docs_e/legal_e/ldc2_512.htm>).

[63] See *supra* (nn 46, 48, 50, 58).

[64] Global Europe (2006), p. 2 ('The WTO remains the most effective way of expanding and managing trade in a rules-based system, and a cornerstone of the multilateral system.'); Trade, Growth and World Affairs (2010), p. 9, para 3.1 ('Despite the slow progress, completing the Doha Round remains our top priority. The potential benefits are simply too important to ignore.'); Trade for All (2015), p. 25, para 5.1 ('The multilateral system must remain the cornerstone of EU trade policy. The WTO rulebook is the foundation of the world trading order').

[65] European Commission, Speech by the European Commissioner for Trade, Cecilia Malmström (Brussels, 28 May 2018) <http://trade.ec.europa.eu/doclib/docs/2018/may/tradoc_156894.pdf>.

[66] Candidate for President of the European Commission, Ursula von der Leyen, A Union that Strives for More. My Agenda for Europe, Political Guidelines for the Next European Commission 2019-2024 <https://ec.europa.eu/commission/sites/beta-political/files/political-guidelines-next-commission_en.pdf>.

[67] EU Commission, An Open, Sustainable and Assertive Trade Policy, pp. 4, 6, 11.

It is clear that the EU is consistent in expressing its intention to support the international multilateral trading regime and follow the multilateral trading rules while developing fruitful bilateral preferential trading relations in both its constitutional treaties and trade agendas; this position is reiterated in the speeches of European Commission officials. The fact that the EU is a champion of FTAs and a declared staunch supporter of multilateralism means that it needs to balance its two directions of trade policy. Accordingly, the EU needs to take all due care when concluding FTAs to ensure that it does not undermine its credibility as a multilateralist.[68] This makes the study of interactions between EU FTA DSMs and the WTO DSM particularly compelling because these interactions should ensure harmonious coexistence of FTAs and the WTO, so that the EU's multilateral approach is not contradicted.

2.2.3 The Choice in Favor of EUKFTA, CETA, EUJEPA, EUSFTA, and EUVFTA

The present book will specifically show how the DSMs contained in the EUKFTA, CETA, EUJEPA, EUSFTA, and EUVFTA interact with the WTO DSM. These FTAs were not chosen randomly, but for specific reasons. This section will justify the choice to study the DSMs of these particular FTAs to analyse the interactions between the FTA and the WTO DSMs.

First, these FTAs reflect the most recent and advanced trends in the EU Trade Policy, including those with respect to dispute settlement. As the chosen FTAs are new generation EU FTAs, they also have a wide scope of coverage, regulating not only trade in goods or services, but also many other areas that may also be enforceable. Second, these FTAs have significant commercial importance, and are, therefore, of special interest to their parties. EUKFTA is the first new generation FTA that the EU concluded and it was with Korea, the EU's eighth largest export destination for goods.[69] When concluded, CETA was regarded as the EU's 'most ambitious trade agreement'.[70] The EUJEPA is considered an 'ambitious, balanced and progressive'[71] trade agreement and 'the biggest ever negotiated by the EU' that covers almost one third of the world's GDP.[72] Without a region-to-region

---

[68] Weiss and Furculita (2020), p. 6.

[69] EU Commission, Countries and Regions. South Korea (Brussels, 23 April 2020) <https://ec.europa.eu/trade/policy/countries-and-regions/countries/south-korea/>.

[70] EU Commission, European Commission Proposes Signature and Conclusion of EU-Canada Trade Deal (Brussels, 5 July 2016) <https://ec.europa.eu/luxembourg/news/european-commission-proposes-signature-and-conclusion-eu-canada-trade-deal_fr>.

[71] EU Commission, Factsheet: A New EU Trade Agreement with Japan (Brussels, 6 July 2018) <http://trade.ec.europa.eu/doclib/docs/2017/july/tradoc_155684.pdf>.

[72] EU Commission, EU and Japan sign Economic Partnership Agreement (Tokyo, 17 July 2018) <http://trade.ec.europa.eu/doclib/press/index.cfm?id=1891>.

agreement, the EU has pursued bilateral agreements, such as the EUSFTA and EUVFTA, with members of the Association of Southeast Asian Nations (ASEAN), it being the EU's third largest trading partner outside Europe. Singapore and Vietnam are some of the EU's major partners from the ASEAN, with the former being the EU's largest trading partner in the Southeast Asian region and a hub for the whole Pacific region, and the latter being the EU's second largest trading partner in ASEAN.[73]

Therefore, all these FTAs are certainly of top priority to their parties, and they call for effective enforcement to ensure that the agreements live up to their expectations and for the parties to be able to take full advantage of the norms they have negotiated, including those on issues outside the coverage of the WTO. The EU is also negotiating other FTAs of a comparable calibre to the above new generation EU FTAs, such as the EU–Australia, EU–New Zeeland, and EU–MERCOSUR FTAs. However, with no final legal text at the moment of writing, it would be mere speculation to discuss the interactions between the DSMs contained in these FTAs and the WTO DSM. Thus, the DSMs within the EUKFTA, CETA, EUJEPA, EUSFTA, and EUVFTA deserve appropriate academic attention. Their practical importance increases the likelihood that these FTA DSMs would actually be used by their parties, in contrast to other FTA DSMs,[74] especially the older, less ambitious, and less comprehensive ones. At least one party (the EU) to these FTAs, or even both (in the case of the EUKFTA, CETA, and EUJEPA) are major users of the WTO DSM, with the EU, South Korea, Canada, and Japan being among the top ten active users.[75] These states often litigate their disputes in an international setting and have vast experience in this respect. Therefore, it can be expected that these states would not shy away from using the FTA dispute settlement provisions to enforce their bilateral rights enshrined in these ambitious agreements.

As argued in the previous section, the study of the interactions of the EU FTAs and the WTO DSMs is especially important given that the EU should minimise the tensions between its bilateral and multilateral agreements to prevent the undermining of its multilateral approach. This section further argued why, among all the EU FTAs, the choice was made specifically in favour of EUKFTA, CETA, EUJEPA, EUSFTA, and EUVFTA. The recency of the chosen EU FTAs and the high importance of these agreements and the DSMs contained therein in ensuring the enforcement of these agreements, as well as the likelihood that the DSMs analysed would be used in practice, lead to the conclusion that there is a high probability of

---

[73] EU Commission, Trade: EU-Singapore Agreement to Enter into Force on 21 November 2019 (Brussels, 11 November 2019) <https://trade.ec.europa.eu/doclib/press/index.cfm?id=2078& title=Trade-EU-Singapore-agreement-to-enter-into-force-on-21-November-2019>; EU Commission, Countries and Regions. Vietnam (Brussels, 7 May 2020) <https://ec.europa.eu/trade/policy/countries-and-regions/countries/vietnam/>.

[74] See *supra* (n 35).

[75] The EU is the second most active user of the WTO DSM, Canada is in third place, Japan in seventh, and Korea in eighth (for a list of disputes by WTO Members, *see* WTO, Disputes by Member <www.wto.org/english/tratop_e/dispu_e/dispu_by_country_e.htm>).

interactions between the DSMs of the EUKFTA, CETA, EUJEPA, EUSFTA, and EUVFTA and the WTO DSM. Consequently, this book researches the interactions between the DSMs of the EUKFTA, CETA, EUJEPA, EUSFTA, and EUVFTA (hereafter, 'the new generation EU FTAs') and the WTO mechanism.

2.3   General Description of the WTO and the New Generation EU FTA DSMs

As the interactions between the DSMs of the WTO and the new generation EU FTAs are at the centre of the present book, this section will introduce these mechanisms. It will first briefly describe the WTO mechanism, and then present the MPIA under which arbitration appeal proceedings may take place between some WTO Members. The section will conclude with a brief introduction to the new generation EU FTA DSMs.

2.3.1   Dispute Settlement Under the WTO DSU

Before facing criticism and being in a crisis that threatens its existence, the mechanism of settling disputes provided by the WTO DSU was thought to be performing well and seemed to be endorsed by the WTO Members that made and are still making extensive use of it.[76] This section will provide a brief overview of the current WTO procedures; more detailed descriptions of the WTO dispute settlement proceedings will follow in the course of the following parts.

The procedures under the WTO DSU are administered by the Dispute Settlement Body (DSB)—a political body composed of representatives of all the Members.[77] The WTO DSM aims to provide security and predictability to the multilateral trading system, preserve the rights and obligations of Members under WTO agreements, clarify the provisions of the agreements, and promptly settle disputes in a way that satisfies the Members.[78] The WTO procedures commence with mandatory consultations during which parties to the dispute attempt to resolve their dispute.[79] A mutually agreed solution ('MAS') by the parties is to be preferred during all stages.[80] If consultations fail, the complainant may request the establishment of a panel

---

[76] *See*, for example, Davey (2014), p. 687.

[77] According to Art IV:3, Marrakesh Agreement, '[t]he General Council shall convene as appropriate to discharge the responsibilities of the Dispute Settlement Body provided for in the Dispute Settlement Understanding'.

[78] DSU, Art 3.2, 3.3, 3.4.

[79] DSU, Art 4.

[80] DSU, Art 3.7.

normally composed of three panelists,[81] almost automatically established by the WTO Secretariat.[82] The alternative dispute resolution (ADR) means, such as good offices, conciliation and mediation, are available and can be voluntarily undertaken by the parties at any time with a view to settling their disputes and can also continue to be used during the panel proceedings.[83] Following the panel examination that involves written submissions and oral arguments, the panel shall issue the descriptive section of its draft report, receive the parties' comments, and issue an interim report containing the descriptive section and the findings and conclusions.[84] If the parties do not submit requests for review, the interim report is considered final, is circulated to the Members, and then adopted by the DSB, unless the DSB rejects the report by consensus or an appeal is filed against it.[85] The DSU provides the possibility of having an appeal stage during which three of the seven members of the standing AB conduct a review limited to issues of law covered in the panel report. The AB reports shall be adopted by the DSB, unless it decides by consensus not to adopt the reports.[86]

When the final panel (un-appealed) or AB reports establish that a measure is inconsistent with the WTO covered agreements, the respondent shall bring it into conformity promptly, or when that is not possible, within a reasonable period of time proposed by the respondent, agreed by both parties, or established by an arbitration panel.[87] If the Member in violation does not bring its measures into conformity (the presence or lack of conformity can be established through arbitration in case of disagreement between the parties) within a reasonable period of time, it can be required to enter into consultations to agree on compensation. If such agreement cannot be reached, the initial complainant may request temporary suspension of concessions or other obligations, subject to certain conditions, until the measure is brought into conformity.[88] Subject to mutual agreement of the parties, including on the procedures to be followed, expeditious arbitration can also be used as a means for dispute settlement under Article 25 of the DSU.

With the paralysis of the AB since December 2019, the way WTO proceedings take place may, however, change. While appealed panel reports risk being sent into limbo, some Members have decided to use appeal arbitration for the appellate stage.[89] This change in the context could potentially also change the way in which

---

[81] DSU, Arts 6, 8.

[82] The WTO Secretariat assists parties in composing panels (DSU, Art 8). It provides panels with legal and technical support, and once they are composed, assists WTO Members with dispute settlement, and conducts special training courses (DSU, Art 27).

[83] DSU, Art 5.

[84] DSU, Art 15.

[85] DSU, Arts 15, 16.

[86] DSU, Art 17.

[87] DSU, Art 21.

[88] DSU, Art 22.

[89] *See infra* Sects. 2.3.2 and 4.2.

the WTO mechanism does and could interact with new generation EU FTA DSMs, an aspect that will be considered in the following parts.

2.3.2   The Multi-Party Interim Appeal Arbitration Arrangement Pursuant to Article 25 of the DSU

In the wake of an inoperative AB, the EU together with other WTO Members jointly decided to establish the MPIA. The EU, Canada, and Singapore, states that are parties to the new generation EU FTAs, are also among the signatories to this arrangement that builds upon the bilateral interim appeal arbitration arrangements signed earlier between the EU and Canada[90] and EU and Norway.[91] As appeal arbitration proceedings under the MPIA may represent the change that could offer a satisfactory alternative within the WTO DSM to the regular WTO appeal proceedings, the MPIA will be introduced in this section.

According to Article 25.1 of the DSU, expeditious arbitration can be used as an alternative means of dispute settlement to 'facilitate the solution of certain disputes that concern issues that are clearly defined by both parties'. Such arbitration, as well as the procedures to be followed, are subject to the mutual agreement of the parties and 'shall be notified to all Members sufficiently in advance of the actual commencement of the arbitration process'.[92] Other Members may become parties to arbitration proceedings only upon the agreement of the disputing parties.[93] The arbitration award does not require adoption by consensus by the DSB, it only needs to be notified to the DSB, whereas the parties shall agree to abide by it.[94] The award can be implemented according to the rules applicable to any final panel or AB report, and is subject to the rules on compensation and suspension of concessions.[95] While it is outside the scope of this study to analyse the requirements of Article 25 of the DSU and the MPIA's compliance with them, this section will introduce the main characteristics of the arrangement.

Any WTO Member can join the MPIA at any time by notifying the DSB, and participating Members may decide to cease their participation also by notification.[96] The MPIA expressly provides that it has been established with the purpose of 'preserv[ing] the essential principles and features of the WTO dispute settlement

---

[90] WTO, Communication from Canada and the European Union, 'Interim Appeal Arbitration Pursuant to Article 25 of the DSU', JOB/DSB/1/Add.11, 25 July 2019.

[91] WTO, Communication from Norway and the European Union, 'Interim Appeal Arbitration Pursuant to Article 25 of the DSU', JOB/DSB/1/Add.11/Suppl.1, 21 October 2019.

[92] DSU, Art 25.2.

[93] DSU, Art 25.3.

[94] DSU, Art 25.3.

[95] DSU, Art 25.4.

[96] MPIA, paras 12, 14.

system which include its binding character and two levels of adjudication through an independent and impartial appellate review of panel reports'.[97] Thus, arbitration under Article 25 of the DSU will be used only for the appeal stage. It will apply to any future dispute between any two or more participating Members, including the compliance stage of such disputes.[98] To render the arrangement operational, participating Members undertake to enter into arbitration agreements when specific disputes arise.[99] Parties, notified of the anticipated date of circulation of the final panel report, are able to request, prior to circulation, the suspension of the panel proceedings with a view to initiating appeal arbitration.[100] The request by any party is to be deemed a joint request for suspension and before suspension takes effect, the final panel report is to be transmitted to the arbitrators upon the filling of a Notice of Appeal according to the Working Procedures for Appellate Review.[101] The MPIA also has a limited no-appeal pact (NAP), establishing that 'where the arbitration has not been initiated under these agreed procedures, the parties shall be deemed to have agreed not to appeal the panel report'.[102] Hence, whenever the parties to a dispute do not avail themselves of the appeal arbitration arrangements, it is deemed that the parties have decided not to appeal the report and it is adopted automatically by the DSB.

Under the MPIA, arbitration appeals should be heard by three appeal arbitrators selected from a pool of ten standing appeal arbitrators, according to the principle of rotation used to form a division of the AB.[103] The MPIA also has detailed rules on the composition of the pool of arbitrators. The Members shall endeavor to compose it by consensus within 3 months following the communication of the MPIA and, except for current or former AB Members,[104] following the preselection of candidates proposed by any participating Member.[105] The preselection process shall be carried out by the WTO Director General (DG), the DSB Chair and the Chairpersons of the Goods, Services, TRIPS, and General Councils in order to ensure that the arbitrators are 'persons of recognized authority, with demonstrated expertise in law, international trade and the subject matter of the covered agreements generally'.[106] The MPIA recognises the importance of consistency and coherence and, hence, establishes that according to the principle of collegiality, the 'arbitrators may discuss their decisions [...] with all of the other members of the pool of arbitrators, without prejudice to the exclusive responsibility and freedom of the arbitrators with respect

---

[97] MPIA, Preamble, recital 5.

[98] MPIA, para 9.

[99] MPIA, para 10; Annex 1, para 1.

[100] MPIA, Annex 1, paras 3, 4.

[101] MPIA, Annex 1, paras 4, 5.

[102] MPIA, Annex 1, para 6.

[103] MPIA, paras 4, 6; Annex 1, para 7.

[104] MPIA, Annex 2, fn 12.

[105] MPIA, Annex 2, paras 1, 3, 4.

[106] MPIA, para 4; Annex 2, para 3.

to such decisions and their quality'.[107] In addition, it stresses that the awards cannot add to or diminish the rights and obligations of the parties to the covered agreements, and that the appeals shall be limited to issues of law and legal interpretations developed by the panels, addressing only those issues necessary for the resolution of the disputes that have been raised by the parties or of a jurisdictional nature.[108]

The appeal arbitration procedures, unless the parties to a specific dispute mutually agree otherwise without prejudice to the principles of the MPIA,[109] are modelled to replicate the AB procedures as closely as possible.[110] Similar to the AB procedures, the MPIA allows participation of third parties that have notified the DSB of a substantial interest in the matter before the panel.[111] Like the AB, the appeal arbitrators should benefit from administrative and legal support. However, this support will not be provided by the AB Secretariat, but by a separate support structure whose availability is to be ensured by the WTO DG, responsible only to the appeal arbitrators.[112] Unlike the DSU, and clearly, addressing some of the US concerns, the MPIA requests that the arbitrators issue the award in 90 days, unless the parties agree to extend this period on a proposal from the arbitrators.[113] To ensure that the deadline is met, the arbitrators may streamline the proceedings by taking appropriate organisational measures, such as 'decisions on page limits, time limits and deadlines as well as on the length and number of hearings required'.[114] Furthermore, the arbitrators may propose substantive measures to the parties, 'such as an exclusion of claims based on the alleged lack of an objective assessment of the facts pursuant to Article 11 of the DSU'.[115] Finally, as in Article 25 of the DSU, the MPIA establishes that parties agree to abide by the arbitration award, which is final, only notified to the DSB, and to which Articles 21 and 22 of the DSU on compliance are applicable *mutatis mutandis*.[116] Parties shall resort to appeal arbitration only as long as the AB is not able to hear appeals, the arrangement itself underlying its interim nature.[117]

The description of the MPIA, as an alternative within the WTO framework to the regular appeal proceedings under the DSU, will be useful for examining how it could shape the interactions between the WTO and the new generation EU FTA DSMs in case of FTA parties that signed this arrangement.

---

[107] MPIA, para 5; Annex 1, para 8.

[108] MPIA, Preamble, recital 6; Annex 1, paras 9, 10.

[109] MPIA, para 11.

[110] MPIA, para 3; Annex 1, para 11.

[111] MPIA, Annex 1, para 16.

[112] MPIA, para 7.

[113] MPIA, paras 12, 14.

[114] MPIA, para 12.

[115] MPIA, para 13.

[116] MPIA, Annex 1, paras 15, 17.

[117] MPIA, paras 1, 2; Annex 1, para 2.

2.3.3 Dispute Settlement Under the New Generation EU FTAs

The new generation EU FTAs all dedicate a separate chapter to the settlement of disputes between parties concerning the interpretation and application of their provisions, except where it is expressly provided otherwise.[118] The process of dispute settlement in the new generation EU FTAs consists of several stages.

The process begins with consultations, a mandatory stage, during which the parties shall attempt to reach an MAS for their dispute.[119] If the consultations fail because of the reasons described in the agreements, the complainant is entitled to request the establishment of an arbitration panel.[120] The arbitration panels in the new generation EU FTAs are composed of three arbitrators. The agreements provide specific procedures for the process of selection of arbitrators.[121] The panels analyse the facts of the dispute and make determinations with respect to the compliance of the contested measures with the obligations undertaken in the agreements. The descriptive parts of facts and the law, as well as the findings and recommendations, are included in an interim report on which the parties can comment. After considering the comments, the panels may or may not review the interim reports and then issue the final reports.[122] This is followed by the compliance stage, during which the parties shall take any necessary measures to comply with the findings and recommendations of the panel immediately or within a reasonable period of time notified by the complainant, or in case of disagreement, established through arbitration.[123] If the responding party does not comply with the final report or the measures taken are still inconsistent and this was established by the arbitration panel, the original complainant is entitled to temporarily suspend obligations or to receive compensation.[124] The party complained against shall then take measures to comply with the report, as a result of which the suspension of obligations or compensation shall be terminated. If there is no agreement on whether the respondent is in conformity, the

---

[118]EUKFTA, Art 14.2; CETA, Art 29.2; EUJEPA, Art 21.2; EUSFTA, Art 14.2; EUVFTA, Art 15.2.

[119]EUKFTA, Art 14.3; CETA, Art 29.4; EUJEPA, Art 21.5; EUSFTA, Art 14.3; EUVFTA, Art 15.3.

[120]EUKFTA, Art 14.4; CETA, Art 29.6; EUJEPA, Art 21.7; EUSFTA, Art 14.4; EUVFTA, Art 15.5.

[121]EUKFTA, Art 14.5, 14.18; CETA, Art 29.7-29.8; EUJEPA, Art 21.8, 21.9; EUSFTA, Art 14.5, 14.20; EUVFTA, Art 15.7, 15.23.

[122]EUKFTA, Art 14.6, 14.17; CETA, Art 29.9, 29.10; EUJEPA, Art 21.18, 21.19; EUSFTA, Art 14.7, 14.8, 14.19; EUVFTA, Art 15.10, 15.11, 15.22.

[123]EUKFTA, Art 14.8, 14.9; CETA, Art 29.12, 29.13; EUJEPA, Art 21.20; EUSFTA, Art 14.9, 14.10; EUVFTA, Art 15.12, 15.13.

[124]EUKFTA, Art 14.10, 14.11; CETA, Art 29.14; EUJEPA, Art 21.21, 21.22; EUSFTA, Art 14.11, 14.12; EUVFTA, Art 15.14, 15.15.

arbitration panel will decide on this issue.[125] The parties, however, are encouraged to reach an MAS at any time (sometimes also subject to domestic approval), as a result of which the FTA dispute settlement procedures are terminated.[126] The new generation EU FTAs also provide for possibility to have recourse to mediation procedures at any time, even during panel proceedings, in order to reach an MAS with the assistance of the mediator.[127]

At first glance, the procedural stages of the new generation EU FTA DSMs analysed are very similar to those prescribed by the WTO DSU; however, there is no second, appeal stage. This section briefly introduced the new generation EU FTA DSMs. The differences and commonalities between these FTA DSMs, as well as their comparison with the WTO mechanism, including when the MPIA is used, and the importance for their interactions will be addressed in more detail later.[128]

References

Allee T, Elsig M (2015) Dispute settlement provisions in PTAs: new data and new concepts. In: Dür A, Elsig M (eds) Trade cooperation: the purpose, design and effects of preferential trade agreements. Cambridge University Press, Cambridge, pp 319–354

Bercero IG (2006) Dispute settlement in European Union free trade agreements: lessons learned. In: Bartels L, Ortino F (eds) Regional trade agreements and the WTO legal system. Oxford University Press, New York, pp 383–405

Chase C et al (2016) Mapping of dispute settlement mechanisms in regional trade agreements: innovative or variations on a theme? In: Acharya R (ed) Regional trade agreements and multilateral trading system. Cambridge University Press, New York, pp 608–702

Choi WM (2010) Defragmenting fragmented rules of origin of RTAs: a building block to global free trade. J Int Econ Law 13(1):111–138

Davey WJ (2014) The WTO and rules-based dispute settlement: historical evolution, operational success, and future challenges. J Int Econ Law 17:679–700

de Mestral ACM (2013) Dispute settlement under the WTO and RTAs: an uneasy relationship. J Int Econ Law 16:777–825

Dür A, Baccini L, Elsig M (2014) The design of international trade agreements: introducing a new dataset. Rev Int Organ 9(3):353–375

Forere MA (2015) The relationship of WTO law and regional trade agreements in dispute settlement. Kluwer Law International, Alphen aan den Rijn

Johnston AM, Trebilcock MJ (2013) Fragmentation in international trade law: insights from the global investment regime. World Trade Rev 12(4):621–652

---

[125] EUKFTA, Art 14.12; CETA, Art 29.14; EUJEPA, Art 21.23; EUSFTA, Art 14.13; EUVFTA, Art 15.16.

[126] EUKFTA, Art 14.13; CETA, Art 29.19; EUJEPA, Art 21.26; EUSFTA, Art 14.15; EUVFTA, Art 15.19.

[127] EUKFTA, Annex 14-A (only for non-tariff measures); CETA, Annex 29-C; EUJEPA, Art 21.6; Decision No 1/2019 of 10 April 2019 of the Joint Committee of the EU-Japan EPA [2019/1035], L 167/81 (Decision of the Joint Committee of the EUJEPA), Annex 2; EUSFTA, Chapter 15; EUVFTA, Annex 15-C; *See infra* 7.5 Likelihood of Reaching Mutually Agreed Solutions.

[128] *See infra* Chap. 6.

Lee YS (2011) Reconciling RTAs with the WTO multilateral trading system: case for a new sunset requirement on RTAs and development facilitation. J World Trade 45(3):629–651

McDougall R (2018) Regional trade agreement dispute settlement mechanisms: modes, challenges and options for effective dispute resolution. ICTSD RTA Exchange, Issue Paper, pp 1–15

Melo Araujo BA (2016) The EU deep trade agenda: law and policy. Oxford University Press, New York, pp 13–49

Payosova T, Hufbauer GC, Schott JJ (2018) The dispute settlement crisis in the World Trade Organization: causes and cures. Peterson Institute for International Economics Policy Brief 18-5, pp 1–14

Porges A (2011) Dispute settlement. In: Chauffour JP, Maur JC (eds) Preferential trade agreement policies for development: a handbook. The World Bank, Washington, pp 467–501

Porges A (2018) Designing common but differentiated rules for regional trade disputes. ICTSD RTA Exchange, Issue Paper, pp 1–11

Shlomo Agon S (2019) International adjudication on trial. The effectiveness of the WTO dispute settlement system. Oxford University Press, New York

Siles-Brügge G (2013) The power of economic ideas: a constructivist political economy of EU trade policy. J Contemp Eur Res 9(4):597–617

Weiss W, Furculita C (2020) Introduction: EU trade policy facing unprecedented challenges. In: Weiss W, Furculita C (eds) Global politics and EU trade policy: facing the challenges to a multilateral approach. Springer, Heidelberg, pp 1–13

WTO (2011) World Trade Report 2011: the WTO and preferential trade agreements: from co-existence to coherence, Geneva

Chapter 3
Conceptual Framework

3.1 Fragmentation and Other Concepts

This section will introduce the concept of fragmentation, its causes, and the debate around it. It will then explain how the concept of fragmentation is understood for the purpose of the present book and the underlying assumptions that are made will be acknowledged. Finally, the concepts of 'forum shopping' and 'limited coherence' will be presented.

3.1.1 'Fragmentation' and Its Causes

The 'so-called' phenomenon of fragmentation is a phenomenon that has its roots in the increase in diversity of international law, both in substance and in procedure.[1] During the last decades, the number of multilateral regulations on the international arena has multiplied.[2] After the Second World War, states signed multiple specialised treaties and, as a result, created many legal regimes regulating different international relationships. These regimes were specialised to reflect the different areas of interest of the states in international relationships.[3] The international sphere came to be covered by specialised regimes dealing with issues such as international trade, human rights, and environmental concerns. The regionalisation trend also

---

[1] Pauwelyn (2008), para 1.

[2] International Law Commission (ILC) Study Group on the Fragmentation of International Law, 'Fragmentation of International Law: Difficulties Arising from the Diversification and Expansion of International Law', Report of the Study Group of the International Law Commission (ILC Report), Finalized by Martti Koskenniemi, A/CN.4/L.682 and add 1 and corr 1 (International Law Commission, 13 April 2006) 10, para 7.

[3] Delimatsis (2011), p. 88.

C. Furculiță, *The WTO and the New Generation EU FTA Dispute Settlement Mechanisms*, EYIEL Monographs - Studies in European and International Economic Law 19, https://doi.org/10.1007/978-3-030-83118-9_3

contributed to the multiplication of regimes.[4] Regional regimes are aimed at the promotion of common objectives in different issue areas shared by several states from a region or from different regions. Every regime created, with its own norms, institutions, and mechanisms of enforcement, was perceived as threatening public international law because it could cause overlaps, conflicts, and inconsistencies.[5]

Certain causes of fragmentation stem from the nature of international law and the way norms are created on the international arena. International law is essentially different from domestic law. Compared to domestic systems, there is no international legislator to adopt norms that would regulate international relationships. International norms are created by states that are also the subjects of the norms that they are creating. Pauwelyn concludes that the 'consent-based nature' of international law leads 'inevitably' to the creation of as many international regimes as there are problems faced by states in international law.[6] States adopt different treaties and create multiple regimes containing DSMs through their own will. It may be a form of reaction to globalisation and the increased demand for regulation of different issue areas of global importance, such as climate change or the migration crisis.[7] The ILC Study Group also determined that new regimes do not emerge by mistake, but because they correspond to the needs and concerns of the states that sign new treaties.[8] Thus, states as sovereign entities choose to create new regimes and to design mechanisms of enforcement that they consider to be necessary. Although a state is a single entity, different departments negotiate different treaties.[9] Thus, the same state may adopt treaties that address the same or a similar issue differently. In addition, there may be political considerations behind the choice of states to create multiple regimes, such as the impossibility of reaching political consensus on treaties covering several issue areas or the deliberate decision to create alternative regimes that would better suit the interests of the states depending on the situation, including offering better mechanisms of enforcement.[10]

This section introduced the concept of fragmentation and detailed the causes behind it. Both the concept and causes will help in the further analysis of fragmentation and in adopting a particular approach towards it.

---

[4] de Chazournes (2017), p. 30.

[5] ILC Report (n 2) 11, para 8.

[6] Pauwelyn (2004), p. 903.

[7] Zürn and Faude (2013), p. 126; Peters (2017), p. 674.

[8] ILC Report (n 2) 14–15, paras 15–16.

[9] Ibid.

[10] For a description of political causes, *see* Peters (2017), pp. 674–675.

3.1.2 The Debate on Fragmentation

Among international practitioners and scholars, the new developments have brought fears of multiple regimes that would challenge and threaten existing principles and institutions by reversing 'established legal hierarchies in favor of the structural bias in the relevant functional expertise'.[11] This section will introduce the debate on fragmentation by listing arguments brought both in favour and against it.

Concerns about the negative effects of fragmentation were voiced by the International Court of Justice (ICJ) Presidents in their speeches to the United Nations General Assembly more than two decades ago. In 1999, President Schwebel praised the development of new international tribunals and, at the same time, warned about the threat of possible conflicts between them and the 'evisceration of the docket of the International Court of Justice'.[12] If President Schwebel's speech was more 'moderate' in his statement that certain precautions were necessary when designing new courts, his successor, Judge Guillaume, talked about serious uncertainty, distortions, and conflicting judgments that can be caused by forum shopping.[13] In the wake of discussions on fragmentation, in 2000, the ILC created a 'Study Group' that focused on substantive fragmentation.[14] The work of the study group resulted in the consolidated report on 'The Fragmentation of International Law',[15] and in the 'Conclusions of the Work of the Study Group on the Fragmentation of International Law'.[16]

Initially, fragmentation was perceived mostly as a negative phenomenon that needed to be eliminated. It was argued that having different sets of rules governing the same or similar situations could lead to conflicts between norms and different international courts and tribunals dealing with the same or similar questions, thereby generating conflicts between the jurisdictions of international courts. Each enforcement mechanism may consider itself committed to its own standards because it may have to apply only its own substantive law to disputes.[17] This in turn may pose the risk of divergent solutions being provided for the same dispute. Disparate solutions may jeopardise the unity and coherence of public international law and affect the

---

[11] Koskenniemi (2007), p. 4.

[12] Koskenniemi and Leino (2002), pp. 553–554; Lindroos (2005), p. 31.

[13] H.E. Judge Gilbert Guillaume, President of the International Court of Justice, 'Speech to the General Assembly of the United Nations', 30 October 2001 <www.icj-cij.org/files/press-releases/3/2993.pdf>.

[14] Young (2012a), p. 3.

[15] ILC Report (n 2).

[16] ILC Study Group on the Fragmentation of International Law, 'Fragmentation of International Law: Difficulties arising from the Diversification and Expansion of International Law', Conclusions of the Work of the Study Group (ILC Conclusions), A/CN.4/L.702 (International Law Commission, 18 July 2006).

[17] Hafner (2004), p. 857.

credibility and authority of the adjudicative bodies resolving these disputes.[18] In this context, authority is to be understood as 'the power to take binding decisions or to prescribe binding rules'.[19] Conflicting binding rulings leave a dispute unresolved, since there is no clear solution for it. Accordingly, the states would face the difficulty of deciding which ruling to comply with and which one to disregard, thereby undermining the authority of the international courts or tribunals issuing such rulings. Furthermore, even without a conflict of jurisdictions, the presence of multiple adjudicating bodies that can rule on equal or similar norms could lead to incoherent interpretations of those norms. Therefore, a potential consequence of fragmentation is the lack of legal certainty and predictability.[20] It may not be clear which rule is applicable for resolving the dispute, which ruling to follow in the case of two different ones, or which interpretation to expect for equal or similar norms in the context of dispute settlement. The legitimate expectations of the states may also be affected, since the adjudicative bodies issuing conflicting rulings would not deliver what is expected by the states.

It was even feared that fragmentation would put under question the entire existence of international law. The concept of a legal system is associated with order, harmony, and coherence, and their loss may mean that international law is merely a set of rules and not a system of law.[21] Besides the concerns related to the dangers it poses to international law and international dispute settlement mechanisms, fragmentation has also been criticised for favouring stronger states. Benvenisti and Down have argued that fragmented international law provides more powerful states the opportunity to abandon institutions that are not advantageous to them and seek other venues. At the same time, it may be harder for weaker states to form coalitions on different issues within the different regimes created by diverse treaties to be able to effectively bargain with stronger states.[22]

As Anne Peters states, 'the heydays of the academic fragmentation debate were the first decade of the millennium'.[23] Over time, fragmentation became no longer perceived as an existential threat to international law.[24] Fragmentation has been normalised, and a consistent amount of recent literature finds positive aspects, in addition to the negative, in the diversity in international law. Competition between legal regimes has been identified as one of the positive effects of fragmentation that

---

[18] Ibid, p. 858.

[19] Wolfrum (2008), p. 6. Authority may be *narrow* if only parties to a particular dispute comply with an adjudicating body's decision; *intermediate* if other similarly situated actors and future litigants, such as the WTO Membership, comply; or *extensive* when the audience represents a larger group of actors, beyond the compliance partners, such as other international courts, civil society, industry, or legal academics (Alter et al. 2016, pp. 9–11).

[20] Peters (2017), p. 679.

[21] Ibid.

[22] Benvenisti and Downs (2007), p. 597.

[23] Peters (2017), p. 674.

[24] Broude (2013), p. 2.

may lead to better norms,[25] with these regimes becoming 'laboratories and boosters for further progressive development'.[26] Accordingly, when designing new regimes or updating the existing ones, states can use the lessons that they have learnt from other regimes. More specialised norms can respond better to the specific needs of the states and modern complexities.[27] For example, an FTA can provide more specialised norms that would respond better to the parties' needs compared to the WTO. Competition can help to improve not only the legal norms, but also the decisions made by competing institutions. It has been suggested that tribunals would probably be more careful in making decisions, and would issue decisions that would ensure that states choose it over others.[28] Moreover, the proliferation of international dispute settlement fora could be celebrated instead of feared by public international lawyers, since the more mechanisms there are, the more accepted they are, and international law can be perceived as a true system of law.[29] The increased number of DSMs is also said to contribute to greater accountability, since states have more venues to enforce their rights and to challenge the practices that they think are violating international rules.[30] Another invoked positive aspect of fragmentation is that it may increase the transparency of the system. Competition may incentivise international DSMs to become more transparent because of their desire to be followed and their need to prove trustworthiness.[31]

To conclude, fragmentation has been much debated in the last decades. It was at first perceived as a negative phenomenon and an existential threat to international law, but gradually became more accepted, treated with less fear, and even praised for some of its aspects.

3.1.3 The Meaning of the Term 'Fragmentation'

This section will explain the exact meaning of the term 'fragmentation', as used in this book, and why it was chosen, since the term itself has sparked debate. The term 'fragmentation' seems to be perceived as having a negative connotation, as opposed to other terms used to describe the same phenomenon, such as 'diversity' or 'pluralism'.[32] However, the term 'fragmentation' will be used as a value-free one,

---

[25]Pauwelyn (2004), p. 904; Biermann et al. (2009), p. 27.

[26]Simma (2009), p. 276.

[27]Hafner (2004), p. 859.

[28]Worster (2008), pp. 140–146.

[29]Charney (1996), p. 74.

[30]Peters (2017), p. 681.

[31]Worster (2008), p. 144.

[32]van Asselt (2014), p. 31.

as advanced by the international relations scholar Harro van Asselt in his book[33] and in the article he co-authored with Fariborz Zelli.[34]

Van Asselt begins by looking into the ordinary meaning of the term 'fragmentation' as defined by Oxford Dictionaries: 'the process or state of breaking or being broken into fragments'.[35] This definition includes the assumption that there was once a 'whole' or 'unity'.[36] This in turn leads to the question of whether there should be unity in international law. The notion of 'whole' can be interpreted differently. 'Under a more neutral interpretation, however, "the whole" could also simply be seen as the sum of its (fragmented) parts, irrespective of whether that is an ideal situation.'[37] Thus, the whole does not necessarily describe a perfect order that was or should be.

Notions like 'fragmentation' and 'unity' could, indeed, be used to promote a certain rhetoric and agenda, especially if promoted by general international lawyers afraid of their practice area losing relevance.[38] However, notions like 'plurality' or 'diversity' have a positive subtext that would make them also suitable for advancing a particular perspective on the state of international law. Therefore, both types of terms could potentially be used to support a certain position. However, a choice is still to be made between one or the other. This book uses the term 'fragmentation' because it is a 'longstanding and widespread concept used across disciplines by both scholars and practitioners'.[39] In this author's opinion, this notion, without attaching any value to it, still describes well the existing situation of international law that consists of different fragments. Although using this term presupposes the existence in the past or the future of a 'whole', in the context of international law, 'this whole does not need to be some form of absolute unity, comparable to domestic legal systems'.[40] Accordingly, a merely descriptive, value-free notion of 'fragmentation' is adopted, meaning that it is not perceived as a positive or negative phenomenon, but rather as a neutral one describing the normal state of international law that resulted from the causes described above.[41]

This section explained why a value-free, merely descriptive notion of fragmentation is adopted and what this means. Since, the concept of fragmentation is linked to certain underlying assumptions, the next section will acknowledge and explain them.

---

[33] Ibid, pp. 31–35.

[34] Zelli and van Asselt (2013), pp. 1–13.

[35] van Asselt (2014), citing Oxford Dictionaries.

[36] Ibid, p. 32.

[37] Ibid, p. 33.

[38] Koskenniemi and Leino (2002), pp. 576–577.

[39] Zelli and van Asselt (2013), p. 3.

[40] Ibid, p. 34.

[41] *See supra* Sect. 3.1.1.

3.1.4 Assumptions Underlying 'Fragmentation'

As stated in the previous section, the term 'fragmentation' implies the existence of a 'whole'; therefore, the question arises whether international law is a system. This book subscribes to the position that international law *is* a system, a conclusion also reached by the ILC Report.[42]

At first sight, this may seem at odds with the fact that the term 'fragmentation' is not ascribed to a negative connotation, which was used to protect the existence of the international law as a system.[43] However, for international law to be considered a system of law, perfect unity is not required. Instead, fragmentation is just a characteristic of the international legal system that describes its actual state. Therefore, this assumption is in harmony with the value-free notion of fragmentation under which absolute unity and order are not required for international law to be considered a 'whole'. International law as a legal system does not have the same characteristics as domestic legal systems because its nature is inherently different.[44] 'Even a limited degree of coherence, in some systematic features might suffice to transform an assortment of legal elements into a system, albeit of a loose nature.'[45] Thus, the lack of absolute unity does not preclude international law being considered a system, although a sui generis one. 'A new type of international legal system is emerging – one that is neither fully fragmented nor completely unitary.'[46]

International law is considered a legal system because all the regimes are still linked and governed by general international law, unless they expressly depart from it. Therefore, international law is not merely a collection of completely unrelated norms. These norms form a whole, while the glue holding them together is general international law. This book adopts the conclusion reached by the ILC Report that no regime is a 'closed legal circuit',[47] an approach that is generally supported by legal doctrine.[48] Thus, it considers that general international law applies to relationships regulated by different international regimes, as long as 'no special derogation is provided or can be inferred from the instrument(s) constituting the regime'.[49] 'Legal subsystems coexisting in isolation from the remaining bulk of international law are inconceivable.'[50] Therefore, the term 'self-contained regime' will not be used, since it has been also associated with arguments in favour of completely detached

---

[42] ILC Conclusions (n 16), 2(a) General (1).

[43] See *supra* (n 21).

[44] See *supra* Sect. 3.1.1.

[45] Shany (2004), p. 94.

[46] Burke-White (2005), p. 977.

[47] ILC Report (n 2) 81, para 152(3).

[48] For example, Bartels (2001), p. 499; Pauwelyn (2003), pp. 25–40; Simma and Pulkowski (2006), p. 492; Matz-Lück (2012), p. 207.

[49] ILC Report (n 2) 81, para 152(3).

[50] Simma and Pulkowski (2006), p. 492.

subsystems from general international law.[51] Instead, the unqualified term 'regime' will be used.

'Regime' is an interdisciplinary concept and has been extensively dealt with by both legal and international relations doctrines. However, there is no consensus on the exact definition of this term,[52] as it can be defined in various ways. In this book, the term 'regime' is used to reflect both a generic and a more specific understanding. In the generic approach, 'regime' means a collection of norms related to a specific functional subject area, such as the law of the sea, international trade law, and human rights law.[53] When defined in a more specific manner, 'regime' is understood as, 'in addition to a catalogue of norms of behavior, a structured and institutionalized process of communication in which norms are molded and collective decisions made'.[54] Therefore, this narrower definition covers both regional and global regimes addressing the same issue areas, such as the WTO and FTA regimes. Accordingly, for the purpose of the present book, the notion of 'regime' is used generally in relation to the collection of all international trade norms, as well as specifically with respect to the WTO and FTAs that offer a structured and institutionalised process of communication and decision-making, in addition to a collection of norms.

This section addressed the underlying assumptions of the term 'fragmentation'. It explained the position adopted in this book with respect to these assumptions which will help in further explaining other relevant concepts.

3.1.5 Forum Shopping

Another concept closely linked to the way fragmentation is perceived is 'forum shopping'. Forum shopping, like fragmentation, is usually used with a negative connotation. This section will deal with the concept of 'forum shopping'. It will explain why forum shopping is considered, in and of itself, a reasonable consequence of fragmentation without necessarily having a negative connotation and asks what type of forum shopping should, nevertheless, be condemned.

Forum shopping is usually portrayed as a negative phenomenon in which more powerful states engage, being involved in creating different fora and choosing the most convenient ones for advancing their claims in each case.[55] However, weaker

---

[51] Ibid.

[52] Kim (2016), p. 14.

[53] ILC Conclusions (n 16) (c) Special ("self-contained") Regimes (12). The ILC Conclusions distinguish between three types of special regimes—the third type comprises 'all the rules and principles that regulate a certain problem area [...] collected together so as to express a "special regime"'; for criticism of this approach, *see* Crawford and Nevill (2012), pp. 258–259; Kim (2016), p. 15.

[54] Gehring and Oberthür (2004), p. 248.

[55] Biermann et al. (2009), p. 30; Zürn and Faude (2013), p. 120.

states could also use forum shopping as a strategy to promote their own agenda.[56] The choice is available to all states, as it stems from their sovereignty, unless they have restricted themselves from this choice by agreement. Therefore, forum shopping could serve the interests of all the states. This book adopts the position that forum shopping, in and of itself, should not be considered a negative phenomenon. Having multiple fora in different regimes is necessary to ensure that special multilateral and regional norms are enforced and that states can benefit from them. Moreover, competition between international tribunals and courts may also result in positive outcomes, such as learning lessons from each other which leads to improved proceedings, increased transparency, and better-drafted judgements.[57] Regarding forum shopping as a negative phenomenon would contradict a value-free, merely descriptive notion of 'fragmentation'. Forum shopping is just another inherent development that comes from the need for expansion of international law to respond to the specific needs of states. 'If forum shopping is considered a problem, then the solution would be to prohibit states from creating any new tribunals, perhaps even ones on a bilateral or regional basis.'[58] Consequently, for the purpose of this book, 'forum shopping' is considered a reasonable consequence of fragmentation that allows benefits to be reaped by offering the possibility of enforcing multiple norms from existing regimes. The definition given by Franco Ferrari, developed in the context of international commercial arbitration, will be borrowed. Thus, forum shopping is defined as 'the choice in favour of a given forum, based on the conviction that the chosen forum is the most favourable one for the purpose of reaching a given result'.[59]

If forum shopping, by its very nature, is a reasonable consequence of fragmentation and has no negative connotation per se in this book, it is 'improper' forum shopping that is considered to be a matter of concern. 'Improper' forum shopping should be understood as commencing sequential or overlapping proceedings before international tribunals on the same dispute, especially when both fora have asserted their jurisdiction over them, and parties have agreed in their treaties that this should be avoided, this creating the risk of conflicting jurisdictions and conflicting rulings. Commencing subsequent proceedings is not to be considered 'improper' forum shopping if the first DSM declined its jurisdiction and never ruled on the case or suspended its proceedings. In these cases, forum shopping is not problematic, as there is no risk of conflicting rulings.

Accordingly, choosing a more appropriate forum from those available on the international arena, in and of itself, is perceived as a reasonable consequence that flows from the value-free concept of fragmentation. Still, engaging in improper forum shopping by bringing the same dispute to multiple fora, which may cause conflicting outcomes, is regarded as a negative phenomenon, and should be

---

[56] Peters (2017), p. 681.

[57] *See supra* Sect. 3.1.2; Shany (2004), p. 144.

[58] Worster (2008), pp. 140–141.

[59] Ferrari (2013), p. 16.

addressed by considering the concept of limited coherence described in the next section.

3.1.6   Limited Coherence in a Fragmented International Legal System

Although the term 'fragmentation' is considered value-free, it does not mean that fragmentation is considered as having no consequences. Rather, it is considered that it can have both positive and negative consequences for the system of public international law. Fragmentation in itself is neither bad nor good; it is an inherent characteristic of international law that has to be treated as such. Hence, whether fragmentation would have overall positive or negative consequences depends mostly on which one is heightened. This section will explain why the concept of 'limited coherence' is necessary in an inherently diverse international legal system.

The increasing number of regimes and institutions should not be restricted and, as argued, these regimes need enforcement mechanisms for different norms, which is why forum shopping is only a reasonable consequence stemming from the inherently fragmented international law. Nonetheless, the interactions between regimes and their DSMs can take place in a more coherent way, so that the negative consequences of fragmentation are diminished, while making it possible to benefit from the positive ones. Specialisation and regionalisation are not antagonist to uniformity.[60] Thus, it is not fragmentation per se, 'but rather the coordination (or lack of it) of fragmented or differentiated institutions that becomes the most important issue'.[61]

As argued by those who are against fragmentation, lack of coherence can lead to the loss of predictability and certainty in public international law.[62] Therefore, in a fragmented international law system, coherence should be sought to ensure that states know what to expect and have a better understanding of their rights.[63] In addition, coherence encourages respect for international law in general, not only for some rules that are advantageous for some states.[64] Were the same or similar disputes to be treated differently, it would also raise questions about the fairness of the international law system.[65] Different regimes disregarding each other and general international law may lead to a perceived 'win' for the prevailing regime. However, this represents a 'loss' for public international law as a system in general, since it gives the signal to states that international rules can be ignored. If states use multiple international regimes to avoid existing rules, instead of creating new rules

---

[60] Matz-Lück (2012), p. 207.

[61] Zürn and Faude (2013), p. 120.

[62] See *supra* (n 20).

[63] van Asselt (2007), p. 3; Kim (2016), p. 47; de Chazournes (2017), p. 36.

[64] De Chazournes (2017), p. 35.

[65] Webb (2013), p. 6.

that advance progress, this may undermine their credibility as trustworthy international partners.[66] The authority of institutions could also suffer, as the norms of their regimes might not be enforced, for example, because of conflicting rulings. Being part of the international law system, international courts derive their legitimacy from it,[67] and if the entire system suffers from incoherence and instability, this also reflects on international courts. The legitimacy of international adjudicative bodies is understood as the justification of their authority to rule.[68] Therefore, international courts have an impulse for cooperation also for the sake of their legitimacy.

The importance of consistency and coherence in international law is not merely a theoretical question, it was also acknowledged recently in the context of ISDS reforms:[69]

> Consistency and coherence would support the rule of law, enhance confidence in the stability of the investment environment and further bring legitimacy to the regime. It was also said that inconsistency and lack of coherence, on the other hand, could negatively affect the reliability, effectiveness and predictability of the ISDS regime and its credibility.[70]

Although this book argues in favour of coherence in a fragmented international law system, it does not view coherence as the ultimate goal. Achieving total uniformity in the international legal system is unrealistic.[71] There are certain conditions under which coherence *can* and *should* be limited. In an unjust legal system, there is no added value by coherence; rather, reform and change should be sought.[72] Thus, coherence should be pursued where there are similar issues in fact and in law; however, this should not be an impediment to deviating from coherence when necessary. These deviations should be accompanied by caution and also an explanation why a departure was necessary.[73] In the context of UNCITRAL discussions on ISDS reform, it was also noted that consistency and coherence are not objectives

---

[66] Oberthür (2016), p. 95.

[67] De Chazournes (2017), p. 35.

[68] Wolfrum (2008), p. 6. Legitimacy should be distinguished from the concept of authority. '[A] court can do everything normative theorists might expect of a legitimate international judicial body and still not have authority in fact. The converse scenario—authority in fact, without normative legitimacy—is also possible.' (Alter et al. 2016, p. 7). For more on the concept of 'legitimacy', *see infra* Sect. 7.6.

[69] United Nations Commission on International Trade Law (UNCITRAL), Working Group III (Investor-State Dispute Settlement Reform) 'Possible Reform of Investor-State Dispute Settlement (ISDS): Consistency and Related Matters: Note by the Secretariat' (Vienna, 29 October–2 November 2018), A/CN.9/WG.III/WP.150, para 5.

[70] UNCITRAL, 'Report of Working Group III (Investor-State Dispute Settlement Reform) on the work of its thirty-fourth session' (Vienna, 27 November–1 December 2017) Part II, A/CN.9/WG.III/WP.150, para 11.

[71] Webb (2013), p. 5.

[72] ILC Report (n 2) 248, para 491.

[73] De Chazournes (2017) pp. 36 and 44.

in themselves,[74] and that they should not be achieved to the detriment of correctness, only unjustified inconsistencies being a matter of concern.[75] Coherence is limited by the sovereignty of states and existing legal framework. Its pursuit should be based on the legal framework created by states. Seeking coherence while ignoring the will of the states expressed in international legal norms would give rise to concerns about the legitimacy of the system.[76]

In conclusion, coherence should be sought to ensure that the 'good fruits' of fragmentation are reaped while the 'bad fruits' are discarded. Coherence should not be regarded as against diversity and multiplication of international regimes, but instead as contributing to positive co-existence of the regimes within the system of public international law. This section listed the benefits of coherence and the disadvantages of the lack of it. However, it also established that coherence should not be considered an absolute goal, and that there are certain limits within which it should be sought; therefore, the international legal system should strive towards limited coherence. The concept of limited coherence will serve as a standard of evaluation throughout the book.

3.2 Fragmentation of the International Trade Law Regime

While the general debate on fragmentation has already been introduced, the discussion on fragmentation in the international trade regime and how it will be tackled will be presented below.

3.2.1 Types of Fragmentation

This section will tackle the issue of different types of fragmentation that can be identified in international law. It will analyse different classifications and will specify the types of fragmentation the present book addresses. By establishing the types of fragmentation caused by proliferation of FTA DSMs within the international trade law regime, this section further defines the scope of the study.

The first types are the fragmentation of norms and the fragmentation of authority.[77] This typology is based on the differentiation between substance and procedure.

---

[74] UNCITRAL, 'Report of Working Group III (Investor-State Dispute Settlement Reform) on the work of its thirty-fourth session' (n 70) para 11.

[75] UNCITRAL, Working Group III (Investor-State Dispute Settlement Reform) 'Possible reform of investor-state dispute settlement (ISDS): Consistency and related matters: Note by the Secretariat' (n 69) para 7, 8. For more on the concept of unjustified inconsistencies, *see infra* Sect. 11.5.

[76] Young (2012b), p. 92.

[77] Lindroos (2005), p. 32; ILC Report (n 1) 13, para 13; Pauwelyn (2008), para 5; Broude (2008), pp. 176–179; Ajevski (2014), p. 88.

As stated previously, fragmentation of international law has been caused by the growing number of treaties and various regimes.[78] As a result, there is a myriad of international norms and, whenever a factual situation occurs, the question arises which substantive norm from the multitude is applicable to it and which one prevails in case there is a conflict between two or more norms—this representing fragmentation of norms.[79] In addition, there is also fragmentation of authority, or the so-called 'institutional fragmentation'. Almost every international regime has its own institutions for law making and enforcement. Therefore, the question arises which of the institutions is competent. This issue is especially acute when there are several international courts and tribunals and they are requested to rule on the same disputes, with the risk of conflicting jurisdictions and the potential emergence of conflicting rulings. The concept of jurisdiction can be used with different meanings,[80] a common feature being that it refers to the power to do something.[81] 'Jurisdiction' is understood as determining the claims or the class of claims that an international court or tribunal is entitled to rule on, also known as 'substantive', 'field', 'principal', or 'original' jurisdiction.[82] This book will deal with fragmentation of authority, since it studies the interactions between different DSMs that have proliferated within the international trade regime.

Joost Pauwelyn further classifies fragmentation of norms and fragmentation of authority, each into three corresponding categories.[83] The first category is functional fragmentation, which in the case of fragmentation of authority, refers to the situations when tribunals have overlapping jurisdictions, each based on its own specialised areas, such as international environmental and international trade law. Since both FTAs and the WTO mainly deal with international trade issues, this type of fragmentation will not be considered. The second category is regional fragmentation which refers to the interactions between norms or institutions of two different regional regimes, for example, the interactions between two different FTAs and their DSMs. The third category is fragmentation of the same issue area. This type of fragmentation occurs in the case of parallel norms or overlapping jurisdictions of the courts and tribunals of the same issue area, for example between the DSMs of FTAs and the WTO.[84] Accordingly, the focus of this book will be this third category, as it

---

[78] See *supra* (n 3, 4).

[79] Broude (2008), p. 176.

[80] For example, some authors refer to the concept of 'inherent powers', described in Sect. 9.3.4.1, as 'inherent jurisdiction' (Pauwelyn and Salles 2009, p. 99). Trachtman also uses the expression 'jurisdiction to apply law' referring to the question of applicability of law (Trachtman 2005, pp. 132–143). On applicable law within WTO proceedings, *see* Sect. 9.3.3.

[81] Salles (2014), p. 114.

[82] Pauwelyn and Salles (2009), p. 98; Salles (2014), p. 115 ('It is also often described through reference to the personal, the material, the temporal, and the territorial elements of jurisdiction (jurisdiction *ratione personae*, *ratione materiae*, *ratione temporis*, and *ratione loci*)'.).

[83] Pauwelyn (2008), paras 2–5.

[84] Ibid.

deals with the interactions between multilateral and regional DSMs in the same issue area and not with the relationship between multiple FTA DSMs.

The level of governance is another criterion used for classifying the types of fragmentation. Fragmentation occurring between the same levels of regulation is horizontal fragmentation; if the levels are different, then fragmentation is vertical.[85] Different scholars perceive these levels of regulation differently. Some view horizontal fragmentation as taking place within the public international law system, between different regimes, whether multilateral or regional, while vertical fragmentation is the one taking place between the international and the domestic or the soft-law levels.[86] Other scholars consider horizontal fragmentation as that appearing in the case of functional and regional fragmentation,[87] since they involve regimes that are at the same level, either of specialised areas or of regions, while vertical fragmentation as that taking place in the same area between multilateral and regional levels.[88] Therefore, vertical fragmentation can occur either between the international and domestic level, as well as between multilateral and regional levels within international law. This research will be limited to vertical fragmentation, understood as occurring between multilateral and regional levels. It will not devote attention to vertical fragmentation between international and domestic law.

To conclude, this section identified different types of fragmentation and established the types that will be further dealt with. It helped to precisely define the scope of the research. Thus, this book will consider the relationship between FTA and WTO DSMs which causes fragmentation of authority and vertical fragmentation within the same issue area between regional and multilateral levels.

3.2.2 Judicial Interactions: The Original Contribution

This section will explain the original contribution this book makes to the general discourse on fragmentation of the international trade regime, compared to the existing literature. Thus, it will provide justification for the relevance of the research conducted.

The relationship between the FTA and WTO DSMs is not a novel subject. It has been researched extensively by international trade law academics. However, the subject has been mostly treated only from the perspective of conflicts between

---

[85] Cottier et al. (2011), p. 4.

[86] Trachtman (2008), p. 206; Delimatsis (2011), p. 97; Cottier et al. (2011), p. 4; Jacobs (2012), p. 327.

[87] See (n 83).

[88] Pauwelyn (2008), para 4; Pellet (2012), pp. 83–84.

regional and multilateral DSMs.[89] Thus, the existing literature mainly investigates conflicting jurisdictions and attempts to identify international norms and principles that could solve these and prevent conflicting rulings, but overlooks other types of interactions. This book joins this discussion on the complicated relationship between FTA and WTO DSMs. It will also analyse conflicts considering the most recent case law, but will also supplement the discussion with new perspectives, including in light of the changing context of the international trade regime.

As argued previously,[90] the concept of fragmentation used is merely descriptive, without specific connotations, and it is considered that its overall effect can be mostly positive or negative depending on how it is dealt with. The book will have a comprehensive approach and will not limit its analysis only to conflicting interactions between the FTA and the WTO DSMs that can result in negative consequences. It will look at how coherence can be enhanced, while also reaping the benefits of multiple international DSMs. Putting too much emphasis on the negative consequences of fragmentation in international law and focusing only on the problems, at the expense of possible synergies and cooperation, has recently been criticised by international lawyers,[91] but mostly by a new strand of literature in international relations on the interactions between international regimes, especially environmental ones.[92] Different terms are used by different international relations researchers, such as 'interactions', 'inter-linkages', 'interplay', 'linkages', and 'overlap'; however, they all refer to 'connections between overlapping institutions or regimes',[93] and do not focus only on conflicts and negative consequences.

The present book strives to analyse the interactions between the FTA and WTO DSMs from a more complex perspective. Consequently, it enquires into how the DSMs of the WTO and the new generation EU FTAs interact, in general, and not only conflict. The term 'interaction' is adopted with the meaning developed by international relations scholars, referring broadly to the situation when one regime may influence another.[94] An interaction considered here is, however, not between entire regimes, but between DSMs belonging to regimes. Thus, it is understood as the influence one DSM can have on another DSM. The term interaction is, therefore, not limited to conflicting influences one DSM might wield on another, it concerns all kinds of interactions. Zang distinguishes between 'judicial interactions' and 'judicial dialogue'. The first, according to him, indicates 'the action initiated by the adjudicator referring, discussing and assessing the norms and judicial decisions from

---

[89]For example, Henckels (2008), pp. 571–599; Nguyen (2008), p. 136; Pauwelyn and Salles (2009); Hillman (2009), p. 208; Marceau and Wyatt (2010), pp. 67–95; de Mestral (2013), pp. 777–825; Mbengue (2016), pp. 207–248.

[90]See supra Sect. 3.1.3.

[91]De Chazournes (2017), pp. 34–35; Peters (2017), pp. 702–703.

[92]Gehring and Oberthür (2006), pp. 315–316; van Asselt (2007), pp. 2–3; Oberthür (2016), pp. 90–92.

[93]van Asselt (2014), p. 45.

[94]Oberthür and Gehring (2006), p. 4.

another jurisdiction' and usually takes the form of a monologue, while the latter 'refers to a communicative exchange in a responsive manner'.[95] As stated previously, a broad interpretation of 'interaction' is adopted; hence, it encompasses both monologues and dialogues between DSMs as a form of judicial communication, as well as other forms of interactions.

The present book brings additional value to the existing literature by focusing on the interactions between the DSMs of the WTO and, particularly, the new generation EU FTAs. While the new generation EU FTA DSMs reflect the most recent approach to bilateral dispute settlement adopted by the EU—a self-declared multilateralist with the most ambitious bilateral trade agenda in the world—they have not been subject to a thorough analysis to date. Furthermore, the interactions between the new generation EU FTA and the WTO DSMs are researched in the context of the most recent developments in the international trade regime, including the AB crisis and the alternative interim appeal arbitration mechanism in which some Member States participate.

Judicial interactions between the DSMs of FTAs and the WTO are considered to encompass all types of influences one mechanism exerts on another. This approach makes this research different from all the other existing studies that analyse the relationship between the DSMs of FTAs and the WTO. It explores these interactions from a complex perspective, analysing the entire picture without focusing only on disruptive effects or monologues or dialogues between DSMs. Furthermore, the originality of the research also derives from its focus on the interactions between the WTO and in particular—the new generation EU FTA DSMs in the context of the most recent events and changes.

3.2.3   The Critique of the Judicial Interactions Perspective

Analyzing regime interactions from the judicial perspective has been highly criticised by Jeffrey Dunoff, who suggests that international litigation is an atypical form of regime interaction, while international judges lack the necessary tools to solve the tensions that arise from regime overlaps.[96]

Regime interaction does not only take place at the dispute settlement stage, it also occurs during other stages, such as law making or implementation of existing obligations without dispute settlement.[97] Despite this critique and the acknowledgment of other types of regime interactions, this book still focuses on judicial interactions, because it considers that the prominent focus on adjudication was and is worth researching.

---

[95] Zang (2018), p. 433.
[96] Dunoff (2012), p. 137.
[97] Young (2012b), p. 92.

The judicial perspective deserves particular attention, especially since the fear of fragmentation emerged as a result of the rising number of regimes and, in particular, of the DSMs.[98] Moreover, most of the advantages of fragmentation stem from and positively affect the enforcement of norms from different regimes by different international adjudicating bodies.[99] Most of the fears and advantages of fragmentation are related to DSMs because equal norms can be enforced by distinct DSMs in a conflicting matter, and even the issue of conflicting norms becomes more evident when enforced by a jurisdictional body.[100] Furthermore, international adjudicating bodies become 'missionaries conveying the message of autonomy' of international regimes.[101] Therefore, one of the most compelling, difficult, and crucial form of regime interaction, even though maybe not the most common, as Dunoff asserts, is that between different DSMs. Consequently, the question of regime interaction is worth analysing from the judicial perspective.

Judicial actors may not have the necessary tools to solve regime overlaps, as Dunoff asserts—a statement researched in the context of the interactions between the WTO and the new generation EU FTA DSMs. Yet, judicial actors are still the ones expected to be aware of fragmentation and act as guardians of coherence (albeit, limited). Moreover, this book will analyse not only judicial interactions from the perspective of conflicts and the tools that international adjudicators may employ for solving them, but also how judicial interactions are and could be shaped by states, as the legislators.

This section addressed the critique of the judicial perspective on regime interactions. It acknowledged the existence of other forms of regime interactions and their importance. At the same time, it justified the judicial perspective adopted for researching the interactions between the WTO and the new generation EU FTA DSMs.

3.2.4   Types of Judicial Interactions Between the DSMs of the FTAs and the WTO

This section discusses the types of judicial interactions between the WTO and FTA DSMs that will serve as a basis for the structure of the book. The typology proposed is a 'response' to the criticism of a purely conflict-based perspective adopted in the literature on the interactions between international adjudicating bodies in general, and in the field of international trade law in specific.

---

[98] See *supra* (nn 12, 13, 17).

[99] See *supra* (nn 28–31).

[100] Broude (2008), pp. 178–179.

[101] Delimatsis (2011), p. 89.

There are manifold typologies of regime interactions, not only judicial interactions, developed by international relations scholars.[102] The typology developed by Oberthür and Gehring for environmental regime interactions, based on their outcomes, is of particular importance for this study.[103] According to Gehring and Oberthür, beneficial effects of interactions result in synergy and adverse effects in disruptions.[104] International legal academics also stress that judicial interactions actually take place more often as judicial communication than as conflicts.[105] Inspired by the typology developed in international relations scholarship pointing towards types of interactions other than the conflicting ones and taking into consideration the claim that there is cooperation between courts on the international arena, this book distinguishes between conflicting and cooperative judicial interactions.

According to the literature, a conflict of jurisdictions appears when the same dispute could be brought entirely or partly under two or more different DSMs.[106] However, for the purpose of the present book these are considered only a precondition for conflicts. An actual conflict between an FTA DSM and the WTO mechanism materialises when the two DSMs are actually triggered with respect to the same dispute (entirely or partly) before either of the fora issues a definite decision, or subsequently, when there is already a definite decision issued by one forum and a discontented disputing party brings the same dispute to the other. Therefore, the conflicting interactions between jurisdictions are directly linked to improper forum shopping. Moreover, the issue of conflicting jurisdictions may also come into play when only one DSM, multilateral or bilateral, is triggered, but the respondent invokes the jurisdiction of another adjudicating body as being the appropriate one.

The cooperative type of judicial interactions is designed to capture the potential synergies of the interactions between the DSMs of the WTO and FTAs. The adjective 'cooperative' is defined by Oxford Dictionaries as 'involving mutual assistance in working towards a common goal'.[107] Since FTA and WTO DSMs both share a common objective, the potential for cooperation is greater than in the instances when the institutions' objectives point in different directions.[108] Cooperation can take place in various forms, such as one-time information exchange or a more ambitious structural form that establishes ongoing interactions.[109] Moreover, although in its perfect form cooperation takes place as a 'mutual' assistance, attempts

---

[102] See, for example, Young (1996), pp. 2–6; Stokke (2001).

[103] Oberthür and Gehring (2006), p. 5.

[104] Gehring and Oberthür (2006), pp. 310–311 ('If the effects of a case of institutional interaction support the objectives of the target institution, they therefore create synergy between the two institutions involved. If they contradict the target's objective, they result in disruption and conflict.').

[105] de Chazournes (2017), p. 34.

[106] Marceau (2001), p. 1108; Kwak and Marceau (2006), p. 467; Graewert (2008), p. 290; Lanyi and Steinbach (2014), p. 375.

[107] Oxford Dictionaries <https://en.oxforddictionaries.com/definition/cooperative>.

[108] van Asselt (2007), p. 10.

[109] Stokke (2001), p. 12; van Asselt (2014), pp. 71–72.

at cooperation can also take place in a unilateral way.[110] One DSM could, for example, have regard to the jurisprudence of another, while the other DSM could disregard the jurisprudence of the first DSM. Therefore, an incipient form of cooperation would be established, that could become full cooperation if the other side also begins to collaborate.

The first two types of judicial interactions mentioned in this section were developed based on the existing international legal and international relations scholarship. This book proposes a third type of interactions, the competing but non-conflicting judicial interactions (hereafter, 'competing interactions'). Similar to conflicting interactions, the precondition for competing interactions is that the same dispute could be brought to multiple fora. Competing judicial interactions, however, describe the choice faced by the disputing parties to which of available fora a dispute can be brought. Thus, the parties will engage in forum shopping since it implies choosing the most favourable forum for adjudication. As previously argued, forum shopping per se is a logical consequence of the fragmented nature of international law, ensuring enforcement of both multilateral and regional norms. In general, forum shopping takes place within the context of competing interactions between DSMs. At the stage of commencing dispute settlement proceedings, from the perspective of disputing parties, the DSMs of the WTO and FTAs will be competing for jurisdiction over the dispute—a competition that will be 'won' by the chosen forum. Two DSMs can *genuinely compete* if parties perceive them as being viable alternatives to each other,[111] and there is an actual choice to be made, at least with respect to some disputes or categories of disputes ('partial alternatives'). The competition between DSMs is considered to be a judicial interaction because one DSM may influence the frequency of use of another. Moreover, as stated in the context of discussions on fragmentation, competition between DSMs can lead to positive outcomes and changes.[112] Thus, competition is not only about the choice in favor of a DSM, but also about the broader consequences of this type of interactions as well as about improving and learning during the process of competing.

The third type of judicial interactions is proposed to provide a complete typology of judicial interactions, as it addresses interactions that are overlooked by the first two types. Judicial competition takes place at the stage when a state considers adjudicating a dispute and it has two or more fora to which it can be brought. If a state faced with a choice initiates proceedings in parallel in all available fora, and after choosing a mechanism the complainant subsequently initiates proceedings on the same dispute in another forum, or the respondent invokes the jurisdiction of another DSM as being the appropriate one, the interaction between the DSMs of the WTO and the FTAs, besides being a merely competing one, also becomes a conflicting one. Moreover, after one DSM is chosen, cooperative judicial interactions are also possible. Therefore, there can be several types of judicial interactions

---

[110] van Asselt (2014), p. 71.

[111] In this respect, *see* also Shany (2004), p. 21.

[112] See *supra* (n 31).

in the process of adjudicating the same dispute simultaneously or at different stages, one type of interactions not being exclusive of others.

The conflicting and competing types of interactions are distinguished and treated separately because they are considered fundamentally different in nature, although in both cases, there are two DSMs exercising their jurisdiction over the same dispute. Even if competing interactions can become actual conflicts, the question is not how to deal with conflicts and which conflicting tools to apply in merely competing interactions. Instead, a competing interaction is shaped by the preferences of the states and is considered from their perspective. States choose one DSM over another based on their own considerations, without the direct involvement of a judicial body. While the way adjudicators might solve the dispute could influence the choice, it is still the states that decide to which forum to bring the dispute. By contrast, in case of conflicting interactions, the direct involvement of international adjudicators may be requested to establish the prevailing jurisdiction.

Based on this typology, the judicial interactions between the DSMs analysed will be approached as three distinct types in three different parts of the book. The first part will deal with competing interactions, since they occur usually before the other types, at the stage of choosing between DSMs, and the other two parts will address conflicting and cooperative judicial interactions.

3.2.5 The Issue of the 'Same Dispute'

As stated previously, the presence of the 'same dispute' is a necessary precondition for a conflict of jurisdictions to materialise and for competing interactions.[113] This section will, therefore, define the concept of 'same dispute'.

According to the literature, for the same dispute to exist, it should arise from the same factual situation between the same parties and should be based on the same or similar grounds.[114] Accordingly, disputes arising from the same factual situation as such do not necessarily lead to a conflict or competition of jurisdictions, as they may be different disputes related to distinct aspects of the same situation.[115] In a narrow interpretation associated with the conditions for application of the principles of *res judicata* and *lis alibi pendens*,[116] only provisions from the exact same agreement can qualify as 'the same legal grounds'. By contrast, according to a broad approach, obligations within two different treaties could also qualify as the same legal grounds.[117] For establishing whether two DSMs and their jurisdictions can conflict or compete, the broad approach is, clearly, the only one feasible, as conflicting and

[113] *See supra*, Sect. 3.2.4.

[114] Lanyi and Steinbach (2014), p. 377.

[115] Linton and Tiba (2009), p. 427.

[116] *See infra* Sect. 9.2.1.1.

[117] Lanyi and Steinbach (2014), p. 377.

competing jurisdictions always deal with claims having legal grounds from different treaties. Therefore, if the same factual situation between the same parties leads to the violation of identical or similar obligations from different treaties, the dispute may be considered the same.

Nonetheless, conflicts of jurisdictions may also materialise in some situations when claims concern at the same time WTO norms and FTA norms that are WTO-plus or WTO-minus and deal with the same issues. WTO-plus norms are those that 'come under the current mandate of the WTO, where the parties undertake bilateral commitments going beyond those they have accepted at the multilateral level',[118] while WTO-minus norms roll back WTO rights and allow measures between parties that would otherwise be illegal under the WTO.[119] Therefore, legal grounds do not necessarily need to be identical or similar; they can also be correlated, regulating the same issues in a somewhat different manner, as it happens in case of the WTO and WTO-plus or WTO-minus FTA norms. Marceau refers to overlaps of jurisdictions in cases in which an obligation included in an RTA is the same as or similar to that of a covered agreement; in a footnote she also mentions that 'there is an overlap even if the 'applicable law' between WTO and RTA are strictly speaking not the same: for example, WTO law on remedies is different from most RTA law on remedies.'[120]

Therefore, for a conflict of jurisdictions between the DSMs of the FTAs and the WTO to materialise and for these DSMs to compete, the concept of 'same dispute' will be defined by the following elements: the same factual situation; the same parties; and the same, similar, or corresponding WTO and FTA norms. Consequently, it will also cover claims related to WTO-plus and WTO-minus FTA norms, as they can, likewise, lead to jurisdictional conflicts and competition between the FTA DSMs and the WTO mechanism.

References

Ajevski M (2014) Fragmentation in international human rights law – beyond conflict of laws. Nordic J Hum Rights 32(2):87–98

Alter KJ, Helfer LR, Madsen MR (2016) How context shapes the authority of international courts. Law Contemp Probl 79(1):1–36

Bartels L (2001) Applicable law in WTO dispute settlement proceedings. J World Trade 35:499–519

Benvenisti E, Downs GW (2007) The empire's new clothes: political economy and the fragmentation of international law. Stanf Law Rev 60(2):595–631

Biermann F, Pattberg P, van Asselt H (2009) The fragmentation of global governance architectures: a framework for analysis. Glob Environ Polit 9(4):14–40

---

[118] Horn et al. (2009), p. 4.

[119] *See infra*, Sect. 5.1.

[120] Marceau (2013), fn 4.

Broude T (2008) Principles of normative integration and the allocation of international authority: the WTO, the Vienna Convention on the Law of Treaties, and the Rio Declaration. Loyola Univ Chic Int Law Rev 6(1):173–207

Broude T (2013) Keep calm and carry on: Martti Koskenniemi and the fragmentation of international law. Research Paper No. 10-13, International Law Forum of the Hebrew University of Jerusalem Law Faculty 2013. https://papers.ssrn.com/sol3/papers.cfm?abstract_id=2297626##

Burke-White WW (2005) International legal pluralism. Mich J Int Law 25:963–979

Charney JI (1996) The implications of expanding international dispute settlement systems: the 1982 Convention on the Law of the Sea. Am J Int Law 90(1):69–75

Cottier T et al (2011) Fragmentation and coherence in international trade regulation: analysis and conceptual foundations. In: Cottier T, Delimatsis P (eds) The prospects of international trade regulation: from fragmentation to coherence. Cambridge University Press, Cambridge, pp 1–66

Crawford J, Nevill P (2012) Relations between international courts and tribunals: the "Regime Problem". In: Young MA (ed) Regime interaction in international law: facing fragmentation. Cambridge University Press, Cambridge, pp 235–260

de Chazournes LB (2017) Plurality in the fabric of international courts and tribunals: the threads of a managerial approach. Eur J Int Law 28(1):13–72

de Mestral ACM (2013) Dispute settlement under the WTO and RTAs: an uneasy relationship. J Int Econ Law 16:777–825

Delimatsis P (2011) The fragmentation of international trade law. J World Trade 45(1):87–116

Dunoff JL (2012) A new approach to regime interaction. In: Young MA (ed) Regime interaction in international law: facing fragmentation. Cambridge University Press, Cambridge, pp 136–174

Ferrari F (2013) Forum shopping in the international commercial arbitration context: setting the stage. In: Ferrari F (ed) Forum shopping in the international commercial arbitration context. Sellier European Law Publishers, München, pp 1–21

Gehring T, Oberthür S (2004) Exploring regime interaction: a framework of analysis. In: Underdal A, Young OR (eds) Regime consequences: methodological challenges and research strategies. Kluwer Academic Publishers, Dordrecht, pp 247–279

Gehring T, Oberthür S (2006) Comparative empirical analysis and ideal types of institutional interaction. In: Gehring T, Oberthür S (eds) Institutional interaction in global environmental governance: synergy and conflict among international and EU policies. The MIT Press, Cambridge, pp 307–371

Graewert T (2008) Conflicting laws and jurisdictions in the dispute settlement process of the regional trade agreements and the WTO. Contemp Asia Arbitr J 287(1):287–334

Hafner G (2004) Pros and cons ensuing from fragmentation of international law. Mich J Int Law 25 (4):849–863

Henckels C (2008) Overcoming jurisdictional isolationism at the WTO–FTA nexus: a potential approach for the WTO. Eur J Int Law 19(3):571–599

Hillman J (2009) Conflicts between dispute settlement mechanisms in regional trade agreements and the WTO - what should the WTO do? Cornell Int Law J 42:193–208

Horn H, Mavroidis PC, Sapir A (2009) Beyond the WTO? An anatomy of EU and US preferential trade agreements. Bruegel Blueprint Series, Brussels

Jacobs D (2012) Puzzling over amnesties: defragmenting the debate for international criminal tribunals. In: van den Herik L, Stahn C (eds) The diversification and fragmentation of international criminal law. Martinus Nijhoff, Leiden, pp 305–345

Kim H (2016) Regime accommodation in international law: human rights in international economic law and policy. Brill Nijhoff, London

Koskenniemi M (2007) The fate of public international law: between technique and politics. Mod Law Rev 70(1):1–30

Koskenniemi M, Leino P (2002) Fragmentation of international law? Postmodern anxieties. Leiden J Int Law 15:553–579

Kwak K, Marceau G (2006) Overlaps and conflicts of jurisdiction between the WTO and RTAs. In: Bartels L, Ortino F (eds) Regional trade agreements and the WTO legal system. Oxford University Press, New York, pp 465–524

Lanyi PA, Steinbach A (2014) Limiting jurisdictional fragmentation in international trade disputes. J Int Dispute Settlement 5:372–405

Lindroos A (2005) Addressing norm conflicts in a fragmented legal system: the doctrine of lex specialis. Nordic J Int Law 74:27–66

Linton S, Tiba FK (2009) The international judge in an age of multiple international courts and tribunals. Chic J Int Law 9(2):407–470

Marceau G (2001) Conflicts of norms and conflicts of jurisdictions: the relationship between the WTO agreement and MEAs and other treaties. J World Trade 35:1081–1131

Marceau G (2013) The primacy of the WTO dispute settlement. Questions Int Law J 23:3–13

Marceau G, Wyatt J (2010) Dispute settlement regimes intermingled: regional trade agreements and the WTO. J Int Dispute Settlement 1(1):67–95

Matz-Lück N (2012) Norm interpretation across international regimes: competences and legitimacy. In: Young MA (ed) Regime interaction in international law: facing fragmentation. Cambridge University Press, Cambridge, pp 201–234

Mbengue MM (2016) The settlement of trade disputes: is there a monopoly for the WTO? Law Pract Int Courts Tribunals 15:207–248

Nguyen TS (2008) Towards a compatible interaction between dispute settlement under the WTO and regional trade agreements. Macquarie J Bus Law 5:113–135

Oberthür S (2016) Regime-interplay management: lessons from environmental policy and law. In: Blome K et al (eds) Contested regime collisions: norm fragmentation in world society. Cambridge University Press, New York, pp 88–108

Oberthür S, Gehring T (2006) Institutional interaction in global environmental governance: the case of the Cartagena Protocol and the World Trade Organization. Glob Environ Polit 6(2):1–31

Pauwelyn J (2003) Conflict of norms in public international law: how WTO law relates to other rules of international law. Cambridge University Press, New York

Pauwelyn J (2004) Bridging fragmentation and unity: international law as a universe of interconnected islands. Mich J Int Law 25(4):903–916

Pauwelyn J (2008) Fragmentation of international law. In: Wolfrum R (ed) Max Planck Encyclopedia of public international law. Oxford University Press, Oxford

Pauwelyn J, Salles LE (2009) Forum shopping before international tribunals: (real) concerns, (im)possible solutions. Cornell Int Law J 42(1):77–118

Pellet A (2012) Less is more: international law of the 21st century – law without faith. In: Crawford J, Nouwen S (eds) Select proceedings of the European Society of International Law, International Law 1989-2010: a performance appraisal, vol 3. Hart, London, pp 81–88

Peters A (2017) The refinement of international law: from fragmentation to regime interaction and politicization. Int J Constitutional Law 15(3):671–704

Salles LE (2014) Forum shopping in international adjudication. The role of preliminary objections. Cambridge University Press, Cambridge

Shany Y (2004) The competing jurisdictions of international courts and tribunals. Oxford University Press, New York

Simma B (2009) Universality of international law from the perspective of a practitioner. EJIL 20 (2):265–297

Simma B, Pulkowski D (2006) Of planets and universe: self-contained regimes in international law. Eur J Int Law 17(3):483–529

Stokke OS (2001) The interplay of international regimes: putting effectiveness theory to work. Report No. 14/2001, Fridtjof Nansen Institute, Lysaker

Trachtman JP (2005) Jurisdiction in WTO dispute settlement. In: Yerxa R, Wilson B (eds) Key issues in WTO dispute settlement. The first ten years. Cambridge University Press, New York, pp 132–143

Trachtman JP (2008) The economic structure of international law. Harvard University Press, Cambridge

van Asselt H (2007) Dealing with the fragmentation of global climate governance. Legal and political approaches in interplay management. Working Paper 30. https://doi.org/10.2139/ssrn. 1335082

van Asselt H (2014) The fragmentation of global climate governance. Edward Elgar, Cheltenham

Webb P (2013) International judicial integration and fragmentation. Oxford University Press, Oxford

Wolfrum R (2008) Legitimacy in international law from a legal perspective: some introductory considerations. In: Wolfrum R, Röben R (eds) Legitimacy in international law. Springer, Heidelberg, pp 1–24

Worster WT (2008) Competition and comity in the fragmentation of international law. Brooklyn J Int Law 34(1):119–149

Young OR (1996) Institutional linkages in international society: polar perspectives. Glob Gov 2 (1):1–24

Young MA (2012a) Introduction: the productive friction between regimes. In: Young MA (ed) Regime interaction in international law: facing fragmentation. Cambridge University Press, Cambridge, pp 1–19

Young MA (2012b) Regime interaction in creating, implementing and enforcing international law. In: Young MA (ed) Regime interaction in international law: facing fragmentation. Cambridge University Press, Cambridge, pp 85–110

Zang MQ (2018) Judicial interaction of international trade courts and tribunals. In: Howse R et al (eds) The legitimacy of international trade courts and tribunals. Cambridge University Press, New York, pp 432–453

Zelli F, van Asselt H (2013) The institutional fragmentation of global environmental governance: causes, consequences, and responses. Glob Environ Polit 13(3):1–13

Zürn M, Faude B (2013) On fragmentation, differentiation, and coordination. Glob Environ Polit 13 (3):119–130

Part II
Competing Interactions Between the WTO and the New Generation EU FTA DSMs

Chapter 4
The Changing Context

4.1 The Rare Use of RTA DSMs Until Recently

The information on RTA disputes is incomplete, as many of these agreements, especially the older ones, do not require public disclosure of consultation and panel requests, or even panel reports.[1] Hence, this section will reflect only on the disputes known to the public. Based on the existing public data, it can be affirmed that RTA DSMs have been rarely used by their parties for the resolution of trade disputes.

Between 1996 and 2001, three disputes were successfully adjudicated under NAFTA's state-to-state DSM for benefits available only at the FTA level. However, since the US blocked the panel selection process in 2000, no panel has been established and no dispute has been resolved.[2] Several other disputes were litigated under other RTAs. For example, in the Mercosur[3] ten awards were issued under the Brasilia Protocol[4] from 1993 to 2005, and another six were awarded between 2005 and 2008 under the Protocol of Olivos[5] that created a Permanent Mercosur Tribunal.[6] After the last award issued in 2008, only one request was submitted under the

---

[1] Porges (2018), p. 3.

[2] Lester et al. (2019), p. 64. For the list of disputes, *see* Porges Trade Law (Updated 11 January 2019) <www.porgeslaw.com/rta-ds-north-america>.

[3] Southern Common Market Agreement, established by the Treaty Establishing a Common Market (Asunción Treaty) between the Argentine Republic, the Federal Republic of Brazil, the Republic of Paraguay and the Eastern Republic of Uruguay, 29 November 1991.

[4] Protocol of Brasilia for the Solution of Controversies, 17 December 1991, 36 ILM 3, repealed by the Protocol of Olivos.

[5] Protocol of Olivos for Dispute Settlement in Mercosur, 10 February 2004, 42 ILM 2.

[6] Porges Trade Law (Updated 11 January 2019) <www.porgeslaw.com/rta-ds-latin-america>.

© The Author(s), under exclusive license to Springer Nature Switzerland AG 2021   61
C. Furculiță, *The WTO and the New Generation EU FTA Dispute Settlement Mechanisms*, EYIEL Monographs - Studies in European and International Economic Law 19, https://doi.org/10.1007/978-3-030-83118-9_4

Mercosur DSM in 2012, but it was found inadmissible.[7] In the last decade, one trade dispute and one labour dispute were successfully adjudicated under the Dominican Republic–Central America FTA (DR–CAFTA) in 2014.[8]

Based on the publicly available information, it can be concluded that FTA DSMs have been rarely used, especially in the last decades, compared to the WTO mechanism under which more than 350 rulings were issued since 1995.[9] The FTA disputes initiated frequently concerned WTO-plus and WTO-x[10] provisions that could not have been brought to the WTO. The older FTAs contained few commitments that went further than the those assumed at the WTO level. Moreover, many of the WTO-plus and WTO-x provisions in FTAs were excluded from the scope coverage of FTA DSMs. Therefore, more FTA disputes may be expected with the growth in the number of FTAs that include more WTO-plus and WTO-x provisions and do not merely mirror the WTO provisions. Furthermore, many FTAs have been concluded relatively recently, including the new generation EU FTAs, and they may still be in their implementation phase.[11] Once the time comes for the parties to deliver their promises, the number of disputes on non-implementation could be expected to increase.[12] Moreover, the initiation of disputes may also depend on the commercial importance of the FTAs. As more FTAs of considerable commercial importance are concluded between major trading countries, such as the new generation EU FTAs, there is also more interest in their implementation. Before the EUKFTA, relatively few important FTAs were concluded by the EU, and there was little incentive to initiate disputes.[13] However, as more and more FTAs of significant importance have already been concluded and are in the implementation phase, more disputes may occur. At the same time, there is evidence that some FTA parties did have disputes to resolve between them, but they were brought to the WTO DSM instead of FTA DSMs.[14] Therefore, when a choice was available, FTA parties seemed to prefer to adjudicate their disputes under WTO rules. However, there are signs that this may already be changing.

---

[7]Vidigal (2017), p. 930. Between 2012–2016, parties 'dealt directly and informally with the many problems that Argentina's licensing regime caused for stakeholders in Mercosur partners' (Porges 2018, p. 4).

[8]Informe Final del Grupo Arbitral, *Costa Rica vs El Salvador – Tratamiento Arancelario a Bienes Originarios de Costa Rica*, 18 November 2014 (CAFTA-DR/ARB/2014/CR-ES/17); Final Panel Report, *In the Matter of Guatemala – Issues Relating to the Obligations Under Article 16.2.1(a) of the CAFTA-DR*, 14 June 2017.

[9]*See supra* (n 33).

[10]WTO-x provisions are those that concern issues lying outside the coverage of the WTO agreements. *See infra* (n 18).

[11]During the implementation phase, if one party fails to fulfil the obligations it undertook, the other side can withhold implementation of its concessions. As such scenarios may occur without public notice, it is difficult to assess how often this happens (Porges 2018, p. 3).

[12]Porges (2018), p. 8.

[13]Interview 2.

[14]Vidigal (2017), pp. 931–932, Table 1 WTO disputes between FTA partners 2007–2016.

In 2018, Canada initiated a dispute against US measures on Canadian solar panels,[15] while the EU requested formal consultations with the Republic of Korea concerning labour commitments undertaken in the EUKFTA.[16] In January 2021, the panel of experts issued their final report.[17] Dispute settlement with respect to labour commitments under the EUKFTA, as well as under other new generation EU FTAs, takes place under special dispute settlement provisions that are outside the scope of this book. In 2019, the US requested consultations with Peru under the Environment Chapter from the US–Peru Trade Promotion Agreement,[18] and the EU requested consultations with Ukraine under the EU–Ukraine Association Agreement (AA) over export restrictions on wood.[19] While labour and environmental issues are not covered by WTO agreements and can be enforced only at the FTA level, the requests under NAFTA and EU–Ukraine AA show that FTA parties turn to FTA DSMs even with respect to areas regulated at the multilateral level. Moreover, the FTA obligation that the EU alleges was violated by the Ukrainian measures replicates Article XI of GATT.[20] Therefore, the same dispute could have been brought to the WTO, but the EU, an international actor that had no previous experience of regional dispute settlement, preferred to use the FTA DSM. In the EU-Ukraine dispute, the panel issued its final report in December 2020.[21] In 2019 and 2020,

---

[15] *See* the request for consultations by Canada <https://static1.squarespace.com/static/5521d064e4b0d8eff6331957/t/5c39720870a6ad9840b2fbf9/1547268617512/2018_0723-Canada-consreq-Solar-201-Ch8.pdf>.

[16] EU Commission, 'EU Steps up Engagement with Republic of Korea Over Labour Commitments Under the Trade Agreement' (Brussels, 17 December 2018) <http://trade.ec.europa.eu/doclib/press/index.cfm?id=1961>.

[17] Report of the Panel of Experts, 20 January 2021 <https://trade.ec.europa.eu/doclib/docs/2021/january/tradoc_159358.pdf>.

[18] Office of the United States Trade Representative, USTR Requests First-Ever Environment Consultations Under the U.S.–Peru Trade Promotion Agreement (PTPA) <https://ustr.gov/about-us/policy-offices/press-office/press-releases/2019/january/ustr-requests-first-ever>.

[19] EU Commission, EU Requests Bilateral Dispute Settlement Consultations with Ukraine Over Wood Export Ban (Brussels, 16 January 2019) <http://trade.ec.europa.eu/doclib/press/index.cfm?id=1968>.

[20] According to Art 35 of the AA, '[n]o Party shall adopt or maintain any prohibition or restriction or any measure having an equivalent effect [. . .] on the export or sale for export of any good destined for the territory of the other Party'. With almost identical wording, Art XI of GATT states that '[n]o prohibitions or restrictions other than duties, taxes or other charges, whether made effective through quotas, import or export licences or other measures, shall be instituted or maintained by any contracting party [. . .] on the exportation or sale for export of any product destined for the territory of any other contracting party'.

[21] Final Report, *Restrictions Applied by Ukraine on Exports of Certain Wood Products to the European Union*, 11 December 2020.

the EU has also initiated disputes under the EU–Southern African Development Community (SADC) EPA[22] and under the EU–Algeria AA.[23]

As the way in which the FTA and the WTO DSMs compete seems to be changing, the next section will investigate what could be the context for this potential change.

4.2   The Unprecedented Crisis of the WTO DSM

Despite its success[24] and states' seeming preference for it over FTA DSMs, the WTO DSM is currently in an unprecedented crisis. As the crisis does and could directly influence the way in which the DSMs of the WTO and the FTAs compete, this section will present in more detail the challenges that the WTO DSM is currently facing.

According to Ujal Singh Bhatia, the Chair of the AB, the WTO mechanism was faced with the 'burgeoning pressure of increasingly complex disputes at various stages',[25] even before the blocking of the appointment and reappointment of AB Members. The increased number of cases brought for adjudication under the WTO DSM, also characterised by their increased complexity and sophistication, has made it difficult for the proceedings to be held within the required timelines and has also put a strain on the Secretariat with its limited resources.[26] It may be said that the WTO DSM became a 'victim of its own success'.[27] Dealing with more and more disputes with a high degree of complexity has made it impossible for both panels and the AB to issue high quality reports within established timelines.[28] Therefore, the WTO DSM has been unable to provide prompt settlement of disputes which, according to the DSU, is 'essential to the effective functioning of the WTO and the maintenance of a proper balance between the rights and obligations of Members'.[29]

The second challenge the WTO DSM faces comes from the US Trump Administration which has blocked the appointment of AB Members, a challenge that is

---

[22] Note Verbale, NV/2019, 14 June 2019 <https://trade.ec.europa.eu/doclib/docs/2019/june/tradoc_157928.pdf>.

[23] Note Verbale, 24 June 2020 <https://trade.ec.europa.eu/doclib/docs/2020/november/tradoc_159037.pdf>.

[24] On how the AB's authority until the current crisis seemed to be accepted by Member States, *see* Howse (2016), pp. 9–77.

[25] AB Chair Ujal Singh Bhatia's Speech at the Presentation of the AB's Annual Report 2017, 22 June 2018 <www.wto.org/english/news_e/news18_e/ab_22jun18_e.htm#>.

[26] Sacerdoti (2018), p. 89.

[27] Ibid.

[28] *See infra* Sect. 6.3.1.

[29] DSU, Art 3.3.

more 'worrying and pervasive'.[30] The DSU establishes that the AB shall be composed of seven Members, three of whom shall sit on a specific dispute.[31] Therefore, at least three Members are needed for the AB to be able to hear appeals. The AB Members are appointed for 4-year terms that can be renewed by a decision of the DSB taken by consensus.[32] As the DSB is composed of all WTO Members, appointments can be blocked by any of them. The US has been blocking the appointment and reappointment of AB Members since August 2017.[33] Since December 2019, it is impossible to form a division of three Members to hear appeals.

The current blockage of appointments to the AB is not a complete novelty. This is not the first time the US has employed this strategy. The US refused to name panelists under NAFTA DSM rules, effectively blocking the establishment of panels and paralysing the dispute settlement proceedings under this FTA.[34] At the WTO level, the Bush Administration decided not to reappoint an American AB Member (Professor Jennifer Hillman), reportedly on the grounds that she did not uphold the US measures challenged at the WTO. Later, the Obama Administration went further and blocked the reappointment of another country's judge, Professor Seung Wha Chang of South Korea, on the grounds that AB Members should be held responsible for the views endorsed by them while deciding on disputes.[35] These actions already posed concerns about the pressure the US has put on AB Members and the way this could affect their independence.[36] Although previous refusals to reappoint AB Members were more targeted to specific Members and the US subsequently agreed to the appointment of new Members, these actions still set a precedent.[37]

Apart from blocking appointments to the AB, the US has also objected to the activity of the AB in general. The former US President Donald Trump declared that the WTO has treated US 'very badly',[38] and that it loses 'almost all of the lawsuits in the WTO',[39] despite statistics demonstrating that it has been more successful than the rest of the Membership, both as complainant and defendant.[40] Moreover, the US always had a national seat in the AB, unlike other Members.[41] The US argued that its blocking of appointments is due to concerns it has voiced for years with respect to the AB's disregard of the rules set in the DSU and that the AB is 'adding and diminishing rights and obligations under the WTO Agreements' contrary to

---

[30] Sacerdoti (2018), p. 95.

[31] DSU, Art 17.

[32] DSU, Arts 2.4, 17.2.

[33] Miles (2018).

[34] Lester et al. (2019), pp. 63–79; *See infra* Sect. 6.4.2.

[35] Charnovitz (2016).

[36] Miles (2018).

[37] Vidigal (2019).

[38] Micklethwait et al. (2018).

[39] Schwarz (2017).

[40] Shaffer et al. (2017).

[41] Ibid.

Article 3.2 of the DSU.[42] While the US has indeed expressed concerns about this over the years, they were elevated to entirely new heights,[43] leading to the dysfunctionality of the AB. The US submitted the following examples as instances in which the AB exceeded its mandate: disregard of the 90-day deadline for AB reports; continued service by AB Members with expired terms; issuing of advisory opinions on matters not relevant to dispute resolution, facts and de novo reviews of domestic law; and the treatment of AB reports as precedents.[44] As the US slowly asphyxiated the AB, international trade scholars,[45] as well as WTO Members,[46] came up with solutions and reform proposals to overcome this impasse. In addition, an informal process on the functioning of the AB facilitated by H.E. Dr. David Walker of New Zealand was begun. The US still considered that its concerns had not been addressed and asked, 'Why did the Appellate Body feel free to disregard the

---

[42] Office of the United States Trade Representative, The President's 2018 Trade Policy Agenda (March 2018), pp. 22–23 <https://ustr.gov/sites/default/files/files/Press/Reports/2018/AR/2018%20Annual%20Report%20I.pdf>; Office of the United States Trade Representative, 2019 Trade Policy Agenda and 2018 Annual Report of the President of the United States on the Trade Agreements Program (March 2019), p. 148 <https://ustr.gov/sites/default/files/2019_Trade_Policy_Agenda_and_2018_Annual_Report.pdf>.

[43] McDougall (2018), p. 1.

[44] Office of the United States Trade Representative, The President's 2018 Trade Policy Agenda, pp. 24–28; Office of the United States Trade Representative, 2019 Trade Policy Agenda and 2018 Annual Report of the President of the United States on the Trade Agreements Program, p. 148.

[45] See Andersen et al. (2017); Charnovitz (2017); Kuijper (2017); Salles (2017); Gantz (2018), pp. 11–14; Raina (2018), pp. 376–386; McDougall (2018); Hillman (2018).

[46] General Council, Communication from Canada, Strengthening and Modernizing the WTO: Discussion Paper, JOB/GC/201, 24 September 2018; General Council, Communication from the European Union, China, Canada, India, Norway, New Zealand, Switzerland, Australia, Republic of Korea, Iceland, Singapore and Mexico to the General Council, WT/GC/W/752, 26 November 2018; General Council, Communication from the European Union, China and India to the General Council, WT/GC/W/753, 26 November 2018; General Council, Communication from Australia, Singapore, Costa Rica, Canada and Switzerland to the General Council, Adjudicative Bodies: Adding to or Diminishing Rights or Obligations Under the WTO Agreement, WT/GC/W/754/Rev.2, 11 December 2018; General Council, Communication from Honduras, Fostering a Discussion on the Functioning of the Appellate Body, WT/GC/W/758, 21 January 2019; General Council, Communication from Honduras, Fostering a Discussion on the Functioning of the Appellate Body, WT/GC/W/759, 21 January 2019; General Council, Communication from Honduras, Fostering a Discussion on the Functioning of the Appellate Body Addressing the Issue of Alleged Judicial Activism by the Appellate Body, WT/GC/W/760, 29 January 2019; General Council, Communication from Honduras, Fostering a Discussion on the Functioning of the Appellate Body Addressing the Issue of Precedent, WT/GC/W/761, 4 February 2019; General Council, Communication from the Separate Customs Territory of Taiwan, Penghu, Kinmen and Matsu, Guideline Development Discussion, WT/GC/W/763/Rev.1, 8 April 2019; General Council, Communication from Brazil, Paraguay and Uruguay, Guidelines for the Work of Panels and the Appellate Body, WT/GC/W/767/Rev.1, 25 April 2019; General Council, Communication from Japan, Australia and Chile, Informal Process on Matters Related to the Functioning of the Appellate Body, WT/GC/W/768/Rev.1, 26 April 2019; General Council, Communication from Thailand, General Council Decision on the Dispute Settlement System of WTO, WT/GC/W/769, 26 April 2019; General Council, Communication from the African Group, Appellate Body Impasse, WT/GC/W/776, 26 June 2019.

clear text of the agreements?'; the US claimed that the answer to this question, which is crucial to finding a solution—has not been answered.[47] With the elections of the US President Biden, hopes have emerged that the crisis will be solved. Nevertheless, at the moment of writing, the AB is still inoperative.

A dysfunctional AB does not mean that the entire WTO DSM is also dysfunctional. Panels are still able to hear cases and issue reports. However, according to the DSU, parties can appeal the panel reports: 'If a party has notified its decision to appeal, the report by the panel shall not be considered for adoption by the DSB until after completion of the appeal'.[48] Therefore, if an appeal is filed and there is no AB to hear it, the panel report would not be adopted and it would have no legal force. Unadopted appealed panel reports remain in limbo for an indefinite period,[49] and the disputes remain unresolved. Hence, there is a risk that the automatic adoption of the final WTO reports would also be endangered, with the losing party having, in practice, a veto right reminiscent of the GATT-era procedures.[50] While a majority (71%) of the GATT panel reports were adopted,[51] a more gloomy prospect may be expected for the panel reports issued while the AB is inoperative. In the early GATT years, disputes were between like-minded states that could easily reach a consensus for adoption. In contrast, in the last 5 years, GATT panel reports were adopted only in 41% of the disputes, with the diversity of parties growing and disputes becoming more and more complex.[52] In some instances, Members could be satisfied with the outcome of the disputes, fear retaliation or that other parties would emulate the same behaviour, be concerned about the WTO DSM's overall effectiveness or about their own reputation and refrain from appealing into the void panel reports.[53] Nevertheless, as the WTO is currently very diverse and the disputes are more and more complex, discontented disputing parties may appeal into the void the panel reports,[54] unless these parties bilaterally, as a group, or all the Members find broader solutions to avert this.

In the event that the blockage of appointment and reappointment of AB Members is not lifted and the DSU is not reformed, several temporary solutions have been proposed by academics. Some of them, such as the MPIA,[55] have already been

---

[47] For more on the US position, see Ambassador Dennis Shea's Statement, Matters Related to the Functioning of the Appellate Body, WTO General Council Meeting, 9 December 2019, <https://geneva.usmission.gov/2019/12/09/ambassador-shea-statement-at-the-wto-general-council-meeting/>.

[48] DSU, Art 16.4.

[49] Vidigal (2019), p. 21.

[50] Pauwelyn (2019), p. 304.

[51] Ibid, p. 305.

[52] Ibid.

[53] Ibid, pp. 306–307.

[54] As of May 2021, there are 19 notified appeals (<https://www.wto.org/english/tratop_e/dispu_e/appellate_body_e.htm#fnt-1>), including by the EU, with no AB to hear these appeals. Accordingly, the appealed panel reports in these disputes are floating into the void.

[55] See supra Sect. 2.3.2.

adopted by multiple Members. The suggested temporary solutions that states could have resorted to or still can make use of are (1) the AB amending its own Working Procedures to prevent new appeals;[56] (2) parties signing procedural agreements on an *ad hoc* basis not to resort to appeal;[57] (3) 'plurilaterally' establishing a distinct agreement based on DSU rules with few changes among like-minded states;[58] and (4) 'plurilaterally' agreeing to make use of the arbitration rules established by Article 25 of the DSU for the appeal process.[59] The first option is not be feasible anymore, as the term of the last sitting AB Member expired in November 2020.[60] This option would have required a bold move from the AB that could have been accused once again of exceeding its mandate. The second option would provide solutions only for specific cases in which an agreement would be reached by the disputing parties, but the disputes could be easily blocked by a party filing an appeal in other cases. For example, Indonesia and Viet Nam have signed an Understanding according to which they would not appeal the Panel Report under Article 21.5 of the DSU, if on the date of circulation, the AB has fewer than three Members available to serve on an appeal division.[61] The third option would have to be agreed *ex ante* between parties, thus providing greater security that a dispute would be resolved. However, this option would require substantial support from the Members and significant time for conclusion. Moreover, this would mean that the US and possibly other parties would not participate in such plurilateral agreement and not recognise the authority of decisions issued under it.[62] The last option was chosen by the EU and other WTO Members, additionally incorporating a limited model of an NAP that was described in the second chapter.[63]

The unprecedented crisis of the WTO DSM represents a change in the context for competition with the FTA DSMs. In the absence of satisfactory solutions and alternatives within the WTO framework and with the perspective that the WTO panel reports could be sent into the void and disputes left unresolved under WTO rules, an increase in the use of FTA DSMs becomes more likely. Therefore, this change in the context provides the possible necessary impetus for Members to turn to FTA DSMs as potential alternatives. Even in the case of a fully functioning AB or a viable alternative within the WTO framework, it can be expected that the number of FTA disputes will rise due to substantive considerations analysed further.[64] Thus, although many disputes under the new generation EU FTAs may be on issues that

---

[56] Charnovitz (2017).

[57] Salles (2017).

[58] Kuijper (2017).

[59] Andersen et al. (2017).

[60] Charnovitz (2019).

[61] Understanding between Viet Nam and Indonesia on the Sequencing of Proceedings, WT/DS496/14, 27 March 2019, para 7.

[62] Vidigal (2019), p. 24.

[63] *See supra* Sect. 2.3.2.

[64] *See infra* Sect. 5.3.

cannot be brought to the WTO forum, the analysis presented is relevant in general for understanding how the new generation EU FTA DSMs, and FTA DSMs in general, would operate and what could be their drawbacks as well as attractive features.

References

Andersen S et al (2017) Using arbitration under Article 25 of the DSU to ensure the availability of appeals. CTEI working papers CTEI-2017-17, pp 1–10

Charnovitz S (2016) The Obama administration's attack on Appellate Body independence shows the need for reforms. International Economic Law and Policy Blog. https://worldtradelaw.typepad.com/ielpblog/2016/09/the-obama-administrations-attack-on-appellate-body-independence-shows-the-need-for-reforms-.html

Charnovitz S (2017) How to save WTO dispute settlement from the Trump administration. International Economic Law and Policy Blog. https://worldtradelaw.typepad.com/ielpblog/2017/11/how-to-save-wto-dispute-settlement-from-the-trump-administration.html

Charnovitz S (2019) The missed opportunity to save WTO dispute settlement' International Economic Law and Policy Blog. International Economic Law and Policy Blog. https://ielp.worldtradelaw.net/2019/12/the-missed-opportunity-to-save-wto-dispute-settlement.html

Gantz DA (2018) An existential threat to WTO dispute settlement: blocking appointment of Appellate Body members by the United States. Arizona Legal Studies Discussion Paper 18-26, pp 1–15

Hillman J (2018) Three approaches to fixing the World Trade Organization's Appellate Body: the good, the bad and the ugly?. Institute of International Economic Law, Georgetown University Law Center. https://georgetown.app.box.com/s/966hfv0smran4m31biblgfszj42za40b

Howse R (2016) The World Trade Organization 20 years on: global governance by judiciary. Eur J Int Law 27(1):9–77

Kuijper PJ (2017) Guest Post from Pieter Jan Kuijper on the US Attack on the Appellate Body. International Economic Law and Policy Blog. https://worldtradelaw.typepad.com/ielpblog/2017/11/guest-post-from-pieter-jan-kuiper-professor-of-the-law-of-international-economic-organizations-at-the-faculty-of-law-of-th.html

Lester S, Manak I, Arpas A (2019) Access to trade justice: fixing NAFTA's flawed state-to-state dispute settlement process. World Trade Rev 18(1):63–79

McDougall R (2018) Crisis in the WTO restoring the WTO dispute settlement function. 194 CIGI Papers 194. www.cigionline.org/sites/default/files/documents/Paper%20no.194.pdf

Micklethwait J, Talev M, Jacobs J (2018) Trump threatens to pull U.S. out of WTO if it doesn't 'Shape Up'. Bloomberg. www.bloomberg.com/news/articles/2018-08-30/trump-says-he-will-pull-u-s-out-of-wto-if-they-don-t-shape-up

Miles T (2018) U.S. blocks WTO judge reappointment as dispute settlement crisis looms. Reuters. www.reuters.com/article/us-usa-trade-wto/u-s-blocks-wto-judge-reappointment-as-dispute-settlement-crisis-looms-idUSKCN1LC19O

Pauwelyn J (2019) WTO Dispute Settlement Post 2019: what to expect? J Int Econ Law 22:297–321

Porges A (2018) Designing common but differentiated rules for regional trade disputes. ICTSD RTA Exchange, Issue Paper, pp 1–11

Porges Trade Law (2019). www.porgeslaw.com/rta-ds-north-america

Raina A (2018) Meditations in an emergency: the Appellate Body deadlock – what it is, why it is a problem, and what to do about it. Glob Trade Customs J 13(9):376–386

Sacerdoti G (2018) The WTO dispute settlement and the challenges to multilateralism: consolidating a 'Common Global Good'. In: Prévost D, Alexovicova I, Pohl JH (eds) Restoring trust in trade: Liber Amicorum in Honour of Peter Van Den Bossche. Hart, Oxford, pp 87–104

Salles LE (2017) Guest Post on bilateral agreements as an option to living through the WTO AB crisis. International Economic Law and Policy Blog. https://worldtradelaw.typepad.com/ielpblog/2017/11/guest-post-on-bilateral-agreements-as-an-option-to-living-through-the-wto-ab-crisis.html

Schwarz I (2017) Full Lou Dobbs Interview: Trump asks what could be more fake than CBS, NBC, ABC, and CNN. Real Clear Politics. www.realclearpolitics.com/video/2017/10/25/full_lou_dobbs_interview_trump_asks_what_could_be_more_fake_than_cbs_nbc_abc_and_cnn.html

Shaffer G, Elsig M, Pollack M (2017) The slow killing of the World Trade Organization. Huffpost. www.huffingtonpost.com/entry/the-slow-killing-of-the-world-trade-organization_us_5a0ccd1de4b03fe7403f82df

Vidigal G (2017) Why is there so little litigation under free trade agreements? Retaliation and adjudication in international dispute settlement. J Int Econ Law 20:927–950

Vidigal G (2019) Living without the Appellate Body: hegemonic, fragmented and network authority in International Trade. Amsterdam Law School Legal Studies Research Paper No. 2019-15, Amsterdam Center for International Law No. 2019-04. https://papers.ssrn.com/sol3/papers.cfm?abstract_id=3343327

Chapter 5
Substantive Coverage and Considerations

5.1 Areas Covered by the New Generation EU FTAs

The new generation EU FTAs cover a wide range of areas that are also regulated by the WTO agreements. They contain chapters on national treatment (NT) and market access to goods,[1] technical barriers to trade (TBT),[2] sanitary and phytosanitary measures (SPS),[3] trade defence instruments,[4] customs and trade facilitation,[5] subsidies,[6] state

---

[1] EUKFTA, Chapter Two; CETA, Chapter Two; EUJEPA, Chapter 2, Section B; EUSFTA, Chapter Two; EUVFTA, Chapter 2. Within the WTO framework, trade in goods is regulated by all the WTO agreements contained in the Marrakesh Agreement, Annex 1A, U.N.T.S 1867, 1868, 1869.

[2] EUKFTA, Chapter Four; CETA, Chapter Four; EUJEPA, Chapter 7; EUSFTA, Chapter Four; EUVFTA, Chapter 5; also regulated by the Agreement on Technical Barriers to Trade (TBT Agreement), 15 April 1994, Marrakesh Agreement, Annex 1A, 1868 U.N.T.S 120.

[3] EUKFTA, Chapter Five; CETA, Chapter Five; EUJEPA, Chapter 6; EUSFTA, Chapter Five; EUVFTA, Chapter 6; also regulated by the Agreement on the Application of Sanitary and Phytosanitary Measures (SPS Agreement), 15 April 1994, Marrakesh Agreement, Annex 1A, 1867 U.N.T.S. 493.

[4] EUKFTA, Chapter Three; CETA, Chapter Three; EUJEPA, Chapter 5; EUSFTA, Chapter Three; EUVFTA, Chapter 3; also regulated by the Agreement on the Implementation of Article VI of GATT 1994 (Antidumping Agreement), 15 April 1994, Marrakesh Agreement, Annex 1A, 1868 U.N.T.S. 201, and the Agreement on Subsidies and Countervailing Measures (SCM Agreement), 15 April 1994, Marrakesh Agreement, Annex 1A, 1869 U.N.T.S. 14.

[5] EUKFTA, Chapter Six; CETA, Chapter Six; EUJEPA, Chapter 4; EUSFTA, Chapter Six; EUVFTA, Chapter 4; also regulated by the Agreement on the Implementation of Article VII of GATT 1994 (Customs Valuation Agreement), 15 April 1994, Marrakesh Agreement, Annex 1A, 1868 U.N.T.S. 279.

[6] EUKFTA, Chapter Eleven, Section B; CETA, Chapter Seven; EUJEPA, Chapter 12; EUSFTA, Chapter Eleven, Section C; EUVFTA, Chapter 10, Section B; also regulated by the SCM Agreement.

C. Furculiță, *The WTO and the New Generation EU FTA Dispute Settlement Mechanisms*, EYIEL Monographs - Studies in European and International Economic Law 19, https://doi.org/10.1007/978-3-030-83118-9_5

trading enterprises,[7] trade in services,[8] public procurement,[9] intellectual property,[10] and transparency obligations.[11] The FTA norms that regulate these areas can be WTO-equal and incorporate, reference, or replicate the text of existing WTO commitments.[12] For example, Articles III and XI of GATT are incorporated into all the new generation EU FTAs,[13] and Article VIII of GATT is referenced in CETA, EUJEPA, EUSFTA, and EUVFTA,[14] while Article 19.4(1) of CETA has similar wording to that of Article IV:1 of GPA.[15]

The new generation EU FTAs contain multiple WTO-plus norms on issues also covered by the WTO agreements, but that go beyond the commitments undertaken at the multilateral level.[16] Examples of WTO-plus norms included in EU FTAs are the extensive provisions on regionalisation in Article 6, Annex II of CETA that provide a list of animal diseases to which the principles of zoning apply.[17] The new generation EU FTAs also cover a wide range of issues 'lying outside the current

[7] EUKFTA, Art 2.13; CETA, Chapter Eighteen; EUJEPA, Chapter 13; EUSFTA, Art 2.12; EUVFTA, Chapter 11; also regulated by Art XVII of GATT and the Understanding on the Interpretation of Article XVII of the General Agreement on Tariffs and Trade 1994.

[8] EUKFTA, Chapter Seven; CETA, Chapters Nine, Ten, Eleven, Thirteen, Fourteen, Fifteen, Sixteen; EUJEPA, Chapter 8; EUSFTA, Chapter Eight; EUVFTA, Chapter 8; also regulated by the General Agreement on Trade in Services (GATS), 15 April 1994, Marrakesh Agreement, Annex 1B, 1869 U.N.T.S. 183, 33 I.L.M. 1167.

[9] EUKFTA, Chapter Nine; CETA, Chapter Nineteen; EUJEPA, Chapter 10; EUSFTA, Chapter Nine; EUVFTA, Chapter 9; also regulated by the Agreement on Government Procurement (GPA), 15 April 1994, Marrakesh Agreement, Annex 4, 1869 U.N.T.S. 508 (Text available at 1915 U.N.T.S. 103), Revision of the Agreement on Government Procurement as at 8 December 2006, GPA/W/297, 11 December 2006.

[10] EUKFTA, Chapter Ten; CETA, Chapter Twenty; EUJEPA, Chapter 14; EUSFTA, Chapter Ten; EUVFTA, Chapter 12; also regulated by the General Agreement on Trade-Related Aspects of Intellectual Property (TRIPS), 15 April 1994, Marrakesh Agreement, Annex 1C, 1869 U.N.T.S. 299, 33 I.L.M. 1197.

[11] EUKFTA, Chapter Twelve; CETA, Chapter Twenty-Seven; EUJEPA, Chapter 17; EUSFTA, Chapter Thirteen; EUVFTA, Chapter 14; also regulated by *inter alia* Art X of GATT, Art III of GATS, Art 63 of TRIPS, Art 6 of Antidumping Agreement, Art 12 of SCM Agreement, Art 10 of TBT Agreement, Art 7 of SPS Agreement.

[12] It should be noted that when parties 'affirm' their WTO rights and obligations, the WTO norms do not become part of the FTAs and cannot be enforced through the FTA DSMs. This was confirmed by the EU and Canada in their reply during review of CETA (Committee on Regional Trade Agreements, Comprehensive Economic and Trade Agreement between Canada and the European Union (Goods and Services): Questions and Replies, 6 June 2018, WT/REG389/2, Question 1.11).

[13] EUKFTA, Art 2.8, 2.9; CETA, Art 2.3(1), 2.11(1); EUJEPA, Art 2.7, 2.15(1); EUSFTA, Art 2.3, 2.9(1); EUVFTA, Art 2.4, 2.14(1).

[14] CETA, Art 2.9(1); EUJEPA, Art 2.16(1); EUSFTA, Art 2.10(1); EUVFTA, Art 2.18(1).

[15] *See infra* (n 66).

[16] Horn et al. (2009), p. 4.

[17] Villalta Puig and Dalke (2016), p. 66.

WTO mandate',[18] the so-called WTO-x norms, concerning issues such as competition,[19] environment,[20] labour,[21] investment,[22] movement of capital,[23] intellectual property rights (IPR) related to compliance and accession to treaties outside the scope of TRIPS,[24] cultural cooperation,[25] small and medium enterprises (SMEs),[26] corporate governance,[27] and agricultural cooperation.[28] Finally, WTO-minus are those norms that allow measures between parties that would otherwise be illegal under the WTO.[29] FTA norms that seem WTO-minus at first sight, but could be justified under other GATT provisions, such as Article XX of GATT, would be WTO-consistent and thus, should not be considered WTO-minus. In CETA, for example, Article 2.11:4(a) permits export restrictions with respect to logs of all species, which contravenes Article XI:1 of GATT that expressly prohibits imposing restrictions on exports and does not contain any special exception in the case of logs. This provision, unless justified under other GATT provisions such as Article XX, would be considered WTO-minus.

The new generation EU FTAs cover a wide range of issues that fall both under and outside the current WTO mandate. The next section will investigate which of these areas are covered by the DSMs contained in the FTAs analysed and with respect to which they compete with the WTO DSM.

---

[18] Horn et al. (2009), p. 4.

[19] EUKFTA Chapter Eleven, Section A; CETA, Chapter Seventeen; EUJEPA, Chapter 11; EUSFTA, Chapter Eleven, Section A; EUVFTA, Chapter 10, Section A.

[20] EUKFTA, Chapter Thirteen; CETA, Chapter Twenty-Four; EUJEPA, Chapter 16; EUSFTA, Chapter Twelve; EUVFTA, Chapter 13.

[21] EUKFTA, Chapter Thirteen; CETA, Chapter Twenty-Three; EUJEPA, Chapter 16; EUSFTA, Chapter Twelve; EUVFTA, Chapter 13.

[22] EUKFTA, Chapter Seven, Section C; CETA, Chapter Eight; EUJEPA, Chapter 8. The EU is signing separate Investment Protection Agreements with Singapore and Vietnam.

[23] EUJEPA, Chapter Eight; EUJEPA, Chapter 9.

[24] For example, EUKFTA, Art 10.16; CETA, Art 20.13; EUJEPA, Art 26.3(3)(c); EUSFTA, Art 10.12; EUVFTA, Art 12.17(3) requiring parties to comply with the Singapore Treaty on the Law of Trademarks (2006); CETA, Art 20.24; EUJEPA, Art 26.3(3)(d); EUVFTA, Art 12.34 providing that parties shall make reasonable efforts to accede to the Geneva Act of the Hague Agreement; EUKFTA, Art 10.33; CETA Art 20.26; EUJEPA, Art 14.3(3)(a); EUSFTA, Art 10.29 requiring parties to make all reasonable efforts to comply with the Patent Law Treaty (2000) or specific articles within it.

[25] EUKFTA, Protocol on Cultural Cooperation.

[26] EUJEPA, Chapter 20.

[27] EUJEPA, Chapter 15.

[28] EUJEPA, Chapter 19.

[29] Flett (2015), p. 557; Pauwelyn and Alschner (2015), p. 502.

5.2 Substantive Coverage of the New Generation EU FTA DSMs

Although the EU FTAs analysed have broad coverage of issues under and outside the current mandate of the WTO, it is essential to establish which of these areas are enforceable through the DSMs contained in these agreements. The substantive coverage of the new generation EU FTA DSMs will be correlated to that of the WTO DSM, to determine the areas with respect to which they compete.

The dispute settlement chapters of the new generation EU FTAs state that unless otherwise provided, they apply to any dispute between the parties concerning the interpretation and/or application of the provisions of the respective agreements.[30] Therefore, the new generation EU FTA DSMs can each enforce only the provisions from the agreements they are contained in. The possibility to enforce norms outside respective FTAs through bilateral dispute settlement proceedings, such as WTO norms that are not reproduced in the agreements, is excluded.[31] The DSU, in its turn, establishes that it 'shall apply to disputes brought pursuant to the consultation and dispute settlement provisions of the agreements listed in Appendix 1 to this Understanding (referred to in this Understanding as the "covered agreements")' and 'to consultations and the settlement of disputes between Members concerning their rights and obligations under the provisions of the Agreement Establishing the World Trade Organization'.[32] Thus, the DSU applies only to disputes on WTO and not FTA provisions. Therefore, the new generation EU FTA DSMs can compete with the WTO DSM only with respect to disputes concerning FTA norms that regulate the same areas as does the WTO.

Disputes on FTA norms that are WTO-equal always also concern WTO norms. Consequently, provided that these norms fall under the coverage of the FTA DSMs, these FTA mechanisms will be in competition with the WTO one. As WTO-plus norms regulate the same issue areas as the WTO agreements, by going beyond them, a disputed measure could be in violation of both agreements at the same time or of only one of them, depending on each case. Therefore, competing relationships between the WTO and the new generation EU FTA DSMs may emerge only in the event of a dispute allegedly concerning violations of both multilateral and corresponding bilateral provisions. Since WTO-x areas lie inevitably outside the scope of the WTO DSM, it is clear that only FTAs offer fora for their enforcement and, hence, in cases concerning WTO-x norms, the FTA DSMs do not compete with the WTO DSM. Although this part is concerned particularly with the competitive relationships between the EU FTA and the WTO DSMs, the analysis is also relevant to the functioning of the new generation EU FTA DSMs with respect to all areas and disputes, including those on WTO-x norms. In fact, a rise is likely in the use of the

---

[30] EUKFTA, Art 14.2; CETA, Art 29.2; EUJEPA, Art 21.2; EUSFTA, Art 14.2; EUVFTA, Art 15.2.

[31] Schill (2017), p. 123.

[32] DSU, Art 1.1. The question of jurisdiction will be analysed in detail in Sect. 9.3.1.

new generation EU FTA DSMs for enforcement of WTO-x provisions, since without competing with the WTO DSM, these are the only mechanisms available for enforcement of these norms.[33]

Regulation of the same areas and simultaneous violations of both multilateral and bilateral provisions do not lead automatically to competition between EU FTA and the WTO DSMs. As stated previously, these norms shall fall under the coverage of these DSMs. The DSU applies to *all* disputes brought under the WTO covered agreements. The DSU itself, the Marrakesh Agreement, and multilateral agreements are covered agreements.[34] Moreover, plurilateral trade agreements, such as the GPA, are also covered agreements and the DSU applies to disputes arising from them within the terms established.[35] New generation EU FTA DSMs, however, generally apply to all disputes on interpretation and application of the agreements, unless the agreements provide otherwise. An analysis of these agreements shows that they provide carve-outs for many areas.

All the new generation EU FTAs exclude the following areas from their dispute settlement chapters: trade defence instruments (anti-dumping, countervailing measures, and global safeguards),[36] labour and environment commitments,[37] and competition.[38] Apart from these areas, each new generation EU FTA excludes additional areas or specific provisions from application of the dispute settlement chapters. The EUKFTA further excludes all SPS measures[39] and matters covered by Article 9.1 of the Protocol on Mutual Administrative Assistance in Customs Matters.[40] CETA additionally carves out consultations on subsidies[41] and decisions under the Investment Canada Act,[42] while the EUJEPA does so with respect to certain provisions related to SPS measures,[43] disputes concerning exclusively TBT-incorporated

---

[33] Interview 2.

[34] DSU, Appendix 1.

[35] DSU, Appendix 1; GPA, Art XX.

[36] EUKFTA, Art 3.7(5), 3.15; CETA, Art 3.7; EUJEPA, Arts 5.9(2), 5.11(2); EUSFTA, Arts 3.5, 3.8; EUVFTA, Arts 3.5, 3.8.

[37] EUKFTA, Art 13.16; CETA, Arts 23.11, 24.16; EUJEPA, Art. 16.17; EUSFTA, Art. 12.16; EUVFTA, Art. 13.16. For disputes arising under these chapters, special procedures are to be followed.

[38] EUKFTA, Art 11.8; CETA, Art 17.4; EUJEPA, Art 11.9; EUSFTA, Art 11.14; EUVFTA, Art 10.13.

[39] EUKFTA, Art. 5.11.

[40] CETA, Art 6.14(2).

[41] CETA, Art 7.9.

[42] CETA, Annex 8-C.

[43] EUJEPA, Art 6.16(1). These provisions concern risk assessment according to Art 5 of SPS Agreement (EUJEPA, Art 6.6), the arbitrariness or unjustifiability of import procedures (EUJEPA, Art 6.7(4)(b)), publication and communication of processing period of import procedures (EUJEPA, Art 6.7(4)(c)), information requirements for import procedures (EUJEPA, Art 6.7(4)(d)), and equivalence of SPS measures (EUJEPA, Art 6.14).

provisions (unless there are also claims on other norms in the dispute),[44] specific subsidies that have or could have negative effects and are not prohibited,[45] cooperation on intellectual property,[46] corporate governance,[47] good regulatory practices and regulatory cooperation,[48] cooperation in agriculture,[49] and SMEs.[50] The EUSFTA additionally carves out subsidies, except prohibited ones.[51]

The areas excluded from the coverage of the analysed EU FTA DSMs mostly concern WTO-x areas, for which the FTAs are the only forum for enforcement. A few WTO-x areas are left for enforcement through FTA dispute settlement proceedings. All the new generation EU FTAs allow the enforcement of provisions concerning IPR and capital movement through interstate DSMs, while the EUKFTA also does so with respect to cultural cooperation.[52] The exclusion of many WTO-x areas from FTA DSMs coverage may be explained by the fact that states are reluctant to commit, as these leading-edge provisions are still controversial.[53] Had these provisions been covered by the dispute settlement chapters, the FTAs risked not being signed. While the EU may be in favour of subjecting many WTO-x areas to FTA dispute settlement, the same cannot be said for the EU's partners.[54] Although many FTA norms that go beyond the WTO ones are excluded from FTA DSMs coverage, they often contain only transparency and cooperation obligations that are difficult to enforce and not of much interest to the parties.[55]

Most of the areas covered by the new generation EU FTAs concern issues that are also covered by the WTO. However, many of these areas are still excluded from the scope of the bilateral DSMs, leaving the WTO DSM as the only available forum. These areas were most likely excluded in order not to undermine the authority of the WTO DSM.[56] It may even be said that the new generation EU FTAs elevate the WTO to primacy when it comes to areas that may be politically more sensitive.[57] Thus, disputes on trade defence instruments in all the new generation EU FTAs, as well as those on some specific subsidy-related provisions and TBT and SPS provisions in the majority of the agreements, seem to be left exclusively to the WTO

---

[44] EUJEPA, Art 7.3(3).

[45] EUJEPA, Art 12.10.

[46] EUJEPA, Art 14.52.

[47] EUJEPA, Art 15.7.

[48] EUJEPA, Art 18.19.

[49] EUJEPA, Art 19.8.

[50] EUJEPA, Art 20.4.

[51] EUSFTA, Art 11.14.

[52] Unless parties agree otherwise (EUKFTA, Protocol on cultural cooperation, Art 3 bis).

[53] Froese (2016), p. 581.

[54] Interview 2.

[55] Ibid.

[56] Schill (2017), p. 124. Also *see infra* Sect. 5.4.

[57] Froese (2016), p. 576. Bown asserts with respect to the TPP that it elevates the WTO system to primacy by design when it concedes traditional areas to it (Bown 2016, p. 4).

DSM. It is, therefore, clear that these bilateral DSMs cannot operate as alternatives to the WTO DSM with respect to these issues even in the context of the AB crisis. As more than 60% of the WTO cases are about trade defence rules,[58] the new generation EU FTA DSMs will not be able to emerge as alternative fora for a vast category of disputes. Conceding potential disputes to the WTO mechanism also indicates that parties may be looking for more coherence and predictability in the outcomes of these disputes, and might prefer avoiding conflicting interpretations. The texts of the new generation EU FTAs are clearly formulated, and when they exclude provisions, sections, or entire chapters from application of the dispute settlement chapters, they do so in an explicit manner.[59]

To conclude, it is possible to bring claims for an important group of potential disputes only to the WTO forum and, therefore, the new generation EU FTA DSMs cannot compete with it in relation to these disputes. Moreover, the FTAs seem to recognise the primacy of the WTO mechanism for multiple areas. However, many areas are left under the jurisdiction of the new generation EU FTA DSMs that are also covered by the WTO DSM, such as NT and market access obligations, TBT measures (in the EUJEPA only TBT-plus and disputes involving claims on TBT-incorporating norms if there are also claims on other norms in the dispute), most of the SPS measures (except in the EUKFTA in which all are excluded), certain provisions related to subsidies, state enterprises, customs valuation, services, intellectual property, and public procurement. Consequently, only when a dispute arises in respect to these areas, the new generation EU FTA DSMs could compete with and be potentially viable, although only partial alternatives to the WTO DSM.

5.3   Substantive Aspects Affecting the Competition Between the New Generation EU FTA and the WTO DSMs

In the case of areas that are covered by both the new generation EU FTA and the WTO DSMs, the choice of forum may be influenced by the competition between substantive WTO and FTA norms.

With FTAs being the 'focal point of the development of new trade rules', at least for now, it is expected that they would grow in importance and frequency of use.[60] Therefore, besides the changing context that is caused by the AB crisis, the increase in use of FTA DSMs is anticipated because of the desire of FTA parties to benefit

---

[58] De Baere (2019).

[59] To show that provisions, sections, or chapters are not covered by the dispute settlement chapter, the EUKFTA uses the expression 'neither Party may have recourse'; CETA uses expressions such as 'is/are not subject to', 'do not apply', or 'nothing in this Chapter shall be subject'; the EUJEPA adopts the phrase 'shall not be subject'; the EUSFTA uses 'shall not be subject', 'no Party may have recourse to', and 'do not apply'; the EUVFTA uses 'shall not be subject' and 'no Party shall have recourse to dispute settlement under this agreement', and 'does not apply'.

[60] McDougall (2018), p. 1.

from the more advanced provisions contained in their bilateral agreements. If a dispute concerns a violation of WTO-plus or WTO-x norms, the FTA parties would have to initiate proceedings in FTA fora to enforce these norms contained in the FTAs rather than the corresponding WTO norms. In these cases, FTA DSMs would not be in genuine competition with the WTO DSM, as they would emerge not as alternatives, but as the *only* available fora, since the WTO DSM would not even have jurisdiction over them.[61] However, there may be measures that would be simultaneously in violation of both WTO norms and the corresponding WTO-plus FTA norms. At the same time, WTO-plus FTA norms may frequently be applied in conjunction with WTO norms.[62] Hence, violations of some FTA exclusive norms would also imply violation of WTO norms. In such cases, the states would have to choose between the WTO and the FTA DSMs. If FTA parties wished to enforce the FTA provisions going beyond the WTO ones, they would need to use FTA DSMs. However, even in these situations, states may still prefer enforcing the WTO norms, instead of the more far-reaching WTO-plus norms, just to be able to use the WTO DSM, if it is perceived as being more advantageous. Furthermore, the same measures could simultaneously violate FTA norms that are WTO-x and WTO norms, prompting states to choose whether to enforce the WTO-x norm at all by using the FTA DSM or to make use of the WTO mechanism alone for the sole enforcement of WTO norms. Despite the fact that FTAs contain WTO-plus and WTO-x norms that can be enforced only through bilateral DSMs, paradoxically, these mechanisms have rarely been used in practice, in contrast to the WTO DSM,[63] showing that substantive considerations are not the only ones that matter, but there are also considerations of a procedural or political nature.

For measures allegedly in violation of WTO-minus norms, similar to the case of WTO-plus and WTO-x norms, only FTA DSMs can be used as means of enforcement. Nevertheless, the complainant may choose the WTO to challenge the FTA norm itself that rolls back the parties' rights compared to the WTO norms.[64] Moreover, from the point of view of the complainant, it may seem more advantageous to bring a claim on the violation of a WTO norm rather than on a WTO-minus FTA norm that rolls back its rights.[65]

For FTA norms that do not merely incorporate, but replicate WTO norms in a slightly different language,[66] their clarity and unambiguity may be a relevant

---

[61] *See supra* (n 32).

[62] Bercero (2006), pp. 403–404.

[63] McDougall (2018), p. 10.

[64] For example, in *Peru – Agricultural Products* (Appellate Body Report, *Peru – Additional Duty on Imports of Certain Agricultural Products (Peru – Agricultural Products)*, WT/DS457/AB/R, 20 July 2015), Peru and Guatemala signed an FTA that did not enter into force, in which Guatemala had allegedly agreed to a WTO inconsistent measure applied by Peru, the legality of which Guatemala contested in a WTO dispute.

[65] Porges (2018), p. 5.

[66] For example, Art 19.4(1) of CETA on General Principles for Government Procurement replicates Art IV:1 of GPA. The article in CETA is, however, formulated differently. Art 19.4(1) of CETA

factor.[67] A clearer and less ambiguous norm may be preferred over another seemingly equivalent norm that could raise questions on interpretation. In addition, the slightly different language may also indicate that parties purposely drafted the norms differently and wished to depart from the existing WTO approach.[68] Accordingly, despite this potentially leading to inconsistencies in how similar provisions are interpreted, as argued in the conceptual framework,[69] coherence should be sought only within the limits set by the states' will.[70] Moreover, even two identically worded norms could still be interpreted differently. Broude and Shany have argued that two norms from different agreements can never be fully equivalent because of their different contexts.[71] According to Article 31 of the Vienna Convention on the Law of Treaties (VCLT),[72] interpretation of terms should take place in their context and in light of the object and purpose of the treaties. Therefore, an FTA and WTO norm belonging to different treaties, potentially offering different contexts and having different objects and purposes, may be interpreted differently. For example, the context of the TBT provisions incorporated into the new generation EU FTAs[73] is different from that of the same norms included in the TBT Agreement. In the EU-Ukraine dispute over the wood export ban, when Ukraine argued that Art 35 of the AA incorporating Art XI GATT should be interpreted differently, the panel also considered whether the broader objectives of the AA would justify a more restrictive interpretation.[74] Consequently, the context provided by the WTO or FTA

---

contains an extra clarification: '[f]or greater certainty, such treatment includes: (a) within Canada, treatment no less favourable than that accorded by a province or territory, including its procuring entities, to goods and services of, and to suppliers located in, that province or territory; and (b) within the European Union, treatment no less favourable than that accorded by a Member State or a sub-central region of a Member State, including its procuring entities, to goods and services of, and suppliers located in that Member State or sub-central region, as the case may be'. Thus, Art 19.4(1) can be considered clearer than the corresponding GPA norm, as it provides a more detailed rule.

[67] Pierola and Horlick (2007), p. 890.

[68] Porges (2018), p. 7.

[69] *See supra* Sect. 3.1.6.

[70] In EU-Ukraine dispute over the wood export ban the panel, for example, had to assess whether the parties incorporated Art XI GATT entirely in Art 35 of the AA (Final Report, *Restrictions Applied by Ukraine on Exports of Certain Wood Products to the European Union*, 11 December 2020, [185]–[193].

[71] Broude and Shany (2011), pp. 7–9.

[72] United Nations, Vienna Convention on the Law of Treaties, 23 May 1969, United Nations, Treaty Series, vol. 1155, p. 331.

[73] EUKFTA, Art 4.1; EUSFTA, Art 4.3 and EUVFTA, Art 5.1 incorporate the TBT Agreement entirely. CETA, Art 4.2(1) and EUJEPA, Art 7.3(1) incorporate Arts 2–9, Annex 1 and Annex 3 of the TBT Agreement. However, the EUJEPA excludes the incorporated TBT norms from the applicability of the Dispute Settlement Chapter. *See* (n 44).

[74] Final Report, *Restrictions Applied by Ukraine on Exports of Certain Wood Products to the European Union*, 11 December 2020, [203].

agreements to a particular provision and their different objectives could also influence the states' choice of a specific mechanism for solving disputes.

To conclude, substantive considerations will play a role in the competition between the new generation EU FTA and the WTO DSMs. The possibility that the new generation EU FTA DSMs would genuinely compete with and become alternatives to the WTO DSM may, however, be additionally affected by considerations other than the substantive ones.

5.4 Conclusions: Wider Consequences Resulting from the Substantive Coverage Considerations

This chapter established the influence of substantive coverage of the new generation EU FTA DSMs on their competition with the WTO mechanism. It found that the FTAs analysed cover a wide range of areas. It further concluded that despite this wide range, the DSMs can genuinely compete only with respect to areas that are covered by both multilateral and bilateral agreements. Several meaningful areas are excluded from the scope of application of the new generation EU FTA DSMs, making them only partial alternatives to the WTO DSM. However, multiple areas are left in which they can compete with the WTO mechanism and be viable partial alternatives. Finally, it established that substantive considerations can also influence the choice of forum when these DSMs compete.

The proliferation of FTAs and their DSMs has been claimed as threats to the authority of the WTO DSM as a multilateral mechanism.[75] However, analysis of the substantive coverage of the new generation EU FTA DSMs suggests otherwise for the wider consequences resulting from substantive considerations. First, as the majority of the WTO-x provisions, such as those on sustainable development, are excluded from the substantive coverage, the ability of the WTO and its DSM to deal with these new areas in the future is not threatened.[76] Second, the exclusion of important aspects from the substantive coverage of the new generation EU FTA DSMs, such as trade defence instruments, provisions incorporating TBT, and some specific SPS measures, shows that FTA DSMs do not necessarily undermine the authority of the WTO DSM. In fact, these exclusions indicate that the FTAs need a functional WTO DSM; otherwise, provisions related to important aspects cannot be enforced through dispute settlement proceedings. Moreover, when it comes to the areas covered by both the new generation EU FTA DSMs and the WTO mechanism, according to the jurisdictional clauses within the FTAs analysed,[77] the parties are clearly allowed to choose the WTO DSM.[78] As the new generation EU FTAs

---

[75] Schill (2017), p. 113; Vidigal (2019), p. 20.

[76] Schill (2017), p. 122.

[77] *See infra* Sect. 10.2.1.

[78] Marceau (2019).

themselves recognise, through exclusions and jurisdictional clauses, the importance of the WTO DSM, this chapter confirmed the claim made in the discussion of the conceptual framework that the interactions between the new generation EU FTA DSMs and the WTO mechanism do not necessarily result in negative consequences. Hence, in certain cases, FTA DSMs may be alternatives to the WTO DSM in the context of the AB crisis, but they also rely on a functional way of solving disputes at the WTO, without which certain provisions within the FTAs cannot be enforced. Moreover, parties could, in fact, be discouraged from initiating disputes under FTA rules because of the fear of multiple proceedings at both multilateral and bilateral levels,[79] given that WTO panels and the AB have never taken into consideration the jurisdictional clauses within the FTAs.[80] Hence, the authority of the WTO DSM should not be regarded as threatened by competition with the FTA mechanisms analysed.

This chapter considered the influence of the substantive aspects on the competition between the DSMs analysed. However, other aspects may also influence this decision.

References

Bercero IG (2006) Dispute settlement in European Union free trade agreements: lessons learned. In: Bartels L, Ortino F (eds) Regional trade agreements and the WTO legal system. Oxford University Press, New York, pp 383–405

Bown CP (2016) Mega-regional trade agreements and the future of the WTO. Discussion paper series on global and regional governance, Council on Foreign Relations, pp 1–14. https://www.piie.com/system/files/documents/bown201609cfr.pdf

Broude T, Shany Y (2011) The international law and policy of multi-sourced equivalent norms. In: Broude T, Shany Y (eds) Multi-sourced equivalent norms in international law. Hart, Oxford, pp 1–16

De Baere P (2019). In: WTI, WTO appellate review: reform proposals and alternatives: proceedings of the 24 May 2019 World Trade Institute Workshop held at the World Trade Organization, Geneva. www.wti.org/media/filer_public/58/3b/583bcf87-075e-4698-9a8b-66600ffe8091/24_may_appellate_review_workshop_final_document.pdf

de Mestral ACM (2013) Dispute settlement under the WTO and RTAs: an uneasy relationship. J Int Econ Law 16:777–825

Flett J (2015) Referring PTA disputes to the WTO dispute settlement system. In: Dür A, Elsig M (eds) Trade cooperation: the purpose, design and effects of preferential trade agreements, World Trade Forum. Cambridge University Press, New York, pp 555–579

Froese MD (2016) Mapping the scope of dispute settlement in regional trade agreements: implications for the multilateral governance of trade. World Trade Rev 15(4):563–585

Horn H, Mavroidis PC, Sapir A (2009) Beyond the WTO? An anatomy of EU and US preferential trade agreements. Bruegel Blueprint Series, Brussels. https://www.bruegel.org/wp-content/uploads/imported/publications/bp_trade_jan09.pdf

---

[79] de Mestral (2013), p. 821.
[80] For a detailed analysis of this issue, *see infra* Sects. 9.3 and 9.4.

Marceau G (2019) Presentation during World Trade Forum 'Multilateralism at Risk', Geneva, 25–26 October 2019

McDougall R (2018) regional trade agreement dispute settlement mechanisms: modes, challenges and options for effective dispute resolution. ICTSD RTA Exchange, Issue Paper 1, pp 1–15

Pauwelyn J, Alschner W (2015) Forget about the WTO: the network of relations between PTAs and "Double PTAs". In: Dür A, Elsig M (eds) Trade cooperation: the purpose, design and effects of preferential trade agreements, World Trade Forum. Cambridge University Press, New York, pp 497–532

Pierola F, Horlick G (2007) WTO dispute settlement and dispute settlement in the "North-South" agreements of the Americas: considerations for choice of forum. J World Trade 41(5):885–908

Porges A (2018) Designing common but differentiated rules for regional trade disputes. ICTSD RTA Exchange, Issue Paper, pp 1–11

Schill SW (2017) Authority, legitimacy, and fragmentation in the (envisaged) dispute settlement disciplines in mega-regionals. In: Griller S, Obwexer W, Vranes E (eds) Mega-regional trade agreements: CETA, TTIP, and TiSA: new orientations for EU external economic relations. Oxford University Press, New York, pp 111–150

Vidigal G (2019) Living without the Appellate Body: hegemonic, fragmented and network authority in international trade. Amsterdam Law School Legal Studies Research Paper No. 2019-15, Amsterdam Center for International Law No. 2019-04. https://papers.ssrn.com/sol3/papers.cfm?abstract_id=3343327

Villalta Puig G, Dalke ED (2016) Nature and enforceability of WTO-plus SPS and TBT provisions in Canada's PTAs: from NAFTA to CETA. World Trade Rev 15(1):51–83

Chapter 6
Competing Procedural Considerations

6.1 Preliminary Remarks

The changing context in the international trade arena, as argued previously, provides, in general, the necessary impetus for FTA DSMs to be used more often. The previous chapter on substantive coverage established the areas with respect to which the new generation EU FTA DSMs could compete with the WTO DSM, the role substantive considerations could play in the competition between them and the wider consequences of competition resulting from substantive considerations. However, it is also necessary to analyse whether the new generation EU FTA DSMs could genuinely compete procedurally with the WTO DSM to be considered viable alternatives for solving trade disputes. The procedural aspects dealt with in this chapter may also explain why the WTO DSM has historically been the preferred forum and whether that could change in the current context.

Exclusive or preferential jurisdictional clauses requiring the use of a particular DSM, generally or at the request of a party, could directly influence choice in favour of the forum mentioned in the clause. However, as it will be shown,[1] the new generation EU FTAs allow parties to choose between the WTO DSM and FTA DSMs, and the WTO's exclusive jurisdiction on WTO-only claims cannot prohibit the adjudication of FTA norms that are WTO-equal under FTA rules.[2] Hence, jurisdictional clauses will not be considered a procedural factor influencing the preference of the new generation EU FTA parties for one DSM over another.

The analysis of the procedural features of the new generation EU FTA DSMs presented in this chapter is relevant not only to the context of competing interactions, but also to the functioning of these DSMs with respect to all areas and disputes that

---

[1] *See infra* Sect. 10.2.1.

[2] *See infra* Sect. 9.3.1.

they cover, including those on WTO-x and WTO-plus norms for which the FTA DSMs are the only available fora for enforcement.

6.2   Types of Complaints

The types of complaints and the measures that they address are closely related to the issue of substantive coverage. Under the DSU, three types of complaints—violation, non-violation and situation—are available to WTO Members.[3] All three categories are based on the concept of 'nullification or impairment of benefits' accruing to Members under WTO agreements.[4] Violation complaints constitute, by far, the majority of complaints. They cover nullification or impairment of benefits or impediment of the attainment of any objective of the covered agreements as a result of a failure of a Member to carry out obligations prescribed by these agreements.[5] Non-violation complaints imply that benefits are nullified or impaired, or objectives impeded from being attained, whether or not there is a violation of the agreements.[6] Nullification and impairment are used in the present tense, indicating that the measure is applied and is currently 'nullifying and impairing the benefits'.[7] If a non-violation claim succeeds, there is no obligation to withdraw the measure impairing the benefits; rather, the panel or the AB should recommend a mutually satisfactory adjustment.[8] While there were five successful GATT non-violation complaints,[9] all WTO non-violation complaints have been rejected, except in the case of a dispute in which the elements of a non-violation complaint were found, but the panel exercised judicial economy and did not rule on it.[10] Moreover, the AB also established that non-violation complaints 'should be approached with caution and should remain an exceptional remedy'.[11] Lastly, situation complaints apply to any other situation in which benefits are nullified or impaired or objectives are impeded

---

[3] GATT, Art XXIII:1; DSU, Art 26; GATS (Art XXIII) provides for violation and non-violation complaints.

[4] GATT, Art XXIII:1.

[5] GATT, Art XXIII:1(a).

[6] GATT, Art XXIII:1(b). Non-violation claims cannot be brought under the TRIPS Agreement, as Members set a moratorium on them in Art 64.2 TRIPS for 5 years that was subsequently extended on several occasions and is still in place (Cook 2018, p. 14).

[7] Panel Report, *Japan – Measures Affecting Consumer Photographic Film and Paper*, WT/DS44/R, 31 March 1998, [10.57]–[10.59].

[8] DSU, Art 26.1(b).

[9] Cook (2018), p. 3.

[10] WTO Analytical Index, DSU, Art. 26, para 1.2.3 <www.wto.org/english/res_e/publications_e/ai17_e/dsu_art26_jur.pdf>.

[11] Appellate Body Report, *European Communities – Measures Affecting Asbestos and Products Containing Asbestos (EC – Asbestos)*, WT/DS315/AB/R, 12 March 200, [186].

from being attained.[12] Nevertheless, they do not apply to GATS and TRIPS Agreements,[13] and are not subject to the negative consensus rule. Thus, panel reports that consider such complaints would have to be adopted by the consensus of all Members.[14] Therefore, the use of this type of complaint is very limited; this is also confirmed by the fact that it has never been used in practice under WTO rules. As arbitration is used at the appeal stage under the MPIA, the arbitrators would hear the same complaints as the panels, hence the same type of complaints, as those under regular appellate procedures, would be heard.

Violation complaints, which are used in almost all cases, target a 'measure' that directly or indirectly impaired the benefits under the agreements.[15] While the DSU does not define the term 'measure', it was clarified in practice by existing jurisprudence that it can refer to any act or omission attributable to a WTO Member.[16] The measure can be binding or not,[17] and it can be challenged 'as such', independent of its application or 'as applied'.[18]

In new generation EU FTAs, the dispute settlement chapters apply with respect to disputes on 'interpretation and application of the provisions' of the agreements.[19] While this concept is broad, there are other provisions that clarify the type of complaint that can be brought under these agreements. Thus, the request for the establishment of the panels shall identify the measure at issue and also explain how it constitutes a breach of or is inconsistent with the provisions of the agreement.[20] Therefore, the provisions for dispute settlement make clear that only violation complaints can be subject to arbitration under the new generation EU FTAs DSMs.[21] This conclusion is further supported by other provisions in these agreements. CETA provides that the interim report shall contain determinations on whether the respondent has conformed with its obligations.[22] The EUJEPA

---

[12] GATT, Art XXIII:1(c).

[13] GATS, Art XXIII; TRIPS, Art 64.2.

[14] DSU, Art 26.2.

[15] DSU, Art 3.3.

[16] Appellate Body Report, *United States – Sunset Review of Anti-Dumping Duties on Corrosion-Resistant Carbon Steel Flat Products from Japan*, WT/DS244/AB/R, 15 December 2003, [81].

[17] Appellate Body Report, *Guatemala – Anti-Dumping Investigation Regarding Portland Cement from Mexico*, WT/DS60/AB/R, 2 November 1998, fn 47.

[18] Appellate Body Report, *United States – Sunset Review of Anti-Dumping Duties on Corrosion-Resistant Carbon Steel Flat Products from Japan*, WT/DS244/AB/R, 15 December 2003, [60]–[61].

[19] EUKFTA, Art 14.2; CETA, Art 29.2; EUJEPA, Art 21.2; EUSFTA, Art 14.2; EUVFTA, Art 15.2.

[20] EUKFTA, Art 14.4(2); CETA, Art 29.4(2); EUJEPA, Art 21.7(2)(b); EUSFTA, Art 14.4(2); EUVFTA, Art 15.5(2).

[21] By contrast, under the Comprehensive and Progressive Agreement for Trans-Pacific Partnership (CPTPP) rules (Art 28.3.1(c)), non-violation complaints brought in relation to certain chapters are allowed (*see* McRae 2019, pp. 542–543).

[22] CETA, Art 29.9(1)(b).

expressly provides that one of the functions of the panels is to make objective assessment of the conformity of measures with the covered provisions.[23] In addition, the EUJEPA, EUSFTA and EUVFTA include terms of reference for panels according to which panels shall decide on the conformity of the measure with the covered provisions.[24]

On the other hand, mediation procedures seem to cover a wide range of issues, including violation and non-violation complaints. The mediation mechanisms under the new generation EU FTAs apply to measures that *adversely affect* trade between the parties,[25] without mentioning that such adverse effects shall be caused by the breach of provisions in the agreements. In the request for mediation, the requesting party shall identify only the measure at issue, the adverse effects on trade and the link between the two.[26] Therefore, while parties cannot initiate arbitration proceedings against non-violating measures that, nevertheless, adversely affect trade between the parties, they can make use of the mediation procedures to facilitate the finding of an MAS. Under CETA, EUSFTA and EUVFTA mediation rules, the effect of the measure can be prospective, as they establish that the requesting party shall provide a statement of the alleged adverse effects that it believes the measure 'has, or will have'.[27] While the mediation mechanisms do not ensure that there will be enforceable binding rulings, they still offer the parties the means to address non-violation complaints. Given that under WTO rules non-violation complaints have been extremely rarely brought and never succeeded, allowing the use of mediation instead of confrontational mechanisms may prove to be an optimal solution for these cases.

The new generation EU FTAs do not expressly list the nature of measures that may be targets of arbitration complaints. While it is not yet clear how the FTA panels would define the term 'measure', due to the provisions requiring the panel to take into account or adopt relevant WTO interpretations,[28] it may be expected to be interpreted in line with existing WTO jurisprudence. In addition, CETA contains a provision that expressly allows consultations on a 'proposed measure', but not mediation and panel procedures for such a measure.[29] Allowing claims on proposed measures is a notable feature of Canada's FTAs.[30] Establishing a panel to consider a measure that might never come into effect would be a waste of resources, while at the same time, addressing such a measure early on could prevent or limit the potential

---

[23] EUJEPA, Art 21.12(a).

[24] EUJEPA, Art 21.13; EUSFTA, Annex 14-A, para 11(a); EUVFTA, Art 15.6.

[25] EUKFTA, Annex 14-A, Art 2 (applicable only to measures 'related to any matter falling under market access in goods including under Chapter Two (National Treatment and Market Access for Goods) and the Annexes pertaining thereto'); CETA, Art 29.5; EUJEPA, Art 21.6(1); EUSFTA, Art 15.1; EUVFTA, Art 15.4.

[26] EUKFTA, Annex 14-A, Art 3(1); CETA, Annex 29-C, Art 2(1); EUSFTA, Art 15.3(1); EUVFTA, Annex 15-C, Art 3.1.

[27] CETA, Annex 29-C, Art 2(1)(b); EUSFTA, Art 15.3(1)(b); EUVFTA, Annex 15-C, Ar. 3.1(b).

[28] *See infra* Sect. 11.8.5.3.

[29] CETA, Art 29.4(8).

[30] Chase et al. (2016), p. 634.

damage caused by it.[31] Subjecting proposed measures only to consultations seems a balanced way of addressing them, and would ensure that not too many resources would be invested, while the measures would be eliminated earlier without causing too much damage.

To conclude, under the WTO rules, different types of complaints can be brought for adjudication. However, the new generation EU FTAs allow violation complaints, the type that is almost always used in WTO proceedings. Therefore, the absence of the other types should not negatively affect the likelihood of the new generation EU FTAs to be used more often and to emerge as potential alternatives to the WTO DSM. Moreover, under the new generation EU FTAs, non-violation complaints are not completely absent, as they can be subject to mediation. Neither of the DSMs expressly defines the measures that are targeted in complaints. However, under the WTO, there is a vast jurisprudence indicating which measures would qualify.[32] Under the new generation EU FTAs, the same interpretation as the one offered by WTO case law is anticipated. In addition, it is already clear that CETA allows consultations on proposed measures in a balanced way that would make the CETA DSM a suitable setting for raising the question of consistency of a proposed measure with the agreements.

6.3   Time Frames

The length of the expected proceedings may be an essential factor for a complainant considering which DSM to choose. Generally, the expeditiousness of the procedures is opportune for prompt dispute settlement.[33] Although speedy proceedings may be on their face more favourable, lengthier proceedings could be associated with other advantages. This section will look at the time frames of the dispute settlement procedures under the WTO and the new generation EU FTAs and their implications for the competition between them.

6.3.1   Time Frames in the WTO DSM

The prompt settlement of disputes is regarded as 'essential to the effective functioning of the WTO and the maintenance of a proper balance between the rights and obligations of Members'.[34] The DSU provides that the establishment of a panel may

---

[31] Donaldson and Lester (2009), p. 404.

[32] *See supra* (nn 16–18).

[33] Pierola and Horlick (2007), p. 895.

[34] DSU, Art 3.3.

be requested after 60 days from the request of consultations.[35] The establishment and composition of the panel shall take place within a maximum of 45 days.[36] The period from the moment of composition of the panel to the circulation of the panel report shall in no case exceed 9 months.[37] After the panel report is issued, the Members are given 20 days for its consideration before it can be adopted by the DSB.[38] If there is no appeal, including in the case of NAPs, the DSB adopts the report within 60 days from the date of its circulation to the Members.[39] If a party decides to appeal the report, the appellate stage in no case shall exceed the term of 90 days.[40] The adoption of the AB report shall occur within 30 days.[41] Thus, it should take a maximum of 15 months from consultations to the adoption of panel reports, and 18 months for AB reports. In cases of urgency the parties, panels, and the AB shall make every effort to accelerate proceedings,[42] and there are also shorter deadlines for specific stages.[43] The time frames of the WTO dispute settlement procedures are quite strict and quasi-automatic.[44]

However, the issue in WTO proceedings is not the time frames as set in the DSU, but the fact that they are not respected. The procedures under WTO rules take considerably longer in practice than envisaged in the DSU. From the outset, the average duration of proceedings exceeded that prescribed by the DSU[45] and only continued to increase. The WTO DSM became very popular and overloaded, and eventually had to deal with highly complex disputes.[46] This led to WTO disputes taking twice as long as envisaged by the DSU's 18-month time frame (including the

---

[35] DSU, Art 4.7.

[36] DSU, fn 5 provides that the meeting of the DSB shall be convened within 15 days of the request of the complaining party. According to Art 8.7, parties have 20 days from the establishment of the panel to agree on the panelists. If they do not reach an agreement, the WTO DG, in consultation with the Chairman of the DSB and the Chairman of the relevant Council or Committee, shall determine the composition of the panel within 10 days. Therefore, the establishment and composition of the panel should take a maximum of 45 days.

[37] DSU, Art 12.9.

[38] DSU, Art 16.1.

[39] DSU, Art 16.4: 'Within 60 days after the date of circulation of a panel report to the Members, the report shall be adopted at a DSB meeting'.

[40] DSU, Art 17.5.

[41] DSU, Art 17.4.

[42] DSU, Art 4.9.

[43] DSU, Art 4.8 establishes that if consultations fail within 20 days, the establishment of the panel can be requested. Art 12.8 provides that the panel aims to issue its report in 3 months in cases of urgency.

[44] Todeschini-Marthe (2018), p. 402.

[45] On average, it took approximately 23 months for disputes that started between 1995 and 1999, and approximately 28 months for those that started between 2007 and 2011. This average includes disputes that did not go through the appeal stage (Reich 2017, p. 23).

[46] WTO, 'Farewell speech of Appellate Body Member Ricardo Ramírez-Hernández' 28 May 2018 <www.wto.org/english/tratop_e/dispu_e/ricardoramirezfarwellspeech_e.htm>.

appeal stage).[47] The legal support offered by the secretarial staff might have also contributed to the extension of the deadlines. First, staff members are usually busy with more than one dispute at a time. Second, when more persons are assigned to the same dispute, as happens at the WTO, much time is spent on reviewing the work by those involved, including by the person in charge of the process.[48] Finally, with all the information on old cases available electronically at the fingertip,[49] the secretarial staff invest time to produce documents of many pages, that once written, tend to be incorporated into the reports.[50]

According to the US administration, one of the main reasons for its blockage of the appointment and reappointment of the AB Members is that the appellate stage regularly takes longer than the specified period of 90 days.[51] The US administration stated that until 2011, the AB respected the 90-day rule, and when it deviated, it asked for the disputing parties' approval, but this practice has changed and the appeals last on average 149 days.[52] The US administration even asserted that a report issued after 90 days would make it unfit for qualifying as an AB report that can be adopted by the DSB.[53] While the US concerns seem justified, if judged on the basis of existing data, it should be pointed that the AB and the Secretariat are not the only ones to blame for the extensive delays. When Members agree to a deadline, they do so in abstract; however, in practice, when a real dispute arises, Members tend to ask for extension of the deadline.[54] The defendant often needs more time to prepare, but even the complainant that can prepare usually in advance may want an extension.[55] Although the parties had their share of guilt, the AB took for granted its ability to extend deadlines without asking the parties—an attitude that sovereign states may find difficult to accept.[56]

---

[47] Porges (2018), p. 6.

[48] Interview 4.

[49] Interview 5.

[50] Interview 4.

[51] Office of the United States Trade Representative, The President's 2018 Trade Policy Agenda (March 2018), pp. 24–28 <https://ustr.gov/sites/default/files/files/Press/Reports/2018/AR/2018% 20Annual%20Report%20I.pdf>; Office of the United States Trade Representative, 2019 Trade Policy Agenda and 2018 Annual Report of the President of the United States on the Trade Agreements Program (March 2019), p. 148 <https://ustr.gov/sites/default/files/2019_Trade_ Policy_Agenda_and_2018_Annual_Report.pdf>.

[52] WTO, DSB Meeting, Statements by the United States at the Meeting of the WTO Dispute Settlement Body Geneva 22 June 2018, 5. Statement by the United States Concerning Article 17.5 of The Understanding on Rules and Procedures Governing the Settlement of Disputes 1, 11 <https://geneva.usmission.gov/wp-content/uploads/sites/290/Jun22.DSB_.Stmt_.as-delivered. fin_.public.rev_.pdf>.

[53] Ibid, p. 20.

[54] Interview 4; Interview 5.

[55] Interview 2; For example, if the EU were the complainant, it would likely ask for an extension in August, due to the holiday period (Interview 4).

[56] Interview 5.

As the issue of respecting deadlines has been in the spotlight in the context of the current crisis, the MPIA seems to attempt to address this issue. To deal with the problem of deadlines, including the parties' contribution to extensions, the MPIA establishes that arbitrators may take organisational measures, such as 'decisions on page limits, time limits and deadlines as well as on the length and number of hearings required', or substantive measures, including the proposal to exclude claims 'based on the alleged lack of an objective assessment of the facts pursuant to Art. 11 of the DSU'.[57] Accordingly, the MPIA proposes, among other things, measures that would limit the amount of work for the AB and streamline the proceedings. Another MPIA provision that may help to that end, and is aimed at tackling one of the US concerns, provides that '[t]he arbitrators shall only address those issues that are necessary for the resolution of the dispute' and 'shall address only those issues that have been raised by the parties, without prejudice to their obligation to rule on jurisdictional issues.'[58] Moreover, the pool of appeal arbitrators comprising ten individuals,[59] compared to the AB consisting of only seven Members, may address the issue of overloading individuals deciding the dispute and help to meet deadlines. Under the MPIA, any extension of the 90-day deadline should be proposed by the arbitrators and agreed by the parties.[60] Therefore, the MPIA signals the will of the parties to have faster proceedings, and when that is not possible, with due consideration of the sovereignty of the states, to extend the deadline only with their approval. It remains to be seen how long the procedures conducted under the MPIA rules would take. In practice, the appeal arbitration proceedings, similar to the regular AB proceedings, could be routinely extended by the parties. However, with the parties' agreement, such extensions may prove less contentious for some Members.

In practice, the WTO proceedings take much longer than envisaged in the DSU without the parties' agreement, which may be perceived as a serious disadvantage from the perspective of states looking for an expeditious way to resolve their disputes. Moreover, these delays threat the existence of the AB which is accused of ignoring deadlines and exceeding its mandate. The MPIA, also endorsed by some new generation EU FTA parties, may address this issue, at least with respect to obtaining the agreement of disputing parties before an extension.

---

[57] MPIA, Annex 1, paras 12, 13. Fn 9 to Annex 1, para 13 establishes that '[f]or greater certainty, the proposal of the arbitrators is not legally binding and it will be up to the party concerned to agree with the proposed substantive measures. The fact that the party concerned does not agree with the proposed substantive measures shall not prejudice the consideration of the case or the rights of the parties.'

[58] MPIA, Annex 1, para 10.

[59] MPIA, para 4; Annex 1, para 7.

[60] MPIA, Annex 1, para 14.

6.3.2   Time Frames in New Generation EU FTA DSMs

This sub-section will proceed with an analysis of the time frames for dispute settlement procedures provided under the new generation EU FTAs to determine whether they are shorter and, thus, possibly more attractive to the parties.

According to the new generation EU FTAs, before requesting the establishment of a panel, the parties to a dispute shall try to solve it through consultations concluded within 30,[61] 45,[62] or 60 days[63] from the date of the receipt of the request for consultations. After the request for consultations, parties have 10 days to agree on the composition of the panel,[64] and if parties do not reach an agreement, special procedures have to be followed that will be analysed in detail in the next section. In the case of EUKFTA, there is no deadline established for such procedures, while the other FTAs establish time frames ranging from 5 to 15 days.[65] After the establishment of the panels, the final report should be issued within a maximum of 150 days under the EUKFTA and EUVFTA,[66] 180 days under CETA and EUSFTA,[67] and 210 days under EUJEPA.[68]

Therefore, dispute settlement procedures, from consultations to the issuing of the final panel report, should last about six and a half months under the EUKFTA (although there are no clear deadlines for the panel selection process), about 8 months under CETA, EUSFTA, and EUVTA, and about 9 months under EUJEPA. All these agreements also provide reduced timelines for urgent cases.[69] All time limits in the

---

[61] EUKFTA, Art 14.3(3).

[62] CETA, Art 29.6(1)(a); EUJEPA, Art 21.5(4); EUJEPA, Art 21.7 provides that in case the other party does not respond to the request within 10 days, or does not enter into consultations within 30 days, the request for the establishment of the panel can be made earlier; EUVFTA, Art 15.3(3).

[63] EUSFTA, Art 14.3(3); if, however, the party to which the request for consultations was made does not respond within 10 days, the complainant can request the establishment of the panel without waiting for the required 60 days to pass.

[64] EUKFTA, Art 14.5(2); CETA, Art 29.7(2) specifies that these 10 days are working days; EUJEPA, Art 21.8; EUSFTA, Art 14.5(3) mentions that this term is to be calculated from the moment parties actually enter into consultations, compared to other agreements in which it is calculated from the date of receipt of the request to establish the panel; EUVFTA, Art 15.7(2).

[65] EUKFTA, Annex 14-B, Art 3.1(a) establishes that 'the chair of the Trade Committee, or the chair's delegate, shall select the arbitrators within five days'; CETA, Art 29.7(4) requires them to take place 'normally within five working days' after the request of one of the parties; EUJEPA, Art 21.8(3) provides 5 days for the parties, each to appoint its own arbitrators, and if they do not manage to do so, another 5 days for their selection by lot, making it a total of 10 days; Art 21.9(4) also establishes 5 days for selection of a chairperson by lot; EUSFTA, Art 14.5, paras (3)–(4) establish a time frame of a maximum of 10 days for the selection of a chairperson and arbitrators; EUVFTA, Art 15.7 establishes a maximum of 15 days.

[66] EUKFTA, Art 14.7(1); EUVFTA, Art 15.11.

[67] CETA, Art 29.9(1), Art 29.10(2); EUSFTA, Art 14.8(1).

[68] EUJEPA, Art 21.18(1), Art 21.19(1).

[69] EUKFTA, Arts 14.3(4), 14.6(3), 14.7(2); CETA, Arts 29.6, 29.11; EUJEPA, Arts 21.5(4), 21.18(3), 21.19(2); EUSFTA, Arts 14.3(4), 14.7(3), 14.8(2); EUVFTA, Arts 15.3(3), 15.10(2), 15.11(2).

dispute settlement chapters may be modified by agreement of the parties at their own initiative or, in the EUJEPA and EUVFTA, at the request of the panels.[70] In the EUJEPA, the panels may themselves decide to modify the deadline for submission of written comments, stating the reasons for their decision, at the request of only one party.[71] At the same time, under all the FTAs analysed, according to the rules of procedure, the time limits applicable to the proceedings may be modified by the arbitration panel alone, by notifying the parties of the modification and the reasons for it.[72] In these cases, extensions would apply only with the panels' involvement and parties would only be informed of the modifications and the reasons for them, except under CETA rules, according to which, parties need to be consulted on the changes.[73] The provisions contained in the rules of procedure may give the impression that the panel has discretion over all extensions. However, as the dispute settlement chapters provide that extensions are to be agreed by the parties, it is clear that the panels can modify only the time limits within the rules of procedure. Thus, the main deadlines, such as those for consultations and the issuance of the interim or final reports will have to be extended only with the agreement of the parties. This interpretation is expressly confirmed in the EUJEPA and EUVFTA, where it is mentioned that the panels may modify the time limits other than those set in the dispute settlement chapters.[74] Therefore, under the new generation EU FTAs, panels should deliver final reports swiftly, extending the deadline only with the agreement of the parties.

6.3.3   Implications of the Time Frames for the Competition Between the New Generation EU FTA and the WTO DSMs

Based on the timelines described above, it can be inferred that the proceedings under the new generation EU FTAs take almost less than half the time of the proceedings prescribed by the DSU, which in reality last even longer.

---

[70]EUKFTA, Art 14.20(2); CETA, Annex 29-A, para 19; EUJEPA, Art 21.28(2); EUSFTA, Art 14.22(2); EUVFTA, Art. 15.25(2).

[71]EUJEPA, Art 21.28(2).

[72]EUKFTA, Annex 14-B, Art 5.6 (however, the timelines on arbitration panel ruling in urgent cases cannot be modified by the panel alone); CETA, Annex 29-A, para 18; Decision of the Joint Committee of the EUJEPA, Annex 2, para 14; EUSFTA, Annex 14-A, para 18; EUVFTA, Annex 15-A, para 19.

[73]CETA, Annex 29-A, para 18.

[74]Decision of the Joint Committee of the EUJEPA, Annex 2, para 14; EUVFTA, Annex 15-A, para 19.

The time frame may be a less important factor if the proceedings concern a claim on a measure in force that in practice has not been applied yet.[75] However, the expeditiousness of proceedings could become especially critical when the negative effects of the measure allegedly in violation of the agreements increase rapidly as time passes.[76] Since trade remedies do not usually have a retrospective effect, if the complainant is supported by industry representatives, it may be important to solve the dispute sooner, in order to curb the amount of losses.[77] Therefore, if a complainant were interested in solving a dispute faster, the new generation EU FTA DSMs could be perceived as attractive alternatives. However, for the respondent, it would be more opportune, on occasion, to give more time to its industry to adjust to the potential withdrawal of the measure at issue in a dispute. Nonetheless, if it takes too long to settle disputes, parties or Members may be incentivised to take inconsistent measures.[78] Given that the complainant would have to choose where to initiate a dispute, it may find expeditious proceedings more attractive.

It is, however, difficult to say what would be the actual duration of the procedures under the new generation EU FTA DSMs, as none of them has been applied in practice and the deadlines have not been tested in actual cases.[79] For instance, under NAFTA, deadlines have been extended regularly at each stage of the process. Although the most significant source of delay has been caused by the panel establishment process,[80] other deadlines have also been routinely exceeded.[81] The panel report in EU-Ukraine dispute on the wood export ban was issued in 319 days from panel composition, despite the limit of maximum 150 days.[82] Considering the pandemic that caused delays and the tight time frames, the panel report was still issued quite fast in comparison with the last reports issued under WTO rules.[83]

The EUKFTA, for example, does not provide a period in which parties have to establish a panel if they cannot agree on its composition. This could cause considerable delays to the seemingly 'expeditious' dispute settlement proceedings under the EUKFTA. Other delays may also occur at different stages under FTA rules. Therefore, similar to the WTO proceedings that in practice take much longer than established by the DSU, the proceedings under the new generation EU FTAs could also suffer from considerable delays. Nevertheless, under the new generation EU FTA rules, the time frames established in the dispute settlement chapters cannot be modified without the agreement of the parties. Hence, the disputing parties have

---

[75] Pierola and Horlick (2007), p. 895.

[76] Ibid.

[77] Interview 2.

[78] Molina-Tejeda (2019), p. 24.

[79] Chase et al. (2016), p. 610; Todeschini-Marthe (2018), p. 402.

[80] On the issue of panel composition in NAFTA, *see infra* Sect. 6.4.2.

[81] VanDuzer (2020), p. 14.

[82] EU–Ukraine AA, Art 310.1.

[83] For example, in case of two recent panel reports, from panel establishment and until the panel reports were circulated it took 972 days and, respectively, 969 days (DS 537 and DS539).

control over the extensions, and when a party would hold on to the strict deadlines, it could prevent them. Similarly, under the MPIA, the time frames for the appellate stage should be either respected or extended with the parties' agreement. Yet, even the MPIA procedures may last longer because of potential delays at the panel stage and because of the interim appeal stage that adds extra time.

Even though the appeal stage adds to the length of the proceedings, it is also associated with a guarantee of the legality of the process.[84] The lengthier procedures because of appeal within the WTO, are perceived as of better quality—since a good report requires the investment of more time—and of greater consistency and legal security.[85] It may be difficult to have speedy proceedings that are both low cost and produce good quality reports.[86] Given the importance of high quality reports and the stability ensured by appeals, the repercussions of adding time and costs could be viewed as less significant, even from the perspective of the representatives of the businesses that may be behind the complaint.[87] Nevertheless, the parties may still prefer having only a panel stage, as they would retain more control over the proceedings.[88] Panel reports should be shorter so that the panels are able to meet the deadlines established in the new generation EU FTAs. Since all the agreements analysed establish that panel reports should be drafted exclusively by the arbitration panels, they seem to send the message that parties would accept shorter reports.[89] At the same time, rapid proceedings may not be possible in evidence-intensive cases involving numerous claims and defences and thousands of pages of written submissions.[90] In such cases, the parties themselves would most likely ask for extensions, and the swiftness of the proceedings may not influence the forum choice of states. Therefore, the implication of time frames for the competition between the new generation EU FTA DSMs and the WTO mechanism would be contingent on the kind of dispute at issue and how the states view the appeal stage. Furthermore, even with delays FTA proceedings might be considerably shorter.

If the parties would be interested in solving the dispute the fastest way possible, the speedier proceedings under the new generation EU FTAs could be an attractive characteristic from their perspective, provided that the deadlines are respected or much shorter in practice. However, if FTA parties would be seeking a mechanism that provides the advantages associated with an appeal stage like that under WTO rules, the seemingly shorter deadlines may become less meaningful when choosing a forum. Moreover, under MPIA rules, the parties would be able to benefit from the

---

[84] Pierola and Horlick (2007), p. 897.

[85] Pauwelyn (2004), p. 258.

[86] Sacerdoti (2019), p. 10.

[87] Interview 3.

[88] For more on the advantages and disadvantages of the presence of an appeal stage, *see infra* Sect. 6.8.

[89] Interview 4.

[90] Posner (2019).

advantages of an appellate stage while retaining control over meaningful extension of time frames.

6.4   The Panel Composition Process

The selection of panelists may be another important aspect to consider by the parties when choosing a forum. For the new generation EU FTA DSMs to be considered viable alternatives to the WTO DSM, the panel selection process should be 'automatic';[91] in other words, it should be designed to ensure that the proceedings cannot be delayed or blocked by one party. The potential difficulties in the process of panel composition have been declared one of the main reasons behind the preference for the WTO DSM over the FTA DSMs.[92] Thus, since FTA parties were not certain that an FTA panel would even be established, they preferred to go straight to the WTO.

6.4.1   The Composition of WTO Panels and the AB

The composition of WTO panels takes place on an *ad-hoc* basis for each dispute. The panel is composed of three panelists, unless parties agree to a panel of five.[93] Citizens of the disputing Members cannot serve on panels associated with the dispute.[94] The nominations for the panel are made by the Secretariat,[95] which maintains a list of indicative names from which it can draw candidates and propose them to the parties to obtain their agreement.[96] Nevertheless, other names can also be proposed.[97] The list is complemented periodically with new names proposed by Member States, the DSB approving them without debate almost all the time.[98] The proposed nominations by the Secretariat shall not be opposed by the parties to the dispute, except for 'compelling reasons'.[99] Once appointed, the panelists are supposed to control the staff assisting them, but they may feel controllable by the

---

[91] Chase et al. (2016), p. 643 ('The notion of "automaticity", in relation to the composition of an *ad hoc* adjudicatory panel refers, essentially, to the extent to which the composition of a panel can proceed without being blocked or paralysed by the actions or omissions of a party to a dispute.').

[92] Vidigal (2017), p. 933; McDougall (2018), p. 11.

[93] DSU, Art 8.5.

[94] DSU, Art 8.3.

[95] DSU, Art 8.6.

[96] DSU, Art 8.4.

[97] WTO Secretariat (2017), p. 72.

[98] Ibid.

[99] DSU, Art 8.6.

Secretariat because it plays an important role in panel selection and can decide whether or not to propose them as panelists again.[100]

In practice, it is generally understood that the parties are free to agree on the composition of a panel even without asking the Secretariat for assistance. Moreover, when the parties ask for the Secretariat's assistance, they disclose the profiles of the desired candidates.[101] For example, parties often ask that the panelists have previous adjudication experience, be former or current government officials, or former Ministers or Ambassadors to the WTO, and can oppose academics with no other experience.[102] If the parties do not agree with the first proposals of the Secretariat, they usually request further proposals that can be tabled, as long as they find this process beneficial.[103] However, if the parties are opposing and cannot agree on the composition of the panel within 20 days from the establishment of the panel, at the request of any party, 'the Director-General, in consultation with the Chairman of the DSB and the Chairman of the relevant Council or Committee, shall determine the composition of the panel by appointing the panelists whom the Director-General considers most appropriate' after consultations with the parties.[104] At this stage, the parties have the opportunity to voice once more their preferred criteria for the panelists to comply with. However, they cannot impose any constraint on who can be appointed by the DG.[105] The DG makes this decision at the recommendation of or in close consultation with the Secretariat.[106] Thus, if parties cannot agree, an independent third party determines the composition of the panel.[107] Therefore, the DSU provides an automatic selection process that ensures that a responding party would not be able to block the entire procedures by delaying panel selection process.

Whereas panels are established on an *ad-hoc* basis, the AB is a standing body composed of seven Members appointed for 4-year terms. Hence, the AB was designed to hear all appeals regardless of the dispute. This means that there is no risk that a party would block its composition for a specific dispute. However, the process for selection or reappointment of AB Members can be blocked not only for the proceedings of a single dispute, but for all appeal proceedings under the WTO rules—a problem that is all too evident now.[108] Under MPIA rules, appeal arbitrators are selected from a pool of ten arbitrators based on the same principle of rotation for

---

[100] Pauwelyn and Pelc (2019), p. 7.

[101] Shoyer (2003), p. 205; Malacrida (2015), pp. 312–315.

[102] Pereyra (2019), p. 10.

[103] Malacrida (2015), p. 315.

[104] DSU, Art 8.7.

[105] Malacrida (2015), p. 316.

[106] Pauwelyn and Pelc (2019), p. 7.

[107] According to Art VI:4 of the Marrakesh Agreement, the responsibilities of the DG shall be exclusively international in character. In the discharge of his or her duties, the DG shall not seek or accept instructions from any government or any other authority external to the WTO.

[108] *See* Sect. 4.2.

the composition of an AB division.[109] Hence, as in the case of regular appeals, as long as there are more than three arbitrators in the pool, an appeal arbitration can take place. The pool of arbitrators has been already composed.[110] However, it will also be re-composed at any time or in case the crisis lasts longer—periodically, starting 2 years after the initial composition.[111] The composition and re-composition of the pool of arbitrators is carried out by consensus of the participating Members.[112] Therefore, a participating Member could block the re-composition of the pool of arbitrators. Nonetheless, as the participating Members are like-minded states that wish to have an alternative appeal mechanism, it is expected that consensus on the updated composition would be reached.

In conclusion, the process for selection of WTO panelists ensures that the composition stage proceeds smoothly, and a party cannot block the process. The AB, on the other hand, is a standing body, and there is no issue with its composition for particular cases. However, the appointment and reappointment of AB Members has proved to be a cause of serious problems in practice, threatening the entire mechanism. The pool of appeal arbitrators under the MPIA has been composed and the selection of arbitrators for single disputes should not pose a problem.

6.4.2 The Precedent Set by NAFTA

NAFTA is an example of a DSM that has become effectively idle because of the blockage of the process of panel selection by one of the parties.[113] After successfully resolving three disputes under NAFTA rules, the US blocked the panel composition process in a dispute that began in the late 1990s, and no panel has been established since then.[114] One of the main reasons behind the preference for the WTO mechanism over the NAFTA DSM might have been the latter's panel composition process susceptible to blockages.[115]

Chapter 20 of NAFTA on interstate dispute settlement established that the parties should endeavour to agree on the chair of the panel, with each party selecting two more panelists.[116] If disputing parties could not agree on the chairperson or other panelists, they were selected by lot.[117] Panelists were normally selected from a

---

[109]MPIA, para 4; Annex, para 7.

[110]Lester (2020a).

[111]MPIA, Annex 2, para 5.

[112]MPIA, Annex 2, para 4.

[113]Lester et al. (2019), pp. 63–79.

[114]Ibid, p. 64.

[115]Interview 4.

[116]NAFTA, Art 2011(2).

[117]NAFTA, Art 2011(2).

roster[118] consisting of up to thirty individuals willing and able to serve as panel-ists.[119] If an individual not on the roster was proposed as a panelist, any party could exercise a 'peremptory challenge' against that candidate.[120] If the roster was not complete and the respondent exercised its right to a peremptory challenge, it could block the panel composition process. Since the roster members were appointed by consensus for terms of 3 years, a party could also block the update of the roster, and there were no rules in place to regulate the panel composition process if there was no roster. The US used this unintentional or purposeful flaw to block the composition of the panels by refusing to agree on a roster. The original United States–Mexico–Canada Agreement (USMCA) rules failed to fix the roster problem, but it is probably addressed by the 2019 Protocol of Amendment.[121] Thus, under the updated USMCA rules, if parties do not manage to achieve consensus within 1 month on a roster of up to 30 individuals, with each party designating up to ten of them, the roster would be composed of the designated individuals.[122] The roster shall remain in effect for a minimum of 3 years or until a new roster is constituted. In case a party fails to designate its individuals, panels can still be established according to the Rules of Procedure that shall specify how to compose a panel in such circumstances.[123] Consequently, the roster problem is likely to have been solved.[124] Furthermore, the USMCA parties managed to agree on a full roster of thirty individuals.[125]

Therefore, NAFTA rules intentionally or by carelessness allowed a party to block the panel composition—a loophole that the US fully exploited. Having analysed the precedent established by NAFTA, it will be investigated whether the DSM rules of the new generation EU FTAs are designed in a manner to ensure that the panel composition processes cannot be blocked by one party, but are more automatic.

---

[118] NAFTA, Art 2011(3).

[119] NAFTA, Art 2009(1).

[120] NAFTA, Art 2011(3).

[121] Protocol of Amendment to the Agreement Between the United States of America, the United Mexican States, and Canada (Protocol of Amendment), Mexico City, Mexico, 10 December 2019.

[122] Protocol of Amendment, 7, C.

[123] Ibid.

[124] Gantz and Puig (2019). For other potential problems that could cause delays even under the amended USMCA rules, *see* Congressional Research Service (2020).

[125] Lester (2020b).

6.4.3 Panel Composition Under the New Generation EU FTA DSMs

6.4.3.1 Composing Panels When Lists of Arbitrators Are Established and Complete

All the new generation EU FTAs establish that parties shall consult in order to reach an agreement on the composition of the arbitration panels.[126] Panels shall be composed of three arbitrators, one of whom will be the chairperson.[127] Every FTA provides procedures for panel composition in the event of the parties not reaching an agreement.

Under the rules of all the new generation EU FTAs, the Trade Committees in EUKFTA, EUSFTA, and EUVTA or Joint Committees in CETA and EUJEPA (together referred to as Committees), co-chaired by the Member of the European Commission responsible for Trade and the respective representatives of the other parties at ministerial levels,[128] shall establish lists of individuals able and willing to serve as arbitrators for each party and non-nationals of the parties to act as chairpersons.[129] Depending on the FTA, the lists of arbitrators should be established within 6 months of entry into force of the agreement,[130] at the first meeting of the Committees,[131] or upon entry into force of the agreement.[132] Moreover, the Committees should ensure that the lists are maintained at the required minimum level.[133] Therefore, lists should be updated whenever the number of arbitrators drop below the threshold.

Under the EUKFTA and CETA, in the event that parties are unable to agree on the panel composition, either party to the dispute may request the chair of the Committees or their delegates to select by lot two arbitrators from the sub-lists of each party and another from the sub-list of chairpersons.[134] If parties agree only on some, but not all, arbitrators, any remaining arbitrator shall be selected by lot from

---

[126]EUKFTA, Art 14.5(2); CETA, Art 29.7(2); EUJEPA, Art 21.8(2); EUSFTA, Art 14.5(3); EUVFTA, Art 15.7(2).

[127]EUKFTA, Art 14.5(1); CETA, Art 29.7(1); EUJEPA, Art 21.8(1); EUSFTA, Art 14.5(1); EUVFTA, Art 15.7(1).

[128]EUKFTA, Art 15.1(2); CETA, Art 26.1(1); EUJEPA, Art 22.1(3); EUSFTA, Art 16.1(2); EUVFTA, Art 17.1(2).

[129]EUKFTA, Art 14.18(1); CETA, Art 29.8(1); EUJEPA, Art 21.9(1); EUSFTA, Art 14.20(1)(2); EUVFTA, Art 15.23(1).

[130]EUKFTA, Art 14.18(1); EUSFTA, Art 14.20(2)—on the lists of arbitrators not acting as chairpersons; EUVFTA, Art 15.23(1).

[131]CETA, Art 29.8(1); EUJEPA, Art 21.9(1).

[132]EUSFTA, Art 14.20(1)—on the list of chairpersons.

[133]EUKFTA, Art 14.18(1); CETA, Art 29.8(1); EUJEPA, Art 21.9(1); EUSFTA, Art 14.20(3); EUVFTA, Art 15.23(2).

[134]EUKFTA, Art 14.5(3); CETA, Art 29.7(3).

the respective sub-list.[135] Thus, in theory, as long as there are established lists of arbitrators, it is guaranteed that the panels will be composed. CETA establishes an additional condition—if the parties agree on an arbitrator other than the chairperson who is not a national of either party, the other arbitrator who is not a chairperson shall be selected from the sub-list of chairpersons.[136] This addition should be commended, as it ensures that there will be only balanced panels, in which both parties have a sitting national, or neither of them.

Yet, the success of selection by lot procedures also hinges on who is performing it. This default mechanism may be seriously weakened if the respondent can claim the power for selection.[137] As the chair of the Committees under the EUKFTA and CETA is held by representatives of both parties to the agreement, one of the co-chairs could potentially refuse to cooperate. The co-chairs are political appointees of the parties, one of which will be the respondent in a dispute. While this may involve bad faith, it is not difficult to imagine how one of the co-chairs might be interested in delaying the panel composition process.[138] The EUKFTA does not establish any measure that a complainant could use in the event of a co-chair being uncooperative, this raising concerns about the automaticity of the composition process under this agreement. The EUKFTA establishes that selection by lot should be performed within 5 days of the request for selection and in the presence of representatives of each party, unless a party fails to appoint its representative.[139] Thus, it establishes a strict deadline and gives representatives of each party the opportunity to observe the process to ensure fairness, unless they forego this right. However, in the case of one of the co-chairs not cooperating, there is no mechanism to compel it to select panelists by lot. Thus, despite the strict deadline, the mechanism is prone to potential delays.

CETA, on the other hand, establishes that selection by lot should take place 'as soon as possible and normally within five working days'.[140] This deadline concerned with the swiftness of the procedures should be commended. However, if it is not possible for the co-chairs, which act together, to select within this deadline, it could be overlooked, as the agreement uses the term 'normally'. The representatives of each party are also given a reasonable opportunity to be present during selection by lot and monitor the process. The use of the expression 'reasonable opportunity' may offer a motive for the respondent to object to the process of selection, since it is difficult to define what 'reasonable' means.[141] This could be an additional reason for the selection process to take more than 5 days. However, any extension would take place only if both co-chairs agree to it, ensuring that the interests of both parties are

[135] EUKFTA, Art 14.5(3); CETA, Art 29.7(3).

[136] CETA, Art 29.7(3).

[137] Chase et al. (2016), p. 645.

[138] Lester et al. (2019), p. 74.

[139] EUKFTA, Annex 14-B, Art 3.1(a).

[140] CETA, Art 29.7(4).

[141] Ibid.

protected. If one of the chairpersons is uncooperative, the other chairperson could 'perform the selection by lot alone if the other chairperson was informed about the date, time and place of the selection by lot and did not accept to participate within five working days of the receipt of the request'.[142] This provision has been criticised by Lester et al as being unclear about the meaning of 'did not accept' and whether mere silence, instead of a formal acknowledgement, would be enough.[143] Since CETA sets a deadline of 5 days in which the co-chairs have to accept to participate, mere silence seems to be enough to proceed to selection by lot performed by only one of them. A narrow interpretation of the norm that would require formal expression of unwillingness to participate has no textual basis and would defeat the purpose of the norm—to ensure that the panel selection process is not unilaterally blocked. Selection by lot performed by only one chairperson should not be treated as threatening the fairness of the process as this is only a measure of last resort, the other party and its co-chair being given the opportunity to participate. Thus, if lists are established, CETA generally provides automatic procedures for panel composition.

Under EUJEPA, EUSFTA, and EUVFTA rules, if parties do not reach an agreement on the composition of the panels, each party shall appoint an arbitrator from its own sub-lists within 5 (EUJEPA, EUSFTA) or 10 (EUVFTA) days.[144] This approach allows parties, even in case of disagreement, to choose from the lists that were agreed on by the representatives of both parties chairing the Committees and to have more control over who would decide their disputes. If parties do not agree on the chairperson or fail to select their own arbitrators, they shall be selected by lot from the corresponding sub-lists.[145] These agreements also set clear deadlines within which selection by lot should take place: within 5 days of the request for selection in the EUJEPA and EUVFTA,[146] and within 20 days of entering into consultations in the EUSFTA.[147] Incorporation of deadlines is meant to ensure that panels can be composed promptly, even when one party is not cooperative.

Under the EUVFTA, the party complained against can be present during selection by lot, if it so chooses, or the selection is carried out only with the party that is present;[148] it can also be performed by only one chairperson if the other chairperson or his delegate does not accept to participate.[149] In view of the deadline established for selection by lot and the fact that another interpretation would defeat the purpose of the norm, the expression 'does not accept' in the EUVFTA should be interpreted

---

[142] Ibid.

[143] Lester et al. (2019), p. 74.

[144] EUJEPA, Art 21.8(3); EUSFTA, Art 14.5(4); EUVFTA, Art 15.7(3).

[145] EUJEPA, Art 21.8(3) and (4); EUSFTA, Art 14.5(3) and (4); EUVFTA, Art 15.7(3) and (4).

[146] EUJEPA, Art 21.8(3) and (4); EUVFTA, Art 15.7(5).

[147] EUSFTA, Art 14.5(3) and (4).

[148] EUVFTA, Annex 15-A, para 8.

[149] EUVFTA, Annex 15-A, para 9.

in a similar way to that in CETA.[150] Under EUSFTA rules, parties are entitled to be present during selection by lot;[151] however, the chair of the Trade Committee that performs the procedure can delay it[152] and may act in bad faith. As in the case of the EUKFTA, there is no opportunity for one of the co-chairs to perform the selection alone; this may potentially cause considerable delays to the selection process.

In the EUJEPA, selection by lot is performed only by the co-chair of the Joint Committee from the complaining party or its representative.[153] This, certainly, ensures the automaticity of the procedures, but could raise concerns about its credibility and fairness. Yet, the Rules of Procedure provide that representatives of both parties may be present when lots are drawn, both co-chairs being informed with due anticipation about the date, time and venue by the designated office by the complaining party pursuant to the rules of the agreement.[154] Accordingly, the respondent, if it wishes so, can oversee the drawing of lots to alleviate potential concerns.

To conclude, CETA, EUJEPA, and EUVFTA ensure the automaticity of the procedures when lists of arbitrators are established by the Joint Committees; in contrast, the EUKFTA and EUSFTA may be prone to unwanted delays and blockages caused by the bad faith of the co-chairs of the Committees.

6.4.3.2 Composing Panels When the Lists of Arbitrators Are Not Established or Are Incomplete

If lists of arbitrators are not established or the lists do not have enough names, the procedures described above are not applicable. Although lists should ideally be established and updated, it is entirely possible that this may not be the case in practice, especially if parties do not act in good faith.

The EUKFTA text does not have procedures to follow when lists are not established or include an insufficient number of names. However, in 2013, the Trade Committee under the EUKFTA established by agreement a list of likely arbitrators.[155] Therefore, there is no current risk of lack of an established list. Nevertheless, there is no assurance for the parties that the list has enough names on each of the sub-lists to compose panels in the future. For example, two individuals

---

[150] See supra (nn 142, 143).

[151] EUSFTA, Annex 14-A, para 10, a).

[152] EUSFTA, Art 14.5(3) and (4).

[153] EUJEPA, Art 21.8(3) and (4).

[154] Decision of the Joint Committee of the EUJEPA, Annex 3, para 2.

[155] Decision No 2 of the EU–Korea Trade Committee of 23 December 2011 on the establishment of a list of arbitrators referred to in Article 14.18 of the Free Trade Agreement between the European Union and its Member States, of the one part, and the Republic of Korea, of the other part, 1 March 2013, OJ L58/13.

proposed as chairpersons have died since the list was established.[156] Since there seem to be no restrictions on the composition of the panels to take place despite the sub-list of chairpersons consisting of only three names, for the time being (only), the EUKFTA panel composition process is expected to progress without delays, except for the potential delays caused by uncooperative co-chairs.

In CETA, when the list of arbitrators 'is not established or if it does not contain sufficient names [. . .] the three arbitrators shall be drawn by lot from the arbitrators who have been proposed by one or both of the Parties.'[157] Hence, as long as the parties have proposed their own arbitrators and they are still available, panel composition is technically assured. Nonetheless, it is not clear from which sub-list the nominated arbitrators and chairpersons should be selected, within which deadline, and who should perform the selection. Whether the Chair of the Joint Committee or only one co-chair should select arbitrators is not specifically mentioned; therefore, this may enable the respondent acting in bad faith to use leverage to delay the proceedings. Reference to the rules for selection by lot applicable to the situation when there are established and complete lists of arbitrators may remediate this drawback. Moreover, CETA does not give preference to arbitrators proposed by both parties on incomplete lists over those proposed by only one party. Thus, a panel could, in theory, be composed of arbitrators proposed by only a single party, although there would be candidates agreed by both parties, which may raise concerns about the impartiality of the panel.

Under EUVFTA rules, if there are no established lists of arbitrators or the lists are incomplete, 'the arbitrators shall be drawn by lot from among the individuals who have been formally proposed by both Parties or by a Party in the event that only one Party has made a proposal.'[158] Hence, similar to CETA, it does not establish the exact sub-lists for selection, yet it has some improvements. According to the Rules of Procedures under the EUVFTA, selection by lot should be carried out at a time and place decided by the complainant, the respondent being only notified of this.[159] With the complainant being in charge of setting the time for selection by lot, the respondent is given fewer opportunities to delay this process. Furthermore, the EUVFTA clearly establishes that candidates proposed by both parties are preferred to those proposed by only one of them, thereby increasing the degree of impartiality of the potential panels.

For chairpersons, the EUJEPA establishes that (1) whenever there are at least two individuals on the sub-list, the co-chair of the Joint Committee from the complainant shall select the chairperson by lot within 5 days of the request to select; (2) if there is only one individual on the sub-list, that individual should act as a chairperson; (3) if there is no individual on the sub-list, 'the Co-chair of the Joint Committee from the complaining party shall, no later than five days after the date of delivery of the

---

[156] Florentino Feliciano died in 2015 and Virachai Plasai in 2019.

[157] CETA, Art 29.7(6).

[158] EUVFTA, Art 15.7(7).

[159] EUVFTA, Annex 15-A, para 8.

request referred to in paragraph 4, select by lot the chairperson from the individuals who had been formally proposed by a party as chairperson at the time of establishing or updating the list of arbitrators'.[160] The procedure for selection of arbitrators not acting as chairpersons is similar: (1) if a party's sub-list contains two individuals, that party shall select one of them within 5 days of the period allocated for the parties to agree on panel composition; (2) if there is only one individual on the sub-list, that individual should act as arbitrator; and (3) if there are no individuals on the lists, the co-chair of the Joint Committee from the complainant should apply *mutatis mutandis* the procedures used for selection of the chairperson, meaning that the arbitrators shall be selected by lot within 5 days of the request, from the individuals formally proposed by a party to act as arbitrators.[161] Therefore, the EUJEPA has clear procedures with clear deadlines if the list of arbitrators is not established or is incomplete. If a party has proposed individuals for its own sub-list, even though the other party has not proposed any individual at all, it can be assured that a panel will be composed.[162] Preference is always given to individuals on the sub-lists established by the Joint Committee over those proposed by one party and not agreed on, thus guaranteeing that the interests of both parties are protected. Moreover, the selection by lot is performed by the co-chair from the complainant, thus securing the swiftness of the selection procedures.

The EUSFTA, like the EUJEPA, has separate procedures for selection of chairpersons and the other arbitrators. For selection of arbitrators not acting as chairpersons: (1) if both parties proposed individuals, each party shall select one within 15 days of entering into consultations to compose the panels, and if a party fails to select an arbitrator, the chair of the Trade Committee or its delegate shall select the arbitrator by lot from among the individuals proposed by the party that failed to select its arbitrator; and (2) where only one party proposed individuals, each party shall select one arbitrator from those proposed, and if a party fails to do so, the arbitrator shall be selected by lot by the chair of the Trade Committee or its delegate. These procedures ensure that if one party proposed its own candidates, arbitrators other than chairpersons will be selected from these individuals. However, there is no timeline for the selection by lot procedures, and they could be delayed by an uncooperative co-chair of the Trade Committee acting in bad faith. When the list of potential chairpersons is not established, 'the chairperson shall be selected by lot from among former Members of the WTO Appellate Body, who shall not be a person of either Party.' This is a unique provision compared to those in other new generation EU FTAs. It secures that the chairperson would always be a non-national of the parties and that it would not have the support of one single party. Moreover, former AB members have tremendous expertise in the field of international trade law. However, there is no deadline for selection of chairpersons, nor is it established who should be responsible for this selection, which could cause significant delays.

---

[160] EUJEPA, Art 21.8(5)(a).

[161] EUJEPA, Art 21.8(5)(b).

[162] Lester et al. (2019), p. 76.

To conclude, the EUKFTA may suffer from blockages in the event its list of arbitrators is incomplete. CETA and EUVFTA (with some improvements) offer procedures that technically ensure that the selection process can take place even without established and complete lists; however, the vague procedures could cause delays. Furthermore, CETA procedures may raise concerns about the impartiality of the panels. The EUSFTA has selection procedures for arbitrators not acting as chairpersons that could be delayed by uncooperative co-chairs of the Trade Committee and are not constrained by any timelines, while the unique procedures for selecting chairpersons could be delayed because of ambiguity. The EUJEPA, in contrast, offers automatic procedures to ensure that there are no blockages.

6.4.4 Implications of the Panel Composition Process for the Competition Between the New Generation EU FTA and the WTO DSMs

The panel selection process in WTO is automatic, and it ensures that it is not blocked or delayed, even if one party is not cooperative. Moreover, the authority proposing candidates and establishing the composition of the panel is an independent third party. The formation of divisions of AB Members and appeal arbitrators is not prone to blockages in single disputes, but the AB has already been rendered dysfunctional by the blocking of appointments and reappointments of AB Members.

The new generation EU FTAs also have mechanisms in place to ensure that when parties cannot agree on the composition of panels, they would be composed with the help of lists of arbitrators established by the parties. While CETA, EUJEPA, and EUVFTA ensure that panel composition at this stage will not be blocked, the EUKFTA and EUSFTA are prone to potential delays because the authority entitled to selecting the panelists might act in bad faith. In comparison, the EUJEPA ensures that the entitled authority will not block selection; however, this authority is only affiliated to one of the parties which raises concerns about the credibility of the process. When there are no lists established, only the EUJEPA offers automatic procedures. The EUKFTA does not regulate this situation at all, while the EUSFTA, EUVFTA and CETA (with respect to the chairpersons' selection) have ambiguous provisions that could cause undesirable delays, were the parties to act in bad faith.

While some of the new generation EU FTAs might be more exposed than others to potential blockages at the panel composition stage, amid the AB crisis, the amended Enforcement Regulation[163] addresses how the EU could enforce its rights not only in case the AB is dysfunctional, but also in case a third country does not cooperate, as necessary, for the composition of panels under bilateral or regional

---

[163] Regulation (EU) 2021/167 of the European Parliament and of the Council of 10 February 2021 amending Regulation (EU) No 654/2014 concerning the exercise of the Union's rights for the application and enforcement of international trade rules, OJ L 49, 12.2.2021, pp. 1–5.

agreements.[164] According to the proposal for the amendment,[165] the general public international law as codified in the International Law Commission Draft Articles on Responsibility of States for Internationally Wrongful Acts (ILC articles on state responsibility)[166] establishes that 'a party taking countermeasures is not relieved from fulfilling its obligations under any applicable dispute settlement procedure'— obligations that are *lex specialis* in relation to general public international law on countermeasures.[167] The Commission argued that 'when one Party "fails to implement the dispute settlement procedures in good faith" or "where a State party fails to cooperate in the establishment of the relevant tribunal"', 'the possibility to resort to countermeasures in accordance with the requirements of general public international law necessarily revives'.[168] Accordingly, the amended Regulation allows the EU, in case another FTA party would not cooperate in good faith for the panel composition, to impose countermeasures.[169] Whereas the analysis of the legality of the amendments under general public international law and international trade law rules is outside the scope of this section,[170] if adopted and used by the EU, it could compel other FTA parties to be more cooperative at the stage of panel composition, due to the threat of EU countermeasures.

The panel composition processes under the new generation EU FTAs do not seem to offer the same degree of automaticity, which may imperil their likelihood of becoming viable alternatives to the WTO DSM. Nevertheless, if parties act in good faith and establish lists of arbitrators, panel composition processes would not be threatened by blockages and undesirable delays. The newly amended Enforcement Regulation may also serve as a stimulus for FTA parties, other than the EU, to compose the panels. Moreover, the FTA panel composition processes offer the

---

[164] Ibid, Preamble, Recitals (4) and (6), Art 1.

[165] Proposal for a Regulation of the European Parliament and of the Council amending Regulation (EU) No 654/2014 of the European Parliament and of the Council Concerning the Exercise of the Union's Rights for the Application and Enforcement of International Trade Rules ('EU Commission Proposal to Amend the Enforcement Regulation'), Brussels, 12.12.2019, COM(2019) 623 final, 2019/0273 (COD).

[166] Text adopted by the International Law Commission at its 53rd session, in 2001, and submitted to the General Assembly as a part of the Commission's report covering the work of that session (A/56/ 10). The report, which also contains commentaries on the draft articles, appears in the Yearbook of the International Law Commission, 2001, vol. II, Part Two, as corrected.

[167] EU Commission Proposal to Amend the Enforcement Regulation referring to ILC Articles on state responsibility, Arts 50.2(a) and 55 in the Explanatory Memorandum, footnotes 7 and 8.

[168] EU Commission Proposal to Amend the Enforcement Regulation referring to ILC Articles on state responsibility, Arts 52(3)(b) and 52(4) and commentaries (2), (8) and (9) in the Explanatory Memorandum, fn 9.

[169] Regulation (EU) No 654/2014 concerning the exercise of the Union's rights for the application and enforcement of international trade rules and amending Council Regulation (EC) No 3286/94 laying down Community procedures in the field of the common commercial policy in order to ensure the exercise of the Community's rights under international trade rules, in particular those established under the auspices of the World Trade Organization (Consolidated version), Art 3 (ba).

[170] In this respect see Weiss and Furculita (2020).

parties greater control over the procedures and the choice of arbitrators. By appointing *ad-hoc* arbitrators, the parties can exercise *ex-ante* control over who would decide the dispute, and the arbitrators are more likely to adopt less activist interpretations.[171] Compared to the WTO, where the selection process is conducted with the involvement of third parties such as the Secretariat and the DG when there is no agreement between the parties, under the rules of the new generation EU FTAs, the parties are more involved. While the indicative list of individuals maintained by the WTO Secretariat contains names that can be proposed by any Member State, and the Secretariat can propose candidates outside the indicative list, the lists under the new generation EU FTAs have only names proposed and selected by the two parties, offering greater control over who would adjudicate disputes. Furthermore, the EUJEPA, EUSFTA and EUVFTA entitle the parties to choose arbitrators from their own lists, even if they do not agree on the panel composition.

To conclude, potential blockages at the stage of panel selection may serve as a reason for FTA parties to choose the WTO DSM. Nevertheless, the new generation EU FTAs could still provide attractive alternative DSMs, if the parties seek greater control over the procedures, and provided that they act in good faith and establish lists of arbitrators.

6.5 Qualifications and Obligations of Panelists, Arbitrators and AB Members

When states entrust a third party with resolving disputes between them and making binding decisions, the panels must be composed of competent and confidence-inspiring people.[172] Therefore, the independence, qualifications, and expertise of the selected panelists are also aspects that could determine the ways in which DSMs compete. One of the reasons for the states' steady choice of the WTO DSM might have been their perception of the WTO panels as being more neutral and fairer.[173]

6.5.1 Qualifications and Obligations of Panelists and AB Members

WTO panels shall be composed of 'well-qualified governmental and/or non-governmental individuals' with experience in WTO litigation or in serving as representatives of Members of GATT 1947 or a Council or Committee of a covered agreement or as senior trade officials of Members, or in teaching and publishing on

---

[171] Pauwelyn and Elsig (2013), p. 463.

[172] Porges (2011), p. 484.

[173] Interview 1; Interview 4.

international trade and policy.[174] In the process of selection of panelists, their independence, diverse background, and wide spectrum of experience shall be ensured.[175] In practice, however, the requirements for qualifications are not always implemented and they are difficult to check.[176] There is a 'general feeling that most panelists lack experience'.[177] Thus, the majority of panelists have served on panels only once, and most of those who served were 'low key diplomats'.[178] It has been noted that once a person has voiced opinions in previous cases or has authored works with views in favour of or against trade or trade protectionism, it is unlikely that the parties would reach an agreement that the individual is selected as a panelist.[179] Thus, while scholars have criticised the lack of experience of the panelists, the states, nevertheless seem to have preferred less experienced panelists with a governmental background.

The DSU also provides requirements for AB Members. They should be persons of 'recognized authority, with demonstrated expertise in law, international trade and the subject matter of the covered agreements generally', 'unaffiliated with any government', and 'broadly representative of membership in the WTO'.[180] Hence, compared to panelists, AB Members are required to have expertise in law. Furthermore, AB Members, being part of a standing body and hearing appeals over the course of 4 or even 8 years, if reappointed, gain significant experience in the field.[181] To protect the independence and impartiality of AB Members, any professional activity inconsistent with their duties and taking any instructions from any organisation (international, governmental, or non-governmental) or private source are prohibited.[182] They should also not participate in cases that raise direct or indirect conflicts of interest.[183] More detailed rules that aim to ensure the independence, impartiality, and integrity of both panelists and AB Members are provided in the Rules of Conduct.[184] The MPIA requires the same qualifications for the appeal arbitrators as for AB Members.[185] It also stipulates that the DSU provisions and other rules and procedures applicable to appellate review are applicable *mutatis*

---

[174] DSU, Art 8.1.

[175] DSU, Art 8.2.

[176] Busch and Pelc (2009), p. 581; Pauwelyn (2015), p. 792.

[177] Cottier (2003), p. 193.

[178] Pauwelyn (2015), p. 792.

[179] Roessler (2003), p. 233; Pauwelyn (2015), p. 787.

[180] DSU, Art 17.3.

[181] Todeschini-Marthe (2018), p. 400.

[182] Appellate Body, Working Procedures for Appellate Review, WT/AB/WP/6, 16 August 2010, Part I, 2 paras (2) and (3).

[183] DSU, Art 17. 3.

[184] Rules of Conduct for the Understanding on Rules and Procedures Governing the Settlement of Disputes, WT/DSB/RC/1, 11 December 1996; Rules of Conduct for the Understanding on Rules and Procedures Governing the Settlement of Disputes, Annex II, WT/AB/WP/6, 16 August 2010.

[185] MPIA, paras 4, 5; Annex 2, para 3.

mutandis.[186] Therefore, the provisions on impartiality and independence in the Working Procedures for Appellate Review and the Rules of Conduct are applicable to appellate arbitrators in the same way as to AB Members.

In its DSU reform proposal, the EU proposed organising meetings between the AB and WTO Members where the latter could express their views, but it also proposed several DSU amendments to enhance the independence and impartiality of the AB. Thus, the independence and impartiality of the AB Members is of particular importance to the EU.[187] While the EU might desire the means to ensure that the AB Members stay true to the intention of the parties when interpreting WTO agreements, it does not wish to undermine their independence and impartiality. The possibility of blocking the reappointment of AB Members by any state that dislikes the way a Member contributed to AB rulings, or to generally block any appointment and reappointment of AB Members because of the entire activity of the body, could seriously compromise the independence and impartiality of AB Members.[188] Such blockages could be considered a serious drawback by WTO Members who could perceive the mechanism as being prone to undesirable interference and outside pressure.

6.5.2   Qualifications and Obligations of Arbitrators Under the New Generation EU FTAs

Arbitrators appointed under the rules of the new generation FTAs shall have specialised knowledge of international trade law, be independent, serve in their individual capacities, and not take instructions from any organisation or government, or be affiliated with the government of any party.[189] The EUVFTA also requires experience of law and international trade for all arbitrators,[190] while CETA additionally asks from chairpersons experience as counsel or panelist in dispute settlement proceedings on subject matters covered by the agreements.[191] Similar to the requirements for WTO panelists, it would be difficult to check the requirements on knowledge and experience in the field for arbitrators under the new generation EU FTAs. Moreover, vast experience will not be required, except from chairpersons under CETA. Therefore, whether or not arbitrators under these agreements have greater experience than WTO panelists will depend mostly on the will of the parties that either appoint them by agreement or propose names from which the panellists

---

[186]MPIA, Annex 2, para 11.

[187]Interview 1; Interview 2.

[188]Sacerdoti (2018), p. 95.

[189]EUKFTA, Art 14.18(2); CETA, Art 29.8(2); EUJEPA, Art 21.10; EUSFTA, Art 14.20(4); EUVFTA, Art 15.23(3).

[190]EUVFTA, Art 15.23(3).

[191]CETA, Art 29.8(2).

are selected by the chairs or one of the co-chairs of the Committees.[192] Therefore, the extent of panelists' experience in adjudication will depend on the parties and, as the WTO's practice shows, it is very likely that parties would prefer individuals who are not outspoken about their views on trade matters. Nevertheless, as panel rulings under the new generation EU FTAs will not be subject to appeals conducted by experienced AB Members, it may well be that parties would prefer more experienced individuals. However, only practice will show how qualified and experienced the selected arbitrators will be under the new generation EU FTAs.

In addition, all the new generation EU FTAs prescribe that arbitrators should comply with their Codes of Conduct.[193] The Codes of Conduct prescribe duties to preserve the fairness and diligence, include disclosure obligations to avoid conflicts of interest, and regulate activities that may impair the independence and impartiality of the arbitrators.[194] Moreover, arbitrators shall not only actually be independent, but also avoid creating an appearance of bias, and shall not be influenced by self-interest, outside pressure, political considerations, public clamour, loyalty to a party or fear of criticism.[195] The new generation EU FTAs allow arbitrators not acting as chairpersons to have the nationality of the parties, and in some cases when there are no established or complete lists, even chairpersons can be nationals of the parties.[196]

To sum up, the new generation EU FTAs require that arbitrators have knowledge or even experience in international trade law, and include detailed rules aimed at ensuring their impartiality and independence.

6.5.3   *Implications of Qualifications and Obligations of Arbitrators, Panelists and AB Members on the Preference for a DSM*

WTO rules should, in theory, ensure that the panelists and AB Members are well qualified in the field of international trade law and that they act in an independent and impartial manner. Yet, practice shows that panels have little experience in the field and WTO Members can attempt to exert pressure on the AB. The new generation EU FTAs also require arbitrators to be qualified in international law and prescribe rules

---

[192] *See supra* Sect. 6.4.

[193] EUKFTA, Art 14.18(2); CETA, Art 29.8(2); EUJEPA, Art 21.10; EUSFTA, Art 14.20(4); EUVFTA, Art 15.23(3).

[194] EUKFTA, Annex 14-C; CETA, Annex 29-B; Decision of the Joint Committee of the EUJEPA, Annex 4; EUSFTA, Annex 14-B; EUVFTA, Annex 15-B.

[195] EUKFTA, Annex 14-C, Art. 5.1; CETA, Annex 29-B, para 11; EUSFTA, Annex 14-B, para 10; EUVFTA, Annex 15-B, para 10.

[196] EUKFTA, Art 14.18(1); CETA, Ar. 29.8(1); EUJEPA, Art 21.9(1); EUVFTA, Art 15.23(1). For more on the selection process when the lists are incomplete or not established, *see supra* Sect. 6.4.3.2.

to ensure their independence and impartiality. Thus, the requirements are quite similar in terms of expertise in international trade law, independence, and impartiality. Moreover, as with WTO panelists, the arbitrators' actual degree of experience in international trade litigation may be limited. Thus, from the perspective of competition, the new generation EU FTAs potentially offer the possibility of having cases heard by arbitrators with qualifications similar to those of WTO panelists. Nonetheless, the same cannot be said about AB Members and appellate arbitrators who would have more experience in adjudication. If parties would seek more experienced panels, but no agreement could be reached between the parties on selecting highly experienced arbitrators, they may perceive the panels under the new generation EU FTAs as not being comparable to the AB or appeal arbitrators in terms of experience and regard the WTO DSM as more appropriate. However, the greater control that parties have over the selection of panelists under FTA rules may be appealing to them in certain cases, if this possibility is balanced with the preservation of the independence and impartiality of arbitrators.

Under the new generation EU FTAs, parties should not, in theory, be concerned about the impartiality and independence of arbitrators. At the same time, having nationals of both parties on the panel, despite the arbitrators' impartiality and independence obligations, implies that the panel may be less independent and the burden to decide would rest *de facto* on the chairperson,[197] as reaching consensus may be more difficult when two panelists are nationals of the two disputing parties. Panelists that are nationals of the parties could be accused of bias and favouritism. Even very few cases in which allegations of bias would be made about FTA panelists, could affect the credibility of the DSMs of these agreements.[198]

The fact that the parties themselves designed the mechanisms and enshrined in the agreements that nationals of their parties can serve as arbitrators (except chairpersons) may indicate that the parties preferred mechanisms that would offer them more control over who will decide FTA disputes. Therefore, the parties could ultimately perceive the new generation EU FTA DSMs as attractive alternatives to the WTO DSM in terms of who would serve as arbitrators, in case they desired greater control over the selection of panelists; however, they may still prefer the WTO DSM if it had a functional experienced AB or if the FTA disputing parties were participating Members of a functional MPIA.

6.6   Rules of Procedure

Once the panels are established under the WTO and the new generation EU FTAs, they can start their work as a body. This section will analyse whether there are specific rules of procedure that should be followed for all disputes or whether the

---

[197] Pauwelyn (2004), p. 251.

[198] Davey (2006), p. 355.

course of procedures is established on an *ad-hoc* basis or if there are rules that prescribe it, and finally, what the implications are for the competition between the WTO DSM and the new generation EU FTA DSMs.

6.6.1 WTO Rules of Procedure

WTO panels, after their establishment, shall set the working procedures and the timetable for their work. The panel should follow the working procedures and timetables described in Appendix 3 of the DSU on Working Procedures; however, the rules are flexible and, after consulting the parties at the first organisational meeting, panels can follow different procedures.[199] In practice, panels generally follow the procedures and time frames prescribed in Appendix 3, while including rules and timelines for specific situations that may arise in every dispute, such as consultations with experts, confidential business information, preliminary rulings, etc.[200]

  The panels shall also set clear deadlines for written submissions.[201] The first written submissions containing the facts of the case and the parties' arguments should be filed before the first substantive meeting by each party and within the deadline, the complainant filling first, unless the panel decides that the submissions should be filed simultaneously.[202] The submissions shall be deposited to the WTO Secretariat that shall transmit them to the panel and the parties.[203] In practice, however, parties serve copies to each other directly and deposit the submissions for panel access at the Dispute Settlement Registry.[204] Third parties receive the parties' submissions for the first meeting[205] and file their own submissions afterwards. After the first exchange of written submissions, the first substantive meeting takes place, during which parties orally present their views, followed by presentation of the third parties' views.[206] The first substantive meeting is followed by submission of written rebuttals in which parties respond to each other's first submissions, and then by the second substantive meeting during which parties present factual and

---

[199] DSU, Art 12.1, 12.2, 12.3; Appendix 3, para 11.

[200] WTO Secretariat (2017), p. 74.

[201] DSU, Art 12.5.

[202] DSU, Art 12.6, Appendix 3, para 4.

[203] DSU, Art 12.6.

[204] In 2002, the Secretariat established a dispute settlement registry which receives and files the submissions and maintains the official record of every dispute at the panel stage (WTO, 'The process – Stages in a typical WTO dispute settlement case' <www.wto.org/english/tratop_e/dispu_e/disp_settlement_cbt_e/c6s3p3_e.htm#fnt2>.

[205] DSU, Art 10.3.

[206] DSU, Appendix 3, paras 5, 6.

oral arguments as rebuttals, with the complainant presenting first.[207] The oral presentations at both the first and second substantive meetings shall be accompanied by written versions submitted to the panel.[208] The panel may at any time address questions to the parties and ask for explanations either in the course of the meetings or in writing afterwards.[209] The parties can answer these questions, as well as questions from other parties during the meetings to the extent that such questions can be answered orally and later also in written form within a set deadline.[210] The panels can suspend their work any time, at the request of the complainant, for a maximum of 12 months to allow parties to reach an MAS. However, if the suspension exceeds 12 months and the dispute remains unresolved, the complainant would need to initiate new proceedings.[211]

To ensure that panels can exercise their function appropriately, especially because they recognise their own limits of expertise in specific areas,[212] WTO panels enjoy the right to seek information and technical advice from any individual or body, including from individual experts or expert review groups.[213] Experts are chosen by the panels in consultation with the parties only for disputes arising under the SPS Agreement.[214] As experts provide technical advice that panels may rely on, it is indispensable that they are independent and impartial. Experts, as well as panelists, are subject to the Rules of Conduct that should ensure their independence and impartiality.[215] Moreover, Appendix 4 on Expert Review Groups, which also indicates the requirements for individual experts, establishes that nationals of the parties cannot serve as experts unless parties jointly agree otherwise or the panel considers that the need for specialised expertise cannot be fulfilled otherwise. Furthermore, government officials of the parties shall not serve as experts in any case. Therefore, WTO rules strive to ensure that experts will act impartially.

As appeals should be limited only to legal questions[216] and the AB should deal with allegations of legal errors in the panel reports, the AB's rules of procedure are different from those at the panel level and will only be briefly addressed here. The procedures at the appellate stage are very similar to those of the panels;[217] however,

---

[207] DSU, Appendix 3, para 7.

[208] DSU, Appendix 3, para 9.

[209] DSU, Appendix 3, para 8.

[210] WTO, 'The process – Stages in a typical WTO dispute settlement case' <https://www.wto.org/english/tratop_e/dispu_e/disp_settlement_cbt_e/c6s3p3_e.htm#fnt2>.

[211] DSU, Art 12.12.

[212] Marceau and Hawkins (2012), pp. 494, 504.

[213] DSU, Art 13; Appellate Body Report, *EC – Hormones*, WT/DS26/AB/R, 16 January 1998, [148].

[214] SPS Agreement, Art 11.2.

[215] Rules of Conduct for the Understanding on Rules and Procedures Governing the Settlement of Disputes, WT/DSB/RC/1, 11 December 1996, IV.1(d).

[216] DSU, Art 17.6. The delimitation of issues of law from those of facts is a contentious issue that is outside the scope of this book.

[217] Working Procedures for Appellate Review, Rules 27, 28.

written submissions and any other communication are filed with the AB Secretariat and directly sent to other parties, third parties, participants, and third participants.[218] Moreover, there is usually only one hearing that is similar to substantive meetings of the panel, but during which oral statements are quite short and parties cannot address questions to each other.[219] In addition, if a procedural question arises that is not covered by the Rules of Procedure for Appellate Review, a division may adopt appropriate procedures for the purposes of that appeal only, provided that it is not inconsistent with the DSU, the other covered agreements, and the Rules of Procedure.[220] The AB used this provision for such cases as adopting special procedures to protect confidential business information[221] or to deal with *amicus curiae* briefs.[222] Finally, *ex parte* communications with both panels and the AB about matters under consideration are prohibited.[223] The rules of procedure under the MPIA for the appeal arbitration stage are similar to those applicable to regular appellate proceedings. The DSU and Working Procedures for Appellate Review apply *mutatis mutandis*, unless by mutual agreement the parties to a specific dispute decide to depart from them without prejudicing the principles set in the arrangement.[224]

The description in this section shows that the WTO rules, also applicable under the MPIA, prescribe in detail how the dispute settlement procedures should take place. In addition, many procedural questions, such as those related to evidence, standard of review, or burden of proof, have been developed in the practice of the WTO's adjudicating bodies.[225] Therefore, the WTO DSM can provide predictability of rules of procedure, with disputing parties having clarity in how different issues could be approached.

---

[218] Working Procedures for Appellate Review, Rule 18(1), (2). According to the Working Procedures, a '"participant" means any party to the dispute that has filed a Notice of Appeal pursuant to Rule 20, a Notice of Other Appeal pursuant to Rule 23 or a submission pursuant to Rule 22 or paragraph 4 of Rule 23', and '"third participant" means any third party that has filed a written submission pursuant to Rule 24(1); or any third party that appears at the oral hearing, whether or not it makes an oral statement at that hearing'.

[219] WTO Secretariat (2017), p. 118.

[220] Working Procedures for Appellate Review, Rule 16(1).

[221] Appellate Body Report, *European Communities and Certain Member States – Measures Affecting Trade in Large Civil Aircraft (EC – Aircraft)*, WT/DS316/AB/R, 18 May 2011, Annex III, [26].

[222] Appellate Body Report, *EC – Asbestos,* [52].

[223] DSU, Art 18.1.

[224] MPIA, para 11, Annex 1, paras 5, 11.

[225] In this respect, *see* Malacrida and Marceau (2018), pp. 35–43.

6.6.2 Rules of Procedure Under the New Generation EU FTAs

The new generation EU FTAs include detailed rules of procedure for arbitration. The rules establish the means of notification and communication between the panel and the parties and also between the parties.[226] There are also rules that address corrections of possible minor errors of a clerical nature, as well as deadlines for the cases in which the last day is a holiday of a party.[227]

The parties shall meet the panel within 7 days (or 10 days in the EUVFTA) of its establishment to determine matters that the panel or the parties deem appropriate, such as the remuneration and expenses of the arbitrators.[228] This meeting seems similar to the first organisational meeting that WTO panels hold with the parties, as it also has only an organisational purpose. After this initial meeting, the phase of written submissions follows, similar to that in WTO panel proceedings, during which the complainant and then the respondent deliver their submissions.[229]

The hearings take place after this stage. The dates and times of the hearings are fixed by the chairperson in consultation with the parties and other arbitrators.[230] The new generation EU FTAs also establish rules for the city in which hearings should be held depending on who initiated the proceedings or by alternating between the parties, unless they agree otherwise.[231] The agreements also specify who may attend the hearings, the names of the persons making oral arguments or delivering presentations to the panel, and (with the exception of the EUJEPA) that only the representatives and advisers of the parties can address the panel.[232] As in WTO panel proceedings, parties present their submissions and rebuttals verbally. However, under the new generation EU FTAs, the initial statements and rebuttals take place within one single hearing, the rules of procedure providing the order of

---

[226]EUKFTA, Annex 14-B, Art 2.1; CETA, Annex 29-A, para 3; Decision of the Joint Committee of the EUJEPA, Annex 3, paras 5–7; EUSFTA, Annex 14-A, para 4; EUVFTA, Annex 15-A, paras 3, 4.

[227]EUKFTA, Annex 14-B, Arts 2.4, 2.5; CETA, Annex 29-A, paras 5, 6; Decision of the Joint Committee of the EUJEPA, Annex 3, paras 8, 9; EUSFTA, Annex 14-A, paras 7, 8; EUVFTA, Annex 15-A, paras 6, 7.

[228]EUKFTA, Annex 14-B, Art 3.1(b); CETA, Annex 29-A, para 8; Decision of the Joint Committee of the EUJEPA, Annex 3, para 4; EUSFTA, Annex 14-A, para 10(a); EUVFTA, Art 15.8(2).

[229]EUKFTA, Annex 14-B, Art 4; CETA, Annex 29-A, para 10; Decision of the Joint Committee of the EUJEPA, Annex 3, para 10; EUSFTA, Annex 14-A, para 12; EUVFTA, Annex 15-A, para 14.

[230]EUKFTA, Annex 14-B, Art 7(1); CETA, Annex 29-A, para 26; Decision of the Joint Committee of the EUJEPA, Annex 3, para 15; EUSFTA, Annex 14-A, para 26; EUVFTA, Annex 15-A, para 25.

[231]EUKFTA, Annex 14-B, Art 7(2); CETA, Annex 29-A, para 27; EUJEPA, Art 21.15(2); EUSFTA, Annex 14-A, para 27; EUVFTA, Art 15.8(3).

[232]EUKFTA, Annex 14-B, Art 7(5), 7(6); CETA, Annex 29-A, paras 30, 31; Decision of the Joint Committee of the EUJEPA, Annex 3, paras 21, 22; EUSFTA, Annex 14-A, paras 30, 31; EUVFTA, Annex 15-A, paras 28, 29, 30.

presentation, ensuring that parties are afforded equal time, while the complainant presents first during both submissions and rebuttals.[233] During the hearing, the panel can direct questions to any party at any time.[234] Although there should be only one hearing, the parties are entitled afterwards to submit supplementary written submissions on any matter that arose during the hearings.[235] Therefore, parties can still respond to questions that they could not respond to during the hearings. As in WTO panel proceedings, under the new generation EU FTAs, the panels can address questions in writing to the parties at any time. Moreover, the new generation EU FTAs provide that such questions, as well as the answers to them, shall be made available as copies to the other party which is also entitled to providing written comments on the first party's reply.[236] Therefore, this process ensures that every party is given the opportunity to comment on the same matters as the other party.

Except for the EUKFTA, the rest of the new generation EU FTAs, like the DSU, provide that panels can suspend their work. In the EUJEPA, EUSFTA, and EUVFTA, the procedures can be suspended for a maximum period of 12 months at the request of both parties, and panels can resume their work at the end of the period at the written request of any party or, specifically, the complaining party (in the case of the EUSFTA) or before the expiry of the agreed suspension period at the joint request of the parties.[237] In contrast, CETA establishes that a suspension of a maximum of 12 months as well as resumption shall take place at the request of the complainant only, but there is no maximum set for the period which parties can request for suspension of equivalence proceedings and for compliance post-retaliation proceedings.[238] In all these agreements, if the specified period in the request lapses and no request for resumption is made, the proceedings shall be terminated.[239] Therefore, if the dispute is not resolved and the proceedings are not resumed, parties would have to initiate a new dispute as under WTO rules.

As in the WTO panel procedures, the panels established under the new generation EU FTAs may seek information and advice from any source they deem appropriate,

---

[233] EUKFTA, Annex 14-B, Art 7(8); CETA, Annex 29-A, para 32; Decision of the Joint Committee of the EUJEPA, Annex 3, para 23; EUSFTA, Annex 14-A, para 33; EUVFTA, Annex 15-A, para 31.

[234] EUKFTA, Annex 14-B, Art 7(9); CETA, Annex 29-A, para 33; Decision of the Joint Committee of the EUJEPA, Annex 3, para 24; EUSFTA, Annex 14-A, para 34; EUVFTA, Annex 15-A, para 32.

[235] EUKFTA, Annex 14-B, Art 7(11); CETA, Annex 29-A, para 35; Decision of the Joint Committee of the EUJEPA, Annex 3, para 26; EUSFTA, Annex 14-A, para 36; EUVFTA, Annex 15-A, para 34.

[236] EUKFTA, Annex 14-B, Art 8; CETA, Annex 29-A, paras 36, 37; Decision of the Joint Committee of the EUJEPA, Annex 3, paras 28, 29; EUSFTA, Annex 14-A, paras 37, 38; EUVFTA, Annex 15-A, paras 35, 36.

[237] EUJEPA, Art 21.24; EUSFTA, Art 14.14(1); EUVFTA, Art 15.18(1).

[238] CETA, Annex 29-A, para 20. *See also infra* Sect. 6.12.2.3.

[239] CETA, Annex 29-A, para 20; EUJEPA, Art 21.24; EUSFTA, Art 14.14(1); EUVFTA, Art 15.18 (1).

including from experts.[240] Similar to panels in SPS disputes, the panels under the EUSFTA and EUVFTA shall consult the parties before choosing experts.[241] Moreover, all new generation EU FTAs provide that any information obtained by the panels shall be disclosed to the parties and they can comment on it.[242] Therefore, the agreements ensure that even when the panel seeks information from other sources, parties are still involved and can have a say on this information, while the final assessment is still left to the panel. Nevertheless, the new generation EU FTAs provide no rules of conduct or other rules that would ensure the impartiality of the experts as WTO rules do. Therefore, it seems possible that nationals of parties, governmental officials, or experts with conflicts of interest could serve as experts, and there are no procedures that a party could use when it considers that an expert is not impartial.

Similar to the Working Procedures for Appellate Review, the new generation EU FTAs establish that when a procedural question arises that is not covered by the provisions of the agreements, the panels may adopt appropriate procedures compatible with the agreements.[243] Except for the EUKFTA, the new generation FTAs also mention that such procedures can be adopted only after consulting with the parties,[244] offering greater control to the parties over the procedures. Finally, like panels and the AB under the DSU, the panels under the new generation EU FTAs are not allowed to have *ex parte* contacts with the parties, aiming to ensure that the parties are treated equally and that the procedures are fair.

Therefore, the new generation EU FTAs include quite detailed and clear procedural rules with some variations across these agreements. However, there might still be less clarity about some grey areas that are not expressly regulated, and there is also no jurisprudence on those matters. For example, there are no clear rules on evidence or standard of proof. The panels composed under the new generation EU FTAs could make use of the existing WTO jurisprudence under the FTA rules of interpretation requiring FTA panels to take into account/adopt the WTO jurisprudence in some cases prescribed by these agreements.[245] How panels would deal with procedural issues not covered by FTA rules, while also respecting the established time frames, remains to be seen in practice.

---

[240] EUKFTA, Art 14.15; CETA, Annex 29-A, para 42; EUJEPA, Art 21.17; EUSFTA, Art 14.17; EUVFTA, Art 15.20.

[241] EUSFTA, Art 14.17; EUVFTA, Art 15.20.

[242] EUKFTA, Art 14.15; EUJEPA, Art 21.17; CETA, Annex 29-A, para 42; EUJEPA, Art 21.17(4); EUSFTA, Art 14.17; EUVFTA, Art 15.20.

[243] EUKFTA, Annex 14-B, Art 5(5); CETA, Annex 29-A, para 17; Decision of the Joint Committee of the EUJEPA, Annex 3, para 13; EUSFTA, Annex 14-A, para 17; EUVFTA, Annex 15-A, para 18.

[244] CETA, Annex 29-A, para 17; Decision of the Joint Committee of the EUJEPA, Annex 3, para 13; EUSFTA, Annex 14-A, para 17; EUVFTA, Annex 15-A, para 18.

[245] CETA, Art 29.17; EUJEPA, Art 21.16; EUSFTA, Art 14.18; EUVFTA, Art 15.21.

6.6.3 Implications of the Rules of Procedure for the Competition Between the WTO and the New Generation EU FTA DSMs

Rules of procedure have become very detailed in order to facilitate the process once a dispute is initiated and to ensure that procedures are predictable for the parties.[246] Establishing procedural rules only once a dispute is initiated may lead to significant delays and uncertainty.

The new generation EU FTAs rules of procedure for arbitration are quite similar to the WTO panel proceedings, albeit different in some respects such as the number of hearings, and regulate in detail the stages of the arbitral procedure. Thus, similar to WTO rules, the new generation EU FTAs include rules on notification and delivery of documents, organisational meetings, written submissions, hearings, suspension of procedures, seeking of information and advice from other sources, and *ex parte* contacts. These detailed regulations should ensure that, once a panel is established in a dispute, the rules of procedure are clear and the parties know what to expect. They aim to guarantee that the procedures would not be delayed. Furthermore, the rules of procedure under the new generation EU FTAs are designed to ensure at different stages that the proceedings are fair, parties are treated equally, and are given certain control over aspects that could influence the outcome of their dispute. Despite being detailed, the rules of procedure cannot address every issue, for example the requirements that experts need to comply with or the standard of proof. Therefore, the panels under the new generation EU FTAs, similar to the AB, are entitled to adopt, after consulting the parties, new procedural rules to address the issues that are not covered. However, the WTO's proceedings have the advantage of offering greater predictability, since they have addressed various procedural issues in their vast jurisprudence. *Au contraire*, FTA panels would still have to face different issues not regulated expressly in the agreements and inspiration for solving them could be found in the WTO jurisprudence.

To conclude, the detailed rules of procedure for arbitration contained in the new-generation EU FTAs may weigh in their favour as viable alternatives to the WTO DSM, especially when the disputing parties would do not participate in the MPIA and would face the risk of panel report being in limbo by an appeal.

6.7 Decisions and Reports

Once the panels and the AB complete their assessments, they deliberate and issue their reports containing the final results. Whether there is an interim review stage, how reports are adopted, whether individual opinions are allowed, and whether the

---

[246]Porges (2011), p. 480; McDougall (2018), p. 8.

reports are binding could play a role, along with other considerations, in influencing the competition between the WTO DSM and the new generation EU FTA DSMs.

6.7.1 WTO Panel and AB Reports and MPIA Arbitral Awards

WTO panels and the AB prepare their reports after the oral hearings are concluded. The AB Members from the division hearing the dispute first exchange their views on the issues raised in the appeal with the other Members, following which the AB report is drafted.[247] The panel and AB deliberations are confidential and the reports shall be drafted without the presence of the parties.[248]

The DSU does not expressly regulate this issue, but in practice, panels strive to decide by consensus. The Working Procedures for Appellate Review expressly urge the division sitting on a dispute to 'make every effort to take their decisions by consensus'.[249] Where such consensus is not achieved, the division shall decide by majority vote.[250] At both panel and AB stages, individual panelists or AB Members may anonymously express individual opinions, including separate opinions, in the reports.[251] Thus, the opinion of a panelist or AB Member disagreeing with the majority view can be found in both panel and AB reports without mention of the dissenting person's name. In practice, however, individual opinions have rarely been used at both panel and appellate review stages.[252] Moreover, not all individual opinions dissent from the majority view, with some stating concurrent views or adding observations.[253] The effort of panels and the AB to act consensually and to avoid individual opinions is said to have been motivated by the desire of arbitrators and AB Members to ensure that the WTO DSM speaks as one voice and proves its independence and legitimacy.[254] Individual opinions may be considered valuable for being able to improve majority opinions by providing alternative approaches and useful reference points for future disputes and highlighting ambiguities in the law.[255]

---

[247] Working Procedures for Appellate Review, Rule 4(1).

[248] DSU, Arts 14.1, 14.2, 17.10.

[249] Working Procedures for Appellate Review, Rule 3(2).

[250] Working Procedures for Appellate Review, Rule 3(2).

[251] DSU, Arts 14.3, 17.11.

[252] As of December 2019, there were 18 separate opinions at the panel stage and 10 at the appellate review stage (WTO Analytical Index, DSU Arts 14 and 17). <www.wto.org/english/res_e/publications_e/ai17_e/dsu_art14_jur.pdf> and <www.wto.org/english/res_e/publications_e/ai17_e/dsu_art17_jur.pdf>.

[253] See, for example, Appellate Body Report, *United States – Continued Existence and Application of Zeroing Methodology (US – Continued Zeroing)* WT/DS350/AB/R, 4 February 2009, [304–313]; Panel Report, *United States – Laws, Regulations and Methodology for Calculating Dumping Margins (Zeroing) (US – Zeroing (EC))*, WT/DS294/R, 31 October 2005, [7.285].

[254] Kolsky Lewis (2006), p. 904; Kolsky Lewis (2012), pp. 3–4.

[255] Kolsky Lewis (2006), pp. 916–918.

Nevertheless, even supporters of individual opinions agree that the right to express such opinions should be exercised sparingly,[256] as they can be disadvantageous by diminishing the authority of the DSM, creating legal uncertainty,[257] and eroding cohesiveness.[258]

The arbitration awards issued under the MPIA should also be issued after appeal arbitrators discuss among themselves matters of interpretation, practice, and procedure.[259] As the DSU rules applicable to appellate review and Working Procedures for the Appellate Review apply *mutatis mutandis* to appeal arbitration procedures,[260] appeal arbitrators' deliberations, the drafting of reports, and individual opinions are governed by the same rules as those in regular appeals.

The final reports of WTO panels are preceded by an interim stage. Initially, the panel issues the descriptive sections containing factual findings and the arguments of their draft reports to the parties of the dispute on which they can comment in writing within a deadline set by the panels.[261] Once the panel receives the comments and the established deadline lapses, it issues an interim report containing the descriptive part (possibly changed because of the parties' comments) and the panel findings and conclusions.[262] As in the case of the descriptive part, the parties can comment on the interim report within a deadline set by the panel and request in writing to review certain aspects of the interim review. The parties can also ask for a further meeting held by the panel with the parties.[263] If no comments are received, then the interim report is considered the final report, but if there are comments then the final panel report shall include a discussion of the arguments made at the interim review stage and whether or not the report is actually modified.[264] Without a functional AB, in disputes between Members not participating in the MPIA, it could be expected that the interim review stage may gain greater importance and may turn into a mini-appeal.[265] There is no similar interim review stage for the AB reports, nor for appeal arbitration awards issued under the MPIA which follows the same rules in this respect as the regular appellate review.[266] In 2003, during the negotiations on DSU reform, Chile and the US proposed the introduction of interim reports at the appellate

---

[256] Ibid 919.

[257] Flett (2010), pp. 312–313.

[258] Kolsky Lewis (2006), p. 916.

[259] MPIA, para 5.

[260] MPIA, Annex 1, para 11.

[261] DSU, Art 15.1.

[262] DSU, Art 15.2.

[263] DSU, Art 15.2.

[264] DSU, Art 15.3.

[265] Pauwelyn (2019), p. 309.

[266] MPIA, Annex 1, para 11.

review stage,[267] which, according to some Members, would allow parties to express their views on issues on which they never comment and would enhance Member's control over dispute settlement.[268] Clearly, as no agreement was reached regarding DSU reform, no change was introduced.

If the parties do not reach an MAS, the final panel report is issued containing the descriptive part, the comments of the parties on the interim report and the panel's response to it, the findings (possibly amended after the interim stage), the conclusions, and recommendations if a violation is found. The panel report is initially issued to the parties only, and once it is available in the three official languages of the WTO, it is circulated to all Members.[269] The AB Report includes the arguments of the participants and third parties, an overview of the measures at issue and findings, and concludes whether the panel decisions are upheld, modified or reversed.[270] Once the AB reports are translated into the official languages, they are circulated to all Members and also received by the parties. An interim appeal arbitration report may uphold, modify, or reverse the legal findings and conclusions of the panel, and where applicable, shall include recommendations. 'The findings of the panel which have not been appealed shall be deemed to form an integral part of the arbitration award together with the arbitrators' own findings.'[271]

Panel and AB reports become binding only when they are adopted by the DSB. Panel reports shall be adopted within 60 days after their circulation, unless they are not appealed,[272] and AB reports shall be adopted within 30 days of circulation.[273] The DSB adopts the panel reports by negative consensus, making their rejection almost impossible. Therefore, panel and AB reports are adopted almost automatically and become binding. Nevertheless, when there is no functional AB and the disputing parties are not participants in the MPIA that would allow the hearing of arbitration appeals or have no NAP in place, the appealed panel reports go into the void for an indefinite period of time and there is no final decision on the dispute. According to the DSU, 'if a party has notified its decision to appeal, the report by the panel shall not be considered for adoption.'[274] Appeal arbitration awards, in contrast to panel and AB reports, do not require adoption by the DSB. Pursuant to the DSU and MPIA, parties agree to abide by arbitration awards, which shall be final and only notified to, but not adopted by, the DSB.[275] Therefore, the bindingness of appeal

---

[267] DSB Special Session, Negotiations on Improvements and Clarifications of the Dispute Settlement Understanding on Improving Flexibility and Member Control in WTO Dispute Settlement: Textual Contribution by Chile and the United States, TN/DS/W/52, 14 March 2003.

[268] Lockhart and Voon (2005), fns 46, 47; Weiss (2008), p. 288.

[269] WTO Secretariat (2017), p. 103.

[270] Ibid 121.

[271] MPIA, Annex 1, para 9.

[272] DSU, Art 16.4.

[273] DSU, Art 17.14.

[274] DSU, Art 16.4. On the risk of having panel reports being sent into the void, *see* Sect. 4.2.

[275] DSU, Art 25.3; MPIA, Annex 1, para 15.

arbitration awards is automatic and cannot be hindered by the actions of other WTO Members. Nevertheless, a paralysed AB may lead to non-adoption of the appealed panel reports in the absence of other arrangements to avert it.

6.7.2   Decisions and Panel Reports in the New Generation EU FTAs

Similar to the Working Procedures for the Appellate Review adopted by the AB,[276] the new generation EU FTAs provide that arbitration panels should take decisions by consensus and when that is not possible, to decide by majority vote.[277] This ensures that adoption of decisions will not be subject to consensus that may be difficult to attain, considering that two of the panelists would be appointed by the two disputing parties and even could be their nationals. Therefore, in such cases, it is most likely that the burden would be on the chairperson to decide the outcome by siding with one of the other two arbitrators.[278] The EUKFTA, EUJEPA, and EUVFTA provide that dissenting opinions shall not be disclosed and published.[279] CETA, in a slightly different language, establishes in the Rules of Procedures that '[a]rbitrators may not issue separate opinions on matters not unanimously agreed'.[280] These provisions make clear that arbitrators cannot publish or issue opinions separately to express their own views not supported unanimously by the arbitration panel. Hence, it appears that the new generation EU FTAs, except the EUSFTA which does not address this issue, prohibit the publication and issuance of dissenting and separate opinions as happens in the ICJ.[281] However, these FTAs do not expressly prohibit inclusion of individual anonymous opinions in the panel reports, similar to those that the DSU allows.

As in WTO panel proceedings, an interim report is issued before the final panel report under the rules of the new generation EU FTAs.[282] Deliberations of the panels shall be confidential and take place in the presence of the arbitrators and their

---

[276] See supra (n 249).

[277] EUKFTA, Art 14.17(1); CETA, Annex 29-A, para 15; EUJEPA, Art 21.15(7); EUSFTA, Art 14.19(1); EUVFTA, Art 15.22(1).

[278] See supra (n 197).

[279] EUKFTA, Art 14.17(1); EUJEPA, Art 21.15(7); EUVFTA, Art 15.22(1).

[280] CETA, Annex 29-A, para 16.

[281] United Nations, Statute of the International Court of Justice (ICJ Statute), 18 April 1946, (33 UNTS 993, UKTS 67 (1946) Cmd 7015, 3 Bevans 1179, 59 Stat 1055, 145 BSP 832, TS No 993), OXIO 95, Art 57.

[282] Note that the EUKFTA, EUSFTA, and EUVFTA use the term 'ruling' for what is called a final report under CETA and EUJEPA.

assistants, if allowed by the panel.[283] The drafting of the interim and final panel reports shall remain the exclusive responsibility of the arbitration panel and shall not be delegated to other individuals.[284] The interim reports shall be issued by the panels to the parties and should set the findings of facts, the legal findings, and conclusions.[285] Parties may submit written requests to review precise aspects of the reports within certain time limits,[286] as a result of which final reports may be modified.[287] The new generation EU FTAs, except CETA, also require, in any case, that the arguments made at the interim stage shall be discussed in the final report,[288] ensuring that the panels will not merely ignore them, but thoroughly analyse and make the analysis known to the parties.

After the interim report, the panels shall issue their final 'report', so called in the EUJEPA, EUVFTA and CETA, or 'rulings' as mentioned in the EUKFTA and EUSFTA, that set the findings of facts, the applicability of the relevant provisions, and the rationale behind the findings and conclusions.[289] Once issued, the final reports and rulings are binding and shall be accepted unconditionally by the parties.[290] There is no other body, similar to the DSB, that would need to adopt the reports for them to become binding.

6.7.3 Implications of the Rules on Decisions and Reports for the Competition Between the WTO and the New Generation EU FTA DSMs

The decisions under the new generation EU FTAs, similar to the WTO reports and MPIA awards, should be made by consensus, unless that is not possible and majority voting is applied. In case of majority voting, individual opinions are allowed only within the reports. Thus, the WTO and the new generation EU FTA DSMs balance,

---

[283] EUKFTA, Annex 14-B, Art 5(3), Annex 14-C, Art 7(3); CETA, Annex 29-A, para 13, Annex 29-B, para 19; EUJEPA, Art 21.15(6), (4); EUSFTA, Annex 14-A, paras 15, 39; EUVFTA, Art 15.8(7).

[284] EUKFTA, Annex 14-B, Art 5(4); CETA, Annex 29-A, para 19; EUJEPA, Art 21.15(6); EUSFTA, Annex 14-A, para 16; EUVFTA, Annex 15-A, para 17.

[285] EUKFTA, Art 14.6(1); CETA, Art 29.9(1); EUJEPA, Art 21.18(1); EUSFTA, Art 14.7(1); EUVFTA, Art 15.10(1).

[286] EUKFTA, Art 14.6(2); CETA, Art 29.9(2); EUJEPA, Art 21.18(2); EUSFTA, Art 14.7(2); EUVFTA, Art 15.10(2).

[287] EUKFTA, Art 14.6(4); CETA, Art 29.9(2); EUJEPA, Art 21.18(2); EUSFTA, Art 14.7(4); EUVFTA, Art 15.10(4).

[288] EUKFTA, Art 14.6(4); EUJEPA, Art 21.19(3); EUSFTA, Art 14.7(4); EUVFTA, Art 15.11(3).

[289] EUKFTA, Art 14.17(2); CETA, Art 29.10; EUJEPA, Art 21.15(8); EUSFTA, Art 14.19(2); EUVFTA, Art 15.22(2).

[290] EUKFTA, Art 14.17(2); CETA, Art 29.10; EUJEPA, Art 21.12(b); EUSFTA, Art 14.19(2); EUVFTA, Art 15.22(2).

in a like manner, the advantages of allowing individual opinions within certain limitations with the benefits of decisions taken by consensus.

Since panel reports are preceded by interim reports under the DSMs of the WTO and the new generation EU FTAs, this ensures that parties have the opportunity to become familiar with the content of the reports and correct what they consider to be errors, as well as prepare for the decision.[291] Interim reports offer the parties additional control over the outcomes of the disputes and allow them to provide input, including on what they see as unacceptable interpretations of their agreements.[292] The automatic binding nature of the reports issued under the new generation EU FTAs is generally comparable to the almost-automatic adoption of the final panel and AB reports and MPIA awards.

The new generation EU FTA and WTO rules on adoption of decisions and reports are very similar. Therefore, from this particular perspective, the new generation EU FTA DSMs are potential alternatives to the WTO mechanism. Still, the automatic binding character of the final FTA reports may become a decisive factor for choosing FTA DSMs in the context of the AB crisis and the risk of appealed panel reports being sent into the void when the disputing parties have no NAP in place and are not participants in the MPIA. Hence, from the perspective of the automatic binding character of the reports, the DSMs contained in the EUKFTA, EUJEPA, and EUVFTA are more likely to be preferred to the WTO DSM in the current circumstances.

6.8 Appellate Stage

Under the WTO rules, the parties to the dispute may appeal a panel report—the appeals being heard by three Members of the standing AB.[293] The new generation EU FTA DSMs do not offer such a possibility. The absence of an appeal stage at the FTA level is considered one of the main reasons for the prevailing preference for the WTO DSM and the rare use of FTA DSMs, at least until recently.[294]

The possibility of appeals against panel reports being heard by Members of a standing AB is associated with certain benefits. First, appealing panel reports represents an opportunity to correct potential mistakes in them.[295] Without appeals, parties may have to live with bad reports.[296] The AB's reports may also contain errors and there would be no other authority to correct them; but panel reports subject to potential review by the AB are said to be more rigorously drafted, as the

---

[291] Allee and Elsig (2015), p. 334.

[292] Schill (2017), p. 128.

[293] DSU, Art 16.4, 17.1, 17.4.

[294] Interview 4; Interview 5.

[295] Hillman (2016), p. 102; Todeschini-Marthe (2018), p. 401; Interview 3.

[296] Gao (2018), p. 3.

scrutiny exercised by the AB incentivises panels to be more careful and thoughtful.[297]

Review of panel reports by the AB also brings greater coherence and predictability to the WTO rendered decisions.[298] Article 3.2 of the DSU stipulates that '[t]he dispute settlement system of the WTO is a central element in providing security and predictability to the multilateral trading system'. The AB interpreted this norm as implying that 'absent cogent reasons, an adjudicatory body will resolve the same legal question in the same way in a subsequent case'.[299] Moreover, the Working Procedures for Appellate Review provide that all Members of the AB regularly convene to discuss matters of policy, practice, and procedure in order to ensure consistency and coherence in decision-making.[300] It ensures that AB Members exchange their views with other Members, despite only three Members sitting on a case. According to a former AB Member, this is the bedrock of the uniformity in the decision-making process of the AB.[301] 'A larger group might also assure greater coherence and continuity of decision-making over time than divisions of three with constantly varying membership.'[302] In practice, the AB regularly cites earlier reports.[303] A coherent and predictable dispute settlement system provides Member States with valuable guidance for future cases. Coherence brings stability and predictability, which is crucial not only to disputing states, but also to their business communities.[304]

The AB has grown to be an important and authoritative body.[305] Although some WTO Members have voiced some criticism, they were generally satisfied with the AB's activity,[306] until the recent discontent and actions of the US paralysed it. The EU has expressly identified the increased coherence that the WTO proceedings offer as one of the main features that make them more attractive than the FTA proceedings.[307] Moreover, from the EU's perspective, keeping a two-stage dispute settlement process has been extremely important and one of its red lines when it

---

[297] Pauwelyn (2004), p. 260.

[298] Pierola and Horlick (2007), p. 899; McDougall (2018), p. 8.

[299] Appellate Body Report, *United States – Final Anti-Dumping Measures on Stainless Steel from Mexico (US – Stainless Steel)*, WT/DS344/AB/R, 30 April 2008, [160].

[300] Working Procedures for Appellate Review, Rule 4(1); also *see supra* (n 247).

[301] Ganesan (2015), p. 529.

[302] Ehlermann (2002), p. 612.

[303] According to an empirical study conducted by Joost Pauwelyn, of 108 AB reports issued between 1996 and 2013, 'all but the very first Appellate Body report contains citations to earlier reports' (Pauwelyn 2016, p. 152).

[304] Interview 3.

[305] *See* Shaffer et al. (2016), pp. 237–273; Howse (2016), pp. 9–77.

[306] Ganesan (2015), p. 543.

[307] European Commission, Report from the Commission to the European Parliament, the Council, the European Economic and Social Committee and the Committee of the Regions on Implementation of Free Trade Agreements, Brussels, COM(2019) 455 final, p. 37.

looked for alternatives within the WTO in the context of the AB crisis.[308] Accordingly, the EU was the initiator of the MPIA negotiations. The participating Members of the MPIA, including the EU, Canada, and Singapore, can, therefore, still benefit from a two-stage dispute settlement process. Nonetheless, as long as the AB is paralysed, WTO Members that are not parties to the MPIA and do not make use of appeal arbitration can either sign NAPs or risk facing panel reports being sent into limbo; in either of these two scenarios, these states would not be able to benefit from the advantages of having an appellate review. Consequently, there would be no advantages associated with having an appellate review by Members of a standing body offered by the WTO DSM from the perspective of these states.

Under the MPIA, the participating Members are able to appeal against panel reports to correct potential errors, with appeal arbitrations being heard by three arbitrators who are selected from the pool of arbitrators composed by the participating Members and should have qualifications similar to those of AB Members.[309] It could be expected that the arbitration awards issued under the MPIA will also provide the participating Members with a degree of coherence. First, as the DSU is applicable *mutatis mutandis* to the appeal procedures,[310] Article 3(2) of the DSU on dispute settlement, ensuring the security and predictability of the system is also applicable. The participating Members of the MPIA also enshrined in its preamble that they reaffirm 'that consistency and predictability in the interpretation of rights and obligations under the covered agreements is of significant value to Members.'[311] Moreover, to promote consistency and coherence in decision-making, the appeal arbitrators, similar to AB Members, will discuss with all the other members of the pool of arbitrators matters of interpretation, practice and procedure, to the extent practicable.[312] However, it remains to be seen in practice if this will ensure coherence across all issued awards. Unlike the Working Procedures for Appellate Review, the MPIA also stipulates that arbitrators shall discuss among themselves, but 'without prejudice to the exclusive responsibility and freedom of the arbitrators with respect to such decisions and their quality'.[313] In addition, the MPIA reaffirms in its preamble that the awards 'cannot add to or diminish the rights and obligations provided in the covered agreements'.[314] It also remains to be seen whether the appeal arbitrators would not depart, in practice, from the existing precedents.[315] Considering that unlike the interim appeal arbitration arrangements between the

---

[308] Lukas (2019), p. 56.

[309] MPIA, para 4, Annex 2.

[310] MPIA, Annex 1, para 11.

[311] MPIA, Preamble, recital 5.

[312] MPIA, para 5, Annex 1, para 8.

[313] MPIA, Annex 1, para 8.

[314] MPIA, Preamble, recital 5.

[315] Dreyer (2020).

EU–Canada and EU–Norway,[316] the MPIA does not require appeal arbitrators to be former AB Members, and in light of the criticism of the AB, the appeal arbitrators may feel the need to depart from certain case law in order for the appeal arbitration mechanism to have the support of other WTO Members.

In contrast to these first two interim appeal arbitration arrangements signed by the EU separately with Canada and Norway, the MPIA does not state that 'awards of other arbitrators under similar appeal arbitration procedures shall be deemed to constitute Appellate Body reports adopted by the DSB for the purposes of interpretation of the covered agreements'.[317] The MPIA does not contain any provision with respect to the effects of appeal arbitration awards for the purpose of interpretation. Therefore, it remains to be seen how panelists, non-participating Members, and even other appeal arbitrators will treat the arbitral awards and whether they give any consideration to them. Without the AB in place as the guarantee of coherence, panels could start diverging from existing jurisprudence by endeavouring to please some parties. Non-participating Members might also ignore the interim awards and not refer to them in their submissions. How the arbitral awards will be treated will depend on their persuasiveness and the perception of the MPIA's results. Hence, the MPIA is expected to offer a considerable degree of consistency, but it remains to be seen in practice if it will be as high as in case of the AB reports.

Although having appeals heard by the AB, as currently regulated by the DSU, appears to be an evident advantage of the WTO DSM, with the current paralysis of the AB, it is likely that the appellate stage and the entire WTO DSM would undergo certain changes in order to overcome it. Changes can be expected as there is no solution to the crisis yet, considering that the MPIA was designed only as a temporary solution and not all WTO Members are participating in it.[318] The US criticised the AB for its acquired independence and going beyond its mandate by offering overreaching interpretations, ignoring the 90-days deadline for appeals, deciding that AB Members with expired terms can continue serving, expressing obiter dicta and undertaking de novo reviews, and establishing precedents.[319] Thus, it may be said that the US accused the AB of judicial activism, defined as the 'tendency to impose on states legal limits or constraints not justified by the strict rule

---

[316] Interim Appeal Arbitration Pursuant to Article 25 of the DSU between Canada and the EU, para 3, Annex, para 7; Interim Appeal Arbitration Pursuant to Article 25 of The DSU between Norway and the EU, para 3, Annex, para 7.

[317] Interim Appeal Arbitration Pursuant to Article 25 of the DSU between Canada and the EU, Annex, para 8; Interim Appeal Arbitration Pursuant to Article 25 of The DSU between Norway and the EU, Annex, para 8.

[318] MPIA, paras 1, 2; Annex 1, para 2.

[319] Office of the United States Trade Representative, The President's 2018 Trade Policy Agenda (March 2018), pp. 24–28 <https://ustr.gov/sites/default/files/files/Press/Reports/2018/AR/2018%20Annual%20Report%20I.pdf>; Office of the United States Trade Representative, 2019 Trade Policy Agenda and 2018 Annual Report of the President of the United States on the Trade Agreements Program (March 2019), p. 148 <https://ustr.gov/sites/default/files/2019_Trade_Policy_Agenda_and_2018_Annual_Report.pdf>.

of international law'.[320] This activism is claimed to be against Article 3.2 of the DSU that additionally establishes that '[r]ecommendations and rulings of the DSB cannot add to or diminish the rights and obligations provided in the covered agreements.'[321] Some American practitioners have also accused the AB of creating a chilling effect on future negotiations, arguing that Member States choose to obtain through dispute settlement what was never negotiated, while being afraid of negotiating ambiguous agreements that will be subject to AB interpretation.[322]

Whether or not the AB overstepped its mandate is beyond the scope of this book. Yet, it should be noted that the negative consensus rule, according to which the DSB decides by consensus not to adopt a report,[323] made it essentially impossible to overrule an AB report, since the respondent in a dispute, at the least, will not join the consensus. Moreover, changing the WTO agreements or adopting 'authoritative interpretations' that would have an effect of overriding AB reports also proved to be impossible because of the required positive consensus of all Members.[324] In the context of the AB crisis, some Member States, including the EU, submitted proposals for holding annual meetings between AB Members and the DSB, where Members could express their views regarding some AB approaches[325] or entitling some other authority to be responsible for the review of reports to establish that AB overstepped its mandate.[326] Too much predictability and stability may result in the rights and obligations of WTO Members being diminished.[327] While complete disregard of all existing case law in all WTO disputes is unlikely to be the outcome of potential DSU reform, very infrequent deviations from existing jurisprudence may be allowed in order to balance between the strive towards security and predictability and protection of Members' rights and their intentions underpinning the norms.

The possibility of appeals against panel reports and hearings conducted by the AB under WTO rules seems to present a clear advantage compared to the procedures

---

[320] Howse (2003), p. 35.

[321] Office of the United States Trade Representative, The President's 2018 Trade Policy Agenda (March 2018), pp. 22–23 <https://ustr.gov/sites/default/files/Press/Reports/2018/AR/2018% 20Annual%20Report%20I.pdf>; Office of the United States Trade Representative, 2019 Trade Policy Agenda and 2018 Annual Report of the President of the United States on the Trade Agreements Program (March 2019), p. 148 <https://ustr.gov/sites/default/files/2019_Trade_ Policy_Agenda_and_2018_Annual_Report.pdf>.

[322] Stewart et al. (2013), pp. 406–407.

[323] DSU, Art 17.14.

[324] Howse (2016), p. 12.

[325] General Council, Communication from the European Union, China, Canada, India, Norway, New Zealand, Switzerland, Australia, Republic of Korea, Iceland, Singapore and Mexico to the General Council, WT/GC/W/752, 26 November 2018.

[326] Communication from Honduras, Fostering a Discussion on the Functioning of the Appellate Body Addressing the Issue of Alleged Judicial Activism by the Appellate Body, WT/GC/W/760, 29 January 2019. For more details on the proposal, see Sect. 7.1.

[327] Hillman (2019), p. 40.

under new generation EU FTA DSMs. The MPIA is likely to provide the advantages of a two-stage procedure, but it has not been tested in practice yet. Besides the lengthier proceedings caused by the appellate review stage, maintaining a standing AB or pool of arbitrators is also very expensive.[328] Instituting a standing appellate body for FTA DSMs that have been rarely used until now may seem an unjustified expenditure. Furthermore, at times states may be reluctant to offer too much authority to a third-party adjudicating body that, sometimes against their will, develops and follows its own jurisprudence.[329] Accordingly, parties may want to avoid far-reaching interpretations of norms. In addition, in specific situations, FTA parties may prefer swifter procedures with the fewest institutional impediments to obtaining compliance.[330] Moreover, if there is no functional AB and disputing parties are not MPIA participants, the WTO DSM can no longer be preferred due its two-stage proceedings, and FTA DSMs may be considered alternatives even in other instances.

Although the new generation EU FTAs do not offer appellate reviews, they still offer the stage of interim review similar to the WTO panel stage, in which parties can express their views on possible errors. *Ad-hoc* panels, like those that can be established under the new generation EU FTAs, can be expected to develop less consistent jurisprudence and offer a lower degree of security and predictability than the WTO procedures. The new generation EU FTAs may offer a certain degree of coherence because of the interpretation rules establishing that FTA panels shall adopt/take into account WTO jurisprudence in certain instances. Nevertheless, since some of these provisions are more limited in either scope or weight than others,[331] the degree of coherence of the FTA reports with the WTO reports remains to be seen. The new generation EU FTAs also do not contain a provision establishing that dispute settlement should ensure security and predictability. Therefore, FTA panels have no legal basis for following their own reports. However, these agreements still expressly provide that panel rulings should not 'add to or diminish the rights and obligations' contained therein.[332] Thus, while parties to the agreements reproduced this part of Article 3.2 of the DSU, they chose not to replicate the one that would have ensured coherence and predictability in panel rulings and implied less control. Therefore, it appears that parties to the new generation EU FTAs purposely designed their DSMs to offer them greater control and the panels the opportunity to deviate from existing jurisprudence, when needed.

To conclude, the second stage of procedures in the form of regular appeals or interim appeal arbitration (that have still to be tested) offer more coherence, security and predictability, and, possibly, higher quality reports. With a functioning AB or when the disputing parties are MPIA participants, the new generation EU FTA

---

[328] McDougall (2018), p. 8.

[329] Schill (2017), p. 119.

[330] Leal-Arcas (2011), p. 25.

[331] *See infra* Sect. 11.8.5.3.

[332] EUKFTA, Art 14.16; CETA, Art 29.18; EUJEPA, Art 21.15(8); EUSFTA, Art 14.18; EUVFTA, Art 15.21.

DSMs are generally not likely to be perceived as offering the same level of guarantees to become actual alternatives to the WTO DSM. For WTO Members that do not participate in the MPIA, the WTO DSM would not provide appellate review advantages with a paralysed AB, making the FTA DSMs similarly attractive from this perspective. In some limited circumstances, states could prefer the new generation EU FTA DSMs, even if the WTO offered two-stage proceedings, to avoid prolongation of the procedures by an appeal, to use mechanisms that could provide parties with more control over the outcome of the disputes, and to increase the chances of departing from WTO established jurisprudence.

6.9 Administrative and Legal Support

The administrative and legal support provided by the WTO and AB Secretariats that the WTO panels and the AB can rely on has been named as one of the decisive reasons for the frequent favouring of the WTO DSM over FTA mechanisms.[333]

6.9.1 Support Provided by the WTO and AB Secretariats

Both WTO panels and the AB benefit from legal and administrative support provided by the WTO and AB Secretariats. According to the Marrakesh Agreement, the WTO Secretariat is headed by the WTO DG who appoints the Secretariat staff and determines their duties and service conditions.[334] The WTO Secretariat is composed of over 600 highly qualified individuals specialising in international trade policy with economic, legal, and other backgrounds.[335] In the area of dispute settlement, the WTO Secretariat has the responsibility to assist panels on legal, historical, and procedural aspects, as well as to provide secretarial and technical support.[336] The AB benefits from the administrative and legal support provided by the AB Secretariat,[337] which is separate from the WTO Secretariat and has its own budget to ensure the independence of the AB.[338] As the AB is inoperative, the AB Secretariat's funding has also been cut drastically at the insistence of the US.[339]

---

[333] Interview 2; Interview 4; Interview 5.

[334] Marrakesh Agreement, Art VI:2, VI:3.

[335] WTO, 'Overview of the WTO Secretariat' <www.wto.org/english/thewto_e/secre_e/intro_e. htm>.

[336] DSU, Art 27.1.

[337] DSU, Art 17.7.

[338] WTO Secretariat (2017), p. 33.

[339] Baschuk (2019).

Under MPIA rules, legal and administrative support should be offered by a structure that is entirely separate from the WTO Secretariat staff and its divisions supporting the panels, and be answerable only to the appeal arbitrators regarding the substance of their work to ensure the necessary guarantees of quality and independence.[340] Since the MPIA only provides that the availability of a structure meeting these criteria is to be ensured by the WTO DG, there are many grey areas left, such as how this structure should be created, whether it should have a permanent or *ad-hoc* nature,[341] whether it would be funded from the WTO budget or the funds of the participating Members,[342] whether it should be a new WTO division or completely separate from the WTO Secretariat,[343] and whether the support structure would report to the arbitrators collectively or individual staff would provide support to specific arbitrators.[344] The US has already objected to both the establishment of a new WTO Division and allocation of staff for the exclusive use of the MPIA participants.[345] It stated that: '[i]f Members desire a separate support staff for their dispute resolutions, those Members (and not the WTO Membership as a whole) should finance it.'[346] Considering the lack of clarity about the nature of this structure, including whether it would be permanent or *ad-hoc* and whether it would be responsible collectively to the AB, the degree of influence on appeal awards is also unclear. Therefore, once the secretarial support would be actually offered to appeal arbitrators at the second stage of proceedings under MPIA rules, some questions will be answered.

The administrative support involves help with document exchange and management, roster coordination, translation and interpretation services, renting of places for the hearings, information services, and capacity building.[347] Provision of legal support implies helping the panels and the AB with substantive and procedural aspects related to issues arising out of the dispute. The WTO Secretariat, in particular, is a key player that acts behind the scenes in panel proceedings.[348] Panelists deal with cases on a part-time basis; therefore, they may not be able to allocate the time necessary to grasp the details of cases.[349] Moreover, the average panelist does not have the necessary substantive and procedural knowledge and experience to be

---

[340] MPIA, para 7.

[341] For example, a letter dated 5 June 2020 from Ambassador Dennis C. Shea stated that '[a] permanent support structure would be particularly inappropriate in light of the limited expected use of the procedures set forth in the arrangement.' (<https://drive.google.com/file/d/1QIhcAoqU8pmdR6nKz0LNmfx8GR6s1lr3/view>).

[342] Dreyer (2020); Interview 4.

[343] For interpretations of the MPIA in this respect, *see* Lester (2020c).

[344] Kreier (2020).

[345] Letter dated 5 June 2020 from Ambassador Dennis C. Shea (n 341).

[346] Ibid.

[347] Porges (2011), p. 479.

[348] Nordström (2005), p. 819.

[349] Flett (2015), p. 558.

able to have full control over the dispute settlement proceedings.[350] The WTO Secretariat, on the other hand, comprises well-experienced staff that can provide legal support to ensure that the legal and factual arguments are adequately developed and that high-quality reports are issued.[351] In practice, the WTO Secretariat has a crucial role. Legal advisers from the Secretariat are present throughout the entire proceedings as well as during deliberations. Moreover, after the panelists listen to the oral arguments, conduct hearings with experts, and discuss the case with the Secretariat advisers, the actual drafting of the panel reports is delegated to the Secretariat.[352]

In addition to ensuring that the panel reports are well grounded in WTO law,[353] the WTO Secretariat also guarantees the promotion of consistency and coherence among all panel reports by acting as the repository of the institutional memory.[354] The secretarial staff that was also tasked with providing legal support to panels in previous disputes, including at the stage of drafting, would be inclined to cite past reports issued with their involvement.[355] At the same time, the legal secretarial support could partly be responsible for the regular extensions of the WTO deadlines for the proceedings.[356] As the WTO Secretariat has the attribution to appoint panelists, because of its influence on panel rulings, it might be inclined to propose individuals who would agree with its position and might be reluctant to appoint and reappoint candidates with their own strong opinions and a tendency not to follow its advice.[357] However, the parties have a considerable say in the candidates proposed by the Secretariat and can always oppose their appointment.[358]

The presentation of the WTO Secretariat shows that it plays a central role during the panel stage. However, the AB Secretariat, while providing assistance to the AB, is thought to have less influence on its decisions. As the AB is a standing body of seven Members meeting regularly to express their views and hear multiple disputes, the AB Secretariat has fewer reasons and opportunities to intervene in the process.[359] Thus, the final decision is made by the AB, with the AB Secretariat supporting it as the law prescribes. There is no clarity thus far about the potential influence of the structure that is envisaged to offer support to appeal arbitrators under the MPIA.

---

[350] Nordström (2005), p. 828. *See supra* Sect. 6.5.1.

[351] Davey (2006), p. 354; Pierola and Horlick (2007), p. 898; Todeschini-Marthe (2018), p. 402.

[352] Weiler (2001), p. 197; Nordström (2005), p. 828. Pauwelyn and Pelc argue that the WTO Secretariat exerts significantly greater influence on the writing of WTO panel reports than the panelists themselves (Pauwelyn and Pelc 2019).

[353] It has been contended by an interviewee that it is the Secretariat that ensures the high quality of panel reports—quality that is sometimes even higher than that of the AB reports (Interview 1).

[354] Weiler (2001), p. 205; Goldstein and Steinberg (2008), p. 261; Interview 4.

[355] Pauwelyn and Pelc (2019), p. 30.

[356] *See supra* Sect. 6.3.1.

[357] Pauwelyn (2015), p. 796.

[358] *See supra* (nn 104–107).

[359] Nordström (2005), p. 829.

6.9.2 Administrative and Legal Support to Panels Under the New Generation EU FTAs

The DSMs established by the EUKFTA, CETA, EUSFTA and EUVFTA do not expressly stipulate that panels can benefit from any kind of support offered by an entity similar to the WTO and AB Secretariats. Unless otherwise agreed, parties themselves seem to be responsible for dealing with logistical and administrative matters, such as locating well-equipped venues, organising hearings, and taking care of translations.[360] Therefore, parties would have to assign the function of providing logistical support in case of FTA Disputes to specific divisions of their national authorities. While some of the designated authorities might be more familiar with international state-to-state dispute settlement, others might have no relevant experience. Although the above-mentioned EU FTAs are silent on the possibility of using an external secretariat, these FTAs appear to allow parties to depart from the provision that logistical support for the hearings shall be insured by the defendant when parties agree otherwise.[361]

The EUJEPA provides expressly that each party shall designate an office responsible for dispute settlement administration, for which it bears the costs and which shall be notified to the other party.[362] In addition, this agreement contains a very innovative provision. It establishes that notwithstanding the obligation to designate offices, 'the Parties may agree to jointly entrust an external body with providing support for certain administrative tasks for the dispute settlement procedure under this Chapter.'[363] This provision entitles parties to agree to outsourcing the administration of the disputes to already established secretariats. Yet, the agreement seems to envisage the possibility of having only *administrative* but no *legal* support from an external body. It is unpredictable yet whether the EUJEPA parties would make use of an external body for administrative assistance at all, whether this would happen on a regular basis, which external body would be used, or whether the same external body would be used in all instances. Parties could make use of the WTO Secretariat itself (although the consent of all WTO Members would be needed)[364] or of other bodies, such as the Permanent Court of Arbitration (PCA) or the International Court of Arbitration. Using the support of already established courts could be beneficial, as it would also mean using the established authority of these bodies.[365] It remains to be seen how the provision contained in the EUJEPA on external assistance would be used (if ever) in practice.

---

[360] For more about provisions on logistical support, *see infra* Sects. 12.1.2 and 12.1.3.

[361] EUKFTA, Annex 14-B, Art 1.2; CETA, Annex 29-A, para 2; EUSFTA, Annex 14-A, para 3; EUVFTA, Annex 15-A, para 2.

[362] EUJEPA, Art 21.25(1). For more, *see infra* Sect. 12.1.2.

[363] EUJEPA, Art 21.25(2).

[364] For more on the possibility of using the WTO Secretariat's legal support in the new generation EU FTA disputes, *see infra* Sect. 12.1.3.

[365] Vidigal (2018).

The Rules of Procedures of the new generation EU FTAs make clear that arbitrators can have assistants that are natural persons who, under the terms of appointment of arbitrators, conduct research for and provide assistance to them and are entitled to assist during deliberations and hearings.[366] Therefore, the arbitrators will benefit from limited legal assistance to deal with the vast amount of work in a dispute. Nevertheless, even with assistants, without an experienced secretariat, the burden on FTA panels would be greater than that on WTO panels.[367] All new generation EU FTAs expressly provide that the drafting of any ruling shall remain the exclusive responsibility of the arbitration panel and it shall not be delegated to any other person or body,[368] therefore not even to assistants. Such a provision is not found in the DSU or the Working Procedures for the Appellate Review. While assistants would likely still draft legal memoranda for the arbitrators that could even be replicated in the final reports, the parties probably wanted to emphasise with this provision that, in contrast to the WTO panel reports, the FTA reports should be drafted by and be the exclusive responsibility of the arbitrators.[369]

6.9.3 Implications for the Competition Between the DSMs of the WTO and the New Generation EU FTAs

Parties could attribute significant importance to the absence of secretariats and be more hesitant in perceiving the new generation EU FTA DSMs as real alternatives to the WTO DSM.[370] While arbitrators under the new generation EU FTAs can benefit from the help of *ad-hoc* assistants, such support is not comparable to that offered by a secretariat comprising experienced staff that deal with disputes on a regular basis. For example, former NAFTA arbitrators disclosed that they lacked legal support from staff with knowledge of and expertise in the field.[371] Without the administrative and legal support provided by secretariats, FTA panels may not be able to deliver reports of a quality comparable to that of WTO reports. Moreover, with no legal support from a body similar to the WTO Secretariat, these reports could be less coherent, and the outcomes of dispute settlement less predictable for the parties.

---

[366] EUKFTA, Annex 14-B, Arts 1.1, 5.3, 7.5(d); CETA, Annex 29-A, paras 1, 13, 30(d); Decision of the Joint Committee of the EUJEPA, Annex 3, paras 2, 21, 27; EUSFTA, Art 14-A, paras 1, 15, 30(d); EUVFTA, Annex 15-A, paras 1(d), 28(e).

[367] Interview 4. *See infra* Sect. 12.1.2.

[368] EUKFTA, Annex 14-B, Art 5(4); CETA, Annex 29-A, para 14; EUJEPA, Art 21.15(6); EUSFTA, Art 14-A, para 16; EUVFTA, Annex 15-A, para 17.

[369] Interview 4.

[370] Interview 5.

[371] Robertson et al. (2018), p. 19.

Having secretariats involves high financial costs.[372] It might not seem worth investing in support for DSMs that only rarely deal with cases, like the ones established under FTA rules. The absence of legal support from an established secretariat, nonetheless, could also be a positive aspect in specific instances when the parties would be bothered by the strong authority that a secretariat could gain. An authoritative secretariat could promote policies inconsistent with the parties' views. The EUJEPA's unique provision that expressly entitles parties to entrust an external body with the supply of administrative support may be a signal that parties themselves prefer a mechanism for settling bilateral disputes that would indirectly allow 'greater interpretative divergence'.[373] Delegation of administrative support to an external body would make it possible to benefit from advantages that secretariats entail, while avoiding the burdensome financial costs that permanent secretariats necessitate and ensuring that a body composed of bureaucrats does not take control of the outcomes of dispute settlement. It is unlikely that the parties would want the panels to always diverge from established jurisprudence, since this would affect the business representatives not knowing how to act. However, a certain degree of divergence, which would ensure that the interpretations issued are according to the will of the states, could be sought—an objective that is also in line with the concept of limited coherence proposed in this book.

To conclude, the new generation EU FTAs do not provide internal or external bodies to offer *legal* support to the panels. From this specific perspective, this lack may hamper the likelihood of new generation EU FTA DSMs emerging as viable alternatives. Still, it may not affect these DSMs being seen as alternatives to the WTO AB in certain cases when parties consider the absence of legal support an advantage. The EUJEPA expressly provides the possibility of having purely *administrative* support for the panels. Thus, this DSM model may sometimes be perceived as a balanced way of panels benefitting from administrative support of an established body, while not empowering another body with too much interpretative power.

6.10 Transparency

In this age, transparency is gaining more and more attention and has become an already established international value.[374] This section will assess the level of transparency of proceedings under WTO and new generation EU FTA rules, and will establish its possible influence on the likelihood of the new generation EU FTA DSMs becoming alternatives to the WTO mechanism.

---

[372] Chase et al. (2016), p. 44.

[373] Vidigal (2018).

[374] Marceau and Hurley (2012), p. 20.

6.10.1 Transparency of the WTO Proceedings

The WTO dispute settlement proceedings were associated with a high degree of secrecy and confidentiality, especially initially.[375] In spite of the built-in confidentiality of the mechanism, a great deal has been done to increase the transparency of WTO proceedings.

The level of transparency in WTO proceedings varies depending on its different stages. At the first stage of dispute settlement—consultations—the WTO publishes the request for consultations in which the contested measures and the legal basis for the complaints are identified.[376] The requests for establishment of panels or notices of appeal are also public. The consultations themselves are confidential.[377] Nevertheless, the confidentiality of consultations causes little concern, potentially because their disclosure could imperil the amicable resolution of the dispute.[378] The parties' submissions (including those of third parties) are kept confidential by default. However, according to the second sentence of Article 18.2, '[n]othing in this Understanding shall preclude a party to a dispute from disclosing statements of its own positions to the public'.[379] The confidentiality of submissions has been criticised especially by those who would like to submit *amicus curiae* briefs, but have no access to submissions in order to know how to supplement the arguments advanced.[380] The US and the EU, for example, make their statements public by uploading full electronic versions on the websites of the relevant public authorities. Moreover, they have broadly interpreted the provision allowing public disclosure of the 'statement of its own position' and also publish, in addition to their written submissions, the responses to questions and oral statements delivered during panel and AB hearings. Neither the parties nor the WTO Secretariat can publish the submissions of other parties. Nevertheless, when a party publishes its own submission, it will indirectly reveal the positions of the other parties.[381] However, according to the third sentence of Article 18.2 of the DSU, '[m]embers shall treat as confidential information submitted by another Member to the panel or the Appellate Body which that Member has designated as confidential'. Therefore, when disclosing their own submissions, parties must be cautious not to divulge information designated as confidential. Even if submissions are not made public, the arguments within them

---

[375] McRae (2004), p. 11.

[376] Following the adoption of the 'Procedures for the Circulation and Derestriction of WTO Documents' Decision of 14 May 2002, WT/L/452, 16 May 2002, adopted by the General Council that provides that 'All official WTO documents shall be unrestricted'.

[377] DSU, Art 4.6.

[378] Marceau and Hurley (2012), p. 25.

[379] DSU, Art 18.2; DSU, Appendix 3, Working Procedures, para 3.

[380] Marceau and Hurley (2012), p. 26.

[381] Cook (2019), p. 6.

are, however, ultimately reflected in the panel and AB reports that are made public.[382]

The closed hearings at both the panel and AB level have been the subject of active debate. The issue proved to be controversial among Member States, as some states, such as the EU and the US, were in favour of having the possibility to have open hearings, while others resisted the idea.[383] The first open hearings took place during panel proceedings in 2005, at the request of the disputing parties (the US, Canada, and the EU) in the *US – Continued Suspension (Hormones)* and *Canada – Continued Suspension (Hormones)* cases.[384] Notwithstanding that the DSU Working Procedures prescribe that '[t]he panel shall meet in closed session',[385] the panel used other provisions to justify its decision in favour of open panel hearings. It used Article 12.1 of the DSU, according to which the Working Procedures shall be followed 'unless the panel decides otherwise after consulting the parties to the dispute', and the second sentence of Article 18.2 of the DSU, according to which parties can disclose the statements of their own positions as legal bases for its decision.[386] Moreover, Article 14.1 of the DSU prescribes that only 'panel deliberations shall be confidential', and according to the panels, it suggests that the term 'deliberation' was not intended to cover the exchange of arguments between the parties, but rather the internal discussion of the panel with a view to reaching its conclusions.[387]

The AB decided to open the appeal hearings in the same disputes after a joint request of the parties. It did so despite Article 17.10 of the DSU stating that the AB proceedings 'shall be confidential'. Although compared to Article 14.2 of the DSU, Article 17.10 specifically refers to proceedings, not only to deliberations, the AB stated that it should be interpreted in the context offered by the second sentence of

---

[382] WTO, 'Dispute Settlement System Training Module: Chapter 6. The Process – Stages in a Typical WTO Dispute Settlement Case' <www.wto.org/english/tratop_e/dispu_e/disp_settlement_cbt_e/c6s3p3_e.htm#txt3>.

[383] Ehring (2008), p. 1022. For more on the positions of different states on transparency, *see* 'Statement by the United States at the Meeting of the WTO Dispute Settlement Body, Geneva, 22 July 2019' <https://geneva.usmission.gov/wp-content/uploads/sites/290/July22.DSB_.Stmt_.as_.delivered.Item_.4.Trans_.fin_.pdf>.

[384] DS320, *United States – Continued Suspension of Obligations in the EC – Hormones Dispute (US – Continued Suspension (Hormones))*; DS321, *Canada – Continued Suspension of Obligations in the EC – Hormones Dispute (Canada – Continued Suspension (Hormones))*.

[385] DSU, Appendix 3, Working Procedures, para 2.

[386] Panel Report, *US – Continued Suspension (Hormones)*, WT/DS320/R, 31 March 2006, [7.46–7.50]; Panel Report, *Canada – Continued Suspension (Hormones)*, WT/DS321/R, 31 March 2008, [7.44–7.48].

[387] Panel Report, *US – Continued Suspension (Hormones)*, [7.49]; Panel Report, *Canada – Continued Suspension (Hormones)*, [7.47].

Article 18.2 of the DSU. It concluded that 'Article 18.2 provides contextual support for the view that the confidentiality rule in Article 17.10 is not absolute'.[388]

Although decisions to open both panel and AB hearings were at first not taken lightly by the third parties,[389] there have been several cases in which parties opted for public hearings.[390] Nevertheless, the openness of panel and AB hearings is dependent on the will of both parties, since the general rule is still that hearings take place behind closed doors. Moreover, even when the hearings are open, they are broadcast in a separate room, sometimes even days after the actual hearing has taken place, because parties are given the opportunity to review the recordings and ensure that information designated as confidential by them is not disclosed.[391] Since the broadcast takes place only through a closed circuit in a room at the WTO premises, and there is no webcast, only people physically present in Geneva can observe the hearings.[392]

The negotiations on the DSU included talks about transparency during dispute settlement and the possible publication of submissions and making the hearings public.[393] During negotiations, not every Member supported these initiatives,[394] and with no successful conclusion of the negotiations on DSU reform, the level of transparency of the WTO proceedings remains as that enshrined in the DSU and developed by panel and AB interpretations. Considering that the MPIA does not have any specific rules on transparency and the DSU rules on appellate review apply *mutatis mutandis*,[395] appeal arbitration is likely to have the same degree of transparency as regular appeals.

6.10.2   Levels of Transparency in the New Generation EU FTAs

As in the case of WTO procedures, the level of transparency in the new generation EU FTAs varies depending on the stages of the procedures.

---

[388] Appellate Body Report, *US – Continued Suspension (Hormones)*, WT/DS320/AB/R, Annex IV, 10 July 2008, para 4; Appellate Body Report, *Canada – Continued Suspension (Hormones)*, WT/DS321/AB/R, Annex IV, 10 July 2008, para 4.

[389] Ehring (2008), pp. 1024, 1029.

[390] According to the WTO Analytical Index, Art 18.2 of the DSU, as of April 2020, there have been 19 open panel hearings, and according to the WTO Analytical Index, Art 27 of the Working Procedures for Appellate Review, there have been 12 open AB hearings.

[391] Cook (2019), p. 9.

[392] Ibid 11.

[393] Dispute Settlement Body, 'Special Session of the Dispute Settlement Body, Report by the Chairman, Ambassador Ronald Saborío Soto, to the Trade Negotiations Committee', TN/DS/25, 21 April 2011, A-37–A-38.

[394] Ibid. Weiss (2008), pp. 286, 290.

[395] MPIA, Annex 1, para 11.

None of the new generation EU FTAs provides explicit rules for publicity of the requests for consultations. The agreements only provide that the requests shall be transmitted in written form to the other party.[396] Moreover, if parties fail to reach an MAS during consultations, the FTAs also do not require the requests for establishment of panels to be made public. There is, however, no provision interdicting the publication of these requests. Therefore, it will remain at the discretion of the parties whether to make them public. On the contrary, it is expressly provided that consultations are confidential.[397] Therefore, the entire consultation procedures, starting with the request, may be held confidentially, without the public being aware of the existence of a dispute.

In the case of parties' submissions, CETA expressly prescribes that 'each party shall make its submission publicly available', provided that the information designated as confidential is not disclosed.[398] The other new generation EU FTAs do not include a similar requirement. Similar to the second sentence of Article 18.2 of the DSU, other new generation EU FTAs establish that nothing shall preclude a party from disclosing its own statements to the public to the extent that it does not disclose information designated as confidential by the other party.[399] Therefore, publication of submissions under these agreements will be subject to the will of the parties as it happens under WTO rules, and it is not an obligation. Therefore, only CETA provides a higher degree of transparency in respect to the publication of parties' submissions. According to the rules of all the new generation EU FTAs analysed, the final panel rulings shall be made public, unless it is decided otherwise as a result of the condition that confidential information shall not be disclosed.[400]

The general rule applicable to the hearings is that they are open to the public, unless parties agree otherwise, or the submissions include confidential information and the hearings are partially or completely closed.[401] Therefore, hearings under the new generation EU FTAs are open to the public by default, the DSMs contained in these agreements having an increased level of transparency. Nonetheless, the EUSFTA has a unique provision according to which '[e]xceptionally, the panel shall have the right to conduct the hearings in a closed session at any time on its own initiative or at the request of either Party.' The agreement does not establish what an exceptional circumstance may be that would justify the action of a panel, on its own initiative, or at the request of a single party, to hold closed hearings. This provision,

---

[396] EUKFTA, Art 14.3(2); CETA, Art 29.4(1); EUJEPA, Art 21.5(2); EUSFTA, Art 14.4(2); EUVFTA, Art 15.3(2).

[397] EUKFTA, Art 14.3(3); CETA, Art 29.4(6); EUJEPA, Art 21.5(6); EUSFTA, Art 14.3(3); EUVFTA, Art 15.3(3).

[398] CETA, Annex 29-A, paras 38, 39.

[399] EUKFTA, Annex 14-B, Art 9; Decision of the Joint Committee of the EUJEPA, Annex 3, para 35; EUSFTA, Annex 14-A, para 39; EUVFTA, Annex 15-A, para 37.

[400] EUKFTA, Art 14.17; CETA, Art 29.10(3), Annex 29-A, para 39; EUJEPA, Art 21.19(4); EUSFTA, Art 14.19(2); EUVFTA, Art 15.22(2).

[401] EUKFTA, Annex 14-B, Art 7.7; CETA, Annex 29-A, paras 38, 39; EUJEPA, Art 21.15(1); EUSFTA, Annex 14-A, para 32; EUVFTA, Art 15.8(4), Annex 15-A, para 37.

therefore, presents the possibility of having closed hearings that could be abused by one party in different cases that may undermine the intended transparency of the proceedings. Moreover, compared to the rest of the agreements that are silent on how viewings take place, the EUSFTA specifically establishes that 'public viewing shall take place via simultaneous closed circuit television broadcast to a separate viewing room at the venue of the arbitration', and even requires registration for it.[402] Therefore, similar to WTO public hearings, at least in the case of the EUSFTA, only people that would be in Brussels or, respectively, Singapore (the designated places for hearings)[403] would be able to view the hearings.

6.10.3   The Influence of Transparency on Choosing a DSM

It is not clear whether the parties to the new generation EU FTAs would disclose their requests for initiation of consultations, requests for establishment of arbitration panels, or their submissions (except under CETA rules that require the publication of submissions). Nevertheless, the rules in these agreements allow public access to hearings that are usually of great public interest. Thus, the new generation EU FTAs expressly provide in their texts what was achieved through the help of jurisprudence in the WTO. Moreover, hearings are public by default, not only when parties agree to it.

While transparency would likely play a more limited role when states choose between fora,[404] it may still have a certain significance. Transparency may influence how dispute settlement mechanisms are perceived by the public and the national constituencies of the states involved. The fact that WTO proceedings have taken place behind closed doors most of the time raised doubts about the fairness of the procedures and caused misconceptions about how they occur.[405] Publicity of the proceedings allows civil society representatives to see how hearings are conducted and foster the understanding of how things work.[406] Moreover, public scrutiny could prevent or reveal abuses, such as the incompetence of the arbitrators. Consequently, increased transparency of the hearings could help build a more trustworthy, credible, and fair mechanism.[407] By opening the proceedings to the public, constituencies can see that the outcomes of the dispute are the result of a fair and adequate process,

---

[402] EUSFTA, Annex 14-A, para 32.

[403] According to EUSFTA, Annex 14-A, para 27, '[u]nless the Parties agree otherwise, the hearing shall be held in Brussels if the complaining Party is Singapore and in Singapore if the complaining Party is the Union.'

[404] Interview 2.

[405] Ehring (2008), p. 1023.

[406] United States at the Meeting of the WTO Dispute Settlement Body, Geneva, 22 July 2019 (n 383) 1.

[407] Ehring (2008), p. 1024.

which could facilitate the acceptance and implementation of the outcomes.[408] Transparency cannot completely eradicate potential wrong perceptions or distrust, but it can help improve the situation.

In addition to helping gain the support of society, transparency may have other advantages for states. A complainant that brings a case on a politically sensitive issue may seek support from civil society.[409] Without transparency, civil society is kept out of the procedures and cannot exert pressure in the case. Of course, there may be cases in which states might want to avoid publicity and the involvement of civil society. Since the general rule in the WTO is that hearings are closed, unless both parties agree to public hearings, the will of a single state might not be enough. In the new generation EU FTAs, the default rule is openness; therefore, the agreements are designed to offer greater transparency. Nevertheless, as the EUSFTA rules of procedure seem to indicate, the proceedings could still be open only to a limited number of persons. The exact means of broadcasting the hearings under the rest of the agreements remains to be seen, but they certainly go further with respect to transparency than WTO rules. Increased transparency could also be associated with increased accountability of the arbitrators, as they would be under public scrutiny. In transparent proceedings, arbitrators are under pressure to render decisions and justify them in a way that is 'understandable to all involved constituencies, and in principle acceptable to them as a proper construction of the agreement.'[410] Therefore, increased transparency can serve as a mechanism of tightening control over the authority of the arbitrators.[411] Finally, increased transparency also increases the legitimacy of the DSMs.[412]

To conclude, governments looking for greater transparency for the reasons mentioned above, may choose to bring a dispute to the new generation EU FTA DSMs, while those that wish to avoid publicity may prefer the WTO DSM.

6.11 *Amicus Curiae* Briefs

To submit an *amicus curiae* brief, access to the documents of the proceedings and arguments brought by the parties is needed. Therefore, the possibility of submitting *amicus curiae* briefs during the proceedings is closely related to the issue of transparency.

---

[408] United States at the Meeting of the WTO Dispute Settlement Body, Geneva, 22 July 2019 (n 383) 2.

[409] Pierola and Horlick (2007), p. 898.

[410] Schill (2017), p. 128.

[411] Ibid.

[412] For more on the legitimacy of the DSMs, *see infra* Sect. 7.6.

6.11.1   Amicus Curiae *Briefs in WTO Proceedings*

The issue of *amicus curiae* briefs has proved to be one of the most contentious in dispute settlement proceedings under WTO rules, since it has raised fears that the AB overreached its mandate and was involved in law-making.[413]

Neither the DSU nor the Working Procedures for Appellate Review specifically address this issue. However, according to the AB report from *US – Shrimp*, panels' right to seek information provided in Article 13 of the DSU and their right to depart from the Working Procedures established by Article 12.1 of the DSU are wide enough to entitle panels to accept, consider and reject information whether requested or not.[414] However, the AB did not address the issue of unsolicited *amici* at the appellate stage in this dispute, the question being responded to in a subsequent case, *US – Lead and Bismuth II*.[415] When the AB received unsolicited *amicus curiae* briefs not part of the parties' submissions, it established that 'nothing in the DSU or the Working Procedures specifically provides that the AB may accept and consider submissions or briefs from sources other than the participants and third participants in an appeal', but there is also nothing that 'explicitly prohibits' such acceptance or consideration.[416] Furthermore, the AB relied on Article 17.9, which endows it with the authority to draw working procedures, to conclude that 'as long as we act consistently with the provisions of the DSU and the covered agreements, we have the legal authority to decide whether or not to accept and consider any information that we believe is pertinent and useful in an appeal'.[417]

In *EC – Asbestos*, the AB anticipated that *amicus* briefs would be submitted, and adopted additional working procedures that established conditions for such submissions, including requirements for length, deadlines, and disclosure.[418] However, while the procedures seemed to organise the process of submitting *amicus curiae* briefs, this initiative was highly criticised and attacked by the Membership, as it was perceived as judicial activism.[419] Since then, no procedures have been adopted and there are no clear rules for submission of *amicus* briefs. Many submissions are presented by industry associations or corporate actors[420] that may have a direct interest in a specific outcome of the dispute and 'lobby' for it. However, there are no conditions establishing who can submit *amicus curiae* briefs and what information

---

[413] Howse (2016), p. 40; Squatrito (2017), pp. 65–89.

[414] Appellate Body Report, *United States – Import Prohibition of Certain Shrimp and Shrimp Products (US – Shrimp)*, WT/DS58/AB/R, 12 October 1998, [106–108].

[415] Appellate Body Report, *United States – Imposition of Countervailing Duties on Certain Hot-Rolled Lead and Bismuth Carbon Steel Products Originating in the United Kingdom (US – Lead and Bismuth II)*, WT/DS138/AB/R, 10 May 2000.

[416] Ibid [39].

[417] Ibid.

[418] Howse (2016), p. 40.

[419] Ibid.

[420] Cook (2019), p. 14.

should be provided in the submissions. The MPIA does not regulate in any way the submission of *amicus curiae* briefs, the relevant DSU and Working Procedures for Appellate Review rules being applicable *mutatis mutandis* to the appeal arbitration procedures.[421]

Although the AB interpreted the DSU as allowing it and panels to consider *amicus* submissions, the issue is no longer as contentious as it was, and *amicus curiae* briefs are submitted and accepted for consideration, in practice, there have been no cases in which the AB relied on *amicus* briefs in its rulings and almost no cases in which panels did so.[422] However, there are cases in which panels and the AB could have relied on *amicus* submissions, but have not expressly stated so.

6.11.2 Amicus Curiae *Briefs Under the New Generation EU FTA DSMs*

The new generation EU FTAs include detailed rules applicable to the submission of *amicus curiae* briefs. Under all the new generation EU FTAs, unsolicited written submissions from natural and legal persons of the parties may be received by the panels.[423] They also expressly establish that even though *amicus curiae* briefs may be submitted, this is so unless parties agree otherwise.[424] Therefore, exceptionally, parties can agree to prohibit this type of submission. When the default rule applies and *amicus curiae* briefs are allowed, they are subject to strict time and size limits and content requirements. Unsolicited written submissions shall be made within 10 days of the establishment of the panel and shall be no longer than 15 typed pages, including any annexes.[425] In addition, these submissions must be directly relevant to the issues under consideration by the panels. CETA mentions in general that they should be relevant to the 'issue under consideration', thus seemingly referring to the dispute without specifying whether the submissions should be relevant to either factual or legal issues.[426] On the other hand, the EUKFTA, EUJEPA, and EUVFTA explicitly refer to both factual and legal issues. The EUSFTA has a more restricted

---

[421] MPIA, Annex 1, para 11.

[422] Ibid 17.

[423] EUKFTA, Annex 14-B, Art 11.1; CETA, Annex 29-A, para 44; Decision of the Joint Committee of the EUJEPA, Annex 3, para 38; EUSFTA, Annex 14-A, para 42; EUVFTA, Art 15.8(4), Annex 15-A, para 40.

[424] EUKFTA, Annex 14-B, Art 11.1; CETA, Annex 29-A, para 44; Decision of the Joint Committee of the EUJEPA, Annex 3, para 38; EUSFTA, Annex 14-A, para 42; EUVFTA, Art 15.8(4), Annex 15-A, para 40.

[425] EUKFTA, Annex 14-B, Art 11.1; CETA, Annex 29-A, para 44; Decision of the Joint Committee of the EUJEPA, Annex 3, paras 38, 39; EUSFTA, Annex 14-A, para 42; EUVFTA, Annex 15-A, para 40.

[426] CETA, Annex 29-A, para 44.

scope: the submission shall only be relevant to the 'factual issue'.[427] Thus, the EUSFTA has stricter rules and provides that *amicus curiae* briefs may be submitted only on factual issues.

Under these agreements, the submission shall also contain detailed information about the person making it, such as whether the person is natural or legal, the person's place of establishment, activity, source of financing, and the nature of the person's interest.[428] Requiring this type of information addresses the concern that groups and lobbyists may influence the outcome of the dispute to satisfy the interests they represent.[429] Therefore, the FTAs ensure that arbitrators are aware of and more cautious about the interests the submitting persons might represent. In addition, CETA, EUJEPA, and EUVFTA expressly require that submissions are made only by non-governmental organisations,[430] and, consequently independent from government officials,[431] thereby introducing a guarantee that parties do not use additional means to influence the outcome of the dispute.

Although the new generation EU FTAs explicitly allow the submission of *amicus briefs*, panels are not obliged to address in their rulings the arguments contained in such submissions.[432] They shall only list the submissions that conform to the requirements provided in the Rules of Procedure and submit them to parties for comment. However, there is no obligation to argue why a submission in conformity with the rules was not taken into consideration, listing them being sufficient.[433] The EUJEPA and EUVFTA additionally prescribe that the arbitration panels 'shall take into consideration' the comments of the parties on *amicus curiae* briefs.[434] Therefore, even if the panels are not obliged to consider *amicus curiae* briefs that conform to conditions, under the EUJEPA and EUVFTA, there is an obligation to take into account possible comments of the parties on these submissions.

It is not yet clear how often in practice FTA arbitration panels would take into account *amicus curiae* briefs. The provisions of the Rules of Procedure technically

---

[427] EUKFTA, Annex 14-B, para 11.1; Decision of the Joint Committee of the EUJEPA, Annex 3, para 39; EUSFTA, Annex 14-A, para 42; EUVFTA, Annex 15-A, para 40.

[428] EUKFTA, Annex 14-B, Art 11.2; CETA, Annex 29-A, para 45; Decision of the Joint Committee of the EUJEPA, Annex 3, para 39; EUSFTA, Annex 14-A, para 43; EUVFTA, Annex 15-A, para 41.

[429] Pusceddu (2016), p. 29.

[430] CETA, Annex 29-A, para 43.

[431] Decision of the Joint Committee of the EUJEPA, Annex 3, para 38; EUVFTA, Annex 15-A, para 40.

[432] EUKFTA, Annex 14-B, Art 11.3; CETA, Annex 29-A, para 46; EUSFTA, Annex 14-A, para 44; EUVFTA, Annex 15-A, para 42.

[433] EUKFTA, Annex 14-B, Art 11.3; CETA, Annex 29-A, para 46; Decision of the Joint Committee of the EUJEPA, Annex 3, para 40; EUSFTA, Annex 14-A, para 44; EUVFTA, Annex 15-A, para 42.

[434] Decision of the Joint Committee of the EUJEPA, Annex 3, para 40; EUVFTA, Annex 15-A, para 42.

allow panels to ignore on a regular basis *amicus curia* briefs that conform to the conditions with no need to provide arguments for doing so.

6.11.3   Implications of the Rules on Amicus Curiae *Briefs* for the Competition Between the WTO and the New Generation EU FTA DSMs

The possibility of submitting *amicus curiae* briefs in trade disputes means that civil society interested in the outcome of the cases can also express and make known its opinions to the panelists. These submissions become especially important in disputes that concern subjects of special interest for civil society, such as environmental or human health protection.[435] Allowing civil society representatives to express their opinions on matters that might affect them directly, could increase their trust in the institutions. Moreover, having civil society weighing in on politically sensitive matters could also be in the interest of the disputing parties because they could seek support from it.

Compared to WTO rules which do not expressly regulate *amicus curiae* briefs, leading panels and the AB to interpret the existing rules, thereby putting themselves at risk of attack, the new generation EU FTAs explicitly regulate unsolicited submissions. The drafters of the new generation EU FTAs seemed to have learned lessons from the history of the WTO dispute settlement. Therefore, the explicit regulation of submission of *amicus curiae* briefs should be considered an improvement in the dispute settlement rules of the FTAs. Moreover, while within the WTO the existing rules were interpreted in the jurisprudence as allowing submissions of *amicus curiae* briefs, there are no clear rules to follow when submitting them. By contrast, the new generation EU FTAs establish conditions for submissions and ensure that relevant information about the submitting persons is disclosed and that possible interests and biased opinions can be more easily detected.

Therefore, the more developed rules for *amicus curiae* briefs in the new generation EU FTAs could be considered an advantage that would tip the scales in favour of their use. Nevertheless, FTA rules permit arbitration panels to completely ignore *amicus curiae* submissions, except for possible comments from the parties under the EUJEPA and EUVFTA. Thus, the effect of these rules in practice might not be different from that of WTO rules, and their influence could be insignificant. Finally, the regulation of *amicus curiae* briefs, despite its advantages, is unlikely to play a decisive role in the choice of a forum.

---

[435] As happened in *US – Shrimp* in which environmental concerns were at issue, and *EC – Asbestos* in which the products under analysis could have affected human health.

6.12   Implementation

Once the panel or the AB issues its final rulings in which measures are found to be inconsistent under WTO or FTA rules, the wrongdoing Member/party has to bring the measures into conformity. The way compliance proceedings take place is another procedural aspect that could influence the selection of one forum over another, this being the stage at which actual change or withdrawal of the measures of another state is sought.

6.12.1   Implementation of Panel and AB Recommendations and Rulings Under the DSU

6.12.1.1   Implementation Procedures Under the DSU

According to Article 19.1 of the DSU, where a panel or AB concludes that a measure is inconsistent with the WTO covered agreements, it recommends that the concerned Member brings its measure into conformity and additionally suggests ways in which to do so. According to Article 21.2 of the DSU, prompt compliance with recommendations is essential 'to ensure the effective resolution of disputes'. Compliance means that the inconsistent measure is either withdrawn or modified to comply with WTO rules.[436]

If prompt or immediate compliance is impracticable, which in most of the cases it is or it is alleged to be so,[437] the respondent shall do that in a reasonable period of time (RPT) that is (1) proposed by it and approved by the DSB; (2) mutually agreed by the parties; or (3) determined through binding arbitration within 90 days of the adoption of the recommendations and rulings.[438] 'If the parties cannot agree on an arbitrator within ten days after referring the matter to arbitration, the arbitrator shall be appointed by the Director-General within ten days, after consulting the parties'.[439] The DSU also prescribes a guideline for the arbitrator, by stipulating that the RPT should not exceed 15 months from the date of the panel or AB report; however, the period can also be shorter or longer depending on the circumstances.[440] By interpreting this guideline on the length of the RPT in light of the context and the object and purpose of the DSU, the arbitrator in *EC – Hormones (Article 21.3(c))*

---

[436] Award of the Arbitrator, *Argentina – Measures Affecting the Export of Bovine Hides and the Import of Finished Leather (Article 21.3(c))*, WT/DS155/10, 31 August 200, [40]–[41]; Award of the Arbitrator, *Japan – Countervailing Duties on Dynamic Random Access Memories from Korea (Article 21.3(c))*, WT/DS336/16, 5 May 2008, [37].

[437] Lester et al. (2018), p. 158.

[438] DSU, Art 21.3.

[439] DSU, Art 21.3(c), fn 12.

[440] DSU, Art 21.3.

concluded that it 'should be the shortest period possible within the legal system of the Member to implement the recommendations and rulings of the DSB.'[441] The average RPT established through arbitration is about 11 months, with the minimum being 6 months and the maximum approximately 15 months.[442] However, parties can agree on longer periods and can extend the RPT agreed by them or determined by the arbitrator.[443] The period from the date of establishment of the panel to the date of determination of the RPT should not exceed 15 months, unless the parties agree otherwise, or if the panel or the AB extends the time of issuing reports, in which case it should not exceed 18 months.[444] In practice, however, arbitration lasts on average 157 days from the date of adoption of the reports and 22 months from panel establishment.[445]

If there is disagreement between the parties on the consistency of the measures taken to comply with the reports, it shall be decided through recourse to dispute settlement procedures (compliance proceedings), if possible by resorting to the original panel which should circulate its report within 90 days of the referral of the matter to it or, if impossible, within another deadline notified to the DSB.[446] In practice, however, the average length of compliance proceedings is almost 400 days from the referral.[447] The scope of the compliance procedures has also been clarified by jurisprudence. Article 21.5 of the DSU specifically refers to 'measures taken to comply' that, according to the AB, are 'measures which have been, or which should be, adopted by a Member to bring about compliance with the recommendations and rulings of the DSB.[448] However, the AB has also stated that compliance proceedings are not limited to establishing whether the adopted measures are consistent with the DSB recommendations and rulings, but that they should also determine whether they are consistent with the relevant provisions of the covered agreements.[449] Whether or not consultations are required before compliance panel procedures is an issue that has not been settled yet.[450] Although Article 21.5 of the DSU does not regulate these

---

[441] Award of the Arbitrator, *European Communities – Measures Concerning Meat and Meat Products (Hormones) (EC – Hormones (Article 21.3(c))*, WT/DS26/15, 29 May 1998, [25]–[26].

[442] WTO Analytical Index, DSU, Art 21. Based on data available up to 31 December 2019, para 25 <www.wto.org/english/res_e/publications_e/ai17_e/dsu_art21_jur.pdf>.

[443] WTO Secretariat (2017), p. 135.

[444] DSU, Art 21.4.

[445] WTO Analytical Index, DSU, Art 21. Based on data available up to 31 December 2019, paras 115, 117 <www.wto.org/english/res_e/publications_e/ai17_e/dsu_art21_jur.pdf>.

[446] DSU, Art 21.5.

[447] WTO Analytical Index, DSU, Art 21. Based on available data till 31 December 2019, para 205 <https://www.wto.org/english/res_e/publications_e/ai17_e/dsu_art21_jur.pdf>.

[448] Appellate Body Report, *Canada – Measures Affecting the Export of Civilian Aircraft, Recourse by Brazil to Article 21.5 of the DSU (Canada – Aircraft (Article 21.5 – Brazil))*, WT/DS70/AB/RW, 21 July 2000, [36].

[449] Appellate Body Report, *Canada – Aircraft (Article 21.5 – Brazil)*, [41, 42].

[450] WTO, 'The Process – Stages in a Typical WTO Dispute Settlement Case' <www.wto.org/english/tratop_e/dispu_e/disp_settlement_cbt_e/c6s7p2_e.htm>.

aspects explicitly, some Members have repeatedly resorted to it,[451] and regular appeals of panel reports from compliance proceedings have also been used.[452] Since the MPIA provides that it applies to any future disputes between participating Members, including at the compliance stage,[453] in case of appeals during compliance proceedings for such disputes, the appeals will be heard by appeal arbitrators as envisaged in the arrangement. Since Articles 21 and 22 of the DSU apply *mutatis mutandis* to arbitration awards issued under Article 25 of the DSU,[454] the procedures for implementation of the arbitration awards issued under the MPIA are the same as for panel and AB reports.

The issue of implementation of the recommendations or rulings shall be placed on the DSB meeting agenda after 6 months following the date of establishment of the RPT. It can be raised by any Member and shall remain on the DSB's agenda until the issue is resolved.[455]

6.12.1.2 Temporary Remedies Under the DSU

In the event that the recommendations and rulings are not implemented within the RPT, temporary measures are available—compensation and suspension of concessions or other obligations[456] (the so-called retaliation). Neither of these remedies is preferred to full implementation.[457] Compliance remedies under the DSU are of a prospective nature and are not meant to provide reparation. Since the goal of the dispute settlement procedures is to ensure the withdrawal of the inconsistent measure, remedies apply only while the breach persists.[458] A reform of the system of remedies has been suggested that would allow retroactive remedies.[459] According to its proponents, it would ensure that violations are not free of consequences and would prevent Members from foot-dragging and encourage prompt compliance.[460]

If implementation fails within the RPT, the Member failing to comply, shall enter into consultations, if so requested, to agree on compensation.[461] Compensation, a rarely used remedy, is only voluntary and should be consistent with the covered agreements, including with the MFN principle that requires extension of the

---

[451] For example, in *Brazil – Export Financing Programme for Aircraft (Brazil – Aircraft)*, DS46, parties have availed themselves of DSU, Art 21.5 on several occasions.

[452] WTO, 'The Process – Stages in a Typical WTO Dispute Settlement Case' (n 450).

[453] MPIA, para 9, Annex 1, fn 4.

[454] DSU, Art 25.4; MPIA, Annex 1, para 17.

[455] DSU, Art 21.6.

[456] DSU, Art 22.1.

[457] DSU, Art 22.1.

[458] Bronckers and Baetens (2013), p. 289; Vidigal (2013), pp. 517, 521.

[459] Davey (2009), Brewster (2011) and Bronckers and Baetens (2013).

[460] Davey (2009), p. 126; Brewster (2011), p. 149; Bronckers and Baetens (2013), p. 308.

[461] DSU, Art 22.2.

compensation to the entire Membership.[462] Moreover, compensation is generally understood to refer only to trade concessions and benefits, not monetary payments.[463] Introducing monetary compensation as an alternative remedy has been advocated by some scholars[464] and Members.[465] While financial compensation entails advantages such as not being trade restrictive, not affecting the aggrieved party even more, and offering possible support for the aggrieved sector,[466] it could also help Members to buy their way out of violations.[467]

If no agreement on compensation is reached within 20 days after expiry of the RPT, authorisation for retaliation may be requested from the DSB, which shall decide by negative consensus within 30 days of expiry of the RPT.[468] Retaliation entails many disadvantages: it is trade destructive; it affects not only the respondent, but also the state making use of it by 'shooting itself in the foot'; and it also negatively affects other bystanders. Moreover, retaliation does not alleviate any of the damage suffered because of the violation.[469] Therefore, it does not come as a surprise that according to Article 3.7 of the DSU, retaliation is 'the last resort' to which Members can have recourse. The proposed suspension of the obligations shall take into account the qualitative and quantitative principles set in the DSU. In terms of quality, the obligations proposed for suspension shall be from the same sector in which the violation was found, unless it is not practicable, in which case the suspension is allowed in another sector from the same agreement or the last resort—even from another agreement.[470] The quantitative requirement is that the level of suspended concessions shall be equivalent to that of the nullification or impairment caused by the violation.[471] The requirement of equivalence ensures that retaliation is only used to *induce compliance* and does not have a *punitive* aim.[472]

According to Article 22.6 of the DSU, if the respondent objects to the proposed level of suspensions, or claims that the qualitative principles were not complied with, the matter shall be referred for arbitration to the original panel, if possible (if not, to an arbitrator appointed by the DG), which should issue its ruling within 60 days from

---

[462] Mercurio (2009), pp. 324–325.

[463] Ibid, 328.

[464] Davies (2006), p. 40; Bronckers and Baetens (2013), pp. 281–311; Davey (2014), p. 699.

[465] DSB, Contribution of Ecuador to the Improvement of the Dispute Settlement Understanding of the WTO, TN/DS/W/9, 8 July 2002; DSB, Proposal by Mexico: Improvements and Clarifications of the Dispute Settlement Understanding, TN/DS/W/91, 16 July 2007.

[466] Bronckers and Baetens (2013), pp. 299–301.

[467] Mercurio (2009), pp. 334–335.

[468] DSU, Arts 22.2, 22.6.

[469] Bronckers and Baetens (2013), p. 282.

[470] DSU, Art 22.3(a)–(c).

[471] DSU, Art 22.4.

[472] Decision by the Arbitrators, *European Communities — Regime for the Importation, Sale and Distribution of Bananas (EC – Bananas III (US) (Article 22.6 – EC))*, WT/DS27/ARB, 9 April 1999 [6.3]; Decision by the Arbitrators, *EC – Hormones (Article 22.6 – Canada)*, WT/DS26/ARB, 12 July 1999, [39].

the expiry of the RPT (equivalence proceedings).[473] In practice, equivalence proceedings begin long after the expiry of the RPT. Therefore, it takes about 700 days on average from the expiry of the RPT for a ruling to be issued.[474] The DSB cannot authorise retaliation until arbitration on its compliance with qualitative and/or quantitative requirements is complete. Retaliation shall be temporary and applied only until the inconsistent measure has been removed, or the respondent provides a solution to the nullification or impairment of benefits, or a mutually satisfactory solution is reached.[475] As Article 22 of the DSU on temporary trade remedies applies likewise to arbitration awards, the same trade remedies governed by the same rules will be available for implementation of arbitral awards issued under the MPIA.

6.12.1.3   Sequencing and Compliance Post-Retaliation Under the DSU

The implementation procedures under the DSU have already been described in detail, but there are some issues that have arisen in practice, which will be addressed in this sub-section.

Retaliation is only allowed when there is a failure to implement compliance measures; a failure that in case of disagreement between the parties is decided through compliance proceedings.[476] However, the sequence of these two procedures is problematic because of the conflicting time frames provided for them in the DSU.[477] The DSB has to grant authorisation for retaliation within 30 days of the expiry of the RPT, while the compliance procedures should take 90 days.[478] These time frames would require the DSB to authorise retaliation before the failure to implement compliance measures was determined. This seems to contradict the requirement in Article 23.1 of the DSU that prohibits a Member from deciding unilaterally if a measure nullifies or impairs its benefits under the WTO agreements.[479] As the DSU does not provide a solution for this issue, in practice, states began to sign *ad-hoc* voluntary agreements to establish that before suspending concessions or other obligations, the compliance procedures are to take place first or that when two concurrent procedures are initiated, the procedure on retaliation should be suspended until that on compliance is completed.[480] Yet, these voluntary agreements do not remedy the contradictory text of the DSU that would become

---

[473] DSU, Art 22.6 (according to fn 15, '[t]he expression "arbitrator" shall be interpreted as referring either to an individual or a group.').

[474] WTO Analytical Index, DSU, Art 22. Based on the data available up to 31 December 2019, para 4 <www.wto.org/english/res_e/publications_e/ai17_e/dsu_art22_jur.pdf>.

[475] DSU, Art 22.7.

[476] DSU, Art 21.5.

[477] Van den Bossche and Zdouc (2017), p. 290.

[478] The contradictory time frames are in Arts 21.5 and 22.6 of the DSU.

[479] Lester et al. (2018), p. 167.

[480] Ibid.

problematic if parties do not manage to agree on the sequence of the proceedings. As the DSU rules on implementation apply to appeal arbitration awards issued under the MPIA, the same issue of sequencing would arise.

Another problem that arises at the implementation stage is the compliance post-retaliation. The DSU does not provide any procedure for terminating or withdrawing the remedies imposed, which may be problematic if the complainant is still unhappy with the measures taken to comply by the respondent.[481] When this issue occurred in *EC – Hormones*, the EU initiated new proceedings against the retaliation imposed by the US and Canada. In dealing with this case, the AB established that although the DSU does not provide procedures for handling disagreement over compliance after retaliation, this does not mean that Members need to stay passive. The parties to the dispute have the responsibility to make sure that the remedies are imposed on a 'temporary' basis.[482] It then established that:

> [R]ecourse to Article 21.5 panel proceedings is the proper course of action within the procedural structure of the DSU in cases where, as in this dispute, a Member subject to the suspension of concessions has taken an implementing measure and a disagreement arises as to whether 'the measure found to be inconsistent with a covered agreement has been removed' within the meaning of Article 22.8.[483]

Moreover, it concluded that initiating procedures under Article 21.5 of the DSU is not limited only to the original complainant, but it is also available to the original respondent,[484] ensuring that regardless of the failure of the original complainant, the retaliation has to be a temporary measure. Therefore, WTO panels and the AB had to develop a solution to the 'post-retaliation' problem that can appear when using existing rules, even though the DSU text is silent on it. Considering that the MPIA stipulates that the DSU rules on implementation apply to appeal arbitration awards *mutatis mutandis*, without providing other new rules, the issue of compliance post-retaliation would remain unresolved when this alternative mechanism is used.

6.12.2   Implementation of Panel Reports and Rulings Under the New Generation EU FTAs

6.12.2.1   Implementation Procedures Under the New Generation EU FTAs

The new generation EU FTAs, similar to the DSU, describe in detail the procedures that ensure a party's compliance with the final panel reports and rulings. Except for the EUKFTA in which compliance measures should be taken initially within a

---

481 Van den Bossche and Zdouc (2017), p. 291.

482 Appellate Body Report, *Canada – Continued Suspension (Hormones)*, [310].

483 Ibid [345].

484 Ibid [347].

RPT,[485] the rest of the new generation EU FTAs require prompt or immediate compliance first, and only if that is not possible, compliance shall take place within a RPT.[486] Under CETA rules, the respondent shall additionally notify the other party and the Joint Committee of its intention to comply within 20 days of receipt of the panel report.[487] The complainant proposes and notifies the other party of the time it will require for compliance.[488] As with DSU rules, parties shall first endeavour to reach an agreement on the RPT, but in the event of disagreement, the party complained against shall request the arbitration panel to establish the length of the RPT within 20 days of notification of the proposed RPT by the complainant.[489] There is no guideline, similar to the one established by the DSU, on the length of the RPT. Thus, there is no indication of what is expected from the panels ruling on this issue. The arbitration panel shall notify its ruling on the length of the RPT in 20 days of the request for arbitration under the EUKFTA, EUSFTA, and EUVFTA rules, and 30 days under CETA and EUJEPA.[490] All new generation EU FTAs, except CETA, expressly specify that this should be the original panel. The RPT can be extended by mutual agreement of the parties.[491]

Before the end of the RPT, the respondent shall notify the other party and the Committees (in the EUJEPA only the other party shall be notified) of any measures taken to comply.[492] When there is disagreement between the parties on the existence of any measure taken to comply or its consistency with the agreements, the complaining party, as under DSU rules, may request the original panel to rule on the matter within 45 days of the request under the EUKFTA, EUSFTA and EUVFTA, and within 90 days under CETA and EUJEPA.[493]

6.12.2.2 Temporary Remedies Under the New Generation EU FTAs

As with DSU rules, in the event that the respondent fails to notify any measure taken to comply or if the arbitration panel established that such a measure does not exist or

---

[485] EUKFTA, Art 14.8.

[486] CETA, Art 29.13(1); EUJEPA, Art 21.20(1); EUSFTA, Art 14.10(1); EUVFTA, Art 15.13(1).

[487] CETA, Art 29.12.

[488] EUKFTA, Art 14.9(1); CETA, Art 29.13(1); EUJEPA, Art 21.20(2); EUSFTA, Art 14.10(1); EUVFTA, Art 15.13(1).

[489] EUKFTA, Art 14.8, 14.9(2); CETA, Art 29.13(2); EUJEPA, Art 21.20(2); EUSFTA, Art 14.10 (2); EUVFTA, Art 15.13(2).

[490] EUKFTA, Art 14.9(2); CETA, Art 29.13(2); EUJEPA, Art 21.20(2); EUSFTA, Art 14.10(2); EUVFTA, Art 15.13(2).

[491] EUKFTA, Art 14.9(5); CETA, Art 29.13(3); EUJEPA, Art 21.20(3); EUSFTA, Art 14.10(5); EUVFTA, Art 15.13(5).

[492] EUKFTA, Art 14.10(1); CETA, Art 29.13(5); EUJEPA, Art 21.21(1); EUSFTA, Art 14.11(1); EUVFTA, Art 15.14(1).

[493] EUKFTA, Art 14.10(2); CETA, Art 29.14(4)–(5); EUJEPA, Art 21.21; EUSFTA, Art 14.11(2); EUVFTA, Art 15.14(2)–(3).

is inconsistent with the agreements, the complainant is entitled to have recourse to temporary remedies.[494] CETA and EUJEPA have additional reasons for recourse to trade remedies by the complainant at an earlier stage, which provide greater flexibility for the complainant. Under CETA rules, if the respondent fails to notify its intention to comply within 20 days after receipt of the final panel report, even without establishing the RPT and without the ruling of the panel, the complainant can have recourse to temporary remedies.[495] Under EUJEPA rules, if the respondent notifies that it is impracticable to comply within the RPT, without waiting for its expiry, the complainant can make use of trade remedies.[496] Therefore, the rules of CETA and EUJEPA could be perceived as being more advantageous from the perspective of the complainant because of the measures to pressure the respondent into compliance sooner.

The complainants under the new generation EU FTAs have available the same remedies as under the DSU: compensation and the suspension of obligations.[497] The EUJEPA offers additional remedies which are termed 'any arrangement'.[498] Thus, it offers flexibility to the parties, as the term 'arrangement' seems to encompass any possible arrangement that parties agree on, including monetary compensation which is not possible under the DSU but has been advocated by many.[499] The EUSFTA requires parties to first attempt to agree on compensation, and if no agreement is reached within 30 days from the expiry of the RPT or from the ruling on the consistency of the measure, the complainant is entitled to suspend obligations.[500] Under the new generation EU FTAs, a compensation offer (or in the EUJEPA, an offer for any alternative arrangement) is made by the respondent if requested by the complainant.[501] CETA, EUJEPA, and EUVFTA have more flexible rules according to which the complainant can suspend obligations without consultations on compensation if the respondent does not request them. Accordingly, disputing parties can skip the stage of consultations on compensation, a remedy rarely used in practice under the DSU.[502] If a request for compensation is made, consultations should take place within 30 days under the EUKFTA and EUVFTA and 20 days under the EUJEPA before obligations can be suspended.[503] CETA provides more flexible

---

[494] EUKFTA, Art 14.11(1); CETA, Art 29.14(1); EUJEPA, Art 21.22(1); EUSFTA, Art 14.12(1); EUVFTA, Art 15.15(1).

[495] CETA, Art 29.14(1)(a).

[496] EUJEPA, Art 15.15(1).

[497] EUKFTA, Art 14.11(1)–(2); CETA, Art 29.14(1); EUJEPA, Art 21.22(1)–(2); EUSFTA, Art 14.12(1)–(2); EUSFTA, Art 15.15(1)–(2).

[498] EUJEPA, Art 21.22(1).

[499] *See supra* (nn 464–466).

[500] EUSFTA, Art 14.12(1)–(2).

[501] EUKFTA, Art 14.11(1); CETA, Art 29.14(10); EUJEPA, Art 21.22(1)–(2); EUVFTA, Art 15.15 (1)(2).

[502] CETA, Art 29.14(1); EUJEPA, Art 21.22(2); EUVFTA, Art 25.15(2).

[503] EUKFTA, Art 14.11(2); EUJEPA, Art 21.22(2); EUVFTA, Art 15.15(2).

rules: a request for an offer of compensation can be made by the complainant at any time and there is no deadline for consultations, meaning that it can be made even after suspension of obligations.[504]

If the complainant makes use of the suspension-of-obligation remedy, such a suspension is subject to a quantitative requirement similar to that established by the DSU. The suspension shall be at a level equivalent to the nullification or impairment caused by the violation.[505] Only CETA and EUJEPA have qualitative requirements establishing that suspension of obligations shall be applied to any sector covered by the dispute settlement chapters.[506] Therefore, even the new generation EU FTAs that include qualitative requirements are flexible and do not require that retaliation be first applied in the same sector. The complainant shall notify the other party (and the Committees under CETA, EUSFTA and EUVFTA) about the suspension of obligations and the level at which it intends to suspend them.[507] If the respondent considers that the level of suspension is not equivalent to the nullification or impairment caused by the violation, it may request the original panel to rule on the matter within 30 days of the request for arbitration; the same is true under the DSU.[508] Obligations shall not be suspended until the panel issues a ruling on equivalence.[509] Suspension of obligations, as well as compensation, is only a temporary remedy and shall be applied only until compliance is achieved or until parties reach a solution that settles the dispute.[510] Suspension of obligations pursuant to the new generation EU FTAs rules shall not be hampered by a party invoking the WTO agreements.[511]

The new generation EU FTAs do not expressly mention whether compliance with trade remedies should be only prospective in nature. However, this can be deduced from the fact that they are temporary and only have the aim of inducing compliance, similar to the WTO remedies. Nonetheless, under CETA rules, the level of nullification and impairment should be calculated starting from the date of notification of the final report to the parties.[512] Thus, CETA provides partial retrospective effects of retaliation. While it does not have effects of reparation and is still meant to be used

---

[504]CETA, Art 29.14(10).

[505]EUKFTA, Art 14.11(2); CETA, Art 29.14(3); EUJEPA, Art 21.22(4)(a); EUSFTA, Art 14.2(2); EUVFTA, Art 15.15(2).

[506]CETA, Art 29.14(3); EUJEPA, Art 21.22(4)(b).

[507]EUKFTA, Art 14.11(2); CETA, Art 29.14(2); EUJEPA, Art 21.22(2); EUSFTA, Art 14.12(2); EUVFTA, Art 15.15(2).

[508]EUKFTA, Art 14.11(4); CETA, Art 29.14(5); EUJEPA, Art 21.22(6); EUSFTA, Art 14.12(3); EUVFTA, Art 15.15(3).

[509]EUKFTA, Art 14.11(4); CETA, Art 29.14(8); EUJEPA, Art 21.22(6); EUSFTA, Art 14.12(3); EUVFTA, Art 15.15(3).

[510]EUKFTA, Art 14.11(6); CETA, Art 29.14(9); EUJEPA, Art 21.22(5); EUSFTA, Art 14.12(5); EUVFTA, Art 15(4).

[511]For an analysis of the relevant provisions regarded as being additional jurisdictional clauses, *see* *infra* Sect. 10.2.4.

[512]CETA, Art 29.14(1).

only to induce compliance, it may incentivise parties to comply more promptly and deter foot-dragging in conforming to the final ruling.

6.12.2.3   Addressing the Issues of Sequencing and Compliance Post-Retaliation

Since the DSU rules raise questions about the sequence in which compliance proceedings and the right to impose temporary remedies takes place, as well as compliance post-retaliation, this section will investigate whether the new generation EU FTAs address these issues.

The new generation EU FTAs do not provide any conflicting time frames that would raise questions about the sequence of compliance and the right to use trade remedies. Moreover, one of the reasons for imposing remedies in all new generation EU FTAs is the presence of the panel ruling issued in compliance proceedings establishing inconsistency.[513] Therefore, it is clear that compliance proceedings should always take place before parties negotiate compensation and also before the complainant can notify the other party of its intention to impose trade remedies. There is also no question about the sequence of compliance and equivalence proceedings. Even if both should take place before the actual suspension of obligations, the equivalence proceedings should take place only after notification of suspension of obligations that follows the compliance proceedings.[514] Under CETA rules, the same arbitration panel can deal with both compliance and equivalence proceedings, and it expressly provides that '[i]n case of disagreements on both compliance and on equivalence, the arbitration panel shall rule on the disagreement on compliance before ruling on the disagreement on equivalence'.[515] Therefore, the new generation EU FTAs do not include conflicting time frames and provisions that would raise questions about the sequence of compliance and the right to impose trade remedies.

With respect to the post-retaliation compliance, all the new generation EU FTAs have express rules that regulate this phase. After temporary remedies are applied in case of non-compliance, the responding party should notify any measure taken to comply, as a result of which temporary remedies should cease.[516] If the parties do not come to an agreement within 30 days (in CETA in 60 days) on whether the notified measure is consistent, the complaining party should request the original panel to rule on the matter in 45 days (in CETA in 90 days).[517] If the arbitrators of the original panel are not available, the standard procedures for panel composition

---

[513] *See supra* (n 494).

[514] EUKFTA, Art. 14.11.

[515] CETA, Art. 29.14(6).

[516] EUKFTA, Art. 14.12(1); CETA, Art. 29.15(1); EUJEPA, Art. 21.23(1); EUSFTA, Art. 14.13 (1); EUVFTA, Art. 15.16(1).

[517] EUKFTA, art 14.12(2); CETA, art 29.15(2); EUJEPA, art 21.23(2); EUSFTA, art 14.13(2); EUVFTA, art 15.16(2)–(3).

should apply under EUKFTA rules, and the time frame for issuing a ruling should be 60 days.[518] Therefore, in contrast to the DSU, the new generation EU FTAs expressly regulate what the procedures should be when there is disagreement on post-retaliation compliance.

6.12.3   The Implications for the Competition Between the WTO and the New Generation EU FTA DSMs

Clarity about the implementation procedures and trade remedies to induce compliance is important for both states and business representatives that need to know what measures can be used in order to address their continued losses, in addition to the findings of violations or other nullification or impairment.[519] Based on the description provided above, it is evident that the WTO and the new generation EU FTAs have very similar compliance mechanisms that first require prompt compliance or compliance within the RPT, potentially followed by compliance proceedings, equivalence proceedings, and imposition of trade remedies. In addition, under the MPIA, the same DSU rules on compliance are applicable. Nevertheless, there are certain differences in compliance between WTO (including MPIA) rules and FTA rules that may influence the way in which these mechanisms compete.

The compliance mechanism of the WTO is under the general surveillance of the DSB, an aspect that matters more from the political rather than procedural perspective, given the negative consensus rule according to which the DSB functions. This will be treated in the following chapter on political aspects.[520] One of the procedural differences that could influence the competition between the mechanisms analysed is the greater flexibility provided by the new generation EU FTAs, for examples with rules on reasons for imposing trade remedies (under CETA and EUJEPA rules), the absence or less strict qualitative requirements for retaliation, and no requirement to conduct consultations on compensation before retaliating (under CETA, EUJEPA, and EUVFTA rules).

Therefore, the new generation EU FTA rules might be perceived as more advantageous from the complainant's point of view and offering more space for pressuring the respondent into compliance from a procedural perspective. These FTAs also offer speedier procedures that could be perceived as more efficient, if respected in practice. However, as these deadlines have not been tested, the procedures could last significantly longer in practice, as happens under the DSU. Hence, parties could be sceptical about the speediness of the procedures. Moreover, as there is no recommended length for the RPT, panels could establish periods that are

---

[518] EUKFTA, Art. 14.12(3).

[519] Interview 3 on the importance of clarity with respect to trade remedies for business representatives.

[520] *See infra* Chap. 7, Sect. 7.2.

considerably longer than under the DSU. In the case of trade remedies, the EUJEPA offers an additional remedy, while CETA allows suspensions of obligations with a partial retrospective effect. The parties that want to induce compliance more effectively could perceive these procedural differences as advantages compared to the DSU, for which such changes have been advocated. Not the least, the new generation EU FTAs expressly address the issue of sequencing and compliance post-retaliation and are, thus, more developed in this respect. Therefore, it is apparent that certain aspects that were problematic at the WTO level have been accounted for during negotiations for the new generation EU FTAs.

To conclude, from a procedural perspective, because of the more flexible, better developed, and potentially faster compliance mechanisms, the new generation EU FTAs could be preferred to the WTO DSM.

6.13   Conclusions: Learning Lessons

This section analysed procedural considerations that could influence the competition between new generation EU FTA and the WTO DSMs. It also identified the considerations that might have been behind the persistent preference for the WTO DSM until recently. Although the analysis was performed in the specific context of competing interactions, it is also valuable for the purpose of understanding, in general, how dispute settlement proceedings under the new generation EU FTAs would take place, as there is currently no such detailed analysis in the field.

First of all, the competition between the new generation EU FTA and the WTO DSMs is limited by the types of complaints that may be brought, with bilateral arbitral proceedings available only for violation complaints. Furthermore, it still remains to be seen what types of measures can be challenged under the FTAs. While the new generation EU FTA DSMs and the WTO mechanism (including MPIA rules) are very similar in some respects, such as the qualifications and obligations of the panelists, the rules of procedure, the way the panels make decisions, or the compliance proceedings, there are still many differences that could influence the preferences of the states for one mechanism or another.

The presence of an appeal stage and the support offered by the WTO and AB Secretariats are evident advantages of the WTO proceedings, making the emergence of the new generation EU FTAs as potential viable alternatives less likely for settlement of the majority of trade disputes. In general, the WTO DSM offers greater predictability and coherence, possibly higher quality reports, and automatic rules that do not entail any risk of delays or even blockages during the panel selection process. Therefore, the new generation EU FTAs hardly undermine the authority of the WTO DSM, which offers secretarial support and a two-stage dispute settlement process. However, if parties to the new generation EU FTAs are not participants in the MPIA, the advantages associated with the presence of an appeal stage are no longer available. Furthermore, if there is no MPIA and no NAP signed between Member States, appealed panel reports would be sent into the void and disputes would remain unresolved. Therefore, the new generation EU FTA DSMs, offering automatic adoption rules for panel reports, could become viable alternatives to the WTO DSM for states with no arrangements between them that would avert this undesirable outcome. In addition, some aspects under MPIA rules, such as secretarial support or the degree of coherence between arbitral awards, remain to be tested and clarified in practice for this arrangement to offer interim appeal proceedings comparable to the regular appeals.

Even states participating in the MPIA or that have signed NAPs between them could prefer using new generation EU FTA DSMs in some instances, as they provide speedier procedures (if timelines are respected and proceedings take considerably less time in practice), greater control and means to battle judicial activism, increased transparency and participation of civil society, more flexible and developed compliance proceedings, and temporary remedies that could help with inducing compliance. There are indications that parties could occasionally prefer greater control over trade dispute settlement and more interpretative divergences in case law. Nevertheless, the automaticity of the panel selection processes could work against the use of new generation EU FTA DSMs even in these instances. The panel selection processes of CETA and EUVFTA, if there are established lists of arbitrators, and of EUJEPA, with or without such lists, ensure that the procedures would not be delayed or blocked. However, potential blockages and delays at the panel selection stage in other cases may reduce the likelihood of new generation EU FTAs being perceived as viable options for solving trade disputes.

As argued in the conceptual framework, the competition between different mechanisms can also have a broader impact. The competing mechanisms can lead to improvements and learning lessons from each other. The competition could become a race to the top with the aim of providing the best rules, including procedural rules. This emphasises again the fact that interactions between DSMs can also result in positive outcomes. This section clearly showed how the FTA parties have extracted lessons from WTO dispute settlement. While the FTA DSMs build on the DSU rules, they also improve them when it comes to aspects that have proved to be problematic during WTO proceedings, such as sequencing and compliance post-retaliation. The new generation EU FTA DSMs also explicitly and in detail regulate aspects, such as publicity of hearings and submission of *amicus curiae* briefs, that are not covered by DSU rules and have only been developed in WTO jurisprudence. Furthermore, new possibilities for DSU reforms that have been debated for years at the multilateral level by WTO Members, for example monetary compensation as a form of compliance remedy or conferring a somewhat retrospective effect to compliance trade remedies, are included in certain new generation EU FTAs. Hence, the WTO DSM could also be improved based on the lessons learned from the FTAs which may prove to be useful models. To conclude, the competition between the DSMs of the EU FTAs and the WTO may result in improvements to these mechanisms, especially if both of them learn lessons from each other.

References

Allee T, Elsig M (2015) Dispute settlement provisions in PTAs: new data and new concepts. In: Dür A, Elsig M (eds) Trade cooperation: the purpose, design and effects of preferential trade agreements. Cambridge University Press, Cambridge, pp 319–354

Baschuk B (2019) A U.S. offer to keep the WTO alive comes with conditions. Bloomberg. www.bloomberg.com/news/articles/2019-11-26/a-u-s-offer-to-keep-the-wto-alive-comes-with-painful-conditions

Brewster R (2011) The remedy gap: institutional design, retaliation, and trade law enforcement. George Wash Law Rev 80(1):102–158

Bronckers M, Baetens F (2013) Reconsidering financial remedies in WTO dispute settlement. J Int Econ Law 16(2):281–311

Busch ML, Pelc KJ (2009) Does the WTO need a permanent body of panelists? J Int Econ Law 12 (3):579–594

Chase C et al (2016) Mapping of dispute settlement mechanisms in regional trade agreements: innovative or variations on a theme? In: Acharya R (ed) Regional trade agreements and multilateral trading system. Cambridge University Press, New York, pp 608–702

Congressional Research Service (2020) USMCA: a legal interpretation of the panel-formation provisions and the question of panel blocking. https://fas.org/sgp/crs/row/IF11418.pdf

Cook G (2018) The legalization of the non-violation concept in the GATT/WTO System https://papers.ssrn.com/sol3/papers.cfm?abstract_id=3272165

Cook G (2019) Confidentiality and transparency in the WTO's party-centric dispute settlement system. In: Huerta-Goldman J, Molina-Tejeda MT (eds) Practical aspects of WTO litigation. Kluwer. https://papers.ssrn.com/sol3/papers.cfm?abstract_id=3301863

Cottier T (2003) The WTO Permanent Panel Body: a bridge too far? J Int Econ Law 6(1):187–202

Davey WJ (2006) Dispute settlement in the WTO and RTAs: a comment. In: Bartels L, Ortino F (eds) Regional trade agreements and the WTO legal system. Oxford University Press, New York, pp 343–357

Davey WJ (2009) Compliance problems in WTO dispute settlement. Cornell Int Law J 42 (1):119–128

Davey WJ (2014) The WTO and rules-based dispute settlement: historical evolution, operational success, and future challenges. J Int Econ Law 17:679–700

Davies A (2006) Reviewing dispute settlement at the World Trade Organization: a time to reconsider the role/s of compensation? World Trade Rev 1(5):31–67

Donaldson V, Lester S (2009) Dispute settlement. In: Lester S, Mercurio B (eds) Bilateral and regional trade agreements: commentary and analysis. Cambridge University Press, New York, pp 385–433

Dreyer I (2020) Leap of faith: the new 16-member alternative appeals tribunal at the WTO. Borderlex. https://www.borderlex.eu/2020/04/22/leap-of-faith-the-new-16-member-alternative-appeals-tribunal-at-the-wto/

Ehlermann CD (2002) Six years on the bench of the "World Trade Court": some personal experiences as member of the Appellate Body of the World Trade Organization. J World Trade 36(4):605–639

Ehring L (2008) Public access to dispute settlement hearings in the World Trade Organization. J Int Econ Law 11(4):1021–1034

Flett J (2010) Collective intelligence and the possibility of dissent: anonymous individual opinions in WTO jurisprudence. J Int Econ Law 13(2):287–320

Flett J (2015) Referring PTA disputes to the WTO dispute settlement system. In: Dür A, Elsig M (eds) Trade cooperation: the purpose, design and effects of preferential trade agreements, World Trade Forum. Cambridge University Press, New York, pp 555–579

Ganesan AV (2015) The Appellate Body in its formative years: a personal perspective. In: Marceau G (ed) A history of law and lawyers in the GATT/WTO: the development of the rule of law in the multilateral trading system. Cambridge University Press, New York, pp 517–546

Gantz DA, Puig S (2019) The scorecard of the USMCA protocol of amendment. EJIL:Talk. https://www.ejiltalk.org/the-scorecard-of-the-usmca-protocol-of-amendment

Gao H (2018) The WTO dispute settlement mechanism: a trade court for the world. ICTSD RTA Exchange, Think Piece, pp 1–8

Goldstein JL, Steinberg RH (2008) Negotiate or litigate? Effects of WTO judicial delegation on U.S. trade politics. Law Contemp Probl 71:257–282

Hillman J (2016) Dispute settlement mechanism. In: Schott JJ, Cimino-Isaacs C (eds) Assessing the trans-pacific partnership, vol 2: Innovations in trading rules. Peterson Institute for International Economics Briefing 16-4, pp 101–114

Hillman J (2019) In: What kind of dispute settlement for the World Trade Organization? Proceedings of the Conference organized by the World Trade Institute, World Trade Organization, Geneva, 4 February 2019

Howse R (2003) The most dangerous branch? WTO Appellate Body jurisprudence on the nature and limits of the judicial power. In: Cottier T, Mavroidis PC (eds) The role of the judge in International Trade Regulation. University of Michigan Press, Michigan, pp 11–42

Howse R (2016) The World Trade Organization 20 years on: global governance by judiciary. Eur J Int Law 27(1):9–77

Kolsky Lewis M (2006) The lack of dissent in WTO dispute settlement. J Int Econ Law 9 (4):895–931

Kolsky Lewis M (2012) Dissent as dialectic: horizontal and vertical disagreement in WTO dispute settlement. Stanf J Int Law 48:1–45

Kreier J (2020) The MPIA and the WTO Secretariat. International Economic Law and Policy Blog. https://ielp.worldtradelaw.net/2020/05/the-mpia-and-the-wto-secretariat.html

Leal-Arcas R (2011) Comparative analysis of NAFTA's Chapter 20 and the WTO's dispute settlement understanding. Queen Mary University of London, School of Law Legal Studies Research Paper 94/2011, pp 1–25

Lester S (2020a) The MPIA pool of arbitrators has been announced. International Economic Law and Policy Blog. https://ielp.worldtradelaw.net/2020/08/the-mpia-pool-of-arbitrators-has-been-announced.html

Lester S (2020b) The USMCA Chapter 31 dispute settlement roster is set. International Economic Law and Policy Blog. https://ielp.worldtradelaw.net/2020/07/usmca-dispute-settlement-roster.html

Lester S (2020c) Who's going to pay for supporting the MPIA? International Economic Law and Policy Blog. https://ielp.worldtradelaw.net/2020/06/whos-going-to-pay-for-the-mpia.html

Lester S, Mercurio B, Davies A (2018) World trade law: text, materials and commentary, 3rd edn. Hart, Oxford

Lester S, Manak I, Arpas A (2019) Access to trade justice: fixing NAFTA's flawed state-to-state dispute settlement process. World Trade Rev 18(1):63–79

Lockhart J, Voon T (2005) Reviewing appellate review in the WTO dispute settlement system. Melbourne J Int Law 6(2):474–484

Lukas M (2019) In: What kind of dispute settlement for the World Trade Organization? Proceedings of the conference organized by the World Trade Institute, World Trade Organization, Geneva, 4 February 2019

Malacrida R (2015) WTO panel composition. In: Marceau G (ed) A history of law and lawyers in the GATT/WTO: the development of the rule of law in the multilateral trading system. Cambridge University Press, New York, pp 311–333

Malacrida R, Marceau G (2018) The WTO adjudicating bodies. In: Howse R et al (eds) The legitimacy of international trade courts and tribunals. Cambridge University Press, New York, pp 20–69

Marceau G, Hawkins JK (2012) Experts in WTO dispute settlement. J Int Dispute Settlement 3 (3):493–507

Marceau G, Hurley M (2012) Transparency and public participation in the WTO: a report card on WTO transparency mechanisms. Trade Law Dev 4(1):19–44

McDougall R (2018) Regional trade agreement dispute settlement mechanisms: modes, challenges and options for effective dispute resolution. ICTSD RTA Exchange, Issue Paper 1, pp 1–15

McRae D (2004) What is the future of WTO dispute settlement? J Int Econ Law 7(1):3–21

McRae D (2019) State-to-state dispute settlement in megaregionals. In: Kingsbury B et al (eds) Megaregulation contested. Global economic ordering after TPP. Oxford University Press, New York, pp 537–550

Mercurio B (2009) Why compensation cannot replace trade retaliation in the WTO dispute settlement understanding. World Trade Rev 8(2):315–338

Molina-Tejeda MT (2019) In: What kind of dispute settlement for the World Trade Organization? Proceedings of the conference organized by the World Trade Institute, World Trade Organization, Geneva, 4 February 2019

Nordström H (2005) The World Trade Organization secretariat in a changing world. J World Trade 39(5):819–853

Pauwelyn J (2004) Going global, regional, or both? Dispute settlement in the Southern African Development Community (SADC) and overlaps with the WTO and other jurisdictions. Minn J Glob Trade 13:231–304

Pauwelyn J (2015) The rule of law without the rule of lawyers? Why investment arbitrators are from mars, trade adjudicators from Venus. Am J Int Law 109(4):761–805

Pauwelyn J (2016) Minority rules: precedent and participation before the WTO Appellate Body. In: Jemielniak J, Nielsen L, Palmer Olsen H (eds) Establishing judicial authority in international economic law. Cambridge University Press, New York, pp 141–172

Pauwelyn J (2019) WTO dispute settlement post 2019: what to expect? J Int Econ Law 22:297–321

Pauwelyn J, Elsig M (2013) The politics of treaty interpretation: variations and explanations across international tribunals. In: Dunoff JL, Pollack MA (eds) Interdisciplinary perspectives on international law and international relations: the state of the art. Cambridge University Press, New York, pp 445–473

Pauwelyn J, Pelc KJ (2019) Who writes the rulings of the World Trade Organization? A critical assessment of the role of the secretariat in WTO dispute settlement. https://papers.ssrn.com/sol3/papers.cfm?abstract_id=3458872

Pereyra M (2019) In: What kind of dispute settlement for the World Trade Organization? Proceedings of the conference organized by the World Trade Institute, World Trade Organization, Geneva, 4 February 2019

Pierola F, Horlick G (2007) WTO dispute settlement and dispute settlement in the "North-South" agreements of the Americas: considerations for choice of forum. J World Trade 41(5):885–908

Porges A (2011) Dispute settlement. In: Chauffour JP, Maur JC (eds) Preferential trade agreement policies for development: a handbook. The World Bank, Washington, pp 467–501

Porges A (2018) Designing common but differentiated rules for regional trade disputes. ICTSD RTA Exchange, Issue Paper, pp 1–11

Posner T (2019) Is USMCA's dispute settlement mechanism up to the task of addressing complaints under its labor chapter? www.american-leadership.org/blog-posts/is-usmcas-dispute-settlement-mechanism-up-to-the-task-of-addressing-complaints-under-its-labor-chapter

Pusceddu P (2016) State-to-state dispute settlement provisions in the EU-Canada comprehensive economic and trade agreement. Transnational Dispute Manag 13(1):1–29

Reich A (2017) The effectiveness of the WTO dispute settlement system: a statistical analysis. European University Institute Working Paper LAW 2017/11, pp 1–29. http://cadmus.eui.eu/bitstream/handle/1814/47045/LAW_2017_11.pdf?sequence=1

Robertson B, Falls S, Novacefski A (2018) Secretariat support for ad hoc panels under Canada's free trade agreements: challenges and options. Trade Lab Memorandum, pp 6–93. www.tradelab.org/single-post/2018/06/14/Secretariat-Support-for-Ad-Hoc-Panels-under-Canadas-Free-Trade-Agreements-Challenges-and-Options

Roessler F (2003) The cobra effects of the WTO panel selection procedures. J Int Econ Law 6 (1):230–235

Sacerdoti G (2018) The WTO dispute settlement and the challenges to multilateralism: consolidating a 'Common Global Good'. In: Prévost D, Alexovicova I, Pohl JH (eds) Restoring trust in trade: Liber Amicorum in honour of Peter Van Den Bossche. Hart, Oxford, pp 87–104

Sacerdoti G (2019) In: What kind of dispute settlement for the World Trade Organization? Proceedings of the conference organized by the World Trade Institute, World Trade Organization, Geneva, 4 February 2019

Schill SW (2017) Authority, legitimacy, and fragmentation in the (envisaged) dispute settlement disciplines in mega-regionals. In: Griller S, Obwexer W, Vranes E (eds) Mega-regional trade agreements: CETA, TTIP, and TiSA: new orientations for EU external economic relations. Oxford University Press, New York, pp 111–150

Shaffer G, Elsig M, Puig S (2016) The extensive (but fragile) authority of the WTO Appellate Body. Law Contemp Probl 79:237–273

Shoyer AW (2003) Panel selection in WTO dispute settlement proceedings. J Int Econ Law 6 (1):203–209

Squatrito T (2017) Amicus Curiae briefs in the WTO DSM: good or bad news for non-state actor involvement? World Trade Rev 17(01):65–89

Stewart TP et al (2013) The increasing recognition of problems with WTO Appellate Body decision-making: will the message be heard? Glob Trade Customs J 8(11) & (12):390–412

Todeschini-Marthe C (2018) Dispute settlement mechanisms under free trade agreements and the WTO: stakes, issues and practical considerations: a question of choice? Glob Trade Customs J 13(9):387–403

Van den Bossche P, Zdouc W (2017) The law and policy of World Trade Organization: text, cases and materials, 4th edn. Oxford University Press, New York

VanDuzer JA (2020) State-to-state dispute settlement under the USMCA: better than NAFTA?. https://papers.ssrn.com/sol3/papers.cfm?abstract_id=3341662

Vidigal G (2013) Re-assessing WTO remedies: the prospective and the retrospective. J Int Econ Law 16(3):505–534

Vidigal G (2017) Why is there so little litigation under free trade agreements? Retaliation and adjudication in International Dispute Settlement. J Int Econ Law 20:927–950

Vidigal G (2018) Making regional dispute settlement attractive: the "Court of Arbitration" option. RTA Exchange, ICTSD. www.ictsd.org/opinion/making-regional-dispute-settlement-attractive-the-

Weiler JHH (2001) The rule of lawyers and the ethos of diplomats: reflections on the internal and external legitimacy of WTO dispute settlement. J World Trade 35(2):191–207

Weiss W (2008) Reforming the dispute settlement understanding. In: Hohmann H (ed) Agreeing and implementing the Doha Round of the WTO. Cambridge University Press, New York, pp 269–293

Weiss W, Furculita C (2020) The EU in search for stronger enforcement rules: assessing the proposed amendments to trade enforcement regulation 654/2014. J Int Econ Law 23 (4):865–884

WTO (2018) Farewell speech of Appellate Body Member Ricardo Ramírez-Hernández, 28 May 2018. www.wto.org/english/tratop_e/dispu_e/ricardoramirezfarwellspeech_e.htm

WTO Secretariat (2017) A handbook on the WTO dispute settlement system, 2nd edn. Cambridge University Press, New York

Chapter 7
Competing Political Considerations

7.1 The Value of Jurisprudence

One of the factors that could influence whether new generation EU FTAs become viable alternatives to the WTO DSM is the value of jurisprudence at the bi- and multilateral levels.

Making use of the WTO would mean resolving a dispute at the multilateral level and establishing a possible multilateral precedent.[1] As previously stated, in practice, the AB has followed its own jurisprudence and has also stated that, absent cogent reasons, the same legal question in a subsequent case should be resolved in the same way as in past cases.[2] Therefore, a ruling issued in a dispute resolved under WTO DSM rules may be relied on in future disputes by any Member.[3] Indeed, some disputes, besides having a bilateral character, could have multilateral importance.[4] The possibility of having third parties in WTO proceedings confirms the potential multilateral effect of a WTO ruling in a dispute between only two or a few Members. According to Article 10 of the DSU '[a]ny Member having a substantial interest in a matter before a panel [...] shall have an opportunity to be heard by the panel and to make written submissions to the panel.' While some Members may seek to become third parties in a dispute due to direct interest, such as ensuring that the dispute would not be resolved in a manner that would have a discriminatory effect on them, third parties could also participate due to concerns about how similar issues would be

---

[1] Interview 3.

[2] Appellate Body Report, *United States – Final Anti-Dumping Measures on Stainless Steel from Mexico (US – Stainless Steel)*, WT/DS344/AB/R, 30 April 2008, [160].

[3] Pauwelyn (2004), p. 261.

[4] Van Damme (2019), p. 65.

© The Author(s), under exclusive license to Springer Nature Switzerland AG 2021
C. Furculiță, *The WTO and the New Generation EU FTA Dispute Settlement Mechanisms*, EYIEL Monographs - Studies in European and International Economic Law 19, https://doi.org/10.1007/978-3-030-83118-9_7

solved in future disputes.[5] WTO Members clearly see a reason for participating as third parties, as the number of such parties regularly outnumbers that of main parties by a sizeable margin.[6] According to the data available for 2019, the average number of third parties in a WTO dispute has risen to 18.[7] As stated by Shaffer, Elsig, and Puig, 'there would be no reason for Members to join as third parties if they had no systemic concerns that such decisions would matter for future cases'.[8]

Moreover, WTO jurisprudence could influence not only the outcomes of WTO disputes, but also those of the disputes under new generation EU FTAs, considering the rules of interpretation requiring FTA panels to take into account/adopt WTO jurisprudence in certain cases prescribed by these agreements.[9] Hence, by bringing a dispute to the WTO, a 'precedent' is established not only at the multilateral, but also at the bilateral level. As the new generation EU FTAs do not have a provision analogous to that of Article 3.2 of the DSU requiring security and predictability in FTA dispute settlement that could serve as a basis for referring to past FTA jurisprudence, bringing the dispute to the WTO may be more helpful even from the perspective of establishing a precedent for FTA proceedings. Still, the rules of interpretation on WTO jurisprudence are limited only to identical WTO and FTA obligations under some FTAs, and panels would still retain certain latitude in assessing whether the WTO case law is relevant and whether to follow it (except for the EUKFTA).[10]

Using political science methodology, Busch explains that the choice between the FTAs and the WTO DSMs will depend on whether states want to establish a precedent that may affect only a small set of relationships—the bilateral ones—or a multilateral precedent affecting the relationships with all WTO Members.[11] A complainant can be strategic were he wants to set a precedent. If the complainant seeks to set a precedent at the multilateral level, it can then be used in future disputes also against other Members. If, however, the complainant is afraid that a ruling could potentially be used against it in future WTO disputes, it may prefer setting only a bilateral precedent.[12] Moreover, not setting a precedent at the multilateral level may be preferred by Members looking for greater control over dispute settlement and a certain degree of interpretative divergence.[13] However, if EU FTA parties prefer

---

[5] For example, in *Canada – Periodicals* (*Canada – Certain Measures Concerning Periodicals*, DS31), the US is said to have taken the dispute to the WTO instead of to NAFTA to set a multilateral precedent (Leal-Arcas 2011, pp. 19–20).

[6] Busch and Reinhardt (2006), p. 446.

[7] WTO, Ambassador Sunanta Kangvalkulkij (Thailand), 2018 DSB Chair and 2019 GC Chair, 'WTO Dispute Settlement Body – Developments in 2018' <www.wto.org/english/tratop_e/dispu_e/sunata_19_e.htm>.

[8] Shaffer et al. (2016).

[9] *See infra* Sect. 11.8.5.3.

[10] *See infra* Sect. 11.8.5.3.

[11] Busch (2007), pp.735–761.

[12] Ibid, p. 736.

[13] *See supra* Sect. 6.8; Vidigal (2018).

setting a precedent at the multilateral level that they could use in their future relationships with *all* WTO Members and with Members with whom they have an FTA in place containing interpretative rules on the use of WTO case law, the EU FTA DSMs would not be perceived as an equivalent substitute for the WTO DSM.

However, it is worth mentioning that the value ascribed to precedent in WTO jurisprudence has been subject to US criticism in the context of the AB crisis. The US claimed that the AB's approach of treating past reports as precedents is not consistent with WTO rules, as only WTO Members can adopt binding interpretations.[14] The US declared that '[b]y purporting to create binding precedent, the Appellate Body has affected WTO Members' rights and obligations without their consent' and has removed 'the incentive for Members to negotiate new trade agreements'.[15] As a reaction to the concerns on treating past AB reports as precedents, some WTO reform proposals tabled by the Members attempted to address this issue. Thus, as previously stated, the reform proposals of the EU, China, Canada, and nine other Members suggested annual meetings between the AB and WTO Members during which Members could express their view on reports.[16] Honduras suggested other alternatives, such as (1) expressly prohibiting WTO panels and the AB relying on previous reports; (2) in each case, Members considering whether the reference to the notion of 'absent cogent reasons' could/should be expunged from a report, where it is used to justify reliance on previous reports; (3) subjecting to positive consensus by Members the question of legal interpretation in the report and whether it can become a precedent and form part of WTO law; or (4) legal interpretations of the AB taking the form of precedent only once they have been repeated a given number of times in similar contexts.[17] However, none of these reform proposals was received with approval by the US which blocks the appointment and reappointment of AB Members. These developments show that in the future, due to the current AB crisis, there could be a certain revision of the role ascribed to WTO jurisprudence.

While a high degree of consistency across interim arbitration awards is expected under the MPIA than across FTA reports, it still remains to be seen whether it would be comparable to the degree of consistency offered by the AB and whether, in practice, appeal arbitrators would refer to past reports with the same regularity as the

---

[14] Office of the United States Trade Representative, The President's 2018 Trade Policy Agenda (March 2018), p. 28 <https://ustr.gov/sites/default/files/files/Press/Reports/2018/AR/2018%20Annual%20Report%20I.pdf>.

[15] United States Trade Representative, 'Report on the Appellate Body of the World Trade Organization' (February 2020) 55 <https://ustr.gov/sites/default/files/Report_on_the_Appellate_Body_of_the_World_Trade_Organization.pdf#page60>.

[16] General Council, Communication from the European Union, China, Canada, India, Norway, New Zealand, Switzerland, Australia, Republic of Korea, Iceland, Singapore and Mexico to the General Council, WT/GC/W/752, 26 November 2018.

[17] General Council, Communication from Honduras, Fostering a Discussion on the Functioning of the Appellate Body Addressing the Issue of Alleged Judicial Activism by the Appellate Body, WT/GC/W/760, 29 January 2019.

AB. Furthermore, the effect of interim appeal arbitration awards for interpretative purposes during panel processes should also be observed in practice.[18] Accordingly, the case law established under the MPIA might not have the same jurisprudential value as the AB reports. Although appeal arbitration awards might not be regarded by all panels, non-participating Members, and even all appeal arbitrators, they would, nevertheless, have a broader interpretative effect than a panel report issued under a merely bilateral agreement.

If FTA parties wished to establish precedents for use in future relations with all WTO Members, FTA DSMs may not currently seem satisfactory alternatives to the WTO DSM from the perspective of the value of jurisprudence. The jurisprudential value of arbitration awards issued under MPIA rules might not compare with that of AB or even panel reports, but it would still be greater than that of reports issued under new generation EU FTAs. Nevertheless, FTA DSMs could be attractive for states that would rather avoid setting a multilateral precedent. Moreover, the approach to existing case law at the WTO is evolving, and WTO panels could discontinue the practice of systematically following past jurisprudence.

7.2   Pressure to Induce Compliance

Important political considerations stem from the fact that the WTO is a multilateral organisation allowed to exert multilateral pressure, while the EU FTAs have a bilateral character that entails limited pressure. The pressure that can be exerted at the multilateral level to induce compliance has been associated with the regular preference for the WTO DSM.[19]

The WTO DSM allows other WTO Members to join a dispute as co-complainants by filing parallel claims,[20] or as third parties without directly confronting the respondent but expressing their interest in and position on the dispute.[21] The new generation EU FTAs, on the other hand, allow only FTA parties to participate in dispute settlement. Thus, at the WTO, Members can form a common front with the co-complainants and third parties to amplify their case and exercise pressure together in a dispute.[22] The presence of multiple complainants in the same proceedings may prevent the alleged violator from having to defend itself in numerous cases. Therefore, adjudicating the dispute at the multilateral level may also be in the interest of

---

[18] For a detailed analysis of the coherence across appeal awards, as well as on the precedential value that may be ascribed to these awards, *see* Sect. 6.8.

[19] Interview 2; Interview 4.

[20] DSU, Art 9(2): 'Where more than one Member requests the establishment of a panel related to the same matter, a single panel may be established to examine these complaints taking into account the rights of all Members concerned. A single panel should be established to examine such complaints whenever feasible.'

[21] DSU, Art 10.

[22] Interview 2; Interview 3.

the defendant, as this would avoid the need for going through a series of proceedings under the rules of different FTAs, if there are such agreements in place with the complainants, and, eventually, even adjudicating under the WTO agreements if there is no FTA concluded with one of the complainants.[23] Furthermore, if there are more original complainants, the aggregate effect of their retaliatory measures to achieve compliance would also be greater.

Almost all conventional studies agree that the participation of third parties can affect rulings.[24] Indeed, according to Article 10.2 of the DSU, third parties shall have the opportunity 'to be heard by the panel and to make written submissions to the panel' which 'shall be reflected in the panel report'. If the opinion of third parties (or their majority) is likely to coincide with that of the complaining party, the latter may find it advantageous to bring the dispute to the WTO. However, if the complaining party is aware that the majority of WTO Members that could become third parties would bring arguments against its position, it may find it more favourable to resolve the dispute in a bilateral setting. Moreover, as shown later, third parties participating in dispute settlement proceedings reduce the likelihood of reaching an MAS, which may be seen as a disadvantage of the WTO DSM.[25]

If parties refrain from participating in the proceedings, they are still entitled to put pressure by voicing their opinions during DSB meetings.[26] Since the reports are adopted by the DSB, the decisions are perceived as collective. Therefore, a respondent in WTO proceedings is subject to peer pressure and multilateral surveillance that may gain importance, especially during the implementation stage. The DSU establishes that the DSB keeps under surveillance the implementation of the adopted recommendations or rulings and that the issue of implementation can be raised by any Member, at any time following their adoption.[27] Therefore, any WTO Member out of the 164 can request that rulings and recommendations are implemented, thus bringing pressure on the Member found in violation of the WTO agreements.

> [T]he issue of implementation of the recommendations or rulings shall be placed on the agenda of the DSB meeting after six months following the date of establishment of the reasonable period of time pursuant to paragraph 3 and shall remain on the DSB's agenda until the issue is resolved.[28]

If a panel report is sent into the void by an appeal, because there is no AB to hear the appeal and the disputing parties are not participants in the MPIA, the report is not final and binding. Therefore, neither the parties to the dispute, be they complainants or third parties, nor other Members can request implementation of the report under the DSU rules. The EU might be able to use the amended Enforcement Regulation to impose countermeasures commensurate with the breach found in a panel report in

---

[23] Pauwelyn (2004), p. 250.

[24] Busch and Reinhardt (2006), p. 447.

[25] *See infra* Sect. 7.5.

[26] Vidigal (2017), p. 935.

[27] DSU, Art 21.6.

[28] Ibid.

order to enforce its WTO rights in case of an appeal that cannot be completed and the other disputing party is not an MPIA participant.[29] However, no multilateral pressure would be possible, and it is not clear yet whether other Members would accept such measures and also have recourse to them. Nevertheless, if the disputing parties are MPIA participants, the arrangement establishes that it applies 'to any future dispute between any *two or more* participating Members'[30] (emphasis added). Thus, under the MPIA, it seems that there may also be co-complainants, if multiple participating Members initiate appeals under these arrangements on the same matter. However, the same panel report could be appealed under the MPIA by one co-complainant and appealed into the void by another that took part at the panel stage but is not participating in the MPIA. Article 25.3 of the DSU on arbitration provides that '[o]ther Members may become party to an arbitration proceeding only upon the agreement of the parties which have agreed to have recourse to arbitration'. Under the MPIA, the parties seem to have agreed to allow third party participation in the same way as during the standard appeal procedures.[31]

The question arises whether WTO Members can exert the same collective pressure to induce compliance with appeal awards issued under the MPIA as in case of AB rulings. The awards issued under Article 25 of the DSU are binding because the parties agree to abide by them,[32] without the need for the DSB to adopt the awards. While the awards are not collective decisions, Article 25.4 of the DSU still establishes that Article 21 on surveillance of implementation and Article 22 on compensation and retaliation apply *mutatis mutandis* to arbitration awards. Hence, as in the case of adopted panel and AB reports, co-complainants may together use the threat of retaliation to achieve compliance with the award and, additionally, any Member may exert extra pressure by requesting that the award be implemented.

FTAs also have political decision-making bodies that can surveille the implementation stage. The EUKFTA, CETA, EUSFTA, and EUVTA establish that the Joint or Trade Committees shall be notified at every stage of the compliance procedures.[33] The Joint Committee of the EUJEPA is not assigned similar functions. However, this difference is unlikely to make the other DSMs better alternatives to the WTO DSM. The Joint and Trade Committees are composed of representatives of the two parties that are also the parties to the dispute, and it is unlikely that they

---

[29] For more on the amended Enforcement Regulation, *see* Sect. 6.4.4.

[30] MPIA, para 9.

[31] 'Third parties which have notified the DSB of a substantial interest in the matter before the panel pursuant to Article 10.2 of the DSU may make written submissions to, and shall be given an opportunity to be heard by, the arbitrators. Rule 24 of the Working Procedures for Appellate Review shall apply *mutatis mutandis*' (MPIA, Annex 1, para 16).

[32] DSU, Art 25.3.

[33] EUKFTA, Arts 14.9(1), (2), 14.10(1), 14.11(2), (4), 14.11(1), (2); CETA, Arts 29.12, 29.13(1), (2), (5), 29.14(2), (6), (7), 29.15(1), (2); EUSFTA, Arts 14.10(1), (2), 14.11(1), 14.12(2), (3), 14.13 (1), (2); EUVFTA, Arts 15.13(1), (2), 15.14(1), (2), (3), 15.15(1), (2), (3), 15.16(1), (2), (3).

would have the ability to exercise more pressure or pressure similar to that exerted by the WTO DSB composed of representatives of all Members.[34]

As a tool to urge compliance, retaliation works in a similar way at both the multilateral and the FTA level. Its usefulness to pressure compliance is related more to the size of the economy of the party using retaliation than to the setting within which it is used. Retaliation seems to mostly serve big economies that can impose retaliatory measures that could influence the behaviour of the offender. Hence, retaliation or the threat of it remains a useful tool for inducing compliance in the context of FTAs involving large economies such as the EU,[35] Canada, or Japan. Even so, '[f]ailure to comply with an RTA dispute settlement ruling is an irritant in bilateral relations; failure to comply with a WTO ruling is not only a bilateral irritant, but has multilateral consequences.'[36] Scholars have attributed considerable importance to the collective pressure put on a Member in violation to ensure compliance with international law.[37] Collective pressure would allow especially developing and least developed countries, that cannot pose a credible threat to the respondent by themselves, to build a common front with other states to exert significant pressure. Proving that the community has been the impetus for compliance with WTO reports is an impossible task, as Members do not state the reasons for their compliance with WTO rulings and recommendations. In practice, compliance was achieved in several cases, although the complainants could not, by themselves, pose serious retaliatory threats, for example in *US – Gasoline*,[38] *US – Shrimp*[39] and *EC – Bananas*.[40] These cases are indicative of factors other than the threat of retaliation that could induce compliance with WTO panels and AB rulings. The significant pressure exerted by other Members and the considerable reputational damage due to the multilateral character of the WTO have been directly linked to the high compliance rate in WTO disputes, including in cases in which the defendant was a small developing economy.[41]

At the multilateral level, Members can jointly exert pressure when arguing a case and during the implementation phase of reports and arbitral awards, while at the FTA level, pressure can be applied only by a single state. Consequently, states, notably smaller economies, seeking the support of other states in a dispute may find the DSMs contained in the new generation EU FTAs less suitable alternatives to the

---

[34] Vidigal (2017), p. 943.

[35] Interview 2.

[36] Davey (2006), p. 356.

[37] Vidigal (2017), p. 940, citing Hudec (2000); Maggi (1999), pp. 191–192; Hudec (1999), p, 9; Pauwelyn (2008), p. 128.

[38] *United States – Standards for Reformulated and Conventional Gasoline,* DS2. The complainant in the dispute was Venezuela.

[39] *United States – Import Prohibition of Certain Shrimp and Shrimp Products*, DS58. Compliance Proceedings in this case were initiated by Malaysia against the US.

[40] *European Communities – Regime for the Importation, Sale and Distribution of Bananas*, DS27. Compliance Procedures against the EC were initiated by Ecuador.

[41] Maggi (1999), pp. 191–192; Vidigal (2017), p. 941.

WTO DSM. The putative ability of multilateral pressure to cause significant reputational damage in case of non-compliance and its importance for the competition between the WTO and the new generation EU FTA DSMs will be covered in detail in the next section.

7.3 Reputation

The ability of non-compliance to cause reputational damage to a state is closely related to considerations of pressure to induce compliance. The multilateral character of the WTO not only allows exertion of significant pressure to induce compliance, it also leads to extensive reputational damage in case of non-compliance.

7.3.1 *Reputational Costs and the Risk of Immediate Retaliation*

The importance of reputation has been stressed in particular by international relations authors that adopt a rationalistic approach to the analysis of compliance with international law. The rationalist theory perceives governments as being rational and acting in their self-interest, hence complying only when the total benefits of doing so outweigh the costs.[42] According to rationalists, such costs could stem from the reputational damage caused by non-compliance.

When international obligations are not respected, other states take note of this, which could affect future relationships and negotiations by making new commitments less credible.[43] Thus, a reputation for compliance represents a judgement about a state's past actions with respect to international obligations that may be used to predict its future behaviour.[44] The reputational damage caused by non-compliance with a multilateral treaty like the WTO agreements would be more severe than that caused by non-compliance with single bilateral FTAs, such as the new generation EU FTAs. The degree to which other governments are aware of the violation would also affect the extent of reputational loss.[45] If other states are not aware of violations, they cannot affect the reputation of the offenders. As the next section will show, WTO rulings and arbitral awards issued under the MPIA are more likely to receive global attention than reports issued under the new generation EU FTAs. Nevertheless, since the EU FTAs under analysis generally require that the final panel rulings are made public, unless it is otherwise decided due to the presence of confidential

---

[42]Burgstaller (2007), pp. 55–56.

[43]Guzman (2002), pp. 1849–1850; Mushkat (2011), p. 711.

[44]Guzman (2008), p. 1.

[45]Raustiala (2000), p. 402; Guzman (2002), p. 1863.

information,[46] the violations would be known by the international community and be able to cause reputational damage.

Another reason why the damage may be more serious in the WTO than the FTA context is the value of these agreements. States are expected to assess the reliability of other states' commitments based on previous actions with respect to agreements and interactions that are valued the same or less by the offenders.[47] If a state does not comply with the norms of an agreement that is perceived as being less important, this might not affect its reputation for compliance with more valuable agreements. Therefore, non-compliance with FTA rulings might not affect the reputation of a state for compliance with the WTO agreements because they are perceived as of greater, multilateral importance. It would, nevertheless, affect the reputation of that state for complying with FTAs in general, as agreements that could have comparable value. Therefore, non-compliance with the new generation EU FTA rulings should have a reputational impact. Moreover, the new generation EU FTAs cannot be regarded as insignificant; they are among the top priorities on the trade agenda of the parties.[48] The importance of FTAs in general is also confirmed by the rising number of these agreements. If states consider them unimportant, it would be difficult to explain the effort and time invested in concluding such an impressive number of FTAs. It is submitted in this section that non-compliance with an FTA would affect the reputation of a government for complying with this type of agreement, and may potentially threaten future FTA negotiations with other countries. These consequences could act as an incentive to comply with rulings issued under the new generation EU FTAs, especially given that these agreements are currently the only engine driving the development of new trade rules.

Vidigal maintains that without a community to back up adjudicatory decisions, FTA DSMs would not only be less interesting than the WTO DSM, but also possibly less interesting than immediate retaliation,[49] and thus, could not become alternatives to the WTO DSM. Although non-compliance in a multilateral context could cause more extensive reputational damage than in a bilateral one, this should not be regarded as indicating that unilateral retaliation will be imposed without the use of mandatory FTA DSMs. While retaliation or the threat of it might remain a useful tool to induce compliance for such large economic players such as the EU, Canada, or Japan, even for these states, retaliation might not be an attractive option, as it involves certain costs.

Retaliatory measures are trade destructive measures from which the party using them could also suffer and might be regarded as 'shooting itself in the foot'.[50] The reluctance to use retaliation is also observed in the WTO. Members do not rush to

[46]EUKFTA, Art 14.17; CETA, Art 29.10(3), Annex 29-A, para 39; EUJEPA, Art 21.19(4); EUSFTA, Art 14.19(2); EUVFTA, Art 15.22(2).

[47]Downs and Jones (2002), pp. 108–111; Guzman (2008), p. 33; Brewster (2012), p. 533.

[48]See supra Sect. 2.2.3.

[49]Vidigal (2017), p. 943.

[50]Bronckers and Baetens (2013), p. 282; Van den Bossche and Zdouc (2017), p. 205.

obtain authorisation to impose retaliatory measures, and even when they were authorised, there are multiple instances in which such measures were not imposed.[51] Furthermore, by using dispute settlement procedures, actual violations can be distinguished from mistaken ones. By going through dispute settlement proceedings before retaliating, parties ensure that they impose justified, optimal, less disruptive, and sound measures.[52] Accordingly, retaliation based on authorisation obtained through DSMs ensures that sanctions are confined by a set of rules constraining arbitrary unilateral actions. If the mandatory dispute settlement procedures that authorise retaliation are not used, the alleged violator could perceive the retaliatory measures as a breach and could counter-retaliate, thereby escalating the conflict.[53] In addition, non-compliance with dispute settlement rules that mandate their use before using retaliation could cause considerable reputational damage to the complainant for ignoring the rules that it agreed to in the first place.[54] Moreover, imposing unilateral retaliation without the mandatory dispute settlement procedures could affect the private sectors that rely on a stable trading environment. Hence, imposing unilateral retaliatory measures by circumventing FTA DSMs might not be perceived by governments as an attractive alternative. It causes reputational damage to the complainant, rather than to the offending party.

If FTA parties constantly disregarded FTA rulings and remained non-compliant, or even forwent the dispute settlement proceedings prescribed in the agreements by imposing immediate retaliation, it would undermine dispute settlement and could even threaten the existence of the FTAs.[55] As FTA parties conduct business together, imposing unilateral retaliation and disregarding FTA rulings would harm their relationships. Therefore, it is unlikely that FTA parties would choose this strategy.[56] Moreover, the fear of emulation would also deter a party from such behaviour.[57] Once a party decides to regularly ignore the rules set in an FTA, the other party has no reason to continue to abide by that bilateral agreement.

To conclude, non-compliance with new generation FTA rulings will have a more limited reputational influence than non-compliance with WTO reports and arbitral awards issued under the MPIA. Yet, the parties might consider using the FTA DSMs, as there would still be reputational costs incurred and incentives for compliance. Furthermore, non-compliance may not be attractive to states that use FTAs to advance their trade agenda. Neither does it mean that FTA DSMs would be generally circumvented and unilateral retaliatory measures applied immediately without making use of the mandatory dispute settlement.

---

[51] Vidigal (2017), pp. 945–948.

[52] Guzman (2002), pp. 1871–1872.

[53] Vidigal (2017), p. 939.

[54] Brewster (2012), p. 538.

[55] Interview 1; Interview 4.

[56] Interview 1; Interview 4.

[57] Pauwelyn (2008), p. 87.

7.3.2 Limited Role of Reputation: Other Important Factors for Compliance

To further substantiate the claim that FTA parties might be less concerned about the limited reputational costs when using FTA DSMs, it will be argued that there are also other factors that could induce compliance which may work at the WTO and FTA levels in a similar manner. While the importance of reputation has been recognised by advocates of rationalist theories, as well as by proponents of other theories of international relations and public international law compliance theories (for example, Chayes and Chayes,[58] Keohane,[59] and Burgstaller[60]), the role of reputational damage as the main factor driving compliance might have been exaggerated.[61]

There seems to be broad consensus that states may have multiple reputations across different issue areas.[62] This would signify that non-compliance with a treaty would impact less the negotiations for other treaties in a different issue area, and that the actual effects of a violation on the overall reputation of a state would be less than initially thought. According to Guzman, 'a decision to violate a trade agreement will, first and foremost, affect a state's reputation in trade',[63] thus confirming the proposition above that non-compliance with an FTA ruling might affect the reputation of a state with respect to other FTAs. Moreover, it could also affect the reputation for compliance with WTO agreements, as they also concern trade issues. States might worry not only about their reputation for compliance with commitments, but also about other aspects, such as a reputation for being tough, retributive, or willing to bully weaker states.[64] In addition, a reputation for compliance could be attached to a specific government, meaning that the governments close to the end of their time in office might be less concerned about the success of future negotiations for other agreements and the reputational damage that non-compliance could cause.[65] The limits of reputation to compel compliance indicate that reputational incentives may not be the sole reason for the high rates of compliance in international law. Other important factors have been proposed by international law and international relations theories that may also play a role in ensuring compliance with international law generally, and FTAs and rulings issued under their DSMs specifically.

While the rationalist theory has been developed by international relations scholars, international legal scholars have advanced their own theories on compliance. The international legal literature mostly explains compliance using

---

[58] Chayes and Chayes (1995).

[59] Keohane (2002).

[60] Burgstaller (2007).

[61] Downs and Jones (2002), pp. 102–112; Burgstaller (2007), pp. 66–71.

[62] Downs and Jones (2002), pp. 97, 102–109; Burgstaller (2007), pp. 70–71; Guzman (2008), pp. 34–36; Brewster(2009), p. 329.

[63] Guzman (2008), p. 32.

[64] Keohane (2002), p. 125; Guzman (2008), p. 39.

[65] Brewster (2009), pp. 327–328.

norm-driven theories that are based on the assumption that norms and ideas influence states' behaviour.[66] Several variants of these theories have been developed, some of the most outstanding being legitimacy, transnational legal process, and managerial theories. According to the legitimacy theory developed by Thomas Franck, states comply with their international obligations because of a 'right process' of norm creation and, mainly, procedural aspects[67] that could make norms be perceived by states as legitimate.[68] Franck suggests that legitimate norms by themselves exercise a 'compliance pull' on governments.[69] Koh has proposed the theory of transnational legal process according to which compliance is determined by, among other things, the actions of public and private actors that internalise international norms legally, socially, and politically into the national domestic system.[70] Hence, according to these theories, some of the factors that may induce compliance relate to the nature of international norms themselves and the processes through which they are created or internalised, rather than to their multilateral or bilateral nature. Therefore, when panels apply FTA norms perceived as legitimate and are already internalised, states may be stimulated to comply, regardless of the absence of collective pressure.

The managerial theory relies on the assumption that states have a general propensity to comply with international obligations.[71] According to the theory, diplomats and governmental officials devote enormous time and effort to conclude and monitor treaties, which reflects the desire of the states to comply with them.[72] The assumption of a general propensity to comply is supported by the considerations that (1) it is more efficient to comply, rather than to constantly calculate whether it is more advantageous to violate the rules; (2) treaties are consensual and the states decided to enter into the treaty in the first place because it was in their interest to do so; and (3) treaties are acknowledged as having legally binding force.[73] Therefore, according to the managerial theory, there is an assumption that FTA parties would tend to comply with FTA rulings despite their ability to cause more limited reputational costs. It should be noted that the managerial theory argues the significance of the *personal* reputation of the individuals who represent a state. As diplomats interact between themselves within international organisations, reporting non-compliance at meetings with other informed colleagues would harm the personal reputation of the diplomats representing the offending state.[74] The damage caused to personal reputations within a multilateral versus bilateral context may be

---

[66] Footer (2007), p. 71.

[67] Franck argues that legitimacy is defined by four elements: determinacy, symbolic validation, coherence, and adherence (Franck 1988, pp. 706–759).

[68] Franck (1988), pp. 706–759; Franck (1995), p. 24.

[69] Franck (1988), p. 712.

[70] Koh (1997), pp. 2599–2659.

[71] Chayes and Chayes (1995), pp. 3–9.

[72] Ibid 3.

[73] Ibid 4–9.

[74] Ibid 166.

different in case of non-compliance. Constant contact in different WTO bodies with other trade officials of all WTO Members in Geneva, in different WTO bodies, makes the personal reputation of a trade official of particular importance.[75] While the personal reputation of diplomats would also be affected in a bilateral setting, the meetings under the new generation EU FTA Joint and Trade Committees composed of the two parties' most senior national trade officials and other bodies, such as committees and working groups on different subjects,[76] would likely play a less important role compared to the multilateral setting where many representatives of all WTO Members meet on different occasions.

International relations scholars, similar to legal scholars, have developed more than one theory of compliance that argue that compliance is underpinned by factors other than reputational costs. Thus, in addition to the rationalist theory, international relations scholars have proposed the institutionalist and the liberal theory. According to the institutionalists, states' behaviour can be constrained by institutions that enhance compliance with international law by promoting cooperation because they provide a platform for, *inter alia*, continuous interactions, exchange of information, and surveillance techniques.[77] Hence, the institutionalist theory states that institutions, including those created at bilateral level like the new generation EU FTAs, can be a factor for inducing compliance. Lastly, pursuant to the liberal theory, domestic liberal democratic institutions may promote compliance with international law.[78] Therefore, compliance with international law might be determined by the types of governments that are parties to the treaties. Liberal democracies would be more likely to comply with both FTA and WTO norms.

To conclude, while the personal reputation of diplomats may suffer more in a multilateral context, other factors inducing compliance, identified by international law and international relations theories, should operate similarly at the WTO and the FTA level. Although the reputational damage caused to the states and their diplomats is greater at the multilateral level, other important factors promoting compliance with FTA rulings may motivate parties to use the FTA DSMs in the first place. The value of each of these factors is difficult to ascertain and there are no theories that disentangle their effects. Therefore, it remains to be seen in practice whether the threat of more limited reputational damage caused by non-compliance with FTA rulings, together with other factors, would promote compliance. Hence, whether FTA DSMs become an attractive option would also depend on compliance being achieved in the first disputes brought to these mechanisms. Finally, this author believes that parties would be especially motivated by the desire to maintain their FTAs. Disregarding FTA rulings could make the other parties emulate this behaviour, leading to the escalation of the conflict. This would endanger the existence of

---

[75] Vidigal (2017), p. 941.

[76] EUKFTA, Art 15.2, 15.3; CETA, Art 26.2; EUJEPA, Art 22.3, 22.4; EUSFTA, Art 16.2; EUVFTA, Art 17.2, 17.3.

[77] Aceves (1997), pp. 250–252.

[78] Slaughter (1995), pp. 503–538.

these agreements which seem to be highly valued by states that are concluding more and more FTAs rather than renouncing them.

7.4 Public Opinion

The possibility of attracting the attention of the general public may also influence the preference for one DSM over another. When initiating proceedings, a complainant could be looking for the support of public opinion, especially if a dispute concerns sensitive issues.

The WTO offers public awareness at the global level,[79] since it is an organization that is in the sight of all the Members and that of media outlets from all over the world. Therefore, WTO disputes receive more publicity and gain more importance, which could make panelists, the AB Members or even appeal arbitrators under the MPIA feel that their activity is scrutinised by the public, prompting them to be more considerate when issuing their reports. The support of the public becomes especially important when the measure at issue relates to sensitive matters of concern to the general public.[80] For example, WTO cases involving environmental and health concerns, such as *EC – Hormones*,[81] *EC – Asbestos*,[82] *US – Tuna II (Mexico)*,[83] and *EC – Seals*,[84] attracted considerable public attention. However, it is impossible to prove that this attention in practice had any actual influence on the outcomes of these disputes.

Disputes under bilateral FTAs, such as the new generation EU FTAs, may not gain the same global attention. The influence of public opinion on the procedures may be less significant, thus making them less attractive to states seeking global support in a dispute. However, parties may consider some disputes to have mere regional importance or not to concern sensitive issues and be of less political significance.[85] Furthermore, by not attracting global attention, it could be easier for the parties to reach an MAS before a panel issues a ruling. If the public becomes aware of the existence of a dispute that gains significant media attention and attracts increased scrutiny of the general public, a state might be prompted to posture to show that it is an effective bargainer and be tempted to avoid reaching an MAS.

---

[79] Todeschini-Marthe (2018), p. 403; Interview 4.

[80] Interview 2.

[81] *European Communities – Measures Concerning Meat and Meat Products (Hormones)*, DS26.

[82] *European Communities – Measures Affecting Asbestos and Products Containing Asbestos*, DS135.

[83] *United States – Measures Concerning the Importation, Marketing and Sale of Tuna and Tuna Products (US – Tuna II (Mexico))*, DS381.

[84] *European Communities – Measures Prohibiting the Importation and Marketing of Seal Products*, DS401.

[85] Pierola and Horlick (2007), p. 890.

Otherwise, it might be difficult for states to explain to their constituencies why they agreed on a solution before a ruling was issued.[86]

While the lesser effect of public opinion could be considered a disadvantage of FTA DSMs in disputes concerning issues of general public interest, this would not necessarily prevent states from making use of these mechanisms. The degree of public attention is unlikely to hamper the use of the new generation EU FTAs as alternative mechanisms, especially since it is not clear whether public opinion can have a significant impact during dispute settlement. Moreover, in some cases, parties may even seek less attention from the public to their dispute.

7.5 Likelihood of Reaching Mutually Agreed Solutions

When looking for a DSM to resolve a dispute with an FTA party, a factor that could play a role in shaping the perception that FTA DSMs are good alternatives to the WTO mechanism is the possibility of reaching an MAS with the other party.

In the same way that firms regularly doing business with each other tend not to litigate, FTA parties are expected to desire the fostering of cooperative relationships with an FTA partner and be less inclined to litigation.[87] The FTAs provide a framework for repeated and close interactions between the parties that can help to avoid disputes.[88] However, a considerable number of the disputes pursued at the WTO are between FTA parties.[89] Therefore, despite their close economic relationships, FTA parties still litigate. Both at the WTO (also if the appeal stage takes place under the MPIA) and the FTA level, dispute settlement proceedings formally begin with consultations. According to the data available up to 31 December 2018, 40% of the disputes did not reach the panel stage,[90] indicating that in many cases, parties reached a settlement. At the WTO, consultations can be 'bilateral' if initiated under Article XXIII:1 of GATT or 'multilateral', involving the participation of third parties, if initiated under Article XXII:1 of GATT. According to Article 4.1 of the DSU, Members with substantial trade interest can participate as third parties in consultations initiated under Article XXII:1 of GATT, provided that the defendant

---

[86]Stasavage (2004), p. 673.

[87]Flett (2015), p. 557.

[88]The Joint Committees under the new generation EUFTA shall seek to solve the disputes that arise under these agreements (EUKFTA, Art 15.1(3)(e); CETA, Art 26.1(4)(c); EUJEPA, Art 22.1(4)(c); EUSFTA, Art 16.1(3)(e); EUVFTA, Art 17.1(3)(e)). Moreover, there are many specialised Committees during whose meetings the parties interact and may solve their differences (EUKFTA, Art 15.2; CETA, Art 26.2; EUJEPA, Ar. 22.3; EUSFTA, Art 16.2; EUVFTA, Art 17.2) On the importance of the Committees in solving FTA disputes, *see* Melillo (2019), pp. 95–128.

[89]Vidigal (2017), pp. 929–932.

[90]WTO, 'Dispute Settlement Activity – Some Figures' <www.wto.org/english/tratop_e/dispu_e/dispustats_e.htm>.

agrees that the claim of substantial trade interest is well founded.[91] According to several authors,[92] reaching an MAS during consultations in which third parties take part is significantly less likely than without their involvement. The participation of third parties during consultations implies multiplication of voices and opinions, which could make reaching a pre-trial agreement more difficult. Moreover, with a larger audience composed of future litigants, disputing parties might be reluctant to retreat from their initial positions to look tough and deter potential future litigants.[93] While initiating consultations under Article XXII:1 of GATT would open the door to third parties and may decrease the likelihood of reaching a pre-trial MAS, WTO Members can choose to initiate consultations under Article XXIII:1 of GATT, a choice, according to the WTO website, that 'is a strategic one, depending on whether the complainant wants to make it possible for other Members to participate.'[94] Thus, by initiating consultations under Article XXIII:1 of GATT, 'the complainant is able to prevent the involvement in the consultations of third parties.'[95]

Even when consultations fail, the parties may still be motivated to reach an MAS. The DSU and the new generation EU FTAs encourage parties to reach an MAS, where possible, during every phase of their dispute settlement procedures.[96] For WTO Members wishing to take a less confrontational approach when settling disputes, the DSU mentions the possibility of using ADR procedures to voluntarily reach an MAS, on a confidential basis, at any time, before or parallel to panel procedures—in the last case only if the parties expressly agree.[97] The DSU, however, only mentions in passing these alternative mechanisms without detailing how they should take place.[98]

In contrast to the DSU, the new generation EU FTAs provide elaborate rules for the mediation mechanisms. These mechanisms are generally available only for the disputes that fall under the coverage of the dispute settlement chapters, except in the EUKFTA in which mediation is additionally limited to disputes on non-tariff measures.[99] The agreements establish comprehensive rules on initiation of

---

[91] In practice, defendants usually agree to the participation of third parties for two reasons. 'First, any country denied third party participation may initiate its own dispute. Second, the same country could join the dispute during the panel stage' (Johns and Pelc 2012).

[92] Stasavage (2004); Busch and Reinhardt (2006); Kucik and Pelc (2015), p. 861.

[93] Busch and Reinhardt (2006), p. 456; Johns and Pelc (2012), pp. 2, 7.

[94] WTO, 'The Process – Stages in a Typical WTO Dispute Settlement Case' <www.wto.org/english/tratop_e/dispu_e/disp_settlement_cbt_e/c6s2p1_e.htm>.

[95] Ibid.

[96] DSU, Arts 3.7, 11, 22.2; EUKFTA, Art 14.1, 14.13; CETA, Art 29.1, 29.19; EUJEPA, Art 21.1, 21.12(c), 21.26; EUSFTA, Art 14.1, 14.15; EUVFTA, Art 15.1, 15.19.

[97] DSU, Art 5.

[98] Mediation has been successfully used at the WTO only in one dispute, between Thailand and the Philippines on one side and the EC on the other, although Art 5 of the DSU was not explicitly mentioned (Lester et al. 2018, p. 169; Weiss 2021).

[99] Under CETA, EUJEPA, and EUVFTA, the mediation mechanisms are broadly regulated in Art 29.5, Art 21.6, and Art 15.4, respectively, and in more detail in the Annexes to the Dispute

mediation,[100] selection of mediators and requirements that they have to comply with (the Code of Conduct for arbitrators applying *mutatis mutandis*),[101] procedures with well-defined timelines,[102] confidentiality,[103] costs,[104] and implementation of an MAS reached as a result of mediation.[105] In addition, the new generation EU FTAs establish that the mediation mechanisms shall be without prejudice to the parties' rights and obligations under the dispute settlement provisions of these agreements, with CETA, EUJEPA, and EUVFTA also mentioning *any other agreement*.[106] As the choice of forum clauses in the EUKFTA and EUSFTA would only apply to situations in which disputes under these agreements are initiated by the request for panel establishment rather than for mediation,[107] the procedures for mediation under these FTAs would also not prejudice the dispute settlement rights and obligations under other agreements, such as the DSU. Hence, a party could pursue mediation procedures under all the new generation EU FTAs analysed, while simultaneously or consequently also pursuing FTA or WTO adjudicative proceedings. In addition to the significantly more detailed rules at the new generation EU FTA level, the more limited level of global awareness of the disputes could also help with reaching an MAS.[108] Furthermore, the detailed rules on mediation contained in the new generation EU FTAs could be suggestive of the fact that parties may seek ways to strengthen their control over the settlement of disputes.[109] As mediation

---

Settlement Chapters, indicating that the substantive coverage is the same. The EUSFTA has a separate chapter dedicated to the mediation procedures. However, throughout the agreement, the same areas that are excluded from the coverage of the dispute settlement chapter are also excluded from the coverage of the chapter on mediation. Lastly, the EUKFTA's mediation mechanism in Annex 14-A is expressly called 'Mediation Mechanism for Non-Tariff Measures', and its coverage is expressly limited by Art 1 of the Annex, according to which '[t]he objective of this Annex is to facilitate the finding of a mutually agreed solution to non-tariff measures'.

[100] EUKFTA, Annex 14-A, Art 3; CETA, Annex 29-C, Art 2; Decision of the Joint Committee of the EUJEPA, Annex 2, para 3; EUSFTA, Art 15.3; EUVFTA, Annex 15-C, Art 3.

[101] EUKFTA, Annex 14-A, Art 4, Annex 14-C, Art 8; CETA, Annex 29-C, Art 3, Annex 29-B, para 21; Decision of the Joint Committee of the EUJEPA, Annex 2, para 6–11; EUSFTA, Art 15.4, Annex 14-B, para 20; EUVFTA, Annex 15-C, Art 4.

[102] EUKFTA, Annex 14-A, Art 5; CETA, Annex 29-C, Art 4; Decision of the Joint Committee of the EUJEPA, Annex 2, paras 12–19; EUSFTA, Art 15.5; EUVFTA, Annex 15-C, Art. 5.

[103] EUKFTA, Annex 14-A, Art 7.1; CETA, Annex 29-C, Art 6; Decision of the Joint Committee of the EUJEPA, Annex 2, para 20; EUSFTA, Art 15.7(2); EUVFTA, Annex 15-C, Art 7.

[104] EUKFTA, Annex 14-A, Art 9; CETA, Annex 29-C, Art 8; Decision of the Joint Committee of the EUJEPA, Annex 2, paras 25, 26; EUSFTA, Art 15.9; EUVFTA, Annex 15-C, Art 9.

[105] EUKFTA, Annex 14-A, Art 6; CETA, Annex 29-C, Art 5; EUSFTA, Art 15.6; EUVFTA, Annex 15-C, Art 6.

[106] EUKFTA, Annex 14-A, Art 7.2; CETA, Annex 29-C, Art 6.2; Decision of the Joint Committee of the EUJEPA, Annex 2, para 21; EUSFTA, Art 15.7(1); EUVFTA, Annex 15-C, Art 7.2.

[107] For a detailed analysis of the moment of selection under the new generation EU FTA choice of forum clauses *see infra* Sect. 10.2.3.

[108] Stasavage (2004), p. 673.

[109] Schill (2017), p. 130.

procedures are aimed at reaching an MAS, parties have direct control over the outcome of disputes. Hence, efforts to strengthen mediation as an alternative to third-party adjudication concur with other features of the new generation EU FTAs that enhance the parties' control over the procedures.

Therefore, the new generation EU FTA DSMs may potentially serve as better fora for reaching an MAS. In addition, these FTAs provide attractive detailed mediation mechanisms that could increase the likelihood of reaching an MAS with an FTA party in a dispute covered by the mechanisms, while also retaining control over the dispute. However, these mediation mechanisms should not necessarily be regarded as alternatives to the WTO DSM, since they can be used simultaneously with or before the WTO dispute settlement procedure. Finally, the detailed mediation mechanisms contained in the new generation EU FTAs may serve as future inspiration to the WTO Membership, if the ADR mechanisms are to be reformed.

7.6 Legitimacy

The high degree of legitimacy of the WTO DSM has been suggested as one of the reasons for its success and for being preferred to the FTA DSMs by the Member States.[110] The fact that states are emulating the WTO DSM in their FTAs and that numerous disputes have been solved under WTO rules is also proof that it is perceived by states as having a high degree of legitimacy. However, with the AB in crisis and the criticism voiced by some Members, although the AB did not completely lose its legitimacy,[111] it might have been affected.[112] This section will compare the legitimacy of EU FTA and the WTO DSMs to ascertain whether the former could become an alternative to the latter.

The term legitimacy has been defined in various ways.[113] However, the legitimacy of international adjudicative bodies has mostly been understood as the justification of the authority to rule.[114] Thus, a legitimate court is mostly interpreted as being a court that possesses a justifiable right to issue judgments, opinions, or

---

[110] Davey (2006), p. 355; Nguyen (2008), p. 119; Froese (2014), p. 383; Kolsky Lewis and Van den Bossche (2014), p. 15; Todeschini-Marthe (2018), p. 403.

[111] Interview 1.

[112] *See* for example, the US claims that '[t]he Appellate Body's failure to follow the agreed rules has undermined confidence in the World Trade Organization and a free and fair rules-based trading system' (United States Trade Representative, 'Report on the Appellate Body of the World Trade Organization' February 2020, Introduction).

[113] *See*, for example, Føllesdal (2007), pp. 211–228; Grossman (2009), p. 115; Bodansky (2013), pp. 321–341.

[114] Wolfrum (2008), p. 6. Legitimacy should be distinguished from the concept of authority. '[A] court can do everything normative theorists might expect of a legitimate international judicial body and still not have authority in fact. The converse scenario—authority in fact, without normative legitimacy—is also possible.' (Alter et al. 2016, p. 7).

decisions that should be obeyed or, at least, considered by those addressed.[115] Legitimacy can be approached from a normative or sociological perspective. Normative legitimacy is concerned with *the right to rule* according to predefined standards, while sociological legitimacy derives from the *perception or beliefs* of external actors about such a right.[116] In this section, legitimacy will be approached from a normative perspective, as sociological legitimacy implies an empirical measurement of the actual support for a body and can vary depending on the external audience chosen.[117] As this section adopts a normative approach and intends to analyse how legitimacy could affect the *preference of states* for a DSM, legitimacy will adopt an insiders' approach. The beliefs of the outsiders are associated with sociological legitimacy. However, in certain cases, they may also influence states' perception. Therefore, the beliefs of other actors will be considered only insofar as they may also affect the preference of states as the insiders.[118] Accordingly, the legitimacy of the DSMs analysed will be appreciated only from the perspective of states.

The assessment of the legitimacy of an international judicial body involves a number of elements. This book follows the theory developed by Wolfrum,[119] supported and adopted by many others,[120] according to which there are source, procedure, and result-oriented elements that induce legitimacy. The source of legitimacy can be found in the consent of the states to the constitutive treaties of the adjudicative bodies. Thus, states have the ability to negotiate and adhere to international treaties and can also commit themselves to the jurisdiction of an international adjudicative body.[121] In the case of the WTO and the new generation EU FTAs, the DSMs can find their source of legitimacy in the consent of the states. Thus, as these DSMs have been initiated lawfully, they are infused with an initial source capital of legitimacy.[122] Since participating Members consented to the MPIA, it also has an initial legitimacy capital from the perspective of these states.[123] While the initial capital represents an asset, it can be increased or decreased by the other elements that constitute building blocks of the overall legitimacy capital, with strengths in some aspects compensating for weaknesses in others.[124]

The procedures of an international court, therefore, are the next elements that could influence how the legitimacy of the new generation EU FTA DSMs compares

---

[115] Cohen et al. (2018), p. 4.

[116] Buchanan and Keohane (2008), p. 25; Cohen et al. (2018), p. 4; Howse et al. (2018), p. 5.

[117] Howse et al. (2018), p. 5.

[118] As Grossman states, 'the views of these various actors are relevant to legitimacy to the extent [that] they are reflected in state preferences.' (Grossman 2009, p. 115).

[119] Wolfrum (2008), pp. 6–7.

[120] *See*, for example, Howse et al. (2018); Malacrida and Marceau (2018); Føllesdal (2020), p. 481.

[121] Wolfrum (2008), p. 6; Føllesdal (2020), p. 482.

[122] Shany (2018), p. 357.

[123] Interview 4.

[124] Ibid.

with the legitimacy of the WTO mechanism. The process of selection of arbitrators, as well as their independence, impartiality, and qualifications, influence the procedural element of legitimacy.[125] As argued above,[126] the requirements for qualifications, independence, and impartiality of EU FTA DSM arbitrators are very similar to those prescribed for WTO DSM panelists. Yet, the fact that the arbitrators and, in limited circumstances, the chairpersons could have the nationality of one of the parties[127] may negatively affect the legitimacy of the new generation EU FTA panels from the perspective of outsiders, which could also have a negative influence on the preferences of the states. Still, the ability to directly appoint the desired arbitrator with the nationality of the parties may also be perceived as a factor boosting the legitimacy of the panel from the perspective of the states. As Marceau and Malacrida suggest, when the disputing parties are directly involved in the appointment of arbitrators, legitimacy is greater from their perspective.[128] Under the new generation EU FTAs, if the disputing parties cannot agree on the composition process, a selection by lot could be performed by the representative of a single party which may raise questions about the legitimacy of the selection process, compared to that under the DSU in which the appointment decision in case of disagreement is made by a third party—the WTO DG.[129] Still, in case of the new generation EU FTAs, selection by lot by one party is only a contingency measure which is supposed to ensure successful formation of the panel. The possibility that one single party could block the panel formation, as could happen in certain circumstances under the EUKFTA, CETA, EUSFTA, and EUVFTA, may negatively affect the legitimacy of these DSMs. The opportunity to support panels by experienced WTO Secretariat staff and appeals reviewed by highly qualified AB Members also has a bearing on the greater legitimacy of the WTO DSM. Yet, AB Members need to ensure the support of the Membership to be reappointed, which gives rise to questions about their independence. As discussed before, the appointment and reappointment of AB Members can be blocked by any Member. These aspects may negatively affect the legitimacy of the WTO DSM, especially that of the AB. Given that the AB is currently dysfunctional, the legitimacy of the WTO DSM might have been affected, especially due to the ability of one disputing party to appeal a report into the void.

Under the MPIA, appeal arbitrators should comply with the same requirements as those for AB Members and undergo a pre-selection process to ensure that they meet these requirements, unless they are former or current AB Members.[130] The appeal arbitrators have been appointed by consensus and the composition is supposed to

---

[125] On the importance of these aspects for legitimacy, *see* von Bogdandy and Venzke (2011), pp. 1356–1361; von Bogdandy and Venzke (2012), p. 32.

[126] *See supra* Sect. 6.5.3.

[127] *See supra* Sect. 6.5.3.

[128] Malacrida and Marceau (2018), p. 27.

[129] DSU, Art 8.7 and Sect. 6.4.3.

[130] MPIA, Annex 2, paras 2, 3, fn 12.

ensure an appropriate balance.[131] These provisions are likely to increase the legitimacy of the procedures under this arrangement. As there are uncertainties about the secretarial support offered to appeal arbitrators,[132] it remains to be seen if this aspect would add to or subtract from the legitimacy capital of the MPIA proceedings.

For the legitimacy of a DSM, the fairness of the procedures, which should provide equal opportunities to the disputing parties to present their views, also plays a significant role.[133] Similar to the WTO DSM, the procedures under the new generation EU FTAs, as shown previously,[134] offer equal opportunities to the parties throughout the different stages. In case of using the MPIA to resolve appeals, a certain degree of legitimacy would be instilled by the replication (almost) of the standard appeal procedures. However, its procedural legitimacy will also depend on how these procedures work in practice as they contain certain innovations. Procedural rules, such as those on evidence, standard of review, and burden of proof, have been developed in practice by the WTO adjudicating bodies and have contributed to the legitimacy capital of the WTO DSM.[135] It remains to be seen how the panels under the new generation EU FTAs would deal with these questions in practice and how their practice would influence the legitimacy capital of their DSMs.

Increased transparency and openness to civil society could play an important role in enhancing legitimacy from an outsider's perspective,[136] which may also indirectly positively influence how states perceive the DSMs. As the opinion and support of constituencies are important for states, the more transparent DSMs are likely to be perceived as having greater legitimacy also from a state perspective. As shown above, the procedures under the new generation EU FTAs are more transparent and allow access to outsiders through the of *amicus curiae* briefs,[137] which could increase the procedural legitimacy of these DSMs. The express regulation of the openness of the proceedings, as well as submission of *amicus curiae* briefs, could also avoid unnecessary damage to their legitimacy capital. Given that these aspects were not regulated in the DSU, panel and AB jurisprudence developed relevant rules—an activity that has not been received with approval by all Members and might have negatively affected the WTO DSM's legitimacy from the perspective of some Members. The effectiveness of jurisdictional clauses could also compromise the procedural legitimacy of the DSMs.[138] As the next part will show,[139] the new generation EU FTAs include jurisdictional clauses that could potentially

---

[131]MPIA, Annex 2, para 4.

[132]*See supra* Sect. 6.9.1.

[133]Grossman (2013), p. 67.

[134]*See supra* Sect. 6.6.3.

[135]In this respect *see* Malacrida and Marceau (2018), pp. 35–43.

[136]Grossman (2009), pp. 153–155.

[137]*See supra* Sects. 6.10.3 and 6.11.3.

[138]On the choice of forum and legitimacy in the context of the WTO and MERCOSUR DSMs, *see* Malacrida and Marceau (2018), pp. 53–56; Wojcikiewicz Almeida (2018), pp. 230–233.

[139]*See infra* Sect. 10.8.

successfully solve the conflicts of jurisdiction with the WTO DSM. However, due to the strict requirements established by the WTO jurisprudence, it remains to be seen if the clauses achieve their aim in practice. The legitimacy capital of the FTA DSMs may be negatively affected if FTA parties are concerned that they would have to adjudicate the same dispute again at the WTO, after doing so at the FTA level.

The last element influencing the legitimacy of an adjudicative body is the results produced by its activity. Since the new generation EU FTAs have not yet been tested in practice and there are no outcomes, the results-oriented element is absent and does not contribute to the legitimacy of these DSMs. Results may refer to their judgments and interpretations or compliance with these judgments.[140] Because the rules of interpretation of the new generation EU FTAs provide that relevant WTO jurisprudence should be taken into account or adopted (generally or in case of identical obligations),[141] interpretations similar to those of the WTO DSM and, hence, with a similar degree of legitimacy, could be expected. The legitimacy of an adjudicative body could suffer if it is considered to engage in law-making, or so-called judicial activism, without the support of the states.[142] Thus, some of the AB's interpretative approaches have been criticised by the US and accusations of judicial activism have been brought at AB's activity,[143] potentially affecting its legitimacy. It remains to be seen in practice how the activity of the new generation EU FFTA panels would be appreciated and whether it would add to or subtract from their legitimacy capital. In the meantime, the legitimacy of the WTO DSM could also suffer. With the AB being dysfunctional, the panels will be aware that the reports may or may not be adopted depending on their findings. This could make them decide in such a way so as not to upset either party too much, rather than taking an objective approach.[144] The 'panel reports may also become more political or power-influenced, skew results in favour of the strongest party',[145] undermining the legitimacy of the DSM. The MPIA procedures have also not yielded any results yet. Appeal arbitrators are likely to follow existing jurisprudence and issue appeal awards with legitimacy comparable to that of AB reports, but they may also diverge from existing jurisprudence in some instances. Furthermore, arbitral awards may not be given the same consideration as that given to AB reports by panels.[146] Consequently, the legitimacy capital of appeal

---

[140] Føllesdal (2020), pp. 486–487.

[141] For a more detailed analysis of these provisions and their effects, *see* Sect. 11.8.5.3.

[142] The traditional view is that judicial law-making always negatively affects the legitimacy of an adjudicative body (*see*, for example, Bodansky 1999, p. 605). However, as argued by Helfer and Alter, the degree of controversy surrounding the decision of an adjudicatory body would depend on the degree of its coincidence with the preferences of the majority of the states, and when this does not happen, states could object to the rulings by invoking the mantra of judicial activism. Hence, claims of judicial activism affecting legitimacy will mostly rise if the decision is not supported by the states and the key domestic actors (Helfer and Alter 2013, p. 502).

[143] For more on US discontent, *see* Weiss (2020), p. 18.

[144] Pauwelyn (2019), p. 309.

[145] Ibid.

[146] In this respect, *see* Sect. 6.8.

arbitration under the MPIA may differ from that of the AB, depending on the results delivered by appeal arbitrators.

Finally, the legitimacy of an adjudicative institution could be affected by the degree of compliance with its decisions.[147] Hence, the legitimacy of the new generation EU FTAs could be impaired if a lack of community pressure leads to lower levels of compliance. The level of legitimacy, in turn, can also influence the degree of compliance. Hence, the limited legitimacy of an adjudicative body may be invoked as an excuse for non-compliance.[148] The WTO compliance rate is very high.[149] Because the same implementation mechanism will be used in appeal arbitral awards, their compliance rate is also expected to be high. Due to the lack of results, both with respect to judgments and the compliance rate with them, the legitimacy capital of the DSMs under the new generation EU FTAs will be defined by ongoing evaluation of their performance by the parties.

Currently, the FTA DSMs studied seem to have a decent starting legitimacy capital that may score in favour of their use, even though it is lower than that of the WTO DSM. Whether they are seen as alternatives to the WTO DSM, will depend on how they perform in the first cases to further build their legitimacy capital. As the legitimacy of the WTO DSM is currently being challenged, there are some open questions about how the panels will perform in the absence of a functional AB. Although there are many uncertainties in this respect, the MPIA mechanism is anticipated to be perceived by the participating Members as having significant legitimacy capital, which could influence these Members to choose the WTO DSM.

7.7 Previous Experience and Financial Costs

The decision whether or not to choose a forum for settlement of trade disputes could also be affected by the fact that the parties have no previous experience of using the new generation EU FTA DSMs. The financial costs associated with FTA DSMs may also have an impact.

After adjudicating multiple disputes at the WTO over some decades, the WTO Members are familiar with the proceedings at the multilateral level and know what to expect from them.[150] On the other hand, the new generation EU FTA DSMs have not yet been used, and starting to use them would mean to test the rules, potentially resulting in unexpected delays, reports of lower quality than those produced at the

---

[147] Wojcikievicz Almeida (2018), p. 235; Føllesdal (2020), pp. 481, 486.

[148] Fukunaga (2009), p. 85.

[149] '[T]he compliance rate with dispute settlement rulings is very high, at around 90%' (WTO, 'MC11 in Brief: Dispute Settlement' <www.wto.org/english/thewto_e/minist_e/mc11_e/briefing_notes_e/bfdispu_e.htm>).

[150] Malacrida and Marceau (2018), p. 57; Interview 5.

WTO level,[151] or unwanted blockages of panel formation. Accordingly, the initial deployment of the FTA DSMs may be associated with a higher degree of undesired unpredictability. The unpredictability of the procedures under the FTA DSMs, as well as that of the possible interpretations of substantive FTA norms, would involve substantial investment of time and other resources.[152] At the WTO level, many procedural and substantive issues have already been clarified in past disputes. By contrast, the FTA parties would need to invest time and effort to build their cases in an attempt to cover various possible interpretations of FTA norms. Moreover, even though some FTAs may be very similar to others, they are still distinct agreements, and would need separate attention dedicated to each of them.[153] While the new generation EU FTAs provide that, in certain cases, the panels shall take into account or adopt the relevant WTO jurisprudence, it still remains to be tested how these provisions would be applied in practice in relation to both procedural and substantive issues. Even for states with substantial resources that regularly participate in WTO dispute settlement, separately building the considerable capacity necessary to deal with FTA dispute settlement may be a disadvantage,[154] due to the need to increase human resources and the high financial costs involved. For example, in its 2018 FTA implementation report, the EU Commission expressly stated that 'the WTO remains a well-tested [. . .] dispute settlement system of first choice.'[155] The risk of appealed panel reports being sent into the void in the context of the AB crisis and of disputes being left unresolved may encourage states to test the DSMs contained in their FTAs. However, if the FTA parties are also MPIA participants, they may be more inclined to initiate WTO proceedings as the MPIA largely follows DSU rules and other rules applicable to appellate review that are familiar to the parties. The MPIA introduces some innovations and deviations from rules on appellate review, such as suspension of panel proceedings, deeming the panel findings not appealed a part of the award, and measures to streamline the proceedings. Nevertheless, the MPIA procedures would still provide a greater degree of familiarity than the unknown FTA procedures.

While dealing with FTA disputes would mean building capacity, which involves financial costs, it would be difficult to estimate in advance the exact amount of employed financial resources. There may also be other costs, with the final amount depending on each dispute. Therefore, the use of FTA DSMs may be associated with unpredictable costs.[156] The costs can be diverse such as the costs for organising hearings, remuneration of arbitrators and assistants, and lawyers' and translation

---

[151] Vidigal (2017), p. 933.

[152] Flett (2015), p. 559.

[153] Interview 1.

[154] Flett (2015), p. 559.

[155] European Commission, Report from the Commission to the European Parliament, the Council, the European Economic and Social Committee and the Committee of the Regions on Implementation of Free Trade Agreements, Brussels, COM(2019) 455 final, p. 37.

[156] Ibid 574.

fees.[157] On the one hand, the new generation EU FTAs provide that the parties shall share the administrative expenses of arbitration proceedings, including remuneration and travel expenses of arbitrators and their assistants.[158] On the other hand, at the WTO, a Member's contribution covers the costs associated with dispute settlement, including the services of the Secretariat, panelists, and the AB.[159] Hence, by commencing WTO proceedings, Members do not have to support extra costs, while each additional FTA dispute initiated implies additional financial resources. Moreover, developing countries such as Vietnam[160] can benefit from the legal advice and litigation assistance offered by the Advisory Centre on WTO Law (ACWL). Issues related to financial costs of MPIA proceedings, such as how the structure offering secretarial support would be funded, remain to be clarified.

To conclude, previous experience with the WTO DSM may act as an incentive to choose it over FTA DSMs when possible, also in case of states that are MPIA participants. Once the FTA DSMs are tested and the experience is positive, states may be more inclined to use these mechanisms. However, the use of the FTA DSMs is also associated with extra financial costs which may be difficult to predict. Thus, the financial costs associated with the FTA proceedings may act as a deterrent for Members with a choice between different DSMs. The extra costs associated with the use of the MPIA have not yet been elucidated. Nonetheless, parties may not be dissuaded by the costs associated with the MPIA due to the advantages of the appellate stage.

7.8 Conclusions on Political Aspects

This section dealt with the political aspects that may influence the competition between the new generation EU FTA and the WTO mechanism. There are several factors that could tip the scales in favour of using the WTO DSM and make the new generation EU FTAs less attractive. Thus, the WTO DSM allows states to establish multilateral precedents and avoid unnecessary disputes against multiple complainants in different fora. While the jurisprudential value of MPIA awards might be lower than that of AB reports, they are nevertheless likely to have a broader impact

---

[157] Porges (2011), p. 474; Todeschini-Marthe (2018), p. 402.

[158] EUKFTA, Annex 14-B, Art 1(2); CETA, Annex 29-A, para 2; EUJEPA, Art 21.29; EUSFTA, Annex 14-A, para 3; EUVFTA, Annex 15-A, para 2. Remuneration of arbitrators shall be in accordance with WTO standards (EUKFTA, Annex 14-B, Art 3(1)(b); CETA, Annex 29-A, para 8; Decision of the Joint Committee of the EUJEPA, Annex 3, para 4(a); EUVFTA, Annex 15-A, para 12) or as agreed by the parties based on the standards of comparable international dispute resolution mechanisms in bilateral or multilateral agreements (EUSFTA, Understanding 2 in Relation to the Remuneration of Arbitrators). For more on expenditure on translation, *see infra* Sect. 12.1.2.

[159] Porges (2018), p. 6.

[160] ACWL, 'Members' <www.acwl.ch/members-introduction/>.

than FTA reports. Under DSU rules, states would also have the opportunity to exercise common pressure and make use of the mechanism of multilateral surveillance to induce compliance. Non-compliance with AB reports and even arbitral awards could cause extensive reputational damage. Moreover, the WTO DSM, including when using the MPIA, would offer a greater level of legitimacy and publicity—a factor important for disputes on sensitive issues. Finally, using the new generation EU FTA DSMs would involve a certain degree of unpredictability due to states' lack of previous experience of them and the need for additional time, financial, and human resources to implement them.

Although the WTO DSM is expected to be preferred from a political point of view, the new generation EU FTA DSMs could nevertheless be viable alternatives to the former. It is unlikely that parties would prefer resorting to unilateral retaliation and disregard mandatory FTA rules. In addition, non-compliance with FTA DSM reports would still cause reputational damage, and there would still be other factors that could help to induce compliance. The FTA DSMs have a good initial legitimacy capital that will adjust once these mechanisms are tested in practice. Moreover, the FTA DSMs could even be the first choice, if states wanted to avoid setting a multilateral precedent and attract public attention to their disputes. The new generation EU FTA DSMs could also be chosen if parties would wish to increase the likelihood of reaching an MAS, meaning that they would have more control over the outcome of the dispute. The mediation mechanisms provided in these FTAs could, nevertheless, be used simultaneously with or before the adjudicatory FTA and WTO proceedings. Hence, when mediation is used, the bilateral and multilateral mechanisms are not necessarily in competition; they can both work towards their purpose of reaching a solution acceptable to both parties. The WTO Members could also learn lessons from the new generation EU FTAs, and in potential discussions on DSU reform with respect to mediation, they could use the model offered by the FTAs analysed as an example. Their fear of having panel reports sent into the void is likely to motivate WTO Members who are not MPIA participants to resort to FTA DSMs if the matter at issue falls under their coverage, and especially if procedural aspects do not play against them.

References

Aceves WJ (1997) Institutionalist theory and international legal scholarship. Am Univ Int Law Rev 12(2):227–266

Alter KJ, Helfer LR, Madsen MR (2016) How context shapes the authority of international courts. Law Contemp Probl 79(1):1–36

Bodansky D (1999) The legitimacy of international governance: a coming challenge for international environmental law? Am J Int Law 93(3):596–624

Bodansky D (2013) Legitimacy in international law and international relations. In: Dunoff JL, Pollack MA (eds) Interdisciplinary perspectives on international law and international relations: the state of the art. Cambridge University Press, New York, pp 321–341

Brewster R (2009) The limits of reputation on compliance. Int Theory 1(2):323–333

Brewster R (2012) Reputation in international relations and international law theory. In: Dunoff JL, Pollack MA (eds) Interdisciplinary perspectives on international law and international relations: the state of the art. Cambridge University Press, New York, pp 524–541

Bronckers M, Baetens F (2013) Reconsidering financial remedies in WTO dispute settlement. J Int Econ Law 16(2):281–311

Buchanan A, Keohane RO (2008) The legitimacy of global governance institutions. In: Wolfrum R, Röben V (eds) Legitimacy in international law. Springer, Heidelberg, pp 25–62

Burgstaller M (2007) Amenities and pitfalls of a reputational theory of compliance with international law. Nordic J Int Law 76:39–71

Busch ML (2007) Overlapping institutions, forum shopping, and dispute settlement in international trade. Int Organ 61(4):735–761

Busch ML, Reinhardt E (2006) Three's a crowd: third parties and WTO dispute settlement. World Polit 58(3):446–477

Chayes A, Chayes AH (1995) The new sovereignty: compliance with international regulatory agreements. Harvard University Press, Cambridge

Cohen HG, Føllesdal A, Grossman N, Ulfstein G (2018) Legitimacy and international courts – a framework. In: Grossman N, Cohen HG, Føllesdal A, Ulfstein G (eds) Legitimacy and international courts. Cambridge University Press, New York, pp 1–40

Davey WJ (2006) Dispute settlement in the WTO and RTAs: a comment. In: Bartels L, Ortino F (eds) Regional trade agreements and the WTO legal system. Oxford University Press, New York, pp 343–357

Downs GW, Jones MA (2002) Reputation, compliance, and international law. J Leg Stud 31 (1):95–114

Flett J (2015) Referring PTA disputes to the WTO dispute settlement system. In: Dür A, Elsig M (eds) Trade cooperation: the purpose, design and effects of preferential trade agreements, World Trade Forum. Cambridge University Press, New York, pp 555–579

Føllesdal A (2007) Legitimacy deficits beyond the state: diagnoses and cures. In: Hurrelmann A, Schneider S, Steffek J (eds) Legitimacy in an age of global politics. Transformations of the state. Palgrave Macmillan, New York, pp 211–228

Føllesdal A (2020) Survey article: the legitimacy of international courts. J Polit Philos 28 (4):476–499

Footer ME (2007) Some theoretical and legal perspectives on WTO compliance. Netherlands Yearb Int Law 38:61–112

Franck TM (1988) Legitimacy in the international system. Am J Int Law 82(4):705–759

Franck TM (1995) Fairness in international law and institutions. Oxford University Press, Oxford

Froese MD (2014) Regional trade agreements and the paradox of dispute settlement. Manchester J Int Econ Law 11:367–396

Fukunaga Y (2009) Civil society and the legitimacy of the WTO dispute settlement system. Brooklyn J Int Law 34(1):85–117

Grossman N (2009) Legitimacy and international adjudicative bodies. George Wash Int Law Rev 41:107–180

Grossman N (2013) The normative legitimacy of international courts. Temple Law Rev 86:61–105

Guzman AT (2002) A compliance-based theory of international law. Calif Law Rev 90 (6):1823–1887

Guzman AT (2008) Reputation and international law, UC Berkeley Public Law Research Paper No. 1112064. https://papers.ssrn.com/sol3/papers.cfm?abstract_id=1112064

Helfer LR, Alter KJ (2013) Legitimacy and lawmaking: a tale of three international courts theoretical inquiries in law 14:479–503

Howse R, Ruiz-Fabri H, Ulfstein G, Zang MQ (2018) Introduction. In: Howse R, Ruiz-Fabri H, Ulfstein G, Zang MQ (eds) The legitimacy of international trade courts and tribunals. Cambridge University Press, New York, pp 3–19

Hudec RE (1999) The new dispute settlement procedure: an overview of the first three years. Minn J Glob Trade 8(1):1–53

Hudec RE (2000) Broadening the scope of remedies in WTO dispute settlement. In: Weiss F, Wiers J (eds) Improving WTO dispute settlement procedures. Cameron May, London, pp 345–376

Johns L, Pelc KJ (2012) On the strategic manipulation of audiences in WTO dispute settlement. Paper presented at annual conference on the political economy of international organizations, 23 June 2011. www.peio.me/wp-content/uploads/2014/04/Conf5_Pelc-28.07.11.pdf

Keohane RO (2002) Power and governance in a partially globalized world. Routledge, London

Koh HH (1997) Why do nations obey international law? Yale Law J 106:2599–2659

Kolsky Lewis M, Van den Bossche P (2014) What to do when disagreement strikes? The complexity of dispute settlement under trade agreements. In: Frankel S, Kolsky Lewis M (eds) Trade agreements at the crossroads. Routledge, London, pp 9–25

Kucik J, Pelc KJ (2015) Measuring the cost of privacy: a look at the distributional effects of private bargaining. Br J Polit Sci:861–889

Leal-Arcas R (2011) Comparative analysis of NAFTA's Chapter 20 and the WTO's dispute settlement understanding. Queen Mary University of London, School of Law Legal Studies Research Paper 94, pp 1–25

Lester S, Mercurio B, Davies A (2018) World trade law: text, materials and commentary, 2nd edn. Hart, Oxford

Maggi G (1999) The role of multilateral institutions in international trade cooperation. Am Econ Rev 89:190–214

Malacrida R, Marceau G (2018) The WTO adjudicating bodies. In: Howse R et al (eds) The legitimacy of international trade courts and tribunals. Cambridge University Press, New York, pp 20–69

Melillo M (2019) Informal dispute resolution in preferential trade agreements. J World Trade 53 (1):95–128

Mushkat R (2011) State reputation and compliance with international law: looking through a Chinese lens. Chinese J Int Law 10(4):703–737

Nguyen TS (2008) Towards a compatible interaction between dispute settlement under the WTO and regional trade agreements. Macquarie J Bus Law 5:113–135

Pauwelyn J (2004) Going global, regional, or both? Dispute settlement in the Southern African Development Community (SADC) and overlaps with the WTO and other jurisdictions. Minn J Glob Trade 13:231–304

Pauwelyn J (2008) Optimal protection of international law: navigating between European absolutism and American voluntarism. Cambridge University Press, New York

Pauwelyn J (2019) WTO dispute settlement post 2019: what to expect? J Int Econ Law 22:297–321

Pierola F, Horlick G (2007) WTO dispute settlement and dispute settlement in the "North-South" agreements of the Americas: considerations for choice of forum. J World Trade 41(5):885–908

Porges A (2011) Dispute settlement. In: Chauffour JP, Maur JC (eds) Preferential trade agreement policies for development: a handbook. The World Bank, Washington, pp 467–501

Porges A (2018) Designing common but differentiated rules for regional trade disputes. ICTSD RTA Exchange, Issue Paper, pp 1–11

Raustiala K (2000) Compliance & effectiveness in international regulatory cooperation. Case West Reserve J Int Law (32)3:387–440

Schill SW (2017) Authority, legitimacy, and fragmentation in the (envisaged) dispute settlement disciplines in mega-regionals. In: Griller S, Obwexer W, Vranes E (eds) Mega-regional trade agreements: CETA, TTIP, and TiSA: new orientations for EU external economic relations. Oxford University Press, New York, pp 111–150

Shaffer G, Elsig M, Puig S (2016) The extensive (but fragile) authority of the WTO Appellate Body. Law Contemp Probl 79:237–273

Shany Y (2018) Stronger together? Legitimacy and effectiveness of international courts as mutually reinforcing or undermining notions. In: Grossman N, Cohen HG, Føllesdal A, Ulfstein G (eds) Legitimacy and international courts. Cambridge University Press, New York, pp 354–371

Slaughter AM (1995) International law in a world of liberal states. Eur J Int Law 6:503–538

Stasavage D (2004) Open-door or closed-door? Transparency in domestic and international bargaining. Int Organ 58(4):667–703

Todeschini-Marthe C (2018) Dispute settlement mechanisms under free trade agreements and the WTO: stakes, issues and practical considerations: a question of choice? Glob Trade Customs J 13(9):387–403

Van Damme I (2019) In: What kind of dispute settlement for the World Trade Organization? Proceedings of the conference organized by the World Trade Institute, World Trade Organization, Geneva, 4 February 2019

Van den Bossche P, Zdouc W (2017) The law and policy of World Trade Organization: text, cases and materials, 4th edn. Oxford University Press, New York

Vidigal G (2017) Why is there so little litigation under free trade agreements? Retaliation and adjudication in international dispute settlement. J Int Econ Law 20:927–950

Vidigal G (2018) Making regional dispute settlement attractive: the "Court of Arbitration" option. RTA Exchange, ICTSD. www.ictsd.org/opinion/making-regional-dispute-settlement-attractive-the-

von Bogdandy A, Venzke I (2011) On the democratic legitimation of international judicial lawmaking. German Law J 12(5):1341–1370

von Bogdandy A, Venzke I (2012) In whose name? An investigation of international courts' public authority and its democratic justification. Eur J Int Law 23(1):7–41

Weiss W (2020) EU multilateral trade policy in a changing, multipolar world: the way forward. In: Weiss W, Furculita C (eds) Global politics and EU trade policy: facing the challenges to a multilateral approach. Springer, Heidelberg, pp 17–39

Weiss W (2021) Art. 5 DSU: good offices, conciliation and mediation. In: Stoll PT, Herstermeyer HP (eds) Commentaries on world trade law, 2nd edn, vol 1. Brill, Leiden

Wojcikievicz Almeida (2018) The case of MERCOSUR. In: Howse R, Ruiz-Fabri H, Ulfstein G, Zang MQ (eds) The legitimacy of international trade courts and tribunals. Cambridge University Press, New York, pp 227–254

Wolfrum R (2008) Legitimacy in international law from a legal perspective: some introductory considerations. In: Wolfrum R, Röben R (eds) Legitimacy in international law. Springer, Heidelberg, pp 1–24

Chapter 8
Conclusions on the Competing Interactions Between the WTO and the New Generation EU FTA DSMs

This part dealt with the competing interactions between the new generation EU FTA DSMs and the WTO mechanism. When the same dispute can be brought to different fora, the complainant is able to choose where to initiate it. As established in the conceptual framework, for two mechanisms to be in genuine competition, an actual choice has to be made at least with respect to some categories of disputes, and states should perceive them as viable alternatives. The part assessed whether the FTA DSMs analysed could be viable alternatives from the perspective of substantive, procedural, and political considerations. It argued that in light of the changing context—the AB crisis and in particular in case of absence of an alternative within the multilateral regime in which all FTA parties participate—there are reasons to believe that more FTA disputes could be initiated and that FTA DSMs may emerge as potential alternatives to the WTO DSM. Even with a fully functional AB or an alternative mechanism within the WTO DSM, it was argued that due to substantive considerations the number of FTA disputes is expected to increase. Analysis of the new generation EU FTA DSMs, in the context of competition with the WTO DSM, is relevant in general to understand their functioning, advantages, and disadvantages.

The substantive considerations showed that the new generation EU FTA DSMs compete with the WTO DSM only with respect to some substantive areas, due to the fact that multiple areas are excluded from the coverage of the first. Therefore, these FTA DSMs can only be partial genuine alternatives to the WTO DSM. The substantive content of the FTA norms could work both in favour of and against their use as fora of first choice, but they could also make them the only available mechanisms for enforcement.

The analysis of procedural and political considerations showed that the WTO DSM is associated with several advantages that could make it the forum of choice for states, leading to the emergence of the new generation EU FTA DSMs as viable and regular alternatives less likely. Compared to the EU FTA DSMs, the WTO DSM is associated with greater coherence and predictability, reports of higher quality, automatic establishment of panels, increased legitimacy and public awareness,

C. Furculiță, *The WTO and the New Generation EU FTA Dispute Settlement Mechanisms*, EYIEL Monographs - Studies in European and International Economic Law 19, https://doi.org/10.1007/978-3-030-83118-9_8

multilateral value of its jurisprudence, multilateral pressure, potentially greater reputational damage in the event of non-compliance, more familiar rules, and lower financial costs. Nonetheless, if the disputing parties are neither MPIA participants nor signatories to an NAP, the appealed panel reports risk being sent into the void because of the non-functional AB. When states face a choice between the WTO DSM that may not provide a solution to the dispute and the FTA DSMs that may, the scales could tip in favour of the latter, especially if there is no risk of the FTA panel selection process being blocked. Moreover, if disputing parties are not MPIA participants, many advantages of the WTO DSM, such as increased predictability, coherence, or higher quality reports, will no longer be present. In addition, the new generation EU FTA DSM procedures are very similar to the WTO ones in many respects, and there are reasons to believe that, despite the more limited reputational costs, FTA parties would be motivated to comply with panel rulings. By contrast, if disputing parties are MPIA participants, there are no risks of appealed panel reports being sent into the void and the arrangement would provide most of the advantages associated with appellate review to the same or to a more limited degree, even though, some issues related to the MPIA are yet to be clarified and tested. Therefore, if FTA parties are also MPIA participants, the new generation EU FTAs are less likely to be in a constant genuine competition with the WTO DSM with respect to all the disputes under the coverage of both WTO and FTA mechanisms.

In certain circumstance, all the new generation EU FTA DSMs even in case of a functional AB or other alternative arrangements within the WTO DSM, could still be perceived as viable partial alternatives to the WTO DSM, considering some of the advantages associated with them. The two main factors that may influence the preference for new generation EU FTA DSMs, and can be correlated to several of their features, are the increased control parties have over these mechanisms and the outcome of the disputes and the potentially greater interpretative divergence of FTA panel reports. Apart from that, the new generation EU FTAs could offer speedier procedures, increased transparency and participation of civil society, developed and flexible compliance proceedings and temporary remedies, higher likelihood of reaching an MAS, limited public awareness, and possible avoidance of setting an inconvenient multilateral precedent.

Although the new generation EU FTAs could become viable partial alternatives to the WTO DSM, especially in the context of the current AB crisis, they also call for a functional mechanism to resolve disputes at the WTO level. While the new generation EU FTAs provide the only available fora for enforcement of the WTO-plus and WTO-x norms they incorporate, they should not be considered as undermining the authority of the WTO DSM. In fact, as argued in this part, the new generation EU FTAs recognise the importance of a functional way of solving disputes at the WTO level and depend on it for enforcement of many replicated or incorporated WTO norms. The FTA parties may even be discouraged from using the FTA DSMs by the potential jurisdictional conflicts. Furthermore, the competition between the new generation EU FTA DSMs and the WTO mechanism does and could generate positive results, if and when they use the opportunity to learn lessons from each other. The new generation EU FTAs provide improved rules based on the

WTO experience, and the WTO could benefit from certain provisions tested at the FTA level for DSU reform.

To conclude, the new generation EU FTA DSMs could represent a solution for states seeking alternatives in the context of the AB crisis and in the absence of other arrangements, but a functioning WTO DSM remains essential. In certain circumstances, when states perceive them as viable partial alternatives, the new generation EU FTA DSMs are and could be in a genuine competition with the WTO DSM.

Part III
Conflicts of Jurisdiction Between the WTO and the New Generation EU FTA DSMs

Chapter 9
Conflicts of Jurisdiction Between the DSMs of the WTO and FTAs in General

9.1 Introduction

According to the conceptual framework,[1] conflicts of jurisdiction between DSMs may appear when the same dispute between the parties can be brought entirely or partly before two or more distinct DSMs. The conflicts materialise when these DSMs are triggered in parallel or subsequence to deal with that dispute or when a party invokes the jurisdiction of the other DSM as being the appropriate one. The concept of conflicting jurisdictions is closely related to improper forum shopping, which may cause conflicting outcomes for a single dispute and is associated with risks, such as loss of coherence, security and predictability of the system, undermined authority and credibility of the DSMs, unresolved disputes, and increased litigation costs.[2] As argued in the conceptual framework, limited coherence should be sought for international law.

Although the chapters on state-to-state DSMs did not raise controversies during negotiations of the new generation EU FTAs, in contrast to the investor-to-state dispute settlement provisions,[3] the possible occurrence of conflicts of jurisdiction with the WTO DSM should not be overlooked. The issue of conflicts of jurisdiction between the WTO and FTA DSMs is not only theoretical; it has occurred in practice, although only exceptionally. For example, in *Argentina – Poultry*,[4] Brazil initiated a WTO case after an unsuccessful claim was first brought to the MERCOSUR DSM.[5] In *Brazil – Retreaded Tyres*, MERCOSUR countries were exempted from the application of a ban imposed on retreaded tyres as a result of a MERCOSUR

---

[1] *See supra*, Sect. 3.2.4.
[2] *See supra* Sect. 2.1.4.
[3] Lester (2016).
[4] *Argentina – Definitive Anti-Dumping Duties on Poultry from Brazil (Argentina – Poultry)*, DS241.
[5] Panel Report, *Argentina – Poultry*, WT/DS241/R, 22 April 2003, [7.17].

C. Furculiță, *The WTO and the New Generation EU FTA Dispute Settlement Mechanisms*, EYIEL Monographs - Studies in European and International Economic Law 19, https://doi.org/10.1007/978-3-030-83118-9_9

panel ruling; this exemption was subsequently found to be in violation of the chapeau of Article XX(b) of GATT in WTO proceedings.[6] In *US – Tuna II (Mexico)*, the US argued that the Mexican request for panel establishment constituted a violation of Article 2005, Chapter 20 of NAFTA, which provided the opportunity for the respondent in a dispute on environmental issues to require exclusive recourse to the FTA DSM. Nevertheless, the US did not raise this issue after the panel was established within the WTO, and the panel and the AB did not face this question in *US – Tuna II (Mexico)*.

The constant increase in the number of FTAs containing DSMs leaves open the possibility of new cases of conflicting jurisdictions. Moreover, as an increase in the use of FTA DSMs has recently been noted,[7] the risk of conflicting jurisdictions may be more imminent. The issue of conflicting jurisdictions continues to be relevant in the context of the current AB crisis[8] as panels are still able to issue reports that will be final and subject to adoption by the DSB, if not appealed, or if appealed, will remain un-adopted or could be subject to appeal arbitration if the disputing parties are MPIA participants. If states initiate parallel or subsequent WTO and FTA proceedings for the same dispute, there may be an FTA ruling and an appealed panel report, but no AB to hear the appeal. Hence, a conflict of jurisdictions involving a dysfunctional AB may lead to a dispute being unresolved for an indefinite period, regardless of the fact that the dispute would be settled under the FTA DSM. Thus, the role of FTA DSMs would be undermined, as the dispute would still remain unresolved under WTO rules. Moreover, a conflict of jurisdictions may also hamper the possibility of initiating FTA disputes after appealed panel reports are sent into limbo in the absence of a functional AB or another alternative appeal arrangement, leaving disputes unsettled.[9]

9.2   Tools Available to Deal with Conflicting Jurisdictions

This section will investigate the tools available to address the issue of conflicting jurisdictions. It will first present the existing general principles of public international law, as well as principles from international commercial law, and will then introduce jurisdictional clauses as a tool to avoid and resolve conflicting jurisdictions. The later sections of this chapter will analyse whether the WTO legal framework permits the use of these tools.

---

[6]Appellate Body Report, *Brazil – Measures Affecting Imports of Retreaded Tyres (Brazil – Retreaded Tyres)*, WT/DS332/AB/R, 3 December 2007, [217–234].

[7]*See supra* Sect. 4.1.

[8]*See supra* Sect. 4.2.

[9]For more on the new generation EU FTA jurisdictional clauses in the context of the current AB crisis, *see* Sect. 10.7.

9.2.1 Public and Private International Law Tools

The following sub-sections will present the principles of public international and international commercial law that may be used to address the issue of conflicting jurisdictions between tribunals.

9.2.1.1 Res Judicata and Lis Alibi Pendens

Res judicata and *lis alibi pendens* are rules that have been used in private international law to address cases in which the same dispute is brought more than once to the same or to more tribunals. *Res judicata* is the rule according to which the final judgement issued by a competent court on the merits of the case is definitive and constitutes, therefore, a bar to re-litigating the same dispute in the same or another forum.[10] Accordingly, if a dispute has been decided by a tribunal, it cannot be decided subsequently by the same or another tribunal. The *lis alibi pendens* rule establishes that once proceedings have been initiated for a dispute, no parallel proceedings may be pursued on the same dispute.[11] While *res judicata* addresses the issue of subsequent proceedings, *lis alibi pendens* deals with parallel proceedings on the same dispute. Thus, according to these rules, if a tribunal finds that the same dispute is being decided or has already been decided by it or another tribunal, it refrains from deciding it in parallel or subsequently.

 Res judicata is widely accepted as a general principle of law recognized by the civilised nations, which, according to Article 38(1) of the ICJ Statue represents a source of international law since it is recognised in the law of most states and has also been recognised as a principle in several instances by international tribunals.[12] It has been argued that despite the more limited recognition of the *lis alibi pendens* principle by international tribunals, it would be difficult to claim that it should not be regarded as a general principle,[13] since it has the same roots as *res judicata* and is also found in many national jurisdictions.[14] Even if *res judicata* and *lis alibi pendens* are considered general principles of international law, their usefulness in dealing with jurisdictional conflicts mainly depends on the conditions for their application.

 It is generally agreed that *res judicata* and *lis alibi pendens* apply only when the 'same dispute' is brought to tribunals, which implies three conditions: the identity of the parties, the same object, and the identity of the legal claims.[15] While not

---

[10] *See* Kwak and Marceau (2006), pp. 480–481; Kuijper (2010), p. 32; Kolsky Lewis and Van den Bossche (2014), p. 20.

[11] *See* Kwak and Marceau (2006), p. 480.

[12] Kuijper (2010), pp. 32–33; For instances in which it was recognized by international tribunals *see* Reinisch (2004), pp. 44–48.

[13] McLachlan (2009), p. 357.

[14] Shany (2004), p. 244.

[15] Kwak and Marceau (2006), p. 480; Kolsky Lewis and Van den Bossche (2014), p. 20.

confirming the status and applicability of the *res judicata* principle, even with respect to subsequent WTO disputes, the panel in *India – Autos* established that it 'requires identity between both the measures and the claims pertaining to them. There is also, for the purposes of *res judicata*, a requirement of identity of the parties.'[16] Although in a case of conflicting jurisdictions between the DSMs of the WTO and FTAs the parties may be the same and the dispute could arise out of the same factual situation, it is the last criterion on the identity of the claims that could make *res judicata* and *lis alibi pendens* of little help in solving this issue.

The identity of claims has been interpreted narrowly in the context of these principles of international law, leading to a narrow interpretation of the concept of 'the same dispute', in contrast to the broader approach adopted for this concept here.[17] Thus, even if an FTA provision is similar or identical in substance to a WTO norm, the legal claims would be technically different, as the tribunals would be faced with a claim of an FTA violation and one of a WTO violation.[18] Such an approach may be criticised for being overly restrictive and 'highly artificial' according to Reinisch who argued in favour of constructing a broader interpretation of the identity of claims.[19] Nevertheless, there is currently no reason to believe that such a broad interpretation would be adopted and that international tribunals would interpret differently these international law principles. This is especially so, since even for cases involving identical FTA and WTO norms, these norms' meaning could be different. As argued by Broude and Shany, two norms from different agreements can never be fully equal.[20] Moreover, remedies available in two different treaties may also differ[21] and affect the identity of the claims.

To conclude, the current narrow interpretation of the conditions for application of *res judicata* and *lis alibi pendens* would seriously affect their potential utility in resolving conflicting jurisdiction between international tribunals in general, and between the DSMs of the WTO and FTAs in particular.

9.2.1.2 *Forum Non Conveniens* and Comity

The doctrines of *forum non conveniens* and comity, both stemming from the common law system, have been suggested as potential private international law

---

[16] Panel Report, *India – Measures Affecting the Automotive Sector (India – Autos)*, WT/DS146/R, 21 December 2001, [7.66].

[17] *See supra* Sect. 3.2.5.

[18] Kwak and Marceau (2006), p. 481; Davey and Sapir (2009), p. 14; Kolsky Lewis and Van den Bossche (2014), p. 20.

[19] Reinisch (2004), pp. 64–65.

[20] Broude and Shany (2011), pp. 7–9.

[21] *See* how temporary remedies in CETA and EUJEPA, for example, differ from those in the WTO DSM in Sect. 6.12.2.2.

tools that could be employed by international tribunals to resolve conflicting jurisdictions.[22]

The doctrine of comity 'allows a court to decline to exercise jurisdiction over matters that would be more appropriately heard by another tribunal' and it is based on the discretionary power, mutual respect, and cooperation between courts.[23] In a similar manner, the *forum non conveniens* doctrine relies on the discretion of courts to stay or terminate a proceeding when another forum is considered more 'convenient', based on connecting factors such as the availability of experts, the residence place of the parties, governing law, expenses, and the general interest of justice.[24] These connecting factors are, however, of little importance in international law,[25] which raises questions about the use of this doctrine to deal with conflicting jurisdictions of public international DSMs.

The advantage of these doctrines is that they are not restricted by a narrow identity test,[26] as that required by *res judicata* and *lis alibi pendens* principles. Therefore, in case of a conflict of jurisdiction between the WTO and an FTA DSMs, it would not matter whether or not the claims are identical; the tribunals could consider whether another tribunal should hear a dispute without any strict condition being attached. The problem with these doctrines, however, is that it has not been settled yet whether they have attained the status of general principles of international law to be a source of public international law.[27] However, even if they were, they entail considerable discretion on the part of tribunals.[28] Thus, the decision would be left entirely to the discretion, intuition, and beliefs of tribunals, without any fixed criteria, making them increasingly prone to accusations of judicial activism. Moreover, as stated by Marceau, it is difficult to imagine an international tribunal finding that it is not the appropriate forum when it has jurisdiction according to its constituent treaty.[29]

The role of comity and *forum non conveniens* within the WTO and whether they could be used as tools to address conflicting jurisdictions between the DSMs of the WTO and FTAs will be determined in the sections that follow.[30]

---

[22] *See* Henckels (2008), pp. 594–597; Pauwelyn and Salles (2009), p. 110; Nguyen (2016), pp. 101–102.

[23] Henckels (2008), pp. 584–585. On mutual respect and comity, *see MOX Plant case, Request for Provisional Measures Order (Ireland v. United Kingdom)*, Order No 3 Suspension of Proceedings on Jurisdiction and Merits, and Request for Further Provisional Measures, 2003, para 28.

[24] Kwak and Marceau (2006), p. 480; Pauwelyn and Salles (2009), pp. 110–111; Lanyi and Steinbach (2014), p. 386.

[25] Kwak and Marceau (2006), p. 480.

[26] Lanyi and Steinbach (2014), p. 387.

[27] Henckels (2008), p. 584; Graewert (2008), p. 315; Lanyi and Steinbach (2014), p. 388.

[28] Henckels (2008), p. 584.

[29] Marceau (2001), p. 1112.

[30] *See infra* Sect. 9.3.4.2.

9.2.1.3 Good Faith, Abuse of Process, and Estoppel

While good faith is a widely recognised general principle of international law,[31] and some argue that it is also a customary rule of interpretation,[32] it is a highly abstract and vague notion, making it impossible to define it concisely.[33] In the absence of particularisation of the principle and of its analysis as a specific manifestation, good faith is conceived as a value-oriented concept encompassing elements such as honesty, fairness, reasonableness, trust, and loyalty.[34] As all these elements are highly vague, good faith manifests itself in various other more concrete principles and concepts,[35] *inter alia*, the abuse of rights or process and estoppel.

The doctrine of abuse of rights is broadly recognised as a principle of international law or as customary international law.[36] It prevents a state from exercising a right either in a way that would impede the enjoyment of other states' own rights or for a purpose other than the one the right was created for, thereby causing injury to another state.[37] The doctrine of abuse of rights can materialise in different instances. When it is used as relating to procedural irregularities, it is usually referred to as abuse of process.[38] Kolb defines abuse of process as

> the use of procedural instruments or rights by one or more parties for purposes that are alien to those for which the procedural rights were established, especially for a fraudulent, procrastinatory or frivolous purpose, for the purpose of causing harm or obtaining an illegitimate advantage, for the purpose of reducing or removing the effectiveness of some other available process or for purposes of pure propaganda. To these situations, action with a malevolent intent or with bad faith can be added.[39]

Thus, initiation of second proceedings on the same matter by a state could be argued as an abuse of process. It has been invoked multiple times in ICJ procedures; nevertheless, the threshold for admitting an abuse of process has been set very high as the necessary conditions have never been fulfilled.[40]

Another manifestation and expression of the good faith principle is in the concept of estoppel. There is a considerable weight of authority that views estoppel as a general principle of international law based on the general principle of good faith.[41] For estoppel to be found, according to the doctrine and ICJ case law, it can be concluded that there should be a clear and unequivocal representation made,

---

[31] Mitchell (2006), p. 341; Ziegler and Baumgartner (2015), p. 10.

[32] *See*, for example, Mitchell (2006), pp. 342–344.

[33] Kolb (2006a), p. 13.

[34] *See* O'Connor (1991), pp. 118–199; Ziegler and Baumgartner (2015), p. 11.

[35] Kolb (2006a), p. 19; Mitchell (2006), p. 345; Ziegler and Baumgartner (2015), p. 10.

[36] Byers (2002), p. 397; Mitchell and Heaton (2010), p. 615.

[37] Kiss (2006).

[38] Ziegler and Baumgartner (2015), p. 32.

[39] Kolb (2006b), p. 904, para 49.

[40] For a list of cases, *see* Ziegler and Baumgartner (2015), fn 164.

[41] Brownlie and Crawford (2012), p. 420.

voluntarily and unconditionally, by one state to another that the other state relied on in good faith, and as a result of which was prejudiced or the state making the representation benefitted from.[42] A similar definition was adopted by the WTO panel in *Guatemala – Cement II*, according to which 'where one party has been induced to act in reliance on the assurances of another party, in such a way that it would be prejudiced were the other party later to change its position, such a change in position is "estopped", that is precluded'.[43] Thus, estoppel has the objective of holding a state to the representation it has made when another state relied on it, ensuring that the legitimate expectations, as well, as the security and predictability of the relations are protected.[44] Similar to the abuse of rights principle, estoppel can have both a substantive and a procedural dimension.[45] Therefore, a violation of the principle of estoppel is when one party created legitimate expectations for another party to act procedurally in a particularly way, on which the other party relied on, and subsequently changed its position to the detriment of that other party or its own advantage. It could be argued that if one party agreed in an FTA that the FTA DSM should be used for disputes arising out of FTA claims, and then initiated WTO proceedings contrary to what it has agreed to, that party could be estopped.

Good faith obligations and the principles deriving from it—abuse of rights and estoppel—make the ability of parties to rely on their treaty rights contingent on their own conduct.[46] Therefore, a party initiating parallel or subsequent proceedings could be regarded as acting contrary to its good faith obligations, being estopped or accused of abusing the process—this could bar it from enjoying its right to initiate proceedings.

While good faith is a general principle, it could be also expressly enshrined in the texts of the treaties. Article 3.10 of the DSU establishes that 'if a dispute arises, all Members will engage in these procedures in good faith in an effort to resolve the dispute'. Thus, in *US – FSC*, the AB affirmed that Article 3.10 is a 'specific manifestation of the principle of good faith which [...] is at once a general principle of law and a principle of general international law'.[47] Since it refers to engaging in good faith in dispute settlement proceedings, it could be considered to enshrine also procedural good faith. In *EC – Export Subsidies on Sugar*, the AB confirmed that the good faith obligation covers 'the entire spectrum of dispute settlement, from the

---

[42] *Temple of Preah Vihear (Cambodia v Thailand) (Merits)* [1962] ICJ Rep 6, 143–144 (Spender J); *Land, Island and Maritime Frontier Dispute (El Salvador v Honduras: Nicaragua Intervening), Application by Nicaragua for Permission to Intervene* (1990) Rep 92, 118, para 63; Brownlie and Crawford (2012), p. 420.

[43] Panel Report, *Guatemala – Definitive Anti-Dumping Measure on Grey Portland Cement from Mexico (Guatemala – Cement II)*, WT/DS156/R, 24 October 2000, [8.23].

[44] Mitchell and Heaton (2010), p. 608; Ziegler and Baumgartner (2015), p. 20.

[45] Kolb (2006b), p. 906, para 69.

[46] Lanyi and Steinbach (2014), p. 385.

[47] Appellate Body Report, *United States – Tax Treatment for "Foreign Sales Corporations" (US – FSC)*, WT/DS108/AB/R, 24 February 2000, [166].

point of initiation of a case through implementation'.[48] In addition, Article 3.7 of the DSU establishes that '[b]efore bringing a case, a Member shall exercise its judgement as to whether action under these procedures would be fruitful'. While Article 3.7 of the DSU does not expressly refer to 'good faith', by considering it in light of Article 3.10 which provides the relevant context, it may be said that good faith is also embedded in Article 3.7.[49] The AB established in *Mexico – Corn Syrup (Article 21.5 – US)* that Article 3.7 'reflects a basic principle that Members should have recourse to WTO dispute settlement in good faith, and not frivolously set in motion the procedures contemplated in the DSU'.[50]

Since abuse of process and estoppel arise from the principle of good faith, it may be argued that they are also, implicitly, covered by Articles 3.7 and 3.10 of the DSU. When estoppel was invoked in *EC – Export Subsidies on Sugar*, the AB stated that there is 'little in the DSU that explicitly limits the rights of WTO Members to bring an action' and continued by referring to Articles 3.7 and 3.10 of the DSU.[51] It concluded that 'assuming arguendo that the principle of estoppel could apply in the WTO, its application would fall within these narrow parameters set out in the DSU'.[52] Therefore, it appears that if applicable in the WTO context, estoppel would be considered within the confines of Articles 3.7 and 3.10 of the DSU.

The conditions for application of good faith and its other manifestations and how WTO panels and the AB interpreted and approached them in cases relevant to conflicting jurisdictions will be treated in more detail in the sections that follow. The implications and usefulness of these principles and concepts in dealing with potential conflicts of jurisdiction between the WTO and new generation EU FTAs DSMs, specifically, will also be assessed in this chapter.

9.2.2 Jurisdictional Clauses

9.2.2.1 Definition, Types, and Implications of Jurisdictional Clauses

This section introduces jurisdictional clauses as tools to address conflicting jurisdictions between international tribunals. It describes the different types of jurisdictional clauses in various FTAs and their implications.

---

[48] Appellate Body Report, *European Communities – Export Subsidies on Sugar (EC – Export Subsidies on Sugar)*, WT/DS265/AB/R, WT/DS266/AB/R, WT/DS283/AB/R, adopted 19 May 2005, [312].

[49] Mitchell (2006), p. 356.

[50] Appellate Body Report, *Mexico – Anti-Dumping Investigation of High Fructose Corn Syrup (HFCS) from the United States, Recourse to Article 21.5 of the DSU by The United States (Mexico – Corn Syrup (Article 21.5 – US))*, WT/DS132/AB/RW, 22 October 2001, [73].

[51] Appellate Body Report, *European Communities – Export Subsidies on Sugar*, [312].

[52] Ibid.

Jurisdictional clauses are treaty clauses that expressly establish whether one jurisdiction should prevail over another or if different jurisdictions may or may not be exercised simultaneously or in parallel and the cases in which this is required or permitted. The WTO agreements contain no express rules on how to deal with potential conflicting jurisdictions. However, when drafting FTAs and their DSMs to resolve disputes arising out of their application and interpretation, parties are aware of the potential overlap with the WTO DSM,[53] and the lack of WTO rules to deal expressly with this issue. Therefore, FTAs can be drafted to include jurisdictional clauses. In contrast to other jurisdictional tools of public international law or international commercial law that can sometimes be abstract, vague, or not entirely suitable for solving conflicting jurisdictions,[54] jurisdictional clauses can more clearly reflect the parties' intention regarding the chosen forum for FTA disputes.

The first type of jurisdictional clause offers exclusive jurisdiction to a specific forum.[55] Therefore, an exclusive FTA jurisdictional clause may designate the FTA or the WTO DSM as the exclusive forum for solving disputes. Exclusive jurisdictional clauses can be found for courts with supranational features, such as in the case of the EU itself and the Andean Community.[56] As will be shown below,[57] according to Article 23.1 of the DSU, the WTO DSM also has exclusive jurisdiction over claims based on WTO norms; however, this does not affect the jurisdiction of the FTA DSMs over norms that are identical or similar to those of the WTO.[58] Exclusive jurisdictional clauses may cover all disputes arising under the agreement or only a specific category.[59] NAFTA, for example, provides that the parties shall have recourse to dispute settlement only under its DSM when disputes concern measures taken to protect human, animal or plant life or health, or to protect the environment of a party and the responding party requests in writing that the matter be considered under NAFTA.[60] The EU–Chile FTA gives exclusive jurisdiction to the WTO DSM with respect to obligations 'equivalent in substance to WTO obligations', unless the parties agree otherwise.[61] Since NAFTA's exclusive jurisdictional clause applies

---

[53] Kolsky Lewis and Van den Bossche (2014), p. 14.

[54] *See supra* Sect. 9.2.1.

[55] Kolsky Lewis and Van den Bossche (2014), pp. 14–15.

[56] Art 344, TFEU ('Member States undertake not to submit a dispute concerning the interpretation or application of the Treaties to any method of settlement other than those provided for therein.'); Treaty Creating the Court of Justice of the Andean Community, Art 42 ('Member Countries shall not submit any dispute that may arise from the application of provisions comprising the legal system of the Andean Community to any court, arbitration system or proceeding whatsoever except for those stipulated in this Treaty.').

[57] *See infra* Sect. 9.3.1.

[58] However, this would not preclude FTA DSMs from adjudicating claims on FTA norms that incorporate or reproduce WTO norms, because these claims would be based on FTA norms.

[59] Kolsky Lewis and Van den Bossche (2014), pp. 14–15.

[60] NAFTA, Art 2005(4)(a).

[61] Agreement Establishing an Association between the European Community and its Member States, of the one part, and the Republic of Chile, of the other part (EU–Chile FTA), Art 189.4(c).

only at the request of the respondent and the parties can depart by agreement from the clause in the EU–Chile FTA, these clauses may also be viewed as preferential jurisdictional clauses, as parties could still depart from them if they preferred to do so.[62]

Another type of jurisdictional clause allows parties to choose on a case-by-case basis where to bring their disputes, called 'choice-of-forum clauses'. The jurisdictional clauses that allow a choice to be made between different DSMs and prescribe that once a forum has been selected, the chosen forum has exclusive jurisdiction, are known as 'fork-in-the-road' clauses.[63] Such a clause can be found in KORUS, according to which '[o]nce the complaining Party has requested the establishment of, or referred a matter to, a dispute settlement panel under an agreement referred to in paragraph 1, the forum selected shall be used to the exclusion of other fora'.[64] Similarly, CPTPP provides that '[o]nce a complaining Party has requested the establishment of, or referred a matter to, a panel or other tribunal under an agreement referred to in paragraph 1, the forum selected shall be used to the exclusion of other fora'.[65] However, limited fork-in-the-road clauses prohibit only parallel proceedings,[66] while allowing subsequent recourse to DSMs. For example, the EU–Cariforum FTA provides that a party 'may not institute a dispute settlement proceeding regarding the same measure in the other forum until the first proceeding has ended'.[67] Furthermore, there are fork-in-the-road clauses that can be departed from when parties expressly agree to use more than one dispute settlement forum in respect to that particular dispute, as in case of China–Singapore FTA.[68]

The purpose of exclusive jurisdictional and fork-in-the road clauses, not those that are limited or can be departed from, is to guarantee that disputes under FTAs will be adjudicated only by the FTA or WTO DSMs. Therefore, they ensure that there will technically be no conflicting jurisdictions with respect to disputes that fall under these clauses. In case of proceedings initiated in both the WTO and FTA fora, the WTO proceedings being the first, the FTA panels would find a violation of the respective jurisdictional clause and the negative consequence of conflicting jurisdictions would be averted. If an FTA party brings a dispute to the FTA forum first and then initiates WTO proceedings for the same dispute, the FTA party against which these claims are brought could claim the violation of the exclusive or fork-in-the-road clause before an FTA panel and follow the FTA procedures that would entitle it

---

[62] *See*, for example, Hillman (2009), pp. 195–196.

[63] Hillman (2009), p. 15; Pusceddu (2016), p. 6.

[64] Free Trade Agreement between the United States of America and the Republic of Korea ('KORUS') Art 22.6.

[65] CPTPP, Art 28.4(2).

[66] Lanyi and Steinbach (2014), p. 395.

[67] Economic Partnership Agreement between the CARIFORUM States, of the one part, and the European Community and its Member States, of the other part (EU–Cariforum FTA), Art 222(2).

[68] Free Trade Agreement Between the Government of the People's Republic of China and the Government of the Republic of Singapore (China–Singapore FTA), Art 92.7.

to retaliation comparable in value to the benefits gained by the other party by initiating WTO procedures.[69] Although the defending party would reduce its material losses by claiming a violation of the exclusive or fork-in-the-road clause in front of an FTA panel, this would not effectively address the issue of conflicting jurisdictions, as there could still be two conflicting rulings for the same dispute. Moreover, the dispute could still remain unresolved, since with two conflicting rulings for the same dispute, the parties would be confused about which one to follow in that particular dispute, as well as which solution should be followed when adopting new measures. Therefore, there would be no stability and predictability, nor would lengthy procedures in multiple fora be avoided. Thus, claiming a violation of FTA jurisdictional clauses in front of an FTA arbitration panel only partially addresses the issue of conflicting jurisdictions. Hence, for the FTA jurisdictional clauses to fully achieve their goal of preventing and resolving conflicts of jurisdiction, they should also be given consideration and effect by WTO panels and the AB when raised in WTO proceedings initiated after the FTA proceedings on the same disputes.

This section introduced different types of jurisdictional clauses and their possible implications for conflicting jurisdictions between the DSMs of the WTO and FTAs. Further, the possible avenues through which they could become relevant in the WTO forum and whether the WTO legal framework allows their enforcement and applicability in WTO proceedings will be analysed.

9.2.2.2 Legal Avenues for Jurisdictional Clauses

Jurisdictional clauses contained in FTAs and other agreements present in and by themselves tools to deal with conflicting jurisdictions when they are considered, for example, within RTAs. However, within other fora they could be considered through other legal avenues.

9.2.2.2.1 Article 45(a) of the ILC Articles on State Responsibility

A legal avenue for invoking jurisdictional clauses could be Article 45(a) of the ILC articles on state responsibility. It provides that '[t]he responsibility of a State may not be invoked if: (a) The injured State has validly waived the claim'. A waiver is the manifestation of the intention to renounce a right or a claim and is, therefore, an expression of the consent, as a principle that runs as a common thread through international law.[70] Thus, it could be argued that a party has waived its right to invoke the responsibility of a state and to initiate WTO disputes by including an

---

[69] Marceau and Tomazos (2008), p. 60.
[70] Crawford (2014), p. 70.

exclusive jurisdictional or a fork-in-the-road clause when the dispute is first brought to the FTA DSM.[71]

While there is no final decision on the form that the ILC draft articles should take, they are already being referred to largely as a 'persuasive source of guidance' and 'an authoritative statement of the rules on State responsibility' by states and the international courts that treat them.[72] The WTO panels and the AB have also cited the ILC articles on state responsibility multiple times when interpreting WTO norms.[73] Therefore, the ILC draft articles on state responsibility may be considered customary international law. The AB stated that 'ILC Articles are not binding by virtue of being part of an international treaty. However, insofar as they reflect customary international law or general principles of law, these Articles are applicable in the relations between the parties'.[74] Nevertheless, the ILC articles on state responsibility have never been regarded as applicable law within WTO proceedings, but have been used merely for interpretative purposes.[75]

Even if Article 45(a) of the ILC draft articles on state responsibility is considered a customary rule applicable between the parties, a pertinent question is whether these articles, which are non-WTO rules, could be enforced and applied by WTO panels; this question will be addressed further in this chapter.

9.2.2.2.2   Using International Rules on Conflicts of Norms

The second legal avenue for invoking jurisdictional clauses within the WTO DSM could be application of international rules on substantive conflicts of norms to resolve the issue of conflicting jurisdictions.[76] As jurisdictional clauses are treaty norms, a jurisdictional conflict could be treated in the same way as any conflict between other norms that is resolved by applying rules on conflicting norms. For example, by applying these rules, it could potentially be claimed that in case of

---

[71] Lanyi and Steinbach (2014), pp. 401–403.

[72] General Assembly of the United Nations, Sixth Committee (Legal)—65th Session (2010), Responsibility of States for Internationally Wrongful Acts <www.un.org/en/ga/sixth/65/RespStatesWrong.shtml>; General Assembly of the United Nations, Sixth Committee (Legal)—68th Session (2013), Responsibility of States for Internationally Wrongful Acts <www.un.org/en/ga/sixth/68/StateRes.shtml>.

[73] See, for example, Appellate Body Report, *United States – Transitional Safeguard Measure on Combed Cotton Yarn from Pakistan (US – Cotton Yarn)*, WT/DS192/AB/R, 8 October 2001, [120]; Panel Report, *United States – Measures Affecting the Cross-Border Supply of Gambling and Betting Services (US – Gambling)*, WT/DS/385/R, 10 November 2004, [6.128].

[74] Appellate Body Report, *United States – Definitive Anti-Dumping and Countervailing Duties on Certain Products from China (US – Anti-Dumping and Countervailing Duties (China))*, WT/DS379/AB/R, 11 March 2011, [309].

[75] For a discussion on the ILC Articles on State Responsibility, *see* Sánchez (2012), p. 292.

[76] Shany (2004), pp. 266–267; Kwak and Marceau (2006), p. 476.

conflicts between WTO and FTA jurisdictional norms, the FTA jurisdictional clauses should prevail and be applied to the dispute.

Before using international rules on conflicts of norms, the question would arise what a conflict of norms is. There are two basic approaches, narrow and broad, adopted by the doctrine for defining conflicts of norms. Although this dichotomy is overly simplistic, as Bartels mentions, it still represents the general framework of the academic debate.[77] The advocates of a narrow definition identify conflicts of norms only in the situation when there is a conflict between obligations. Thus, according to them, when a state is party to two different treaties that include conflicting obligations and it cannot comply with one of them because of another, there is a conflict of norms.[78] While there are some authoritative opinions that support narrow definitions, there are also equally authoritative opinions, especially the most recent ones, that define conflict of norms more broadly so that it also encompasses inconsistencies between rights and obligations.[79] Besides being supported by many doctrinaires, the broad definition has been also backed by the ILC Study Group. It stated that it adopts a 'wide definition' where conflict is understood 'as a situation where two rules or principles suggest different ways of dealing with a problem'.[80] Therefore, the broader approach seems to have become the dominant position in the last decade.

The narrow definition would lead to the automatic recognition of the superiority of mandatory norms over permissive norms,[81] reducing the latter to inutility.[82] Moreover, entire agreements could be reduced to inapplicability, if an agreement is based on a permission that contradicts an obligation from another treaty.[83] When parties agreed on a norm or an agreement containing an obligation, they might have, specifically, intended to detract from that obligation in certain circumstances.[84] Therefore, for the purpose of this book, a broad definition of conflict of norms is adopted. Hence, there could be a conflict of norms involving an exclusive jurisdictional clause providing the *obligation* to resort to that jurisdiction and a choice of forum clause providing the *right* to choose between two fora. There could also be a

---

[77] Bartels (2008), p. 131.

[78] *See* Jenks (1953), pp. 425–256; Karl (1984), p. 468; Czaplinski and Danilenko (1990), p. 12; Wolfrum and Matz (2003), p. 6; Marceau (2001), pp. 1083–1086.

[79] *See* Lauterpacht (1936), p. 58; Aufsricht (1952), p. 656; Pauwelyn (2003a), pp. 175–176; Weiss (2003), p. 202; Vranes (2006), p. 395; Milanovic (2009), pp. 72–74; Chase (2012), pp. 802–806.

[80] International Law Commission (ILC) Study Group on the Fragmentation of International Law, 'Fragmentation of International Law: Difficulties Arising from the Diversification and Expansion of International Law', Report of the Study Group of the International Law Commission (ILC Report), Finalized by Martti Koskenniemi, A/CN.4/L.682 and add 1 and corr 1 (International Law Commission, 13 April 2006) 10, para 25.

[81] Pauwelyn (2003a), p. 197; Vranes (2006), p. 405; Chase (2012), p. 804; Jeutner (2017), pp. 29–30.

[82] Vranes (2006), p. 404; Chase (2012), p. 803.

[83] Davey (2008), p. 110.

[84] Pauwelyn (2003a), p. 174; Vranes (2006), p. 404; Davey (2008), p. 111.

conflict between the obligation not to resort to other fora contained in an exclusive jurisdictional clause and the prohibition to resort to another forum once a choice has been made contained in a fork-in-the-road clause. Considering that the WTO exclusive jurisdiction provided by Article 23 of the DSU covers only WTO obligations and it is considered as not affecting the rights of FTA panels to deal with FTA norms that may incorporate or replicate WTO norms,[85] a conflict of norms between Article 23 of the DSU and other jurisdictional FTA clauses should not occur. Nevertheless, this section will further consider how it could be dealt with, in case it is argued by others that there is such a conflict.

Parties can agree on rules dealing with potential conflicts between their and other agreements and expressly enshrine in their international agreement which norm should prevail in case of a conflict.[86] If a conflict between jurisdictional clauses were found, and there would be no specific rules provided in the treaties that stipulated how to deal with conflicts, traditional conflict of norms rules would apply. The most prominent one can be found in Article 30 of the VCLT containing the *lex posterior* rule, also constituting customary international law,[87] under which 'a later rule is presumed to trump an earlier rule'.[88] By favouring the most recent treaty provision, the *lex posterior* rule is considered to show the evolving intent of the parties.[89] It applies to successive treaties, even if not all the parties to the first treaty are parties to the later one, as in the case of FTAs and the WTO. Article 30 (4) of the VCLT provides that in such situations, the later treaty prevails only as between the parties to both treaties.

Lex specialis is another conflict of norms principle. While it has not been included in the VCLT, it has been used in practice largely by international courts and is recognised as an international principle.[90] According to this principle, 'if a matter is being regulated by a general standard as well as a more specific rule, then the latter should take precedence over the former'.[91] Similar to the *lex posterior* rule, it is based on the idea of giving consideration to parties' intent. It would seem pointless

---

[85] *See infra* Sect. 9.3.1.

[86] The new generation EU FTAs under analysis provide either that parties 'affirm their rights and obligations to each other under the WTO Agreement' (CETA, Art 1.5) or that nothing in the agreements shall be construed to require the parties to act in a manner inconsistent with the WTO obligations (EUKFTA, Art 15.14(4); EUJEPA, Art 1.9(2); EUSFTA, Art 16.18(2); EUVFTA, 17.22(3)). The second paragraph of Art 30 of the VCLT establishes that 'when a treaty specifies that it is subject to, or that it is not to be considered as incompatible with, an earlier or later treaty, the provisions of that other treaty prevail'. Therefore, the new generation EU FTAs may be interpreted as giving preference to the WTO agreements in case of conflicts of norms, as they could also be interpreted as requiring not to be construed as incompatible with the WTO agreements.

[87] Kuijper (2010), p. 8.

[88] Michaels and Pauwelyn (2012), p. 354.

[89] Borgen (2005), p. 587; Michaels and Pauwelyn (2012), p. 354.

[90] Marceau (2001), p. 1092; ILC Report (n 80), para 65.

[91] ILC Report (n 80), para 56.

to apply a more general norm to a set of circumstances already regulated by the parties in a more specific manner.[92]

According to these conflict of norms rules, provisions of FTAs that have been mostly concluded after the creation of the WTO are, assumingly, more specific because they are usually created with the aim of going further than the WTO norms. Therefore, they can be presumed to have priority over WTO rules.[93] Nevertheless, the solution may not be that simple. Sometimes, it may be difficult to establish which treaty is earlier in time[94] and the application of the *lex posterior* rule may lead to absurd results.[95] For example, in case of a conflict between the WTO and FTA norms, if the WTO agreements are updated, the more specific FTAs would be technically earlier treaties and the WTO norms would prevail. Moreover, there are FTAs, such as NAFTA, that are earlier in time. In this case, would the WTO prevail?[96] What is more, the relationship between *lex specialis* and *lex posterior* rules and the hierarchy between them are not entirely clear when their application leads to contradictory results. For example, some claim that *lex specialis* should have priority when treaties have different levels of detail,[97] while Pauwelyn argues that *lex specialis* should be applicable as a second resort, when *lex posterior* cannot be invoked because it is impossible to define the treaty as either 'earlier' or 'later' in time.[98] Even when according to the *lex specialis* and *lex posterior* rules a jurisdictional clause from another treaty prevails, the question would arise whether the relevant international court or tribunal can apply a jurisdictional clause from a treaty outside its jurisdiction.

In addition, for the purpose of *inter se* agreements concluded only between some parties of the earlier treaty, such as in the case of FTAs, Article 41 of the VCLT is relevant. It establishes that two or more parties to a multilateral treaty may modify it solely between themselves by concluding another agreement if this possibility is either provided or not prohibited in the earlier multilateral treaty and the modification does not affect the enjoyment of rights of other parties and does not relate to a provision, derogation from which is incompatible with the object and purpose of the multilateral treaty. If an *inter se* agreement does not comply with the requirements of Article 41 of the VCLT, then it is an illegal agreement whose validity is nonetheless unaffected. However, states concluding such illegal *inter se* agreements bear international responsibility.[99] In the relationship between the multilateral treaty and the *inter se* agreement, there is broad consensus that the legal *inter se* agreement prevails

---

[92] Lindroos (2005), p. 36.

[93] Gao and Lim (2008), p. 919; Pauwelyn and Alschner (2015), p. 523.

[94] ILC Report (n 80), para 232.

[95] Pauwelyn (2003a), pp. 375–378.

[96] Gao and Lim (2008), p. 919.

[97] Kuijper (2010), p. 9.

[98] Pauwelyn (2003a), p. 378.

[99] Mus (1998), p. 225; ILC Report (n 80), para 319; von der Decken (2018), p. 779.

either by virtue of Article 41 itself or of Article 30(4) of the VCLT.[100] Hence, if an FTA is found to be a legal inter se agreement, it would technically prevail over the WTO agreements.

Whether the WTO agreements permit or prohibit *inter se* agreements and the norms within them, other than those complying with the requirements of Article XXIV of GATT, Article V of GATS and the Enabling Clause on RTAs, has been part of academic debate. Some claim that WTO agreements indirectly prohibit *inter se* agreements under Article 41 of the VCLT because of the explicit provisions on waiver and amendments of WTO agreements contained in the Marrakesh Agreement[101] or that it may not be possible to conclude such agreements without violating third party rights.[102] Thus, according to this strict approach, WTO Members can depart from the WTO agreements only under the WTO norms and requirements such as those contained in Art. XXIV GATT. Others argue that the possibility of signing *inter se* agreements cannot be limited only to Article XXIV of GATT and its conditions, since the WTO agreements do not expressly prohibit other types of modifications, and that the presence of this article should not be perceived as precluding other *inter se* agreements or FTA norms that do not further liberalize trade between the parties, but rather restrict it.[103]

In *Peru – Agricultural Products*, the Appellate Body addressed the question of whether Members can modify the WTO agreements *inter se* and concluded that since WTO agreements include specific provisions on amendments, waivers, or exceptions for RTAs, these provisions prevail over Article 41 of the VCLT. Hence, according to it, the proper route to assess if an FTA provision can depart from WTO rules is the WTO rules on FTAs: Article XXIV of GATT, Article V of GATS, and the Enabling Clause.[104] The AB's analysis may be faulted for not contemplating the requirements of Article 41 of the VCLT. It did not establish whether Article XXIV of GATT represents an express permission to modify as provided in Article 41, and did not explain the relevance for the question at issue of the WTO provisions on waiver and amendments which are only briefly invoked.[105] In fact, the AB's invocation of Article IX of the Marrakesh Agreement on unilateral waivers granted to a Member by the Membership and Article X of the same

---

[100] Some claim that Art 30(4) of the VCLT is applicable only to an illegal *inter se* agreement as Art 30(5) establishes that paragraph 4 is without prejudice to Art 41 and any question of responsibility, while in the case of a legal agreement, Art 41 will simply prevail over the latter as a legitimate modification (*see* Mus 1998, pp. 226–227; Aust 2018, p. 242; von der Decken 2018, p. 779). On the contrary, others claim that Art 30(4) further governs the relationship between an earlier multilateral treaty and a legal *inter se* agreement (*see* Villiger 2009, p. 537, paras 14–15; Pauwelyn 2003a, p. 382). Nevertheless, there is consensus that a legal *inter se* agreement prevails over an earlier multilateral one.

[101] Trachtman (2004), p. 859.

[102] Marceau (2001), p. 1105; Trachtman (2004), p. 860.

[103] Kuijper (2010), p. 10; Shaffer and Winters (2017), p. 321.

[104] Appellate Body Report, *Peru – Agricultural Products*, [5.112].

[105] Mathis (2016), p. 103.

agreement on treaty amendments affecting all Members to prove that WTO Members have contracted out of Article 41 of the VCLT seems misplaced, as these norms do not concern modification of a multilateral agreement *inter partes*.[106]

While this author concurs with other doctrinaires that the AB's argumentation related to Article 41 of the VCLT seems flawed and lacks clarity, it is submitted that when non-WTO norms are invoked in the context of dispute settlement, the first questions to be posed should have been different. While Article 41 of the VCLT and the WTO agreements may not restrict the right of Members to conclude *inter se* agreements, the first questions should have been related to the jurisdiction and applicability of non-WTO law: whether Article 41 of the VCLT and potential non-WTO *inter se* agreements could be considered and applied within dispute settlement procedures by WTO panels and the AB. The decisive question of whether non-WTO law can be enforced and applied by WTO panels will be considered in the next section.

9.2.2.2.3   Other Legal Venues

In addition to the avenues described above, jurisdictional clauses in FTAs could become relevant within the WTO through other important venues. First, they could be considered under Article XXIV of GATT that regulates the formation of FTAs. Second, good faith, abuse of process and estoppel, as general principles or as principles enshrined in Articles 3.7 and 3.10 of the DSU,[107] may be violated if, contrary to what a party has agreed to in an FTA exclusive jurisdictional or fork-in-the-road clause (if FTA proceedings were commenced first), it still initiated WTO proceedings. Therefore, jurisdictional clauses could also serve as a basis of and provide evidence for claims on good faith related violations. The next sections will detail the possibility of considering FTA jurisdictional clauses under Article XXIV of GATT[108] and for the purpose of bringing good faith related violation claims.[109]

9.3   Using Tools on Conflicting Jurisdictions Within the WTO

After analysing the tools available to deal with conflicting jurisdictions, this section will further investigate which of them could be successful if invoked during WTO proceedings.

---

[106] In this respect, *see* Shaffer and Winters (2017), p. 320; Shadikhodjaev (2017), p. 121.

[107] *See supra*, Sect. 9.2.1.3.

[108] *See infra*, Sect. 9.3.2.

[109] *See infra*, Sect. 9.4.

9.3.1   Jurisdiction of the WTO Panels

For the purpose of studying conflicting jurisdictions between the WTO and the new generation EU FTAs and investigating solutions to them, the jurisdiction of the WTO panels is one of the most relevant factors. The question of jurisdiction of the WTO panels determines whether rules of international law other than those of the WTO, such as international law principles, customary norms or jurisdictional clauses, which are potential tools to deal with conflicting jurisdictions, could be enforced directly by WTO panels and the AB.

Article 1.1 of the DSU establishes that the rules and procedures of the Understanding shall apply to 'disputes brought pursuant to the consultation and dispute settlement provisions of the agreements listed in Appendix 1 to this Understanding (referred to in this Understanding as the "covered agreements")'. Since there is nothing in the text of this article that indicates otherwise, this author agrees with the doctrinaires, according to whom Article 1.1 of the DSU clearly establishes that the WTO panels have jurisdiction to decide only on claims brought under the covered agreements.[110] This interpretation of Article 1.1 is also supported by other DSU articles. Article 4.2 of the DSU provides that consultations are about 'representations made by another Member concerning measures affecting the operation of any *covered agreement* taken within the territory of the former' (emphasis added). Therefore, consultations are initiated on allegations of violations of WTO covered agreements. In addition, Article 7.1 of the DSU provides that, unless parties to the dispute agree otherwise, the terms of reference of panels are

> to examine, in the light of the relevant provisions in (name of the covered agreement(s) cited by the parties to the dispute), the matter referred to the DSB by (name of party) in document . . . and to make such findings as will assist the DSB in making the recommendations or in giving the rulings provided for in that/those agreement(s).

Therefore, the findings of the AB should help in making recommendations and issuing rulings, again, specifically on covered agreements. Moreover, Article 11 of the DSU also supports the interpretation that the jurisdiction of the WTO panels and the AB is only limited to finding violations under the WTO covered agreements. It establishes that

> a panel should make an objective assessment of the matter before it, including an objective assessment of the facts of the case and the applicability of and conformity with the relevant covered agreements, and make such other findings as will assist the DSB in making the recommendations or in giving the rulings provided for in the covered agreements.

Thus, the conformity of the matter before the panels is established according to the covered agreements, and the findings shall assist, again, in making recommendations and issuing rulings related to the covered agreements. Therefore, in accordance with Article 1.1 of the DSU, supported also by Articles 4.2, 7.1 and 11 of the DSU, WTO panels have limited jurisdiction on only WTO covered agreements.

---

[110]Bartels (2001), pp. 502–503; Marceau (2002), p. 814; Pauwelyn (2003b), p. 1000.

They have no jurisdiction to decide on the conformity of a matter with other international rules, such as general principles and customary rules of international law or FTA jurisdictional clauses that may deal with conflicting jurisdictions. Therefore, such tools cannot be enforced within WTO proceedings, and the question remains whether they could be, at least, applicable within these proceedings.

Apart from the fact that the WTO Panels and the AB have jurisdiction only on claims related to covered agreements, this jurisdiction is also exclusive. Article 23.1 establishes that

> [w]hen Members seek the redress of a violation of obligations or other nullification or impairment of benefits under the covered agreements or an impediment to the attainment of any objective of the covered agreements, they shall have recourse to, and abide by, the rules and procedures of this Understanding.'

While some have claimed that the *raison d'être* of Article 23.1 is to prevent Members from adopting unilateral measures without making use of the WTO DSM,[111] the AB confirmed that '[a]rticle 23.1 establishes the WTO dispute settlement system as the *exclusive* forum for the resolution of such disputes and requires adherence to the rules of the DSU'[112] (emphasis added). Article 23.2(a) further specifies that no determination of a violation or nullification of benefits under covered agreements can be made 'except through recourse to dispute settlement in accordance with the rules and procedures of this Understanding'. This could be interpreted as a prohibition to bring WTO-related disputes to any other forum; adjudication of such a dispute by the FTA DSM would be, thus, a violation of Article 23 of the DSU.[113] The WTO panel in *EC – Commercial Vessels* confirmed that Article 23 is violated when 'Members submit a dispute concerning rights and obligations under the WTO Agreement to an international dispute settlement body outside the WTO framework'.[114] However, this would not preclude EU FTA DSMs from adjudicating on FTA norms that incorporate or reproduce WTO norms because these claims would no longer be claims under covered agreements,[115] but would already be claims based on EU FTA norms. Article 23 of the DSU cannot prohibit other adjudicators from other international fora, such as FTA DSMs, from exercising their jurisdiction over claims arising out of FTA norms that overlap with those of the WTO.[116]

To conclude, the jurisdiction of the WTO panels is limited to WTO covered agreements. Although the WTO's jurisdiction is exclusive, it cannot affect the

---

[111] Vranes (2005), p. 287; Mbengue (2016), p. 223.

[112] Appellate Body Report, *Canada — Continued Suspension of Obligations in the EC — Hormones Dispute (Canada – Continued Suspension)*, WT/DS321/AB/R, 16 October 2008 [371].

[113] Marceau (2001), p. 1101; Kwak and Marceau (2006), p. 466; Marceau and Tomazos (2008), p. 61.

[114] Panel Report, *European Communities — Measures Affecting Trade in Commercial Vessels (EC – Commercial Vessels)*, WT/DS301/R, 22 April 2005, [7.195].

[115] Lanyi and Steinbach (2014), p. 397; Flett (2015), pp. 557–558.

[116] Zang (2019), p. 37.

jurisdiction of FTA DSMs on WTO-equal norms enshrined in FTAs. Non-WTO international tools dealing with conflicting jurisdictions cannot be enforced directly within WTO proceedings. However, non-WTO international tools could be considered indirectly under WTO norms, such as Article XXIV of GATT, over which WTO panels have jurisdiction.

9.3.2 The Exception Under Article XXIV of GATT

As WTO panels have jurisdiction only over WTO law, some scholars have suggested considering Article XXIV of GATT, Article V of GATS, and the Enabling Clause on the formation of RTAs to address conflicting jurisdictions between the DSMs of the WTO and RTAs.[117] By using these provisions, the question of jurisdiction of WTO panels over non-WTO law would be avoided and the focus would be squarely on the explicitly regulated status of FTAs under WTO law.[118]

A party could invoke Article XXIV of GATT to justify its FTA jurisdictional clause and invoke it within the WTO proceedings. Nevertheless, there are certain impediments to the invocation of such an exception, especially for the purpose considered in this section. Since a jurisdictional clause would likely require justification in relation to WTO norms on dispute settlement, the question arises which violations Article XXIV of GATT could justify and, particularly, whether it could act as an exception to DSU obligations. Some scholars argue that Article XXIV of GATT can act as an exception only to Article I of GATT, allowing Members to depart from the MFN obligation.[119] On the other hand, Article XXIV:5 of GATT itself states in the chapeau that 'the provisions of this Agreement shall not prevent', suggesting that it could be an exception not only to the MFN obligation, but also to other GATT provisions.[120] The *Turkey – Textiles* case may be instructive in this respect. The panel found that Article XXIV of GATT was not an exception to Articles XI and XIII of GATT, suggesting that it could operate as a justification only with respect to Article I violations,[121] but the reasoning of the AB from the same case seems to indicate otherwise. Thus, while not explicitly finding the obligations to which Article XXIV is an exception, the AB stated that 'the chapeau makes it clear that Article XXIV may, under certain conditions, justify the adoption of a measure which is inconsistent with *certain other GATT provisions*'[122]

---

[117] Lanyi and Steinbach (2014), pp. 400–401; Salles (2015), p. 15.

[118] Salles (2015), p. 23.

[119] Pauwelyn and Alschner (2015), p. 499; Shaffer and Winters (2017), p. 320.

[120] Herrmann (2008), p. 6.

[121] Panel Report, *Turkey – Textiles*, WET/DS34/R, 31 May 1999, [9.134; 9.154].

[122] Appellate Body Report, *Turkey – Restrictions on Imports of Textile and Clothing Products (Turkey – Textiles)*, WT/DS34/AB/R, 22 October 1999, [45].

(emphasis added). The AB's reasoning suggests that at least in theory it could serve as a justification for GATT violations other than those of the MFN.[123]

Even if other GATT articles may be covered by the exception established by Article XXIV of GATT, position which is considered here to be supported by the chapeau of the article, it still does not cover obligations contained in the DSU. In *Turkey – Textiles*, the AB considered it to be an exception to an obligation in the Agreement on Agriculture and argued that 'Article XXIV of the GATT 1994 is incorporated in the ATC and may be invoked as a defence to a claim of inconsistency with Article 2.4 of the ATC', since 'Article 2.4 of the ATC provides that "[n]o new restrictions . . . shall be introduced except under the provisions of this Agreement or relevant GATT 1994 provisions."'.[124] This logic was reaffirmed by the panel in *US – Wheat Gluten*, where it stated that '[a]rticle XXIV of the GATT 1994 [. . .] may also provide a defence to a claim of inconsistency with a provision of another covered agreement if it is somehow incorporated into that provision or agreement'.[125] The DSU does not seem to incorporate any substantive exception from the covered agreements; thus, it also does not incorporate Article XXIV of GATT. Hence, it would not be possible to claim that a violation of DSU obligations can be justified by Article XXIV of GATT. Yet, while the exception is not incorporated, Lanyi and Steinbach affirm that it may be argued that the DSU constitutes an elaboration of Articles XXII and XXIII of GATT.[126] Article 3.1 of the DSU affirms adherence to the principles applied under these GATT article and states that the DSU elaborates and further modifies them. Nevertheless, the DSU does not incorporate other GATT articles or exceptions such as Article XXIV of GATT, as it was in the *Turkey – Textiles* case. Even if Article XXIV could be used as a justification for a violation of a WTO norm on dispute settlement, as explained above, it is considered that the FTA jurisdictional clauses applicable to claims on FTA norms should not be viewed as violations of Article 23 of the DSU, as they do not infringe the exclusive jurisdiction of WTO panels over WTO norms. While a jurisdictional clause is not deemed to be in violation of the DSU, and Article XXIV of GATT is not even regarded as a viable justification for DSU violations, the consistency of jurisdictional clauses with the conditions set forth in Article XXIV will be considered *arguendo* in case the justification under Article XXIV would be extended to the DSU as an elaboration of Articles XXII and XXIII of GATT and if Article XXIV of GATT would be invoked as justification for an alleged DSU violation.

Art. XXIV:8 provides that in RTAs 'duties and other restrictive regulations of commerce (except, where necessary, those permitted under Articles XI, XII, XIII, XIV, XV and XX) are eliminated with respect to substantially all the trade'. While there is no consensus yet on the meaning of 'other restrictive regulations of

---

[123] Mathis (2002), p. 96; Brink (2010), p. 833.

[124] Appellate Body Report, *Turkey – Textiles*, fn 13.

[125] Panel Report, *United States – Definitive Safeguard Measures on Imports of Wheat Gluten from the European Communities (US – Wheat Gluten)*, 31 July 2000, WT/DS166/R, [8.180].

[126] Lanyi and Steinbach (2014), p. 401.

commerce' (ORRC),[127] it has never been proposed that such regulations could also encompass dispute settlement rules. Moreover, the bracket list that informs the meaning of ORRC is composed only of substantive obligations, showing that they do not concern dispute settlement rules that are procedural in nature. There seems to be a consensus that Article XXIV is silent on dispute settlement provisions of FTAs and their relationship with the WTO DSM.[128]

According to the AB report on *Turkey – Textiles*, for Article XXIV of GATT to be a justification, two cumulative conditions would have to be fulfilled: (1) the measure at issue should be introduced upon formation of a WTO-consistent RTA; and (2) the formation of the RTA would be prevented if it were not allowed to introduce the measure at issue.[129] For an FTA to be WTO consistent, it has to comply with Article XXIV:5(b) of GATT, according to which duties and other regulations of commerce applicable at the formation of the FTA to third parties by the constituent territories should not be higher or more restrictive than prior to the formation, and Article XXIV:8(b) on elimination of duties and ORRC on substantially all the trade (except, where necessary, those permitted under Articles XI, XII, XIII, XIV, XV and XX).[130] Both requirements established by the AB in *Turkey – Textiles* attracted criticism for being overly demanding and having no textual basis.[131] The first requirement was said to be excessive and absurd as duties or other restrictions between the parties eliminated later would not qualify under it,[132] even though they would facilitate trade between the parties in line with the purpose of RTAs prescribed by paragraph 4 of Article XXIV of GATT.[133] Moreover, according to Pauwelyn, the second requirement is said to be based on an erroneous interpretation of Article XXIV:5 of GATT that uses the word 'prevented' within the context of the relationship between the provisions of the GATT agreement and the formation of the RTA, and not of the necessity of the measure in question and the formation of the RTA.[134] At the same time, Lockhart and Mitchell argue that the second condition based on paragraph 5 of Article XXIV of GATT that addresses the external requirement of RTAs should be understood as applicable only to measures that violate third parties' rights, as it was in the case of the *Turkey – Textiles* dispute, and not on purely internal measures.[135] Notwithstanding the criticism, in *Peru – Agricultural*

---

[127] *See* Mathis (2002), pp. 227–269; Gobbi Estrella and Horlick (2006), pp. 916–920; Herrmann (2008), p. 7.

[128] Kwak and Marceau (2006), p. 477; Yang (2012), p. 298; de Mestral (2013), p. 818; Lanyi and Steinbach (2014), p. 401; de Chazournes (2017).

[129] Appellate Body Report, *Turkey – Textiles*, [45–46; 58].

[130] Appellate Body Report, *Turkey – Textiles*, [52] on the need for a CU to be WTO-consistent for Article XXIV of GATT to be invoked as a defence.

[131] *See* Pauwelyn (2004b), pp. 131–135; Kuijper (2010), p. 21; Salles (2015), p. 24.

[132] Pauwelyn (2004b), p. 132.

[133] Appellate Body Report, *Turkey – Textiles*, [57].

[134] Pauwelyn (2004b), pp. 133–134.

[135] Lockhart and Mitchell (2005), pp. 226–228.

Products, the AB reaffirmed and invoked the two-tier test established in *Turkey –
Textiles*,[136] even though this case concerned an internal measure that did not violate
a third party's rights. Therefore, unless this approach is revised, the same two-tier
test would be applicable to an FTA jurisdictional clause if it was argued that it should
be justified by Article XXIV of GATT.

If, *arguendo*, Article XXIV of GATT would be considered a justification for a
jurisdictional clause, it would have to comply with the two-tier test. The second
condition, requiring demonstration that in the absence of the measure at issue RTA
formation would be prevented, makes justification of a jurisdictional clause highly
unlikely. Nevertheless, a jurisdictional clause could be invoked and considered
together with a substantive FTA norm that falls under the coverage of these FTA
clauses, and for whose justification Article XXIV of GATT would be claimed. It
could be argued that DSM provisions are necessary in general for enforcement of
FTA norms and that the parties would not be ready to assume commitments to
further liberalise trade under an FTA, and hence the formation of the FTA would be
prevented, were it not for the FTA DSM.[137] Yet, this argument is unlikely to be
successful in the case of FTA norms that merely reproduce or incorporate WTO
norms that can be enforced through the available WTO DSM. Even in the context of
the current AB crisis, panels can still be established and cases heard at the WTO.
Hence, while jurisdictional clauses could ensure that FTA parties do not initiate
parallel and subsequent multilateral and bilateral proceedings, with the aim of
safeguarding coherence in the international trade law regime, it may be difficult to
argue that the formation of an FTA would be prevented without them as the WTO
DSM would remain available as a forum, unless the dispute would also concern
obligations available only at the FTA level.[138]

To conclude, the use of Article XXIV to justify a jurisdictional clause for giving
consideration to it does not raise jurisdictional hurdles. Nevertheless, this section
argued that Article XXIV is not an exception to DSU obligations. Even if it were an
exception, there would be no DSU violation by FTA jurisdictional clauses to be
justified, and these clauses would probably not qualify under the two-tier test
established by the AB in its jurisprudence for justification under Article XXIV of
GATT, unless the jurisprudence is deviated from. Therefore, it seems unlikely that
using the avenue of Article XXIV of GATT is the answer to the issue of jurisdictional conflicts.

---

[136] Appellate Body Report, *Peru – Agricultural Products,* [5.115].

[137] Lanyi and Steinbach (2014), p. 401.

[138] Ibid.

9.3.3 Applicable Law Within the WTO DSM

Although WTO panels have no jurisdiction to enforce other rules of international law except the covered agreements, and it is unlikely that Article XXIV of GATT can be used to resolve the issue of conflicting jurisdiction between FTA and WTO DSMs, some authors have advocated for a distinction to be made between the concepts of jurisdiction and applicable law.[139] Thus, while jurisdiction defines the claims that an international court or tribunal can examine and decide on, applicable law refers to the law that such a court may apply when examining and making determinations on the claims.[140] According to this distinction, even if panels do not have jurisdiction to decide on matters other than WTO law, they can nevertheless decide on a claim of violation of WTO law while applying non-WTO international law, such as general principles and customary rules of public international law, which may also act as legal avenues for jurisdictional clauses.

9.3.3.1 Articles 7 and 11 of the DSU

The DSU does not contain an express provision on which norms are applicable within WTO proceedings. For determining what the applicable law is by WTO Panels and the AB, reference is usually made to Articles 7, 11, 3.2, and 19.2 of the DSU. Article 7 establishes in the first paragraph that the terms of reference of the panels are 'to examine, in the light of' the relevant provisions from the covered agreements cited by the parties[141] the matter referred to the DSB, and continues in the second paragraph that '[p]anels shall address the relevant provisions in any covered agreement or agreements cited by the parties to the dispute'. At the same time, Article 11 of the DSU provides that 'a panel should make an objective assessment of the matter before it, including an objective assessment of the facts of the case and the *applicability* of and conformity with the relevant covered agreements' (emphasis added).[142]

These articles have been used to support completely opposite views. Some authors read these provisions narrowly and find support in them for the statement that non-WTO law cannot be applied by the panels, since both Articles 7 and 11 refer only to the covered agreements.[143] This position may be supported by the fact that Article 11 specifically uses the term 'applicability' only with respect to covered agreements.[144] Therefore, according to the narrow interpretation of Articles 7 and 11 of the DSU, as long as the possibility of using non-WTO law is not expressly

---

[139] Bartels (2001), pp. 501–502; Pauwelyn (2004a), p. 910; Vranes (2005), pp. 265–289.

[140] Pauwelyn (2004a), p. 910.

[141] For the full text of Art 7.1 of the DSU, *see supra*, Sect. 9.3.1.

[142] For the full text of Art 11 of the DSU, *see supra*, Sect. 9.3.1.

[143] Trachtman (1999), p. 342; Marceau (2001), p. 1102; Weiss (2003), p. 193.

[144] Trachtman (1999), p. 342.

provided, the DSU does not allow their application. Others interpret these articles more broadly and suggest that they do not present an exhaustive list of applicable norms and that there is nothing in the DSU that would prohibit the application of non-WTO law.[145] Moreover, according to this view, WTO panels may even need to apply non-WTO law 'to make findings as will assist the DSB in making the recommendations or in giving the rulings',[146] as provided by both articles and to 'make an objective assessment of the matter', as required by Article 11 of the DSU.[147] According to this broad approach, there is no need for the DSU to expressly provide that other international law is applicable in WTO proceedings, since the WTO is part of international law and it can apply it, by default, as long as states have not contracted out of it.[148] The statement of the panel in *Korea – Procurement* is also in support of this position:

> Customary international law applies generally to the economic relations between the WTO Members. Such international law applies to the extent that the WTO treaty agreements do not 'contract out' from it. To put it another way, to the extent there is no conflict or inconsistency, or an expression in a covered WTO agreement that implies differently, we are of the view that the customary rules of international law apply to the WTO treaties and to the process of treaty formation under the WTO.[149]

A third group of scholars consider both articles as being inconclusive with respect to the applicable law within the WTO DSM,[150] a position which is also shared by the present author. The requirements to examine 'in the light of' the cited provisions from the covered agreements in Article 7 of the DSU and to make an 'objective assessment [...] of the applicability of and conformity with the relevant covered agreements' in Article 11 of the DSU do not restrict the sources that can be applied.[151] However, they also do not expressly allow it. These provisions are too general to offer textual support for the broader view, but are also too unspecific to back the narrow perspective.[152]

Therefore, these articles are considered inconclusive for the purpose of establishing the applicability of non-WTO law, such as general principles and customary norms of international law, which could also represent legal avenues for jurisdictional clauses. While the broader view would square better with the position in favour of coherent international law adopted in this book, this coherence is limited by the existing legal framework reflecting the will of the states. The

---

[145] Pauwelyn (2003b), p. 1001; de Mestral (2013), p. 806.

[146] Pauwelyn (2003a), pp. 468–469.

[147] Pauwelyn (2003b), p. 1020.

[148] Ibid, pp. 1001–1002.

[149] Panel Report, *Korea – Measures Affecting Government Procurement* (*Korea – Procurement*), WT/DS163/R, 1 May 2000, [7.96].

[150] Bartels (2001), pp. 504–506; Vranes (2005), pp. 284–286.

[151] Bartels (2001), pp. 504–506.

[152] Vranes (2005), p. 286.

concept of 'limited coherence' has been described in detail in the conceptual framework.[153]

9.3.3.2   Articles 3.2 and 19.2 of the DSU

Articles 7 and 11 of the DSU do not restrict the application of international law, as it was rightly pointed out by Pauwelyn and the panel in *Korea – Procurement*.[154] The WTO is part of international law and is, therefore, subject to general international law, including treaty law, to the extent that parties have not contracted out of it. Thus, while the DSU does not impose any express *a priori* restriction on the applicable sources of international law, it does so with respect to application of such law in given cases.[155] It is submitted that such restriction through which WTO Members have to some extent contracted out of public international law rules is found in the last sentence of Article 3.2 and in Article 19.2 of the DSU which establish that recommendations and rulings of the DSB 'cannot add to or diminish the rights and obligations provided in the covered agreements.' There is no complete agreement in the doctrine on the interpretation of these articles.

Some interpret them in a literal way, arguing that their text is unambiguous and generally prohibits WTO panels and the AB from 'add[ing] to or diminish[ing]' the rights and obligations provided in WTO covered agreements.[156] It also depends on whether the last sentence of Article 3.2 of the DSU is read in conjunction with the second or first part of the previous sentence. Pauwelyn, for example, interprets these articles as being only statements against judicial activism during the process of interpretation, since the phrase follows the previous sentence of Article 3.2 of the DSU that stipulates in the second part that the aim of the WTO DSM is 'to clarify the existing provisions of those agreements in accordance with customary rules of interpretation of public international law'.[157] It has also been argued that since all norms of international law could be applicable, their application would not add to or diminish Member's rights and obligations.[158] Moreover, Pauwelyn argues that this also constitutes a clear recognition that the WTO 'frames itself in the wider context of public international law'.[159] Nonetheless, if the last sentence of Article 3.2 of the DSU is read in light of the first part of the preceding sentence establishing that another aim of the WTO DSM is 'to preserve the rights and obligations of Members under the covered agreements',[160] there is no reason to consider that the prohibition

---

[153] *See supra*, Sect. 3.1.6.

[154] Pauwelyn (2003b), p. 1001–1002; Panel Report, *Korea – Procurement*, [7.96].

[155] Bartels (2001), p. 506.

[156] Trachtman (1999), p. 342; Marceau (2001), p. 1102.

[157] Pauwelyn (2003b), p. 1003. This position is also supported in Mitchell (2007), p. 809.

[158] Pauwelyn (2001), p. 566; Mitchell (2007), p. 828.

[159] Pauwelyn (2003b), p. 1001.

[160] *See* Vranes (2005), p. 283, for criticism of such a reading.

'to add to or diminish' WTO rights is only a statement against activism during interpretation.

Article 3.2 of the DSU is deemed here a statement that generally prohibits panels from adding to or diminishing rights and obligations in the covered agreements. This interpretation has been adopted because it is considered to be confirmed by the repetition of the prohibition to 'add to and diminish rights and obligations' in Article 19.2 of the DSU that refers generally to panel and AB findings and recommendations, without specifying that it should be respected exclusively in the process of interpretation. Thus, the prohibition in Article 19.2 of the DSU is not preceded by any reference to the customary rules of interpretation. Furthermore, the argument that potentially applicable international law would not add to or diminish Members' rights cannot be supported, as Article 3.2 of the DSU seems to be concerned with the integrity of the 'rights and obligations provided in the covered agreements' and not with all the rights and obligations of Members. Accordingly, it is submitted that Articles 3.2 and 19.2 of the DSU clearly establish that adding to and diminishing WTO rights and obligations is prohibited and that it is not only a statement against judicial activism.

WTO panels and the AB cannot apply non-WTO international sources of law that diminish Members' rights and obligations provided in the covered agreements. If non-WTO conflicting jurisdiction tools, such as general principles and customary norms of international law that can also serve as avenues for jurisdictional clauses, were applicable within WTO proceedings without having a legal basis in the WTO agreements, the WTO Members' right to WTO proceedings would be added to or diminished. WTO Members have the right to initiate proceedings on WTO claims; this can be deduced from Article 23 of the DSU, which mandates recourse to proceedings under the DSU for WTO claims, as well as from Article 3.3 of the DSU, according to which prompt settlement of disputes is essential when 'a Member *considers* that any benefits accruing to it directly or indirectly under the covered agreements are being impaired by measures taken by another Member' (emphasis added). The fact that recourse to WTO proceedings is mandated and that it can take place whenever a Member considers appropriate has been interpreted by the AB as implying that Members are entitled to a panel ruling.[161] It seems uncontroversial in the doctrine that there is *a right* to initiate WTO proceedings. Application of non-WTO tools that deal with conflicting jurisdictions and lead to the denial or restriction of the WTO DSM jurisdiction would cause a diminution of the right to initiate WTO proceedings and a violation of Articles 3.2 and 19.2 of the DSU. Therefore, the general principles related to good faith without a legal basis in the DSU, Article 45(a) of the ILC articles on state responsibility, and international rules on conflict of norms as legal avenues for FTA jurisdictional clauses cannot be

---

[161] Appellate Body Report, *United States – Sunset Review of Anti-Dumping Duties on Corrosion-Resistant Carbon Steel Flat Products from Japan (US – Corrosion-Resistant Steel Sunset Review)*, WT/DS244/AB/R, 15 December 2003, [89]; Appellate Body Report, *Mexico – Tax Measures on Soft Drinks and Other Beverages (Mexico – Soft Drinks)*, WT/DS308/AB/R, 6 March 2006, [52].

applied by WTO panels and the AB to diminish the Members' right to WTO proceedings.

To conclude, it is submitted that the distinction between jurisdiction and applicability seems to bring no benefit to using the tools identified for addressing the conflicting jurisdictions between the WTO and FTA DSMs.

9.3.3.3   Using International Law Not As Applicable Law

Despite the fact that the applicable law is limited by Articles 3.2 and 19.2 of the DSU and, therefore, non-WTO tools to deal with conflicting jurisdictions cannot be applied within WTO proceedings, these tools could still play a role for a distinct purpose.

First, international law, including FTA norms, could be used within WTO proceedings for interpretative purposes according to Article 3.2 of the DSU. As the use of 'customary rules of interpretation of public international law' to clarify WTO provisions is expressly prescribed by the DSU, this type of use is not controversial. Second, international law could be used as a fact for making legal determinations under WTO law. Reference to rules from other legal regimes may be necessary to establish the relevant facts for determining conformity with WTO rules.[162] Thus, an FTA jurisdictional clause could serve as evidence of non-compliance with a WTO norm.[163] This type of use of non-WTO law is also confirmed by statements made by WTO panels and the AB. For example, the panel in *India – Autos*, referring to the MAS agreement, stated that while a panel cannot consider claims on the violation of such an agreement, '[i]t does not necessarily prove that a panel may not in some circumstances need to consider the terms of such agreed solutions in order to fulfil its duties under the DSU'.[164] More recently, in *Peru – Agricultural Products*, the AB looked into FTA provisions and asserted that 'we are of the view that the consideration of provisions of an FTA for the purpose of determining whether a Member has complied with its WTO obligations involves legal characterizations that fall within the scope of appellate review'.[165] Using non-WTO law, therefore, may be necessary for the panels to 'make an objective assessment of the facts of the case', according to Article 11 of the DSU.[166] How jurisdictional clauses could be used in the context of claims on violation of the good faith obligations enshrined in the DSU will be addressed comprehensively later in this chapter.[167]

---

[162] Marceau (2002), p. 764; Trachtman (2005), p. 136; Bartels 2016, pp. 12–13.

[163] Natens and Descheemaeker (2015), p. 883.

[164] Panel Report, *India – Measures Affecting the Automotive Sector (India – Autos)*, WT/DS146/R, 21 December 2001, footnote 364 to [7.115].

[165] Appellate Body Report, *Peru – Agricultural Products*, [5.86].

[166] For more on different ways of considering non-WTO law when applying WTO law, *see* Weiss (2003), pp. 194–195.

[167] *See infra*, Sect. 9.4.

International law could also be used to fill gaps on procedural issues, allowing proper adjudicative functioning of international courts and tribunals. The concept of 'inherent powers' based on which such a use of international law relies on, as well as the possibility of using tools dealing with conflicting jurisdictions as part of these inherent powers, will be analysed in more detail in the next section.

9.3.4   WTO Panels Declining or Not Exercising Jurisdiction

Despite the fact that WTO panels can decide only on WTO covered agreements and have exclusive jurisdiction to do so and the applicability of non-WTO law is limited, the question arises whether they could decline their jurisdiction as part of their inherent powers when a conflict of jurisdiction arises.

9.3.4.1   Inherent Powers

The DSU does not provide an express right to the panels to decline or decide on their own jurisdiction. However, it may be argued that even without the express conferment of the right to decline their validly established jurisdiction, WTO panels and the AB, similar to other international courts,[168] enjoy some inherent powers.

It is generally recognised that an international court or tribunal enjoys inherent powers[169] merely because of its status, regardless of the presence of a clause in its constitutive treaty texts, based on the presumption that once states consented to the creation of a court or tribunal, they also consented to its inherent powers.[170] Inherent powers are the functional powers necessary for tribunals and courts to be able to carry out their adjudicative function, even in situations in which their constitutive treaties are silent.[171] Thus, inherent powers allow a court or tribunal to react to unforeseen circumstances when matters that are not regulated by their constitutive treaty arise.[172] Under the inherent powers doctrine, principles recognised as customary international law or general principles of law may be used to resolve emerging issues. An unforeseen circumstance that is not expressly regulated in the

---

[168] The ICJ explained what its inherent powers are in *Northern Cameroons (Cameroon v United Kingdom, Preliminary Objections, Judgment,* [1963] ICJ Rep 15, ICGJ 153 (ICJ 1963), 2nd December 1963, International Court of Justice)*, Nuclear Tests (Australia v France, Interim Protection, Order,* [1973] ICJ Rep 99, ICGJ 130 (ICJ 1973), 22nd June 1973, International Court of Justice), and *Legality of Use of Force, Yugoslavia v Belgium, Order, Provisional Measures,* ICJ GL No 105, [1999] ICJ Rep 124, ICGJ 32 (ICJ 1999), 2nd June 1999, International Court of Justice).

[169] Nguyen (2016), p. 282; Lanyi and Steinbach (2014), p. 378; Hartmann (2016), p. 633.

[170] Van Damme (2009), p. 166.

[171] Van Damme (2009), p. 166; Hartmann (2016), p. 622.

[172] Henckels (2008), p. 583.

constitutive treaties and requires the use of inherent powers to respond to it is the situation in which it would be necessary to decline jurisdiction because of international principles on conflicting jurisdictions, such as those introduced earlier.[173]

Although WTO panels and the AB are not called international courts or tribunals and have some atypical diplomatic features in their proceedings,[174] they clearly have a judicial character stemming from the judicial procedures prescribed by the DSU. In addition, practice confirms that they acted from the beginning as if they were courts.[175] Therefore, WTO panels and the AB, as international adjudicative bodies, should also be regarded as possessing certain inherent powers. While most authors recognise that WTO panels enjoy some inherent powers, there is no agreement on their extent. On the one hand, some authors affirm that WTO panels enjoy extensive inherent powers and see nothing in the DSU that limits their power to decline jurisdiction.[176] On the other hand, others claim that WTO panels have inherent powers to the extent that they are implied in the DSU (known as 'implied powers' doctrine).[177] These approaches highlight the tension that exists between the concept of 'inherent powers' and state consent. A more balanced approach is to recognise that inherent powers can be exercised as long as they do not contravene the constitutive agreement. If WTO panels did not possess inherent powers that are necessarily implied in the text, they would be unable to function properly given that there are procedural gaps in the DSU for regulation of all the procedural matters.[178] Nevertheless, inherent powers can be distinguished from implied ones. Thus, in order to exercise their powers under the DSU, it may be necessary for panels to have additional, implied powers to ensure that DSU powers are efficiently exercised.[179] In contrast to inherent powers that are not implied in any way in the DSU, '[a] tribunal relying on implied powers would look to the text of its constitutive document to determine if a particular power or authority exists.'[180]

The scope of the rules that can be used pursuant to inherent powers cannot be exhaustively defined.[181] Therefore, whether an international tribunal makes use of its inherent powers will need to be decided on a case-by-case basis. The conditions developed by Mitchell and Heaton for rules to be applied pursuant to inherent powers will be adopted here. According to Mitchell and Heaton, only international law rules that satisfy the following three conditions can be used as part of inherent

---

[173] For such principles and their status in international law, *See supra*, Sect. 9.2.1.

[174] An atypical feature is the requirement that panel reports must be adopted in order to be binding. Nevertheless, because of the negative consensus rule, adoption becomes quasi-automatic (Mitchell and Heaton 2010, pp. 567–568).

[175] McRae (2004), pp. 7–8.

[176] Henckels (2008), p. 594; Pauwelyn and Salles (2009), p. 101.

[177] Marceau (2002), pp. 764–765.

[178] Hartmann (2016), p. 631.

[179] Van Damme (2009), p. 191.

[180] Hartmann (2016), p. 622.

[181] Mitchell and Heaton (2010), p. 572.

powers: (1) they are necessary for the proper exercise of adjudicative function, (2) they have no substantive content of their own, and (3) they are not inconsistent with the covered agreements.[182] The first and second conditions can be easily complied with by the tools that deal with conflicting jurisdictions. It could be argued that their application would be necessary for panels' judicial functioning in order to establish whether WTO panels should decline their jurisdiction—a matter not explicitly regulated or implied in the DSU. Moreover, these tools either have a procedural nature, as they regulate the jurisdiction of the courts[183] or, in the case of good faith obligations and its manifestations, they have no autonomous substantive content as they affect the ability of states to rely on their rights subject to their own conduct.[184] The third condition is, however, of particular importance for this analysis and has also been confirmed by the ICJ.[185] An international court or tribunal cannot exercise its inherent powers in a way incompatible with the texts agreed by the states and included in the constitutive agreement. While inherent powers are presumed, due to the agreement of the states to create a court or tribunal, states can depart from this presumption by providing express rules in their agreements limiting such powers. In other words, inherent powers are limited by states' consent and cannot be used *carte blanche* by courts and tribunals to do what they want.[186] This approach is in line with the concept of limited coherence developed here, according to which coherence is limited by the existing legal framework reflecting the will of the states.[187]

The AB has stated that it enjoys certain inherent powers. In *US – Lead and Bismuth II*, the AB ascertained that it 'has broad authority to adopt procedural rules which do not conflict with any rules and procedures in the DSU or the covered agreements.'[188] Thus, with this statement, the AB confirmed the last two requirements for application of rules based on inherent powers developed by Mitchell and Heaton and adopted here. Similar to the ICJ and other doctrinaires, the AB seems to adopt a concept of inherent powers that is limited in case of inconsistencies with the WTO covered agreements. In *India – Autos*, the panel also confirmed that 'it is certainly true that certain widely recognized principles of international law have been found to be applicable in WTO dispute settlement, particularly concerning

---

[182]Ibid, p. 566.

[183]*Res judicata, lis alibi pendens, forum non conveniens*, and comity are all by their nature procedural principles as they deal with jurisdictional issues (*See supra*, Sects. 9.2.1.1 and 9.2.1.2).

[184]Mitchell and Heaton (2010), pp. 608, 616.

[185]ICJ, *Nottebohm Case (Liechtenstein v Guatemala) (Preliminary Objection)*, ICJ Reports (1953) 111, 119; ICJ, *Case of Certain Norwegian Loans (France v Norway)*, Separate Opinion Judge Lauterpacht, ICJ Reports (1957) 34, 45.

[186]Brown (2007), p. 78.

[187]*See supra*, Sect. 3.1.6.

[188]Appellate Body Report, *US – Imposition of Countervailing Duties on Certain Hot-Rolled Lead and Bismuth Carbon Steel Products Originating in the United Kingdom, (US – Lead and Bismuth II)*, WT/DS138/AB/R, 7 June 2000, [39].

fundamental procedural matters'.[189] In a different case, *US – 1916 Act,* the AB confirmed that 'it is a widely accepted rule that an international tribunal is entitled to consider the issue of its own jurisdiction on its own initiative, and to satisfy itself that it has jurisdiction in any case that comes before it'.[190] Thus, the AB reaffirmed that it enjoys inherent powers by endorsing the principle of *la compétence de la compétence,* according to which courts and tribunals can decide on their own jurisdiction— a principle that has been referred to as 'perhaps the best known example of an inherent power'.[191] Another example of an expression of inherent powers is the principle of judicial economy, according to which panels may refrain from ruling on one or more claims in a dispute that are not necessary for the resolution of the matter at issue in the case.[192]

This section introduced the concept of inherent powers, presented the conditions under which such powers could be used, and established that WTO panels and the AB enjoy inherent powers.

9.3.4.2 *Mexico – Soft Drinks* and Legal Impediments to the Exercise of Jurisdiction

After introducing the concept of inherent powers, this section continues by investigating whether WTO panels could decline their jurisdiction pursuant to such powers and the conditions attached to such a refusal.

The issue of declining jurisdiction was dealt with in the *Mexico – Soft Drinks* case, in which Mexico argued that, based on their implied jurisdictional powers, the panels should have declined to exercise their jurisdiction because the US claims were 'inextricably linked to a broader dispute' under NAFTA.[193] The broader dispute concerned the regulation of sweeteners under that agreement. Mexico claimed that the US was not complying with its NAFTA obligations, so it took the dispute to the FTA DSM.[194] However, the US blocked the formation of a panel to hear the dispute, in response to which Mexico imposed measures to remedy the alleged non-compliance of the FTA, which were challenged under the WTO rules in *Mexico – Soft Drinks.*[195] While measures were taken unilaterally in *Mexico – Soft Drinks* because FTA panel formation was blocked, countermeasures allegedly in

---

[189] Panel Report, *India – Autos,* [7.57], footnotes omitted.

[190] Appellate Body Report, *United States – Anti-Dumping Act of 1916 (US – 1916 Act),* WT/DS136/AB/R, WT/DS162/AB/R, 28 August 2000, [54] fn 30.

[191] Brown (2007), p. 63.

[192] Van Damme (2009), p. 180. Such an inherent power was also confirmed by the Appellate Body Report, *Mexico – Soft Drinks,* [45].

[193] Ibid [42, 45].

[194] For more on the dispute, *see* Davey and Sapir (2009), pp. 5–23.

[195] Panel Report, *Mexico – Soft Drinks,* WT/DS308/R, 7 October 2005, [4.72].

violation of WTO norms could also have been imposed based on the authorisation of an FTA panel.

According to Mexico, as the dispute arose under NAFTA, it would have been 'inappropriate for this Panel to hear it'.[196] Hence, although not expressly stating it, Mexico's assertion seems to refer to either the doctrine of comity[197] or the doctrine of *forum non conveniens*.[198] In *Mexico – Soft Drinks,* the AB, in line with its previous jurisprudence,[199] expressly recognised that 'WTO panels have certain powers that are inherent in their adjudicative function', notably to 'have the right to determine whether they have jurisdiction in a given case, as well as to determine the scope of their jurisdiction'.[200] However, it continued that it does not mean that it has the authority to decline its validly established jurisdiction and that it cannot modify the substantive provisions of the DSU.[201] According to the AB, by declining their jurisdiction, panels would not be able to fulfil their obligations to 'examine' the claims before them or to 'make findings' on the consistency of the measures, as required by Article 7.1 of the DSU, nor to 'address the relevant provisions in any covered agreement or agreements cited by the parties to the dispute,' according to Article 7.2 of the DSU, and 'to make an objective assessment of the matter before them' and make findings that will assist the DSB, as required by Article 11 of the DSU.[202] Most importantly, the AB stated that this would also be against Articles 3.2 and 19.2 of the DSU, according to which recommendations and rulings of the DSB 'cannot add to or diminish the rights and obligations provided in the covered agreements.' By declining their jurisdiction, panels would diminish the obligation and the right of Members to bring WTO claims to the WTO DSM under Article 23 of the DSU,[203] and would, thus, act against what is prescribed by the DSU. Therefore, based on the AB's report, it can be inferred that WTO panels cannot use their inherent powers to apply principles of international law not contained in the DSU, such as the principles of comity and *forum non conveniens*, if they lead to the refusal of their validly established jurisdiction. The question of using international principles embodied in the DSU is, however, different.

While the interpretation of inherent powers in the AB report in *Mexico – Soft Drinks* has been criticised for being too rigid[204] and the report characterised as

---

[196] Panel Report, *Mexico – Soft Drinks,* [4.71].

[197] Mitchell and Heaton (2010), p. 599, for example, assert that 'Mexico's arguments in Mexico-Soft Drinks amounted effectively to an invocation of comity in all but name'.

[198] Lanyi and Steinbach (2014), p. 388, state that Mexico's claim falls under the *forum non conveniens* doctrine: 'It did not argue that the Panel was legally precluded from ruling, but that the panel shall refrain from exercising jurisdiction based on *forum non conveniens*'.

[199] *See supra,* (nn 188–191).

[200] Appellate Body Report, *Mexico – Soft Drinks*, [45].

[201] Ibid [46].

[202] Ibid [48–51].

[203] Ibid [53].

[204] Henckels (2008), p. 591.

'worrisome' and 'unjust' for giving too little weight to the unfairness of the situation in which one party unlawfully frustrates an available dispute settlement procedure agreed between the parties,[205] as established in the conceptual framework, this author considers that the strive for coherence is limited by the legal framework. As previously stated, this author considers that Article 3.2 of the DSU is not a mere statement against judicial activism and that it would be violated if a Member's right to proceedings were diminished.[206] Therefore, despite the inherent powers that WTO panels generally enjoy, it is submitted that when panels decline their jurisdiction, they would act against the DSU and would not be able to exercise their inherent powers for this purpose, as it would be against the condition not to be inconsistent with the covered agreements.[207]

Although the AB established that WTO panels cannot decline their jurisdiction, it appears to have opened the door to other 'legal impediments' to the exercise of their jurisdiction.[208] The AB stated that it expressed 'no view as to whether there may be other circumstances in which legal impediments could exist that would preclude a panel from ruling on the merits of the claims that are before it.'[209] Although the AB mentioned that it did not express a view on whether such circumstances are legal impediments, it nevertheless specified that 'neither the subject matter nor the respective positions of the parties are identical in the dispute under the NAFTA . . . and the dispute before us', 'no NAFTA panel as yet has decided the "broader dispute" to which Mexico has alluded', and that 'the so-called "exclusion clause" of Article 2005.6 of the NAFTA, had not been "exercised"'.[210] Therefore, the AB seems to imply that had the same dispute been decided by a NAFTA panel and Article 2005.6 been exercised, the outcome of the case could have been different. Article 2005.6 of NAFTA is a fork-in-the-road clause providing that '[o]nce dispute settlement procedures have been initiated under Article 2007 or dispute settlement proceedings have been initiated under the GATT, the forum selected shall be used to the exclusion of the other'.

The AB's reference to 'legal impediments' may seem to contradict the previous conclusion that declining validly established jurisdiction would 'diminish' the rights and obligations of the parties under the DSU. Some authors argue that a distinction should be made between jurisdiction and admissibility as preliminary questions.[211] While jurisdiction refers to the scope of the tribunals' authority, admissibility concerns the conditions for the claims before the tribunal, such as exhaustion of local remedies or the conduct of the parties in the dispute settlement proceedings.[212]

---

[205] Kuijper (2010), pp. 34–35; Forere (2015), p. 84.

[206] See supra, Sect. 9.3.3.2.

[207] See supra, (nn 182–188).

[208] Marceau and Wyatt (2010), p. 71; Mbengue (2016), p. 236.

[209] Appellate Body Report, *Mexico – Soft Drinks*, [54].

[210] Ibid.

[211] See Pauwelyn and Salles (2009), pp. 92–102; Bartels (2016), pp. 8–10; Zang (2019), pp. 35–38.

[212] Pauwelyn and Salles (2009), p. 94; Bartels (2016), p. 9.

Therefore, it may be argued that by finding certain claims inadmissible and suspending and terminating the proceedings, the panel would, nevertheless, retain its jurisdiction.[213] The AB's statement that 'legal impediments could exist that would preclude a panel from ruling on the merits of the claims' may be perceived as supporting the distinction between these concepts. Nevertheless, as Pauwelyn and Salles recognise in their attempt to advocate for using admissibility to address conflicting jurisdictions, in the exercise of its inherent powers, a panel would consider admissibility as a preliminary question.[214] Deciding that a claim is inadmissible because of the jurisdiction of another tribunal and terminating proceedings would still 'diminish' the right of parties to seek redress for a violation of obligations under Article 23 of the DSU.[215] Therefore, while the distinction between jurisdiction and admissibility could be recognised and may even be useful, it can hardly change the fact that by declining their jurisdiction or declaring the claims inadmissible, panels would act against the DSU, and, thus, cannot exercise their inherent powers for this particular purpose.

Nevertheless, the AB clearly stated that there still could be 'legal impediments' to the exercise of a panel's jurisdiction. If declining jurisdiction or declaring claims inadmissible would diminish the rights of Members, such rights would not be diminished if principles of international law incorporated into the DSU, for example in Articles 3.7 and 3.10, were used for this purpose.[216] While the WTO panel and the AB in *Mexico – Soft Drinks* did not describe in detail the so-called 'legal impediments' and requirements that would apply to them, the AB report indicated what such impediments could be in a footnote. In footnote 101, the AB cited its statement from *EC – Export Subsidies on Sugar*, according to which 'there is little in the DSU that explicitly limits the rights of WTO Members to bring an action'.[217] This statement was followed by references to Articles 3.7 and 3.10 of the DSU.[218] Thus, these articles expressly provide requirements for Members when bringing a WTO dispute; by acting against the principle of good faith, they may limit their right to bring an action with their own conduct. If an FTA party agreed in a jurisdictional clause that the FTA DSMs shall be used for disputes arising from FTAs, or that parallel or subsequent WTO and FTA proceedings were prohibited, and afterwards it initiated WTO proceedings contrary to the conditions stated in the FTA clause, this could be argued as being a violation of the good faith obligation enshrined in Articles 3.7 and 3.10 of the DSU. Consequently, such a violation could constitute a legal impediment that would preclude panels from ruling on the merits of the case.

---

[213] Pauwelyn and Salles (2009), p. 96.

[214] Ibid.

[215] Although not making an argument based on the conditions for inherent powers, Bartels concluded that '[t]he Appellate Body can be understood as saying that the DSU overrode the admissibility condition that was advanced by the respondent' (Bartels 2016, p. 10).

[216] *See supra*, Sect. 9.2.1.3.

[217] Appellate Body Report, *European Communities – Export Subsidies on Sugar*, [312].

[218] Appellate Body Report, *Mexico – Soft Drinks*, fn 101 to [52].

Although jurisdictional clauses cannot be applicable law within WTO proceedings, they can be used in the determination of violations of Articles 3.7 and 3.10 of the DSU.[219] Therefore, it is submitted that, in line with the concept of limited coherence developed in the conceptual framework, Articles 3.7 and 3.10 of the DSU could be used together with FTA jurisdictional clauses treated as evidence to address conflicting jurisdictions between the WTO and FTA DSMs.

To conclude, WTO panels cannot use their inherent powers to apply principles of international law that are not enshrined in the DSU, such as the principles of comity and *forum non conveniens*, when they require the panels to decline their validly established jurisdiction. Nonetheless, there may be 'legal impediments' to the exercise of a panel's jurisdiction enshrined in the DSU. The failure of a Member to initiate disputes in good faith could present a situation in which there would be a DSU legal impediment to rule on a case, because the right of a Member to bring a dispute would be affected and limited by its own conduct. Accordingly, the following section will analyse the possibility and conditions for using the principle of good faith enshrined in Articles 3.7 and 3.10 of the DSU as a potential legal impediment to the exercise of the panels' jurisdiction. Articles 3.7 and 3.10 of the DSU could be considered violated based on the evidence provided by FTA jurisdictional clauses.

9.4   WTO Members' Rights to WTO Proceedings Limited by the Breach of DSU Good Faith Obligations[220]

In several cases, without applying non-WTO law, declining their jurisdiction or declaring claims inadmissible based on their inherent powers, WTO panels and the AB had to rule on whether Members were prevented from initiating WTO proceedings because of their own conduct. As mentioned, WTO Members could be in violation of the principle of good faith, as enshrined in Articles 3.7 and 3.10 of the DSU, by initiating proceedings in one forum and then seeking redress for the same claims in another after undertaking not to do so under an FTA jurisdictional clause. Panels' refusal to exercise their jurisdiction based on non-WTO law would diminish a Member's right to WTO proceedings. However, if the exercise of the jurisdiction is limited by the parties' own conduct as expressly established under Articles 3.7 and 3.10 of the DSU, Members' rights would stay intact and a panel's decision not to exercise its jurisdiction would not contravene the DSU, since the decision would only follow the Undertaking to the letter. The following sections will review the relevant WTO case law to confirm that Articles 3.7 and 3.10 of the DSU could serve as available avenues to invoke a jurisdictional clause and resolve the issue of conflicting jurisdictions and identify the conditions with which a claim of good faith violation would have to comply.

---

[219]Zang (2019), p. 41.

[220]This section is based on a previous draft originally published as Furculita (2019).

9.4.1   Argentina – Poultry

In *Argentina – Poultry*, the panel dealt with a claim of violation of the principle of good faith that allegedly also warranted the invocation of the principle of estoppel.[221] According to Argentina, Brazil (the complainant) failed to act in good faith when it unsuccessfully challenged an anti-dumping measure before MERCOSUR and subsequently initiated WTO procedures on the same dispute within the WTO.[222] While Articles 3.7 and 3.10 of the DSU were not invoked in this dispute, the case is suggestive with respect to conditions for a claim of good faith violation as well as the potential role of jurisdictional clauses.

Citing the AB's report from *US – Offset Act (Byrd Amendment)*,[223] the panel established two conditions for a violation of good faith to be found: (1) a violation of a substantive WTO norm; and (2) 'more than a mere violation'.[224] Since Argentina did not invoke any violation of a substantive WTO norm as a basis for its good faith claim, the panel rejected it. The imposition of such conditions would disqualify claims of good faith violations based on statements in FTA jurisdictional clauses, as there would be no violation of a substantive norm. Thus, it seems that the panel applied the test for substantive good faith that was developed in *US – Offset Act (Byrd Amendment)*, a test that was inappropriate for the dispute in question in which good faith was rather of a procedural nature.[225] Nevertheless, these conditions were not decisive for the outcome of the dispute.

The panel continued with the analysis of the estoppel argument, without confirming its application as a principle of public international law within the WTO and the potential legal basis for such an application, or that of the criteria proposed by the complainant. Argentina asserted that 'the principle of estoppel applies in circumstances where (i) a statement of fact which is clear and unambiguous, and which (ii) is voluntary, unconditional, and authorized, is (iii) relied on in good faith.'[226] Thus, the panel's analysis did not contradict the conclusion reached above, that non-WTO law principles cannot be applied if they would lead to a refusal of jurisdiction. However, the panel also did not clarify whether an estoppel claim could be brought under DSU rules, such as Articles 3.7 and 3.10. The panel did not confirm the applicability of estoppel or the criteria for it, but went on to prove that even if the principle applied, the case at issue would not comply with the invoked requirements. With respect to the first criterion, the Panel found that Brazil did not make a 'clear and unambiguous statement to the effect that, having brought a case

---

[221] Panel Report, *Argentina – Poultry*, [7.18].

[222] Ibid, [7.19–7.20].

[223] Appellate Body Report, *United States – Continued Dumping and Subsidy Offset Act of 2000 (US – Offset Act (Byrd Amendment))*, WT/DS217/AB/R, WT/DS234/AB/R, 27 January 2003, [297].

[224] Panel Report, *Argentina – Poultry*, [7.36].

[225] Natens and Descheemaeker (2015), p. 879.

[226] Panel Report, *Argentina – Poultry*, [7.37].

under the MERCOSUR dispute settlement framework, it would not subsequently resort to WTO dispute settlement proceedings'.[227] One of the reasons for reaching this conclusion was that the Protocol of Brasilia, which was in force at the time, included a non-exclusive choice of forum clause that did not prohibit parallel or subsequent proceedings and was interpreted as imposing 'no restrictions on Brazil's right to bring subsequent WTO dispute settlement proceedings in respect of the same measure'.[228] The new Protocol of Olivos did provide a fork-in-the-road clause, but it had not entered into force at the time and was interpreted as showing that parties recognised that parallel proceedings were permitted without it.[229] The panel did not exclude the possibility of refraining from ruling on the claims raised and finding a breach of the estoppel principle had the Protocol of Olivos with its fork-in-the-road clause been in force.[230] Moreover, the panel showed willingness to look at FTA clauses for the purpose of making determinations.[231] Thus, the panel looked at FTA clauses as evidence for the parties' statements in order to establish whether or not estoppel could be found.

Despite not expressly endorsing such a condition, the panel considered whether there was a 'clear and unambiguous statement' to find a violation of estoppel as a manifestation of good faith, a condition also mentioned in international scholarly work and ICJ jurisprudence on estoppel.[232] This condition of clarity is indicative of what would be expected from a successful claim under Articles 3.7 and 3.10 of the DSU. Of greater importance is the panel's suggestion that a mere choice of forum clause would not be enough to comply with the requirement for clarity. Yet, it left the door open to a fork-in-the-road clause to qualify under this condition for a statement that can serve as the necessary evidence for a successful good faith claim.

9.4.2   EC – Bananas III (Article 21.5 – Ecuador II / Article 21.5 – US)[233]

The issue in *EC – Bananas III (Article 21.5 – Ecuador II / Article 21.5 – US)* was whether the two Understandings on Bananas signed by the European Communities

---

[227] Ibid [7.38].

[228] Ibid.

[229] Ibid.

[230] Yang (2014), p. 140.

[231] Pauwelyn (2003b), p. 1013.

[232] *Temple of Preah Vihear (Cambodia v Thailand) (Merits)* [1962] ICJ Rep 6, 143–144 (Spender J); *Land, Island and Maritime Frontier Dispute (El Salvador v Honduras: Nicaragua Intervening), Application by Nicaragua for Permission to Intervene* (1990) Rep 92, 118, para 63; Brownlie and Crawford (2012), p. 420.

[233] Appellate Body Reports, *EC – Bananas III, Recourse to Article 21.5 of The DSU by the United States, Second Recourse to Article 21.5 of the DSU by Ecuador (EC – Bananas III (Article 21.5 –*

(EC) with the US and Ecuador, providing the means for resolving the long-standing dispute on the EC's banana regime, 'prevented the complainants from initiating compliance proceedings pursuant to Article 21.5 of the DSU with respect to the European Communities' regime for the importation of bananas'.[234] Article 21.5 of the DSU provides that in case of disagreements on the implementation of an existing WTO ruling, parties should have recourse to the dispute settlement proceedings. Since the US and Ecuador claimed that the EC's preferential banana import regime provided in the Understandings was against the DSB recommendations and rulings, they initiated compliance proceedings.

The EC argued that the Understandings on Bananas were mutually agreed solutions between the parties through which they settled the dispute.[235] The term 'solution' was interpreted as referring to an 'act of solving a problem'.[236] According to the AB, 'a mutually agreed solution pursuant to Article 3.7 may encompass an agreement to forego the right to initiate compliance proceedings' but 'this need not always be so'.[237] Therefore, the mere presence of an MAS does not imply that the parties relinquished their right to initiate compliance proceedings. The AB concluded that the Understandings would preclude parties from initiating Article 21.5 compliance proceedings only if they 'explicitly or by necessary implication, agreed to waive their right to have recourse to Article 21.5' and would 'reveal clearly that the parties intended to relinquish their rights', a relinquishment which 'cannot be lightly assumed'.[238] Therefore, the AB confirmed the requirement analysed in *Argentina – Poultry* with respect to the clarity of a statement. Although the AB concluded that the parties did not relinquish their right to have recourse to Article 21.5 proceedings in the Understandings,[239] the case confirmed that a DSU right could be relinquished,[240] at least when the case concerns an MAS. However, the AB did not clarify whether its findings could have a more general character to also encompass relinquishments in the form of judicial clauses or whether they were only limited to compliance proceedings in which an MAS was considered.[241]

The AB further addressed the claim of breach of the good faith obligation prescribed in Article 3.10 of the DSU. The AB established that a breach of good faith was a procedural impediment for a WTO Member to start Article 21.5 proceedings and not a substantive one, as in the case of *US – Offset Act (Byrd*

Ecuador   II   /   Article   21.5   –   US)),   WT/DS27/AB/RW/USA,   WT/DS27/AB/RW2/ECU, 26 November 2008.

[234] Ibid [199].

[235] Ibid [34].

[236] Ibid [212].

[237] Ibid.

[238] Ibid [217].

[239] Ibid [220].

[240] Pauwelyn (2017), p. 14.

[241] Gruszczynski (2017), p. 129, fn 58.

Amendment).[242] Thus, the test used in that dispute would not be applicable in cases of procedural good faith. This statement contradicts and corrects the panel's reasoning in *Argentina – Poultry*[243] by refining the test used for procedural good faith.[244] It concluded that there is no need to establish that there was 'more than a mere violation'.[245] Therefore, a claim of violation of procedural good faith based on a statement contained in a jurisdictional clause would not be impaired by the demand for presenting additional claims of substantive violations. The AB also deemed that the EC's claim was an estoppel argument and, by citing the AB report from *EC – Export Subsidies on Sugar*,[246] confirmed once again that there is 'little in the DSU that explicitly limits the rights of WTO Members to bring an action' except Articles 3.7 and 3.10, 'even assuming arguendo that the principle of estoppel could apply in the WTO, its application would fall within these narrow parameters set out in the DSU.'[247]

Therefore, in *EC – Bananas III (Article 21.5 – Ecuador II / Article 21.5 – US)*, the AB confirmed that a DSU right could be relinquished but did not clarify if this was a general conclusion. It also re-affirmed the requirement for 'clarity' necessary for such a relinquishment. Moreover, even though the panel in *Argentina – Poultry* did not clarify the legal basis on which good faith and its manifestations as general principles of public international law could be applied within WTO proceedings, in *EC – Bananas III (Article 21.5 – Ecuador II / Article 21.5 – US)*, it confirmed that application of good faith was possible only if based on Articles 3.7 and 3.10 of the DSU. Thus, the AB's reasoning in this case is consistent with that in *Mexico – Soft Drinks* and backs the conclusion that a violation of good faith obligations as enshrined in the DSU could present a legal impediment to the exercise of a panel's jurisdiction.

9.4.3   Peru – Agricultural Products: *Clarity or More Confusion?*

In *Peru – Agricultural Products*, the AB investigated whether a DSU right can be generally relinquished and described the conditions that should be met by a 'relinquishment of the right to initiate WTO dispute settlement proceedings' for the obligations prescribed by Articles 3.7 and 3.10 of the DSU to be infringed.[248]

---

[242] See *supra*, (nn 223, 224).

[243] See *supra*, (n 225).

[244] Natens and Descheemaeker (2015), p. 880.

[245] Appellate Body Report, *EC – Bananas III (Article 21.5 – Ecuador II / Article 21.5 – US)*, [228].

[246] Appellate Body Report, *European Communities – Export Subsidies on Sugar*, [312].

[247] Ibid [227–228].

[248] Appellate Body Report, *Peru – Agricultural Products*, [5.25].

Peru and Guatemala signed an FTA that did not enter into force, in which Guatemala had allegedly agreed to a WTO-inconsistent measure applied by Peru, the legality of which Guatemala contested in the dispute. Therefore, the AB analysed whether the complainant acted in good faith under Articles 3.7 and 3.10 of the DSU because of an alleged relinquishment of the right to challenge the contested measure.[249] In an earlier dispute, *Mexico – Corn Syrup (Article 21.5 – US)*, the AB interpreted the first sentence of Article 3.7—'Before bringing a case, a Member shall *exercise its judgement* [emphasis added] as to whether action under these procedures would be fruitful.'—as being a 'largely self-regulating' requirement that is to be presumed to have been respected.[250] However, it remained debatable whether this presumption could be rebutted. In *Peru – Agricultural Products*, the AB concluded that Members enjoy discretion in deciding whether bringing a case would be fruitful, as prescribed in Article 3.7 of the DSU; however, the 'considerable deference' that a Member enjoys 'is not entirely unbounded'.[251] Thus, the AB confirmed that the presumption of good faith can be rebutted. With this conclusion, it gave 'real life' to Article 3.7 of the DSU,[252] which would otherwise have remained merely declarative.

In *Peru – Agricultural Products*, Peru contended that parties had already reached a 'positive solution' within the meaning of Article 3.7 of the DSU when they agreed on the contested measure in the FTA.[253] After considering whether Guatemala relinquished through an MAS its right to use the WTO DSM, the AB concluded that while it did not 'exclude the possibility of articulating the relinquishment of the right to initiate WTO dispute settlement proceedings in a form other than a waiver embodied in a mutually agreed solution [. . .] any such relinquishment must be made clearly'.[254] Thus, the AB left the door open to a relinquishment of the right to initiate disputes also in other forms, if it were clear enough.[255] However, it did not specify what those other forms could be and whether a fork-in-the-road clause from an FTA could be considered such a relinquishment. Moreover, almost contradicting itself, it proceeded with the analysis of the FTA provision exclusively in the form of an MAS.[256] Considering that Peru itself argued that the parties had already reached a solution, the AB conducted an analysis on whether the requirements were complied with for a relinquishment in such a form.

Article 3.7 of the DSU requires Members to exercise their judgment on fruitfulness of the action under the DSU *procedures*, and Article 3.10 expressly mandates

---

[249] Ibid.

[250] Appellate Body Report, *Mexico – Corn Syrup (Article 21.5 – US)*, [74].

[251] Appellate Body Report, *Peru – Agricultural Products*, [5.18–5.19]. This statement may be interpreted as showing that a Member's judgment when bringing a dispute can be subject to judicial review (Reyes Tagle and Claros 2016, p. 12).

[252] Raina (2016), p. 74.

[253] Appellate Body Report, *Peru – Agricultural Products*, [5.26] fn 103.

[254] Ibid, [5.25].

[255] Mathis (2016), p. 104; Shaffer and Winters (2017), p. 321.

[256] Raina (2016), p. 79.

that all Members shall engage in these *procedures* in good faith. Thus, neither of these articles suggests that a breach of good faith can be ascertained only in cases in which an MAS was first reached. Since the good faith obligation covers the entirety of the *procedures*, from initiation to implementation,[257] the AB's possible openness to other forms should be commended. It makes less sense to analyse whether a jurisdictional clause constitutes a waiver in the form of an MAS.[258] First of all, a jurisdictional clause is procedural in nature and cannot resolve the dispute between the parties. Moreover, there is a temporal problem that may be a hurdle to the consideration of a jurisdictional clause or an FTA norm in general as an MAS: FTA norms are commonly negotiated before there is even a dispute.[259] When reaching the conclusion that the FTA norm did not constitute an MAS, the AB also argued *en passant* that 'Peru and Guatemala negotiated the FTA before the initiation of the present dispute'.[260]

Based on the reasoning in *EC – Bananas III (Article 21.5 – Ecuador II / Article 21.5 – US)*, the AB stated in *Peru – Agricultural Products* that while relinquishments in forms other than an MAS are not excluded, 'any such relinquishment must be made clearly'.[261] Since the FTA provision at stake only provided that Peru 'may maintain' its PRS, the relinquishment was not found to be clear enough. Therefore, the AB set a high standard of proof for the requirement of 'clarity',[262] a threshold that may be very difficult to pass. Nevertheless, clarity of the relinquishment also ensures that Members are not 'strong-armed or tricked into waiving their rights' against their consent.[263] The Peru–Guatemala FTA had a choice of forum clause that was not exclusive, which, according to the AB, consistent with the conclusion reached in *Argentina – Poultry*, did not procedurally bar Guatemala from bringing a case. In its analysis of this clause, the AB said that 'even from the perspective of the FTA, parties to the FTA have the right to bring claims under the WTO covered agreements to the WTO dispute settlement system.'[264] It is certain, therefore, that a simple choice of forum clause in an FTA would not qualify as a relinquishment of the right to initiate disputes, as it does not clearly relinquish the right to subsequently use the WTO DSM. Still, it is not yet discernible whether a fork-in-the-road or an exclusive clause would relinquish this right, provided that it is clear enough. Nevertheless, the AB was willing to look into an FTA provision to establish whether the right to initiate WTO proceedings was relinquished, which would lead to a violation of Articles 3.7 and 3.10 of the DSU.

---

[257] *See supra*, (n 48).

[258] Hartmann (2016), p. 649.

[259] Ibid.

[260] Appellate Body Report, *Peru – Agricultural Products* [5.26].

[261] Ibid [5.25].

[262] Marceau (2013), p. 12; Shlomo Agon (2019), p. 306.

[263] Natens and Descheemaeker (2015), p. 884.

[264] Appellate Body Report, *Peru – Agricultural Products,* [5.27].

After stating that it did not exclude the possibility of relinquishing the right to initiate WTO dispute settlement procedures in forms other than an MAS, the AB declared '[i]n any event, [...], a Member's compliance with its good faith obligations under Articles 3.7 and 3.10 of the DSU should be ascertained on the basis of actions taken in relation to, or within the context of, the rules and procedures of the DSU.'[265] The meaning of this requirement is not entirely clear as the AB did not provide the reasoning behind it. According to Pauwelyn, this means that a relinquishment should make explicit reference to the DSU provisions,[266] while Shadikhodjaev concludes that it means that a DSU waiver should be 'operationalized during WTO dispute settlement procedures'.[267] Since, in the words of the AB, compliance with good faith under the DSU is ascertained on the basis of actions *related to or within the context of* DSU rules and procedures, the relinquishment does not have to take place only within the DSU procedures, it can also be *related to* a DSU rule. Therefore, a jurisdictional clause should, at least, expressly *relate to* the right to initiate proceedings under the DSU in order to comply with this requirement. In the opinion of this author, this requirement may be understood as complementing the 'clarity requirement'. By taking action in the context of or in relation to DSU rules, it is clear that Members are relinquishing DSU rights and what those rights are.

Another requirement set by the AB for relinquishment of the rights and obligations under the DSU is that it cannot go 'beyond the settlement of specific disputes'.[268] This requirement is problematic because it seems to have no textual basis.[269] The AB recalled in this respect Article 23.1 of the DSU that mandates recourse to and respect of the DSU proceedings.[270] It failed to explain how it derived this requirement from Article 23 of the DSU. In the opinion of this author, there is nothing in Article 23 to suggest that states can relinquish their rights and obligations under the DSU only with respect to specific disputes. While Article 23 mandates recourse to the DSU rules and procedures for claims on covered agreements, it is not clear how it would permit relinquishment of a DSU right for specific disputes and would prohibit extending it beyond such disputes. Hence, it is submitted that this requirement has no legal basis and should not be followed in other instances. Moreover, despite the fact that this requirement has no legal basis, it is also difficult to establish its meaning. It may be argued that relinquishing the right to initiate disputes in case of a certain category of disputes may be enough,[271] while at the

---

[265] Ibid [5.25].

[266] Pauwelyn (2017), p. 19.

[267] Shadikhodjaev (2017), p. 117.

[268] Appellate Body Report, *Peru – Agricultural Products*, fn 106.

[269] Shaffer and Winters (2017), p. 318 ('For example, why must a waiver apply to a specific dispute rather than a general obligation, so long as no other WTO party is harmed?'); Shlomo Agon (2019), pp. 306–307.

[270] Appellate Body Report, *Peru – Agricultural Products*, fn 106.

[271] *See*, for example, Pauwelyn (2017), p. 19, fn 68.

same time it has been advanced that the AB would consider only relinquishments that relate to specific single disputes.[272] If the latter is the case, no jurisdictional clause would comply with this requirement.[273] Notably, there is a temporal problem, as jurisdictional clauses are drafted and signed together with the entire agreement, while specific disputes on FTA norms arise only afterwards. Jurisdictional clauses cannot relinquish the right to use the WTO DSM in relation to specific single disputes that will only materialise later. In this narrow interpretation, only agreements signed between parties after a dispute arises, such as an MAS, would qualify as relinquishments of the rights under the DSU. It may be that this condition was enunciated by the AB only for the purpose of a waiver embodied in an MAS that had the aim of resolving only a particular dispute, a condition that would not be applicable to other forms of relinquishment. Since the narrow interpretation considerably limits other forms of relinquishment and, hence, contradicts the AB's statement that there may be other such forms, it is submitted that even if the requirement on 'specific disputes' is reaffirmed, it should be interpreted broadly.

According to the AB, another condition that applies to a 'waiver embodied in a mutually agreed solution', based on Article 3.7 DSU, is that it has to be 'consistent with the covered agreements'.[274] The AB seems to have specifically enunciated this requirement in relation to an MAS.[275] Article 3.7 of the DSU provides that '[a] solution mutually acceptable to the parties to a dispute and consistent with the covered agreements' is preferred. This requirement should not be applicable to a relinquishment that is embodied in a form other than an MAS, such as a jurisdictional clause, as it has no textual basis. If a substantive FTA norm were analysed as a relinquishment of the right, it could have also been invoked in cases where only one DSM were available. Thus, this situation would not necessarily involve conflicting jurisdictions that are the focus of this part. For that reason, this chapter mainly investigates the possibility of claiming a good faith violation based on a jurisdictional clause. In *Peru – Agricultural Products* when considering the substantive norm as a relinquishment of the right to initiate disputes, the AB nevertheless examined the jurisdictional clause in the FTA to determine whether the Members actually relinquished their right to initiate DSU proceedings. Therefore, the requirement for consistency with the covered agreements could be relevant if a jurisdictional clause

---

[272] *See*, for example, Gruszczynski (2017), p. 123.

[273] Ibid ('Although it may be argued that a decision of the parties to use a specific dispute settlement system is always individualized (as this type of provision only provides for an option), such a consent will not be expressed by both parties').

[274] Appellate Body Report, *Peru – Agricultural Products*, [5.26].

[275] Appellate Body Report, *Peru – Agricultural Products*, [5.25, 5.26] fn 102 ('Thus, we proceed to examine in this dispute whether the participants clearly stipulated the relinquishment of their right to have recourse to WTO dispute settlement by means of a "solution mutually acceptable to the parties" that is consistent with the covered agreements.'; 'the DSU emphasizes that "[a] solution mutually acceptable to the parties to a dispute" must be "consistent with the covered agreements"'; 'The third sentence of Article 3.7 provides that "[a] solution mutually acceptable to the parties to a dispute and consistent with the covered agreements is clearly to be preferred."').

operated within the broader context of a case that involved a substantive FTA norm analysed as an MAS, as was the case in *Peru – Agricultural Products*. Nevertheless, this requirement would refer to the substantive FTA norm that purports to resolve a dispute and not to the jurisdictional clause. In a potential case where a jurisdictional clause would be the main focus of the claim and the relinquishment of the right to initiate procedures would be in a form other than an MAS, this condition should not be enunciated by the AB.

To conclude, the AB report from *Peru – Agricultural Products* established strict conditions for relinquishment of the right to use the WTO DSM, especially if such a relinquishment would be considered in the form of an MAS. The report clarified that the right to initiate DSU proceedings could be relinquished, and if after such a relinquishment a Member still initiates proceedings, it would be in violation of the good faith obligation enshrined in Articles 3.7 and 3.10 of the DSU. Moreover, it confirmed that the AB would be able and willing to examine FTA jurisdictional clauses as evidence for violation claims under Articles 3.7 and 3.10 of the DSU. While the AB should be commended for clarifying these points, the conditions enunciated for finding such a relinquishment have raised more questions than answers. Not all the conditions have a textual basis in the DSU; therefore, it was submitted that groundless conditions should not be reaffirmed in future disputes. It is also uncertain whether some of these conditions would be applicable if the relinquishment of the right to use the WTO DSM were in a form other than an MAS. Furthermore, what these other forms could be and whether a jurisdictional clause could qualify as a form of relinquishment remain unanswered. Nevertheless, similar to the panel in *Argentina – Poultry*,[276] the AB clearly closed the door to non-exclusive choice of forum clauses, while leaving it open to fork-in-the-road ones.

9.5   Evaluation

Jurisdictional clauses in FTAs could address the issue of conflicting jurisdictions with respect to the category of disputes covered by them when invoked in an FTA context. If exclusive or fork-in-the-road clauses were not respected, and the issue was brought within FTA proceedings, the panels would find a violation of the respective jurisdictional clauses, and the negative consequence of conflicting jurisdictions would be avoided. However, the issue of conflicting jurisdictions in this case would only be partially addressed, as the jurisdictional clauses may not be given the same consideration when invoked within WTO proceedings.

It can be concluded that the relevant WTO case law confirms the position that Articles 3.7 and 3.10 of the DSU, together with jurisdictional clauses as evidence, could address jurisdictional conflicts between the DSMs of the WTO and FTAs

---

[276] Panel Report, *Argentina – Poultry,* [7.38].

when invoked within WTO proceedings. WTO panels may rule that Members are in breach of the good faith obligations prescribed in Articles 3.7 and 3.10 of the DSU. Accordingly, this would preclude the parties from commencing WTO proceedings and would result in WTO panels declining to exercise their jurisdiction.

It is promising that even if the AB never found that a WTO Member had been prevented from bringing a dispute to the WTO DSM, none of these cases concerned invocation by the parties of a fork-in-the-road clause that was also in force at the time of the proceedings. Moreover, in all the cases the WTO panels and the AB seemed to leave open the possibility that had there been a fork-in-the-road clause, the conclusion would have been different. This author agrees that a mere choice of forum clause would not qualify as a relinquishment of the right to initiate WTO proceedings. Since the parties expressly agree to allow a choice in a choice of forum clause but do not prohibit proceedings in other fora, it is difficult to see how a Member initiating other proceedings would be acting against good faith. That Member did not make any representations to the other party to which it should have been held. If the FTA parties truly relinquished their right to make use of the WTO DSM, they would mention so expressly and clearly as they do in the case of exclusive and fork-in-the-road jurisdictional clauses.

It is argued that clear jurisdictional clauses should be considered another form of possible relinquishment of the right to initiate disputes, in addition to an MAS. Such an approach would be consonant with the concept of limited coherence adopted in the conceptual framework.[277] It would also give appropriate meaning to the consent of states in both WTO and FTA settings, because it would give consideration to both the WTO and FTA DSMs. As previously argued, WTO panels' jurisdiction is limited to strictly WTO claims and non-WTO law tools cannot be directly applied to prompt panels to decline or limit their jurisdiction. The DSU limits the general possibility of declining jurisdiction, except in the case of Articles 3.7 and 3.10 of the DSU. If WTO panels or the AB declined or did not exercise their jurisdiction in other instances, they would have been accused of exceeding their mandate and 'adding to and diminishing' rights in covered agreements. In case of allegations of violations of good faith under Articles 3.7 and 3.10 of the DSU, rejection of clearly formulated jurisdictional clauses would equally amount to the overstepping of their mandate,[278] especially if WTO adjudicators continue to develop or reaffirm conditions that have no textual support for relinquishment of a DSU right.

The DSU expressly includes provisions that permit divergence from its rigid text and give consideration to other DSMs, especially those contained in FTAs. Giving effect to clear jurisdictional clauses under Articles 3.7 and 3.10 of the DSU would allow panels to reach a balance between respecting what Members agreed in the DSU and considering what Members agreed in their FTAs. For non-WTO law tools to be given direct consideration within WTO proceedings without using Articles 3.7 and 3.10 of the DSU, an amendment of the DSU would be required.

---

[277] See supra, Sect. 3.1.6.
[278] See Raina (2016), p. 79.

While discussions on reform of WTO dispute settlement are ongoing in the context of the AB crisis, there are no discussions thus far on amending the DSU to allow the application of non-WTO law or including a provision that would address conflicts of jurisdiction with other international adjudicatory bodies. Therefore, the drafting of clear FTA jurisdictional clauses that would be considered as relinquishments of the right to initiate WTO proceedings in the course of the analysis of good faith claims under Articles 3.7 and 3.10 of the DSU, currently, has the best chances to address conflicting jurisdictions between the WTO and FTA DSMs.

The analysis in this chapter is equally pertinent to interim appeal arbitration under the MPIA used for the appellate stage. According to Article 1.1 of the DSU, the rules and procedures of the Understanding shall apply to the disputes brought under WTO covered agreements, thus, including in instances when Article 25 of the DSU is used as means of dispute settlement at the stage of appeal.[279] Furthermore, according to the MPIA itself, appeal arbitration shall be generally governed *mutatis mutandis* by DSU provisions and other rules and procedures applicable to the Appellate Review.[280] Thus, the conclusion that FTA jurisdictional clauses have the highest chance of solving jurisdictional conflicts between the new generation EU FTA and the WTO DSMs and the conditions applicable to the clauses would be the same, even if MPIA rules are used at the appeal stage.

References

Aufsricht H (1952) Supersession of treaties in international law. Cornell Law Q 37(2):655–700
Aust A (2018) Modern treaty law and practice, 3rd edn. Cambridge University Press, New York
Bartels L (2001) Applicable law in WTO dispute settlement proceedings. J World Trade 35:499–519
Bartels L (2008) Treaty conflicts in WTO law – a comment on William J. Davey's Paper 'The Quest for Consistency'. In: Griller S (ed) At the crossroads: The World Trading System and the Doha Round. Springer, Heidelberg, pp 129–145
Bartels L (2016) Jurisdiction and applicable law in the WTO. SIEL Working Paper No. 2016/18, pp 1–21
Borgen CJ (2005) Resolving treaty conflicts. George Wash Int Law Rev 37:573–648
Brink T (2010) Which WTO rules can a PTA lawfully breach? Completing the analysis in Brazil – Tyres. J World Trade 44(4):813–846
Broude T, Shany Y (2011) The international law and policy of multi-sourced equivalent norms. In: Broude T, Shany Y (eds) Multi-sourced equivalent norms in international law. Hart, Oxford, pp 1–16
Brown C (2007) A common law of international adjudication. Oxford University Press, New York
Brownlie I, Crawford J (2012) Brownlie's principles of public international law, 8th edn. Oxford University Press, New York
Byers M (2002) Abuse of rights: an old principle, a new age. McGill Law J 47:389–434

---

[279] For more details, *see infra*, Sect. 12.2.1.

[280] MPIA, Annex 1, para 11.

Chase C (2012) Norm conflict between WTO covered agreements – real, apparent or avoided? Int Comp Law Q 61:791–821

Crawford J (2014) State responsibility: the general part. Cambridge University Press, New York

Czaplinski W, Danilenko G (1990) Conflicts of norms in international law. Netherlands Yearb Int Law 21:3–42

Davey WJ (2008) The quest for consistency: principles governing the interrelation of the WTO agreements. In: Griller S (ed) At the crossroads: the World Trading System and the Doha Round. Springer, Heidelberg, pp 101–127

Davey WJ, Sapir A (2009) The Soft Drinks Case: the WTO and regional agreements. World Trade Rev 8(1):5–23

de Chazournes LB (2017) Interactions between regional and universal organizations. A legal perspective. Brill Nijhoff, Leiden

de Mestral ACM (2013) Dispute settlement under the WTO and RTAs: an uneasy relationship. J Int Econ Law 16:777–825

Flett J (2015) Referring PTA disputes to the WTO dispute settlement system. In: Dür A, Elsig M (eds) Trade cooperation: the purpose, design and effects of preferential trade agreements. World Trade Forum. Cambridge University Press, New York, pp 555–579

Forere MA (2015) The relationship of WTO law and regional trade agreements in dispute settlement. Kluwer Law International, Alphen aan den Rijn

Furculita C (2019) Fork-in-the-road clauses in the new EU FTAs: addressing conflicts of jurisdictions with the WTO dispute settlement mechanism. CLLER Paper 2019/1. www.asser.nl/media/5268/cleer19-01_web.pdf

Gao H, Lim CL (2008) Saving the WTO from the risk of irrelevance: the WTO dispute settlement mechanism as a 'Common Good' for RTA disputes. J Int Econ Law 11(4):899–925

Gobbi Estrella AT, Horlick GN (2006) Mandatory abolition of anti-dumping, countervailing duties and safeguards in customs unions and free trade areas constituted between World Trade Organization members: revisiting a long-standing discussion in light of the Appellate Body's Turkey-Textiles Ruling. J World Trade 40(5):909–944

Graewert T (2008) Conflicting laws and jurisdictions in the dispute settlement process of the regional trade agreements and the WTO. Contemp Asia Arbitr J 287(1):287–334

Gruszczynski L (2017) The WTO and FCTC dispute settlement systems: friends or foes. Asian J WTO Int Health Law Policy 12:105–134

Hartmann S (2016) Recognizing the limitations of WTO dispute settlement - the Peru-price bands dispute and sources of authority for applying non-WTO law in WTO disputes. George Wash Int Law Rev 48:617–652

Henckels C (2008) Overcoming jurisdictional isolationism at the WTO–FTA Nexus: a potential approach for the WTO. Eur J Int Law 19(3):571–599

Herrmann C (2008) Bilateral and regional trade agreements as a challenge to the multilateral trading system. EUI Working Papers Law 2008/09, pp 1–17

Hillman J (2009) Conflicts between dispute settlement mechanisms in regional trade agreements and the WTO - what should the WTO do?'. Cornell Int Law J 42:193–208

Jenks CW (1953) The conflict of law-making treaties. Br Yearb Int Law 30:401–453

Jeutner V (2017) Irresolvable norm conflicts in international law: the concept of legal dilemma. Oxford Monographs in International Law, New York

Karl W (1984) Conflicts between treaties. In: Bernhardt R (ed) Encyclopedia of public international law. Max Planck Institute for Comparative Public Law and International Law. Rudolph Bernhard, Amsterdam, pp 467–473

Kiss A (2006) Abuse of rights. In: Max Planck Encyclopedia of Public International Law. Oxford University Press, Oxford. https://opil.ouplaw.com/view/10.1093/law:epil/9780199231690/law-9780199231690-e1371

Kolb R (2006a) Principles as sources of international law (with special reference to good faith). Netherlands Int Law Rev 53(1):1–36

Kolb R (2006b) General principles of procedural law. In: Zimmermman A, Tams CJ, Oellers-Frahm K, Tomuschat C (eds) The Statute of the International Court of Justice: a commentary. Oxford University Press, Oxford, pp 871–908

Kolsky Lewis M, Van den Bossche P (2014) What to do when disagreement strikes? The complexity of dispute settlement under trade agreements. In: Frankel S, Kolsky Lewis M (eds) Trade agreements at the crossroads. Routledge, London, pp 9–25

Kuijper PJ (2010) Conflicting rules and clashing courts: the case of multilateral environmental agreements, Free Trade Agreements and the WTO. ICTSD Issue Paper No. 10, pp 1–64

Kwak K, Marceau G (2006) Overlaps and conflicts of jurisdiction between the WTO and RTAs. In: Bartels L, Ortino F (eds) Regional trade agreements and the WTO legal system. Oxford University Press, New York, pp 465–524

Lanyi PA, Steinbach A (2014) Limiting jurisdictional fragmentation in international trade disputes. J Int Dispute Settlement 5:372–405

Lauterpacht H (1936) The covenant as the "Higher Law". Br Yearb Int Law 17:54–65

Lester S (2016) The ISDS controversy: how we got here and where next. https://www.cato.org/commentary/isds-controversy-how-we-got-here-where-next

Lindroos A (2005) Addressing norm conflicts in a fragmented legal system: the doctrine of Lex Specialis. Nordic J Int Law 74:27–66

Lockhart N, Mitchell AD (2005) Regional trade agreements under GATT 1994: an exception and its limits. In: Mitchell AD (ed) Challenges and prospects for the WTO. Cameron May, London, pp 217–252

Marceau G (2001) Conflicts of norms and conflicts of jurisdictions: the relationship between the WTO agreement and MEAs and other treaties. J World Trade 35:1081–1131

Marceau G (2002) WTO dispute settlement and human rights. Eur J Int Law 13(4):753–814

Marceau G (2013) The primacy of the WTO dispute settlement. Quest Int Law J 23:3–13

Marceau G, Tomazos A (2008) Comments on Joost Pauwelyn's paper: "How to win a WTO dispute based on non-WTO law?". In: Griller S (ed) At the crossroads: the World Trading System and the Doha Round. Springer, Heidelberg, pp 55–81

Marceau G, Wyatt J (2010) Dispute settlement regimes intermingled: regional trade agreements and the WTO. J Int Dispute Settlement 1(1):67–95

Mathis JH (2002) Regional trade agreements in the GATT/WTO: Art. XXIV and the internal trade requirement. T.M.C. Asser Press, The Hague

Mathis JH (2016) WTO Appellate Body, Peru – Additional Duty on Imports of Certain Agriculture Products, WT/DS457/AB/R, 20 July 2015. Leg Issues Econ Integr 43(1):97–105

Mbengue MM (2016) The settlement of trade disputes: is there a monopoly for the WTO? Law Pract Int Courts Tribunals 15:207–248

McLachlan C (2009) Lis Pendens in international litigation. Hague Academy of International Law. Brill, Leiden

McRae D (2004) What is the future of WTO dispute settlement? J Int Econ Law 7(1):3–21

Michaels R, Pauwelyn J (2012) Conflict of norms or conflict of laws? Different techniques in the fragmentation of public international law. Duke J Comp Int Law 22:349–376

Milanovic M (2009) Norm conflict in international law: Whither human rights. Duke J Comp Int Law 20:69–131

Mitchell AD (2006) Good faith in WTO dispute settlement. Melbourne J Int Law 7(2):339–371

Mitchell AD (2007) The legal basis for using principles in WTO disputes. J Int Econ Law 10(4):795–835

Mitchell AD, Heaton D (2010) The inherent jurisdiction of WTO tribunals: the select application of public international law required by the judicial function. Mich J Int Law 31(3):559–619

Mus JB (1998) Conflicts between treaties in international law. Netherlands Int Law Rev 45(2):208–232

Natens B, Descheemaeker S (2015) Say it loud, say it clear – Article 3.10 DSU's clear statement test as a legal impediment to validly established jurisdiction. J World Trade 49(5):873–890

Nguyen TS (2016) The applicability of comity and abuse of rights in World Trade Organisation dispute settlement. Univ Tasmania Law Rev 35(1):95–130

O'Connor JF (1991) Good faith in international law. Dartmouth Publishing, London

Pauwelyn J (2001) The role of public international law in the WTO: how far can we go? Am J Int Law 95(3):535–578

Pauwelyn J (2003a) Conflict of norms in public international law: how WTO law relates to other rules of international law. Cambridge University Press, New York

Pauwelyn J (2003b) How to win a World Trade Organization dispute based on non-world trade organization law? Questions of jurisdiction and merits. J World Trade 37(6):997–1030

Pauwelyn J (2004a) Bridging fragmentation and unity: international law as a universe of inter-connected islands. Mich J Int Law 25(4):903–916

Pauwelyn J (2004b) The puzzle of WTO safeguards and regional trade agreements. J Int Econ Law 7(1):109–142

Pauwelyn J (2017) Interplay between the WTO treaty and other international legal instruments and tribunals: evolution after 20 years of WTO jurisprudence. https://papers.ssrn.com/sol3/papers.cfm?abstract_id=2731144

Pauwelyn J, Alschner W (2015) Forget about the WTO: the network of relations between PTAs and "Double PTAs". In: Dür A, Elsig M (eds) Trade cooperation: the purpose, design and effects of preferential trade agreements, World Trade Forum. Cambridge University Press, New York, pp 497–532

Pauwelyn J, Salles LE (2009) Forum shopping before international tribunals: (real) concerns, (im)possible solutions. Cornell Int Law J 42(1):77–118

Pusceddu P (2016) State-to-state dispute settlement provisions in the EU-Canada comprehensive economic and trade agreement. Transnational Dispute Manag 13(1):1–29

Raina A (2016) "The Day the Music Died": the curious case of Peru-Agricultural Products. Glob Trade Customs J 11(2):71–85

Reinisch A (2004) The use and limits of Res Judicata and Lis Pendens as procedural tools to avoid conflicting dispute settlement outcomes. Law Pract Int Courts Tribunals 3(1):37–77

Reyes Tagle Y, Claros R (2016) The law of regional trade agreements in the WTO dispute settlement system: lessons from the Peru-Agricultural Products Case. SECO/WTI Academic Cooperation Project Working Paper No 04/2016, pp 1–44

Salles LE (2015) A deal is a deal: party autonomy, the multiplication of PTAs, and WTO dispute settlement. Quest Int Law 23:15–29

Sánchez A (2012) What trade lawyers should know about the ILC Articles on state responsibility. Glob Trade Customs J 7(6):292–299

Shadikhodjaev S (2017) The "Regionalism vs Multilateralism" issue in international trade law: revisiting the Peru–Agricultural Products Case. Chinese J Int Law 16:109–123

Shaffer G, Winters A (2017) FTA law in WTO dispute settlement: Peru–Additional Duty and the fragmentation of trade law. World Trade Rev 16(2):303–326

Shany Y (2004) The competing jurisdictions of international courts and tribunals. Oxford University Press, New York

Shlomo Agon S (2019) International adjudication on trial. The effectiveness of the WTO dispute settlement system. Oxford University Press, New York

Trachtman JP (1999) The domain of WTO dispute resolution. Harv Int Law J 40:333–377

Trachtman JP (2004) Book review: conflict of norms in public international law: how WTO law relates to other rules of international law by Joost Pauwelyn. In: Bilder RB (ed) Recent books on international law. The American Journal of International Law 98, pp 855–861

Trachtman JP (2005) Jurisdiction in WTO dispute settlement. In: Yerxa R, Wilson B (eds) Key issues in WTO dispute settlement. The first ten years. Cambridge University Press, New York, pp 132–143

Van Damme I (2009) Treaty interpretation by the WTO Appellate Body. Oxford University Press, New York

Villiger ME (2009) Commentary on the 1969 Vienna Convention on the Law of Treaties. Martinus Nijhoff, Leiden

von der Decken K (2018) Article 41. Agreements to modify multilateral treaties between certain of the parties only. In: Dörr O, Schmalenbach K (eds) Vienna Convention on the Law of Treaties. a commentary, 2nd edn. Springer, Heidelberg, pp 777–786

Vranes E (2005) Jurisdiction and applicable law in WTO dispute settlement. German Yearb Int Law 48:265–290

Vranes E (2006) The definition of "Norm Conflict" in international law and legal theory. Eur J Int Law 17(2):395–418

Weiss W (2003) Security and predictability under WTO law. World Trade Rev 2(2):183–219

Wolfrum R, Matz N (2003) Conflicts in international environmental law. Springer, Heidelberg

Yang S (2012) The key role of the WTO in settling its jurisdictional conflicts with RTAs. Chinese J Int Law 11:281–319

Yang S (2014) The solution for jurisdictional conflicts between the WTO and RTAs: the forum choice clause. Mich State Int Law Rev 23(1):107–152

Zang MQ (2019) When the multilateral meets the regionals: regional trade agreements at WTO dispute settlement. World Trade Rev 18(1):33–61

Ziegler AR, Baumgartner J (2015) Good faith as a general principle of (international) law. In: Mitchell AD, Sornarajah M, Voon T (eds) Good faith and international economic law. Oxford University Press, New York, pp 9–36

Chapter 10
Assessment of the Jurisdictional Clauses in the New Generation EU FTAs

10.1 Areas Presenting the Risk of Conflicting Jurisdictions Between the WTO and the New Generation EU FTA DSMs

The jurisdiction of a court or tribunal defines the scope of the authority granted by the parties to the international tribunal to adjudicate and solve disputes on a matter.[1] As concluded in the section on the substantive coverage of the FTA DSMs analysed, aspects such as NT and Market Access Obligations, TBT measures (in the EUJEPA, TBT incorporated norms only if there are also claims on other norms in the dispute), most SPS measures (except in the EUKFTA in which all are excluded), certain provisions on subsidies, state enterprises, customs valuation, services, intellectual property, and public procurement are covered by both the WTO and the new generation EU FTA DSMs. Therefore, the same measure of the EU or of one of its trading FTA partners could be potentially adjudicated in two different fora in parallel or subsequence, or one forum could be invoked as being the appropriate one, thereby raising the risk of conflicting jurisdictions.

By carving out certain areas, such as trade defence instruments, some or all SPS measures, some measures related to subsidies, and TBT incorporated norms, from the coverage of all or some new generation EU FTA DSMs, the negotiators of these agreements restricted the number of areas with a potential risk of conflicting jurisdictions with the WTO DSM. Thus, it may be said that the negotiators took *preventive* measures against conflicting jurisdictions. Moreover, as argued in the Chap. 5,[2] these exclusions show that the new generation EU FTAs do not undermine the authority of the WTO DSM, but rather need a functional multilateral dispute settlement mechanism. The explicit exclusion of TBT incorporated norms from the

---

[1] *See* Kwak and Marceau (2006), p. 465; Kuijper (2010), p. 25.
[2] *See supra*, Sect. 5.4.

© The Author(s), under exclusive license to Springer Nature Switzerland AG 2021
C. Furculiță, *The WTO and the New Generation EU FTA Dispute Settlement Mechanisms*, EYIEL Monographs - Studies in European and International Economic Law 19, https://doi.org/10.1007/978-3-030-83118-9_10

coverage of the FTA DSMs is a clear illustration of the intention of the parties to avoid conflicting rulings. However, many incorporated, referenced, or reproduced WTO norms in the FTAs, as well as others that are similar to the WTO norms, are still covered by the jurisdiction of the FTA DSMs. For example, Articles III and XI of GATT incorporated in all the new generation EU FTAs, Article VIII of GATT referenced in CETA, EUJEPA, EUSFTA, and EUVFTA, and Article 19.4(1) of CETA with similar wording to Article IV:1 of GPA are not excluded from the coverage of the FTA DSMs. Hence, there is a risk of conflicting jurisdictions with respect to claims under them and the corresponding WTO norms.

In addition to incorporated, referenced, or replicated WTO norms in the FTAs, there are also WTO-plus and WTO-minus norms that deal with the same issues addressed in the WTO agreements.[3] For WTO-plus and WTO-minus norms to be enforced, they need to be applied to the dispute instead of a WTO norm that relates to the same subject. The WTO DSM cannot enforce these norms because of the lack of jurisdiction over them.[4] Therefore, when enforcement of WTO-plus or WTO-minus norms is sought, claims should be brought to the DSMs of the new generation EU FTAs. Nevertheless, as previously argued,[5] WTO-plus norms could be violated along with other WTO norms or the same measure could be in violation of both WTO and the corresponding WTO-plus FTA norms, also causing conflicts of jurisdiction.[6] Thus, the same measure could be challenged in two different fora.

As previously argued,[7] although in such cases a claimant is expected to prefer lodging a complaint in the FTA forum to enforce the WTO-plus norms, because of procedural or political reasons, the complainant could, nonetheless, also initiate proceedings at the WTO to enforce at least the corresponding WTO norms. Measures implementing WTO-minus norms could be challenged under WTO rules, while an FTA panel could find them legal or its jurisdiction could be invoked as being the appropriate one. Moreover, the WTO-minus norms included in the FTAs could be directly challenged at the multilateral level. Such a situation occurred in *Peru – Agricultural Products*; Peru and Guatemala signed an FTA that did not enter into force in which Guatemala had allegedly agreed to a WTO-minus measure applied by Peru, the legality of which Guatemala contested.[8]

Therefore, the same factual situation, between the same parties with claims on similar or corresponding WTO and FTA norms, could be brought both to the multilateral WTO and the bilateral new generation EU FTA DSMs leading to conflicting jurisdictions.

---

[3] Horn et al. (2009), p. 4.

[4] *See supra*, Sect. 9.3.1.

[5] *See supra*, Sect. 5.3.

[6] As argued in Sect. 3.2.5, for a conflict of jurisdiction to materialise, the dispute must be the same, which does not mean that legal grounds need to be identical or similar; they can also be correlated.

[7] *See supra*, Sect. 5.3.

[8] *See supra*, Sect. 9.4.3.

10.2   Introduction to Jurisdictional Clauses in the New Generation EU FTAs

To analyse the jurisdictional clauses in the new generation EU FTAs, they will be first introduced and important aspects related to them will be considered.

10.2.1   Types of Jurisdictional Clauses in the New Generation EU FTAs

The jurisdictional clauses in the new generation EU FTAs are found under the title 'Choice of Forum'[9] or 'Relation with WTO Obligations'.[10] The first title appears to already indicate what type of jurisdictional clause would be within that FTA, although it is yet to be seen whether the clauses also require the choice to be final, being, in fact, fork-in-the-road clauses.

All the new generation EU FTAs, except the EUJEPA, establish in their first paragraphs that '[r]ecourse to the dispute settlement provisions' of the FTA dispute settlement chapters is or shall be 'without prejudice' to recourse to dispute settlement under the WTO agreement.[11] Thus, the general rule applying with respect to redress of all breach of obligations provided in the first paragraph of the relevant article in every FTA is that its dispute settlement chapters do not affect in any way the WTO proceedings. However, this general rule is followed by further jurisdictional clauses applicable to a certain category of disputes. These jurisdictional clauses are introduced in paragraph 2 of these articles by such terms and expressions as 'however' in the EUKFTA,[12] '[n]otwithstanding paragraph 1' in CETA and EUSFTA,[13] and '[b]y way of derogation from paragraph 1' in the EUVFTA,[14] showing that these clauses are exceptions from the first paragraph.

The EUKFTA establishes that

> where a Party has, with regard to a particular measure, initiated a dispute settlement proceeding, either under this Chapter or under the WTO Agreement, it may not institute a dispute settlement proceeding regarding the same measure in the other forum until the first proceeding has been concluded.[15]

The EUSFTA adopts an almost identical language, except that it uses the term 'ended' instead of 'concluded'—an insignificant difference—when referring to

---

[9]CETA, Art 29.4; EUJEPA, Art 21.27; EUVFTA, Art 15.24.

[10]EUKFTA, Art 14.19; EUSFTA, Art 14. 21.

[11]EUKFTA, Art 14.19(1); CETA, Art 29.4(1); EUSFTA, Art 14.21(1); EUVFTA, Art 15.24(1).

[12]EUKFTA, Art 14.19(2).

[13]CETA, Art 29.4(2); EUSFTA, Art 14.21(2).

[14]EUVFTA, Art 15.24(2).

[15]EUKFTA, Art 14.19(2), first sentence.

procedures in another forum.[16] As the EUKFTA and EUSFTA clauses prohibit the initiation of proceedings for the same measures only until other proceedings have not been concluded, it is clear that they aim to prevent only parallel proceedings, not subsequent ones; they are, therefore, limited fork-in-the-road clauses.[17] However, these limited fork-in-the-road clauses are applicable only to WTO and FTA disputes that concern the 'same measures'. Thus, the EUKFTA and EUSFTA aim to prevent parallel disputes on the same measures, even if the claims on them may refer to WTO and FTA norms that are different in substance. Both the EUKFTA and EUSFTA provide further full fork-in-the-road clauses. Thus, the EUKFTA establishes that

[i]n addition, a Party shall not seek redress of an obligation which is identical under this Agreement and under the WTO Agreement in the two forums. In such case, once a dispute settlement proceeding has been initiated, the Party shall not bring a claim seeking redress of the identical obligation under the other Agreement to the other forum, unless the forum selected fails for procedural or jurisdictional reasons to make findings on the claim seeking redress of that obligation.[18]

Thus, once proceedings are initiated, parallel and subsequent proceedings concerning 'identical obligations' in WTO and FTA fora are prohibited. In the EUSFTA, on the other hand, the full fork-in-the-road clause is formulated in a very similar manner, but it covers a broader category of disputes. It establishes that

[m]oreover, a Party shall not initiate dispute settlement proceedings under this Chapter and under the WTO Agreement, unless substantially different obligations under both agreements are in dispute, or unless the forum selected fails for procedural or jurisdictional reasons to make findings on the claim seeking redress of that obligation, provided that the failure of the forum is not the result of a failure of a disputing Party to act diligently.[19]

Hence, while the EUKFTA's full fork-in-the-road clause covers only disputes on strictly 'identical obligations', the EUSFTA's clause covers all disputes concerning obligations that are not 'substantially different'. CETA and EUVFTA contain only full fork-in-the-road clauses, as they provide that once proceedings have been initiated under one agreement, redress under other agreement shall not be sought. CETA establishes that

if an obligation is equivalent in substance under this Agreement and under the WTO Agreement, or under any other agreement to which the Parties are party, a Party may not seek redress for the breach of such an obligation in the two fora. In such case, once a dispute settlement proceeding has been initiated under one agreement, the Party shall not bring a claim seeking redress for the breach of the substantially equivalent obligation under the other agreement, unless the forum selected fails, for procedural or jurisdictional reasons, other than termination under paragraph 20 of Annex 29-A, to make findings on that claim.[20]

---

[16] EUSFTA, Art 14.21(2), first sentence.

[17] As stated in Sect. 9.2.2, limited fork-in-the-road clauses prohibit only parallel proceedings.

[18] EUKFTA, Art 14.19(2), second and third sentences.

[19] EUSFTA, Art 14.21(2), second sentence.

[20] CETA, Art 29.3(2).

The EUVFTA's choice of forum clause has very similar wording to that of CETA. However, while CETA uses two expressions, 'substantially equivalent obligation' and 'obligation equivalent in substance', to refer to the category to which the jurisdictional clause is applicable, the EUVFTA uses only the first one.[21]

The EUJEPA, in contrast to the other EU FTAs analysed, has no paragraph establishing that recourse to DSMs under the FTA is without prejudice to actions under other agreements. Instead, it explicitly regulates in the first paragraph the choice between different fora for dispute settlement 'where a dispute arises with regard to the alleged inconsistency of a particular measure with an obligation under this Agreement and a substantially equivalent obligation under any other international agreement to which both Parties are party'. The EUJEPA expressly states that in these situations 'the complaining party may select the forum'.[22] This paragraph is followed by a full fork-in-the-road clause that establishes

> [o]nce a Party has selected the forum and initiated dispute settlement proceedings under this Chapter or under the other international agreement with respect to the particular measure referred to in paragraph 1, that Party shall not initiate dispute settlement proceedings in another forum with respect to that particular measure unless the forum selected first fails to make findings on the issues in dispute for jurisdictional or procedural reasons.[23]

Thus, similar to CETA and EUVFTA, the EUJEPA contains a full fork-in-the-road clause covering disputes on 'substantially equivalent obligations'. While the other EU FTAs analysed do not *expressly* provide that parties can choose between different fora for certain categories of disputes, this possibility can be inferred from the prohibition to seek redress in two fora in parallel or subsequence, without mentioning in which forum the dispute should be initiated first.[24] Hence, every new generation EU FTA enables its parties seeking redress for a claim to choose between the WTO DSM or EU FTA DSMs for disputes concerning certain categories of disputes.

10.2.2 The Relevance of Choice

The fact that the new generation EU FTAs allow the possibility of using the WTO DSM is not surprising, since EU FTAs often explicitly refer to and incorporate WTO norms or replicate them.

It may be perceived as useful by FTA parties to refer disputes on interpretation and application of the incorporated, referenced, or replicated WTO norms to the

---

[21] EUVFTA, Art 15.24(2).

[22] EUJEPA, Art 21.27(1).

[23] EUJEPA, Art 21.27(2).

[24] EUKFTA, Art 14.19(2); CETA, Art 29.3(2), second sentence; EUSFTA, Art 14.21(2); EUVFTA, Art 15.24(2), second sentence.

WTO DSM.[25] This provides security and predictability to the interpretation of general concepts of international trade law[26] and allows EU FTA parties to benefit from the expertise and practice of WTO panels and the AB. The possibility of choosing the WTO DSM to resolve disputes on certain FTA norms inscribed in the new generation EU FTAs indicates that the parties themselves acknowledge the importance of being able to bring disputes to the WTO DSM. For the parties to actually benefit from the advantages associated with the use of the WTO DSM, it should be functional and render reports or, at least, awards that are final, binding, and enforceable. Therefore, from the perspective of the new generation EU FTAs, it is important to solve the AB crisis. In addition, the choice that parties are allowed to make indicates the fact that the new generation EU FTAs are not intended to undermine the authority of the WTO DSM. At the same time, parties are allowed to bring disputes on these norms to the FTA DSMs because even though they have the same substance, they may nevertheless be different due to the fact that they are located in different contexts that influence the way the norms should be interpreted.[27] Moreover, an incorporated WTO norm could be violated along with other FTA norms that are WTO-plus or WTO-minus by the same measure. In such cases, the parties may prefer to bring the same dispute, together with all the related claims, to the FTA DSM. Lastly, the EU FTA DSMs may also be preferred by the parties because of other political and procedural considerations. As argued in the conceptual framework, non-abusive forum shopping, in itself, should be regarded as a natural phenomenon in international law, rather than a negative one.

In addition to the full fork-in-the-road clauses in the dispute settlement chapter, the EUJEPA has an exclusive jurisdictional clause covering a specific category of disputes provided in its TBT chapter. It stipulates that 'where a dispute arises regarding a particular measure of a Party which the other Party alleges to be exclusively in breach of the provisions of the TBT Agreement referred to in paragraph 2, that other Party shall, notwithstanding paragraph 1 of Article 21.27, select the dispute settlement mechanism under the WTO Agreement'.[28] Since this provision concerns only the category of disputes regarding measures allegedly *exclusively* in violation of TBT provisions incorporated in FTAs, it does not seem to be applicable to potential disputes that may refer to claims on TBT incorporated norms invoked together with claims on other EUJEPA provisions. This clause is of little interest for the purpose of establishing whether WTO panels could consider FTA jurisdictional clauses, as it is in favour of the WTO DSM jurisdiction. Nonetheless, it confirms that FTA parties have considered the coherence of the international trade law regime, would like to avoid causing inconsistencies, and seek stability and predictability in certain cases. Moreover, this clause confirms, again, that the parties prefer some of the disputes to be solved only under DSU rules.

---

[25] Kuijper (2010), p. 28.

[26] Stoll (2019), p. 240.

[27] Broude and Shany (2011), pp. 7–9.

[28] EUJEPA, Art. 7.3.

Hence, from the perspective of the new generation EU FTAs, it is important to have a functional WTO DSM to enforce provisions such as the incorporated TBT provisions in EUJEPA.

To conclude, the choice between the new generation EU FTA DSMs and the WTO mechanism available in certain cases shows the importance of having both multilateral and bilateral functional ways of resolving trade disputes. The new generation EU FTAs allowing a preference for the WTO DSM and the exclusive jurisdictional clause in the EUJEPA demonstrate the reliance of the FTA DSMs on the multilateral DSU proceedings. The fact that a dispute concerning claims that are not exclusively on norms incorporating TBT but also on other norms is excluded from the coverage of the EUJEPA's exclusive jurisdictional clause, and thus allows a choice, shows that choosing to resolve a dispute on WTO-equal norms within FTA fora is, likewise, considered essential by states in certain cases.

10.2.3 The Moment of Selection

For a fork-in-the-road clause to be exercised, a forum should be selected first, since the mere existence of such a clause is insufficient.[29] The question arises when a selection is considered to have been made and, hence, the fork-in-the-road clause exercised.

The moment a selection is considered to have been made is mentioned in all the agreements as the moment proceedings are initiated. Thus, the fork-in-the-road clauses in all the EU FTAs analysed are followed by paragraphs with a definition of the initiation of proceedings, precisely identifying the relevant moment for the exercise of these clauses. The agreements provide that dispute settlement proceedings under the WTO are deemed to be initiated by a request for the establishment of a panel according to Article 6 of the DSU,[30] while those under the FTAs, by the request for establishment of an arbitration panel under the relevant FTA provisions.[31] Consequently, parallel or subsequent consultations under WTO and FTA rules that allow parties to obtain further information about the dispute and their arguments, without requests for establishment of panels, are permitted. In addition, for the limited fork-in-the-road clauses that address only parallel proceedings, there is another decisive moment—the moment the first proceedings are concluded. In this respect, the EUKFTA and EUSFTA expressly regulate that WTO proceedings are deemed concluded when panel or AB reports, as the case may be, are adopted by the

---

[29] Natens and Descheemaeker (2015), p. 881.

[30] EUKFTA, Art 14.19(3)(a); CETA, Art 29.3(3)(a); EUJEPA, Art 21.27(3)(b); EUSFTA, Art 14.21(3)(a); EUVFTA, Art 15.24(3)(a).

[31] EUKFTA, Art 14.19(3)(b); CETA, Art 29.3(3)(b); EUJEPA, Art 21.27(3)(a); EUSFTA, Art 14.21(3)(b); EUVFTA, Art 15.24(3)(b).

DSB, while FTA proceedings are concluded when the arbitration panel issues its ruling to the parties and the Trade Committee.[32]

Thus, the new generation EU FTAs expressly define the relevant moments for operation of the limited and full fork-in-the-road clauses, bringing greater precision to the question of when a fork-in-the-road clause is considered exercised.

10.2.4 Additional Jurisdictional Clauses on Countermeasures

All the new generation EU FTAs under analysis include a clause that addresses the situation in which the legality of countermeasures authorised by FTA or WTO panels may be challenged in front of the other forum.

These clauses provide that nothing in the agreements 'shall preclude a Party from implementing the suspension of obligations authorised' by the DSB.[33] Therefore, claims on violation of FTA norms by the DSB-authorised measures cannot be brought to EU FTA panels. Moreover, the agreements further stipulate that a party 'shall not invoke' the WTO Agreement to prevent the other party from suspending concessions or other obligations under the FTA dispute settlement chapter. Hence, the agreements also deal with potential claims within WTO proceedings of violations of WTO norms by countermeasures authorised by FTA panels.

While the clauses on countermeasures may not seem classic exclusive jurisdictional clauses, they will be considered as potential ones, as they could be interpreted as preventing WTO panels from exercising their jurisdiction over FTA countermeasures that are left solely to the FTA panels under the special procedures of the FTA dispute settlement chapters.

10.2.5 Preliminary Remarks

Based on the provisions described above, it can be concluded that all the new generation EU FTAs include fork in-the-road clauses on certain categories of disputes, such as those on 'identical obligations', not 'substantially different obligations', 'substantially equivalent obligations', or the 'same measure'. They all offer the possibility of a choice between different fora, a choice that is essential. These FTAs also expressly define the relevant moments for the operation of these clauses. In addition, the new generation EU FTAs have potential exclusive jurisdictional

---

[32] EUKFTA, Art 14.19(3)(a) and (b); EUSFTA, Art 14.21(3)(a) and (b).

[33] EUKFTA, Art 14.19(4), first sentence; CETA, Art 29.3(4), first sentence; EUJEPA, Art 21.27(4), first sentence (it used the expression 'suspension of concessions or other obligations'); EUSFTA, Art 14.21(3)(a), first sentence; EUVFTA, Art 15.24(3)(a), first sentence.

clauses for the countermeasures imposed according to the FTA dispute settlement chapters.

The full fork-in-the-road clauses, prohibiting both parallel and subsequent proceedings in the WTO and FTA fora, will prevent conflicts of jurisdiction with respect to the category of disputes covered, when a dispute is initiated first under the WTO rules and then under FTA rules, as FTA panels will give consideration to these clauses. However, the limited fork-in-the-road clauses in the EUKFTA and EUSFTA that refer only to parallel proceedings on disputes concerning the same measures do not adequately address the risks associated with conflicting jurisdictions, since the risk of incoherence and unpredictability, as well as of unnecessary costs, persists because of the possibility of subsequent proceedings. Nevertheless, both the EUKFTA and EUSFTA also include full fork-in-the-road clauses that would appropriately address the risks associated with conflicting jurisdictions if invoked within FTA proceedings with respect to the category of disputes covered by them. The EUKFTA's full fork-in-the-road clause covers only disputes on identical obligations; accordingly, it would not prevent conflicting jurisdictions if proceedings were initiated subsequently with regard to similar obligations. In contrast, the EUSFTA's full fork-in-the-road clause, similar to those in CETA, EUJEPA, and EUVFTA, has wider coverage referring to obligations that are both identical and similar in their substance.[34] The full fork-in-the-road clause addressing not only conflicting jurisdictions with regard to identical FTA and WTO norms, but also similar ones, are designed to ensure greater coherence, and should be used by the EU in its FTAs to better balance its bilateral and multilateral aspirations. The additional jurisdictional clauses on countermeasures, if invoked within FTA proceedings, would prevent claims of violations of FTA norms by DSB-authorised measures, allowing FTA panels to contribute to a more coherent international trading regime.

While jurisdictional clauses in the new generation EU FTAs will be given consideration within FTA proceedings if invoked, the rest of this chapter will analyse the likelihood of these clauses resolving conflicting jurisdictions and being considered if raised within WTO proceedings.

10.3 Conditions for Jurisdictional Clauses

As argued in the previous chapter, WTO panels and the AB left open the possibility of not exercising their jurisdiction in disputes in which fork-in-the-road clauses would be invoked as relinquishments of the right to initiate WTO disputes and a violation of Articles 3.7 and 3.10 of the DSU would be found. Nevertheless, based on WTO case law, there are several conditions that such relinquishments should fulfil: (1) they should be clear and unambiguous; (2) they should relate to DSU rules

---

[34]On the category of disputes covered by the new generation EU FTA jurisdictional clauses and their meaning, *see infra*, Sect. 10.4.2. The Clarity and Unambiguity of the Category of Disputes.

and procedures; and (3) they should not to go beyond the settlement of specific disputes.[35] In addition, when a jurisdictional clause operates within the broader context of a case that involves a substantive FTA norm analysed as an MAS, such a MAS should be consistent with the covered agreements. Although some of these conditions and their interpretations are regarded have been regarded as erroneous in the previous chapter,[36] they will still be considered here, given the high probability that the conditions established in existing jurisprudence would be followed in future disputes

10.4   The Clarity and Unambiguity of the Jurisdictional Clauses in the New Generation EU FTAs

This section will scrutinise the jurisdictional clauses in the new generation EU FTAs to establish whether they clearly relinquish the right to initiate WTO proceedings. It will investigate whether they clearly enunciate that WTO proceedings should not be initiated subsequently or in parallel to FTA proceedings and whether they clearly define the category of disputes with respect to which they are applicable. Since the bar was set very high by WTO case law for being considered clear and unambiguous,[37] it can be expected that every potential ambiguity may be held against the respondent and in favour of the exercise of the jurisdiction of WTO panels.[38] The analysis in this section will be performed in light of this benchmark, which aims to prevent groundless deprivation of WTO Members of their right to use the WTO DSM.

10.4.1   The Clarity and Unambiguity of the Relinquishment of the Right to Initiate WTO Proceedings

All the full fork-in-the-road clauses in the new generation EU FTAs, with slightly different language, provide that once a dispute settlement proceeding has been *initiated* under one agreement for a specific category of disputes under the FTA and the WTO Agreement, the party *shall not* initiate proceedings in another forum and seek redress for claims under other agreements, unless the first forum fails for jurisdictional or procedural reasons to make findings on that claim.[39] Therefore, by

---

[35] *See supra*, Sect. 9.4.

[36] *See supra*, Sect. 9.4.

[37] Marceau (2013), p. 12; Shlomo Agon (2019), p. 306.

[38] Zang (2019), p. 45.

[39] EUKFTA, Art 14.19(2); CETA, Art 29.3(2); EUJEPA, Art 21.27(2); EUSFTA, Art 14.21(2); EUVFTA, Art 15.24(2).

clearly using the mandatory expression *shall not*, these clauses explicitly prohibit the initiation of procedures under other DSMs. As the decisive moment for such a prohibition is the initiation of proceedings in another forum first, it is clear that these provisions address both parallel and subsequent proceedings on the same disputes. Thus, it is not necessary for a case to be finalised under the first proceedings; it is sufficient for the proceedings to be initiated. Nor do they provide that the effect of such a prohibition lasts only until the first proceedings are concluded.[40] Therefore, by introducing these clauses in their FTAs, the parties clearly agreed not to initiate WTO proceedings at any time when they would first initiate FTA proceedings, and that such proceedings would not fail to make findings for jurisdictional or procedural reasons. Moreover, the FTAs provide a further degree of clarity by defining when disputes under the FTA and the WTO are initiated in the paragraphs that follow those that include the fork-in-the-road clauses.[41] Thus, there is no room for ambiguity: the choice is definite, as recourse to WTO proceedings is precluded and the exact moment when it becomes so is also clearly established. Hence, the parties have clearly relinquished their right to initiate WTO proceedings with respect to a certain category of disputes.

The limited fork-in-the-road clauses in the EUKFTA and EUSFTA explicitly provide that when a party has initiated dispute settlement proceedings with regard to a particular measure, it *may not institute* proceedings on the same measure in another forum until the first proceedings are concluded.[42] The word 'may' expresses a possibility or permission.[43] When used together with the negation 'not' this possibility or permission is excluded. The expression 'may not' with the meaning of a prohibition is used in other international treaties. For example, the TBT Agreement, the Customs Valuation Agreement, the Agreement on Import Licensing Procedures, and the Agreement on Trade Facilitation prohibit reservations, by providing that 'reservations *may not* be entered in respect of any of the provisions of this Agreement without the consent of the other Members' (emphasis added).[44] The VCLT also uses the expression 'may not invoke' in Article 27 to establish the prohibition of invocation of internal law as a justification for the failure to perform a treaty obligation. When analysing Article 9.3 of the Anti-Dumping Agreement, which states that the amount of anti-dumping duty is not to exceed the margin of dumping using the expressions 'shall not' and 'may not' interchangeably, the panel in *Argentina – Poultry* stated that 'Article 9.3 provides that a duty *may not* be collected in excess of the margin of dumping' (emphasis added).[45] Similarly, when describing the claimant's arguments in *Argentina – Footwear*, the AB referred to Article 5 of

---

[40]Furculita (2019, pp. 33–34).

[41]*See supra*, Sect. 10.2.3.

[42]EUKFTA, Art 14.19(2) first sentence; EUSFTA, Art 14.21(2) first sentence.

[43]Lexico Powered by Oxford <www.lexico.com/definition/may>.

[44]TBT Agreement, Art 15.1; Customs Valuation Agreement, Art 21; The Agreement on Import Licensing Procedures, 15 April 1994, Marrakesh Agreement, 1869 U.N.T.S. 436, Art 8.1; The Agreement on Trade Facilitation, 22 February 2017, Art 24.9.

[45]Panel Report, *Argentina – Poultry*, [7.355].

the Safeguards Agreement mandating that '[a] Member shall apply safeguard mea-sures only to the extent necessary to prevent or remedy serious injury' and interpreted it as indicating that 'a measure *may not* exceed what is necessary to remedy the injury' (emphasis added).[46] Accordingly, the expression 'may not' has been broadly used in international treaties and WTO jurisprudence to express a prohibition, sometimes interchangeably with the expression 'shall not'. Thus, the clauses from the EUKFTA and EUSFTA clearly establish that parties are not allowed to initiate parallel WTO proceedings.

The limited fork-in-the-road clauses in the EUKFTA and EUSFTA also unam-biguously provide when exactly a dispute is considered concluded under the FTAs and the WTO.[47] Nevertheless, it would be difficult to argue that the right to initiate WTO proceedings was relinquished in these clauses, considering that after the first proceedings are concluded, dispute settlement proceedings can be initiated for the same measures in another forum. It could be argued that the right has been relinquished for the limited period between initiation and conclusion of proceedings in another forum. However, if WTO panels were to consider such a clause, whether the exclusion of parallel proceedings (only) on the same measure is a clear relin-quishment would not be unambiguous. Hence, a limited fork-in-the-road clause, similar to the clauses considered in *Argentina – Poultry* and *Peru – Agricultural Products*, does not seem to entirely relinquish the right to initiate WTO disputes for the category of disputes it covers as it does not restrict the right to bring subsequent WTO proceedings.

Finally, the clarity of potential exclusive jurisdictional clauses with respect to FTA countermeasures will be assessed. These clauses use the mandatory expression 'the WTO Agreement shall not be invoked'. As they prohibit *invocation* of the WTO Agreement, it seems that they also prohibit bringing claims on WTO violations. Nevertheless, it could also be argued that they simply prohibit invocation of WTO norms by the defendant as substantive defences against the imposition of counter-measures within FTA proceedings. Hence, relinquishment of the right to initiate WTO proceedings in this situation may be perceived as ambiguous, compared to the fork-in-the-road clauses that use and define the term initiation of proceedings, making it clear that they refer to the right to initiate proceedings. The fact that these clauses are in the dispute settlement chapters of the EU FTAs and are part of the articles entitled 'Choice of Forum' in the majority shows that they are concerned with the procedural question of whether countermeasures can be contested in the WTO forum, rather than whether the substantive WTO norms could be invoked as a defence. Nevertheless, because of the high bar for clarity of the relinquishment of the right to initiate WTO proceedings, it is advisable to draft jurisdictional clauses on countermeasures so that they unequivocally state that a party *shall not initiate proceedings seeking redress for the breach of WTO obligations* to preclude a party

---

[46] Appellate Body Report, *Argentina – Safeguard Measures on Imports of Footwear (Argentina – Footwear)*, WT/DS121/AB/R, 14 December 1999, [14].

[47] *See supra*, Sect. 10.2.3.

from suspending obligations under the FTA dispute settlement chapters. The ability of the fork-in-the-road clauses in the new generation EU FTAs to successfully resolve conflicts of jurisdiction would be seriously undermined if the exclusive jurisdictional clauses on countermeasures would not prevent WTO proceedings on the FTA countermeasures. If countermeasures imposed in the process of implementation of an FTA ruling would be subject to WTO proceedings, the initial complainant in the dispute might not be able to satisfy its intention of compliance and the purpose of the FTA proceedings and the fork-in-the-road clauses would be defeated, as the final result of the proceedings would be challenged in another forum. Hence, it is of the utmost importance that exclusive jurisdictional clauses on countermeasures are drafted clearly and given consideration within the WTO DSM.

Therefore, while the full fork-in-the-road clauses in all the new generation EU FTAs clearly relinquish the right to initiate WTO proceedings, the limited clauses in the EUKFTA and EUSFTA and the potential exclusive jurisdictional clauses on countermeasures could fail to pass the high benchmark for clarity established by WTO case law. It is advisable that the additional jurisdictional clauses on countermeasures are drafted without any ambiguity, so that the potential successful exercise of the fork-in-the-road clauses is not undermined.

10.4.2   The Clarity and Unambiguity of the Category of Disputes

To establish the clarity and unambiguity of the jurisdictional clauses in the new generation EU FTAs, it is essential to delineate the category of disputes that these clauses cover; otherwise, it cannot be clear with respect to which disputes the right to initiate WTO proceedings is relinquished.

The EUKFTA's full fork-in-the-road clause refers to 'identical obligation under the other agreement' as the category to which it applies.[48] Since it uses the term 'identical', it is clear that the legal bases for the disputes initiated at the two fora have to be formulated identically; therefore, the FTA norm would be identical to the WTO norm if the former either incorporates or faithfully replicates the latter. This provision seems very similar to the *lis alibi pendens* and *res judicata* principles according to which once proceedings are initiated, no other proceedings on the same dispute may be brought in parallel or subsequence. However, unlike these principles under which legal claims identical in substance under different agreements would most likely be considered different,[49] the fork-in-the-road clause from the EUKFTA clearly refers to an identical obligation under *the other agreement*. Therefore, the mere fact that two identical obligations are provided in different agreements does not lessen the usefulness of this clause. While clearly identifying the category of

---

[48] EUKFTA, Art 14.19(2), second sentence.

[49] *See supra*, Sect. 9.2.1.1.

disputes to which it applies, the coverage of the fork-in-the-road clause in the EUKFTA is, nevertheless, very narrow. It would not cover FTA norms with wording different from that of WTO norms, although in substance they would be the same, similar, or would regulate the same matter.

The full fork-in-the-road clauses of CETA, EUJEPA, EUSFTA and EUVFTA cover the category of disputes on WTO and FTA obligations that are *substantially equivalent* or *different*. It is important to establish, first of all, the meaning of the term 'substantially'. The term 'substantially' means 'to a great or significant extent' or 'for the most part, essentially'.[50] In a similar manner, in interpretations of Article XXIV:8 of GATT, the expression 'substantially all trade' has been defined as meaning 'not the same as all the trade' and also 'something considerably more than merely some of the trade'. Therefore, the term 'substantially' refers to the degree or extent of something, whose exact size is difficult to establish. If the term 'substantially' were used in this sense in relation to the fork-in-the-road clauses in the new generation EU FTAs, it would refer to an undefined degree and extent of equivalence or difference between norms that would be rather ambiguous. The interchangeable use of the terms 'in substance' and 'substantially' in CETA,[51] and the fact that the parties to CETA used the expression 'obligation that is equivalent in substance' when referring to the fork-in-the-road clause in the Questions and Replies to the WTO Committee on Regional Trade Agreements,[52] show that the EU refers to the substance of the obligations in its FTAs rather than to the degree of equivalence between the norms. Therefore, it is advisable for the EU to use the expression 'obligations equivalent in substance' when drafting its fork-in-the-road clauses to eliminate possible ambiguities raised against the consideration of these clauses as clear relinquishments of the right to initiate WTO proceedings.

As equivalence and difference between WTO and FTA norms refer to their substance, the next question is how this relationship can be established. Lanyi and Steinbach interpreted the expression 'equivalent in substance' as referring to WTO provisions incorporated or reproduced in the FTAs and those that 'while not identical, are equivalent in substance to WTO rules'.[53] Lanyi and Steinbach, themselves, believe that it may be difficult to establish what equivalent in substance means.[54] In a similar fashion, Broude and Shany identified norms provided in different sources of international law as being equivalent when they are 'similar or identical in their normative content'.[55] Referring to CETA's clause, Kuijper also

---

[50] Oxford Dictionary <https://en.oxforddictionaries.com/definition/substantially>.

[51] CETA, Art 29.3(2).

[52] Committee on Regional Trade Agreements, 'Comprehensive Economic and Trade Agreement Between Canada and the European Union (Goods and Services) – Questions and Replies', WT/REG389/2, 6 June 2018 <https://docs.wto.org/dol2fe/Pages/FE_Search/FE_S_S006.aspx?Query=@Symbol=%20(wt/reg389/*)&Language=ENGLISH&Context=FomerScriptedSearch&languageUIChanged=true#>.

[53] Lanyi and Steinbach (2014), p. 392.

[54] Ibid.

[55] Broude and Shany (2011), p. 5.

concluded that it provides a 'broad formula' that does not require complete identity between the claims and obligations within WTO and FTA fora.[56] Thus, the full fork-in-the-road clauses in CETA, EUJEPA, and EUVFTA seem to refer to broader categories that do not require complete identity between the WTO and FTA obligations, since being only similar would suffice. The EUSFTA fork-in-the-road clause provides that it covers disputes on all obligations unless they are *different* in substance. Therefore, unlike CETA, EUJEPA, and EUVFTA, it uses a negative demarcation for the category of disputes to which it applies. Since it solely requires that the obligations are not different, rather than being identical, it is advanced here that like the *equivalent* norms, it also covers obligations that are both identical and similar in their substance. While these categories are aimed at addressing conflicting jurisdictions that involve not only identical but also similar FTA and WTO norms, thus ensuring greater coherence, precise establishment of their boundaries may be difficult in practice.

For norms that have identical content, such as FTA norms that reproduce or incorporate WTO norms, there should be no problems in establishing their equivalence; the difficulty would arise with norms that are similar, but not identical.[57] Establishing the similarity of norms from different sources involves a process of comparison of their normative content.[58] Such a comparison would need to be performed by the panels investigating the question of whether the fork-in-the-road clauses have been exercised. Similarity cannot be established without comparing two things, such as a WTO and an FTA norm. The similarity between two norms is established when a dispute materialises and the two norms to be compared are identified.[59] Therefore, whether an FTA norm is similar to a WTO one should be established on a case-by-case basis. The scope of application of the fork-in-the road clauses of the new generation EU FTAs fork-in-the road clauses will be contingent on the assessment of specific obligations involved in the disputes in the two different fora. This would imply considerable willingness on the part of WTO panels to look into the substance of non-WTO law for the purpose of making determinations under WTO law.

As the similarity of two norms would have to be assessed for every case, WTO panels may view these jurisdictional clauses as vague and ambiguous. However, this author considers that such a conclusion would be unfounded. Finding the full fork-in-the-road clauses ambiguous would be equal to denying the right to find a good faith violation if the relinquishment of the right would not refer to disputes on identical obligations. As Kuijper concluded in his assessment of CETA's jurisdictional clause and its effect on conflicting jurisdictions, '[n]egotiators have done what they could in order to prevent this from happening and that is the maximum one can reasonably ask for'.[60] There is no clearer and less ambiguous way to address conflicting jurisdictions when they concern similar, but not identical, obligations.

---

[56] Kuijper (2016).

[57] Furculita (2019, p. 35).

[58] Denters and Gazzini (2011), p. 80.

[59] Furculita (2019, p. 35).

[60] Kuijper (2016).

The limited fork-in-the-road clauses in the EUKFTA and EUSFTA refer to a rather broad category of disputes on the *same measure*. The measure could be in violation of WTO and FTA norms that are completely different in substance, as measure, matter, and claim are different notions. This can also be deduced from the AB's reasoning that the matter consists of a specific measure and the legal basis of the complaint.[61] Therefore, the category that the clause covers is clear—it refers specifically to the measure. Moreover, it refers to a concept familiar to WTO panels. In *India – Autos*, the panel evaluated whether the measures in two disputes were the same, albeit both were considered within WTO disputes.[62] There is no ambiguity about the category covered by the potential exclusive jurisdictional clauses on the countermeasures as they explicitly refer to suspension of obligations under the dispute settlement chapters.

In conclusion, it is submitted that all jurisdictional clauses from the new generation EU FTAs should be regarded as clearly defining the category of disputes that they cover. While some doubts could occur about the full fork-in-the-road clauses with a broader coverage, it was argued that it would not be possible to define the category more clearly and less ambiguously than the drafters have already done, if the same broad coverage that is aimed at providing greater coherence is to be preserved. Nevertheless, it is suggested that the term 'in substance' be used instead of 'substantially' to avoid any potential uncertainty about its meaning.

10.5   Relating to DSU Rules and Procedures

The AB's reasoning in *Peru – Agricultural Products* seems to require relinquishment of the right to initiate proceedings in any form other than an MAS to relate to DSU rules and procedures.[63] Although there is no clarity about the legal basis of this requirement enunciated by the AB, it has been argued that it could be regarded as supplementing the clarity requirement.[64] Considering that WTO panels and the AB may affirm this requirement in potential cases dealing with violations of Articles 3.7 and 3.10 of the DSU, it is relevant to examine the consistency of the jurisdictional clauses with the requirement.

The new generation EU FTAs studied do not expressly refer to DSU rules and procedures in the paragraphs that contain the full and limited fork-in-the-road clauses. However, the paragraphs that follow define the moment of initiation of different procedures. They expressly refer to the DSU by establishing that dispute settlement procedures under the WTO are deemed to be initiated when a party

---

[61] Appellate Body Report, *Guatemala – Anti-Dumping Investigation Regarding Portland Cement from Mexico (Guatemala – Cement I)*, WT/DS60/AB/R, 2 November 1998, [72].

[62] Panel Report, *India – Autos*, [7.83-7.86].

[63] Appellate Body Report, *Peru – Agricultural Products*, [5.25].

[64] *See supra*, Sect. 9.4.3.

requests the establishment of a panel under Article 6 of the DSU.[65] Hence, the jurisdictional clauses of the EU FTAs under analysis expressly relate to a specific rule of the DSU. When reading the fork-in-the-road clauses together with their subsequent paragraphs, it becomes clear that the right relinquished in these clauses is that prescribed by Article 6 of the DSU—the right to initiate WTO proceedings. Accordingly, the fork-in-the-road clauses in the new generation EU FTAs should be regarded as complying with the requirement set by the AB in *Peru – Agricultural Products*, if followed in future disputes.

The potential exclusive jurisdictional clauses on countermeasures do not use the term 'initiate', and it is ambiguous whether they relinquish the right to initiate proceedings or merely the right to invoke substantive arguments on WTO agreements within FTA proceedings. Therefore, they cannot be read together with the paragraphs that define when WTO proceedings are initiated and, consequently, are not related expressly to DSU rules and proceedings. This could be remediated by using the draft text recommended to redress potential doubts of clarity[66] that uses the term 'to initiate', thereby linking the clauses to the paragraphs explicitly referring to Article 6 of the DSU. Parties are urged to pay attention to the drafting of potential exclusive jurisdictional clauses on countermeasures, since challenging an FTA-authorised countermeasure in WTO proceedings may render FTA proceedings and fork-in-the-road clauses futile.

Therefore, the fork-in-the-road clauses in the new generation EU FTAs would comply with the requirement to relate to DSU rules on procedures, if followed. Nevertheless, this requirement may be a hurdle for jurisdictional clauses on countermeasures, proposals on how parties could resolve this significant issue being made in this section.

10.6 'Consistent with the Covered Agreements'

If jurisdictional clauses are invoked in a case in which the WTO panel and the AB decide to investigate a waiver in the form of an MAS, the proposed solution needs to be 'consistent with the covered agreements'.[67] It makes little sense to consider applying a requirement specific to an MAS in a case where the analysis is focused merely on a fork-in-the-road clause that is not intended to resolve a dispute. It is also unlikely that countermeasures imposed under FTA dispute settlement chapters could be considered MAS, as they are not 'act[s] of solving a problem'[68] but rather

---

[65] EUKFTA, Art 14.19(3)(a); CETA, Art 29.3 (3)(a); EUJEPA, Art 21.27(3)(b); EUSFTA, Art 14.21(3)(a); EUVFTA, Art 15.24(3)(a).

[66] *See supra*, Sect. 10.4.1.

[67] Appellate Body Report, *Peru – Agricultural Products*, [5.26].

[68] This was the expression used by the AB to define an MAS in *EC – Bananas III (Article 21.5 – Ecuador II/Article 21.5 – US)*, [212].

remedies to induce compliance, nor are they agreed by the parties. Therefore, the requirement to be consistent with the covered agreements should not be considered in the context of jurisdictional clauses on countermeasures.

Nevertheless, the framework of the MAS could potentially be applied if the FTA in question contained a substantive provision that purported to resolve the dispute between the parties and the fork-in-the-road clauses would be considered additional elements for analysis to demonstrate that the intention of the parties was, clearly, to waive their right to bring disputes on that substantive norm, as happened in *Peru – Agricultural Products*. Taking into account established case law, this section analyses the implications of such a requirement for fork-in-the-road clauses of the new generation EU FTAs, which may be regarded as a part of the analysis of a relinquishment, in the form of an MAS, of the right to initiate WTO procedures.

This requirement would be relevant, especially in a dispute concerning WTO-minus norms included in FTAs, which by definition are illegal under the WTO.[69] In addition, WTO-minus norms cannot be justified by Article XXIV of GATT on the creation of FTAs. The AB report from *Turkey – Textiles* establishes that according to Article XXIV:4 of GATT, the purpose of an FTA is to 'facilitate trade'[70] between the parties. The report from *Peru – Agricultural Products* adds that 'the references in paragraph 4 to facilitating trade and closer integration are not consistent with an interpretation of Article XXIV as a broad defence for measures in FTAs that roll back on Members' rights and obligations under the WTO covered agreements'.[71] These reports lead to the conclusion that WTO-minus norms cannot be justified by Article XXIV of GATT. Thus, despite its compliance with the rest of the criteria, a fork-in-the-road clause evaluated in the context of a substantive WTO-minus norm treated as an MAS could be ignored by WTO panels in a situation of conflicting jurisdictions.

Since the full fork-in-the-road clauses in the new generation EU FTAs cover only FTA obligations that are equivalent or identical in substance to WTO norms, the WTO-minus norms do not fall under this category. They would be illegal under the WTO and cannot, therefore, be identical or equivalent to WTO norms. Accordingly, the parties to these FTAs evidently did not relinquish through these clauses their right to initiate parallel or subsequent WTO proceedings with respect to WTO-inconsistent norms. Nevertheless, the limited fork-in-the-road clauses in the EUKFTA and EUSFTA that cover disputes on the 'same measure' could also cover disputes on WTO-minus norms, as well as other inconsistent FTA norms. Therefore, if these jurisdictional clauses are assessed in the context of WTO-inconsistent FTA norms evaluated as MAS, they might not operate as legal impediments to the exercise of the jurisdiction of WTO panels.

To conclude, while the requirement specific for MAS to be consistent with the WTO covered agreements should not affect the operation of the full fork-in-the-road

---

[69] *See supra*, Sect. 5.1.

[70] Appellate Body Report, *Turkey – Textiles*, [57].

[71] Appellate Body Report, *Peru – Additional Products*, [5.116].

clauses in the new generation EU FTAs, it could have an impact on the functioning of the limited fork-in-the-road clauses.

10.7   Not Going 'Beyond the Settlement of Specific Disputes'

The requirement for a relinquishment of the right to initiate WTO proceedings to not go 'beyond the settlement of specific disputes' does not seem to have a textual basis in the DSU.[72] Nonetheless, this section will consider whether the new generation EU FTAs jurisdictional clauses would comply with it, if WTO panels and the AB or an MPIA arbitrator do not depart from case law in future disputes, but instead, reiterate it.

If the requirement to not go 'beyond the settlement of specific disputes' is interpreted narrowly as requesting application to single disputes that have already arisen, then there is no jurisdictional clause that would qualify under it.[73] Drafters of jurisdictional clauses could, nevertheless, try to comply with the broad interpretation that requires mentioning a category of disputes to which the clauses apply. All the new generation EU FTAs studied refer in their jurisdictional clauses to a specific category of disputes on 'identical obligation under the other agreement', 'substantially equivalent obligations under the other agreement', 'unless substantially different obligations under both agreements', 'the same measure', and 'suspension of obligations authorised by the DSB'. According to the Oxford Dictionary, 'specific' means 'clearly defined or identified'.[74]

Since the new generation EU FTAs identify and clearly define categories of disputes with respect to which the right to initiate WTO proceedings could be considered relinquished, the new generation EU FTAs would comply with the broad interpretation of the requirement to not go 'beyond the settlement of specific disputes'.

10.8   Jurisdictional Clauses in the Context of the AB Crisis

The final section of this chapter will examine the operation of fork-in-the-road clauses in the new generation EU FTAs in the context of the AB crisis. It will assess critical aspects that could influence the effects of these clauses if a panel report is sent into limbo by an appeal or if parties sign no appeal pacts or use the MPIA at the appeal stage.

---

[72] *See supra* Sect. 9.4.3.

[73] *See supra*, Sect. 9.4.3.

[74] Oxford Dictionaries <https://en.oxforddictionaries.com/definition/specific>.

The content of the jurisdictional clauses is important not only from the perspective of preventing WTO panels from exercising their jurisdiction, but also for the ability of the FTA panels to exercise their jurisdiction in the context of the AB crisis. These jurisdictional clauses could represent an impediment to FTA parties bringing disputes to FTA DSMs subsequent to WTO proceedings, as the FTA panels would directly apply FTA jurisdictional clauses. While these clauses are aimed at ensuring coherence in the international trade law regime, they might also affect the possibility of bringing FTA disputes after appealed panel reports are sent into the void in the absence of a functional AB to hear the appeals, causing the disputes to remain unresolved. If the disputing parties sign *ex-ante* or *ad-hoc* non-appeal arrangements to avoid panel reports being sent into the void, the reports should be adopted by the DSB without any clear repercussions for the regular exercise of FTA jurisdictional clauses.

Since a dispute is considered initiated but not completed under DSU rules when the appealed WTO panel report is not adopted,[75] both the full and limited fork-in-the-road clauses are likely to prohibit subsequent initiation of proceedings under FTAs. Nevertheless, under the new generation EU FTAs, these clauses have effect unless the selected forums fail for 'jurisdictional or procedural reasons' 'to make findings' on the claim.[76] The issue is whether the WTO panels whose reports are in limbo could be considered as failing to make findings because of jurisdictional or procedural reasons. Clearly, appealed panel reports cannot be regarded as failing for jurisdictional reasons merely because the report was appealed. If the panel confirmed that it had jurisdiction over the claims at issue, the appeal into the void cannot have any jurisdictional impact. The procedural reasons remain unclear and may be considered by some as being the potential legal basis to be invoked to allow parallel or subsequent FTA proceedings if WTO panel reports are in limbo. Nevertheless, the expression 'fail to make findings' clarifies that this cannot be the case. Under DSU rules, findings are set out in panel reports as early as at the interim review stage.[77] Thus, panel reports, even when appealed and not adopted, contain findings,[78] and panels cannot be regarded as failing to make conclusions if their reports are appealed into the void. Therefore, jurisdictional clauses will prevent parties from using FTA DSMs as alternatives to settling disputes on covered norms when the already initiated WTO disputes remain unresolved because of appeals and the absence of an alternative mechanism within the WTO, such as appeal arbitration proceedings. Since an unadopted panel report cannot be viewed as demonstrating a failure to make findings on claims for procedural or jurisdictional clauses, the EU FTA fork-in-the-road clauses will prevent subsequent and parallel FTA adjudication. Accordingly, if the new generation EU FTA DSMs are considered potential alternatives to

---

[75] For the definition of initiated and completed WTO proceedings, *see* (nn 31, 32).

[76] EUKFTA, Art 14.19(2), second and third sentences; EUSFTA, Art 14.21(2), second sentence; CETA, Art 29.3(2); EUJEPA, Art 21.27(2).

[77] DSU, Art 15.2, 15.3.

[78] DSU, Art 12.7.

the WTO mechanism during the AB crisis, FTA parties should initiate disputes under the FTAs immediately, and not subsequent to or in parallel with WTO proceedings.

Another potential question is whether the fork-in-the-road clauses in the new generation EU FTAs are operational and WTO proceedings deemed initiated and not failed in the event of appeal arbitration arrangements. In the event of FTA parties participating in an interim appeal arbitration arrangement, such as the MPIA according to which arbitration should be used solely for the appeal stage, panel proceedings are still initiated according to Article 6 of the DSU. Therefore, the fork-in-the-road clauses in the EU FTAs studied cover the proceedings that use arbitration at the appeal stage, as they would cover proceedings conducted by the AB if it were functional.

The MPIA provides that following the issuance of the final report to the parties and 10 days before it is circulated to the rest of the membership, any party may request that the panel proceedings are suspended with a view to initiating appeal arbitration procedures.[79] The request is deemed a joint request to suspend the panel proceedings for 12 months pursuant to Article 12.12 of the DSU according to which a panel may suspend its work for a maximum of 12 months.[80] Whether suspended panel reports could be viewed as failing to make findings because of jurisdictional or procedural reasons could be an additional confusion. Evidently, final panel reports cannot be regarded as failing to make findings for jurisdictional reasons, as the suspension cannot affect the jurisdiction of the panels in any way. Due to the use of the expression 'fail to make findings' dealt with earlier in this section, as long as the proceedings are suspended *after* the final panel report is issued, as required by the MPIA, even if the 12-month period expires, they cannot also be considered as failed because of procedural reasons.

The application of the additional jurisdictional clauses on countermeasures could also be affected by the AB crisis. If states decide to use unilateral measures to enforce their rights when a panel report is sent into the void by an appeal, and there is no alternative mechanism such as appeal arbitration, these measures could be subject to FTA arbitration provided that the claims are on violations of FTA norms. Thus, potential suspensions of concessions without the DSB's authorisation, as provided under the amended EU Enforcement regulation,[81] in the case of a panel report being appealed into the void and in the absence of an interim appeal arbitration agreement, will not be covered by these additional jurisdictional clauses. Although the EU amendments relies purportedly on customary international law as codified by the ILC articles on responsibility,[82] there would be no authorisation by the DSB as

---

[79] MPIA, Annex 1, para 4.

[80] Ibid.

[81] Regulation (EU) 2021/167 of the European Parliament and of the Council of 10 February 2021 amending Regulation (EU) No 654/2014 concerning the exercise of the Union's rights for the application and enforcement of international trade rules, OJ L 49, 12.2.2021.

[82] The assessment of whether WTO Member States could, indeed, make use of customary international law as a legal basis when imposing countermeasures 'where a State party fails to cooperate in

required by these additional jurisdictional clauses. On the other hand, the additional jurisdictional clauses would cover the countermeasures authorised by the DSB for implementation of appeal arbitration awards. Since Article 22 of the DSU on compensation and suspension of concessions applies *mutatis mutandis* to arbitration awards,[83] countermeasures imposed for non-implementation of an arbitration award would have to be authorised by the DSB. Therefore, jurisdictional clauses on countermeasures would operate in case of the implementation of appeal arbitration awards in the same manner as they would in the implementation of final AB reports.

The way the jurisdictional clauses in the new generation EU FTAs operate in the context of the AB crisis is an essential aspect that deserves special attention. In the case of NAPs and the MPIA, this section concluded that their operation should remain unchanged. Both full and limited fork-in-the-road clauses would not allow initiation of parallel FTA proceedings for the categories of disputes that they cover, in case a WTO panel report is sent into the void in the context of a dysfunctional AB. Finally, while the application of additional jurisdictional clauses on counter-measures will remain unchanged in case of interim appeal arbitration agreements, they would have no applicability over unilateral countermeasures, including those based on customary international law.

10.9   Conclusion

This chapter assessed the jurisdictional clauses in the new generation EU FTAs. It began by identifying the substantive areas with respect to which conflicting juris-dictions between the new generation EU FTA and WTO DSMs could arise—situations in which jurisdictional clauses would be needed. It was established that by excluding certain areas from the coverage of the new generation EU FTA DSMs, the parties likely wanted to prevent conflicts of jurisdiction, an intention that also supports the assertion that the authority of the WTO DSM should not be regarded as undermined by the FTAs analysed and that a functional WTO DSM is necessary from the perspective of the FTAs. The chapter introduced the jurisdictional clauses in the EU FTAs studied and established that each of the agreements has a full fork-in-the-road clause covering a specific category of disputes, as well as, a potential exclusive jurisdictional clause on countermeasures. In addition, the EUKFTA and EUSFTA also provide limited fork-in-the-road clauses addressing only potential parallel disputes on the same measures. As previously argued, the full fork-in-the-road clauses, if invoked within FTA proceedings, would adequately address the risks of conflicting jurisdictions and would bring greater coherence to the international trading regime, especially in the case of clauses with a wider coverage that do not

---

the establishment of the relevant tribunal' is outside the scope of this book. In this respect see Weiss and Furculita (2020).
[83]DSU, Art 25(4).

refer only to identical obligations. Furthermore, the additional clauses on counter-measures would further alleviate the risk of incoherencies, by precluding parties from bringing claims of FTA violation in relation to DSB-authorised measures.

The chapter further assessed the likelihood of EU FTA jurisdictional clauses resolving conflicting jurisdictions if invoked within WTO proceedings, especially in light of the conditions established by the relevant WTO jurisprudence on Articles 3.7 and 3.10 of the DSU. While some of the conditions enunciated by WTO panels and the AB have no legal basis and have been criticized in the previous chapter, given that these conditions might be reiterated in future disputes, this chapter considered the compliance of jurisdictional clauses with all of them.

The limited fork-in-the-road-clauses refer to DSU rules and cover a clear category of disputes. However, since they allow subsequent proceedings, they could be perceived as ambiguously relinquishing the right to initiate WTO proceedings. Moreover, since they cover disputes on the same measure, they might also face hurdles if investigated in the context of an MAS that is not in compliance with the DSU rules. On the other hand, the potential exclusive jurisdictional clauses on compliance, despite clearly establishing the category to which they apply, might fail to pass the high standard of clarity for relinquishment of the right to initiate WTO proceedings. Furthermore, they do not relate to DSU rules. The chapter made suggestions to remediate both these potential deficiencies. Thus, it is advisable to draft jurisdictional clauses on countermeasures so that they unequivocally state that a party *shall not initiate proceedings seeking redress for the breach of WTO obligations* to preclude a party from suspending obligations under the FTA dispute settlement chapters. The importance of having jurisdictional clauses on countermeasures for the successful functioning of FTA proceedings and for meaningful application of the fork-in-the-road clauses was also stressed. If the potential jurisdictional clauses on countermeasures are not given consideration within WTO proceedings, the effect of the fork-in-the-road clauses would be considerably weakened.

The full fork-in-the-road clauses in the new generation EU FTAs proved to establish quite clearly that parallel and subsequent proceedings are prohibited when they concern certain categories of disputes. To fully comply with the requirement for clarity and unambiguity, the use of the term 'in substance' instead of 'substantially' is recommended. The requirement of 'not [going] beyond the settlement of specific disputes' has no legal basis. Nevertheless, the jurisdictional clauses in the new generation EU FTAs should be regarded as in compliance with the broad interpretation of this requirement. These clauses also comply with the requirement for reference to DSU provisions and cover only norms consistent with the WTO covered agreements, as stipulated. Therefore, with a jurisprudence that would reflect the law, the full fork-in-the-road clauses in the new generation EU FTAs may be considered good candidates to qualify as relinquishments of the right to initiate procedures under the WTO and, consequently, for resolving jurisdictional conflicts when invoked within WTO proceedings.

Given that they would adequately address the issue of conflicting jurisdictions when invoked within FTA proceedings and that they have a high likelihood of successfully addressing the same issue when considered within WTO proceedings, the full fork-in-the road clauses show that the EU is striving to balance its multilateral and bilateral trade policy aspirations. To balance the two aspirations to an even greater degree, the modifications suggested in this chapter should be considered, at least when negotiating other FTAs from the EU's ambitious trade agenda.

In its final section, the chapter considered essential aspects that could influence the operation of the fork-in-the-road clauses in the new generation EU FTAs in the context of the AB crisis. While the fork-in-the-road clauses would have a similar effect to that of a functioning AB in case of NAPs and the MPIA, they would likely prevent FTA parties from bringing the same disputes to FTA DSMs as alternative mechanisms if WTO panel reports are sent into the void by appeals. Finally, unilateral countermeasures and those based on customary international law could be subject to FTA adjudication, as they would not be covered by additional jurisdictional clauses on countermeasures. Nevertheless, the operation of the additional jurisdictional clauses on countermeasures would remain unchanged if invoked with respect to countermeasures authorised by the DSB for implementation of appeal arbitration awards.

References

Broude T, Shany Y (2011) The international law and policy of multi-sourced equivalent norms. In: Broude T, Shany Y (eds) Multi-sourced equivalent norms in international law. Hart, Oxford, pp 1–16

Denters E, Gazzini T (2011) Multi-sourced equivalent norms from the standpoint of governments. In: Broude T, Shany Y (eds) Multi-sourced equivalent norms in international law. Hart, Oxford, pp 69–89

Furculita C (2019) Fork-in-the-road clauses in the new EU FTAs: addressing conflicts of jurisdictions with the WTO dispute settlement mechanism. CLLER Paper 2019/1. www.asser.nl/media/5268/cleer19-01_web.pdf

Horn H, Mavroidis PC, Sapir A (2009) Beyond the WTO? An anatomy of EU and US preferential trade agreements. Bruegel Blueprint Series, Brussels

Kuijper PJ (2010) Conflicting rules and clashing courts: the case of multilateral environmental agreements. Free Trade Agreements and the WTO. ICTSD Issue Paper No. 10, pp 1–64

Kuijper PJ (2016) Preface. TDM 1 CETA Special. www.transnational-dispute-management.com/article.asp?key=2309

Kwak K, Marceau G (2006) Overlaps and conflicts of jurisdiction between the WTO and RTAs. In: Bartels L, Ortino F (eds) Regional trade agreements and the WTO legal system. Oxford University Press, New York, pp 465–524

Lanyi PA, Steinbach A (2014) Limiting jurisdictional fragmentation in international trade disputes. J Int Dispute Settlement 5:372–405

Marceau G (2013) The primacy of the WTO dispute settlement. Questions Int Law J 23:3–13

Natens B, Descheemaeker S (2015) Say it loud, say it clear – Article 3.10 DSU's clear statement test as a legal impediment to validly established jurisdiction. J World Trade 49(5):873–890

Shlomo Agon S (2019) International adjudication on trial. The effectiveness of the WTO dispute settlement system. Oxford University Press, New York

Stoll PT (2019) The WTO dispute settlement system and regional trade tribunals: the potential for conflict and solutions. In: do Amaral Júnior A, de Oliveira Sá Pires LM, Carneiro CL (eds) The WTO dispute settlement mechanism: a developing country perspective. Springer, Heidelberg, pp 229–244

Weiss W, Furculita C (2020) The EU in search for stronger enforcement rules: assessing the proposed amendments to trade enforcement regulation 654/2014. J Int Econ Law 23 (4):865–884

Zang MQ (2019) When the multilateral meets the regionals: regional trade agreements at WTO dispute settlement. World Trade Rev 18(1):33–61

Part IV
Cooperative Interactions Between the WTO and the New Generation EU FTA DSMs

Chapter 11
Judicial Communication

11.1 The Concept and Pre-conditions of Judicial Communication

Both international and national judicial bodies across the globe talk to each other. Here, the concept of 'judicial communication' is understood as encompassing the references made by one judicial body in the process of adjudication to the jurisprudence and practice of another.[1] Many scholars describe the reference made by one court or tribunal to the jurisprudence of another as a 'dialogue' between them.[2] Nevertheless, the use of this term has been subject to criticism, as dialogue is defined as an 'exchange of views between two interlocutors on a given subject'.[3] Thus, a dialogue would involve two interlocutors actively engaging in a discussion in a responsive manner, committed to both speaking and listening.[4] The term dialogue can be contrasted to one-sided communication, when only one party communicates with another, an interaction that can be termed a 'monologue'.[5] Since judicial communication rarely involves a dialogue between two judicial entities engaged with each other's views in a responsive manner, this book uses the concept 'judicial communication' to refer to various forms of communication, encompassing both judicial dialogues and monologues, not simply to those implying a responsive exchange of views.

For judicial communication to occur, a set of pre-conditions needs to be fulfilled. First of all, judicial entities engaged in judicial communication should perceive their own judicial nature and recognise the entities to which jurisprudence the reference is

---

[1] Zang (2017), p. 274.

[2] For example, Charney (1998), p. 101; Peters (2017), p. 695.

[3] Tzanakopoulos (2016), p. 73.

[4] Law and Chang (2011), p. 534.

[5] Linton and Tiba (2009), p. 419.

made as international actors with judicial identity, independent of governmental institutions and performing similar functions.[6] Thus, without the perception of one's own judicial identity and recognition of the other side as judicial bodies, there can be no judicial communication. As previously stated,[7] the WTO DSM clearly has a judicial character, which it has recognised itself to possess it when it confirmed that panels can consider their own jurisdiction because international tribunals are entitled to do so.[8] Moreover, there are provisions in the DSU and the Rules of Conduct that should ensure the independence, impartiality, and integrity of both panelists and AB Members.[9] As the same procedures are applicable *mutatis mutandis* to arbitrators under the MPIA,[10] the presumption is that they will bestow judicial identity to the arbitrators and similarly ensure their independence. The panels established under the new generation EU FTA DSMs, with very similar procedures to the WTO DSM and being independent from the parties,[11] should also be regarded as and expected to perceive themselves as judicial bodies. In addition, the new generation EU FTAs expressly recognise WTO panels and the AB as judicial bodies in their texts on various occasions; they refer to them as judicial bodies in the choice of forum clauses and the rules of interpretation.[12] The AB also seems to have recognised that RTA panels can be judicial bodies. For example, in *Brazil – Retreaded Tyres*, the AB referred to the MERCOSUR arbitral tribunal as a 'judicial or quasi-judicial body'.[13] Thus, the first pre-condition in the case of the new generation EU FTAs and the WTO DSMs is met.

Judicial communication cannot occur unless the decisions of the courts are made public, so that other courts are able to refer to them. Hence, judicial communication between the WTO and the new generation EU FTAs can take place, since both, as a rule, publish their final reports.[14] Lastly, judicial communication has to rely on the persuasiveness of the jurisprudence of the other court, rather than on its coercive authority to impose its jurisprudence.[15] In international law, as well as in transnational law,[16] even when there is a hierarchical structure, a body ranked higher has no coercive power to compel adherence to its jurisprudence by those ranked lower. In the case of the WTO, for example, the AB famously established the 'absent cogent

---

[6] Slaughter (1994), pp. 122–126.

[7] *See supra*, Sect. 9.3.4.1.

[8] Appellate Body Report, *United States – Anti-Dumping Act of 1916 (US – 1916 Act)*, WT/DS136/AB/R, WT/DS162/AB/R, 28 August 2000, [54] fn 30; Van Damme (2009), p. 180. Such an inherent power was also confirmed by the Appellate Body Report, *Mexico – Soft Drinks*, [45].

[9] DSU, Arts 8.2, 17.3; Rules of Conduct, II, III, IV:1, VI, VIII.

[10] MPIA, Annex 1, para 11.

[11] *See supra*, Sect. 6.5.2.

[12] *See supra*, Sect. 10.2.1 and *infra*, Sect. 11.8.5.3.

[13] Appellate Body Report, *Brazil – Retreaded Tyres*, [232].

[14] *See supra*, Sect. 6.10.

[15] Slaughter (1994), pp. 124–125.

[16] Ibid, 125.

reasons' standard,[17] and asserted that there is a 'hierarchical structure contemplated in the DSU' where panels and the AB play different roles and that '[t]he Panel's failure to follow previously adopted Appellate Body reports addressing the same issues undermines the development of a coherent and predictable body of jurisprudence' as required by the DSU.[18] Despite these statements and the de facto rule of precedent in the WTO,[19] the AB has no power to coerce the panels to follow its jurisprudence, but has to rely on the persuasiveness of its conclusions, especially since it is settled that AB reports 'are not binding, except with respect to resolving the particular dispute between the parties'.[20]

In any event, there is no hierarchical relationship between the judicial bodies of the WTO and the new generation EU FTAs. Both the WTO and the new generation EU FTAs establish international adjudicatory bodies. As judicial bodies constituted by different international treaties that, as a rule, have equal value because they are based on the consent of states, they should not be regarded as being in a hierarchical relationship, unless the treaties are drafted to establish otherwise. While Article XXIV of GATT regulates the formation of FTAs, neither the WTO agreements nor the FTAs contain any indication that suggests that the FTA DSMs should be inferior to the WTO DSM and follow its jurisprudence.[21] Thus, as adjudicatory bodies with equal status, they do not need to be in a subordinate position, but can cooperate by communicating with each other.

To conclude, this section introduced the concept of judicial communication and argued for preferential use of this term. It also presented the necessary pre-conditions for such communication to take place and confirmed their presence in the interactions between the new generation EU FTA and the WTO DSMs. The following sections will use the concept presented, elaborate on it, and analyse it in the specific context of interactions between the WTO and the new generation EU FTAs.

11.2 Functions of Judicial Communication

Judicial communication can have different functions. This section will present its function of bringing coherence and unity, which is pivotal for the purpose of this part, while also introducing other functions illustrating the potential of judicial communication to enhance synergies as a result of judicial interactions.

---

[17] Appellate Body Report, *United States – Final Anti-Dumping Measures on Stainless Steel from Mexico (US – Stainless Steel)*, WT/DS344/AB/R, 30 April 2008, [160].

[18] Appellate Body Report, *US – Stainless Steel*, [161].

[19] *See supra*, Sect. 7.1.

[20] Appellate Body Report, *Japan – Taxes on Alcoholic Beverages (Japan — Alcoholic Beverages II)*, WT/DS8/AB/R, 4 October 1996, 14.

[21] Forere (2015), p. 117.

Judicial communication can be regarded as a phenomenon that occurs as a natural reaction to counter fragmentation,[22] being the most-discussed avenue of promoting unity in international law.[23] The importance of references to the jurisprudence of other international judicial bodies to deal with the negative effects of fragmentation has also been noted by ICJ judges. In 2000, Judge Guillaume proposed that in the context of the proliferation of international courts and tribunals, international judges 'must inform themselves more fully of the case-law developed by their colleagues, conduct more sustained relationships with other courts and, in a word, engage in constant inter-judicial dialogue'.[24] In 2012, in the *Diallo* Declaration, Judge Greenwood argued that international law 'is a single, unified system of law and each international court can, and should, draw on the jurisprudence of other international courts and tribunals, even though it is not bound necessarily to come to the same conclusions'.[25] The reference to the jurisprudence of other courts and tribunals during legal reasoning, indeed, brings a sense of unity and coherence to international law even though a different conclusion may be reached. Reference to the jurisprudence of the same international judicial bodies by others ensures coherence not only between the jurisprudence of the entities directly engaging in this communication, but also across the judicial bodies that refer to the same jurisprudence. The function of judicial communication to bring coherence and unity to international law is the focus of this part which aims to enhance potential synergies between the DSMs of the WTO and new generation EU FTAs.

Another function of judicial communication is to aid in the process of adjudication. Judicial entities disseminate ideas that can be used as an inspiration for future solutions by other courts and tribunals.[26] While the jurisprudence of another court or tribunal can serve as an inspiration for the interpretation and application of substantive norms, it can also prove useful for solving procedural problems. This gap-filling function refers to the use of external jurisprudence and practice when the statute of an international court is silent on the matter and it relates only to procedural matters.[27] The practice of other international tribunals can also be pertinent to establishing the existence of international customary rules and general principles of international law[28] and could serve as subsidiary sources of international law under Article 38(d) of the ICJ Statute.[29] Moreover, the jurisprudence of one

---

[22] Marceau et al. (2013), p. 482.

[23] Peters (2017), p. 695.

[24] 'The Proliferation of International Judicial Bodies: The Outlook for the International Legal Order', Speech by His Excellency Judge Gilbert Guillaume, President of the International Court of Justice, to the Sixth Committee of the General Assembly of the United Nations, 27 October 2000.

[25] 'Declaration of Judge Greenwood', *Ahmadou Sadio Diallo (Republic of Guinea v. Democratic Republic of the Congo)*, Judgment, 2012 ICJ Rep. 324, 19 June 2012, para 8.

[26] Slaughter (1994), p. 117; Voeten (2010), p. 550.

[27] Zang (2017), p. 291.

[28] ICJ Statute, Art 38(1)(b) and (c); *see* Weiss (2001), p. 409.

[29] This provision will be analysed in more detail Sect. 11.8.3.

international judicial body could also serve as evidence in the procedures of another body serving a factual function. In addition, by citing external jurisprudence, a judicial body could provide additional support and persuasiveness to its own deci-sions.[30] When more international judicial bodies adopt the same or similar interpre-tations for the same norms, this could be perceived as evidence that the decision is correct.[31] Furthermore, using the jurisprudence of an international judicial entity that enjoys greater authority to support a decision may also confer increased weight to that decision. Yet, different interpretations and conclusions can be reached for similar or identical terms or provisions because of various factors that act as limits, which will be detailed below.[32] Similar to bringing coherence and unity, these other functions also highlight that the proliferation of DSMs and their interactions do not only cause negative outcomes, but can also result in positive effects that need to be enhanced.

This section presented and explained the functions of judicial communication. The present book deals with judicial communication between the new generation EU FTA and the WTO DSMs primarily because of its function of bringing coherence and unity to the international trade regime, but also by reason of other functions that have been presented in order to illustrate the potential benefits of judicial communication.

11.3   Factors Encouraging Judicial Communication

This section will list and assess the factors that could encourage judicial communi-cation. It will also establish how they could bolster this phenomenon specifically between the new generation EU FTA and the WTO DSMs.

Judicial communication can be encouraged by different factors. The greater the proliferation of international courts and tribunals, the greater the cross-referencing may be to their jurisprudence. Nevertheless, the level of judicial communication will depend not only on the number of DSMs, but also on the number of cases that were actually brought under their rules. Thus, since only a small number of disputes have been litigated under FTA rules, the number of cross-references to the FTA jurispru-dence made by the WTO adjudicatory bodies would also likely be low. As up to now, no reports have been issued under the new generation EU FTAs, there is no jurisprudence that could be referenced in WTO proceedings. However, once there is jurisprudence under the new generation EU FTAs, the situation could change. On the other hand, as there is a large body of WTO jurisprudence dealing with various procedural and substantive issues, it is expected that new generation EU FTA tribunals would be more likely to refer to WTO jurisprudence.

---

[30] Slaughter (1994), p. 119.

[31] Ibid.

[32] *See infra*, Sect. 11.5.

In addition, when more than one international judicial body deals with similar questions and issues, the probability that they would engage in judicial communication is higher. The reasoning and interpretations of a court or tribunal may be more relevant to a court from the same issue area. The substantive coverage of the WTO and the new generation EU FTAs is very similar, the FTAs containing WTO-equal and WTO-plus norms that regulate in an identical or similar manner issues that also fall under WTO coverage.[33] Furthermore, FTAs often borrow terms or concepts from the WTO agreements, such as 'like' products or 'necessary',[34] and use them in WTO-plus and even WTO-x provisions. These terms can also be found in the new generation EU FTAs.[35] This can be explained by the fact that even when designing new provisions, parties do not start from a blank page, but use already familiar concepts by relying on the existing WTO provisions that serve as an inspiration.[36] Additionally, FTAs frequently expressly adopt definitions for some concepts in accordance with the WTO agreements. For example, the EUKFTA establishes that the concepts 'serious injury and threat of serious injury shall be understood in accordance with Article 4.1(a) and (b) of the Agreement on Safeguards'.[37] The similarity between the WTO agreements and FTAs is not limited to their substantive content; there is similarity also between procedural rules.[38] Therefore, due to the similarity of the issues dealt with and of the provisions in the WTO and FTA context, the likelihood of increased judicial communication between them is higher than between courts or tribunals from different international regimes.

The legal text of the constitutive treaties of international judicial bodies may themselves encourage or even mandate reference to the jurisprudence of another body in certain situations. The new generation EU FTAs include rules on interpretation that make express reference to WTO jurisprudence.[39] Thus, CETA, EUJEPA, and EUVFTA establish in general that panels 'shall also take into account relevant interpretations' in panel and AB reports adopted by the DSB.[40] The EUKFTA provides that the arbitration panel 'shall adopt an interpretation which is consistent with any relevant interpretation established in rulings of the WTO Dispute Settlement Body', with respect to a limited category of obligations—the FTA obligations identical to those of the WTO agreements.[41] Using similar wording and referring to

---

[33] *See supra*, Sect. 5.1.

[34] Lanyi and Steinbach (2017), p. 80.

[35] For example, EUKFTA, Art 3.1(1) and EUJEPA, Art 5.2(1), both on bilateral safeguard measures, and, thus, WTO-plus provisions, use the term 'like' and 'necessary', respectively.

[36] Bercero (2006), p. 401; Pierola and Horlick (2007), pp. 886–887; Lanyi and Steinbach (2017), p. 83.

[37] EUKFTA, Art 3.5.

[38] *See supra*, Chap. 6.

[39] For a detailed analysis of the scope, weight, effects, and importance in the context of the AB crisis, *see infra*, Sect. 11.8.5.3.

[40] CETA, Art 29.17; EUJEPA, Art 21.16; EUVFTA, Art 15.21.

[41] EUKFTA, Art 14.16.

the same limited category of obligations, the EUSFTA provides that the panel 'shall take into account any relevant interpretation established in rulings of the WTO Dispute Settlement Body'.[42]

The behaviour of the parties to a treaty may be another factor that contributes to the increase of cross-referencing across international tribunals. Thus, by referencing WTO and, respectively, FTA jurisprudence in their submissions, parties would make the adjudicatory bodies to treat them as evidence and, potentially, even to rely on them.[43] Given the limited number of disputes under a specific FTA, parties to an FTA dispute that concerns provisions or issues similar to those that have already been dealt with at the WTO level are highly likely to invoke WTO jurisprudence in support of their arguments. Thus, even in the context of the dispute settlement crisis and a paralysed AB, arbitrators under new generation EU FTA DSMs are more likely to inspire themselves from the extensive WTO jurisprudence, since there will only be a few disputes, if any, litigated under the rules of the agreement they would be solving the dispute under or under other similar agreements. Hence, in such cases, the use of WTO jurisprudence would fulfil the function of judicial communication of aiding the process of adjudication and serving as a source of inspiration.

Judicial communication could also be boosted by another factor: the semantic authority of the international judicial body whose jurisprudence is considered for referencing. International judicial entities may be more inclined to cite the case law of other entities that they regard as authoritative.[44] The 'capacity to influence and shape meanings as well as the ability to establish its communications as authoritative reference points in legal discourse' has been termed by Ingo Venzke as 'semantic authority'.[45] It hinges on the belief of others that one should follow what an authoritative court or tribunal says.[46] Hence, wide reference to the jurisprudence of an international court or tribunal can serve as evidence that it is perceived to have high semantic authority. The extensive reference to internal jurisprudence, especially to that of the AB, which explicitly affirmed the need for panels to follow its past reports,[47] shows the extensive semantic authority of the WTO DSM and, particularly, of the AB within the WTO.[48] With the creation of the WTO and the change in design of the DSM to a highly legalised one with almost automatic procedures for adoption of binding reports and high rates of usage and acceptance by both large and emerging economies, the WTO DSM, and especially the AB, rapidly gained extensive authority which is also recognised by other international courts and tribunals.[49]

---

[42] EUSFTA, Art 14.18.

[43] Johnston and Trebilcock (2013), p. 640.

[44] Vidigal (2019), p. 6.

[45] Venzke (2012), p. 63.

[46] Ibid.

[47] Appellate Body Report, *United States – Final Anti-Dumping Measures on Stainless Steel from Mexico (US – Stainless Steel)*, WT/DS344/AB/R, 30 April 2008, [160], [161].

[48] On the extensive semantic authority of the AB within the WTO, *see* Vidigal (2019), pp. 12–14.

[49] Shaffer et al. (2016), pp. 237–273.

Hence, even in the context of the current crisis at the WTO, past and future panel jurisprudence is expected to enjoy the existing semantic authority. Moreover, despite the demise of the AB, its existing jurisprudence still remains authoritative. Hence, because of the extensive semantic authority of the AB and the WTO DSM in general, it is expected that FTA adjudicatory bodies are likely to refer to the existing WTO jurisprudence. Yet, it remains to be seen what the semantic authority would be of the rulings issued under potential alternatives to the AB, such as the MPIA. The appeal arbitration proceedings would be very similar to the regular appeals and should be conducted by arbitrators with comparable authority, knowledge, and experience to that of the AB Members and which should follow the collegiality principle.[50] Hence, a considerable degree of semantic authority is expected to emerge from appeal arbitration awards. Whether the extent of this authority would be comparable to that of the AB reports will also depend on the quality and persuasiveness of the awards. Due to the rare use of the FTA DSMs and their relatively low semantic authority, less cross-referencing to FTA jurisprudence is anticipated.

Finally, there may also be personal factors that would encourage an international judicial body to cite the jurisprudence of another. A certain career background and past professional experience of international judges or arbitrators related to the activity of another international judicial body may make them more inclined to reference the jurisprudence of that body. For example, FTA arbitrators, especially those that previously served as WTO litigators, panelists, or AB Members, may be very familiar with WTO jurisprudence or might even have participated in WTO relevant disputes. They might also be more accustomed to the style of reasoning adopted by WTO panels and the AB reports and be inclined to follow WTO jurisprudence. Given that under the new generation EU FTAs arbitrators should have expertise and knowledge in international trade law[51] and even in settlement of disputes on trade subject matters covered by the agreements,[52] it is reasonable to expect that many would have knowledge of and experience in WTO dispute settlement. The list of arbitrators already established under the EUKFTA illustrates how FTA arbitrators are experienced and knowledgeable in the field of international trade law and, specifically, WTO law. Most of the arbitrators in the list have teaching experience related to international trade, especially WTO law[53] and some have

---

[50] *See supra*, Sect. 2.3.2.

[51] EUKFTA, Art 14.18(2); CETA, Art 29.8(2); EUJEPA, Art 21.10; EUSFTA, Art 14.20(4); EUVFTA, Art 15.23(3).

[52] Under the EUVFTA, panelists can have alternatively 'specialised knowledge of or experience in law and international trade or in the settlement of disputes arising under international trade agreements' (EUVFTA, Art 14.20(4)). Under CETA rules, 'chairpersons must also have experience as counsel or panelist in dispute settlement proceedings on subject matters within the scope of this Agreement' (CETA, Art 29.8(2)).

[53] For example, the following arbitrators from the list all have experience in teaching international trade law: Dukgeun Ahn, Seungwha Chang, Sungjoon Cho, Jaemin Lee, Claus-Dieter Ehlermann, Pieter Jan Kuijper, Ramon Torrent, William Davey, and Merit Janow.

represented or advised their governments on WTO disputes or negotiations,[54] directed the WTO Legal Affairs Division,[55] served as WTO panelists[56] or arbitrators[57] or are former AB Members.[58] Thus, given these arbitrators' experience in and knowledge of WTO law, it is only rational to assume that they are well aware of WTO jurisprudence and may be more predisposed to cross-reference it.

The introduction and analysis of the factors that could encourage judicial communication between the new generation EU FTA and the WTO DSMs showed how they could perform. The scarce jurisprudence, as of yet, under the new generation EU FTAs, their rules on interpretation, the extensive semantic authority of the WTO DSM, and the FTA arbitrators' experience and knowledge of the WTO are factors likely to work unidirectionally at present, encouraging references to WTO jurisprudence by the new generation EU FTA adjudicatory bodies. In time, if the new generation EU FTA DSMs issue more rulings and gain more semantic authority, these factors may also work in the opposite direction.

11.4   Types of Judicial Communication

Judicial communication can be of different types which will be identified in this section to establish under which the communication between the WTO and the new generation EU FTA DSMs could fall.

Judicial communication can be classified into vertical or horizontal depending on the level of the courts between which it takes place.[59] Thus, vertical communication occurs between judicial bodies belonging to different legal orders, such as supranational and national courts, for example, as in the case of the national courts of EU member states and the Court of Justice or the General Court within the EU.[60] On the other hand, horizontal interactions take place between international judicial bodies that are positioned at the same level.[61] Since both the WTO and the new generation EU FTA DSMs provide international tribunals constituted by international treaties that have equal value, the communication between them can be regarded as horizontal. Therefore, this chapter will only deal with horizontal communication.

---

[54] For example, Dukgeun Ahn, Sungjoon Cho, Jaemin Lee, Jacques Bourgeois, Claus-Dieter Ehlermann, Pieter Jan Kuijper, have experience in representing their governments in the context of the WTO.

[55] William Davey and Pieter Jan Kuijper are both former Directors of the Legal Affairs Division.

[56] Seungwha Chang, Jacques Bourgeois, and William Davey acted as panelists or chaired WTO panels.

[57] Claus-Dieter Ehlermann acted as an arbitrator under Art 25 of the DSU.

[58] Giorgio Sacerdoti and Merit Janow are former AB Members.

[59] Slaughter (1994), pp. 103–112.

[60] Kassoti (2015), p. 36.

[61] Tzanakopoulos (2016), p. 6.

Another way of classifying judicial communication is based on the degree of reciprocal engagement between the international judicial bodies.[62] A dialogue takes place when both sides are actively engaged, by one party initiating it and the other responding to the first party. Such communication takes place, for example, in the case of national courts of the EU member states that can request a preliminary ruling from the Court of Justice of the EU to clarify questions on interpretation or validity of EU law. While the request for a preliminary ruling can be made based on Article 267 of the TFEU, there is no similar provision in the WTO agreements or the FTAs studied, nor would this be suitable. As previously stated, judicial communication rarely takes the form of a dialogue,[63] yet the WTO and FTA adjudicators could engage in a more indirect kind of dialogue, compared to that under Article 267 of the TFEU, by acting in a responsive manner when dealing with the same interpretative issues in a sequence of reports and reciprocally considering their jurisprudence on the matter. WTO panels or the AB and FTA panels are even more likely to engage in one-sided judicial communication, without having an ongoing dialogue about a specific dispute or issue. Thus, the new generation EU FTA and WTO DSMs could engage in monologues, without the international judicial body whose jurisprudence is defenced acting in a responsive manner.

Judicial communication can also be classified into different types depending on the initiator of the interaction. Thus, there can be proactive interaction between different courts when the adjudicators on their own initiative analyse and reference the jurisprudence of another judicial entity.[64] On the other hand, there can also be passive interaction when the jurisprudence of another international court is brought to the attention of the adjudicators and, subsequently, referenced at the initiative of the parties to the dispute.[65] Thus, this type of interaction is caused by one of the factors that can contribute to the advancement of judicial communication: the behaviour of the parties. The functions of judicial communication in these two different types of judicial interactions are also likely to be different. When the communication is proactive, it is likely that the adjudicator is concerned about the coherence and unity of international law, and looks for ideas and inspiration for a solution and arguments that would add persuasiveness to their decision.[66] In the case of passive communication, it is more likely that it performs only the function of evidence brought by the parties in support of their claims. The parties also bear the burden of proof of demonstrating the relevance of external jurisprudence, which has to be evaluated by the adjudicators that will either endorse or dismiss it.[67] Thus, the way the adjudicators treat these references will differ. In the case of judicial

---

[62] Slaughter (1994), p. 112.

[63] *See supra*, Sect. 11.1.

[64] Zang (2018), pp. 435–436.

[65] Ibid, 436.

[66] Ibid.

[67] Ibid.

communication between the WTO and the new-generation EU FTAs, both types can occur, depending on who initiates the interaction.

This section presented different ways to classify judicial communication based on various criteria. It established that judicial communication between the new generation EU FTA and the WTO DSMs would be a horizontal monologue or indirect dialogue that could be either proactive or passive depending on its initiator and serving distinct functions.

11.5   Increased Importance of and the Limits to Coherence in Case of the Communication Between the DSMs of the WTO and the New Generation EU FTAs

This section will argue that because of the similarity between the norms and the issues dealt with in the proceedings under the new generation EU FTAs and the WTO agreements, coherence in their interpretation and application gains increased importance. Despite this importance, it will also present the limits to this coherence and will establish the types of incoherencies dealt with here.

The new generation EU FTA and the WTO DSMs may deal with the same or similar disputes, sometimes raising the risk of conflicting jurisdictions addressed in detail in the previous part. Different treatment of the same or similar factual aspects may also affect the predictability of the international trade regime. As the new generation EU FTAs include many norms covered by their DSMs that incorporate, reference or are similar to WTO norms,[68] there is also a risk that they would be interpreted differently in WTO and FTA proceedings. Different interpretations of the same or similar norms can lead to incoherence and the negative consequences associated with it.[69] Moreover, the issue of incoherence could appear not only for FTA norms that are similar or identical to the WTO ones, but also for WTO-plus and WTO-x norms that use terms and concepts similar to those in WTO agreements. Hence, even in the case of WTO-plus and WTO-x provisions, similar concepts or terms, such as 'likeness' or 'necessity', could be interpreted differently in WTO and FTA proceedings. As the WTO and FTA adjudicating bodies also deal with similar procedural issues, a coherent way to deal with these issues may provide predictability for the states as the users of these mechanisms. Thus, if the same procedural matter is resolved in a similar way by both mechanisms, parties would know what to expect from the procedures. Therefore, in all these cases different interpretations and applications of the norms and concepts, both substantive and procedural, within WTO and FTA proceedings can pose a threat to the coherence of the international trade law regime.

---

[68] In this respect, *see supra*, Sect. 5.1.

[69] *See supra*, Sect. 2.1.4.

While different interpretations of similar or identical norms or concepts can negatively affect the international trade regime, coherence is not an end in itself as stated in the conceptual framework. In the context of the ISDS reform there a difference was found between correctness and consistency. The conclusion reached was that it is more important when decisions are interpreted correctly and in line with international rules of public international law, rather than interpreted coherently but at the expense of correctness.[70] As previously argued, coherence should not be an impediment to deviating from existing jurisprudence when necessary.[71] Thus, if an interpretation is not made according to the rules of interpretation, the deviation would be unjustifiable. When a previous ruling is found to contain flawed reasoning, it is justifiable to depart from it.[72] Thus, if application of international rules yields different interpretations of similar or identical norms, these distinctions would be justifiable.

Coherence should not be pursued without a legal basis to do so, since it would mean ignoring the intention of the states that consented to and concluded the agreements with these rules in mind. According to Article 34 of the VCLT, a treaty does not create rights and obligations for a third state without its consent. Thus, it may be argued that by interpreting a treaty in light of the jurisprudence of another judicial body without a legal basis to do so would not be covered by the initial consent of the parties.[73] In addition, if the WTO and FTA judicial bodies engage in judicial communication and use external jurisprudence without legal avenues, they may be accused of adding to or diminishing the rights and obligations contained in the agreements, which is against the text of the WTO agreements and the new generation EU FTAs.[74] Although international judicial bodies frequently cite external jurisprudence without mentioning the legal basis for doing so,[75] engaging in judicial communication without a legal basis could be perceived as a form of judicial activism and excessive exercise of authority by the adjudicators, even if it is done with the aim of achieving coherence. Therefore, coherence should be sought only

---

[70] Report of Working Group III (Investor-State Dispute Settlement Reform) on the Work of its 34th Session (Vienna, 27 November–1 December 2017), A/CN.9/930/Add.1/Rev.1, 25 June–13 July 2018, para 29; Report of Working Group III (Investor-State Dispute Settlement Reform) on the Work of its 36th Session (Vienna, 29 October–2 November 2018), A/CN.9/964, 8–26 July 2019, para 34.

[71] *See supra*, Sect. 3.1.6.

[72] On how the ICJ in the *Bosnia Genocide Case (Case Concerning the Application of the Convention on the Prevention and Punishment of the Crime of Genocide (Bosnia and Herzegovina v Serbia and Montenegro)* (Mar 13, 2006)) rejected the position of the ICTY in the *Tadic* case (*Prosecutor v Tadic, Case No IT-94-1-A*) for being unpersuasive and flawed, *see* Linton and Tiba (2009), pp. 455–456.

[73] For potential legal avenues for judicial communication, including Art 31(3)(c) of the VCLT, *see infra*, Sect. 10.8.

[74] DSU, Art 3.2; EUKFTA, Art 14.16; CETA, Art 29.18; EUJEPA, Art 21.15(8); EUSFTA, Art 14.18; EUVFTA, Art 15.21.

[75] Marceau et al. (2013), pp. 409, 519, 531.

when it is justifiable to do so, while unjustifiable inconsistencies should be considered a matter of concern and avoided.

The difference between justifiable and unjustifiable inconsistencies has also been noted by the states in the context of ISDS reform discussions.[76] Nevertheless, judicial communication brings predictability and stability also in case of justifiable inconsistencies. Thus, by detailing and arguing why a similar norm is interpreted in a different way from the previous interpretation of another adjudicatory body,[77] the difference is justified and explained and does not raise concerns. Hence, judicial communication not only helps with tackling unjustified inconsistencies, it also helps with more easily identifying those that are justified.

Similar and identical norms could be interpreted differently because of the public international law rules of interpretation. As previously argued, two identical norms cannot be fully equivalent due to, for example, the difference in context.[78] The differences in interpretation can stem from the fact that every single treaty is the result of specific negotiations between the parties; the small differences in the text of the interpreted norm and its context should be given the consideration necessary. For example, each new generation EU FTA was part of a distinct process of negotiations with a different party. Thus, it might have been a deliberate choice of the parties to ascribe a specific meaning to a provision. At the same time, since the EU is a party to all these agreements, identical WTO-plus or WTO-x norms can be found in different EU FTAs,[79] showing that they might have been drafted to have the same meaning. Moreover, WTO norms have often been used as a starting point for negotiations and as a source of inspiration for FTAs, hence the similarity between them, especially in the language which can hardly be conceived as 'accidental'.[80] It is reasonable to assume that the parties intended the norms and concepts borrowed from the WTO agreements to have the same meaning, and using WTO jurisprudence for their interpretation would be a logical step. Therefore, each situation needs to be assessed individually to establish whether parties intended similar or identical norms to be interpreted in the same or a different way.

To conclude, FTAs and WTO agreements include many similar or even identical norms that could be interpreted differently, which may lead to negative consequences. Nevertheless, it is worth highlighting that some of the inconsistencies may be justified while others are not. As coherence should be pursued within certain limits, it is submitted that judicial communication should not be undertaken for its function of bringing coherence at the expense of correctness of interpretation.

---

[76] Report of Working Group III (Investor-State Dispute Settlement Reform) on the Work of its 36th Session, A/CN.9/964 (n 70) para 39.

[77] On how the ECtHR interpreted a similar norm in the *Laizidou Case* (*Laizidou vs Turkey*, ECHR, Series A, Vol. 310, 23 March 1995) differently from the ICJ and why it was justified in doing so, *see* Oellers-Frahm (2001), pp. 81–83.

[78] Broude, Shany (2011), pp. 7–9. *See supra*, Sect. 5.3.

[79] *See*, for example, Art 17.2(1) of CETA and Art 11.1 of EUJEPA both of which are on competition and have similar wording.

[80] Stoll (2019), p. 242.

11.6   Judicial Communication Within the WTO DSM

This section will analyse WTO adjudicators' references to RTA jurisprudence, as well as to the jurisprudence of other international tribunals. Such judicial communication could be one-sided, with the WTO DSM conducting monologues, or it could sporadically take the form of an indirect dialogue, with WTO adjudicators referring in a responsive manner to the jurisprudence of another tribunal. This section will also be indicative with respect to the instances of and avenues for future WTO DSM's judicial communication with the new generation EU FTA DSMs, when there is jurisprudence under the rules of the latter. Identifying the avenues for judicial communication is paramount in the wake of the need to pursue coherence within the limits set by the intention of states as expressed in the rules of international law.

11.6.1   General Attitude of the WTO DSM Towards RTAs

Before investigating how the WTO DSM treats RTA jurisprudence, it is useful to understand the attitude of the WTO DSM towards RTAs in general. As previously shown in the second part dedicated to conflicting jurisdictions, the WTO has no jurisdiction over non-WTO norms, nor are FTA jurisdictional clauses applicable within WTO proceedings. *Mexico – Soft Drinks*, *Argentina – Poultry* and *Peru – Agricultural Products* illustrated the arguments that established that FTA jurisdictional clauses cannot lead WTO panels and the AB to decline their jurisdiction and how they can only be perceived as a relinquishment of a DSU right leading to a violation of the good faith obligations prescribed by Articles 3.7 and 3.10 of the DSU.[81] Hence, it was showed how procedural FTA rules on conflicting jurisdictions can be given effect only if they are brought as evidence under DSU rules.

WTO practice also shows that substantive RTA rules have been treated only under existing WTO rules. In *Turkey – Textiles*, the AB confirmed that Article XXIV of GATT could justify the adoption of measures that are inconsistent with certain GATT provisions.[82] Additionally, it established overly demanding conditions that could be difficult to comply with for such a justification to take place.[83] The most recent case that dealt with FTA norms, *Peru – Agricultural Products*, not only re-confirmed these conditions but also established that specific WTO provisions, including the exceptions for regional trade agreements, prevail over general rules of international law, such as those in the VCLT.[84] It concluded that Article XXIV of GATT, the Enabling Clause, and Article V of GATS on the formation of RTAs are

---

[81] *See supra*, Sect. 9.3.

[82] Appellate Body Report, *Turkey – Textiles*, [45].

[83] *See* Pauwelyn (2004), pp. 131–135; Kuijper (2010), p. 21; Salles (2015), p. 24.

[84] Appellate Body Report, *Peru – Agricultural Products*, [5.112].

the 'the proper routes to assess whether a provision in an FTA that may depart from certain WTO rules is nevertheless consistent with the covered agreements'.[85]

In addition, general exceptions in Article XX of GATT have also been invoked in cases involving RTA norms, for example in disputes such as *Mexico – Soft Drinks* and *Brazil – Retreaded Tyres*. In *Mexico – Soft Drinks*, Mexico invoked Article XX (d) of GATT as a defence, claiming that its 'measures are "necessary to secure compliance" by the United States with the United States' obligations under the NAFTA, an international agreement that is a law not inconsistent with the provisions of the GATT 1994'.[86] Nevertheless, the AB reached the conclusion that 'the terms "laws or regulations" [in Art. XX(d) of GATT] refer to rules that form part of the domestic legal system of a WTO Member' and 'do not include obligations of *another* WTO Member under an international agreement'.[87] *Brazil – Retreaded Tyres* concerned a measure imposed because of a MERCOSUR ruling which will be detailed in the following section. Still, it is important to note that in this case the AB did not find that the measure imposed as the result of the RTA ruling was justifiable under Article XX(b) of GATT. Thus, invoking substantive RTA norms was possible only under exceptions expressly contained in the WTO agreements— an outcome that is in line with the conclusion reached in the previous part that non-WTO norms leading to the addition or diminishment of WTO rights, which would occur if RTA norms prevailed over WTO ones, are not applicable within the WTO DSM. Moreover, the invocation of RTA norms has to take place in conformity with the strict conditions of the exceptions.

RTA norms have also been invoked during the process of interpretation of WTO norms. Thus, in *Peru – Agricultural Products*, Peru contented that the WTO provisions at issue should have been interpreted in light of FTA provisions according to Article 31(3)(a) and (c) of the VCLT.[88] Under these VCLT provisions, 'any subsequent agreement between the parties regarding the interpretation of the treaty' and 'any relevant rules of international law applicable in the relations between the parties' should be taken into account together with the context for the purpose of interpretation. However, the AB concluded that interpretation of multilateral treaties, such as the WTO agreements, according to Article 31 of the VCLT, 'is aimed at establishing the ordinary meaning of treaty terms reflecting the common intention of the parties to the treaty, and not just the intentions of some of the parties';[89] thus, FTA rules were not used to reach an interpretation that would be applicable only between FTA parties. Moreover, when interpreting a provision in light of this context, the conclusion reached cannot contradict the textual terms, as it would

---

[85] Ibid [5.113]; For the criticism of this conclusion, *see* Mathis (2016), p. 103; Shaffer and Winters (2017), p. 320; Shadikhodjaev (2017), p. 121.

[86] Appellate Body Report, *Mexico – Soft Drinks*, [59].

[87] Ibid, [69].

[88] Appellate Body Report, *Peru – Agricultural Products*, [5.91].

[89] Ibid, [5.95].

amount to a modification rather than an interpretation.[90] It also rejected the possibility of interpreting WTO norms in light of the FTA ones, as it established that under Article 31(3)(a), the subsequent agreements regarding the interpretation of the treaty are 'agreements bearing specifically upon the interpretation of a treaty'.[91] In addition, the AB established that rules of international law 'must concern the same subject matter as the treaty terms being interpreted' to be considered relevant under Article 31(3)(c),[92] which was not the case with the FTA norms invoked by Peru.[93] The meaning and elements of Article 31(3)(c) will be dealt with in detail when analysing the avenues under which WTO and the new generation EU FTA DSMs could refer to each other's jurisprudence.[94]

A reticent attitude is evident within the WTO DSM towards the use of RTA norms. It may seem so because of the specificities of each dispute, as well as the existing WTO legal framework. The next section will analyse whether the same reticence is expressed towards FTA rulings.

11.6.2 RTA Rulings in WTO Jurisprudence

RTA rulings have been invoked twice during WTO proceedings, in *Argentina – Poultry* and *Brazil – Retreaded Tyres*. The small number of references to RTA rulings may also be due to the factors that could intensify judicial communication being directed mostly towards encouraging communication initiated at the RTA level.[95] These instances in which WTO panels and the AB had to deal directly with

---

[90] Ibid, [5.94], [5.97]. In this respect *see infra*, Sect. 11.8.5.

[91] Appellate Body Report, *Peru – Agricultural Products*, [5.101] with the following original fn 294 stating 'Appellate Body Reports, *EC – Bananas III (Article 21.5 – Ecuador II / Article 21.5 – US)*, para 390. In *US – Clove Cigarettes*, the Appellate Body found that it was not possible to discern a function of paragraph 5.2 of the 2001 Doha Ministerial Decision "*other than* to interpret the term 'reasonable interval'" in the Agreement on Technical Barriers to Trade (TBT Agreement), and it was therefore considered to "*bear[] specifically* upon the interpretation" of that term. (Appellate Body Report, *US – Clove Cigarettes*, para 266 (emphasis original)) In *US – Tuna II (Mexico)*, the Appellate Body found that a TBT Committee Decision could be considered as a "subsequent agreement" within the meaning of Article 31(3)(a) of the Vienna Convention. The Appellate Body considered that the extent to which the Decision would inform the interpretation and application of a term or provision of the TBT Agreement would depend on the degree to which it "bears specifically" on the interpretation and application of a term or provision "in a specific case". (Appellate Body Report, *US – Tuna II (Mexico)*, WT/DS381/AB/R, 16 May 2012, para 372)'.

[92] Appellate Body Report, *Peru – Agricultural Products*, [5.101], original footnote 291 citing 'Appellate Body Reports, *US – Anti-Dumping and Countervailing Duties (China)*, para. 308; *EC and certain member States – Large Civil Aircraft*, para. 846'.

[93] Appellate Body Report, *Peru – Agricultural Products*, [5.103].

[94] *See infra*, Sect. 11.8.5.2.

[95] *See supra*, Sect. 11.3.

RTA rulings indicate how the judicial communication between the WTO and RTAs occurred and how it may take place specifically with the new generation EU FTAs.

As previously described, *Argentina – Poultry* concerned a measure brought to the WTO after it was subject to MERCOSUR proceedings that resulted in a ruling.[96] Argentina argued that 'the Panel is bound by the earlier MERCOSUR ruling on the measure at issue in this case', as it is 'part of the normative framework to be applied by the Panel as a result of Article 31.3(c) of the *Vienna Convention*'.[97] The panel, on the other hand, stressed that Article 3.2 of the DSU and Article 31.3(c) of the VCLT were concerned with the *interpretation* of the treaties, while Argentina had not indicated any specific provision of the WTO agreements that should have been interpreted in a specific way.[98] Thus, the panel concluded that Argentina was arguing that the MERCOSUR ruling required the tribunal to rule and apply the WTO provisions in a particular way, rather than interpreting them in a particular way.[99] Moreover, the panel established that

> there is no basis in Article 3.2 of the DSU, or any other provision, to suggest that we are bound to rule in a particular way, or apply the relevant WTO provisions in a particular way. We note that we are not even bound to follow rulings contained in adopted WTO panel reports, so we see no reason at all why we should be bound by the rulings of non-WTO dispute settlement bodies.[100]

Thus, the panel in *Argentina – Poultry* clearly indicated that panels do not have to follow the jurisprudence of any other dispute settlement, including that of RTA DSMs. Moreover, without clarifying the potential role of an RTA ruling in the interpretation of WTO norms, it differentiated between *interpretation* and *application* of WTO norms in light of these rulings. Thus, this suggests that while WTO agreements are silent on the applicability of rulings of other tribunals, they could play a role in the process of interpretation and lead to judicial communication.

In *Brazil – Retreaded Tyres*, Brazil adopted a measure banning the importation of retreaded tyres into its territory which was aimed at reducing the health and environmental risks associated with them. Uruguay requested arbitral proceedings on this measure under MERCOSUR rules, as a result of which a MERCOSUR tribunal decided that the measure at issue was incompatible with the rules of the customs union that required parties not to introduce new restrictions on commerce among them.[101] As a result of this ruling, Brazil eliminated other MERCOSUR parties from the application of the ban on retreaded tyres, which was challenged by the European Communities under WTO rules as it was allegedly discriminatory.[102] Hence, the measure at issue in the WTO proceedings was introduced because of the RTA ruling

---

[96] *See supra*, Sect. 9.4.1.

[97] Panel Report, *Argentina – Poultry*, [7.40].

[98] Ibid, [7.41].

[99] Ibid.

[100] Ibid.

[101] Panel Report, *Brazil – Retreaded Tyres*, WT/DS332/R, 12 June 2007, [2.13].

[102] Ibid, [2.14, 3.1].

and the question in the dispute was whether the exemption granted only to the RTA parties was justified under the WTO agreements.

According to Brazil, its measure was justified under Article XX(b) of GATT which can exempt measures 'necessary to protect human, animal or plant life or health' from other GATT obligations. The panel accepted Brazil's argument and stated that because of the MERCOSUR ruling which is binding on Brazil, the measure at issue 'does not seem to be motivated by capricious or unpredictable reasons'.[103] Moreover, it also noted that the discrimination arising from the MERCOSUR agreement is not '*a priori* unreasonable', as it occurred in the context of an agreement expressly recognised by Article XXIV of GATT,[104] even though it did not assess the compliance of MERCOSUR with the requirements of that provision.

The AB reversed the panel's finding and reached a distinct conclusion. The examination of a measure under Article XX of GATT is two-tiered; first, the panels must examine whether the measure falls under one of the exceptions listed and, second, analyse whether the measure complies with the requirements of the chapeau,[105] according to which the measure must not be applied in a manner that would constitute 'arbitrary or unjustifiable discrimination' between countries where the same conditions prevail and would not represent 'a disguised restriction on international trade'.[106] After determining that the import ban on tyres was provisionally justified under Article XX(b) of GATT, the panel proceeded to examined whether the MERCOSUR exemption qualifies under the chapeau requirements. Contrary to the panel, the AB reached the conclusion that

> the ruling issued by the MERCOSUR arbitral tribunal is not an acceptable rationale for the discrimination, because it bears no relationship to the legitimate objective pursued by the Import Ban that falls within the purview of Article XX(b), and even goes against this objective, to however small a degree.[107]

While the AB did agree with the panel that '[a]cts implementing a decision of a judicial or quasi-judicial body [. . .] can hardly be characterized as a decision that is "capricious" or "random"', it established that 'discrimination can result from a rational decision or behaviour, and still be "arbitrary or unjustifiable"'.[108] Hence, while the AB recognised that implementing a ruling of an RTA would be rational, this would not grant an exemption from WTO rules. The AB could be criticised for asserting some sort of supremacy over other tribunals and being not cooperative;[109]

---

[103] Ibid, [7.272].

[104] Ibid, [7.273, 7.274].

[105] Appellate Body Report, *United States – Standards for Reformulated and Conventional Gasoline*, WT/DS2/AB/R, 29 April 1996, p. 22; Appellate Body Report, *US – Shrimp*, [119–120]; Appellate Body Report, *Brazil – Retreaded Tyres*, [139].

[106] Appellate Body Report, *Brazil – Retreaded Tyres*, [215].

[107] Ibid, [228].

[108] Ibid, [232].

[109] Lavranos (2008), p. 596.

however, the conclusion shows that when it comes to other international obligations, RTAs constitute no exception to the regular application of WTO law.[110] The AB consistently interpreted the chapeau of Article XX of GATT so as to highlight its importance in constraining abusive protectionist public policies undermining basic 'GATT-like commitments on border measures' and strictly scrutinised how a measure applied in practice causes discrimination.[111] While in this dispute the AB analysed an FTA ruling as a justification for a measure under Articles XX of GATT, it did not engage with the argument that the measure applied as a result of a MERCOSUR ruling could be justified under Article XXIV. The panel exercised judicial economy in this respect and the AB did not find the conditions mentioned in the appeal to complete the analysis.[112]

The AB report in *Brazil – Retreaded Tyres* shows that RTA rulings, similar to RTA norms, are to be analysed only in relation to WTO provisions and in accordance with their requirements. Yet, this dispute also shows that RTA rulings could play a role if brought as evidence and treated as facts. While in this specific dispute the measure at issue was not found to be justifiable under Article XX of GATT, the AB did acknowledge the fact that the MERCOSUR ruling was the reason behind the imposition of the measure at issue and, therefore, Brazil's actions could not be considered capricious. Thus, RTA rulings in a distinct case and potentially under a distinct WTO provision could play a more prominent role if analysed as a fact and treated accordingly.

To conclude, WTO panels and the AB have been reticent not only with respect to substantive and procedural RTA norms, but also with respect to RTA rulings, which have been treated according to the regular application of WTO law and practice of panels and the AB. However, they have left the door open to a potential role for RTA rulings in the process of interpretation of and as evidence under WTO norms, including under Article XXIV of GATT explicitly regulating RTAs. WTO panels and the AB, referring to specific WTO provisions such as Article 3.2 of the DSU and Article XX of GATT, have shown the importance of finding a legal basis for judicial communication and have confirmed that coherence should be limited by the existing relevant international rules. The small number of instances in which WTO adjudicators considered RTA case law can also be explained by the fact that the factors encouraging judicial communication tend to work unidirectionally, stimulating communication initiated within the RTA DSMs.

---

[110]Vidigal (2013), p. 1050.

[111]Howse (2016), p. 51.

[112]Panel Report, *Brazil – Retreaded Tyres*, [7.456]; Appellate Body Report, *Brazil – Retreaded Tyres*, [255, 256].

11.6.3   Reference to Other International Tribunals' Jurisprudence Within WTO Proceedings

While the analysis of WTO jurisprudence in which RTA norms and rulings were treated was indicative of how judicial communication between the DSMs of the WTO and the new generation EU FTA DSMs could take place, analysis of how the WTO adjudicators treat other jurisprudence, such as that of the Permanent Court of International Justice (PCIJ), ICJ or CJEU, may be similarly instructive.

When cross-referencing the jurisprudence of other international judicial bodies, WTO adjudicators have most often referred to PCIJ and ICJ jurisprudence and have quoted it multiple times.[113] On several occasions, PCIJ and ICJ jurisprudence was quoted to fill procedural gaps. For example, in *US – Wool Shirts and Blouses* on the issue of distribution of burden of proof between the parties, the AB stated that

> we find it difficult, indeed, to see how any system of judicial settlement could work if it incorporated the proposition that the mere assertion of a claim might amount to proof. It is, thus, hardly surprising that various international tribunals, including the International Court of Justice, have generally and consistently accepted and applied the rule that the party who asserts a fact, whether the claimant or the respondent, is responsible for providing proof thereof.[114]

As the WTO agreements are silent on the treatment of municipal law, in *India – Patents (US)*, the Appellate Body cited the PCIJ judgment from *Certain German Interests in Polish Upper Silesia* to elucidate the matter.[115] When faced with the procedural issue of the use of private counsels before the panel, the AB concluded in *EC – Bananas III* that it could not find anything in the WTO, the DSU, or the Working Procedures, 'nor in customary international law or *the prevailing practice of international tribunals*, which prevents a WTO Member from determining the composition of its delegation in Appellate Body proceedings' (emphasis added).[116] The AB also referred to the jurisprudence of the PCIJ and ICJ to ascertain its ability to decide on its own jurisdiction (*la compétence de la compétence*).[117]

As Article 3.2 of the DSU provides that dispute settlement serves to clarify the WTO provisions 'in accordance with customary rules of interpretation of public international law', the relevant customary rules of interpretation were also

---

[113]Zang (2017), p. 282.

[114]Appellate Body Report, *United States – Measure Affecting Imports of Woven Wool Shirts and Blouses from India (US – Wool Shirts)*, WT/DS33/AB, 23 May 1997, p. 14.

[115]Appellate Body Report, *India – Patent Protection for Pharmaceutical and Agricultural Chemical Products (India – Patents (US))*, WT/DS50/AB/R, 19 December 1997, [65] (original quote: '[1926], PCIJ Rep., Series A, No. 7, p. 19').

[116]Appellate Body Report, *EC – Bananas III*, WT/DS27/AB/R, 9 September 1997, [10].

[117]Appellate Body Report, *US – 1916 Act*, [54] fn 30. The AB noted that 'it is a widely accepted rule that an international tribunal is entitled to consider the issue of its own jurisdiction on its own initiative, and to satisfy itself that it has jurisdiction in any case that comes before it', and cited several ICJ and PCIJ judgments in support of its statement.

determined by the AB using external jurisprudence, such as that of the ICJ, PCIJ, and the European Court of Human Rights (ECtHR). For example, in *US – Gasoline*, the AB asserted that Article 31 of the VCLT has attained the status of a rule of customary or general international law.[118] Similarly, in *Japan – Alcoholic Beverages II*, the AB confirmed the status of customary or general international law of Article 32 of the VCLT.[119] Moreover, the ICJ and PCIJ jurisprudence has also been used to assert the existence of other rules of customary international law.[120] Thus, external jurisprudence can be used to assert the existence of general principles and customary rules of international law, especially on interpretation.

CJEU jurisprudence has also been referred to in WTO proceedings; however, it was passive judicial communication only, as the jurisprudence was invoked by the disputing parties. For example, in *Korea – Alcoholic Beverages*, the European Communities argued that ECJ jurisprudence could be relevant to the interpretation of a GATT provision,[121] while in *EC – IT Products*, the EU made reference to CJEU jurisprudence with respect to customs classification,[122] and in *EC – Chicken Cuts*, the EU argued that CJEU jurisprudence constituted 'circumstances of conclusion' for the European Communities Schedule.[123] Although the WTO panels or the AB

---

[118] Appellate Body Report, *United States – Standards for Reformulated and Conventional Gasoline (US – Gasoline)*, WT/DS2/AB/R, 29 April 1996, p. 17, (original footnote): 'See, e.g., *Territorial Dispute Case (Libyan Arab Jamahiriya v. Chad)*, (1994), I.C.J. Reports p. 6 (International Court of Justice); *Golder v. United Kingdom*, ECHR, Series A, (1995) no. 18 (European Court of Human Rights*); Restrictions to the Death Penalty Cases*, (1986) 70 International Law Reports 449 (Inter-American Court of Human Rights); Jiménez de Aréchaga, "International Law in the Past Third of a Century" (1978-I) 159 Recueil des Cours 1, 42; D. Carreau, Droit International (3è ed, 1991) p. 140; Oppenheim's International Law (9th ed, Jennings and Watts, eds. 1992) Vol. 1, pp. 1271–1275'.

[119] Appellate Body Report, *Japan – Alcoholic Beverages II*, p. 10, (original footnote): 'See e.g.: Jiménez de Aréchaga, "International Law in the Past Third of a Century" (1978-I) 159 Recueil des Cours 1, 42; *Territorial Dispute (Libyan Arab Jamahiriya/Chad), Judgment*, (1994), I.C.J. Reports, p. 6 at 20; *Maritime Delimitation and Territorial Questions between Qatar and Bahrain, Jurisdiction and Admissibility, Judgment*, (1995), I.C.J. Reports, p. 6 at 18; *Interpretation of the Convention of 1919 Concerning Employment of Women during the Night (1932)*, P.C.I.J., Series A/B, No. 50, p. 365 at 380; cf. *the Serbian and Brazilian Loans Cases* (1929), P.C.I.J., Series A, Nos. 20–21, p. 5 at 30; *Constitution of the Maritime Safety Committee of the IMCO* (1960), I.C.J. Reports, p. 150 at 161; *Air Transport Services Agreement Arbitration (United States of America v. France) (1963)*, International Law Reports, 38, p. 182 at 235–43'.

[120] For example, in *Korea – Procurement*, the panel stated that error in treaty law developed as customary international law through the case law of the ICJ and PCIJ (Panel Report, *Korea – Procurement*, [7.123]). On the applicability of general and customary rules of international law, *see* Sect. 9.3.3.

[121] Panel Report, *Korea – Taxes on Alcoholic Beverages (Korea – Alcoholic Beverages)*, WT/DS75/R, 17 February 1999, [7.4(i)].

[122] Panel Report, *European Communities and Its Member States – Tariff Treatment of Certain Information Technology Products (EC – IT Products)*, WT/DS375/R, 21 September 2010, [7.1395].

[123] Appellate Body Report, *European Communities – Customs Classification of Frozen Boneless Chicken Cuts (EC – Chicken Cuts)*, WT/DS269/AB/R, [327, 336].

did not follow cited jurisprudence in any of these cases,[124] they are indicative of how external jurisprudence is treated in passive judicial communication. As also shown by *Brazil – Retreaded Tyres,* it is clear that within WTO proceedings, external jurisprudence as evidence does not benefit from special treatment, but is treated as any evidence and is subject to adjudicatory verification.[125] CJEU jurisprudence was also used by the panel in *US – Gambling* in a statement that was not referred to by the AB, according to which '[o]ther jurisdictions have accepted that gambling activities could be limited or prohibited for public policy considerations, in derogation of general treaty or legislative rules'.[126] The panel used CJEU jurisprudence as part of the legal reasoning to support its interpretation of a term. Hence, in this dispute, external jurisprudence was used to add persuasiveness to the panel conclusion. It should be mentioned that the status of CJEU jurisprudence is unique, since the EU itself is a WTO Member.[127] Thus, CJEU jurisprudence may be classified as municipal, making judicial communication between the WTO and CJEU adjudicators vertical.

To conclude, during WTO proceedings, external jurisprudence has been used by adjudicators on different occasions to fill procedural gaps. Additionally, external jurisprudence has also been used to assert the status of customary international law rules, especially those on interpretation, as evidence brought by the parties, and to interpret substantive terms. The following section will analyse how RTA panels have communicated with the WTO DSM until now, and reflect on the situations in which WTO jurisprudence was used in RTA proceedings.

11.7   Judicial Communication Within RTA Proceedings

As the previous section looked at judicial communication involving WTO adjudicators, specifically how RTAs and their jurisprudence and the jurisprudence of other tribunals have been treated within WTO proceedings, this section will illustrate instances in which RTA adjudicators engaged in judicial communication and referred to WTO jurisprudence.

In several instances, RTA adjudicatory bodies have referred to WTO jurisprudence and treated it as fact. Thus, in cases when a dispute has been dealt with at both the WTO and RTA levels, RTA adjudicatory bodies have used the facts presented in

---

[124] *See* Zang (2017), p. 289.

[125] Ibid.

[126] Panel Report, *US – Gambling,* [6.473] referring in fn 914 to Case C-275/92, *Her Majesty's Customs and Excise v. Gerhart Schindler and Jörg Schindler, (24 March 1994) and Case C-6/01, Associação Nacional de Operadores de Máquinas Recreativas (Anomar) and Others, (11 September 2003).*

[127] Marceau et al. (2013), p. 483, fn 9; Zang (2017), p. 281.

WTO proceedings. For example, in the Mercosur case, *Retreaded Tyres IV*,[128] the tribunal accepted the physical properties described in the AB report from *Brazil – Retreaded Tyres* as a fact.[129] Similarly, in the NAFTA Chapter 19 dispute, *Review of the Final Antidumping Determination in High Fructose Corn Syrup*, the tribunal relied on the WTO panel report from *Mexico – Corn Syrup* to confirm that the initiation of investigations by the Mexican investigating authorities was consistent under its international obligations prescribed by the Antidumping Agreement.[130] Thus, when the same measure or dispute was brought at the multilateral and bilateral level, RTA adjudicatory bodies referred to WTO jurisprudence as a 'source of undisputed authority'.[131] By referring to WTO jurisprudence and its conclusions as facts, RTA judicial bodies ensured greater coherence between the WTO and RTA rulings that dealt with the same disputes or measures.

WTO jurisprudence was also used within RTA proceedings for the purpose of procedural gap filling in cases where the panels were faced with issues that they had not dealt with before and were not addressed in their statutes.[132] For example, in *Oil Country Tubular Goods*, the NAFTA panel used WTO jurisprudence to decide whether a previous panel created a burden of production that 'would require a party to present evidence sufficient to make a *prima facie* showing of the proposition'.[133] The panel specifically referred to an AB report from a similar case that dealt with a similar issue: *US – Anti-Dumping Measures on Oil Country Tubular Goods*.[134] Reference to WTO jurisprudence for solving procedural issues has also been made in MERCOSUR proceedings. In *Blocking of International Bridges,* the MERCOSUR tribunal was faced with the question of whether the object of the dispute had ceased to exist and referred to WTO jurisprudence to answer it.[135] In *Broom Corn Brooms* the NAFTA panel referred to *Brazil – Desiccated Coconuts*[136]

---

[128]*Disagreement over Compliance of the Award on the 'Reversal of the Award "Prohibition Affecting Imports of Retreaded Tyres"'* (Uru. v. Arg.), MERCOSUR, Permanent Court of Appeal, Judgement 10, 25 April 2008, (*Retreaded Tyres IV*).

[129]Marceau et al. (2013), p. 495.

[130]*Review of the Final Determination of the Antidumping Investigation on Imports of High Fructose Corn Syrup, Originating from the United States of America*, NAFTA, MEX-USA-98-1904-01, Final Decision of the Panel, 3 August 2001, [448–454].

[131]Marceau et al. (2013), p. 495.

[132]Ibid, p. 497.

[133]*Oil Country Tubular Goods from Mexico Final Results of Sunset Review of Antidumping Duty Order*, NAFTA, USA-MEX-2001-1904-03, Decision of The Panel on Remand, 3 February 2006, 10, fn17.

[134]*United States – Antidumping Measures on Oil Country Tubular Goods from Mexico*, WT/DS282/AB/R, 2 November 2005.

[135]Marceau et al. (2013), p. 504.

[136]Panel Report, *Brazil – Measures Affecting Desiccated Coconut (Brazil – Desiccated Coconuts)*, WT/DS22/R, 17 October 1996.

to establish what the request for the establishment of the panel must contain.[137] In the EU-Ukraine dispute over the wood export ban, the panel also referred to the WTO jurisprudence to deal with the question of timelines with respect to a jurisdictional objection.[138] Thus, as both RTA and WTO adjudicatory bodies deal with similar procedural questions, reference to each other's jurisprudence can be a source of inspiration and bring coherence and predictability to procedural issues.

Like WTO panels and the AB, RTA adjudicatory bodies use external jurisprudence to assert the status of customary and general international law rules and establish their interpretation. In the first MERCOSUR *Retreaded Tyres* case, the tribunal referred to WTO cases, such as *Argentina – Poultry*, *Guatemala – Cement II*, and *EC – Asbestos*, to establish the elements of the principle of estoppel.[139] In *Tariffs Applied by Canada to Certain U.S. – Origin Agricultural Products*, the NAFTA panel when faced with the question of interpretation stated that importance is to be attached 'to the trade liberalization background against which the agreements' must be interpreted, and in support of this statement, referred to WTO jurisprudence according to which exceptions to obligations of trade liberalisation must be narrowly construed.[140] In EU-Ukraine dispute over the wood export ban, the panel used WTO jurisprudence when applying the principle of *effet utile* for interpretation.[141] Consequently, a certain degree of coherence seems to be ensured by interpreting general principles of international law consistently across proceedings that deal with international trade law issues.

RTA adjudicatory bodies have also used WTO jurisprudence for interpretation of substantive norms. In *Lobsters from Canada*, the NAFTA panel adjudicating on a claim of violation of Article XI of GATT relied on the relevant GATT jurisprudence.[142] In the *Broom Corn Brooms* dispute, for example, the NAFTA panel referred to and used the WTO panel and AB reports from *Japan – Alcoholic Beverages II* to interpret the term 'like product'.[143] Similarly, in *Cross-Border Trucking Services*,[144] the NAFTA panel had to interpret the term 'necessary' in the context of a provision similar to Article XX of GATT. The panel stated that 'the GATT/WTO jurisprudence proves helpful in determining what "necessary" means' and went on to detail how this term was interpreted in various WTO disputes, such as

---

[137] *The U.S. Safeguard Action Taken on Broom Corn Brooms from Mexico (Broom Corn Brooms)*, USA-97-2008-01, 30 January 1998, [53].

[138] Final Report, *Restrictions Applied by Ukraine on Exports of Certain Wood Products to the European Union*, 11 December 2020, [121].

[139] Ibid 509.

[140] *Tariffs Applied by Canada to Certain U.S. – Origin Agricultural Products*, CDA-95-2008-01, 2 December 1996, [122].

[141] Final Report, *Restrictions Applied by Ukraine on Exports of Certain Wood Products to the European Union*, 11 December 2020, [188].

[142] *Lobsters from Canada*, USA 89-1807-01, Final Report of the Panel, 25 May 1990, [7.16–7.19].

[143] *Broom Corn Brooms*, [66].

[144] *Cross-Border Trucking Services*, USA-MEX-98-2008-01, 6 February 2001.

Canada – Periodicals[145] and *US – Gasoline.*[146,147] It also looked at WTO jurisprudence for the interpretation of the chapeau of Article XX of GATT.[148] The panel in the dispute between EU and Ukraine over the wood export ban, referred to the WTO jurisprudence on numerous occasions for the purpose of interpreting WTO norms referred to in the AA, such as Art. XI and XX GATT.[149]

It may be concluded that WTO jurisprudence is often referenced by RTA adjudicators, which can be owed to the factors that encourage these references: an extensive body of WTO jurisprudence on substantive and procedural issues; high semantic authority of the WTO DSM, and especially of the AB; the experience in and knowledge about international trade law of the RTA arbitrators; and also the explicit legal text of the FTAs requiring that the relevant WTO jurisprudence be taken into account. The examples described in this section illustrate that adjudicatory bodies of RTAs use WTO/GATT jurisprudence in various situations that are to a great extent similar to those in which external jurisprudence is referenced within WTO proceedings. They use WTO jurisprudence as a fact, to fill procedural gaps, to assert the meaning of general and customary rules of international law, and for the purpose of interpreting substantive norms.

11.8   Legal Avenues for Judicial Communication Between the New Generation EU FTA and the WTO DSMs

Taking into consideration the various reasons for which judicial communication has occurred between the DSMs of the WTO and RTAs, this section will analyse the possible legal avenues that could be used for such communication between the WTO and the new generation EU FTA DSMs. Establishing the legal bases for potential judicial communication is necessary, since without a legal basis, the intention of the parties may be disregarded and the DSMs may be perceived as exceeding their authority, engaging in judicial activism, and adding to or diminishing the parties' rights and obligations.[150] Hence, the search for legal avenues for judicial communication is rooted in the need to seek coherence, but within the limits set by the intention of the parties as expressed in international law. Moreover, using legal avenues to argue why a judicial interpretation should depart from the one offered by

---

[145] Panel Report, *Canada – Certain Measures Concerning Periodicals* (*Canada – Periodicals*), WT/DS31/R, 14 March 1997.

[146] Panel Report, *US – Gasoline*, WT/DS2/R, 20 May 1996.

[147] *Cross-Border Trucking Services*, [262–263].

[148] Ibid, [264–269].

[149] For example, Final Report, *Restrictions Applied by Ukraine on Exports of Certain Wood Products to the European Union*, 11 December 2020, [202], [259], [282], [293], [298], [301], [335], etc.

[150] *See supra*, Sect. 11.5.

another judicial body dealing with a similar norm would also help to identify justifiable incoherencies and distinguish them from those that are unjustified. Thus, using legal avenues in the argumentation of judicial bodies would make the public understand how and why a specific conclusion was reached.

11.8.1 *Inherent Powers as Avenues for Judicial Communication*

As the previous section illustrated, the WTO and RTA adjudicatory bodies have used external jurisprudence to fill procedural gaps. Considering that this section argued that judicial communication aiming to enhance coherence should, nevertheless, take place within the limits set by the law, a legal basis for procedural gap filling is needed. The legal avenue for this may be the use of inherent powers possessed by these bodies due to their adjudicatory nature.

Regardless of the presence of specific clauses in the constitutive texts of an adjudicatory body, it enjoys certain inherent powers due to the consent of the parties to create such an international adjudicatory body in the first place. These bodies can use their inherent powers to ensure that they carry out their adjudicative function.[151] Thus, WTO and new generation EU FTA adjudicators, including MPIA appeal arbitrators, when faced with procedural gaps that they need to fill in order to perform their adjudicatory function could turn to the jurisprudence of other tribunals that have already addressed the same issues. Hence, external jurisprudence can serve as a source of inspiration and for establishing procedural principles or rules to be used when the constitutive treaties are silent on some procedural issues, but the international courts and tribunals need to react to these unforeseen circumstances. According to Art. 38(1)(d) of the ICJ Statute judicial decisions represent subsidiary means for the determination of rules of law.[152] Therefore, WTO and new generation EU FTA adjudicators can use external jurisprudence to determine the procedural rules that could fill the procedural gaps in their constituent treaties that prevent them from exercising their judicial functions. However, reference to such external jurisprudence can be made only when it relates to procedural principles and rules, is necessary for the proper exercise of adjudicative functions, does not have substantive content, and does not contravene the constitutive agreement.[153]

While judicial communication could take place based on the inherent powers of international adjudicatory bodies, its role in bringing coherence is limited due to the requirement that it should concern only procedural rules. Hence, inherent powers cannot be used as legal avenues for bringing coherence across WTO and new generation EU FTAs for substantive norms. Nevertheless, coherence in procedural

---

[151] *See supra*, Sect. 9.3.4.1.

[152] For more on Art 38(1)(d) of the ICJ Statute, *see infra* Sect. 11.8.3.

[153] *See supra*, Sect. 9.3.4.1. Mitchell and Heaton (2010), p. 566.

matters (especially when the agreement is silent and does not provide otherwise, as it is required in the case of inherent powers) is also valuable. Solving similar procedural questions in a similar manner brings predictability to the procedures and ensures a sense of fairness that similar procedural issues are treated similarly. It is especially important when procedural issues, such as those of jurisdiction or burden of proof, arise in the same disputes brought simultaneously or subsequently to the WTO and FTA DSMs in case jurisdictional clauses proved unsuccessful in solving conflicting jurisdictions.

The analysis in this sub-section showed that inherent powers of the WTO and new generation EU FTAs international judicial bodies could be used as a legal avenue for initiating judicial communication. However, such judicial communication could take place only if the requirements for inherent powers are met. Hence, it would be only limited to filling procedural gaps and could not have a role in ensuring coherence between substantive norms.

11.8.2 Facts and Evidence

WTO and RTA judicial practice shows that external jurisprudence has been adduced and used as evidence and assessed as facts. Thus, in the WTO context, in *Brazil – Retreaded Tyres*, the AB considered as a fact that Brazil imposed the measure at issue as a result of a MERCOSUR ruling, while the RTA panels used as facts some of the determinations made by WTO panels or the AB. This section will investigate how judicial communication can take place by treating judicial reports as facts and evidence, considering that the strive for coherence is limited by the will of the parties as embedded in public international rules.

First of all, parties themselves could invoke the jurisprudence of another judicial body as evidence in their submissions, giving rise to passive judicial communication.[154] Parties could invoke judicial rulings or awards as evidence to comply with their burden of proof: the complainant to establish the prima facie case and the defendant to rebut it.[155] Neither the DSU nor the texts of the new generation EU FTAs impose limitations on the types of evidence that can be brought. Thus, parties enjoy flexibility in this respect and can also invoke scholarly articles and judicial rulings. As Andersen stated, in the context of WTO proceedings, the type of evidence 'is limited only by the resources and imagination of the litigants'.[156]

According to Article 11 of the DSU, 'a panel should make an objective assessment of the matter before it, including an objective assessment of the facts of the case and the applicability of and conformity with the relevant covered agreements'. Thus, WTO panels enjoy a considerable margin of discretion in assessing evidence and

---

[154] *See supra*, Sect. 11.4.

[155] Andersen (2010), p. 178.

[156] Ibid, p. 184.

ascribing value to it,[157] as the evidence would be attested in the panelists' own process of verification.[158] In *EC – Hormones*, the AB stated that 'it is generally within the discretion of the Panel to decide which evidence it chooses to utilize in making findings'.[159] In *Korea – Alcoholic Beverages*, the AB reiterated that panels enjoy a certain level of discretion when examining and weighing evidence; however, it also pointed out that this discretion is subject to certain limits. Thus, the AB stated, 'A panel's discretion as trier of facts is not [. . .] unlimited. That discretion is always subject to, and is circumscribed by [. . .] the panel's duty to render an objective assessment of the matter before it'.[160] While there are no exact criteria on how to objectively assess the evidence, in *EC – Hormones*, the AB established that an objective assessment entails 'an obligation to consider the evidence presented to a panel and to make factual findings on the basis of that evidence',[161] while

> [t]he willful distortion or misrepresentation of the evidence put before a panel is similarly inconsistent with an objective assessment of the facts. 'Disregard' and 'distortion' and 'misrepresentation' of the evidence, in their ordinary signification in judicial and quasi-judicial processes, imply not simply an error of judgment in the appreciation of evidence but rather an egregious error that calls into question the good faith of a panel.[162]

Accordingly, to comply with Article 11 of the DSU, WTO panels should not disregard, distort, or misrepresent RTA rulings if they are submitted as evidence, but they nevertheless would have considerable discretion in assessing and weighing FTA rulings. While WTO panels and the AB can ascribe evidential value to RTA rulings, we can see from *Brazil – Retreaded Tyres* that the AB did not defer to the results and conclusions of the RTA ruling, but conducted its own assessment under WTO rules. While treating RTA rulings as facts, the AB made no exception to its consistent approach towards Article XX of GATT. Indeed, there is no legal reason for treating judicial rulings as evidence different from other types of evidence. Similarly, WTO panels did not defer to the factual findings from previous WTO panel reports on the same measures. The panel in *US – Shrimp II (Viet Nam)* stated that 'Viet Nam is therefore bound to provide relevant evidence proving the facts it asserts in the present dispute and cannot rely on previous panel and Appellate Body decisions to establish, as a matter of fact, the existence of the zeroing methodology'.[163] Hence, while parties invoking FTA rulings in their submissions will trigger

---

[157] Marceau (2013), pp. 8–9.

[158] Zang (2017), p. 289.

[159] Appellate Body Report, *EC – Hormones*, WT/DS26/AB/R, WT/DS48/AB/R, 16 January 1998, [135].

[160] Appellate Body Report, *Korea – Alcoholic Beverages*, WT/DS75/AB/R, WT/DS84/AB/R, 18 January 1999, [162].

[161] Appellate Body Report, *EC – Hormones*, [133].

[162] Ibid.

[163] Panel Report, *United States – Anti-Dumping Measures on Certain Shrimp from Viet Nam (US – Shrimp II (Viet Nam))*, WT/DS429/R, 17 November 2014, [7.42].

judicial communication, it is highly likely that these rulings would not be ascribed value at all or not a considerable one.

The new generation EU FTAs, except the EUJEPA, do not include a provision similar to Article 11 of DSU that requires an objective assessment of the facts. Thus, it seems that the panels enjoy broader discretion under these agreements, possibly also to disregard invoked evidence. What should be the standard of review under these agreements could be clarified by judicial practice as the texts are silent on this matter. Only the EUJEPA uses language similar to that of the DSU, stating that the panel 'shall make an objective assessment of the matter before it, including an objective assessment of the facts of the case and the applicability of, and conformity of the measures at issue with, the covered provisions'.[164] Hence, by using language similar to that of the DSU, the EUJEPA parties seemingly wanted to set the same standard of review as in WTO proceedings. Since the standard of review under the EUJEPA is likely to be the same as that under the WTO, other new generation EU FTA panels may enjoy greater discretion. WTO rulings or potential appeal arbitral awards invoked as evidence will be subject to the arbitrators' own review. Yet, as practice has shown, RTAs could take WTO factual findings for granted without questioning them,[165] even when an independent assessment might be thought as needed,[166] likely due to the increased semantic authority of WTO rulings, a factor that encourages judicial communication.

For WTO and RTA jurisprudence to be treated as facts, panels themselves could seek information, even when the parties do not reference them in their submissions. Thus, Article 13 of the DSU establishes that '[e]ach panel shall have the right to seek information and technical advice from any individual or body which it deems appropriate'. As Article 11 of the DSU mandates an 'objective' assessment of the facts and law, the panel could itself seek further information that would allow it to fulfil this obligation.[167] When faced with the question of whether the right to seek information covers data from scientific articles, the panel from *Australia – Tobacco Plain Packaging (Cuba)* stated:

> Articles 13.1 and 13.2 of the DSU permit panels to request and obtain information from 'any individual or body which it deems appropriate' and from 'any relevant source' and the Panel did not see any *a priori* restriction on the individual to whom, or body to which, we might direct a request. The Panel therefore considered that the fact that the requested information underlay published articles did not, in itself, shield it from scrutiny under Article 13 of the DSU.[168]

---

[164] EUJEPA, Art 21.12(a).

[165] *See supra*, (n 130).

[166] Marceau et al. (2013), p. 497.

[167] Matsushita et al. (2015), p. 98.

[168] Panel Report, *Australia – Certain Measures Concerning Trademarks, Geographical Indications and Other Plain Packaging Requirements Applicable to Tobacco Products and Packaging (Australia – Tobacco Packaging (Cuba))*, WT/DS458/R, 28 June 2018, [1.91].

Hence, panels enjoy broad authority to inform themselves. 'That authority, and the breadth thereof, is indispensably necessary to enable a panel to discharge its duty imposed by Article 11 of the DSU'.[169] This extensive authority, which covers requests for information from *any source*, could also include the authority to request information about the procedures of another forum from the parties or even about rulings from an FTA panel.[170] However, WTO panels also enjoy broad discretion to decide whether or not to seek information and the value to ascribe to it. In *US – Shrimp*, the AB established that

> [a] panel's authority includes the authority to decide not to seek such information or advice at all. [...] to accept or reject any information or advice which it may have sought and received, or to make some other appropriate disposition thereof. [...] to ascertain the acceptability and relevancy of information or advice received, and to decide what weight to ascribe to that information or advice or to conclude that no weight at all should be given to what has been received.[171]

Therefore, while panels could seek information by themselves, including on the proceedings of and rulings issued by other fora, it remains solely at their discretion to decide whether or not to do so and what value to ascribe to it. The new generation EU FTAs, similar to Article 13 of the DSU, provide that panels can request information on their 'own initiative' from 'any source' or 'any person or body'.[172] Accordingly, panels under the new generation EU FTAs, as well as WTO panels, have broad authority to seek information, including on WTO proceedings, rulings, or arbitral awards. However, as there are no restrictions imposed on the right of FTA panels to seek information, it can be deduced that similar to WTO panels, they enjoy discretion to seek or not to seek information, to accept or reject it, and what value to ascribe to it.

To conclude, under WTO and new generation EU FTA rules, the jurisprudence of another tribunal could be invoked by parties as evidence, or panels on their own initiative could seek information on external proceedings and rulings that would be treated as facts. However, the value that judicial communication through this legal avenue could have for the function of promoting coherence in the interactions between the DSMs of the new generation EU FTAs and the WTO is limited due to the broad discretion that panels have to assess evidence and facts. While the new generation EU FTA panels could defer to the fact findings of WTO jurisprudence by virtue of its higher authority, it is expected that WTO panels would continue to approach RTA rulings as any other evidence and treat them with caution. Finally, using external jurisprudence as evidence or facts has no influence whatsoever on how similar substantive rules are interpreted and applied.

---

[169] Appellate Body Report, *US – Shrimp*, [106].

[170] Hillman (2009), p. 205; Marceau (2013), p. 8.

[171] Appellate Body Report, *US – Shrimp*, [104].

[172] EUKFTA, Art 14.15; CETA, Annex 29-A, para 42; EUJEPA, Art 21.17(2); EUSFTA, Art 14.17 (1); EUVFTA, Art 15.20.

11.8.3 Judicial Decisions Determining Customary Rules and Principles of Interpretation

The review of the WTO and RTA practice of referring to external jurisprudence indicates that it had the purpose to, *inter alia*, assert the meaning and status of international rules, including that of customary rules of interpretation. Incoherent interpretations of identical or similar norms may also result from incoherent interpretation and application of the international rules of interpretation. In line with the concept of limited coherence, a legal basis for the use of judicial decisions for the purpose considered in this section is needed. Article 38(1)(d) of the ICJ Statute could be used as a legal basis to refer to judicial decisions for determining the meaning of general principles of international law and customary international rules, including those of interpretation.

While Article 38(1)(d) of the ICJ Statute could be used in conjunction with the principle of inherent powers as an avenue for judicial communication to establish procedural rules to fill in procedural gaps,[173] it could also be used independently to determine the meaning of international general principles and customary rules. In the first instance, international procedural rules would become applicable within WTO or new generation EU FTA proceedings due to the inherent powers of the panels, and in the second, the customary rules of interpretation are generally applicable to international treaties unless parties departed from them. In the WTO agreements and the new generation EU FTAs, there is express reference in the constitutive treaties that clearly allows the use of these rules. Thus, according to Article 3.2 of the DSU (also applicable in interim appeal arbitration proceedings),[174] Article 14.16 of the EUKFTA, Article 29.17 of CETA, Article 21.16 of the EUJEPA, Article 14.18 of the EUSFTA, and Article 15.21 of the EUVFTA, the WTO and the new generation EU FTA norms are to be interpreted 'in accordance with customary rules of interpretation of public international law'. Hence, using customary rules of international law on interpretation does not violate Article 3.2 of the DSU, as their use is expressly enshrined in the treaty. The new generation EU FTAs additionally specify that these rules include those codified in the VCLT,[175] which, in the case of the WTO agreements, was clarified by jurisprudence.[176]

---

[173] See *supra*, Sect. 11.8.1.

[174] As suggested by Arts 1.1 and 3.5 of the DSU, arbitral awards are subject to the DSU and shall be consistent with the covered agreements, including the DSU and its Art 3.2. MPIA, Annex 1, para 11 also provides that '[u]nless otherwise provided for in these agreed procedures, the arbitration shall be governed, mutatis mutandis, by the provisions of the DSU'.

[175] EUKFTA, Art 14.16; CETA, Art 29.17; EUJEPA, Art 21.16; EUSFTA, Art 14.18; EUVFTA, Art 15.21.

[176] See *supra*, Sect. 11.6.3.

The discussion on Article 38 of the ICJ Statute is mostly focused on what would qualify as a source of international law,[177] and especially whether international judicial decisions could be independent sources. Since Article 38(1)(d) of the ICJ Statute states that 'judicial decisions and the teachings of the most highly qualified publicists' are 'subsidiary means for the determination of rules of law', the debate revolves around the meaning of the term 'subsidiary means'. This author adheres to the view that only the sources listed in Article 38(1)(a)–(c) of the ICJ Statute— treaties, international customary law, and general principles—are independent sources of obligations, while paragraph (d) provides the means for determination of the existence and the state of international rules of law at the relevant time, as well as the proper interpretation of these rules.[178] However, this should not be interpreted as negating the binding nature of judicial decisions *inter se* for the parties of the dispute. Hence, while panel and AB reports, interim appeal awards, and FTA rulings are binding on the disputing parties,[179] they do not represent an independent source of international law for other judicial entities, but merely a source that can be used for the purpose of establishing the existence, status, and interpretation of those primary sources. Thus, adjudicators could give consideration to the fact that for the parties a ruling of another judicial body is an authoritative source in itself, as happened in *Brazil – Retreaded Tyres*, where the AB recognised that the measure implementing a decision of a judicial or quasi-judicial body could not be characterised as being capricious or random.[180] Although consideration may be given to judicial decisions, it would not make them independent sources of international law to be considered on by adjudicators in the proceedings.

This approach is adopted, as the term 'subsidiary', itself suggests two levels of determination of sources, but does not indicate that the subsidiary means are of lesser importance, but rather that they depend on primary sources.[181] Moreover, the drafting history also seems to support this approach. During the Advisory Committee of Jurists' drafting process in 1920 of the Statute of the Permanent Court of International Justice which contains the precursor to Article 38(1)(d) of the ICJ Statute, the mention of 'the use of judicial decisions as a means for the development of the law' was removed and there appeared to be agreement among the drafters that judicial decisions are not primary sources of law.[182] International courts,[183] including a WTO panel, seem to have also endorsed this approach. In *EC –Biotech*

---

[177] For more details on this debate, *see* Zammit Borda (2013), pp. 649–661; Andenas and Leiss (2017), pp. 907–972.

[178] Opinion adopted and justified by de Brabandere (2012), p. 246; Zammit Borda (2013), pp. 651–656; Andenas and Leiss (2017), pp. 927–928.

[179] *See supra*, Sect. 6.7.

[180] Appellate Body Report, *Brazil – Retreaded Tyres*, [232].

[181] Andenas and Leiss (2017), p. 927.

[182] Zammit Borda (2013), pp. 951–952.

[183] On how this approach is generally endorsed by international courts, such as the International Criminal Tribunal for the Former Yugoslavia and the Special Court for Sierra Leone, *see* Zammit Borda (2013), p. 653.

Products, without making express reference to Article 38(1) of the ICJ Statute, but mirroring its paragraphs (a)–(c), the panel identified '(i) international conventions (treaties), (ii) international custom (customary international law), and (iii) the recognized general principles of law' as the 'generally accepted sources of public international law'.[184] As Alain Pellet, former chairperson of the ILC, noted in a lecture, while the teachings are also subsidiary means, '[n]o one would think of asserting that the doctrine could, as such, be a source of international law, even though it certainly helps to discover and formulate the rules of law'.[185]

According to the approach adopted, judicial decisions can be used to determine the existence and content of primary sources, including that of the international customary rules of interpretation. For example, the AB used the jurisprudence of other international courts to establish the status of customary rules of interpretation of Articles 31 and 32 of the VCLT.[186] Likewise, WTO adjudicators, as well as new generation EU FTA panels could use each other's jurisprudence to coherently determine the meaning of these rules. For instance, the panels established under FTAs could make use of the interpretations offered by WTO jurisprudence on the *effet utile* principle according to which '[o]ne of the corollaries of the "general rule of interpretation" in the Vienna Convention is that interpretation must give meaning and effect to all the terms of a treaty'.[187]

In conclusion, by adopting coherent interpretations of the customary rules of interpretation with the help of judicial communication, judicial bodies of the WTO and the new generation EU FTAs are more likely to reach consistent results and avoid unjustified incoherencies. Nevertheless, this would merely represent an indirect way of using external jurisprudence to ensure coherence. Coherently interpreting and applying the rules of interpretation still does not equal to coherently interpreting substantive norms and reaching similar results.

11.8.4   FTA Judicial Decisions Under Article XXIV of GATT

The previous section showed that WTO panels and the AB left the door open to invocation of RTA rulings under specific WTO norms. As Article XXIV of GATT is the provision that expressly regulates the status of RTAs within the WTO and permits their conclusion, it is reasonable to expect that the invocation of an FTA ruling is most likely to take place under it.

---

[184]Panel Report, *European Communities – Measures Affecting the Approval and Marketing of Biotech Products (EC – Biotech Products)*, WT/DS291/R, 29 September 2006, [7.67].

[185]Pellet (2018), p. 34.

[186]*See supra*, Sect. 11.6.3.

[187]Appellate Body Report, *US – Gasoline*, p. 23. The principle of effective interpretation was also reaffirmed *inter alia* in Appellate Body Report, *US – Shrimp,* [131]; Appellate Body Report, *Korea – Definitive Safeguard Measure on Imports of Certain Dairy Products (Korea – Dairy)*, WT/DS98/AB/R, 14 December 1999, [81].

Treating FTA rulings in connection with FTA norms under Article XXIV of
GATT would avoid the issue of jurisdiction and applicable law within WTO proceedings. Although WTO adjudicators would have no jurisdiction over FTA norms,
they can consider FTA norms to determine their consistency with Article XXIV
requirements and whether a GATT violation could be justified.[188] Furthermore,
while application of FTA provisions and rulings within WTO proceedings, instead
of WTO provisions, would most likely not be permitted, as this would diminish or
add to WTO rights and obligations,[189] consideration within the limits set by Article XXIV would comply with Article 3.2 of the DSU because it would be according
to the covered agreements. In *Peru – Agricultural Products*, the AB also clarified in
a footnote that '[a]rticle XXIV of the GATT 1994 [. . .] necessitate[s] consideration
of relevant FTA provisions and thus provide[s] a basis for panels and the Appellate
Body to determine the meaning of the provisions in such FTAs in order to determine
their consistency with WTO law'.[190] Therefore, Article XXIV could represent a
legal avenue to consider whether an FTA measure that violates GATT provisions
could be justified. Moreover, the AB further concluded that the proper routes to
assess whether an FTA provision may depart from certain WTO rules is nevertheless
consistent with the covered agreements are the WTO provisions that permit the RTA
formation, namely Article XXIV of GATT, the Enabling Clause, or Article V of
GATS. However, as previously explained, only violations of Article I of GATT and
certain other GATT violations could be justified under Art. XXIV GATT, due to its
limited scope of coverage.[191]

Since Art. XXIV GATT could justify the adoption of domestic GATT-
inconsistent measures,[192] it is argued that FTA rulings could become relevant in
two ways. First, FTA rulings could be relevant in the examination of a measure
based directly on an FTA provision. FTA rulings interpreting that provision could be
regarded as subsidiary means for determining the interpretation of the provision
under Article 38(1)(d) of the ICJ Statute. Hence, FTA rulings could be taken into
consideration to establish the meaning of an FTA provision that could be justified
under Article XXIV of GATT, despite violating certain other GATT rules. The
determination would, thus, have an informative character with respect to the measure
under consideration. Second, when an FTA measure is introduced because of an
FTA ruling requiring it, as in *Brazil – Retreaded Tyres*, the ruling could have factual
value and be considered under Article 11 of the DSU. Nevertheless, WTO adjudicators would not be bound by the determinations contained in such a ruling and
would have discretion to ascribe a value to it.[193]

---

[188] *See supra*, Sect. 9.3.2.

[189] *See supra*, Sects. 9.3.3.2.

[190] Appellate Body Report, *Peru – Agricultural Products*, fn 276.

[191] *See supra*, Sect. 9.3.2.

[192] Appellate Body Report, *Turkey – Textiles*, [45].

[193] *See supra*, Sect. 11.8.2.

Article XXIV of GATT has an exceptional character; it cannot be invoked as a justification for all FTA-connected measures, but only for those that meet the WTO requirements.[194] Accordingly, both a measure whose meaning could be established with the help of an FTA ruling and a measure imposed as a consequence of such a ruling should comply with the WTO requirements in order to justify a GATT violation. Unless the two-tiered test established in *Turkey – Textiles* is revised, the defendant claiming a justification under Article XXIV of GATT would have to prove (1) that the measure at issue was introduced upon the formation of the FTA that fully meets the requirements of Article XXIV of GATT; and (2) that the formation of that FTA would be prevented if it had not been allowed to introduce the measure at issue.[195] To determine whether an FTA fully meets the requirements of Article XXIV of GATT, the defendant would have to prove that the duties and other regulations of commerce applicable to third parties at the formation of the FTA by the constituent territories to third parties were not higher or more restrictive than those prior to the formation and that duties and ORRC have been eliminated on substantially all the trade (except, where necessary, those permitted under Articles XI, XII, XIII, XIV, XV and XX of GATT). Assessment of the compliance of the new generation EU FTAs with Article XXIV of GATT requirements is outside the ambit of this book, and such an evaluation would represent a task that would require enormous effort.[196] Furthermore, the meaning of 'substantially all' and 'ORRC' and whether the list of exceptions contained in the brackets of Article XXIV is exhaustive are issues that have not been clarified yet and represent controversial topics,[197] making the task of a Member seeking to justify a measure under Article XXIV of GATT more difficult.

As stated previously,[198] the requirements established in *Turkey – Textiles* have been criticised for being overly restrictive and demonstrating that the qualification of a measure under them might be an extremely complicated journey. Thus, a Member trying to justify its measure under Article XXIV of GATT would have to prove that it was introduced upon and necessary for the formation of the FTA. The assessment of compliance with the requirements of GATT exceptions, as demonstrated by the AB's approach in *Brazil – Retreaded Tyres*,[199] would be the same for all measures, even if they were introduced because of an FTA provision or ruling. For example, if an FTA measure is required by an FTA ruling, it would not make it automatically necessary for the formation of the FTA.[200] WTO panels and the AB could analyse in such a case the factual value of an FTA ruling. Nevertheless, whether the formation

---

[194] Marceau and Wyatt (2010), p. 83.

[195] Appellate Body Report, *Turkey – Textiles*, [58].

[196] Marceau and Wyatt (2010), p. 82; For more on whether general review of an FTA is possible within WTO dispute settlement context *see* Herrmann and Würdemann (2017), pp. 51–52;

[197] For more on these issues, *see* Mathis (2002); Matsushita (2004), p. 497; Gobbi Estrella and Horlick (2006); Herrmann and Würdemann (2017), p. 46; Bartels (2013).

[198] *See supra*, Sect. 9.3.2.

[199] *See supra*, Sect. 11.6.3.

[200] Brink (2010), p. 839.

of the FTA would have been prevented without the introduction of the measure will be analysed separately and would not hinge on the existence of the ruling.

It can be concluded that Article XXIV of GATT expressly regulating the status of the FTAs could be a legal avenue for judicial communication initiated by WTO adjudicators to determine the content of an FTA provision or to analyse FTA rulings as a reason behind the introduction of a measure. Yet, such communication would be rather limited, due to Article XXIV of GATT being able to justify only GATT violations, restrictive requirements, and controversial concepts. In addition, judicial communication under Article XXIV of GATT would be able to promote coherence only between FTA provisions when considered by both WTO and FTA adjudicators, but not between FTA and WTO provisions.

11.8.5   Judicial Decisions in the Process of Interpretation

As deduced in previous sections, WTO panels and the AB have used external jurisprudence and RTA panels have referred to WTO case law for the purpose of interpretation of treaty norms. As previously argued, coherence should not be sought at the expense of correctness; therefore, this section will establish the legal basis for using external jurisprudence in the process of interpretation. Judicial communication in such a case can take place with the aim of establishing the ordinary meaning of a term, indicating any relevant rules of international law applicable in the relations between the parties, or be used under express interpretation rules requiring the use of external jurisprudence. All these cases will be analysed in detail bellow.

11.8.5.1   The Ordinary Meaning of Terms

WTO and FTA panels could use each other's jurisprudence to establish the meaning of a term in FTAs and WTO agreements, respectively. Thus, external jurisprudence could be useful in establishing the ordinary meaning of a term in accordance with Article 31(1) of the VCLT which states that '[a] treaty shall be interpreted in good faith in accordance with the *ordinary meaning* to be given to the terms of the treaty in their context and in the light of its object and purpose' (emphasis added). One of the ways to determine the ordinary meaning of a term is with the help of dictionaries. For example, WTO panels and the AB usually start by consulting one or several dictionaries and seem particularly keen to use them to establish the meaning of terms.[201] While dictionaries are by far the most frequently used tools for determining

---

[201] Mitchell (2007), p. 812. On how the AB has been criticised for often relying solely on dictionary definitions and adopting a textual approach, *see* Horn and Weiler (2005), pp. 252–253; Magnuson (2010), pp. 124–129.

the meaning of terms, there are also other ways. In *EC – Biotech Products*, the panel asserted that

> in addition to dictionaries, other relevant rules of international law may in some cases aid a treaty interpreter in establishing, or confirming, the ordinary meaning of treaty terms in the specific context in which they are used.[202]

Thus, the panel stated that it 'may consider other relevant rules of international law [...] if it deems such rules to be informative'.[203] Hence, other international conventions could also be used in a similar way to dictionaries to help establish the ordinary meaning of a term. The panel supported its approach by referring to the *US – Shrimp* case,[204] where, without expressly invoking Article 31(1) of the VCLT, the AB cited other international conventions for the purpose of establishing the meaning of a term.[205] The panel concluded that a convention does not have to be negotiated between all the parties for it to be informative and shed light on the meaning of a term,[206] an issue that emerges when invoking Article 31(3)(c) of the VCLT.[207]

Given the openness of the WTO panel to consider other international rules that can be informative in defining the ordinary meaning of a term, it may be expected that the interpretation offered by other international courts or tribunals could be similarly informative and indicative of the meaning. As the norms of the new generation EU FTAs are also to be interpreted according to the customary rules of international law and, thus, according to Article 31 of the VCLT, reference to WTO jurisprudence, including to appeal arbitral awards, to establish the ordinary meaning of a term would be equally possible. Hence, the use of WTO jurisprudence by NAFTA panels to help establish the meaning of terms such as 'like products' and 'necessary' could have been based on Article 31(1) of the VCLT, even though the panels did not expressly refer to it.[208]

However, in *EC – Biotech*, the panel noted that '[s]uch rules would not be considered because they are legal rules, but rather because they may provide evidence of the ordinary meaning of terms' and because of their 'informative character'.[209] Since other relevant rules of international law would be used in the context of Article 31(1) of the VCLT because of their potentially informative character and not because of their legal nature, the panel would enjoy discretion to decide whether or not to rely on such rules for establishing the ordinary meaning of a term, 'particularly if it considers that the ordinary meaning of the terms of WTO

---

[202] Panel Report, *EC – Biotech Products*, [7.92].

[203] Ibid [7.93].

[204] Ibid [7.94].

[205] Appellate Body Report, *US – Shrimp*, [130].

[206] Panel Report, *EC – Biotech Products*, [7.94].

[207] *See infra*, Sect. 11.8.5.2.3.

[208] *See supra*, Sect. 11.7.

[209] Panel Report, *EC – Biotech Products*, [7.92].

agreements may be ascertained by reference to other elements'.[210] Following this statement, without detailing the reasons, the panel decided that in the case at issue it was not necessary or appropriate to rely on the provisions from international conventions invoked by the European Communities, but it did consider material obtained from several international organisations, such as the World Health Organization (WHO) or the Food and Agriculture Organization of the United Nations (FAO).[211] *EC – Biotech* makes clear that if judicial decisions of another body would be used for establishing the ordinary meaning of a term, they would only have an evidential character. Thus, they would not be considered because of their status as a subsidiary means of international law, but would be used in the same manner as any dictionary.

While there was expressed an openness by a WTO panel towards other sources than dictionaries as evidence of the ordinary meaning of terms,[212] without being constrained by requirements such as, for example, the need that all WTO Members are parties to the international rules considered, reliance on such sources would remain at the complete discretion of the panels. Therefore, other international rules and judicial decisions would not benefit from special treatment. Rather, their impact would be small or no bigger than that of Webster's Dictionary.[213] Moreover, consideration of external jurisprudence in the process of establishing the ordinary meaning of a term would only be an element of the interpretative process.

The process of treaty interpretation logically starts with the text of a particular provision[214] as the authentic expression of the intention of the parties.[215] Nevertheless, the text of the treaty is only the starting point of the process of interpretation. Article 31 of the VCLT provides the following interpretative elements: interpretation in good faith in accordance with the ordinary meaning given to the terms of the treaty in their context (paragraphs 2 and 3 further elucidating what the context is) and in light of its object and purpose, which are part of a single combined operation.[216] Accordingly, interpretation represents a holistic approach during which all elements are to be taken into consideration. The meaning of the terms should not be taken out of context and established in the abstract—they have not been drafted in isolation.[217] The 'raw text' is only a piece of the puzzle, with the context, object and purpose being the other pieces necessary to construct the entire puzzle.[218] In *US – Gambling*, the AB stated that the dictionary definitions of terms 'are not necessarily capable of

---

[210] Ibid [7.93].

[211] Ibid [7.95].

[212] For criticism of the possibility of bringing evidence for legal interpretation of a norm, *see* Flett (2012), p. 296.

[213] Broude (2008), p. 199.

[214] Villiger (2009), p. 426, para 9; Mercurio and Tyagi (2010), p. 304; Gardiner (2015), p. 164.

[215] Dörr (2012), p. 541, para 38.

[216] Frankel (2014), p. 15; Dörr (2012), p. 541, para 39.

[217] Villiger (2009), p. 427, para 10.

[218] Ortino (2006), p. 123.

resolving complex questions of interpretation, as they typically aim to catalogue all meanings of words'.[219] Similarly, rulings of other international judicial bodies could reflect the meaning of a word that does not correspond to the one suggested by elements such as the context, object and purpose of the treaty. Indeed, the same word can have multiple definitions, and to establish which one was intended by the parties, other elements of the interpretative process are necessary. If other elements are not accounted for, the interpretation could lead to erroneous and unjustified results. The AB also expressly recognised the holistic nature of interpretation as described by the VCLT. In *US – Continued Zeroing*, the AB affirmed:

> A word or term may have more than one meaning or shade of meaning, but the identification of such meanings in isolation only commences the process of interpretation, it does not conclude it. [...] Instead, a treaty interpreter is required to have recourse to context and object and purpose to elucidate the relevant meaning of the word or term. [...] treaty interpretation is an integrated operation, where interpretative rules or principles must be understood and applied as connected and mutually reinforcing components of a holistic exercise.[220]

Even within the same agreement, the same term may have different meanings; for example, the concept of likeness has been interpreted differently in GATT articles.[221] Hence, while other international treaties and external jurisprudence could be useful in establishing the ordinary meaning of a term, their role may be more limited since other elements of interpretation would also be taken into account and could provide reasons for justified incoherencies. The principle of effectiveness correlated with the elements of good faith and interpretation in light of object and purpose could represent one of the limitations of the role of external norms and jurisprudence in establishing the ordinary meaning of a term. According to this principle, all provisions of a treaty should be read in a way that gives meaning to all of them, so that the reading would not result 'in reducing whole clauses or paragraphs of a treaty to redundancy or inutility'.[222] Therefore, if one of the meanings suggested by the ruling of another international court reduces a clause to redundancy, such an interpretation should not be adopted.

In conclusion, judicial communication could potentially play a role in ensuring coherence across interpretations by being used in the process of establishing the ordinary meaning of a term under Article 31(1) of the VCLT. However, its role would be limited by the ability of panels to exercise broad discretion during the process, as well as by other interpretative elements.

---

[219] Appellate Body Report, *US – Gambling*, [164].

[220] Appellate Body Report, *United States – Continued Existence and Application of Zeroing Methodology (US – Continued Zeroing)*, WT/DS350/AB/R, 4 February 2009, [268].

[221] The concept of likeness has been interpreted more narrowly under Art III:2 of GATT, first sentence than under Art III:4 of GATT (Lester et al. 2018, pp. 269, 300).

[222] Appellate Body Report, *US – Gasoline*, p. 23.

11.8.5.2   Any Relevant Rules of International Law Applicable in the Relations Between the Parties

Judicial communication between new generation EU FTA and WTO DSMs could also be based on Article 31(3)(c) of the VCLT, according to which for the interpretation of the treaties, together with the context, account should be taken of 'any relevant rules of international law applicable in the relations between the parties'. This section analyses whether the use of WTO and FTA jurisprudence in the process of interpretation by FTA and WTO adjudicators, respectively, could be justified under this provision.

11.8.5.2.1   Article 31(3)(c): Purpose, Elements, and Weight

This sub-section introduces the purpose of Article 31(3)(c) of the VCLT and its elements that have to be complied with and analyses in detail the weight that may be ascribed to other relevant rules of international law under this provision. Determination of whether there is a legal avenue for judicial communication is important due to the argument that coherence should be pursued within the limits established by the relevant law.

Article 31(3)(c) of the VCLT is said to be the expression of the principle of systemic integration, according to which treaties are to be interpreted against the background of all the rules of international law understood as a system and in a manner that would give a sense of 'coherence and meaningfulness'.[223] Consequently, according to this principle, a provision should be interpreted not only in light of the context provided by the treaty that contains it, but also in light of the broader context of international law, confirming the approach of the conceptual framework that international law is a legal system within which norms are not completely unrelated and regimes are not isolated, but form a whole.[224] This principle also stems from the fact that states are presumed to have negotiated their treaties in good faith, implying that they took all their international obligations into account and did not intend to act inconsistently with them; hence, international norms should be read together to avoid conflicts.[225] Thus, the principle of systemic integration reflected in Article 31(3)(c) of the VCLT represents a potentially important tool to enhance likely synergies as consequences of the interactions between the DSMs of new generation EU FTAs and the WTO.

---

[223] International Law Commission (ILC) Study Group on the Fragmentation of International Law, 'Fragmentation of International Law: Difficulties Arising from the Diversification and Expansion of International Law', Report of the Study Group of the International Law Commission (ILC Report), Finalized by Martti Koskenniemi, A/CN.4/L.682 and add 1 and corr 1 (International Law Commission, 13 April 2006), para 413–414; Appellate Body Report, *EC – Aircraft*, [845]; Isabelle Van Damme (2009), p. 360.

[224] *See supra*, Sect. 3.1.4.

[225] Marceau (2001), p. 1089; Villiger (2009), p. 433, para 25.

For Article 31(3)(c) of the VCLT to act as a legal avenue for the purpose of systemic integration, three elements have to be complied with: (1) there has to be 'a rule of international law' that is (2) 'relevant' and (3) 'applicable between the parties'.[226] Before analysing the meaning of the three elements and whether they could be complied with in the context of judicial communication between the DSMs of FTAs and the WTO, it is also important to point out the normative weight that could be ascribed to the rules used as part of the interpretative process under Article 31(3)(c) of the VCLT, which can be deduced from the chapeau of Article 31 (3) specifying that they 'shall be taken into account'.

The use of the imperative word 'shall' indicates that there is an obligation to take into account other rules of international law in the process of interpretation under Article 31(3)(c), provided that other elements are also complied with. In *EC – Biotech*, the panel stated that Article 31(3)(c) 'mandates [...] it does not merely give a treaty interpreter the option of doing so'.[227] This stands in contrast to the flexible provision enshrined in Article 31(1) of the VCLT, where, in the context of using external international sources for the purpose of establishing the ordinary meaning of a term, the panel stated that it only '*may* consider other relevant rules of international law' (emphasis added).[228] The expression 'to take into account' is, however, more flexible and does not prescribe a particular outcome,[229] but rather allows a certain degree of freedom to the interpreter when deciding how to use other international rules.[230] Nevertheless, this freedom is subject to the obligation to interpret a treaty in good faith, meaning that when there are several permissible interpretations, the one in accordance with other international rules should be followed.[231] Moreover, as any other rule of interpretation, Article 31(3)(c) can only serve the purpose of *interpretation*, not *modification* or specific *application* of a provision.[232]

To conclude, the purpose of Article 31(3)(c) of the VCLT is to ensure coherence and it embodies the principle of systemic interpretation. It has three elements that will be analysed in detail in the sections that follow. Due to its wording and other principles envisaged in the VCLT, Article 31(3)(c) could have a greater role in ensuring coherence in international law and enhancing the potential synergies in the interactions between the WTO and FTA DSMs than Article 31(1) of the VCLT, provided that the three elements are complied with and that the article is used specifically for the purpose of interpretation.

---

[226] Appellate Body Report, *EC – Aircraft*, [841]; McGrady (2008), p. 591.

[227] Panel Report, *EC – Biotech*, [7.69].

[228] Ibid [7.93].

[229] Ibid [7.69].

[230] McGrady (2008), p. 606.

[231] Panel Report, *EC – Biotech*, [7.69].

[232] Panel Report, *Argentina – Poultry*, [7.40]; Appellate Body Report, *Peru – Agricultural Products*, [5.97].

11.8.5.2.2 'Rules of International Law' and 'Relevant'

This sub-section will deal with the first two of the three elements of Article 31(3)
(c) of the VCLT that need to be respected for the article to be applicable. The first
element is that there should be 'rules of international law'.

There is no reason for the interpretation of this element to be restrictive. There
seems to be a general consensus in the doctrine that 'rules of international law' can
refer to all accepted sources of international law.[233] Thus, Article 31(3)(c) of the
VCLT can be understood as implicitly referencing Article 38 of the ICJ Statute
containing the sources of international law.[234] While there are no limitations on the
types of sources, it seems that there is general agreement that primary sources are to
be considered rules of international law, but the majority of authors are silent on the
potential role of secondary sources, such as judicial decisions. Thus, the doctrine
generally describes international treaties, international customs, and/or general principles as rules of international law under Article 31(3)(c).[235] Similarly, the panel in
EC – Biotech stated that the expression 'rules of international law' is

> sufficiently broad to encompass all generally accepted sources of public international law,
> that is to say, (i) international conventions (treaties), (ii) international custom (customary
> international law), and (iii) the recognized general principles of law.[236]

Hence, while it is clear that primary sources could be used, the question arises
whether judicial decisions, as supplementary sources according to Article 38 of the
ICJ Statute, could be used for the purpose of judicial communication under Article 31
(3)(c) of the VCLT. As this author already stated, it shares the opinion that supplementary sources under Article 38 of the ICJ Statute cannot represent independent
sources of international law; they are merely the means to determine the existence
and status of rules of law at the relevant time and the proper interpretation of those
rules.[237] Hence, subsidiary means, such as judicial decisions and teachings, are
never used alone, but employed only to establish the existence and meaning of the
primary rules regarded as 'rules of international law' under Article 31(3)(c) of the
VCLT. Similar to Gardiner[238] and Lanyi and Steinbach[239] this author, does not see
an impediment to using judicial decisions to determine the meaning of primary
sources of international law, such as treaties that are going to be taken into account
during the process of interpretation. Therefore, for the purpose of interpretation in

---

[233] Linderfalk (2007), p. 178; Van Aaken (2009), p. 497; Merkouris (2015); Dörr (2012), p. 605,
para 96. For more on a debate that appeared around the question of whether international treaties are
also rules of international law under Art 31(3)(c) of the VCLT, *see* Paparemborde (2014), p. 41;
Gardiner (2015), pp. 300–301.

[234] Dörr (2012), p. 605, para 96.

[235] Marceau (2001), p. 1087; Linderfalk (2007), p. 177; Merkouris (2015), p. 19.

[236] Panel Report, *EC – Biotech*, [7.67].

[237] *See supra*, Sect. 11.8.3.

[238] Gardiner (2015), p. 307.

[239] Lanyi and Steinbach (2017), p. 81.

the case at issue, FTAs as treaties and primary rules of international law could potentially be taken into account by WTO adjudicators as relevant rules of international law. Judicial decisions could also be used as subsidiary rules to determine the content of the FTA norms being evaluated. Similarly, FTA adjudicators could use WTO rulings or awards to determine the meaning of WTO norms. While this position is supported here, it may be perceived as being too broad. Currently, there is no judicial practice that would support or contradict this position, and the doctrine is largely silent on this issue which remains to be clarified. Nevertheless, it should be noted that judicial decisions, such as panel and AB reports, interim appeal awards, and FTA rulings, are binding *inter se* on the parties to the dispute.[240] Accordingly, if the disputing parties within WTO proceedings also adjudicated the same, similar, or related matters under FTA rules, the FTA rulings on those matters are binding on them. While judicial bodies could give factual consideration to the external jurisprudence that is binding on the disputing parties, it would not make this jurisprudence an independent source of international law to be regarded as independent relevant rules of international law by the adjudicators.

Another issue that needs to be raised in relation to 'rules of international law' is intertemporality. The question is which international rules should be used under Article 31(3)(c)—those valid at the time of the conclusion of a treaty or those valid at the time of its interpretation. Since the majority of the RTAs were concluded after the WTO agreements, the former could potentially play a role only if the rules that are valid at the moment of interpretation would be taken into account. There seems to be general agreement in the doctrine that the answer depends on the treaty under interpretation and the intent of the parties.[241] Hence, the treaty itself should be interpreted in order to establish the intent of the parties. For example, if a treaty uses a term that is 'not static but evolutionary' or the obligations are written in very 'general terms', this may indicate that the intention of the parties is that the treaty should be interpreted in accordance with the existing law at the time of interpretation.[242] In *US – Shrimp*, the AB acknowledged 'that the generic term "natural resources" in Article XX(g) is not "static" in its content or reference but is "by definition, evolutionary"'[243] and should be read in light of the provisions valid at the moment of interpretation. Thus, in similar situations, the use of rules valid at the moment of interpretation would be appropriate. In conclusion, whether agreements concluded after the treaty under interpretation, such as many RTAs, could be brought into the process of interpretation under Article 31(3)(c) of the VCLT would depend on the treaty text and the intention of the parties.

Another element whose presence is to be ascertained when using Article 31(3)(c) of the VCLT is that the rules of international law have to be 'relevant'. The

---

[240] *See infra*, Sect. 11.8.3.

[241] ILC Report, para 477; Pauwelyn (2003), p. 265; Merkouris (2015), p. 123; Gardiner (2015), p. 295.

[242] ILC Report, para 478.

[243] Appellate Body Report, *US – Shrimp*, [130].

doctrinaires and WTO jurisprudence seem to share the opinion that for a norm to be relevant, it must concern the same subject matter as the norm under interpretation.[244] While it may seem easy to establish relevance, the definition of 'same subject matter' is in itself vague and the degree of identity of the subject matters is not entirely clear.[245] Hence, the interpreters seem to enjoy rather broad discretion in assessing the relevance of a provision for the interpretation of another. WTO panels and the AB rejected the relevance of the invoked provisions in both *EC – Aircraft* and *Peru – Agricultural Products* as those provisions could not be said to speak to the term under interpretation.[246] Hence, a high bar has been set for a rule of international law to be 'relevant' for the interpretation of another provision. The AB quite convincingly argued in both these disputes that the invoked international rules did not concern the same specific interpretative issues as those arising under the rules subject to interpretation. Although the rules invoked concerned related aspects, they were not the *same* aspects. As the provisions in WTO agreements and FTAs often deal with exactly the same subject matters, it could be expected that those provisions and the judicial decisions that interpreted them could be considered 'relevant' under Article 31(3)(c) of the VCLT. Yet, the provisions that would be informative only with respect to related and not the same matters would not be relevant within the meaning of Article 31(3)(c). The relevance of an international rule for interpretation of another norm should be assessed on a case-by-case basis.[247]

In conclusion, it was argued that the decisions of the judicial bodies established under the WTO agreements and the new generation EU FTAs could be taken into account under Article 31(3)(c) of the VCLT as secondary sources to determine the meaning of the primary sources of international law and would qualify under the first element—'any rules of international law'. It was also explained that the issue of intertemporality depends on the provision under interpretation and it should thus be solved on a case-by-case basis. Likewise, the 'relevance' of a norm should be assessed in individual disputes, but it is clear that the invoked norm should concern the exact same interpretative issue as that arising in the process of interpretation.

11.8.5.2.3   'Applicable Between the Parties'

The third and most controversial element of Article 31(3)(c) is the expression 'applicable between the parties'. The question arises whether it covers only rules applicable between all the parties to the treaty under interpretation or whether it can

---

[244] Appellate Body Report, *EC – Aircraft*, [846]; Appellate Body Report, *Peru – Agricultural Products,* [5.101]; Pauwelyn (2003), p. 263; Villiger (2009), p. 433, para 25.

[245] Merkouris (2015), p. 21; Dörr (2012), pp. 609–610, para 102.

[246] Appellate Body Report, *EC – Aircraft*, [851]; Appellate Body Report, *Peru – Agricultural Products*, [5.101–5.104].

[247] Marceau (2002), pp. 783–784.

also cover treaties applicable between some parties or even only between the disputing parties.[248]

Depending on the interpretation adopted, an FTA norm as a primary source may or may not qualify as a relevant rule of international law applicable between the parties for the purpose of interpreting WTO agreements. Hence, judicial decisions as secondary sources for determining the meaning of an FTA norm would follow the same fate. On the other hand, regardless of the interpretation adopted, WTO agreements could play a role in the interpretation of the new generation EU FTAs, as the parties to these FTAs are all WTO Members. Therefore, the WTO agreements would qualify for all the proposed interpretations.

The first approach is the narrow one, according to which the term 'the parties' should be interpreted as all the parties to the treaty under interpretation. This narrow interpretation seems to have been supported by the panel in *EC – Biotech*. It first noted that Article 31(3)(c) of the VCLT does not refer to 'one or more parties' as Article 31(2)(b) of the VCLT does, nor does it refer to 'the parties to a dispute' as Article 66 of the VCLT does.[249] The panel then referred to the notion of the term 'party' as defined by Article 2(1)(g) of the VCLT, according to which a party is 'a State which has consented to be bound by the treaty and for which the treaty is in force'.[250] Hence, by using an interpretation based on the meaning and the context of the term, the panel concluded that

> [i]t may be inferred from these elements that the rules of international law applicable in the relations between 'the parties' are the rules of international law applicable in the relations between the States which have consented to be bound by the treaty which is being interpreted, and for which that treaty is in force.[251]

It further stated that 'it makes sense to interpret Article 31(3)(c) of the VCLT as requiring consideration of those rules of international law which are applicable in the relations between *all parties* to the treaty which is being interpreted'[252] (emphasis added). This narrow interpretation could also be said to be supported by the principle *pacta tertiis nec nocent nec prosunt* enshrined in Article 34 of the VCLT, according to which '[a] treaty does not create either obligations or rights for a third State without its consent'. Nevertheless, the panel in *EC – Biotech* also cautiously asserted that in the case at issue not even all disputing parties were parties to the treaty invoked for use in interpretation. Hence, they did not take a position regarding the possibility of taking into consideration international rules to which all the disputing parties would be parties to these rules and would argue in favour of the interpretation in light of those rules.[253]

---

[248] Van Damme (2009), p. 362.

[249] Panel Report, *EC – Biotech*, [7.68].

[250] Ibid.

[251] Ibid.

[252] Ibid, [7.69].

[253] Ibid, [7.72].

The arguments in favour of the narrow interpretation based on the ordinary meaning and context of Article 31(3)(c) of the VCLT can be contested. The VCLT uses the expression 'all the parties' on twelve occasions; hence, attributing to it the same meaning as that of 'the parties' could make the use of the term 'all' superfluous.[254] Therefore, the use of the term 'the parties' without any qualification could also be interpreted as meaning less than all the parties to the treaty under interpretation, but more than one party or more than the disputing parties.[255] The term 'the parties' is used in VCLT with three different meanings. It can refer to all the parties to the treaty, as in Article 59 of the VCLT on termination or suspension of a treaty which uses the expression 'all the parties' and 'the parties' interchangeably. In Article 66 of the VCLT governing the resolution of disputes, 'the parties' refers to the disputing parties. Finally, 'the parties' can also refer to only some parties to a treaty as in Article 72 on the suspension of the operation of a treaty.[256] Therefore, interpretation of the unqualified term 'the parties' used in Article 31(3)(c) of the VCLT interpreted within the context offered by other VCLT provisions, in fact, leads to a rather inconclusive result, as it could be interpreted in different ways.

The narrow approach has been criticised by many scholars. Such an interpretation would have a considerable impact on the purpose of Article 31(3)(c) of the VCLT to provide systemic integration and coherence. The requirement that all the parties to the treaty under interpretation are also parties to the treaty to be taken into account during the process would considerably limit the number of treaties that could be used for interpretation and would lead to paradoxical results. Thus, the more the number of parties to a treaty would grow, the greater the isolation of that treaty.[257] It would be especially difficult to find multilateral treaties with congruent membership, so that they become relevant to each other's interpretation.[258] Moreover, a change in membership in an agreement could affect the way it is to be interpreted,[259] leading to the situation where the accession of a new member could mean that another treaty would no longer have weight in interpretation. The narrow approach would also lead to one-way interpretative relationships.[260] For example while WTO agreements could be relevant to the interpretation of an FTA, an FTA could not have a role in the interpretation of a WTO agreement, leading to greater fragmentation rather than greater coherence. Another reason against the narrow interpretation is the fact that some WTO Members are non-sovereign entities, such as Chinese Taipei or Macau, that could not become parties to other treaties and would not qualify under the definition offered by Article 2(1)(g) of the VCLT, according to which a party has to

---

[254] McGrady (2008), p. 594.

[255] Marceau (2002), p. 782.

[256] McGrady (2008), pp. 595–596.

[257] Marceau (2002), p. 781.

[258] ILC Report, para 450.

[259] Weiss (2003), p. 195; McGrady (2008), p. 600.

[260] Ibid 599; Lanyi and Steinbach (2017), pp. 70–71.

be a state.[261] Therefore, this author also backs the critics of this approach and finds it too narrow and contrary to the purpose of the norm itself.

According to the ILC Report, '[a] better solution is to permit reference to another treaty provided that the parties in dispute are also parties to that other treaty'.[262] As the Report itself mentions, this interpretation could lead to divergent interpretations.[263] While the principle *pacta tertiis nec nocent nec prosunt* requires that no new obligations be created without the consent of the states, the rulings have a binding effect only on the parties.[264] Yet, even without a binding effect on parties other than disputing ones, these rulings could affect the legitimate expectations[265] of other parties and affect the security and predictability of trade relations, as the treaty would be interpreted differently depending on the disputing parties. The ILC Report asserted that this should not be a problem, especially since most treaties are reciprocal in nature (where benefits are offered on an individual and reciprocal basis) and can result in different obligations being applied differently to the parties.[266] It stated that this would actually allow the parties' will, as elucidated by other treaties, to be respected.[267] While divergent interpretations may be less problematic in case of reciprocal treaties, it is not clear why it would be considered that Article 31(3)(c) of the VCLT would be applicable only to the interpretation of reciprocal treaties and not to integral treaties (where obligations are owed to all the world) or interdependent treaties (where the obligation of each party is dependent on the corresponding performance by *all* parties), for which coherence of the treaty under interpretation would be necessary.[268] Thus, the argument in the ILC Report does not in fact seem to support the interpretation of the term 'the parties' as referring merely to disputing parties for the purpose of generally interpreting all treaties and not only the reciprocal ones. Article 31 of the VCLT entitled General Rule of Interpretation serves as a general rule of interpretation for all the treaties, not only for a certain type.

As divergent interpretation based on the distinction between reciprocal and other types of treaties has been rebuffed, in the context of the WTO Agreement, there is an extra argument in favour of interpreting the term 'parties' as referring not just to disputing parties. Article IX:2 of the WTO Agreement sets out the requirements for authentic interpretations, according to which, they should be adopted by a three-fourths majority of the Membership; in practice, however, the consensus rule is used

---

[261] Van Damme (2009), p. 372.

[262] ILC Report, para 472.

[263] Ibid.

[264] Appellate Body Report, *Japan – Alcoholic Beverages II*, 14.

[265] In *Japan – Alcoholic Beverages II*, p. 13, the AB stated with respect to panel reports that '[t]hey create legitimate expectations among WTO Members, and, therefore, should be taken into account where they are relevant to any dispute'.

[266] ILC Report. para 472, referring to 'the practices regarding reservations, *inter se* modification and successive treaties' in support of this statement.

[267] Ibid.

[268] For the distinction between different types of treaties, *see* McGrady (2008), p. 602.

in this respect. Based on this provision and how it has been applied in practice, it would be difficult to argue that a treaty concluded only between the disputing parties could be taken into consideration during interpretations.[269] Moreover, Article 31(3) (c) of the VCLT represents a general rule of interpretation, not merely a rule of interpretation if there is a dispute.[270] By understanding the term 'parties' as meaning disputing parties, the interpretation outside disputes would be disregarded, which would not correspond to the general character of this rule of interpretation. Hence, although such an interpretation would allow in a dispute between WTO Members that have also an FTA in place to make reference to the FTA jurisprudence in WTO proceedings and would increase coherence in the international trade regime, it is not supported, due to the fact that the VCLT does not seem to back such an interpretation. The adoption of such an interpretation would go against the position espoused here[271] that interpretations should not be coherent at the expense of correctness.

Finally, the term 'parties' can be understood as referring only to some parties, not necessarily to those in the dispute. As the VCLT uses the unqualified term 'parties', without referring to all the parties or the disputing parties, it seems to permit the interpretation that the term refers to some of the parties. Nevertheless, the question arises in which case another treaty could play a role in the interpretation if the parties to it are only some of the parties to the treaty under interpretation. Both the ILC Report and Pauwelyn propose that other relevant rules of international law are taken into account in the process of interpretation as long as they reflect the 'common intention' of all the parties to the treaty under interpretation by being, at least implicitly, accepted or tolerated by all the parties.[272] Thus, this approach provides some flexibility by not requiring that every single party to the treaty under interpretation is also a party to the treaty that is to be used in this process, while at the same time avoiding divergent interpretations the same treaty and ensuring security and predictability.

Pauwelyn argues that this interpretation is supported by the close proximity of paragraph (3)(c) to paragraphs (3)(a) and (b) of Article 31, according to which account shall be taken of any 'subsequent *agreement* between the *parties* regarding the interpretation of the treaty or the application of its provisions' (emphasis added) and of 'any subsequent *practice* in the application of the treaty which establishes *the agreement of the parties* regarding its interpretation'.[273] The preparatory work and jurisprudence seem to concur that paragraphs (3)(a) and (b) of Article 31 refer only to agreements and practice reflecting the common intention of all the parties to the treaty.[274] Nevertheless, as McGrady noted, the position of paragraph (3)(c) may be of little relevance, since it was moved there because it did not belong anywhere

---

[269] Pauwelyn (2003), pp. 258–259.

[270] Marceau (1999), p. 125; Lennard (2002), p. 37; McLachlan (2005), p. 315.

[271] *See supra*, Sect. 11.5.

[272] Pauwelyn (2003), p. 257; ILC Report, para 472.

[273] Pauwelyn (2003), p. 258.

[274] Ibid.

else.[275] Although paragraphs (3)(a) and (b) may be of little help, this intermediate reading respects the most the legitimate expectations of the parties, while still promoting coherence.

The most recent WTO jurisprudence also seems to support this middle-view interpretation. In *EC – Aircraft*, the AB stated that '[a]n interpretation of "the parties" in Article 31(3)(c) should be guided by the Appellate Body's statement that "the purpose of treaty interpretation is to establish the common intention of the parties to the treaty."'[276] It further continued:

> [A] proper interpretation of the term 'the parties' must also take account of the fact that Article 31(3)(c) of the Vienna Convention is considered an expression of the 'principle of systemic integration' [...] a delicate balance must be struck between, on the one hand, taking due account of an individual WTO Member's international obligations and, on the other hand, ensuring a consistent and harmonious approach to the interpretation of WTO law among all WTO Members.[277]

The AB confirmed this interpretation of the term 'the parties' in *Peru – Agricultural Products*, by asserting that 'the "general rule of interpretation" in Article 31 of the Vienna Convention is aimed at establishing the ordinary meaning of treaty terms reflecting the common intention of the parties to the treaty, and not just the intentions of some of the parties'.[278] Hence, the AB seems to recognise that Article 31(3)(c) of the VCLT should promote coherence—a statement that seems to reject the narrow approach according to which the term 'the parties' refers to *all* the parties. At the same time, it also implies that Article 31 serves as a general rule of interpretation, not only as a rule for the disputing parties, also denying the broad-approach reading of the term 'the parties' as disputing parties. The AB seems to suggest an interpretation that reconciles the broad and narrow approaches.

The *US – Shrimp* case is also often cited in support of the claim that treaties to which not all WTO Members or even not all disputing parties are parties, can be taken into consideration under Article 31(3)(c) of the VCLT.[279] In *US – Shrimp*, when interpreting the meaning of the term 'exhaustible natural resources', the AB used extraneous treaties to which not the entire Membership and not even all disputing parties were parties,[280] yet it did not invoke Article 31(3)(c) of the VCLT for doing so. It is likely that it used extraneous treaties to establish the ordinary meaning of the term and it can be seen that the panel in *EC – Biotech* also interpreted *US – Shrimp* as using extraneous treaties for this purpose, when it

---

[275] McGrady (2008), p. 597.

[276] Appellate Body Report, *EC – Aircraft*, [845], fn 1915 referring to the Appellate Body Report, *EC – Computer Equipment*, [93] (original footnote).

[277] Appellate Body Report, *EC – Aircraft*, [845].

[278] Appellate Body Report, *Peru – Agricultural Products*, [5.95].

[279] *See* Marceau (2002), p. 781; Lanyi and Steinbach (2017), p. 78; Hyams and Villalta Puig (2017), p. 251.

[280] Appellate Body Report, *US – Shrimp*, [130].

referred to this report in support of its statement.[281] Finally, even if supposedly the AB had used Article 31(3)(c) of the VCLT for its analysis in *US – Shrimp*, the definitions from the treaties that it referred to were generally accepted by all the Members.[282]

Given that the AB interpreted Article 31(3)(c) of the VCLT as requiring that the rule used for interpretation reflect the 'common intentions of the parties to the treaty', in both cases in which it stated this standard, it refrained from assessing whether the rules at issue complied with it, but rather preferred to discard them based on the 'relevant' element. Nevertheless, in *Peru – Agricultural Products*, the AB referring to an FTA rule stated that it had 'reservations' about whether a particular FTA provision invoked 'can be used under Article 31(3) of the Vienna Convention in establishing the common intention of WTO Members underlying the provisions of Article 4.2 of the Agreement on Agriculture and Article II:1(b) of the GATT 1994.'[283] It further stated that 'such an approach would suggest that WTO provisions can be interpreted differently, depending on the Members to which they apply and on their rights and obligations under an FTA to which they are parties'.[284] It appears that an FTA provision could not be invoked unless it reflects the common intention of the entire Membership. Thus, an FTA norm can be invoked in interpretation only in limited circumstances under Article 31(3)(c) of the VCLT. Ascertaining whether or not a certain interpretation reflects the common intentions of the parties seems difficult,[285] and WTO jurisprudence does not have guidance on how to do it. In the case of RTAs, it could be argued that if numerous RTAs included the same or similar provisions, this would show the common intention of the parties. In this interpretation, Article 31(3)(c) of the VCLT could serve as a legal basis for judicial communication between the DSMs of the WTO and the new generation EU FTAs if initiated by the latter in FTA disputes, but with only a limited role if initiated by panels or the AB in a WTO dispute.

Based on the analysis above, it can be concluded that the question of how the expression 'applicable between the parties' should be interpreted has no clear answer. While the third middle-way approach, supported by this author, may seem desirable, since it could offset the disadvantages of the two more extreme approaches, it remains unclear whether it would gain the support of the Members, as some of the countries have previously argued in favour of a narrow interpretation.[286] Finally, all three approaches would make Article 31(3)(c) of the VCLT a

---

[281] *See supra*, Sect. 11.8.5.1.

[282] Marceau (2002), p. 783; Pauwelyn (2003), p. 260.

[283] Appellate Body Report, *Peru – Agricultural Products*, [5.106].

[284] Ibid.

[285] Weiss (2003), p. 196.

[286] *See*, for example, the US argument in 2015 that 'the expression "applicable in the relations between the parties" refers to all WTO Members (i.e. the parties to the WTO agreement) and not just the parties to the dispute' (Special Session of the Dispute Settlement Body, Report by the Chairman, Ambassador Ronald Saborío Soto, TN/DS/26, 30 January 2015, para 595).

possible legal basis for judicial communication with the WTO DSM initiated by the new generation EU FTA panels in an FTA dispute. By contrast, only the second approach, and to a much more limited extent the third, could make Article 31(3) (c) an appropriate avenue for the WTO adjudicatory bodies to refer to FTAs and FTA jurisprudence in the process of interpretation. Moreover, even though broader interpretations of the term 'the parties' may be more beneficial for ensuring coherence, by adopting such an interpretation, WTO adjudicatory bodies would only put themselves at risk of being accused of judicial activism and overreach, a criticism that has already paralysed the AB. As this author opts for limited coherence reflecting the will of the states, coherence through interpretation should be achieved only if the legal framework allows it. While current negotiations on WTO dispute settlement are focused mostly on how to salvage the DSM, once the issue is solved, Members could investigate the introduction of an express provision in the DSU that would allow the WTO adjudicatory bodies to refer to FTA jurisprudence in a dispute between Members that have an FTA in place. Such an express provision would avoid the use of Article 31(3)(c) of the VCLT and the inconclusive expression 'applicable between the parties'.

11.8.5.3   FTA Rules on Interpretation Expressly Referencing WTO Jurisprudence

While customary rules of interpretation could be used as a legal basis for judicial communication between different DSMs, there could also be specific rules that expressly require judicial communication between specific adjudicatory bodies. The panel in EU-Ukraine dispute over the wood export ban expressly relied on the AA rule on interpretation expressly referencing the WTO case law on multiple occasions when interpreting WTO provisions referred to in the agreement.[287] The WTO agreements are silent on this issue. However, the new generation EU FTAs include specific rules on the interpretative role of WTO jurisprudence in FTA dispute settlement. While these provisions were introduced earlier in this chapter,[288] this section will analyse in detail their scope, weight, effects, and importance in the context of the AB crisis.

Both the EUKFTA and EUSFTA refer to 'identical obligations' as the category of disputes covered by their rules on the interpretative role of WTO case law.[289] The similar language of the two agreements may be explained by the fact that their negotiations started and concluded earlier than the negotiations for the other

---

[287] Final Report, *Restrictions Applied by Ukraine on Exports of Certain Wood Products to the European Union*, 11 December 2020, [200], fn 193, [203]–[205], [211], [217], [437].

[288] *See supra*, Sect. 11.3.

[289] EUKFTA, Art 14.16; EUSFTA, Art 14.18.

agreements.[290] Thus, it appears that the EUSFTA followed the example of EUKFTA. After the negotiations for CETA, the rest of the new generation EU FTAs have a more general application, providing that panels 'shall also take into account relevant interpretations' in WTO panel and AB reports.[291] Therefore, the provisions in the EUKFTA and EUSFTA have more limited scope, since they concern only relevant jurisprudence for identical FTA and WTO obligations. Accordingly, they would not be applicable to disputes that would concern FTA provisions mirroring WTO norms in a slightly different language. On the other hand, the provisions in the other new generation EU FTAs do not constrain the use of external WTO jurisprudence in disputes concerning only FTA provisions that are identical to WTO norms. The more recent new generation EU FTAs are better designed and provide better tools to ensure consistency between FTA and WTO judicial interpretation and to provide predictability to FTA disputes, showcasing the EU's intention to balance its multilateral and bilateral aspirations. Still, in EUKFTA or EUSFTA disputes on FTA provisions that are not identical to WTO norms, recourse could be had to Article 31(3)(c) of the VCLT to make use of WTO jurisprudence, provided that it would refer to a WTO provision as a rule of international law and would be relevant, since in any case the parties to the new generation EU FTAs are also parties to the WTO agreements.

In addition to the limits to the scope of these provisions, other elements also merit attention. All the new generation EU FTAs confer a certain interpretative role solely to the 'relevant' WTO jurisprudence.[292] It is reasonable to expect that the term 'relevant' would have the same meaning as in Article 31(3)(c) of the VCLT which requires that the jurisprudence concerns the same subject matter as the norm under interpretation, the assessment of the similarity of the subject matter remaining at the discretion of the panel that should make its decision on a case-by-case basis. The weight of these provisions should also be clarified. The EUKFTA states that a panel '*shall adopt* an interpretation that is consistent' (emphasis added) with relevant WTO jurisprudence, which clearly indicates an obligation to do so. The use of the term 'shall' leaves no room for the panel's discretion in this respect. Thus, the panel would be obliged to adopt an interpretation that is *consistent* with those in WTO jurisprudence, meaning that while the interpretation adopted should not necessarily be identical, it cannot contradict that developed by WTO panels and the AB. The

---

[290] The EUKFTA was the first new generation EU FTA that was provisionally applied from 2011 until it was ratified in 2015. EUSFTA negotiations were initiated in 2009 and finalised in 2012 for the trade agreement (https://trade.ec.europa.eu/doclib/docs/2019/february/tradoc_157684.pdf). CETA negotiations were launched in 2009, but were finalised in 2014 (www.europarl.europa.eu/RegData/etudes/IDAN/2014/536410/EXPO_IDA(2014)536410_EN.pdf). EUVFTA negotiations started in 2012 and were finalised in 2018 (https://ec.europa.eu/trade/policy/countries-and-regions/countries/vietnam/). EUJEPA negotiations were launched in 2013 and concluded in 2017 (https://ec.europa.eu/commission/presscorner/detail/en/MEMO_18_3326).

[291] CETA, Art 29.17; EUJEPA, Art 21.16; EUVFTA, Art 15.21.

[292] EUKFTA, Art 14.16; CETA, Art 29.17; EUJEPA, Art 21.16; EUSFTA, Art 14.18; EUVFTA, Art 15.21.

other new generation EU FTAs provide that the panels 'shall take into account' the relevant WTO interpretation, a phrase that is also encountered in Article 31(3)(c) of the VCLT, whose meaning was clarified in this section. Thus, the word 'shall' indicates that panels do not have the option, but are charged with taking into account relevant WTO jurisprudence.[293] Nevertheless, the obligation to consider WTO jurisprudence does not require a specific outcome, as the expression 'take into account' bestows a certain flexibility and discretion on the panels that will have to decide on the weight to ascribe to it.[294] Hence, the provision with the more limited scope in the EUKFTA uses stronger language.

The above analysis indicates that while the EUKFTA and EUSFTA provisions on using relevant WTO jurisprudence are limited to FTA obligations identical to those of the WTO agreements, and all the new generation EU FTAs, except EUKFTA, use language that does not mandate a final outcome consistent with WTO jurisprudence, they nevertheless all represent legal tools for judicial communication that would increase the coherence between FTA and WTO rulings. All these provisions clearly indicate the FTA parties' recognition of the need to preserve coherence in the international trade regime.[295] These rules of interpretation will also bring greater predictability to FTA proceedings, as it seems reasonable for the parties to expect that the same or similar provisions would be interpreted in the WTO and FTA context alike. Moreover, these provisions are also evidence of the high semantic authority of WTO panels and the AB.[296] Therefore, it is apparent that the parties did not intend the FTA proceedings to undermine the WTO DSM; rather, they recognised the high importance of the WTO proceedings and their results in the context of FTA dispute settlement. Consequently, the FTA proceedings appear to have been designed to build on WTO jurisprudence, not against it.

Finally, these provisions could also help in maintaining a certain degree of coherence between FTA rulings, especially at a time when the AB is dysfunctional. In an international trade regime in which states could resort more and more to dispute settlement under FTAs because of the paralysed AB, there is a risk that the international trade regime becomes highly fragmented. If FTA panels use existing WTO jurisprudence with respect to identical terms and norms that incorporate, replicate or are similar to WTO norms and terms, it would bring a degree of coherence across FTA reports, at least with respect to the norms and concepts that are identical or similar to those contained in WTO agreements. Hence, at least initially and with respect to matters already treated in existing WTO jurisprudence,[297] the high semantic authority of WTO jurisprudence reflected in rules of interpretation, such as those in the new generation EU FTAs, could ensure a certain degree of coherence in the international trade regime.

---

[293] On the interpretation of the term 'shall', *see supra*, (n 227).

[294] On the meaning of the expression 'take into account', *see supra*, (n 229, 230).

[295] Lanyi and Steinbach (2017), p. 81.

[296] *See supra*, Sect. 11.3.

[297] Vidigal (2019), p. 25.

It should be noted, however, that the rules of interpretation of the new generation EU FTAs would not cover the interim arbitral awards, as they only refer to rulings of the WTO DSB[298] or panel and AB reports adopted by the DSB.[299] The new generation EU FTA rules do not expressly ascribe any role to arbitral awards and since they are not subject to adoption by the DSB, they do not fall under the coverage of these rules.[300] Therefore, while the FTA rules on interpretation would bring a certain degree of coherence across FTA reports during the AB crisis, they would not address the issue of coherence with the interim appeal awards. Nonetheless, Article 31(3)(c) of the VCLT could be used as a legal basis for judicial communication initiated by FTA panels with appeal arbitrators, when WTO appeal arbitration awards would provide interpretations for a relevant WTO provision that should be taken into account in the process of interpretation. Furthermore, there are multiple factors that could encourage unidirectional judicial communication initiated by FTA panels with the WTO adjudicator under Article 31(3)(c) of the VCLT.

To conclude, the new generation EU FTAs include rules on interpretation expressly referencing WTO jurisprudence that could serve as a legal avenue for judicial communication with the WTO DSM initiated by FTA panels. These provisions, however, vary in their scope and weight and do not cover appeal awards. Nevertheless, Article 31(3)(c) of the VCLT could be used as a legal avenue where the application of FTA rules on interpretation is limited. The express interpretation rules on WTO jurisprudence contained in the new generation EU FTAs are likely to bring a certain degree of coherence across FTA rulings in times of AB crisis and demonstrate the importance of WTO jurisprudence to FTAs.

11.9   Conclusion

This chapter dealt with the question of judicial communication between the DSMs of the new generation EU FTAs and the WTO as a form of interaction embodying potential synergies rather than negative outcomes. It introduced the concept of judicial communication and argued the choice in favor of this term. The chapter established that since the WTO agreements and the new generation EU FTAs perceive themselves and recognise each other as judicial entities, publish their own reports, and have no hierarchical relationship between them, but would rely on each other's jurisprudence based on its persuasiveness, they meet the necessary pre-conditions to engage in judicial communication.

The chapter further introduced the functions of judicial communication and explained that the function to bring coherence and unity is the focus of its analysis. This function together with others, such as aiding the process of adjudication, gap

---

[298] EUKFTA, Art 14.16; EUSFTA, Art 14.18.

[299] CETA, Art 29.17; EUJEPA, Art 21.16; EUVFTA, Art 15.21.

[300] DSU, Art 25.3; MPIA, Annex 1, para 15.

filling of procedural matters, and providing factual evidence, support, and persuasiveness to a decision, showcase the potential positive outcomes of interactions in the form of judicial communication between different DSMs. After pondering the functions of judicial communication, the chapter illustrated the factors that could encourage it. The analysis concluded that, at least for now, the factors mostly encourage the FTA DSMs to unidirectionally initiate judicial communication with the WTO DSM and engage with WTO jurisprudence, potentially including appeal arbitral awards. Further, the chapter identified different types of judicial communication and established that the communication between the DSMs of the new generation EU FTAs and the WTO would be horizontal, take the form of a monologue or an indirect dialogue and could be either proactive or passive depending on the initiator.

After dealing with various aspects related to the concept of judicial communication, the chapter analysed why it is important for the DSMs of the new generation EU FTAs and the WTO to engage in it. It argued that because there are many similar or even identical substantive and procedural rules contained in both the new generation EU FTAs and the WTO agreements, engaging in judicial communication would help maintain coherence and consistency in the international trade regime. Nevertheless, the chapter cautioned that a distinction should be made between justifiable and unjustifiable inconsistencies. Thus, while judicial communication could help distinguish between them, it should not be initiated at the expense of correctness of the interpretation, since only limited coherence should be sought.

The chapter proceeded with the analysis of how the WTO and the new generation EU FTA DSMs treated each other's jurisprudence in practice. First, it analysed judicial communication initiated by WTO panels and the AB. It concluded that they generally had a reticent attitude towards RTA norms and rulings, potentially leaving the door open to judicial decisions of the RTAs to have a role in the process of interpretation and as evidence under WTO norms, including under Article XXIV of GATT. To identify other potential cases in which RTA jurisprudence could be referred to, the chapter analysed the cases in which WTO panels and the AB referred to the jurisprudence of international judicial bodies other than RTA DSMs. It concluded that when WTO adjudicators referred to the jurisprudence of the PCIJ, ICJ, ECtHR, and CJEU, they did so to fill procedural gaps, to establish the status of customary or general rules of international law, to interpret a term, or as a piece of evidence. The chapter proceeded with the analysis of instances in which WTO jurisprudence was referenced by RTA panels. It concluded that WTO jurisprudence was frequently referred to in RTA proceedings, likely due to the factors encouraging such judicial communication. It also determined that the instances in which WTO jurisprudence was used by RTA panels were similar to those in which WTO panels and the AB referred to external jurisprudence. Thus, RTA panels engaged in judicial communication with the WTO DSM to establish facts, fill procedural gaps, ascertain the status of customary and general international rules of law, and to interpret substantive norms.

The chapter identified different situations in which WTO and new generation EU FTA adjudicators could engage in judicial communication with each other, and proceeded to analyse the potential legal avenues for such communication. The need to establish legal avenues for judicial communication is grounded in the call to seek coherence only within the limits set by the intention of the parties as expressed in international law. The chapter established that for the purpose of procedural gap filling, the inherent powers of the adjudicatory bodies of the WTO and the new generation EU FTAs adjudicatory bodies could be used as a legal avenue. However, such use would only be for procedural purposes in limited cases and would not have the broader effect of also ensuring substantive coherence. It further determined that WTO and new generation EU FTA adjudicators could use each other's jurisprudence as evidence brought by the parties or as information sought by panels, as the constitutive treaties contain no limitation on the types of evidence that can be brought or sought. Nevertheless, WTO and new generation EU FTA panels enjoy broad discretion to decide whether to seek information and to assess and ascribe value to external rulings or awards if they themselves seek the information or if the parties invoke it. While the new generation EU FTAs, except the EUJEPA, seem to provide broader discretion to the panels, they might also be inclined to ascribe greater evidential value to WTO jurisprudence due to its high authority. However, as in the case of inherent powers, the avenue provided by provisions on evidence and the right to seek information can only address factual fragmentation, not substantive fragmentation. Article 38(1)(d) of the ICJ Statute was presented as an indirect legal avenue for addressing this issue, being used for establishing the meaning and content of the international rules of interpretation. Nevertheless, this avenue would not be equal to those that could directly ensure coherent interpretations of substantive norms. A logical avenue for WTO adjudicators to consider FTA jurisprudence is Article XXIV of GATT. It was established that Article XXIV could be used as a legal avenue to consider FTA rulings to establish the meaning of FTA measures under analysis in a dispute or as factual evidence if the measure under consideration was introduced as a result of an FTA ruling. Nevertheless, Article XXIV as a legal avenue for judicial communication with FTA DSMs initiated by WTO adjudicators would have limited use due to its restricted application as a justification, the high bar established for the requirements for a measure to be justified under it, and its reference to controversial concepts. Furthermore, judicial communication under Article XXIV of GATT would be able to ensure coherence only with respect to FTA provisions when considered by both WTO and FTA adjudicators, but not between FTA and WTO provisions.

The chapter continued by analysing the legal avenues for judicial communication to deal directly with potential substantive fragmentation between WTO and FTA norms—the rules of treaty interpretation. It reached the conclusion that Article 31 (1) of the VCLT could serve as a legal basis for judicial communication between WTO and new generation EU FTA adjudicators in both directions to help establish the ordinary meaning of a term. However, this avenue would be limited due to the high discretion of the panels and other elements in the interpretative process. Article 31(3)(c) of the VCLT was designed with the aim to promote coherence as it embodies the principle of systemic interpretation. Moreover, panels do not have discretion whether or not to consider external rules, but are mandated to do so. Yet, three elements, 'a rule of international law', 'relevant' and 'applicable between the parties', are required to be met to make use of Article 31(3)(c) of the VCLT.

It was argued that judicial decisions, such as those issued by the adjudicatory bodies of the WTO and the new generation EU FTAs, would comply with the first requirement to constitute 'rules of international law', if they determine the content of primary norms in a binding way. The question of intertemporality and relevance would have to be assessed on a case-by-case basis. The last element does not pose any problem for judicial communication initiated by the new generation EU FTA DSMs with the WTO mechanism, but it could hinder the application of Article 31(3) (c) of the VCLT to cases in which WTO adjudicators initiate communication. Thus, this author supports the interpretation of the term 'the parties' as referring to all or some parties to the treaty under interpretation, as long as the treaty used for interpretation reflects the common intention of the parties, a position also supported by recent WTO jurisprudence. Such an interpretation would only be of limited use for references to RTA norms and jurisprudence in WTO disputes. Moreover, Article 31(3)(c) is ambiguous, and the adoption of a broad or middle way interpretations of this term could have negative consequences for the WTO DSM, only an express clarification in the WTO agreements being able to solve this issue.

Finally, the chapter analysed in detail the express rules of interpretation contained in the new generation EU FTAs on the use of WTO jurisprudence. It reached the conclusion that these provisions, more or less limited in their application or weight depending on the agreement, could greatly increase coherence by offering a clear legal avenue for judicial communication initiated by the new generation EU FTA DSMs with the WTO DSM. They would also help to ensure a certain degree of coherence across FTA rulings in times of AB crisis. The express rules of interpretation referring to WTO jurisprudence also showcase the importance of having a functional WTO DSM and recognition of the authority of WTO jurisprudence by FTA parties. Nevertheless, the rules of interpretation of the new generation EU FTAs would not cover interim arbitral awards and would not ensure coherence of FTA rulings with MPIA awards. Still, in this case, other legal avenues mentioned, especially Article 31(3)(c) of the VCLT, could serve as a legal basis for interpreting FTA norms in light of appeal arbitral awards.

As deduced from the analysis, the available legal avenues could help to ensure a certain degree of procedural and factual coherence within the international trade regime. Article XXIV of GATT could secure to some extent substantive coherence within the international trading regime, but only with respect to the interpretation of FTA norms. In addition, Article 31(1) of the VCLT could have a role within certain limits in ensuring substantive coherence. Article 31(3)(c) of the VCLT together with the express provisions on interpretation in the new generation EU FTAs represent promising legal avenues for communication with the WTO DSM initiated by FTA panels. Judicial communication in the other direction initiated by WTO adjudicators that would result in coherent interpretations has fewer available avenues.

References

Andenas M, Leiss JR (2017) The systemic relevance of "Judicial Decisions" in Article 38 of the ICJ
    Statute. Zeitschrift für ausländisches öffentliches Recht und Völkerrecht 77:907–972
Andersen S (2010) Administration of evidence in WTO dispute settlement proceedings. In:
    Yerxa R, Wilson B (eds) Key issues in WTO dispute settlement. Cambridge University Press,
    New York, pp 177–189
Bartels L (2013) Regional trade agreements. In: Max Planck Encyclopedia of Public International
    Law. https://opil.ouplaw.com/view/10.1093/law:epil/9780199231690/law-9780199231690-
    e1803?prd=EPIL
Bercero IG (2006) Dispute settlement in European Union free trade agreements: lessons learned. In:
    Bartels L, Ortino F (eds) Regional trade agreements and the WTO legal system. Oxford
    University Press, New York, pp 383–405
Brink T (2010) Which WTO rules can a PTA lawfully breach? Completing the analysis in Brazil –
    Tyres. J World Trade 44(4):813–846
Broude T, Shany Y (2011) The international law and policy of multi-sourced equivalent norms. In:
    Broude T, Shany Y (eds) Multi-sourced equivalent norms in international law. Hart, Oxford, pp
    1–16
Broude T (2008) Principles of normative integration and the allocation of international authority:
    the WTO, the Vienna Convention on the Law of Treaties, and the Rio Declaration. Loyola Univ
    Chic Int Law Rev 6(1):173–207
Charney JI (1998) Is international law threatened by multiple international tribunals? Recueil des
    Cours 271:101–382
de Brabandere E (2012) Arbitral decisions as a source of international investment law. In:
    Gazzini T, de Brabandere E (eds) International investment law. The sources of rights and
    obligations. Martinus Nijhoff, Leiden, pp 245–288
Dörr O (2012) Article 31. General rule of interpretation. In: Dörr O, Schmalenbach K (eds) Vienna
    Convention on the Law of Treaties. A commentary, 2nd edn. Springer, Heidelberg, pp 521–570
Flett J (2012) Importing other international regimes into World Trade Organization litigation. In:
    Young MA (ed) Regime interaction in international law. Facing fragmentation. Cambridge
    University Press, New York, pp 261–304
Forere MA (2015) The relationship of WTO law and regional trade agreements in dispute
    settlement. Kluwer Law International, Alphen aan den Rijn
Frankel S (2014) The WTO's application of "The Customary Rules of Interpretation of Public
    International Law" to intellectual property. Victoria Univ Wellington Leg Res Papers 4(1):1–44
Gardiner R (2015) Treaty interpretation, 2nd edn. Oxford University Press, New York
Gobbi Estrella AT, Horlick GN (2006) Mandatory abolition of anti-dumping, countervailing duties
    and safeguards in customs unions and free trade areas constituted between World Trade
    Organization members: revisiting a long-standing discussion in light of the Appellate Body's
    Turkey-Textiles ruling. J World Trade 40(5):909–944
Herrmann C, Würdemann A (2017) Der Wirtschaftsvölkerrechtliche und Unionsrechtliche Rahmen
    für Regionale Integrationsgemeinschaften. In: Felbermayr GJ, Göler D, Herrmann C, Kalina A
    (eds) Multilateralismus und Regionalismus in der EU-Handelspolitik. Nomos, Baden-Baden, pp
    33–60
Hillman J (2009) Conflicts between dispute settlement mechanisms in regional trade agreements
    and the WTO - what should the WTO do? Cornell Int Law J 42:193–208
Horn H, Weiler JWW (2005) European communities – trade description of sardines: textualism and
    its discontent. The WTO Case Law of 2002 4(S1), pp 248–275
Howse R (2016) The World Trade Organization 20 years on: global governance by judiciary. Eur J
    Int Law 27(1):9–77
Hyams A, Villalta Puig G (2017) Preferential trade agreements and the World Trade Organization:
    developments to the dispute settlement understanding. Leg Issues Econ Integr 44(3):237–264

Johnston AM, Trebilcock MJ (2013) Fragmentation in international trade law: insights from the global investment regime. World Trade Rev 12(4):621–652

Kassoti E (2015) Fragmentation and inter-judicial dialogue: the CJEU and the ICJ at the interface. Eur J Leg Stud 8(2):21–49

Kuijper PJ (2010) Conflicting rules and clashing courts: the case of multilateral environmental agreements, Free Trade Agreements and the WTO. ICTSD Issue Paper No. 10, pp 1–64

Lanyi PA, Steinbach A (2017) Promoting coherence between PTAs and the WTO through systemic integration. J Int Econ Law 20:61–85

Lavranos N (2008) Regulating competing jurisdictions among international courts and tribunals. Zeitschrift für Ausländisches Öffentliches Recht und Völkerrecht 68:575–621

Law DS, Chang WC (2011) The limits of global judicial dialogue. Wash Law Rev 86(3):523–577

Lennard M (2002) Navigating by the stars: interpreting the WTO agreements. J Int Econ Law 5 (1):17–89

Lester S, Mercurio B, Davies A (2018) World trade law: text, materials and commentary, 3rd edn. Hart, Oxford

Linderfalk U (2007) On the interpretation of treaties. The modern international law as expressed in the 1969 Vienna Convention on the Law of Treaties. Springer, Heidelberg

Linton S, Tiba FK (2009) The international judge in an age of multiple international courts and tribunals. Chic J Int Law 9(2):407–470

Magnuson W (2010) WTO jurisprudence & its critiques: the Appellate Body's anti-constitutional resistance. Harv Int Law J 51:121–154

Marceau G (1999) A call for coherence in international law: praises for the prohibition against "Clinical Isolation" in WTO dispute settlement. J World Trade 33(5):87–152

Marceau G (2001) Conflicts of norms and conflicts of jurisdictions: the relationship between the WTO agreement and MEAs and other treaties. J World Trade 35:1081–1131

Marceau G (2002) WTO dispute settlement and human rights. Eur J Int Law 13(4):753–814

Marceau G (2013) The primacy of the WTO dispute settlement. Quest Int Law J 23:3–13

Marceau G, Wyatt J (2010) Dispute settlement regimes intermingled: regional trade agreements and the WTO. J Int Dispute Settlement 1(1):67–95

Marceau G, Izaguerri A, Lanovoy V (2013) The WTO's influence on other dispute settlement mechanisms: a lighthouse in the storm of fragmentation. J World Trade 47(3):481–574

Mathis JH (2002) Regional trade agreements in the GATT/WTO: Art. XXIV and the internal trade requirement. T.M.C. Asser Press, The Hague

Mathis JH (2016) WTO Appellate Body, Peru – Additional Duty on imports of certain agriculture products, WT/DS457/AB/R, 20 July 2015. Leg Issues Econ Integr 43(1):97–105

Matsushita M (2004) Legal aspects of free trade agreements: in the context of Article XXIV of the GATT 1994. In: Matsushita M, Ahn D (eds) WTO and East Asia: new perspectives. Cameron May, London, pp 497–514

Matsushita M, Schoenbaum TJ, Mavroidis PC, Hahn M (2015) The World Trade Organization: law, practice, and policy. Oxford University Press, New York

McGrady B (2008) Fragmentation of international law or "Systemic Integration" of treaty regimes: EC – Biotech Products and the proper interpretation of Article 31(3)(c) of the Vienna Convention on the Law of Treaties. J World Trade 42(4):589–618

McLachlan C (2005) The principle of systemic integration and Article 31(3)(c) of the Vienna Convention. Int Comp Law Q 54:279–319

Mercurio B, Tyagi M (2010) Treaty interpretation in WTO dispute settlement: the outstanding question of the legality of local working requirements. Minn J Int Law 19(2):275–326

Merkouris P (2015) Article 31(3)(c) VCLT and the principle of systemic integration: normative shadows in Plato's Cave. In: Fitzmaurice M, Okowa P (eds) Queen Mary studies in international law series, vol 17. Brill Nijhoff, Boston

Mitchell AD (2007) The legal basis for using principles in WTO disputes. J Int Econ Law 10 (4):795–835

Mitchell AD, Heaton D (2010) The inherent jurisdiction of WTO tribunals: the select application of public international law required by the judicial function. Mich J Int Law 31(3):559–619

Oellers-Frahm K (2001) Multiplication of international courts and tribunals and conflicting jurisdictions – problems and possible solutions. In: Frowein JA, Wolfrum R, Philipp CE (eds) Max Planck Yearbook of United Nations Law, vol 5. Kluwer Law International, London, pp 67–104

Ortino F (2006) Treaty interpretation and the WTO Appellate Body report in US – Gambling: a critique. J Int Econ Law 9(1):117–148

Paparemborde EA (2014) Looking back at Canada - Periodicals: autopsy of a missed opportunity to address the problem of conflicting provisions in the World Trade Organization and preferential trade agreements' dispute settlement systems. McGill J Dispute Resolut 1(1):26–46

Pauwelyn J (2003) Conflict of norms in public international law: how WTO law relates to other rules of international law. Cambridge University Press, New York

Pauwelyn J (2004) The puzzle of WTO safeguards and regional trade agreements. J Int Econ Law 7 (1):109–142

Pellet A (2018) Decisions of the ICJ as sources of international law? Gaetano Morelli Lectures Series, vol 2. International and European Papers Publishing, Rome

Peters A (2017) The refinement of international law: from fragmentation to regime interaction and politicization. Int J Constitut Law 15(3):671–704

Pierola F, Horlick G (2007) WTO dispute settlement and dispute settlement in the "North-South" agreements of the Americas: considerations for choice of forum. J World Trade 41(5):885–908

Salles LE (2015) A deal is a deal: party autonomy, the multiplication of PTAs, and WTO dispute settlement. Quest Int Law 23:15–29

Shadikhodjaev S (2017) The "Regionalism vs Multilateralism" issue in international trade law: revisiting the Peru–Agricultural Products Case. Chin J Int Law 16:109–123

Shaffer G, Winters A (2017) FTA law in WTO dispute settlement: Peru–Additional Duty and the fragmentation of trade law. World Trade Rev 16(2):303–326

Shaffer G, Elsig M, Puig S (2016) The extensive (but fragile) authority of the WTO Appellate Body. Law Contemp Probl 79:237–273

Slaughter AM (1994) A typology of transjudicial communication. Univ Richmond Law Rev 29 (1):99–137

Stoll PT (2019) The WTO dispute settlement system and regional trade tribunals: the potential for conflict and solutions. In: do Amaral Júnior A, de Oliveira Sá Pires LM, Lucena Carneiro Cristiane (eds) The WTO dispute settlement mechanism: A developing country perspective. Springer, Heidelberg, pp. 229–244

Tzanakopoulos A (2016) Judicial dialogue as a means of interpretation. In: Aust HP, Nolte G (eds) The interpretation of international law by domestic courts: uniformity, diversity, convergence. Oxford University Press, New York, pp 72–95

Van Aaken A (2009) Defragmentation of public international law through interpretation: a methodological proposal. Indiana J Glob Leg Stud 16(2):483–512

Van Damme I (2009) Treaty interpretation by the WTO Appellate Body. Oxford University Press, New York

Venzke I (2012) How interpretation makes international law: on semantic change and normative twists. Oxford University Press, Oxford

Vidigal G (2013) From bilateral to multilateral law-making: legislation, practice, evolution and the future of inter se agreements in the WTO. Eur J Int Law 24(4):1027–1053

Vidigal G (2019) Living without the Appellate Body: hegemonic, fragmented and network authority in international trade. Amsterdam Law School Legal Studies Research Paper No. 2019-15, Amsterdam Center for International Law No. 2019-04. https://papers.ssrn.com/sol3/papers.cfm?abstract_id=3343327

Villiger ME (2009) Commentary on the 1969 Vienna Convention on the Law of Treaties. Martinus Nijhoff, Leiden

Voeten E (2010) Borrowing and nonborrowing among international courts. J Leg Stud 39 (2):547–576

Weiss W (2001) Allgemeine Rechtsgrundsätze des Völkerrechts. Archiv des Voelkerrechts 39 (4):394–431

Weiss W (2003) Security and predictability under WTO law. World Trade Rev 2(2):183–219

Zammit Borda A (2013) A formal approach to Article 38(1)(d) of the ICJ statute from the perspective of the international criminal courts and tribunals. Eur J Int Law 24(2):649–661

Zang MQ (2017) Shall we talk? Judicial communication between the CJEU and WTO dispute settlement. Eur J Int Law 28(1):273–293

Zang MQ (2018) Judicial interaction of international trade courts and tribunals. In: Howse R et al (eds) The legitimacy of international trade courts and tribunals. Cambridge University Press, New York, p 4

Chapter 12
Prospective Developments for Contemplation

12.1 Using the WTO Secretariat for Supporting WTO Panels

The first ambitious form of cooperation that this chapter will investigate is the possibility of using the WTO Secretariat to support FTA panels. As the new generation EU FTAs, similar to the majority of FTAs, do not have their own secretariats and establishing such permanent institutional structures under every FTA to deal only occasionally with disputes would be costly and implausible, this section considers the opportunity of using the already established WTO Secretariat. The support of a secretariat could ensure better functioning of the FTA DSMs. Considering that the AB is currently paralysed and the WTO-plus and WTO-x norms in FTAs could need enforcement, a rise in the use of FTA DSMs is anticipated. Therefore, assurance of the smooth functioning of FTA DSMs becomes essential. This section will first introduce the WTO Secretariat and will then weigh the advantages and disadvantages of the support it could offer to FTA panels. Finally, it will evaluate the existing legal framework to see how it could accommodate such a prospect and whether this ambitious form of cooperation could materialise in the near future.

12.1.1 Introducing the WTO Secretariat

The WTO Secretariat and its functions in WTO dispute settlement will be presented in detail first to assess the opportunities for using the WTO Secretariat in FTA adjudication.

As previously stated, the WTO Secretariat is composed of staff members highly qualified in international trade policy; they are appointed by the DG who also

C. Furculiță, *The WTO and the New Generation EU FTA Dispute Settlement Mechanisms*, EYIEL Monographs - Studies in European and International Economic Law 19, https://doi.org/10.1007/978-3-030-83118-9_12

determines their duties and service conditions.[1] In the area of dispute settlement, the Secretariat has a clearly defined mandate set by the DSU: 'assisting panels, especially on the legal, historical and procedural aspects of the matters dealt with, and of providing secretarial and technical support'.[2] Thus, the Secretariat has, *inter alia*, administrative and logistical functions. It should be noted in particular how the provision expressly sets the mandate for the Secretariat to also provide support on *legal* aspects to panels. The Secretariat also assists Members at their request, provides additional legal advice and assistance in respect of dispute settlement to developing country Members, and conducts special training courses for interested Members concerning the WTO dispute settlement procedures and practices.[3] Together with a staff member from the division of the Secretariat responsible for the covered agreement at issue, two divisions of the Secretariat, Legal Affairs Division (LAD) and the Rules Division, regularly provide support to panels during dispute settlement proceedings.[4] The LAD has the mission to provide legal advice and information to WTO panels, WTO Members, the WTO Secretariat, and other bodies, while the Rules Division assists panels during disputes on trade defence instruments (i.e. antidumping, subsidies and countervailing measures, and safeguards).[5]

The WTO Secretariat is involved in all stages of the panel proceedings. As part of its administrative and logistical functions, the WTO Secretariat organises the panelists' travel, prepares letters to invite the parties to meetings, receives submissions, deposits them and forwards them to the panelists, ensures translation and interpretation services, and hires venues for hearings.[6] In addition to logistical help, the Secretariat also provides procedural and legal support that can play a more substantive role in the proceedings. Thus, the Secretariat has a crucial role in the selection of the panelists, although in practice, it is agreed that even without the Secretariat the parties have the right to choose them.[7] The Secretariat also prepares the timetables and the working procedures which have to be approved by the panel, sent to the parties, and discussed at an 'organisational meeting'.[8] After the organisational meeting, during which the parties can comment orally on the instructions from the panel, the Secretariat revises the timetable and the working procedures that, in the end, have to be adopted by the panel.[9] The role of the Secretariat in establishing the timetables can be explained by the fact that in order to ensure that it will manage

---

[1] *See supra*, Sect. 6.9.1.

[2] DSU, Art 27.1.

[3] DSU, Art 27.2 and 27.3.

[4] WTO Secretariat (2017), p. 22.

[5] WTO, 'The WTO: Secretariat and Budget. Divisions'. <www.wto.org/english/thewto_e/secre_e/div_e.htm>.

[6] WTO Secretariat (2017), p. 22.

[7] For more on the role of the WTO Secretariat at this stage, *see* Sect. 6.4.1.

[8] Baker, Marceau (2019), p. 83.

[9] Ibid.

to provide the required support, it needs to distribute staff members and coordinate with other ongoing disputes.[10] The Secretariat also provides legal support by writing the 'Issue Paper', based on the submissions of the parties, which summarises the facts and arguments, identifies the issues to be decided and, most importantly, proposes ways in which the maters could be resolved.[11] While the Issue Paper might exert great deal of influence on the way panelists decide, it has only an exploratory and advisory nature and is in no way binding on the panelists.[12] Furthermore, the Secretariat participates in drafting the questions that the parties would be asked at the discretion of the panel during the hearings.[13]

Lastly, the WTO Secretariat is also present during the hearings, taking notes and helping with other issues that may arise,[14] assisting during deliberations,[15] and even drafting the panel reports[16] based on instructions from the arbitrators who retain the final word and the power to make decisions. Thus, while the panelists decide on the case, the Secretariat plays an important role. Although the Secretariat drafts the reports (and it recognises this), it is supposed to be a technical function only,[17] as the drafting is carried out at the direction and close and regular instructions of the panels which retain the final word and review them several times.[18] Hence, the Secretariat staff could draft findings and reasons that they may or not agree with. Moreover, as stated by a former Director of the LAD, the Secretariat maintains its neutrality and ensures that it does not overstep the panels' right to make their own decisions.[19] Therefore, the Secretariat technically has no decision-making power and adjudicatory role, although this could be contested—an issue that will be addressed in the next section.

The analysis of both the technical and legal functions of the Secretariat shows its significance in the dispute settlement process. While the importance of the Secretariat in WTO proceedings is indubitable, the question arises whether similar support could also benefit the panels in the context of FTA proceedings.

---

[10] Pauwelyn and Pelc (2019), p. 8.

[11] Ibid.

[12] Baker and Marceau (2019), p. 83.

[13] Ibid, p. 84; Pauwelyn and Pelc (2019), p. 9.

[14] Baker and Marceau (2019), p. 84.

[15] Howse (2016), p. 20.

[16] Weiler (2001), p. 197; Nordström (2005), p. 828.

[17] Baker and Marceau (2019), p. 84.

[18] Hughes (2015), p. 406.

[19] Ibid, p. 405.

12.1.2   Advantages and Drawbacks of the Potential Use of the WTO Secretariat During FTA Proceedings

This section will weigh the potential advantages and drawbacks of potentially using the WTO Secretariat's support in the context of FTA proceedings. It will also answer the question of which type of support could be more desirable from the perspective of FTA parties.

Using the WTO Secretariat to provide logistical support to FTA panels could be beneficial, since it has extensive experience in organising state-to-state dispute settlement procedures. It could offer well-equipped venues and translation services, handle expenses and payments, and arrange the logistical part of selecting arbitrators by lot. While this support may not seem important and should not necessarily be offered by staff highly qualified in international trade, leaving these responsibilities to the panelists would burden them unreasonably. Hence, secretarial support can ensure that procedures are not delayed because of administrative and logistical issues and that they can progress smoothly. Thus, without a secretariat, parties would need to generate institutional backup *ad-hoc* for every dispute, which could be quite burdensome and lead to unnecessary delays. For example, in the labour dispute under CAFTA-DR,[20] many of the responsibilities that could have been assumed by the Secretariat were borne by the panelists themselves, even translation of documents, which was time-consuming.[21]

Unless parties agree otherwise, in the EUKFTA, CETA, and EUSFTA, the hearings should be held in the capitals of the defendants (Brussels and other cities, respectively)[22] that also have to propose and prepare venues. In the EUVFTA the parties need to first attempt to agree on the place of hearings, and in case of disagreement, the same rule as those in the first three FTAs are followed.[23] Under the EUJEPA, the location should alternate between the parties, with the party hosting the hearing determining the venue.[24] Hence, under the new generation EU FTAs, one of the parties would bear the responsibility to locate a technically equipped venue, which should not represent a problem as long as the party is willing to do so and is not ill-intentioned and interested in delaying or disrupting the procedures. Under the new generation EU FTAs, unless otherwise agreed, the logistical administration of the dispute settlement proceedings, in particular that of the hearings, is the responsibility of the defendant, except in the EUJEPA under which the

---

[20] Informe Final del Grupo Arbitral, *Costa Rica vs El Salvador – Tratamiento Arancelario a Bienes Originarios de Costa Rica*, 18 November 2014 (CAFTA-DR/ARB/2014/CR-ES/17); Final Panel Report, *In the Matter of Guatemala – Issues Relating to the Obligations Under Article 16.2.1(a) of the CAFTA-DR*, 14 June 2017.

[21] Robertson et al. (2018), p. 14.

[22] EUKFTA, Rules of Procedure, Art 7.2; CETA, Rules of Procedure, para 27; EUSFTA, Rules of Procedure, para 27.

[23] EUVFTA, Art 15.8.3.

[24] EUJEPA, Art 21.15, Rules of Procedure, para 16(a).

responsibility is that of the party, either the defendant or the complainant, hosting the hearing.[25] If the party in charge of logistical administration lacks qualified personnel to manage state-to-state international disputes, the proceedings could be delayed. Moreover, if the defendant is in charge, it might be directly interested in delaying the procedures.

If a common language is not agreed by the parties under the EUKFTA and CETA, each party has to ensure translation of its own written submissions.[26] In the same situation under the EUJEPA, submissions have to be translated by a party in a WTO language chosen by the other party,[27] while under the EUVFTA, each party should submit the written submissions in one of the languages chosen from the WTO working languages.[28] Translation of oral arguments under the EUKFTA, CETA, and EUJEPA is the responsibility of the party in charge of organising the hearings,[29] making such arrangements vulnerable, if the defendant is the organiser. Under the EUKFTA, CETA, and EUVFTA, if a common language is not agreed, panel rulings should be issued in the languages chosen by the parties,[30] and in the EUJEPA in the chosen WTO working languages.[31] While the costs are to be borne equally by the parties,[32] the agreements are silent on who should take care of the translation of the reports—the panels or one or both of the parties. Hence, panels may end up being responsible for finding translators or even translating the reports themselves, which in both cases could result in unnecessary delays to the proceedings. Moreover, the EUSFTA is silent on what happens if the parties cannot agree on a common working language and who is responsible for translations in general, while the EUVFTA does not stipulate who is responsible for translating oral arguments, potentially leading to uncertain situations, disagreements, and even delays. Hence, technical support offered by a secretariat, such as the WTO's, could ensure the avoidance of such undesirable situations.

When it comes to the notifications, under the EUKFTA, CETA, EUSFTA, and EUVFTA, the parties communicate directly, without a special body mentioned as being part of the process.[33] Nevertheless, each FTA party, at its discretion, could entrust an existent or new national body with communicating attributions. EUJEPA, by contrast, expressly provides that each party shall establish an office responsible for administration of dispute settlement procedures, for which it shall bear the costs

---

[25] EUKFTA, Rules of Procedure, Art 1.2; CETA, Rules of Procedure, para 2; EUJEPA, Rules of Procedure, para 16(b); EUSFTA, Rules of Procedure, para 3; EUVFTA, Rules of Procedure, para 2.

[26] EUKFTA, Art 13.2; CETA, Rules of Procedure, para 49.

[27] EUJEPA, Rules of Procedure, para 42.

[28] EUVFTA, Rules of Procedure, para 45.

[29] EUKFTA, Art 13.2; CETA, Rules of Procedure, para 49; EUJEPA, Rules of Procedure, para 43.

[30] EUKFTA, Rules of Procedure, Art 13.3; CETA, Rules of Procedure, para 50; EUVFTA, Art 46.

[31] EUJEPA, Rules of Procedure, para 43.

[32] EUKFTA, Art 13.4; CETA, Rules of Procedure, para 51.

[33] EUKFTA, Rules of Procedure, Art 2; CETA, Rules of Procedure, paras 3-7; EUSFTA, Rules of Procedure, para 3; EUVFTA, Rules of Procedure, para 2.

and be responsible of, to receive all notifications.[34] The support offered and independence granted to such bodies could vary depending on the parties[35] since such offices are national. As it seems from the EUJEPA Rules of Procedures, the offices established according to the agreement are expressly attributed only a few functions: to organise the selection by lot of the panelists and to receive all notifications of the necessary documents.[36] The support of a secretariat or an office similar to the one specified in the EUJEPA for organising the logistical part of the meetings for selecting arbitrators by lot could avert undesirable delays in proceedings under the EUKFTA, CETA, and EUSFTA, which are silent in this respect.

While receiving technical support from a secretariat could be beneficial, *legal* support specifically from the WTO Secretariat would have additional advantages. The WTO Secretariat staff, with their knowledge and experience in trade dispute settlement, could offer substantive and procedural help. As the FTAs and the WTO agreements deal with similar issues and contain similar norms and concepts, the advice of the WTO Secretariat staff could help familiarise the arbitrators on how the same issues have already been dealt with under WTO rules. This would be especially helpful in the case of the new generation EU FTA provisions on interpretation that stipulate that WTO jurisprudence should be taken into account by FTA panels, dealt with in the previous chapter.[37] Although the new generation EU FTAs specify that the arbitrators should have knowledge of international trade law, CETA even requiring the chairperson to have experience as counsel or panelist in WTO proceedings,[38] it is probable that the arbitrators' knowledge of WTO jurisprudence would be more limited than that of the WTO Secretariat. Furthermore, despite the arbitrators benefiting from the help of assistants under the new generation EU FTAs, the assistants, similar to the panelists, are appointed only on an *ad-hoc* basis under the terms of appointment of the arbitrators[39] and are not even required to have specialised knowledge of international trade law. Hence, their support cannot be compared to that of the WTO Secretariat staff dealing regularly with trade disputes. In addition, finding highly qualified legal assistants and hiring them for single disputes may also be difficult, especially since their remuneration may not be sufficiently attractive.[40] Under CETA, EUJEPA, and EUVFTA, for example, the

---

[34] EUJEPA, Art 21.25(1); EUJEPA, Rules of Procedure, para 6.

[35] McRae (2019), p. 546.

[36] EUJEPA, Rules of Procedure, para 2, 6.

[37] *See supra*, Sect. 11.8.5.3.

[38] CETA, Art 29.8(2).

[39] EUKFTA, Rules of Procedure for Arbitration, Art 1.1; CETA, Rules of Procedure for Arbitration, para 1; EUSFTA, Rules of Procedure for Arbitration, para 1; EUVFTA, Rules of Procedure, para 1 (d); EUJEPA, Rules of Procedure, para 1.

[40] Robertson et al. (2018), p. 15.

remuneration of an arbitrator's assistant should not exceed 50% of the total remuneration of the arbitrator,[41] but there is no minimum payment set.

As FTA panels would encounter procedural issues, the advice of the WTO Secretariat could also be beneficial in explaining how WTO panels and the AB have dealt with similar issues, resulting in judicial communication for the purpose of procedural gap filling. As Pauwelyn stated in discussions on the CAFTA-DR labour dispute, there is no reason to reinvent the wheel when dealing with procedural issues such as evidentiary rules if the FTA is silent on that.[42] Thus, the legal support of the WTO Secretariat could foster judicial communication within the limits of the existing legal framework. The WTO Secretariat could also assist with reviewing large quantities of documents and the evidence submitted by the parties and ensure better quality reports. Finally, using the support of the WTO Secretariat, as the repository of institutional memory, within FTA proceedings could ensure consistency between reports issued under the same or different FTAs, as well as between FTA and WTO reports. While this consistency could bring predictability to the proceedings, it could also represent a disadvantage.

This section will continue by presenting the drawbacks associated with the potential use of the WTO Secretariat's assistance during FTA proceedings. First of all, the WTO Secretariat is already overloaded with the work stemming from the assistance provided to WTO panels. As it has limited capacity and personnel, the WTO Secretariat would be further overburdened, if requested to provide assistance to FTA panels.[43] This could also make it impossible to comply with the tight timelines under the new generation EU FTAs that could be an advantage compared to the timescales of WTO proceedings. In addition, benefitting from the support of the WTO Secretariat would involve extra costs covered by the Secretariat's budget. It is unlikely that WTO Members would agree that the WTO Secretariat provides assistance to FTA panels while being funded by the WTO budget to which all the Members contribute. Hence, FTA parties could have to pay *ad-hoc* for the services provided by the Secretariat.[44] The costs to use the WTO Secretariat's services for FTA proceedings could be perceived as too high by FTA parties.[45] Still, establishing permanent FTA secretariats might be even more costly. If the WTO Secretariat provided support to FTA panels, it would also have to deal with a greater workload. For that reason, extra staff might be needed *ad-hoc* or on a permanent basis, funded by the FTA parties to assist in FTA proceedings.[46] The drawback is that the hired staff would not have the same experience and knowledge of WTO law as the regular

---

[41] CETA, Rules of Procedure, para 8; EUJEPA, Rules of Procedure, para 4(b); EUVFTA, Rules of Procedure, para 12.

[42] ICTSD (2017).

[43] Porges (2018), p. 6.

[44] Porges (2018), p. 6; Robertson et al. (2018), p. 39.

[45] Robertson et al. (2018), p. 39.

[46] The WTO already hired *ad-hoc* additional Secretariat members in the *Boeing (US) – Airbus (EU)* disputes (Shaffer and Winters 2017, p. 323).

Secretariat staff, and their support could compare to that offered by the assistants that the FTA panelists can already benefit from under the new generation EU FTAs. In addition, as discussed below,[47] it is unlikely that WTO Members would agree in the first place to permit the WTO Secretariat to provide its services externally.

Another potential drawback is that the place of hearings would have to be Geneva, as the WTO Secretariat and its staff would not travel to Brussels or other capitals of FTA parties to provide assistance. Hence, using the help of the WTO Secretariat during FTA proceedings would involve additional costs, as both parties and their representatives would have to travel to Switzerland. However, this issue may be irrelevant considering that FTA parties, as WTO Members, have offices and permanent representation in Geneva.[48]

Finally, the *legal* support can also be perceived as being detrimental. Coherence and consistency are desirable to ensure predictability of the reports, but too much consistency and coherence could mean that unwanted precedents are perpetuated and parties would have less control over their disputes.[49] Although the WTO Secretariat's support could help FTA arbitrators and familiarise them with WTO jurisprudence, it could also promote WTO jurisprudence even when the FTA provisions are similar, but the differences and the context would, nevertheless, require justified inconsistencies. Thus, the intention of the parties to depart from the multilateral rules in their FTAs would be disregarded.

The WTO Secretariat's role may additionally be seen as too invasive of the arbitrators' work and too influential in the final outcomes of disputes. Some doctrinaires, for example, have argued that it is the Secretariat that decides the cases, not the panelists,[50] with some panelists feeling that they could not challenge the view of the assigned secretarial staff on legal issues.[51] While panelists are appointed only on an *ad-hoc* basis, the Secretariat is a standing body with extensive knowledge and experience of the matters in disputes; therefore, it is no surprise that panelists might listen to the Secretariat's views. A recent empirical study conducted by Pauwelyn and Pelc on panel reports issued in disputes DS2 to DS302 showed that the majority could be attributed to the Secretariat.[52] Pauwelyn and Pelc suggest that the increased role of the Secretariat may contribute to 'an increased role for precedent; longer and more convoluted reports and proceedings; rulings that are more ambitious and expansive in scope; and a lower number of dissents, because of pressure to reach consensus decisions'; and reduced legitimacy and compliance pull of the reports— effects that correspond to US concerns about the AB.[53] Although the methodology chosen by Pauwelyn and Pelc is contentious, the fact that the Secretariat drafts

---

[47] *See infra*, Sect. 12.1.3.

[48] Robertson et al. (2018), p. 39.

[49] *See supra*, Sect. 6.9.3.

[50] Nordström (2005), p. 829.

[51] Weiler (2001), p. 205.

[52] Pauwelyn and Pelc (2019), p. 19.

[53] Ibid, p. 25.

reports under panel supervision is already openly acknowledged by it. As previously claimed,[54] WTO panels technically review and have the final word on draft reports. Still, the choice of words in which a decision is conveyed is also important.[55] When reports are treated in practice as precedents, they are often analysed textually and the wording has an influence on future disputes.

All new generation EU FTAs explicitly establish that the drafting of any ruling remains the exclusive responsibility of the arbitration panel and that it should not be delegated to any other person or body.[56] These provisions are clear about the opposition that FTA parties show to the involvement of someone other than the panelists in the decision-making process. Had the parties wanted to attribute a greater role to externals, they would have allowed the assistants to have a role in the drafting of the rulings. The EUJEPA provision on solely administrative support conceivably shows the parties' aversion to legal support provided by an external body.[57] Similarly, under the old NAFTA[58] and the new USCMA,[59] the FTA secretariats were supposed to offer only administrative support. Also, under CPTPP, national offices are designated to provide only administrative assistance to panels.[60] Hence, these provisions are indicative of the fact that the increased legal role of the WTO Secretariat could be conceived as a disadvantage rather than an advantage by the parties in the context of FTA proceedings. Therefore, while administrative support seems to be sought in FTAs, the same cannot be said about legal support. In such a case, FTA parties could make use only of the administrative support of the WTO Secretariat. Nevertheless, if only administrative support is sought, it may not necessarily be provided by the WTO Secretariat. The principal reason for preferring the WTO Secretariat to other institutions able to provide support is its staff who are highly qualified and experienced in international trade policy. If legal support is not contemplated by the FTA parties, the WTO Secretariat staff's knowledge and experience of international trade are less relevant. Other institutions, such as the Permanent Court of Arbitration (PCA) in the Hague, the International Court of Arbitration of the International Chamber of Commerce (ICC) in Paris, the London Court of International Arbitration and the Arbitration Institute of the Stockholm Chamber of Commerce, or the International Centre for the Settlement of Investment Disputes (ICSID), which have facilities and staff

---

[54] *See supra*, Sect. 12.1.1.

[55] Pauwelyn and Pelc (2019), p. 27.

[56] EUKFTA, Rules of Procedure for Arbitration, Art 5(4); CETA, Rules of Procedure for Arbitration, para 14; EUJEPA, Art 21.15(6); EUSFTA, Rules of Procedure for Arbitration, para 16; EUVFTA, Rules of Procedure, para 17.

[57] EUJEPA, Art 21.25(2).

[58] NAFTA, Art 2002(3)(b)(i).

[59] USMCA, Art 30.6(3)(b)(i).

[60] CPTPP, Art 27.6(1)(a).

experienced in dealing with international dispute settlement, could also help with the logistical administration of FTA dispute settlement proceedings.[61]

To conclude, FTA proceedings would clearly gain certain advantages from the WTO Secretariat's administrative support. The legal support of the WTO Secretariat may also provide some benefits; however, the provisions of the FTAs suggest that parties seem to give greater weight to the drawbacks of legal support and do not opt for such assistance in the context of FTA proceedings. Nevertheless, in the context of the AB crisis, if parties contemplate using the FTA DSMs as alternatives to the WTO DSM and would not hold on more control over the disputes, it could be expected that FTA parties would reconsider their preferences and be more prepared to use legal support provided by experienced and knowledgeable secretariats.

12.1.3 The Relevant New Generation EU FTA and WTO Legal Frameworks

Since the desirability of using the WTO Secretariat's support in FTA proceedings is questionable, before considering the legal framework that would allow it, this chapter analysed first whether such support would be wanted by the parties. As the previous section concluded, currently it seems that only secretarial administrative support is contemplated by parties for FTA proceedings. This section will analyse the conditions under which the legal framework of the new generation EU FTAs and the WTO agreements would permit the WTO Secretariat to offer support to FTA panels, the amendments that would be necessary and the likelihood of introducing such changes in the future. This analysis is also relevant in case parties would consider using the legal support of the WTO Secretariat, especially in the context of the AB crisis.

In the first place, the legal provisions in the FTAs should allow FTA panels to make use of the support of an external body. While the EUJEPA includes an express provision on administrative support from an external secretariat, the same cannot be said about the other new generation EU FTAs. Under the EUJEPA, such support would be possible only if the parties jointly agree to it. In addition, Article 21.25 of the EUJEPA provides that support by an external body would be used for '*certain* administrative tasks for the dispute settlement procedure' (emphasis added). Hence, parties would also have to agree the specific tasks to entrust to such an external body. They could agree to entrust it with notifications and selection of panelists by lot—the functions expressly provided by the EUJEPA for national offices—and additional administrative tasks, such as organisation of hearings and translation of documents,

---

[61] As the analysis of the interactions between the new-generation EU FTA DSMs and other institutions is outside the scope of the present book, it will not be treated in detail here. For an analysis of the possibility of using bodies other than the WTO Secretariat for providing administrative support to FTA panels, *see* Vidigal (2018) and Robertson et al. (2018).

tasks for which the responsibility normally lies with the party hosting the hearing. The question also arises when such an agreement should take place and whether an agreement could be signed with respect to all future disputes. As the EUJEPA is silent and contains no requirements with respect to when and which disputes, it appears that such agreements could be signed *ad-hoc* for all future disputes arising under the FTA—once a dispute arises, or even during the proceedings.

Although the other new generation EU FTAs contain no equivalent provision to that of EUJEPA, it still seems possible to entrust the logistical administration of the dispute settlement proceedings to an external body, in particular the organisation of hearings, as the agreements state that the defendant shall be in charge of these responsibilities *unless otherwise agreed*.[62] Hence, parties could agree otherwise, including on entrusting the logistical administration of hearings to an external body, such as the WTO Secretariat or secretariats of other international institutions. As in the case of the EUJEPA, such an arrangement could be agreed for all future disputes or on an *ad-hoc* basis. However, *ad-hoc* signing of agreements on the use of external logistical support could be more difficult because once the dispute materialises, the defendant may be interested in delaying the procedures and could see external support as a factor that would expedite them.[63] Therefore, signing agreements on external administrative support for the organisation of hearings for all future disputes arising under the FTAs, before they have materialised and it is not known which party would be the defendant and which the complainant, would be more advisable.

While the new generation EU FTAs technically permit the use of external bodies for *administrative and logistical* support, especially for organising hearings, when there is agreement between the parties, the FTAs do not seem to have provisions for the possibility that *legal* support is given by an external body. Hence, if parties wanted the panels constituted under these agreements to benefit from the legal support of an external body such as the WTO Secretariat or a secretariat of another international institution, the FTAs would have to be amended according to their provisions on amendments. The new generation EU FTAs provide that the parties may agree in writing to amend the treaties, with amendments entering into force only after the exchange of written notifications certifying that their internal legal requirements and procedures have been complied with.[64] As far as the EU is concerned, when the parties agree to amend the treaties, the ordinary treaty-making procedures, established under Article 218(1)–(6) of TFEU and corroborated with Article 207 of TFEU, should apply, requiring the European Parliament's approval and the decision of the Council.[65] Accordingly, the amendments would require time and effort to go through the EU's ordinary treaty-making procedures. The international requirements

---

[62]EUKFTA, Annex 14-B, Art 1.2; CETA, Annex 29-A, para 2; EUSFTA, Annex 14-A, para 3; EUVFTA, Annex 15-A, para 2.

[63]Robertson et al. (2018), p. 73.

[64]EUKFTA, Art 15.5(1); CETA, Art 30.2(1); EUJEPA, Art 23.2(2); EUSFTA, Art 16.5(1); EUVFTA, Art 17.5(1).

[65]Brown and Record (2015), p. 41.

of the other FTA parties could also necessitate considerable time resources. However, under the EUKFTA, CETA, EUSFTA, and EUVFTA, the Annexes on the Rules of Procedure, regulating who should be in charge of the logistical administration of the dispute, and the dispute settlement chapter under the EUSFTA can be amended through a decision of the Trade or Joint Committees, a decision that should be adopted by the parties or enter into force in accordance with their internal requirements and procedures.[66] When the decision for amendment is made by treaty bodies, at least under the EU internal requirements, the simplified procedure for treaty-making under Article 218(7) and (9) of TFEU is applicable, meaning that the European Parliament's approval would not be required and the Council's decision would only be a preparatory action, addressing exclusively the EU representative within the Committee.[67] From the perspective of EU law, once adopted, the decisions of the Joint or Trade Committee become binding on the parties.[68] Therefore, at least under EU internal rules, the amendment by the Joint or Trade Committees would be a less time-consuming process. In any case, reaching an agreement between the parties, or even between their representatives acting on their behalf within the Trade or Joint Committees, on external legal support may be difficult in practice, due to the drawbacks associated with it.

The second and biggest hurdle for using the technical or legal support of the WTO Secretariat is the WTO legal framework. The WTO is silent on the possibility of the WTO Secretariat contracting out its services. The only article that could be invoked against its use for external purposes is Article VI:4 of the Marrakesh Agreement establishing that 'the Director-General and the staff of the Secretariat *shall not seek or accept instructions from any government or any other authority external to the WTO*' (emphasis added). It could be argued that if the WTO Secretariat were used in FTA proceedings, it would have to accept the instructions of the governments to provide external support and also that of the arbitrators during proceedings. However, the context, according to which the DG and the staff 'shall refrain from any action which might adversely reflect on their position as international officials', 'shall respect the international character of the responsibilities' and 'shall not seek to influence them in the discharge of their duties', sheds light on the purpose of this provision.[69] Hence, it is apparent that this provision has the aim of ensuring that the Secretariat remains neutral and does not submit to potential influence exercised by the Members.[70] Therefore, this provision should not be considered an impediment to the WTO Secretariat providing its services outside the WTO.

While the WTO agreements do not seem to prohibit the WTO Secretariat from providing its services externally, such a possibility would most likely be subject to

---

[66] EUKFTA, Art 15.5(2); CETA, Art 30.2; EUJEPA, Art 23.2(3).

[67] Weiss (2018), p. 540.

[68] For a detailed explanation of the binding force of the CETA Joint Committee's decisions, *see* ibid, pp. 536–537.

[69] Marrakesh Agreement, Art VI:4.

[70] Robertson et al. (2018), p. 38.

the consensus of the WTO Members.[71] In Article 27, the DSU clearly establishes the WTO Secretariat's responsibilities in relation to dispute settlement, suggesting that it was created to offer assistance only to WTO panels. Hence, a different use of the WTO Secretariat could be considered as going against the original intent of the parties. If the WTO Secretariat's support were used without the consensus of the Members, it could cause a significant backlash from them. First of all, Members could be opposed to such a use because of adding to the workload of the Secretariat which is already overburdened, leading to even longer WTO panel proceedings. There seems to be no reason why Members that do not wish to make use of the WTO Secretariat in their own FTA proceedings would agree to the WTO Secretariat's services being provided to other FTAs, especially when the Secretariat struggles with dealing with its own workload. In addition, it is not entirely clear if and how parties would cover the costs and whether extra staff could be employed only for the purpose of assisting with FTA procedures. Moreover, WTO Members could argue against the involvement of the WTO, a multilateral organisation, in Member's RTAs that are separate agreements, even though regulated by Article XXIV of the GATT.

A potential backlash against the use of the WTO Secretariat's services in FTA procedures without the consent of all Members could lead to damaging consequences. The US, for example, expressed its discontent with the EU and other Members using Article 25 interim appeal arbitration agreements as an alternative to the regular appeal proceedings, and has threatened to block the WTO budget for 2020–2021.[72] Ultimately the budget for 2020 was agreed, even though the payment for AB Members was decreased by 87% and the AB's operating fund by 95%.[73] Yet, the US clearly objected to financing the separate support structure envisaged by the MPIA from the WTO budget.[74] Similarly, the WTO Secretariat's services being provided to FTA proceedings without the agreement of the Membership could cause significant discontent and lead to threats to block the formation of the WTO budget. The most dangerous consequence of the WTO Secretariat offering its service without the Membership's consensus may be the threat by some Members to even withdraw from the WTO. Moreover, being aware of the contentiousness of this issue, the Secretariat itself is unlikely to offer its services without the consensus of Members. At a time of the deepest crisis at the WTO that has seen the AB asphyxiated, it would be unreasonable to cause further backlash against the WTO dispute settlement and the Secretariat and threaten the budget and the functioning of panels. Yet, considering the tense atmosphere at the WTO, especially in relation to

---

[71] Vidigal (2018).

[72] Financial Times, 'Saving the WTO', 22 November 2019 <www.ft.com/content/2a888286-0cc9-11ea-b2d6-9bf4d1957a67>.

[73] See Bloomberg, 'WTO Members Agree on a 2020 Budget, Averting Jan. 1 Shutdown', 5 December 2019 <www.bloomberg.com/news/articles/2019-12-05/wto-members-agree-on-a-2020-budget-averting-jan-1-shutdown>.

[74] See supra, Sect. 6.9.1.

dispute settlement, consensus is unlikely to be reached in the foreseeable future.[75] Moreover, until the AB crisis is resolved or a viable multilateral alternative acceptable to all is found, it is unlikely that proposals such as the services of the WTO Secretariat being provided externally would even be considered.

To conclude, the legal framework provided by the new generation EU FTAs seems to expressly or implicitly allow the use of the WTO Secretariat's administrative and logistical support for FTA proceedings. However, the new generation EU FTAs would have to be amended to obtain external legal support. In the case of the WTO legal framework, for the WTO Secretariat to provide both administrative and legal services to external DSMs, the Members' consensus would be required to avoid a backlash, a consensus that is unlikely to be reached in the foreseeable future.

12.1.4 Preliminary Conclusions

This section was dedicated to a more ambitious form of judicial cooperation between the new generation EU FTAs and WTO DSMs. It considered the possibility of making use of the WTO Secretariat's services for supporting FTA panels and sought to invite the reader to reflect on prospective advancements in the area of cooperative interactions.

The section started with an introduction to the WTO Secretariat and how it provides technical and legal support to WTO panels during dispute settlement proceedings. It showed the substantial role of the Secretariat during the panel stage of the proceedings. The chapter then analysed whether similar support would be desired by parties for the panels established under the new generation EU FTAs. The chapter enumerated the advantages and drawbacks associated with the potential support offered by the WTO Secretariat to FTA panels. It concluded that while administrative support offered by an external body, such as the WTO Secretariat or another secretariat, would be desirable, the same conclusion is unlikely to be valid in case of legal support. The provisions of the new generation EU FTAs suggest that currently there is no will for the FTA panels to benefit from legal support from an external body, which may change as the dispute settlement crisis at the WTO unfolds.

Finally, in accordance with the concept of limited coherence adopted here, the WTO Secretariat can provide its services externally only if the legal framework allows it. The new generation EU FTAs currently permit the use of administrative services provided by external bodies, but for legal services, amendments to the provisions would be required. The main impediment to FTA parties choosing the WTO Secretariat as the body providing assistance to FTA panels is obtaining the consensus of the entire WTO Membership. The chapter argued that such consensus

---

[75] Vidigal (2018) also considers that consensus is unlikely to be reached in this respect.

is absolutely important but unlikely to be reached in the foreseeable future and as long as the dispute settlement crisis at the WTO persists.

12.2 Using the WTO DSM to Solve FTA Disputes

The concept of cooperative interactions between DSMs, as established in the conceptual framework, means working towards a common goal. Both the WTO and the new generation EU FTAs DSMs work towards solving trade disputes between their Members/parties. The most ambitious form of such cooperation would be to solve disputes together. Thus, after trying to solve matters in bilateral consultations under FTAs, parties could refer them to WTO panels that would expand their jurisdiction over FTA disputes. Such a progressive structural way of cooperative interactions has been suggested by several academics,[76] and even by the former AB Member Ricardo Ramírez-Hernández in his farewell speech.[77] It has been argued that since FTAs are the main vehicles for progress and change in international trade, but the FTA DSMs are rarely used compared to the WTO DSM—the latter, as a more successful mechanism, should also be used for resolving FTA disputes.[78]

12.2.1 Assessing the Existing WTO Rules

To implement this proposal in practice, WTO rules would have to be amended. It was established that the jurisdiction of WTO panels, as inferred from Article 1.1 and supported by Articles 4.2, 7, and 11 of the DSU, is limited to claims brought under the covered agreements.[79] Of course, claims on FTA norms that replicate or incorporate WTO norms can already be brought under WTO rules, as they can also be regarded as claims under the WTO covered agreements. As the AB indicated in *Turkey – Textiles*,[80] although WTO panels can rule on the consistency of an FTA with the requirements of Article XXIV of GATT (including on the potential inconsistency of a WTO-minus provision), claims on the consistency with FTA norms that are WTO-plus or WTO-x norms cannot be brought under the DSU.

---

[76] *See* Gao and Lim (2008), Hammond (2012), Forere (2015), Shaffer and Winters (2017) and Gao (2019).

[77] 'Given the amount of expertise and knowledge developed over the past decades, the WTO could become the dispute settlement centre for all RTAs. We need to brand the name.' ('Farewell speech of Appellate Body Member Ricardo Ramírez-Hernández', 28 May 2018 <www.wto.org/english/tratop_e/dispu_e/ricardoramirezfarwellspeech_e.htm>).

[78] Hammond (2012), pp. 422, 423; Gao (2019), p. 1.

[79] In this respect, *see* Sect. 9.3.1.

[80] Appellate Body Report, *Turkey – Textiles*, [58–60].

Flett argued that Articles 7.1 and 7.3 of the DSU that allow parties to agree on special terms of reference could be used as a basis for solving FTA disputes without amending the DSU.[81] Article 7.1 of the DSU provides the standard terms of references, unless parties agree otherwise in 20 days,[82] meaning that parties can agree on special terms of reference. According to Article 7.3 of the DSU, such special terms of reference should be drawn by the DSB chairman in consultation with the parties and circulated to all the Members; afterwards, any Member can raise a point in the DSB with respect to the terms of reference. Flett argues that there are no limitations within the DSU that would restrict the use of special terms of reference only to solving disputes arising under the WTO covered agreements and, hence, they could be extended to cover FTAs if there is agreement between disputing parties.[83]

This author, however, does not share this opinion. While the special terms of reference provide panels with a certain degree of flexibility, they cannot extend the jurisdiction of the panels over claims not based on the covered agreements, due to the context in which Articles 7.1 and 7.3 are situated. Article 1.1 of the DSU establishes that DSU rules and procedures apply to 'disputes brought pursuant to the consultation and dispute settlement provisions' of the covered agreements, without providing any exception for special terms of reference. Moreover, this reading is further confirmed by the context provided by other articles. Thus, Article 3.2 of the DSU establishes that '[r]ecommendations and rulings of the DSB cannot add to or diminish the rights and obligations provided in the covered agreements'. If panels ruled on purely FTA claims that could be considered WTO claims, Members' rights and obligations under the covered agreements could be affected. Moreover, the panels would not fulfil their function to make an 'objective assessment of the facts of the case and the applicability of and conformity with the relevant *covered agreements*, and make such other findings as will assist the DSB in making the recommendations or in giving the rulings provided for in the *covered agreements*' (emphasis added), as required by Article 11 of the DSU. Nor would the respect of Article 3.4 of the DSU be ensured, according to which '[r] ecommendations or rulings [. . .] shall be aimed at achieving a satisfactory settlement of the matter *in accordance with the rights and obligations* [. . .] *under the covered agreements*' (emphasis added), as the settlement of the disputes would actually be in accordance with the FTA provisions.[84]

Besides the special terms of references, it has also been argued that Article 25 of the DSU on arbitration could similarly serve as a basis for bringing non-WTO claims. According to Article 25, subject to mutual agreement of the parties on

---

[81] Flett (2015), p. 555.

[82] According to Art 7.1 of the DSU, panels have the following standard terms of reference: 'To examine, in the light of the relevant provisions in (name of the covered agreement(s) cited by the parties to the dispute), the matter referred to the DSB by (name of party) in document . . . and to make such findings as will assist the DSB in making the recommendations or in giving the rulings provided for in that/those agreement(s)'.

[83] Flett (2015), p. 570.

[84] Forere (2015), p. 133.

procedures, which should be notified to the Membership sufficiently in advance, and unless otherwise provided in the DSU, arbitration can be used as an alternative means of dispute settlement for 'issues that are clearly defined by both parties'. It has been argued that except for the requirement that the issues are clearly defined, the DSU does not limit in any way which disputes can be arbitrated.[85] However, Article 25 as a DSU provision is also subject to Article 1.1 that establishes that DSU rules and procedures apply to disputes brought under the covered agreements.[86] While Article 25.2 of the DSU expressly establishes that parties shall agree on the procedures to be followed, due to Article 1.1 of the DSU, it is evident that they cannot depart from the DSU norms relevant for aspects such as jurisdiction or applicable law. Hence, the jurisdiction of arbitrators under Article 25 of the DSU is the same as that of WTO panels. This is also supported by the context and jurisprudence. Article 3.5 of the DSU establishes that solutions to matters 'raised under the dispute settlement provisions of the covered agreements, *including arbitration awards*, shall be consistent with those agreements and shall not nullify or impair benefits' (emphasis added). Therefore, arbitral awards should be issued in accordance with the covered agreements, including the DSU and specifically Article 3.2 that provides that the WTO dispute settlement system should 'preserve the rights and obligations of Members under the covered agreements'. The arbitrators in *US – Section 110(5) Copyright Act (Article 25)* stated that 'it is incumbent on the Arbitrators' to ensure that Article 25 of the DSU is 'applied in accordance with the rules and principles governing the WTO system',[87] hence, including in accordance with Articles 1.1 and 3.2 of the DSU. Moreover, they said that Members may have recourse to arbitration 'whenever necessary *within the WTO framework*' (emphasis added).[88] Nevertheless, if disputing parties were to agree to make use of Article 25 of the DSU to resolve FTA disputes and the arbitrators did not oppose the adjudication of the dispute, other Members would not have the opportunity to block the adoption of the arbitral award as it would not be subject to DSB adoption.[89] Other WTO Members could object when a DSB authorisation is required in implementation proceedings, as Articles 21 and 22 of the DSU apply *mutatis mutandis* to arbitration under Art. 25 of the DSU.[90] However, these objections are unlikely to affect the implementation of an arbitral award issued in a dispute concerning FTA claims as negative consensus would be required.[91] While the DSB would be unable to hinder the use of Art. 25 of the DSU for solving FTA disputes, the lack of a legal basis to do

---

[85] Forere (2015), pp. 134, 135.

[86] Andersen et al. (2017), para 9.

[87] Award of the Arbitrators, *United States – Section 110(5) of the US Copyright Act. Recourse to Arbitration Under Article 25 of the DSU (US – Section 110(5) Copyright Act (Article 25))*, WT/DS160/ARB25/1, 9 November 2001, [2.1].

[88] Ibid [2.4].

[89] DSU, Art 25.3; MPIA, Annex 1, para 15; Interview 4.

[90] DSU, Art 25.4.

[91] Interview 4.

so could cause considerable backlash from many WTO Members, which could bring more damage to the WTO. Members could jeopardize the adoption of the WTO budget or even threaten to leave the WTO. Thus, recourse to arbitration cannot legally take place if it is for the purpose of resolving disputes related to FTAs that are outside the WTO framework.

To conclude, WTO jurisdiction is limited to disputes on covered agreements, and the special terms of reference and Article 25 of the DSU cannot be used as a backdoor to bring FTA disputes under WTO dispute settlement rules, even though some have argued for this possibility. Accordingly, if WTO Members wished to proceed down the path of adjudicating FTA disputes under WTO dispute settlement rules, the DSU would have to be amended.

12.2.2 Assessing the Likelihood of FTA Disputes Being Resolved Under WTO Rules

Extension of WTO jurisdiction over FTA disputes, a proposal advocated by some, has certain advantages, but it is also associated with many hurdles. This section will list them in order to assess the likelihood of FTA disputes being adjudicated under WTO rules in the foreseeable future.

While disputes resolved using the FTA DSMs are not a common phenomenon, due to the need to enforce FTA provisions that are WTO-plus and WTO-x as well as due to the AB crisis, their numbers could soon see an increase. Resolving all FTA disputes under WTO rules would alleviate the fears of negative effects of fragmentation and increase coherence in the international trade law regime.[92] Thus, the use of WTO proceedings to resolve FTA disputes could ensure that relevant WTO jurisprudence would be applied to FTA disputes. This would bring coherence not only between WTO and FTA jurisprudence, but also across disputes that arise under different FTAs or even between disputes arising under the same FTA.[93] In disputes between MPIA participants, a considerable degree of consistency across reports is expected, although it remains to be seen in practice if it would be as high as in case of the AB reports.[94] The experience with the bilateral international investment treaties (BITs) and considerations to create a Multilateral Investment Court to deal with the fragmentation across BITs could serve as an incentive to avoid the same situation in the international trade regime and to subject FTA disputes to a single adjudicating body.[95] Some FTAs, such as the new generation EU FTAs, already have provisions that require that relevant WTO jurisprudence is taken into account.[96] Yet, bringing

---

[92] Hammond (2012), p. 447; Trebilcock (2015), p. 138; Shaffer and Winters (2017), p. 323.

[93] Hammond (2012), p. 447.

[94] See supra, Sect. 6.8.

[95] Trebilcock (2015), p. 138.

[96] For a detailed analysis of these provisions, see Sect. 11.8.5.3.

FTA disputes to the WTO would also mean benefitting from its credibility as an institution, as well as from the WTO Secretariat's and the AB's (if it were functional) knowledge of and familiarity with WTO provisions potentially contributing to the high quality of reports.[97] Even with a dysfunctional AB, in case of disputes between MPIA participants, the selected standing appeal arbitrators are expected to be as qualified as the AB Members and to follow the collegiality principle, ensuring that all ten standing appeal arbitrators will discuss among themselves matters arising out of the disputes under consideration.[98] Settling FTA disputes under WTO rules would also reduce the risk of conflicting jurisdictions, especially given that due to DSU rules and existing jurisprudence, resolving these conflicts when a dispute is brought under an FTA first and then under the WTO agreements could be quite difficult.[99] Moreover, FTA parties could benefit from the certainty and predictability of well-established procedures, including in case of arbitral appeals under the MPIA, according to which DSU rules on appellate procedures apply *mutatis mutandis*.[100] Finally, it has been argued that by using the WTO DSM to resolve FTA disputes, a common body of law related to FTAs could be formed, paving the way for their multilateralisation and minimisation of the negative effects of fragmentation.[101]

Since the idea of consistency as an end in itself is not endorsed by the present book, which promotes the concept of limited consistency within the limits of the states' will and consent, it is utterly important to see if states want this ambitious form of cooperation to materialise. As no FTA, including the new generation EU FTAs, provides the possibility that disputes arising under them being referred to WTO panels, FTA parties should be willing to amend their FTAs and provide that the disputes arising under these agreements should be brought to the WTO. While the process of amending the FTAs could in itself be cumbersome,[102] there are additional reasons why FTA parties may not want to engage in it for the purpose of having their disputes adjudicated by WTO panels.

When negotiating FTAs, parties often use the WTO norms as a starting point[103] and use the same treaty model to initiate negotiations with different parties.[104] Nevertheless, every FTA is the result of specific negotiations and the apparent differences in the wording of the norms at issue, as well as the differences in their context, may be a deliberate choice made by the parties to influence the interpretation of those norms. Hence, parties may not want their apparently similar provisions to be

---

[97] Gao and Lim (2008), p. 922.

[98] MPIA, para 4, 5; Annex 1, para 8; Annex 2, para 3.

[99] For a detailed analysis of the relevant DSU rules and jurisprudence on the issue of conflicting jurisdictions, *see* Chap. 9.

[100] MPIA, Annex 1, para 11.

[101] Gao and Lim (2008), p. 900.

[102] In order to see how the new generation EU FTAs could be amended, *see supra* (nn 64–68).

[103] Bercero (2006), p. 401.

[104] For example, EUKFTA, Art 3.1(1) and EUJEPA, Art 5.2(1) on the application of bilateral safeguard measures have very similar wording.

interpreted consistently when they were intended to have different meanings. Although the new generation EU FTAs require that WTO jurisprudence is taken into account when relevant, FTA panels would be more likely than WTO panels to find that, i.e. because of the context provided by other FTA norms, the WTO jurisprudence is not relevant—leading to justified inconsistencies. Furthermore, the precedential value of past jurisprudence has been questioned by WTO Members in the context of the AB crisis, indicating that within the WTO, there is also resistance to the perpetuation of certain jurisprudence. Additionally, in relation to WTO-x provisions that concern issues outside the WTO mandate, it is likely that the parties would not perceive WTO adjudicators and the Secretariat as having the necessary experience to deal with them.[105] Nonetheless, these areas are already excluded from the coverage of some FTA DSMs, such as those contained in the new generation EU FTAs,[106] indicating that the parties might not wish to subject these disputes to legal DSMs at all. Moreover, with the WTO DSM in the midst of an unprecedented crisis, without DSU reform or an alternative for the appellate stage within the WTO, such as the MPIA, accepted by FTA parties, these parties are unlikely to give preference to the WTO DSM to resolve their FTA disputes. Extending the jurisdiction of the WTO DSM over FTA claims without a functional AB or an alternative in place within the WTO in which disputing parties could participate would lead to the risk of having unadopted reports sent into the void. It seems that the EU, for example, will start using its FTA DSMs more often, potentially even to resolve disputes that could be brought to the WTO, a scenario that was analysed in the first part of the book.

The decision of FTA parties to make use of the WTO DSM is not the only obstacle to the extension of the jurisdiction of WTO panels over FTA disputes. The greatest impediment is the unlikely consensus of the WTO Membership on modifying the DSU and extending the panels' jurisdiction.[107] Thus, to extend the jurisdiction of the WTO panels, Article 1.1 of the DSU together with other articles, such as Articles 3.2, 4.2, 7, and 11 of the DSU, would have to be modified. Gao proposed amending only Appendix 1 of the DSU and adding FTAs to the list of the covered agreements to which Articles 1.1, 3.2, 4.2, 7 and 11 of the DSU refer, while leaving other provisions as they are.[108] However, even in this case, an amendment would still be necessary. Extending the WTO panels' jurisdiction over FTA disputes would also raise a set of other questions leading to potential discussions on further amendments to the DSU rules. Additional discussions could start with respect to questions such as whether WTO Members that are non-FTA parties could participate as third parties in the proceedings, whether the reports on FTA disputes should be

---

[105] Hammond (2012), p. 443; Porges (2018), p. 7.

[106] *See supra*, Sect. 5.2.

[107] Art X:8 of the Marrakesh Agreement establishes that for amendments to the DSU, the decision to approve 'shall be made by consensus and these amendments shall take effect for all Members upon approval by the Ministerial Conference'.

[108] Gao (2019), p. 4.

adopted by the entire Membership by negative consensus, or whether they should be subject to the WTO or FTA rules on remedies.[109] Moreover, such an amendment would also raise questions regarding the funding of the necessary expansions, such as increasing the WTO Secretariat's staff to support panels when dealing with FTA disputes.[110] As in the case of the proposal to make use of the WTO Secretariat's assistance in appeal arbitration and FTA proceedings, it is unlikely that WTO Members would agree that the WTO DSM is used for resolving FTA disputes from the WTO budget to which all Members contribute. Therefore, Members would have to also reach a consensus on funding and how to reform the mechanism, so that it would deal with a heavier workload without more delays. Considering the inability of the WTO Membership to reach consensus on reforms for years, it is unlikely that it would be able to reach a consensus on the many changes necessary to extend WTO jurisdiction over FTA claims, especially considering that many Members may not want this.

Given the current blockage at the WTO and the paralysis of the AB, it is conspicuous that Members would not even consider engaging in a discussion on extending WTO panels' jurisdiction over FTA disputes before resolving the crisis. A solution acceptable to the entire Membership is not expected in the foreseeable future. However, as this section shows, even with the two procedural stages of the WTO DSM fully functional, there are many aspects that would still impede the use of the WTO DSM for settlement of FTA disputes.

In conclusion, taking into consideration that states as FTA parties may not even want to consider using the WTO DSM to resolve their disputes, a consensus on the manifold amendments required would be extremely hard to reach and, above all, as the WTO DSM is currently in crisis, it can be asserted that in the foreseeable time to come it is highly improbable that FTA disputes would be resolved under WTO rules. Rather, it is expected that in the near future, FTA parties could bring more disputes under FTA dispute settlement rules, including those disputes on FTA norms that incorporate or replicate WTO norms. Hence, for a discussion on extending the jurisdiction of WTO panels over FTA claims to even begin, it is crucial that a functional WTO DSM is guaranteed first.

12.3 Conclusion

This chapter adopted an entirely prospective approach to the subject of cooperative interactions between the DSMs of the WTO and FTAs. Its purpose was to provoke the reader to ponder upon eventual future ways of cooperation, particularly the most ambitious approaches that would result not in *ad-hoc*, but in structural judicial interactions.

---

[109]Hammond (2012), pp. 439–441; Forere (2015), pp. 190–192.

[110]Shaffer and Winters (2017), p. 323.

The chapter considered two such forms of ambitious judicial interaction: the use of the WTO Secretariat's support during FTA proceedings, particularly under new generation EU FTA rules, and expanding WTO jurisdiction over FTA disputes. The desirability of the materialisation of these forms, as well as the difficulties in front of them were evaluated and inferences were made. In addition, the chapter assessed the likelihood that the necessary changes to the agreements would actually be made for these interactions to materialise. When it comes to using the WTO Secretariat's support during FTA proceedings, the chapter concluded that only administrative support is likely to be acceptable to FTA parties. However, while such support would be explicitly or implicitly permissible under the new generation EU FTAs, it is implausible that consensus would be reached within the WTO. In the case of the second form of ambitious judicial interaction, FTA parties could be expected to be against it and what is more, the current crisis and the unlikelihood of reaching consensus in this respect makes the perspective of having FTA disputes adjudicated under WTO rules almost fantastical. In practice, for a discussion about this form of interaction to be ignited, a well-functioning WTO DSM should be secured first.

Finally, while the chapter reached the conclusion that the ambitious structural forms of cooperation considered are unlikely to come to fruition in the foreseeable future, they have a theoretical value and should be kept in mind for a time when the context is more favourable for their realisation.

References

Andersen S et al (2017) Using arbitration under Article 25 of the DSU to ensure the availability of appeals. CTEI Working Papers CTEI-2017-17, pp 1–10

Baker DA, Marceau G (2019) The World Trade Organization. In: Baetens F (ed) Legitimacy of unseen actors in international adjudication. Cambridge University Press, New York, pp 70–91

Bercero IG (2006) Dispute settlement in European Union free trade agreements: lessons learned. In: Bartels L, Ortino F (eds) Regional trade agreements and the WTO legal system. Oxford University Press, New York, pp 383–405

Brown CM, Record J (2015) EU – Korea free trade agreement. In: Lester S, Mercurio B, Bartels L (eds) Bilateral and regional trade agreements. Case studies, 2nd edn. Cambridge University Press, New York, pp 39–59

Flett J (2015) Referring PTA disputes to the WTO dispute settlement system. In: Dür A, Elsig M (eds) Trade cooperation: the purpose, design and effects of preferential trade agreements, World Trade Forum. Cambridge University Press, New York, pp 555–579

Forere MA (2015) The relationship of WTO law and regional trade agreements in dispute settlement. Kluwer Law International, Alphen aan den Rijn

Gao H (2019) The WTO dispute settlement mechanism: a trade court for the world. ICTSD RTA Exchange, Think Piece, pp 1–8

Gao H, Lim CL (2008) Saving the WTO from the risk of irrelevance: the WTO dispute settlement mechanism as a 'Common Good' for RTA disputes. J Int Econ Law 11(4):899–925

Hammond F (2012) A balancing act: using WTO dispute settlement to resolve regional trade agreement disputes. Trade Law Dev 4(2):421–450

Howse R (2016) The World Trade Organization 20 years on: global governance by judiciary. Eur J Int Law 27(1):9–77

Hughes V (2015) Working in WTO dispute settlement. Without prejudice. In: Marceau G (ed) A history of law and lawyers in the GATT/WTO: the development of the rule of law in the multilateral trading system. Cambridge University Press, New York, pp 400–423

ICTSD (2017) Talking disputes | The Guatemala – US Labour Enforcement Dispute under CAFTA-DR. www.ictsd.org/themes/trade-law/events/talking-disputes-the-guatemala-us-labour-enforce ment-dispute-under-cafta

McRae D (2019) State-to-state dispute settlement in megaregionals. In: Kingsbury B et al (eds) Megaregulation contested. Global economic ordering after TPP. Oxford University Press, New York, pp 537–550

Nordström H (2005) The World Trade Organization Secretariat in a changing world. J World Trade 39(5):819–853

Pauwelyn J, Pelc KJ (2019) Who writes the rulings of the World Trade Organization? A critical assessment of the role of the secretariat in WTO dispute settlement. https://papers.ssrn.com/sol3/papers.cfm?abstract_id=3458872

Porges A (2018) Designing common but differentiated rules for regional trade disputes. ICTSD RTA Exchange, Issue Paper, pp 1–11

Robertson B, Falls S, Novacefski A (2018) Secretariat support for ad hoc panels under Canada's free trade agreements: challenges and options. Trade Lab Memorandum, pp 6–93. www.tradelab.org/single-post/2018/06/14/Secretariat-Support-for-Ad-Hoc-Panels-under-Canadas-Free-Trade-Agreements-Challenges-and-Options

Shaffer G, Winters A (2017) FTA law in WTO dispute settlement: Peru–Additional duty and the fragmentation of trade law. World Trade Rev 16(2):303–326

Trebilcock M (2015) Between theories of trade and development: the future of the world trading system. J World Invest Trade 16:122–140

Vidigal G (2018) Making regional dispute settlement attractive: the "Court of Arbitration" option. RTA Exchange, ICTSD. www.ictsd.org/opinion/making-regional-dispute-settlement-attractive-the-

Weiler JHH (2001) The rule of lawyers and the ethos of diplomats: reflections on the internal and external legitimacy of WTO dispute settlement. J World Trade 35(2):191–207

Weiss W (2018) Delegation to treaty bodies in EU agreements: constitutional constraints and proposals for strengthening the European Parliament. Eur Constitut Law Rev 14:532–566

WTO Secretariat (2017) A handbook on the WTO dispute settlement system, 2nd edn. Cambridge University Press, New York

Chapter 13
Conclusion

This book dealt with the interactions between the new generation EU FTA DSMs and the WTO mechanism in a fragmented and changing international trade law regime. As established in Part I (Chap. 2), in the last decades, there has been a continuous trend of proliferation of RTAs, especially FTAs, and the DSMs incorporated within them. The proliferation of FTAs and their DSMs has been raising concerns that the international trade law regime is becoming increasingly fragmented. The fragmentation of international trade law regime caused by the presence of multiple fora to adjudicate trade disputes may be associated with risks such as increased incoherence, unpredictability, instability, significant financial and time costs, affected legitimate expectations, and undermined authority and centrality of the WTO DSM. Nevertheless, incorporation of DSMs in FTAs is of utmost importance. FTA DSMs ensure that the norms enshrined in the agreements, especially those that are not contained in WTO agreements, are complied with. They can also strengthen the credibility of the commitments assumed by the parties, avoid escalation of trade conflicts, and even prevent the termination of the agreements due to unresolved conflicts. This book anticipates a rise in the use of FTA DSMs because of the need to enforce more developed FTA provisions as WTO negotiations are stalled and due to the possibility that these mechanisms would be used as alternatives for solving trade disputes in times of AB crisis. Accordingly, in the context of the recent developments, the issue of interactions between the DSMs of the new generation EU FTAs and the WTO gains renewed attention.

The DSMs of the EUKFTA, CETA, EUJEPA, EUSFTA, and EUVFTA were chosen to study their interactions with the WTO mechanism. The new generation EU FTA DSMs analysed reflect the most recent and advanced approach taken by the EU with respect to bilateral dispute settlement in trade. In addition, due to the considerable commercial importance of these FTAs and the dispute settlement experience of the parties, it is highly likely that the particular DSMs analysed would be used in practice. The study of the interactions between the new generation EU FTAs and the WTO DSMs presents particular interest. Given its constant expression of support for

© The Author(s), under exclusive license to Springer Nature Switzerland AG 2021
C. Furculiță, *The WTO and the New Generation EU FTA Dispute Settlement Mechanisms*, EYIEL Monographs - Studies in European and International Economic Law 19, https://doi.org/10.1007/978-3-030-83118-9_13

multilateralism in trade while advancing its ambitious bilateral trade agenda, the EU needs to take care not to undermine its credibility as a multilateralist. Therefore, the interactions between the DSMs of new generation EU FTAs and the WTO should not be perceived as contradicting the declared support for the multilateral trading regime.

An interdisciplinary conceptual framework was developed that served as a starting point for the research presented in the book (Chap. 3). It argued that for the purposes of this study the concepts of fragmentation and forum shopping should be perceived as value-free without having an automatic negative connotation. It acknowledged the assumptions made: that public international law is a legal system and that the regimes within it are governed by general public international law unless they do not derogate from it. In the framework it was also argued why it is considered that coherence should be sought, but only within the limits established by the rules of international law reflecting the will of the states. To more clearly define the scope of the research, the framework established that since it deals with the fragmentation caused by the proliferation of FTA DSMs within the international trading regimes, it only tackles vertical fragmentation of authority within the same issue area. Although the fragmentation of the international trading regime could have been approached from other perspectives, the judicial approach was regarded as of particular importance.

Considering that fragmentation and forum shopping do not necessarily result in negative consequences, using international legal and international relations scholarship, a complex approach was developed to analyse the fragmentation caused by the proliferation of FTA DSMs within the international trade law regime. Thus, the book did not merely study the conflicts of jurisdiction between the DSMs of the new generation EU FTAs and the WTO, it also assessed other types of interactions, such as competing and cooperative, with a potential for synergies. Furthermore, the study is original because it investigated these interactions in light of the most recent changes taking place within the international trading regime. Consequently, it studied how the DSMs of the new generation EU FTAs and the WTO do and could interact in a fragmented and changing international trade regime. It aimed to investigate whether the negative consequences of these interactions could be reduced and the synergies enhanced. Such a complex investigation on how the DSMs of the new generation EU FTAs and the WTO interact adds novelty to the existing scholarship due to the analysis of the interactions in the context of the latest changes and events.

Part II investigated whether the new generation EU FTA DSMs could emerge as potential alternatives to the WTO mechanism for solving trade disputes, especially in the current changing context. It also assessed the broader implications of the competition between the new generation EU FTA DSMs and the WTO mechanism, including whether there are some positive consequences. Chapter 4 argued that due to the AB's paralysis, the context in the international trading regime has changed, and the FTA DSMs that have been rarely used until recently may emerge as potential alternatives to the WTO mechanism. Furthermore, due to the need to enforce WTO-plus and WTO-x provisions and other substantive considerations, it is expected that the new generation EU FTA dispute settlement procedures would be used more often. Part II (Chaps. 5 and 6) established that the new generation EU FTA DSMs can become only partial viable alternatives to the WTO DSM because of their more limited coverage and the possibility of adjudicating only violation complaints.

Whether or not the FTA DSMs studied are and can be viable alternatives to the WTO mechanism depends on various substantive, procedural, and political aspects, as well as on the dispute at issue. While substantive considerations (treated in Chap. 5) could serve as arguments both in favour and against the use of the new generation EU FTA DSMs, in some instances, they will be the only available fora for enforcement of the norms contained only in the FTAs. The WTO mechanism, especially in case there is a regular or arbitral appellate stage, provides some clear procedural and political advantages (Chaps. 6 and 7). Thus, the WTO proceedings would likely offer greater coherence, security and predictability, reports of higher quality, automatic procedures for panel composition, increased value of jurisprudence, multilateral pressure leading to greater reputational costs for non-compliance, and lower financial costs. The MPIA proceedings would likely offer most of the advantages associated with the classical appeal proceedings, although possibly not to the same extent, and although there are some issues needing to be clarified and tested in practice. The main reason for FTA parties preferring the new generation EU FTA DSMs in the current changing context, is the automatic binding character of the reports issued. In case of FTAs with parties that do not participate in the MPIA, there is a risk that panel reports are sent into the void by appeals. Accordingly, it is very likely that FTA parties not participating in the MPIA and with no NAP in place would resort to the FTA DSMs, when possible, to solve their trade disputes, especially if there is no risk of the FTA panel selection process being stalled. In contrast, if there is a functional AB or the FTA parties are MPIA participants, in the majority of the cases the new generation EU FTA DSMs are less likely to become viable alternatives to the WTO DSM. Hence, the authority of a functional WTO mechanism should not be regarded as threatened in any way. Furthermore, when FTA DSMs may emerge as alternative mechanisms because of the risk that WTO panel reports may be sent into the void, FTA DSMs would be a temporary solution for states to resolve their trade disputes while the risk persists, rather than a problem.

In some limited cases, the new-generation EU FTA DSMs could be attractive alternatives even with the possibility of resolving disputes at the multilateral level and when there is no risk of WTO panel reports to being sent into the void. Accordingly, in specific disputes, states could choose the new generation EU FTA mechanisms due to their ability to provide more expeditious proceedings, greater control over the outcomes of the dispute, greater interpretative divergence, increased transparency and civil society participation, more flexible and developed implantation rules and remedies, lower publicity and the opportunity to avoid setting an unwanted multilateral precedent. In addition, it was argued that there should be no reason to anticipate high non-compliance rates with FTA reports and that unilateral retaliation would be regularly preferred over the use of the FTA DSMs.

Therefore, Part II (Chap. 8) concluded that the new generation EU FTA DSMs are and could be in genuine competition with the WTO DSM in the instances described and become partial viable alternatives to the WTO DSM. However, the authority of the WTO DSM is unlikely to be seriously threatened. On the contrary, the substantive coverage of the FTA mechanisms clearly shows that these agreements rely on a functional WTO mechanism to enforce many WTO norms that have been incorporated or replicated in the FTAs. It could even be argued that the FTA DSMs studied elevate the WTO DSM to primacy with respect to enforcement of some provisions. Accordingly, the EU, as a self-declared multilateralist, appears to be striving to balance its trade policy directions by seeking to avoid incoherent interpretations of some norms in different fora and being concerned about the coherence and predictability of the international trade regime. As most WTO-x provisions are not covered by the FTA DSMs studied, it is evident that these agreements do not pose a risk that states would not be motivated to multilateralise the regulation of these areas. The potential jurisdictional conflicts with the WTO DSM could also incentivise FTA parties to prefer the multilateral way of solving trade disputes. The competition between the DSMs of the new generation EU FTAs and the WTO also shows how states have learned lessons from the multilateral dispute settlement and applied them in bilateral settings. Thus, it has resulted in positive outcomes such as improved FTA rules for transparency, *amicus curiae* briefs, implementation proceedings, and temporary trade remedies. Moreover, in case of prospective discussions on DSU reform, the FTA mechanisms could be a source of inspiration for the Members to improve the rules based on their FTA models.

Part III dealt with the potential negative consequences of fragmentation caused by the proliferation of FTA DSMs within the international trade law regime. It analysed conflicts of jurisdiction—the most dealt with type of interactions between DSMs by doctrinaires, and investigated how they could be addressed so that the negative consequences are tackled. Chapter 9 assessed the likelihood of different tools generally dealing with conflicts of jurisdiction between the FTA and WTO DSMs, taking into consideration the concept of limited coherence. It argued how the issue of conflicting jurisdiction continues to remain relevant in the current changing context and explained that the conclusions reached are also relevant if the MPIA is used for the appellate stage. Chapter 9 analysed international tools such as *res judicata, lis alibi pendens, forum non conveniens*, comity, and the good faith principle and its manifestations. While some of these tools might not be useful in addressing the issue of conflicting jurisdiction between the WTO DSM and the FTA mechanisms due to their conditions or status, the question was raised whether WTO panels would even have jurisdiction over them or could apply them in the first place. The chapter proceeded with a presentation of jurisdictional clauses and argued that FTA exclusive or fork-in-the-road jurisdictional clauses, if invoked within FTA proceedings for the category of disputes that they cover, would be given consideration by FTA panels, at least partially solving the issue of conflicting jurisdiction. Thus, if an FTA party initiates WTO proceedings and then brings the same dispute to the FTA DSM and an exclusive or jurisdictional clause is invoked by the other party within the proceedings, the FTA panel would find a violation of that clause. However, to fully address the issue of conflicting jurisdictions, these FTA clauses would have to be given consideration also within the WTO DSM. The chapter established several legal avenues for potentially invoking these clauses; however, all these avenues were non-WTO law, raising the issue again whether WTO adjudicators could consider them.

Due to the WTO's limited jurisdiction over WTO covered agreements, unlikely successful invocation of Article XXIV of GATT as a justification for a jurisdictional clause, applicable law and inherent powers that are confined by Articles 3.2 and 19.2 of the DSU so that they cannot lead to the diminishment of the right to initiate WTO proceedings, it was concluded that non-WTO law cannot be considered by WTO panels to decline or not exercise their jurisdiction unless there is a legal basis in the DSU for doing so. Accordingly, Articles 3.7 and 3.10 of the DSU embodying the principle of good faith could serve as a legal basis for a claim of good faith violation when the right to initiate WTO proceedings is relinquished in a clear FTA jurisdictional clause, making the prospect feasible that WTO panels and the AB would not exercise their jurisdiction. The determination that the invocation of clear FTA jurisdictional clauses to substantiate the claim of a good faith violation under Articles 3.7 and 3.10 of the DSU would be possible was also confirmed by WTO jurisprudence. The jurisprudence studied also showed the willingness of WTO panels and the AB to analyse FTA norms to establish a violation of a WTO provision and it seemed to have left the door open to successful invocation of a fork-in-the-road clause to limit the right of a WTO Member to bring an action. Accordingly, clear jurisdictional clauses were identified as the tool with the highest probability of successfully dealing with jurisdictional conflicts between FTA and the WTO DSMs. However, it was also determined that for successful invocation of a jurisdictional clause, WTO jurisprudence has established some conditions that raise many questions, are quite strict, not all of these conditions have a legal basis, and it is unclear whether some of them would be applicable if the relinquishment of the right to use the WTO DSM was in a form other than an MAS.

Chapter 10 of Part III dealt specifically with the conflicts of jurisdiction between the WTO and the new generation EU FTA DSMs. It analysed the jurisdictional clauses contained in the new generation EU FTAs and assessed how they deal with conflicting jurisdictions. It first established the areas with respect to which conflicts of jurisdiction could appear between the mechanisms studied. It concluded that many areas are carved out from the coverage of the new generation EU FTA DSMs, which could be regarded as a conflict prevention measure, showing once again that these FTAs were not intended to undermine the authority of the WTO DSM. Chapter 10 established that all the new generation EU FTAs contain full fork-in-the-road clauses covering a certain category of disputes as well as additional jurisdictional clauses on countermeasures, while the EUKFTA and EUSFTA also provide limited fork-in-the-road clauses, and the EUJEPA an exclusive jurisdictional clause on TBT-exclusive violations claims. The fork-in-the-road clauses allowing the parties to choose between the new generation EU FTA and the WTO DSMs clearly demonstrate that the parties acknowledge the importance of bringing disputes to the WTO DSM. Therefore, the jurisdictional clauses in the new generation EU

FTAs also show that it is important to have a functional WTO DSM from the perspective of these agreements. Furthermore, the exclusive clause contained in the EUJEPA showcases the concern of the FTA parties about the coherence of the international trade regime.

Chapter 10 determined that if invoked within the FTA proceedings, the full fork-in-the-road clauses would adequately address the issue of conflicting jurisdictions with the WTO mechanism and would deal with its potential negative consequences. This is especially so when these clauses cover not only identical WTO and FTA norms, as in the EUKFTA, but also similar provisions, as in the rest of the FTAs studied. Besides, the additional clauses on countermeasures would further mitigate the risk of incoherencies, as they would impede claims of FTA violations by DSB-authorised countermeasures. The chapter further analysed whether the jurisdictional clauses in the new generation EU FTAs could also address the issue of conflicting jurisdictions if invoked within WTO proceedings. It assessed them in light of the conditions established in Chapter 9 based on the existing jurisprudence. Although the author criticized the conditions and argued that some of them should be departed from in the future, the compliance of the jurisdictional clauses with these conditions was, nevertheless, analysed, as they may be followed in future WTO disputes.

The limited fork-in-the-road clauses and jurisdictional clauses on countermeasures may be less successful if invoked within WTO proceedings. Without successful invocation of the clauses on countermeasures within WTO proceedings, the purpose of the full fork-in-the-road clauses and FTA proceedings might be defeated. The chapter suggested how these clauses could be drafted to remediate this risk. Chapter 5 established that the full fork-in-the-road clauses would likely comply with the conditions established in jurisprudence, if one of the requirements, that should in any case be departed from, is interpreted broadly. Therefore, the full-fork-in-the-road clauses have a high likelihood of qualifying as relinquishments of the right to initiate WTO proceedings, which could be considered under Articles 3.7 and 3.10 of the DSU, and could make panels to decline the exercise of their jurisdiction, thereby addressing the issue of conflicting jurisdictions. Consequently, these clauses could be acceptable tools to balance the EU's bilateral and multilateral endeavours. The chapter ended with an assessment of the influence of the current changing context on the operation of the jurisdictional clauses. It concluded that while the fork-in-the-road clauses would operate in a similar manner in case of NAPs or the MPIA, they would likely hamper the initiation of FTA proceedings if the same dispute is brought to the WTO and the procedures deliver a panel report that is appealed into the void. Finally, if FTA parties intend to make use of unilateral measures not authorised by the DSB to curb the unilateral measures of other Members or to address appeals sent into the void within the multilateral context, these measures would not be covered by the jurisdictional clauses on countermeasures, and claims could be brought on violations of FTA norms by these measures.

Part IV was dedicated to cooperative interactions between the WTO and the new generation EU FTAs. Chapter 11 was specifically focused on judicial communication between the DSMs studied, because of its pivotal function and ability to bring coherence and unity to the international law regime and other functions that can enhance synergies rather than causing negative outcomes. In the case at hand, the chapter established that the preconditions for judicial communication are present and it could take place. Nevertheless, the majority of the factors that could boost judicial communication would mostly encourage unidirectional communication initiated by FTA panels. Based on an analysis of WTO and FTA jurisprudence, the chapter established that unidirectional or responsive communication between the WTO and the new generation EU FTAs is likely to occur to establish facts, fill procedural gaps, determine the status and meaning of customary and general rules of international law, and to interpret substantive norms. In line with the conceptual framework, this chapter argued that there could be justifiable inconsistencies and that coherence should not be sought at the expense of correctness but within the limits established by international rules. Accordingly, it proceeded to evaluate the legal basis under which judicial communication could take place between adjudicators of the new generation EU FTAs and the WTO.

Chapter 11 established that for procedural coherence, the inherent powers doctrine could be used as a legal avenue. Factual coherence could be provided by the WTO and the new generation EU FTA rules that do not limit the right of the parties to invoke and that of the panels to seek information outside their regime, but the considerable discretion enjoyed by the parties could limit the ability of this legal avenue to ensure consistency. Article 38(1)(d) of the ICJ Statute could help to indirectly ensure substantive coherence by allowing FTA and WTO adjudicators to establish the same meaning and status of the customary rules and general principles of interpretation. Article XXIV of GATT could be used in strict and some quite unclear conditions to bring coherence with respect to FTA provisions when considered within both multilateral and bilateral settings. Finally, substantive coherence between WTO and FTA interpretations could be assured with the help of rules of interpretation. Thus, external jurisprudence of another judicial body could be used within certain limits for the purpose of establishing the ordinary meaning of a term under Article 31(1) of the VCLT. The principle of systemic interpretation embodied in Article 31(3)(c) of the VCLT, designed with the specific aim of ensuring coherence in international law together with the rules contained in the new generation EU FTAs on the role of WTO case law represent promising legal avenues for judicial communication initiated by FTA arbitrators. In case of appeal arbitral awards that are not covered by the new generation EU FTA rules expressly referencing WTO jurisprudence, Article 31(3)(c) could serve as the basis for FTA panels engaging with MPIA awards in the process of interpretation. Article 31(3)(c) could also be used as an avenue for judicial communication initiated by WTO adjudicators with FTA panels; however, such use depends on the interpretation of some ambiguous elements and is likely to be restricted. Finally, the express rules contained in the new generation EU FTAs on WTO jurisprudence demonstrate their recognition of its authority and of having a functional way of solving disputes at the WTO level. They confirm that the new generation EU FTAs were designed to build upon WTO jurisprudence, not against it, and, therefore, were not intended to undermine the WTO DSM. Finally, in times of AB crisis and when not all the new generation EU FTA parties are MPIA participants, these FTA rules on interpretation could secure a certain degree of coherence within a fragmented international trading regime where FTA dispute settlement would be used more often.

Chapter 12 considered two highly ambitious, structural forms of cooperative interactions that could take place between the DSMs of the WTO and the new generation EU FTAs. First, it considered the possibility of using the WTO Secretariat's support within WTO proceedings. It established that the FTA legal framework currently permits external administrative secretarial support, but legal support is likely to be undesirable to the parties. Nevertheless, regardless of the type of support, the WTO Membership would need to reach consensus on the WTO Secretariat providing assistance within FTA proceedings—an unlikely event in the foreseeable future. The second form of structural cooperation considered was the extension of the WTO panels' jurisdiction over FTA disputes. Chapter 12 established that because the FTA parties may be against this form of cooperation, due to the current WTO dispute settlement crisis and the need to modify the DSU by consensus, the possibility that this form of cooperation sees the light of the day in the not so distant future seems almost fantastical. Nevertheless, the last chapter with its entirely prospective approach had the aim of engaging in an exercise of imagination, because with a future change in the context, these structural forms of cooperation might appear more feasible.

The analysis of the different forms of interaction between the WTO and the new generation EU FTA DSMs showed that negative consequences of fragmentation could be offset to a certain extent. It showed that although in some instances it could be difficult to deal with negative consequences and enhance the synergies of the interactions analysed, the new generation EU FTAs seem to have been designed with coherence and consistency of the international trade law regime in mind. Drafting suggestions were made for circumstances when the EU, as a self-declared multilateralist, could do even more to balance its bilateral and multilateral aspirations. In case of all three types of interactions, it was established that the new generation EU FTAs are unlikely to undermine the authority and centrality of the WTO DSM. The interactions considered could also result in positive outcomes, such as learning lessons from each other. What is more, from the perspective of the new generation EU FTAs, having a functional way of solving disputes within the WTO context is of utmost importance. Accordingly, it is also important that the current dispute settlement crisis at the WTO is resolved. As shown, the interactions between the DSMs of the new generation EU FTAs and the WTO gain special importance in light of the current changing international trade law regime and are affected by it. If the crisis continues and there is a risk that WTO panel reports are sent into the void, the new generation EU FTAs could provide alternative fora for solving trade disputes and at least initially, WTO jurisprudence could provide some degree of coherence in the changing international trade law regime.

9 783030 831202